THE LAW

OF

CONTRACTS.

BY

J. I. CLARK HARE, LL.D.

THE LAWBOOK EXCHANGE, LTD.
Clark, New Jersey
2003

ISBN 1-58477-311-1

Printed in the United States of America
on acid-free paper

The Lawbook Exchange, Ltd.
33 Terminal Avenue
Clark, New Jersey 07066-1321

Please see our website
www.lawbookexchange.com
for a selection of our other publications and
fine facsimile reprints
of classic works of legal history.

Library of Congress Cataloging-in-Publication Data

Hare, J. I. Clark (John Innes Clark)
The law of contracts / by ii. Clark Hare.
p. cm.
Originally published: Boston: Little, Brown, and Co., 1887.
Includes bibliographical references and index.
ISBN 1-58477-311-1 (cloth: alk. paper)
1. Contracts—United States. 2. Contracts. I. Title.

KF8O1.H26 2003
346.73 02—dc21 2003047461

THE LAW

OF

CONTRACTS.

BY

J. I. CLARK HARE, LL.D.

BOSTON:
LITTLE, BROWN, AND COMPANY.
1887.

University Press:
John Wilson and Son, Cambridge.

PREFACE.

This book originated from a course of lectures delivered in the law school of the University of Pennsylvania; and one object of the author was to trace the doctrine of consideration, and show how large a part it has in the theory of contracts at common law. In doing this, he was led to contrast the Roman Law, where the doctrine of consideration was unknown, or existed only in the germ, and he then passed to the law of sales as being a practical and important application of the principles of both systems.

The work is now submitted to the profession, in the hope that it may cast some light on one aspect of the vast field of jurisprudence, which is continually expanding, and, though continually explored, will ever remain unexhausted.

Philadelphia, Jan. 1, 1887.

CONTENTS.

CHAPTER I.

THE GROWTH OF JURISPRUDENCE.

CHAPTER II.

THE FORMULARY SYSTEM.

CHAPTER III.

JUSTINIAN'S LEGISLATION.

CHAPTER IV.

DEVELOPMENT OF OBLIGATIONS AT ROMAN LAW.

CHAPTER V.

THE CONSENSUAL CONTRACTS.

CHAPTER VI.

MODERN APPLICATION OF THE ROMAN LAW.

CHAPTER VII.

ASSUMPSIT.

CHAPTER VIII.

TRESPASS ON THE CASE.

CHAPTER IX.

ROMAN AND COMMON LAW CONTRASTED.

CHAPTER X.

CONSIDERATION.

CHAPTER XI.

IMPLIED PROMISES.

CHAPTER XII.

ANTECEDENT CONSIDERATION.

CHAPTER XIII.

MORAL OBLIGATION.

CHAPTER XIV.

RATIFICATION AND WAIVER.

CHAPTER XV.

UNILATERAL CONTRACTS.

CHAPTER XVI.

BILATERAL CONTRACTS.

CHAPTER XVII.

MUTUALITY.

CHAPTER XVIII.

SALE OF SPECIFIC GOODS.

CHAPTER XIX.

SALE BY DESCRIPTION.

CHAPTER XX.

SALE BY SAMPLE.

CHAPTER XXI.

WARRANTY.

CHAPTER XXII.

REMEDIES OF THE VENDEE.

CHAPTER XXIII.

PERFORMANCE.

CHAPTER XXIV.

DEPENDENT AND INDEPENDENT COVENANTS AND PROMISES.

CHAPTER XXV.

ENTIRE AND DIVISIBLE CONTRACTS.

CHAPTER XXVI.

IMPOSSIBILITY.

TABLE OF CASES CITED.

A.

B.

C.

D.

H.

I.

L.

M.

N.

O.

Q.

R.

T.

U.

V.

Y.

Z.

THE LAW OF CONTRACTS.

THE LAW OF CONTRACTS.

CHAPTER I.

THE GROWTH OF JURISPRUDENCE.

Law in the Ancient World. — Effects of War and Commerce. — The Roman Law. — Jurisprudence of the Middle Ages. — Relation of the Roman Law to the Common Law.

THE growth of jurisprudence has been influenced by causes that might at first sight appear inadequate to such a result. War and commerce have been the civilizers and instructors of mankind. Without them there would hardly have been a science of the law. In order to appreciate their beneficial influence we must revert to the period when mankind were segregated in clans or tribes. Each district had its peculiar family, which regarded every other with fear or aversion, and "stranger" was so nearly equivalent to "enemy" that the same term served to designate both. The diversity extended to manners, language, religion, laws. Six different tongues were, it is said, spoken in Italy, and not less than four within thirty miles of the gates of Rome. Union seems to have been produced in the first instance by causes which humanity and reason may disapprove, but which were notwithstanding effectual. Some tribe more adventurous than the rest left their native seat in the hope of plunder, or with a view to secure a more fertile soil, and drew others along with them. Such seem to have been the moving springs of the long series of armed migrations which peopled Europe from Asia, and gave the Indo-Germanic race a dominion which, did not China intervene, would be co-extensive with the globe.[1] The fear of aggression induced concert for defence. In whichever way the struggle terminated, the barriers of race and prejudice were broken down. It was, if we may believe tradition, the union of the Greeks against a common enemy that gave rise to the first and greatest of all poems — "the Tale of Troy divine." The desire to record the heroic deeds of his countrymen in resisting the invasion of Xerxes prompted the history of Herodotus. The conquest of Persia by Alexander spread the language and culture of Greece throughout the vast Asian Empire, which he overthrew. Heterogeneous races, creeds the most various, — the monotheism of the Jew, the dualism of the Fire-worshipper, Egyptian symbolism, — were brought beneath a European sceptre, and the philosophers who flourished under the successors of the Macedonian conqueror might find in the diversity of religious belief an argument for scepticism, or reason from its universality to faith. A cosmopolitan city arose in Alexandria, which might boast that as men of all nations gathered in its marts, and its libraries contained the books of every age and clime, so every shade of opinion was represented in its schools; and the mingling of these diverse elements generated ideas which leavened the currents of Judaic and Hellenic thought, and finally made their influence felt throughout the civilized world.[2] The labors of the Seventy rendered the Pentateuch accessible to every one who under-

[1] Some idea of the instability which led to such important results may be formed from Cæsar's account of the Helvetii. We there see a people having a fixed abode, a magistracy, laws, and the spirit and organization requisite for vindicating their liberty and punishing the powerful chief by whom it was assailed, but who yet did not hesitate to devastate and abandon their country, and go forth with their wives and children through hostile tribes, they knew not whither, in the hope that conquest would give them a more fertile territory than that which they left behind. Mad as such an enterprise may appear, it was simply out of date, and might, three centuries earlier, or at a later period, have been as successful as that which gave the Celts Cisalpine Gaul, or like the march of Brennus or of Alaric have ended in the capture of Rome.

[2] See Matter, École d'Alexandrie, i. 228, 272, 286. Stanley, History of the Jewish Church, lect. xlvii.

stood Greek, which then held the place that was filled by the French language during the last century; and the sublime account of the creation in the book of Genesis could not in the then temper of mankind but gain by comparison with the idle cosmogony of Hesiod, or the Epicurean theory that matter has in it the potentiality of all things.[1] The Hebrew Scriptures were thus brought into juxtaposition with the lessons taught by Socrates and Plato, and became a factor in the education of mankind, which grew in importance with the lapse of time.[2] Such intellectual commerce could not but be advantageous to both the nations that have contributed so largely to the development of our race. If the Greek did not readily believe he might at least be compelled to feel that there was more in heaven and earth than had been dreamed of in his philosophy; and the Jew learned to abate the repugnance with which he had regarded the Gentile as common and unclean. A great and predominating power arose in Rome. Unlike most other conquerors her arms were used to establish rather than destroy, and their success was generally followed by the introduction of the Latin tongue. The void which war had made in Africa and Spain was filled from Italy, and the emigration to the East was hardly less numerous. We may judge of the extent of this outflow from what seems to be the well authenticated statement, that eighty thousand — or, according to some authorities, one hundred and fifty thousand — Italians perished in a single day in Asia Minor, by the orders of Mithridates; that a number almost as great were subsequently massacred in the Islands of the Ægean Sea, by the same despotic command; and that notwithstanding these atrocities, a numerous corps of Italian exiles fought in his armies to avenge the wrongs of Samnium and the sufferings which they had endured, during the social war, at the hands of Rome. The obstacle was removed by the downfall of a monarch whose power for a brief period rivalled that which had been wielded

[1] Matter, École d'Alexandrie, i. 212. Stanley, History of the Jewish Church, iii. 268, 283.

[2] Matter, École d'Alexandrie, i. 198, 272.

by the Persian kings, and the Roman dominion was soon afterwards extended in Europe to the Northern Ocean. By an impulse that could not be withstood, the Greek and Latin tongues became the common speech of the civilized world, and an audience might be found in every city that could understand and follow the teachings of the apostles of Christianity. The Mediterranean became a Roman lake, and around it clustered a group of nations which, though differing in manners and origin, read the same books, and were to a great extent imbued with the same principles. Commerce did her part to complete the change that war had inaugurated. The ships which traded to the different parts of the Roman Empire diffused ideas as well as merchandise, and in the search for profit promoted the growth of civilization. The Roman, standing in the centre as the common master, was from the necessity of the case forced to look upon all with an equal eye, and to lay down rules that should be generally applicable. The law ceased to be a bundle of customs or traditions, and became a science. The reason of the rule was sought for, and when it ceased to be applicable, an exception was deduced or a new rule instituted.

Great as was the opportunity of the Romans to civilize and legislate for the nations whom they subdued, it would have signified little had they not been peculiarly fitted for such a task; and we may believe that much as they acquired from their intercourse with other nations, they were still more indebted to their own traditions, which recognized a higher standard of duty than any which prevailed elsewhere, or is practically followed in modern times. It is the fashion to decry the Roman legends as the offspring of patrician vanity credulously accepted by descendants who were ready to propagate any story that added to their family renown; but we should recollect that a myth may have a higher significance than if it were a fact, as being the creature of the popular imagination and what the popular heart approves.

It has been justly said that national character depends on what a people believes of its leaders, rather than on what they really are. If Chevy-Chace were historical, it would prove that a quarrel between feudal chiefs was fought out to the bitter end; viewed as legendary, it confirms what we may learn from Froissart, that chivalric valor was the quality most esteemed on either side of the border. We may therefore feel sure, that whether the Roman traditions were or were not historically true, mankind did not err in looking to them for lessons of constancy, patriotic devotion and unswerving rectitude, nor in regarding those qualities as characteristics of the race which subdued the world. So the story of the expulsion of Tarquin, of the fall of the Decemvirate, of Coriolanus, and of the plebeian's wife who instigated the agitation that led to the Licinian laws, would be a convincing proof of the respect for woman and her influence on the course of events, though the incidents were fabulous, and Lucretia, Volumnia, and Virginia never existed.

No reader of Cicero's dialogues or of Horace can fail to note the grandeur of the Roman ideal, and the reverent regard of both orator and poet for the ancestral virtue of the republic. Such conceptions formed the character of the men who, after liberty had become extinct, and when the other avenues to public life were closed, found a career in the army, at the bar, and in the administration of justice, and could, like Agricola or Papinian, stand erect under a Domitian or Caracalla.

The morals of a people are reflected in their laws, and the lofty tone of the Roman jurists dignified their work and fitted it to endure. A sweeping generalization is rarely accurate; but we may agree with Guizot that, while culture came from Greece, and spiritual lore from Palestine, Rome taught a moral lesson through her jurisprudence and the lives of her great men, as portrayed in her annals, that could not have been learned from any other source. It was characteristic of the Roman, though continually at war, to rate civic virtue above the glory to be acquired in battle; and this trait qualified him not only to legislate for the nations whom he subdued, but to form a code which survived his downfall, and rendered him in effect the lawgiver of the races by whom his empire was overthrown.

It is to these among other causes that we may attribute the amazing growth of the science of jurisprudence, which in the two centuries succeeding the accession of Augustus, attained a height which it was not destined to surpass. For although we now look to the Pandects and the Institutes which date from the reign of Justinian, for the principles of Roman law, these publications are well known to have been compiled from the writings of an earlier period.

The downfall of the Roman Empire was to a great extent a wreck of the accumulated learning of the past, but jurisprudence is a science not easily destructible. It was indeed at one time the received opinion that during the centuries popularly known as the dark ages, the civil law ceased to exist as a guide for the tribunals or to regulate the transactions of mankind. It was to the discovery of the Pandects in the twelfth century, at Amalfi, that historians attributed the revival of a learning that might otherwise have perished. This opinion is now known to have been fallacious. The vestiges of Roman law and civilization were submerged rather than obliterated by the tide of invasion. The steps by which the Provençal and the French grew out of the ruins of the Latin tongue were so gradual as to be almost imperceptible, and the conquered people not only continued to speak the same language but were to a great extent governed by the same laws. Such was especially the case in Southern Europe, where the currents of life and thought were slow to quit the channels that had been worn by time.

Under these circumstances, the knowledge of the Roman law might be obscured but could not wholly disappear, and this inference has been confirmed by the research of modern times. A striking proof is afforded by the codes which were formed and promulgated by the Burgundians on the Rhine, and by the Goths and Lombards in Italy and the south of France. A distinguishing feature of these systems was that every man should obey the rules which had descended from his ancestors. If the barbarian followed the customs which he had brought with him from the forests of Germany, the Roman might still appeal to the refined principles and distinctions of the civil law. It is related in a chronicle of the time that of four men sitting on the same bench each was presumably governed by a different law. The stamp which Rome had set upon the world was too deeply cut to disappear on the breaking of the die. When Charlemagne aspired to universal empire, he claimed as the inheritor of the Cæsars, and the title descended from him in an unbroken line, until the thread was cut by the arms of Napoleon. The belief that Rome was still the pivot upon which the destinies of mankind should hinge may be traced alike in the Divine Comedy of Dante, and in the heroic madness of Rienzi, and contributed to the establishment of that spiritual ascendency which gave the successors of St. Peter a wider sway than Trajan or Augustus.

The jurisprudence of the middle ages was, as might have been expected under such circumstances, a mosaic in which maxims and principles drawn from a refined civilization alternated with customs arising from the necessities of the times, or peculiar to the races which overthrew the Roman Empire. The feudal system was founded on the ownership or possession of land, and the title and succession to real estate are consequently in a great measure regulated, even in our own times, by rules derived from the feudal law. The curious and subtle learning of contingent remainders, executory devises and reversions, of merger, of common recoveries and of estates tail, can only be found in the books of the common law, and we must go to them or to the corresponding treatises in France and Germany if we wish to learn the nature of a feud or comprehend the various and complicated relations between lord and vassal.

If we now turn to the law of chattels personal, we shall find the picture to a great extent reversed. The value of this description of property was, during the period which succeeded the overthrow of the Roman Empire, and until far down in the middle ages, too small to attract attention. A manorial lord, or a prosperous yeoman might have been rich in flocks and herds; granaries may, as the legend of Bishop Hatto intimates, have been stored with grain; hides and fleeces were no doubt accumulated for use or sale; but save in the great commercial and manufacturing towns, the enumeration could hardly be carried further. Even when luxury and wealth were at their height in the Roman world, the labors of the artisan took the direction of grace and elegance rather than utility, and much that men of moderate means now deem indispensable, was then unknown in the palaces of the wealthy. In the confusion and disorder that marked the influx of the barbarians, skilled labor became rare and costly, and if food, fire, and clothing were supplied, mankind looked no higher. A tapestry worked by the ladies of the household, a few coats of mail hanging by the wall, a store of choice weapons from Toledo or Milan, a chest of rich attire for festivals, were an inventory which even a powerful chief might envy. Glass, porcelain, mirrors, carpets, and the multitude of other objects which constant use now makes indispensable, were almost unknown. Rushes strewed the floors, and food and drink were served in earthenware or wooden utensils, on roughly hewn tables.

The commercial transactions of such a period were necessarily few in number, and extremely simple. They seldom went farther than an exchange of the products of the land with some neighboring proprietor, or the purchase of an embroidered robe or suit of armor at the nearest mart, or from a merchant trading under a safe conduct. The law of chattels could not, under these circumstances, have the refinement or complexity which characterized that of land. It did not, even as late as the reign of Elizabeth, afford room for such a treatise as that of Littleton, or for commentaries like those of Coke. At an earlier period it was ignored, and it can hardly be said to have acquired shape and method until the time of Lord Holt. But England presented in this respect a striking contrast to the continent of Europe, where trade had, in the free cities of Germany and the Italian republics, gone hand in hand with liberty, from a date anterior to the Norman conquest. The productions of the East flowed into Europe through Barcelona, Marseilles, Genoa, and Venice, and the revival of trade was attended with a corresponding growth of legal science. The codes which regulated commerce in these states during the middle ages may be consulted with advantage by the modern lawyer. Nor was this all. In northern Italy, in Flanders, and in the prosperous towns which arose in Germany, manufacturing industry kept pace with trade; wealth increased in every form; and the proximity and certainty of a market induced a skilful and thorough cultivation of the soil. The plains of Tuscany and Lombardy were dotted with cities which, though placed almost at each other's gates, and at constant feud, found time to cultivate the arts of peace. A way briefer than that which leads from Philadelphia to Lancaster conducted the militia of Ghent to Bruges, of Florence to Pisa, of Milan to Pavia; and the path was as much worn by the passage of armies as by peaceful travel. In spite of every drawback, prosperity was for a long time exuberant. Men were then, as they are now in the United States, entering into the possession of new and unreaped fields of enterprise, and their success was in a corresponding ratio. There is this difference, that the growth of material prosperity was attended with a thirst for knowledge to which our times afford no parallel. The remains of antiquity were explored with an enthusiasm that resulted in the brilliant literary and artistic development which, though generally known as the Renaissance, was not so much the revival of a dead past as the birth of a new era. For good or evil the world had left its accustomed moorings for the unknown goal towards which it is still moving; and if the currents of thought were colored by lights reflected from antiquity, they tended to ends that had not been dreamed of in Greece or Rome.

Far different was the result in the field of jurisprudence, where by a singular exception mankind not only reverted to the past for instruction, but accepted its teachings as a final and authentic exposition of the truth. As far back as the twelfth century, the Roman law was taught publicly to eager hearers, not for its historical interest nor as an aid to the study of jurisprudence, but as the perfection of human reason, and as such having an indefeasible claim to obedience which no political change could destroy. Europe was then, as I have elsewhere stated, divided between the doctrines of the Institutes and Pandects, and the traditional usages of the Teutonic conquerors as modified by the complicated relations of lord and vassal; but the former system gradually displaced the latter, and not only regained the ground which it had lost at the downfall of the Roman Empire, but became the common law of Continental Europe or the groundwork of its codes. Among the causes that contributed to this result, may be enumerated the claim of the Emperors of Germany as the successors of Charlemagne and Constantine, to exercise the supremacy which had formerly belonged to Rome. It was as *Romanorum imperator semper Augustus* that Frederic Barbarossa asserted his authority in Italy, and was welcomed by the Ghibelins and opposed by the Guelfs; and his grandson and successor Frederic II. did not think that he displaced the seat of empire in establishing himself at Naples. Rulers who claimed as the inheritors of the Cæsars might reasonably adopt the Roman law; and such a course was the more natural on their part because its maxims had been framed under a despotic government, and were eminently favorable to autocratic rule.[1]

The jurists of Italy and Germany were not less ready than their Byzantine predecessors to declare that all men owed implicit obedience to Cæsar, and held their lives and property at his pleasure; and the language of the Institutes, *quod principi placuit legis habet vigorem*, was relied on to sustain this servile doctrine. The authority of the emperors was founded in opinion rather than on military force, and therefore less to be apprehended or liable to abuse; but the dogma of passive obedience was by an almost inevitable sequence invoked on behalf of regal as well as imperial power, and contributed to the growth of the absolutism which supplanted the free institutions of the middle ages. While such was the course of events on the Continent, England adhered instinctively to the manlier precepts of the common

[1] Bryce, Holy Roman Empire, ch. xi. p. 173; Appendix, p. 452; Sismondi, Républiques Italiennes, i. 350; Mackeldey, Roman Law, § 102.

law, and in so doing, maintained the liberty which she was destined to transmit to her numerous progeny throughout the globe.

It has been my object in these remarks to show that if the advance of commerce, the growth of commercial jurisprudence, and a more thorough and scientific study of the civil law, occurred simultaneously during the middle ages, and anticipated the revival of letters, the connection between these results was not fortuitous. The controversies arising from the increase of trade made a demand on the knowledge of the jurist which he could only meet by recurring to the authors who had treated of such subjects in ancient Rome. It would, nevertheless, be erroneous to suppose that the doctrines of commercial law in their present form can be found in the books of the civil law. On the contrary, many of the most important titles are of modern growth, and were little known or studied, until the middle of the seventeenth century. The Institutes and Pandects make no mention of promissory notes and bills of exchange, or of the contract of insurance, which occupy so large a place in our present jurisprudence; and although the outlines of the law of bailment were traced with a masterly hand, the superstructure has been erected almost entirely in our time.

We are, notwithstanding, indebted to the Romans for the foundation of commercial law. Trade is throughout the result of an express or implied contract; and the great lawyers whose precepts were compiled in the reign of Justinian, reduced the law of contracts to a system which, if cramped by the technicality of its origin, and not always broad or philosophic, has yet contributed largely to the development of jurisprudence. Their method is still followed by the Continental jurists and in Scotland, but a different doctrine was evolved in England, and has been adopted in the United States, which, although having some features in common with the civil law, is yet as a whole of native growth.

Few things, notwithstanding, are more difficult than to form a correct estimate of the relation of Roman to English jurisprudence, and few have given rise to a greater difference of opinion.[1] The laws of all civilized nations have in them much that is the same; and when two systems are one of earlier, the other of later growth, it cannot readily be determined whether the principles in which they agree were borrowed, or due to causes which from the nature of things, are everywhere alike and tend to similar results. The Anglo-Saxons were, moreover, by conquest, immigration, commerce, the bond of a common faith and of Papal supremacy, brought into constant intercourse with the nations of Continental Europe, and received through them and the influence of the clergy, the impress of the principles and doctrines which had been bequeathed by Rome. The common law is consequently analogous to the civil law in many points where the conception was original, as well as where the germ was derived from a foreign source. So much is generally conceded: but it has been plausibly contended that the civil law was not only the source whence the English lawyers drew maxims and ideas which rendered the common law less arbitrary and technical, but that it was looked upon as having an authority which, though not legislative, should be regarded where no customary rule or statute stood in the way, and was a guide in determining how property could be acquired and conveyed.[2]

Bracton, who flourished in the middle of the thirteenth century, gives color to this hypothesis by treating the Institutes and Digest, and even the imperial constitutions and rescripts, as of equal weight with the decisions of the English courts and the recognized customs of the realm. His treatise, it has been contended, presents "an indivisible homogeneous whole, in which the Roman elements are no longer merely Roman law, but have become integral parts of the *leges et consuetudines Angliæ*."[3]

This view is accepted by Güterbock, who declares that the historical evidence, as well as the internal evidence of Bracton's work, demonstrate that no inconsiderable part of the Roman law must have been practically applied in England in

[1] See Güterbock, Bracton, p. 56; Reeves' Hist. of the Eng. Law, i. 103, 495; Spence, Eq. Jurisd. i. 119, 121, 235.

[2] Güterbock, Bracton, p. 58.

[3] Güterbock, Bracton, pp. 58, 62.

Bracton's day;[1] and Spence inclines to the same conclusion. The English law however, could not, when Bracton wrote, justly be described as a homogeneous whole, nor was there ever such an incorporation of the Roman law as that above suggested.[2] The laws of England were, prior to the Conquest, a bundle of traditions to which Saxon, Dane and Norseman each contributed his share, and which, although in many respects analogous as coming from a Teutonic stock, differed in some material particulars.

The codes of Ethelbert, of Alfred and of Canute were, as we learn from competent authority, concerned with the preservation of the public peace and the privileges of the great landed proprietors and clergy, and did little to improve or systematize the law of property or of contracts.[3] The forms of grants and contracts were to some extent derived from the civil law as modified by the constitutions of the later emperors and the Teutonic conquest; but the great body of the Anglo-Saxon law remained.[4]

The Norman Conquest added to the discordance by introducing usages which had arisen among the Normans during their long residence in France, or were derived from intercourse and intermarriage with the French. For one hundred and fifty years, foreign ideas and manners, and the French tongue seemed likely to efface the distinctive features of the sturdy race that was the backbone of the nascent English people. The descent, transfer and tenure of land were governed under the Anglo-Norman kings by rules which formed part of the complex machinery of the feudal system;[5] but the other departments of the law presented an increasing array of questions for which there were no certain guides. The legislative authority resided in the king acting with the concurrence of the barons, but was seldom exercised anterior to the reign of Edward III., and the task of moulding as

[1] Güterbock, Bracton, p. 57. [2] Selden, Ad Fletam, ch. ix. §§ 1, 2.

[3] Spence, Eq. Jurisd. pp. 10, 19; Essays in Anglo-Saxon Law, pp. 8, 55; Selden, Ad Fletam, ch. vii. § 1.

[4] Amos, Hist. and Princ. of the Civil Law, p. 444.

[5] Creasy, Eng. Const. pp. 64, 78.

well as administering the law devolved on the courts, which were for the time being disinclined to the usages of the conquered people.

The larger part of all that was powerful, wealthy, or cultured in England, — her barons, prelates, and jurists, — were of Norman birth or extraction, or came from the fertile provinces which formed the dowry of Eleanor of Guienne. It has been computed that from two hundred thousand to three hundred thousand emigrants from the Continent became inhabitants of England under the Conqueror and his sons, and the influx continued during the succeeding reigns.[1]

So great a change could not be without its effect on jurisprudence, and it is not surprising that the legal conceptions of men born in France, and generally French by descent in the maternal line, should have been modified by the study of the civil law, which was enthusiastically pursued in Italy and not unknown in the countries to the north of the Alps. The Institutes and Digest were accordingly regarded during the centuries which immediately succeeded the Conquest, as a repertory of principles which, though having no legislative force, were yet authoritative from their essential reason, and should be followed where there was no established rule.[2] Such a result was the more likely to ensue because the judges were in numerous instances ecclesiastics, versed in the canon law, and inclined, both as priests and jurists, to view Rome as the centre to which mankind should look for guidance.[3]

The aversion of the great body of the people to innovations which were a badge of servitude and certainly not intended for their good, led to an outcry for the laws of Edward the Confessor, that is, for the rules and usages in force during his reign, and William seemed at first inclined to accede to the request, but soon found himself obliged to organize England as a feud, and deprive the Saxons of their laws as well as their lands.[4] The Conquest thus evoked two senti-

[1] Creasy, Eng. Const. p. 67.

[2] Selden, Ad Fletam, ch. iv. p. 1053; ch. vii. p. 1081; Amos, Hist. and Princ. of the Civil Law, p. 447.

[3] Selden, Ad Fletam, ch. viii. § 1.

[4] Spence, Eq. Jurisd. pp. 19, 89.

ments, — one inclined, the other bitterly hostile, to all that savored of imperial or papal Rome;[1] but as the conquerors, with the versatility of their dual descent, came to regard themselves as Englishmen, the latter gained the upper hand, and, when Normans, Danes and Saxons were fused into one people, took the form of a fixed resolve not to suffer any alteration of the English common law by a foreign hand.[2] Accordingly, as Selden observes,[3] the civil law passed through various stages in Britain. Under the Roman rule it was supreme throughout the greater part of the island, as in the other provinces of the empire. Receding before the Anglo-Saxons after the imperial troops were withdrawn, it may have retained some measure of authority among the Britons until Wales was finally subdued.[4] It regained weight and consideration through the Norman Conquest, and was consulted and relied on by the judges during the twelfth and thirteenth centuries,— not as having a conclusive force, but as the Rhodian law was accepted among the Romans where navigation was concerned, and the laws of Oleron may be cited in our courts at the present day.[5] But when the English people were so far consolidated and organized that their voice could be heard, the civil law was repudiated as foreign to the laws and customs of the realm, and ignored in the King's Bench and Common Pleas, although still retaining a foot-hold in the Admiralty, the Marshalsea, and the Ecclesiastical tribunals which took cognizance of the administration of personal property after death and mat-

[1] Amos, Hist. and Princ. of the Civil Law, pp. 446, 449.

[2] Amos, Hist. and Princ. of the Civil Law, p. 450; Selden, Ad Fletam, ch. vii. § 5; ch. viii. § 5; ch. ix. §§ 1, 2, 3.

There can be little doubt that the *lex terræ* guaranteed by Magna Charta is the law of the land, that is, of England, as opposed to the modes of procedure which had been brought from the Continent, and were founded on the civil law. See Amos, Hist. and Princ. of the Civil Law, p. 448; Selden, Ad Fletam, ch. ix. § 3.

[3] Selden, Ad Fletam, ch. iv. § 1.

[4] Selden, Ad Fletam, ch. vii. § 1; Amos, Hist. and Princ. of the Civil Law, pp. 443, 444.

[5] Selden, Ad Fletam, ch. viii. § 3.

ters that concerned the church.[1] These tribunals were kept within bounds by the writ of prohibition, which was unsparingly used by the King's Bench; but the remark is not applicable to the Court of Chancery, which, in its turn controlling the common law courts by enjoining their suitors, and building alike on the civil and on the common law, founded a system unparalleled for breadth, rectitude, and wisdom, and that should be cherished as a valuable part of our inheritance.

We can therefore readily understand why Bracton, writing in the reign of Henry III., and before the consolidation of the English nation which took place under his successor, should give an erroneous impression of the importance of the civil law as a factor in the development of English jurisprudence. His work is an attempt to harmonize doctrines which had little in common that may not be found in all systems of jurisprudence in the earlier stages of their growth.

Delivery is the earliest and generally received mode of passing the title to real or personal property, and if it was essential to the completion of a gift or sale among the Anglo-Normans, as formerly at Rome, and livery of seisin may be likened to mancipation, the feudal is not therefore necessarily to be regarded as founded on Roman law. Assent did not, save exceptionally, impose an obligation under either system independently of form; but the forms were not analogous, and the maxim *ex nudo pacto non oritur actio* was adopted by the Anglo-Norman jurists as the expression of an existing fact, and certainly was not the source of a rule which originated in the needs and manners of the times.

Bracton might well refer to the Institutes for the definition of justice[2] and of jurisprudence,[3] and for the distinction between natural and legal rights, and civil and prætorian obligations;[4] but when he cites the Roman prohibition of nuptial donations as not only invalidating such gifts in England even when made through a third person, but precluding a

1 Selden, Ad Fletam, ch. viii. § 5.

2 Bracton, i. 13 (§ 2, f. 2 b).

3 Bracton, i. 19 (§ 4, f. 3).

4 Bracton, i. 233 (f. 29 b).

man from settling property on his intended wife, save under a constitution of Justinian where the amount did not exceed the third to which she would be entitled as dower,[1] he treats the Roman law as having a force which it did not possess in his age or subsequently. It was not requisite, as Güterbock supposes, to look to a past age for an explanation that lay near at hand.[2] The rule depended on the incorporation of husband and wife in one person, which rendered them technically incapable of conveying to or contracting with each other, and the policy of the feudal law which discouraged any alienation tending to impair the ability of the tenant to fulfil his duty to his lord.[3] Such resemblances are superficial, and do not indicate community of origin, or that the common servilely followed the Roman law.

Bracton not only fails to note the differences between the Roman and English law, but treats them as alike where no such similarity exists. It would be difficult for the most careful student to discover from his treatment that lands and chattels, which stood on the same plane as regards gift sale, and succession at Rome, were as they still are, separated by so wide an interval in England, that an English lawyer can hardly conceive of them as belonging to the same category. A sale was not when he wrote, binding merely *ex consensu*, nor unless reduced to writing and perfected by delivery; and yet his chapter on obligations would convey the idea that the consensual contracts of the Roman law were recognized in England,[4] and it is only on looking under another head that we find that an oral sale was invalid, and left the parties free to act as they thought proper.[5] So a reader who had no other source of information would infer that the *stipulatio* was in use in the reign of Henry II.,[6]

[1] Bracton, i. 233 (f. 29 b). [2] Güterbock, Bracton, p. 110.

[3] "For this reason a man cannot grant anything to his wife, or enter into covenant with her: for the grant would be to suppose her separate existence; and to covenant with her would only be to covenant with himself." Bl. Com. i. 442.

[4] Bracton, ii. 119 (f. 100 b).

[5] Bracton, i. 489, 490; Güterbock, Bracton, p. 144.

[6] Bracton, i. 125 (§ 12, f. 15 b); ii. 111 (f. 99 b).

although it was practically unknown to English jurisprudence, which adopted only so much of the civil law as suited the actual condition of things. The formal interrogation and response of the contract *verbis* were no doubt practised in Britain under the Roman rule, and may have survived in Wales or Cornwall, but were as foreign to the Anglo-Saxons as was Latin or Welsh.[1] Bracton also states that "if it be written that some one has promised, it is the same as if a response had been made to a preceding interrogation,"[2] and "if a person write that he owes money to another, he will be bound, and cannot object that the money was not paid."[3] If this means that a writing under seal had the conclusive force in England which a stipulation or an entry in the creditor's books with the debtor's assent originally possessed at Rome, it is no doubt true although ambiguously expressed; but unexplained it gives an erroneous impression of the Roman law, which treated writings as merely *prima facie* evidence, and liable to be set aside on proof that they did not accurately set forth what had occurred. If as would appear, the contract *literis* was originally an exception and conclusive, it ceased to be so when the plea *non numeratæ pecuniæ* was recognized by the prætor as a defence.[4]

In like manner Bracton treats the Roman rule and a constitution of Justinian which gave the public the right of way along the banks of navigable rivers, and provided that no one should be shut out from access to the sea, as applicable in England. When, however, the question was judicially considered, this passage was cited and overruled, and the judges said in effect that the common law should be sought for in its books, and what was not found there could not be sustained on the authority of the Institutes or an imperial decree.[5]

[1] See Amos, Hist. and Princ. of the Civil Law, p. 444; Selden, Ad Fletam, ch. vii. § 1.

[2] See Institutes, 3. 19. 17.

[3] Bracton, ii. 117, 119 (§§ 8, 10, f. 100, 100 b).

[4] Institutes, Book. iii. 121; Sandars, Justinian, 439; Accarias, Nos. 498, 580, note b.

[5] Ball *v.* Herbert, 3 Term, 253; Blundell *v.* Catterall, 5 B. & Ald. 268.

Whatever doubt may exist as to the magnitude, there can be none as to the reality of the debt due from the English to the Roman law, nor of the benefit to be derived from reading the Institutes and the commentaries by which they have been elucidated in modern times. Complicated as are the problems which jurisprudence has to solve, they yet depend on fundamental principles which can be best understood by viewing them in various aspects and when clothed in different forms. A comparative study is therefore as essential to a scientific knowledge of the law as of anatomy or politics, and can nowhere be pursued to so much advantage as in contrasting the two great systems of jurisprudence which divide the world.

In such a study it seems preferable to begin with the Roman law, not only as being first in date, but because many of its doctrines were incorporated with English jurisprudence, or have been referred to in the courts as affording an illustration or analogy, and the ensuing chapters will therefore contain a summary of obligations *ex contractu* as they existed at Rome, and some account of the procedure through which they were enforced.

CHAPTER II.

THE FORMULARY SYSTEM.

The *jus civile.* — Formulary Procedure. — *Legis actiones.* — The Interdicts. — Roman Criminal Law.

The *jus civile* is literally the civic law or law peculiar to the state or city, and hence, as the authors of the Institutes observe, the laws of Draco or of Solon might properly be termed the civil law of Athens, although when a Roman spoke of the civil law he was to be understood as referring to the laws of Rome. It is in this sense that the term is now employed, as signifying the vast body of law which, expanding as Rome grew, was diffused throughout the Empire, and when that fell was adopted by the conquerors, and became the common law of France, Scotland, Germany, and Italy, and still prevails in those countries except where manifestly inapplicable or superseded by a code. The term *jus civile* had however a narrower meaning, in which it signified the rules and maxims constituting the unwritten or customary law and the statutes by which this was modified, as distinguished from the *jus prætorium* or *honorarium.* The latter was the fruit of a judicial legislation which, operating through a long series of years and not less wise than cautious, corrected the defects of the earlier law, and evolved a system which still excites the admiration of mankind. The *jus civile* and *jus prætorium* were in this sense contrasted as the common law and equity are in England, where the function of the chancellor was in many respects analogous to that of a Roman prætor. The Roman like the common law originated in usages or customs dating from an unknown antiquity and that might seem arbitrary or unsuited to the wants of an advancing civilization, but were long observed with an almost superstitious reverence. In entering into a contract or enforcing it by a suit, it was requisite to adhere rigidly to certain forms; and if they were not observed the agreement was invalid or the suit would fail.[1] We are told by Gaius that the *legis actiones* which were originally in use at Rome followed the letter of the law, and were as fixed as the laws themselves. One who sought to recover for the destruction of his vines and called them by that name, lost his cause, because the XII. Tables, which gave the remedy for such injuries spoke generally of trees.[2] These formularies, and indeed the whole body of the law, in default of writing or at a time when it was little used, were handed down traditionally among the governing class and were inaccessible to the plebeians who constituted the growing bulk of the inhabitants of Rome.

Among the many grievances which the plebeians bore with patience, and redressed with the steadfast moderation that characterized their long struggle for freedom, was the condition of the law, which was the science of the governing class and could only be administered on days that were lawful according to a calendar which they knew, and omens which they interpreted as they thought proper. If the XII. Tables were regarded as a boon of inestimable value, it was not solely for their intrinsic worth, but because they gave publicity to rules and maxims which had previously been the secret of a few. The ritual of procedure and the days on which the *comitia* could lawfully be convened or the magistrates sit for the transaction of public business, were still locked up in the breasts of the patricians; and it was not until the *dies fasti* and *nefasti* and the forms that were essential to the institution of a suit were published after the lapse of two hundred years, by the freedman and secretary of the blind Appius Claudius, who, though proudest among nobles, aimed at popularity, that the great body of the people could feel sure of their equality before the law.[3] It would be erroneous to suppose that the superstitions which were interwoven

[1] Gaius, c. iv. §§ 16, 21, 30. [2] Gaius, c. iv. § 11.

[3] Accarias, ii. No. 740; Amos, Hist. and Princ. of the Civil Law, p. 17.

with the politics and jurisprudence of Rome, were devised to hoodwink or control the masses. Though too often abused, they were long religiously observed by both patricians and plebeians, and as Cicero's treatise De Divinatione indicates were even in his age plausibly defended by believers against the scoffs of sceptics, who declared that two augurs could not look upon each other without laughing.

If we turn to the Norse law as administered in Iceland in the eleventh century, we shall find a similar state of things, and that the mistake of a syllable in the pleadings, in the names of the parties, or the summons by which the defendant was required to appear, might cause the failure of a just claim or the escape of a notorious offender. The English law was hardly less precise in making the fate of the cause depend on the conformity of the declaration to the original writ, and forbidding the slightest variance from the issue when the case came to be tried before a jury. It was a sufficient answer to an action for the breach of a contract that it was made in London and not as alleged, in Oxford;[1] and a variance as to time or amount was not less fatal, and could not after the record had been made up, be cured by an amendment. As society becomes refined and complex the rules and customs of a bygone age appear harsh and inequitable, and the ingenuity of the magistrate or lawgiver is taxed to remedy the defect. New rights arise for which there are no remedies, and an enlightened moral sense recognizes equities which have been ignored or disregarded. Such a transition occurred in Rome, and led to a reform which was in part accomplished by legislation, but to a much greater extent through the *jus prætorium*, which in the language of Papinian was introduced *adjuvandi vel supplendi vel corrigendi juris civilis gratia*, — to aid, supplement, or correct the municipal law; — and was consequently as I have observed, analogous to the jurisdiction of the Court of Chancery. At Rome both systems were administered by the same magistrate; but this difference has been to a great extent effaced in England and generally in the United States, through the operation of the

[1] Y. B. 19 Henry VI. 49.

statutes which confer equitable jurisdiction on the courts of common law.

The legal remedies given by the civil law in the earlier years of the Republic were five in number, — *sacramentum*, *judicis postulatio*, *condictio*, *manus injectio*, and *pignoris capio*,[1] and were known as the *legis actiones*, because they were given by the law and not by the prætor, or because they were cast in legal forms that must be closely followed.[2] The first derived its name from the *sacramentum* or stake, which was its distinctive feature, and seems to have been an ingenious means of substituting a wager of law for the primitive wager of battle. We may believe that the parties originally came ready for either alternative, and might, as in the English writ of right or appeal of murder, insist on the arbitrament of arms. In after years the preparations for combat became symbolical; the litigants grasped the object in dispute, each claimed it as his own by quiritary right, in a set form of words, and touched it with a wand which did duty for the lance of an earlier period. The prætor then commanded them to loose their hold. They obeyed, and each challenged the other to attest the justice of his cause by wagering a sum of money, which was known as the *sacramentum*, because it was deposited with the pontifex and forfeited by the loser to the service of the gods. The prætor then referred the cause to a tribunal styled the centumviri, and composed of citizens chosen by the various tribes, whose decision though nominally of the bet, was conclusive of the demand.[3] If the thing in dispute was insusceptible of transportation, part was brought into court to represent the whole, as, for instance, an oar or a yard arm in the case of a galley, a tile in that of a house, a turf or clod where the subject-matter was a farm. It was from this source that the English jurists derived the use of wagers as a means of bringing a legal controversy to a point, and they are still employed in Pennsylvania in interpleaders, or when a definite fact is in dispute, as, for instance, whether a judgment was confessed in fraud of creditors.

[1] Mackeldey, § 203.

[2] Gaius, c. iv. §§ 11, 12.

[3] Maynz, i. § 43, p. 491.

This method, as Maynz observes, is manifestly inapplicable when the question is one of amount or damages and cannot be answered by a simple Yes or No. A sum certain might be recovered by such means, or a horse, or slave, or farm, but not damages for an injury to real or personal property, or the non-performance of an executory agreement. So long as the *sacramentum* was the only remedy, as it originally seems to have been, contracts for the hire of lands, goods, or services, to build or let, were nugatory, because there was no way in which they could be enforced.

The *sacramentum* was presumably coeval with the *mancipatio* and *stipulatio*, and like them the offspring of an age when intention went for nothing unless clothed with customary or symbolical forms, and the jurisdiction of controversies between individuals that did not endanger the public peace depended on consent. The simulated combat, the wager and deposit of a sum of money, brought a dispute that would otherwise have been private within the scope of the law, and were an irrefragable proof of the agreement of the parties that the question should be referred to the appropriate tribunal, and that they would abide by the decision.

The *judicis postulatio* was introduced or sanctioned by the XII. Tables to provide for cases where the demand was for damages or compensation, and was, as the name imports, a formal application to the prætor to refer the case to an arbiter or *judex*. This remedy had the advantage of enabling the parties to select an expert on whom they could rely, and the *lex Pinaria* subsequently provided that a *judex* might be substituted in the *sacramentum* for the centumviri. The *lex Silia and lex Calpurnia* carried the reform to its logical conclusion, in the fifth century before Christ, by giving a form of action, known as the *condictio*, through which a demand for a specific thing or sum certain might be referred to a judge without going through the cumbrous preliminary of the *sacramentum*.[1] The remaining *legis actiones* were in the nature of process rather than suits in the ordinary acceptance of the term. One who had been sentenced to pay a debt, and was

[1] Maynz, i. § 43, p. 494; Accarias, ii. No. 744.

in default, might be arrested by his creditor without legal process, and brought before the tribunal, where, as the matter had been already adjudged, he was not allowed to make defence in his own person, and unless some one came forward in his behalf and gave bail, was awarded to the creditor who might keep him in bonds for sixty days, and then, if the amount was not forthcoming, sell him into slavery beyond the Tiber.[1] This proceeding, known as the *manus injectio*, was an execution rather than a suit, and may be likened to the *scire facias quare executionem non* of the common law.

The *pignoris capio* was analogous to the common-law distress, by which the holder of certain privileged claims, as, for instance, a collector of the revenue or soldier whose pay was in arrear might seize the property of the defaulter and detain it as a pledge.[2]

Notwithstanding the reform worked by the *lex Silia* and *lex Calpurnia* the *legis actiones* were subject to delays, and so technical that, as we are informed by Gaius, he who failed in a syllable lost his cause. It was moreover essential that both parties should be Roman citizens; and no claim or defence could be admitted that was not in accordance with the strict letter of the civil law.[3] Such a state of things was intolerable in a city whose streets were thronged with persons who, though born in Italy, had no rights under the Roman law, and led (A. U. C. 508) to the appointment of a prætor peregrinus to administer justice among aliens, or where either party was not a Roman citizen.

The new magistrate could hardly take a single step in the performance of his onerous task consistently with the technical requirements of the civil law, and had to choose between disregarding them overtly and evading them by a legal fiction, or rather directing the *judex* to decide as if the obstacle which lay in the path of justice did not exist. If, for instance, the defendant in a suit to recover compensation for the theft of a cup proved to be an alien, the formula or instruction transmitted to the judge would run as follows: "If it appear

[1] Accarias, ii. No. 745.
[2] Accarias, ii. No. 746.
[3] Accarias, ii. No. 748.

that Herenæus was a party or privy to the theft of a gold cup belonging to Titius, for which if he were a Roman citizen he would be answerable in damages, then condemn him for the penalty due in such a case."

When once this method of reaching the merits of a cause without regard to technicalities had become familiar in suits where one or more of the parties were aliens, it would naturally be applied where both parties were citizens; and as the *legis actiones* did not readily admit of such an adaptation, they were abrogated in the first and second centuries B. C., by laws which authorized the submission of the case to a *judex* without the formal steps which had previously been indispensable.

The formulas by which the cause was put at issue and submitted to the *judex* were flexible, and might be moulded into any shape that was requisite to surmount technical obstacles, but the end was generally attained by requiring the judgment to be entered on a given state of facts, or as if a fact existed that would obviate the objection and leave the way open for a decision on the merits.

One who acquired a slave or other *res mancipi* by a sale or gift attended with delivery, was in the position which a buyer who pays the price and goes into possession of land without a deed holds under our system, and could no more maintain a *sacramentum* or *condictio* than such a buyer can recover in an ejectment or writ of entry. Such an equitable title might, however, be perfected at Rome by a year's usucapion, or adverse possession, as against every one who did not show a better right; and hence if the slave in the case above supposed was wrongfully taken from the buyer before the year was out, the *judex* was instructed that if the man who had been so bought and delivered, would, had he been possessed by the purchaser for a year, have been his according to the quiritary law, judgment should be rendered in his favor.[1]

The strictness of the common law was mitigated by like devices in England where the action of trover and conversion is based on a pretended finding, and the rule that the trial must take place before a jury of the neighborhood where the

[1] Poste, p. 429; Gaius, c. iv. § 36; Maynz, i. No. 125, p. 225.

cause of action originated is evaded as regards transitory suits, by the transparent pretence that the place where the contract was made or tort committed, perchance Minorca or Paris, was in the town or county whence the jury is summoned for the trial.[1] Fiction so used is simply a pious fraud devised for the attainment of truth, and bears out the maxim, *in fictione juris, semper existit æquitas.*

Fiction was not the only means through which the prætor mitigated the rigor of the civil law; and when the plaintiff was equitably though not legally entitled to relief, supposing his complaint to be true, the *judex* was instructed to render judgment in his favor, if the facts as set forth in the formula were sustained by the proofs. Such a formula was styled *in factum*, while one which left the case open for decision was said to be *in jus.*[2]

The difference was that in the former the prætor ruled the law beforehand, except in so far as it was necessarily involved in the points submitted to the judge, while the judge might in the latter find that the complaint was true in fact, and decide it adversely on the law.

According to Gaius, the formula was said to be *in jus* when the plaintiff's claim was based on the principles of the civil, as distinguished from the prætorian law, and *in factum* when he relied on equities growing out of the facts, and the *judex* was directed to decide in his favor if these were proved.[3]

Gaius illustrates the distinction by typical instances. The following formula was one of law. "Whereas Aulus Agerius deposited a silver table with Numerius Negidius, which is the matter in dispute. Whatever Numerius Negidius ought on that account in good faith to give or render to Aulus Agerius, to that do thou, Judge, condemn Numerius Negidius to make restitution; if it does not so appear, acquit."[4]

A formula framed as follows was one of fact. "Let Octa-

[1] See Y. B. 19 Henry VI. 49; Mostyn *v.* Fabrigas, Cowper, 161; 1 Sm. L. C. 8 Am. ed. 1040, 1053.

[2] Gaius, c. iv. §§ 45, 46; Poste, p. 436; Mackeldey, § 204.

[3] Gaius, c. iv. §§ 45, 46.

[4] Gaius, c. iv. § 47.

vius be the judge. If it appears that Aulus Ægerius deposited a silver table with Numerius Egidius, and that through the fraud of Numerius Egidius it was not restored to Aulus Ægerius, do thou, Judge, condemn Numerius Egidius to pay Aulus Ægerius as much money as the table is worth; if it does not appear, acquit."[1]

The first of the above forms was *in jus*, because the deposit of the table was set forth as a conceded fact, and the judge was left to draw the inference according to the rules of law and evidence. In the second, two questions of fact were submitted: Had the table been deposited? Was it withheld by fraud? and if both were decided favorably to the plaintiff, he was to have judgment. The formula was consequently said to be *in factum*. It is, notwithstanding, obvious that both formulas presented a mixed question of fact and law, depending on whether the defendant was chargeable with the misconduct or gross negligence which rendered a depositary answerable under the Roman law; and the difference would seem to be that the case turned in the latter on two points: Did the defendant receive the table? Was the failure to return it fraudulent?

Another instance given by Gaius is obviously *in factum*, as making the judgment depend on whether a single thing had occurred, and leaving no discretion to the *judex*, save as to the sufficiency of the evidence. "If it appears that such a patron was summoned by such a freedman against the prætor's edict, do you, recuperators, condemn the freedman to pay ten thousand sesterces; if not, acquit him."[2]

The formula consisted ordinarily of three several parts, each having an appropriate use,—the *demonstratio*, which pointed out the subject-matter (in the instance given above, the bailment or deposit of a silver table); the *intentio*, which set forth the plaintiff's demand (which was, as there stated, for whatever the defendant ought to pay or render, unless the table was restored); and, finally, the *condemnatio*, or sentence to be pronounced, if the case terminated in the plaintiff's favor.

[1] Gaius, c. iv. § 47.

[2] Gaius, c. iv. § 45.

We have seen that compensation in damages could not be recovered in the *sacramentum*, which could only be employed where the demand was for a sum certain or a specific thing. The formulary method might appear to go to the opposite extreme, because it afforded no remedy answering to an ejectment, or replevin, or bill for specific performance, and the judgment was pecuniary for the value of the property wrongfully taken or withheld. Even when the suit was for a farm, a slave, a garment, or a gold or silver vessel, the recovery was not of the property itself, but of as much money as it was worth.[1] The ends of justice might, nevertheless, be attained by ordering the defendant to pay more than the value unless he made restitution; and in the course of time the prætor compelled a surrender, or put the plaintiff in possession.

A suit was instituted at Rome, not as with us by a summons from the court, but through a notification by the plaintiff (*vocatio in jus*), which made it incumbent on the defendant to go with the plaintiff before the prætor, to send some responsible person to represent him, or to give security for his appearance at a future day. If he took none of these steps he might be seized and brought by force; but a judgment could not be entered by default for want of an appearance until both parties were in court personally, or through their duly authorized representatives.[2] The plaintiff then

[1] Gaius, c. iv. § 48.

[2] Accarias, ii. Nos. 749, 750. If the defendant was contumacious the plaintiff asked a bystander to attest what had occurred, and if he consented, haled the defendant before the prætor, followed by the witness, who could testify that it was necessary to have recourse to force. Such scenes were of frequent occurrence in a capital where every man was his own sheriff's officer, and are amusingly portrayed by Horace, in the lines which recount his deliverance from the bore who was talking him to death.

> "Casu venit obvius illi
> Adversarius, et, 'Quo tu, turpissime?' magna
> Inclamat voce, et 'Licet antestari?' Ego vero
> Oppono auriculam. Rapit in jus; clamor utrimque,
> Undique concursus. Sic me servavit Apollo."

It is surprising that a practice which was obviously a survival from the period when men took justice into their own hands, and calculated

laid his claim before the prætor, who considered whether it came within the strict rules of the civil law, or presented equities that could not be disregarded consistently with justice. If his opinion was adverse, the case was dismissed; if favorable, it became his duty to hear the other side. If the defendant admitted the plaintiff's allegations, and made no counter-statement that was valid technically, or according to the more liberal view of the *jus honorarium*, the claim was regarded as confessed, and the prætor proceeded forthwith to a decree.[1] The defendant might, however, allege some matter that would avoid the plaintiff's demand, even if the facts which it set forth were true, — as, for instance, failure of consideration, or that judgment had been rendered for the same matter in a former suit, — and the prætor would then have to determine whether such a defence was so far good that an inquiry should be made as to its truth. It was accordingly during these preliminary steps that the questions which are debated under our practice on a demurrer to the plea or declaration, arose in a less formal way, which may be likened to that taken to evolve the issue in England while the pleadings were still oral.[2] Both parties might concede that the allegations on either side were well-founded in fact, and argue the question simply as one of law, and the case would then presumably be decided on that basis without the intervention of a *judex*. Such a result is not common under our system or in any age, and the parties, no doubt, usually preferred then, as they do now, to have the case decided in the light of the evidence, and not on abstract legal principles.

When this stage had been reached a formula was drawn up embracing the points made on either side, and which the prætor deemed material, and the name of the person to whom the case was referred for adjudication. One judge only was appointed in the same cause; but if one or all of the parties were aliens, the controversy was referred to three or more

to lead to breaches of the peace, should have been tolerated in the Augustan age. Compare Matthew v. 25, which seems, however, to refer to the *injectio manus*.

[1] Maynz, i. §§ 35, 44, 47. [2] Gaius, c. iv. §§ 115–129; Poste, p. 481.

persons known as *recuperators*.[1] The custom originated far back in the history of the republic in a treaty with the Latins, and was subsequently extended to other foreign states. The function of the *recuperator* is not accurately known, and this may also be said of the arbiters who were sometimes appointed instead of a *judex*, except that they were clothed with the larger powers.[2]

It was the privilege of the Roman to choose his judge, or at all events that his cause should not be tried by a man whom he regarded as incompetent or partial.[3] The plaintiff nominated; but the defendant might peremptorily object, and ask that some other name should be suggested. If, however, his opposition was carried beyond reasonable bounds, and intended for delay, the case might be treated as undefended, or a judge chosen by lot or designated by the prætor.[4] Agreeably to Accarias, the parties might by mutual consent select any one whom they preferred as judge, and it was only when they disagreed that the choice was restricted to the official list.[5]

When the formula was settled or agreed on, the judge chosen, and the appointment officially announced, the parties signified their assent by calling on the bystanders to witness their assent; and this act, which was known as the *litis contestatio*, and may be likened to the similiter or joinder in issue of the common law, brought the proceeding before the magistrate (*in jure*) to a close.[6] The cause was then at the appointed time formally laid before the judge, who heard the evidence and argument, and proceeded to a decree, which was always for a fixed sum; although, when the suit was for the recovery of land or chattels, he might give the defendant the alternative of making restitution or paying a larger amount than the property was worth.[7]

The sentence resembled the award of an arbitrator rather

[1] Accarias, ii. No. 737.
[2] Maynz, i. § 100; Accarias, ii. No. 737.
[3] Accarias, ii. No. 737.
[4] Accarias, ii. No. 738.
[5] Accarias, ii. No. 737.
[6] Maynz, i. §§ 47, 54; Accarias, ii. No. 764.
[7] Institutes, 4. 6. 31; Gaius, c. iv. §§ 47, 48, 52; Poste, p. 439.

than a judgment as we now understand the term, because the *judex* was a private citizen, and could not enforce his decree. The right of proceeding to execution consequently devolved on the plaintiff, who arrested the defendant without legal process and brought him before the prætor, where he was not allowed to make defence in person, and unless some one appeared for him and gave bail was delivered to the creditor. His right to freedom, and even to life, thenceforth depended on his ability to pay. He was kept in bonds; and if the debt was not discharged within sixty days might be put to death or sold into slavery beyond the Tiber. Such was the rule as laid down in the XII. Tables; and it was further provided, with a cruel exactitude which anticipated and overruled the point made for the defence in "The Merchant of Venice," that where there were several creditors the debtor might be hewn in pieces and divided among all, and that no one of them should be answerable for cutting more than his share. Such a dividend might have a substantial value in the Fiji Islands or on the coast of New Guinea, but the motive at Rome presumably was to enable each creditor to compel payment through the fear of death, although the others might be inclined to mercy, or to compound the debt.[1]

This right of arrest or *manus injectio* continued in force after the abrogation of the *legis actiones*, and might be exercised without the close adhesion to forms that were originally indispensable. Laws were subsequently passed authorizing the seizure of the debtor's goods and land; and an assignment or sale for the benefit of creditors, under a proceeding analogous to a decree in bankruptcy,[2] was substituted for the incarceration which might gratify vindictive feeling, but could answer no good end.

A like change has been made in England and the United States during the last century, and occurs in the annals of most nations as they advance in civilization and come to regard insolvency as a misfortune rather than a crime.

The common law originally sought to reduce the controversy to a single point of fact or law; and this method, which

[1] Accarias, ii. No. 745. [2] Gaius, c. iv. § 78; Poste, pp. 278, 281.

though logically sound, was objectionable as tending to entangle the cause in the meshes of special pleading, and had fallen into disuse, was revived by the "Rules of Hilary Term," some fifty years ago. Agreeably to the practice which prevailed in England at the beginning of the century, and is still followed in Pennsylvania, the great majority of causes are tried under a broad traverse which puts the entire case at issue, attended if the defendant thinks proper, with a collateral plea in confession and avoidance, — as, for instance, a release, or an accord and satisfaction. Actions on sealed instruments and judgments obey a somewhat different rule; but a like result is attained by concurrent pleas, which together cover the whole ground, and render it incumbent on the plaintiff to make out his case, while leaving the defendant free to show that even if the demand was originally just it has been released or satisfied.

Such was also virtually the result at Rome, where the matter alleged by way of confession and avoidance was known as an *exceptio*, and was embodied in the formula prepared for the guidance of the *judex*. Thus in an action on a stipulation, the direction to condemn on proof of the formal question and response might be accompanied with the qualification,—"if the plaintiff did not act fraudulently,"[1] or if the suit was on an entry charging the defendant with money lent to him or expended on his behalf, unless it appeared that the money was never paid out. The exception might be met with a reply which rendered it unavailing, as, for instance, where the defendant alleged a promise to forgive the debt, the judge might also be directed to inquire whether the defendant did not subsequently agree that it should revive, *si non postea conveniret ut eam pecuniam petere liceret*. The *exceptio* answered to a plea in confession and avoidance, while the *replicatio* is obviously analogous to the modern replication.

It was not requisite that a legal defence should be embodied or set forth in the instruction given to the judge, because he might take cognizance of it under his general authority to try the cause; and hence an *acceptilatio* or formal acknowledgment

[1] *Si in ea re nihil dolo malo factum sit.* Gaius, c. iv. § 119.

that a stipulation had been fulfilled, which answered to the common-law release under seal, might be proved in a suit on a verbal contract, although it was not mentioned in the formula. The *judex* could not, however, take notice of an equitable defence, as for instance fraud, or, where the contract arose *literis*, that the consideration had not been paid, in the absence of an explicit authority to that effect, save in actions *bonæ fidei*, where the mere fact of claiming more than was justly due showed that the plaintiff was wanting in the good faith which was essential to success in such a suit. There is a close analogy between this rule and that which prevails under the common counts of the present day, where everything save a former recovery, which shows that the debt did not exist at the time of action brought, is admissible under *non assumpsit*.

As the *judex* was not a magistrate, and exercised a merely delegated power, he was bound by the letter of the formula even when it was manifestly erroneous, and the effect of leaving the mistake uncorrected was to sacrifice the merits of the cause, and lead to a result that was manifestly unjust or absurd.[1] Hence, where the *intentio* claimed twenty golden pieces, and only nineteen were due, or demanded Falernian wine where the contract was for some other vintage, the issue could not be amended in accordance with the proofs, and a judgment was rendered for the defendant, which was not only conclusive of the existing suit, but debarred the plaintiff from bringing another action in proper form. So, if the stipulation was to pay ten thousand sesterces or render the slave Stichus, and the complainant demanded either, instead of giving the defendant the alternative, there was a fatal variance, or as it was technically termed *plus petitio*, and a subsequent action for the same cause on the same contract might be met by a plea of *res adjudicata*.[2] A false *demonstratio* was equally prejudicial in the existing suit, but did not preclude the plaintiff from bringing another action, because under these circumstances the cause was not actually before the court; and this seems to be the origin of the maxim *falsa demonstratio non nocet*, which is now frequently employed in another sense.

[1] Accarias, ii. No. 775.

[2] Institutes, 4. 6. 34; Gaius, c. iv. §§ 52, 53.

The stringency of this rule was relaxed by the Emperor Zeno after the abolition of the formulary system, and still further by Justinian, but without allowing the freedom of amendment which is perhaps carried to an extreme at the present day.[1]

Such was the course of procedure in common use to obtain compensation for wrongs already done, or protect rights which would not suffer by delay; but there are cases where the march of justice must be accelerated to prevent a threatened injury, or restore the balance which has been wrongfully disturbed. Such an instance occurred when a claimant sought to obtain possession by violence instead of using the remedies prescribed by law, or where a public right was infringed by obstructing a highway or navigable stream, and the prætor might then summarily command the defendant to refrain, or enforce restitution if the wrong had been already done.[2]

Interdicts, as classified by Gaius and in the Institutes, were restitutory, exhibitory, or prohibitory; that is, for restitution, production, or abstention;[3] although some interdicts might serve either as a means of maintaining the existing status, or restoring it when disturbed. Interdicts took different forms, and were adapted to the various instances in which a summary or preventive remedy was requisite; but two of them deserve notice as showing the nicety with which the Roman jurists suited the action to the case. These technically known *uti possidetis* and *utrubi*, related one to immovables and the other to movables, but both, though differing in some particulars, were substantially the same, and directed to like ends. An allegation that the defendant had wrongfully dispossessed the plaintiff, or was about so to dispossess him, might be admitted, or might be met by a counter charge that the wrong lay at the plaintiff's door, and that he and not the defendant was using undue means. In the former case, the defendant would be ordered to make restitution, and abstain from further injury. In the latter, the prætor made an order

[1] Institutes, 4. 6. 34, 35.

[2] Institutes, 4. 15. 4, 7.

[3] Gaius, c. iv. §§ 139, 140; Institutes, 4. 15. 1.

which, in the case of immovables, was as follows: *Uti nunc nec vi nec clam nec precario alter ab altero possidetis quo minus ita possidetis vim fieri veto,* — "whichever of you is in possession without having obtained it violently, clandestinely, or by permission from the other, I forbid his possession to be disturbed by force." Such also was the edict as to movables, save that the question was as to which party was in possession during the greater part of the preceding year *nec vi nec clam nec precario.*[1]

Such interdicts were termed double, as involving the question which party was entitled to the benefit of the decree, and as the inquiry was one of fact and could not consistently be determined by a magistrate, the parties wagered a sum to be forfeited by him who proved to be in the wrong, and the property was then delivered to whichever bid highest for the privilege of possession until the termination of the suit, and gave security for payment if he lost the cause. The controversy was then referred to a judge, whose duty was to decide against him who held contrary to the interdict, that is, by force, secretly, or by permission. The stakes were then awarded to the successful party, while the other was condemned, if he held or retained possession as the highest bidder, to pay the sum which he had agreed to give for the privilege, and to surrender the property together with its fruits or income while in his hands. If this ingeniously contrived mechanism might enable a rich litigant temporarily to dispossess an adversary whose means were inferior to his own, it rendered such a measure too costly to be adopted readily by any one who did not feel secure of the goodness of his cause, and insured an ample indemnity to the party whom he wronged.[2]

The interdict of the Roman is obviously analogous to the injunction of the English law, though covering less ground in some directions, and extending further in others. The main object in both systems is to prevent irreparable injury, or to

[1] Gaius, c. iv. § 150; Accarias, ii. Nos. 965, 968; Poste, p. 505.

[2] Accarias, ii. Nos. 965–968; Gaius, c. iv. §§ 166, 167; Sandars' Justinian, 4. 15. 8, note.

maintain the existing *status* until the right can be determined in due course of law.

The prætor might, however, not only direct that an act should be refrained from, but that it should be performed, as, for instance, the production of a slave or freeman who was unlawfully detained, or that a child should be returned to its father.[1] Such an order had the effect of a *habeas corpus* or *mandamus* rather than an injunction. One who had been ejected by force or fraud might be reinstated without pausing to inquire which party had the title, although such relief would not be afforded if the complainant had acquired the possession which he sought to regain by dispossessing the defendant forcibly or surreptitiously, nor where he had entered with his permission and held over wrongfully.[2]

The Roman criminal law was extremely crude; and acts which are now regarded as offences against the community and visited with imprisonment, were viewed as private wrongs with which the State had no concern, and that simply entitled the injured party to a compensation in excess of the pecuniary loss that might operate as a penalty, but which he was entitled to forego if he thought proper.[3] Theft, robbery and injuries to the person were within this category, and gave rise to obligations that were classed with those arising *ex contractu*, and might be enforced by a suit instituted before the prætor and referred to a single *judex*.[4] On the other hand, offences that threatened the existence of the state or were peculiarly dangerous to the general welfare, as, for instance, treason, deliberate murder, incendiarism, the seduction of a wife or maiden, or even the theft of crops lying ungathered in the fields, were viewed as fit subjects for public justice, and punishable in most instances with death. Such at least was the rule under the monarchy, and in the earlier days of the republic; but the accused might, as did Cicero, Milo and Verres, escape prosecution or evade sentence by a voluntary exile.[5]

[1] Institutes, 4. 15; Gaius, c. iv. § 140; Poste, p. 499, note.

[2] Gaius, c. iv. § 154; Poste, p. 512.

[3] Mommsen, i. 207; Maynz, i. Nos. 17–19, pp. 53–59.

[4] Gaius, §§ 183–209.

[5] Maynz, i. No. 95, p. 182.

This alternative involved no great hardship so long as it was possible for the fugitive to eat figs at Marseilles, or sup with Cleopatra at Alexandria, but assumed a different aspect when the empire became coextensive with the civilized world, and no secure or tolerable refuge could be found without its pale.

Historians differ as to the administration of justice in Rome during the regal period, and while some maintain that it devolved in the last resort on the people,[1] others like Mommsen are not less clear that it was vested exclusively in the king, and that the accused could not appeal to the *comitia* even when the penalty was death.[2]

The inquiry is the more difficult because it is conceded that the king or magistrate made a preliminary investigation and might condemn; and the doubt is whether his sentence was final when the offence was civil, and not against military discipline or martial law. Moreover, it does not follow that the jurisdiction of the king or people was throughout the same; and the right of appeal may have become impracticable or been temporarily withheld during the period of unknown duration which preceded the establishment of the Republic, and amidst the political dissensions which, notwithstanding the Servian reform, enabled the younger Tarquin to subjugate both orders and exercise a despotic rule. When it is considered that the *comitia* were thoroughly organized and frequently convened; that they were the same men who formed the strength of the army when in the field; that the kings did not derive their title by descent, and had no regular or mercenary force that could overawe a people who were at once citizens and warriors,—we may believe that the popular assemblies of the Romans like those of the Teutonic tribes, were always entitled as of right to share in the making and administration of the laws. Such an inference is the more probable because the commentators agree that the authority of the kings devolved on the consuls, with little change save that arising from the limitation of the office to a year and the liability to impeachment when the term expired; and yet it is as generally conceded that these magistrates could not con-

[1] Maynz, i. No. 20, pp. 59, 60. [2] Mommsen, i. 203.

demn a Roman citizen to death, and that the jurisdiction in capital cases lay with the *comitia centuriata*, while minor offences were subsequently prosecuted by the tribunes of the people before the assembled tribes.[1]

The duty of taking the preliminary steps for the discovery of such crimes as from their magnitude concerned the state, was practically discharged in accordance with a long established usage by magistrates known as quæstors, that is, seekers or trackers, who laid the accusation before the *comitia centuriata*, where the case was duly heard, and decided by the popular voice. This simple machinery might suffice for the government of a city; but proved inadequate when Rome extended her dominion at the close of the third Punic war to lands beyond the Alps and sea, and standing commissions were established for the trial of the grave offences, including the extortion, venality, and embezzlement which were then rife among public men in the provinces if not at Rome. The members of these tribunals, though addressed as *judices*, had no official station, and, like the Athenian dicasts and the English jurors, were taken from private life for the trial of such cases as might be brought before them in due course of law. The number of the *judices* varied at different periods and with the nature of the offence, from thirty-two to one hundred, and, if reduced by the challenges on either side was filled up with others taken from the official list.

The prosecution might, as it would seem, be instituted at the instance of the *comitia* or the senate, but the charge was ordinarily made by a private person as in England or the United States. The prosecutor laid the case attested by his oath before the prætor, who considered whether the allegations constituted an offence against the law; and might, where, as in the noted case of Verres, two persons presented the same charge order a preliminary inquiry as to which should proceed. When these preliminaries had been settled, the cause was placed on the trial list of the appropriate court, and a day fixed for the hearing. The prætor presided personally or through a delegate, but as it would seem with-

[1] Maynz, i. Nos. 90, 91, pp. 162–167.

out power to regulate the admission of evidence, declare the law, or confine the advocates to the facts in proof; and the decision was, from these causes, and because the jurors were frequently of the same class as the accused, influenced by baseless allegations, or sympathy for an offender whose case might one day be their own. Each *judex* returned his verdict separately on a tablet which he dropped into an urn, and the ballots were then counted by the presiding magistrate, who declared the result, and if it was unfavorable to the accused, pronounced the sentence which was not left to his discretion but prescribed by law. Unanimity was not requisite, and a majority of all the votes sufficed to condemn; but a *judex* might, as in civil cases, vote *non liquet* — "it doth not appear;" and the Scotch verdict of "not proven" may have been borrowed from this source.

It was a natural consequence of such a system that the nobles who sat as jurors at Rome were no more trustworthy than the dicasts who administered justice at Athens for their daily bread, and gave judgment as self-interest, class prejudice, and the passions of the hour dictated, or in obedience to irrelevant or calumnious suggestions as to the character or past conduct of the accused, or, it might be, of his relatives or friends. The times were exceptional, and full of such temptations as have never beset any other people, unless a parallel can be found in the English conquest in India or that of the New World by Spain.

Notwithstanding the manifold defects of the tribunals known as the *quæstiones perpetuæ*, they savored too much of freedom to be viewed favorably by a despotic government, and their authority was circumscribed under the emperors, and finally abrogated. Augustus conferred the jurisdiction of treason and breaches of public trust on the senate; and the city prefect was finally authorized by Severus to take cognizance of all offences committed in the capital, or within a circuit of a hundred miles; and this edict, followed by another from Diocletian, which worked a like change in civil cases, brought jury trials to a close in the ancient world, fortunately to be revived in a better and more enduring form in England, and the free communities which she has disseminated throughout the globe. By a natural sequence the lenity which had been the boast of the Republic, gave place to a more stringent rule, and criminal offences, including theft, were punished by death, exile, or condemnation to hard labor in the mines.[1]

[1] Maynz, i. Nos. 154, 165, pp. 253, 265.

CHAPTER III.

JUSTINIAN'S LEGISLATION.

Defects of the Formulary System. — The Jurisconsults. — *Responsa prudentum.* — Treatises. — The Code. — The Digest. — The Institutes.

ENGLISH jurisprudence affords no exact analogue to the Roman *judex*, who may be likened to a juror, a master in Chancery, or a referee, and the difficulty of giving a just description of his office is greater because it varied at different periods, and was not the same in criminal as in civil procedure. The method taken to frame an issue at Westminster and send it for trial before a judge holding a court of *nisi prius*, bears a strong resemblance to that by which the vital question was educed by the prætor and submitted to the *judex*, who, like the juror, was chosen, not to administer the law generally, but in the particular cause, and like him also, did not consider the whole controversy, but only the specific formula or issue. His peculiar province was the determination of the facts,[1] and, if he was also required, to apply the law. This occurs whenever a jury is empanelled under a plea of not guilty or *non assumpsit.* The material difference is that while the jury are subordinate to the court, and must take the law from the presiding judge, the prætor framed the issue, but left it absolutely to the *judex.* Moreover, the decision of the *judex* was conclusive, and did not, like a verdict, require to be sanctioned by the entry of a judgment — a difference which was less considerable during the earlier periods of English law, and before the practice of granting new trials. We may, on the whole, believe that the intervention of the *judex* was a security against the abuse of magisterial power, especially in criminal cases where the *judices* sat collec-

[1] Maynz, i. No. 97, p. 187.

tively, and were not only judges of law and fact, but would seem to have been at liberty to receive such evidence as they thought proper.

There were three kinds of delegated judges in civil causes, designated respectively as *judex*, *arbitrator*, and *recuperator*. The *judices* were originally of senatorial rank; but the privilege was transferred to the knights, then divided between both orders, and Augustus finally admitted men of inferior degree. The list is said in his reign to have contained four thousand names, or about half the number that are annually put in the wheel from which jurors are drawn in Philadelphia.

When the circumstances or the nature of the case required the exercise of a larger discretion than that ordinarily conferred, the prætor might with the assent of both parties select such persons as he deemed best fitted from the community at large; and there might consequently be several arbiters,[1] although immemorial usage required that civil cases should be referred to a single judge. The recuperators might be even more numerous, and were, according to usage dating from a compact between Rome and the allied Latin towns, chosen from the whole body of the citizens for the determination of cases where one or more of the parties were aliens, and which consequently did not fall within the letter of the civil law.[2]

The *judex* could not refuse to serve, and was legally answerable for a plain mistake of fact or of law, although committed innocently and without an intention to defraud;[3] but the hardship was less than at first sight might appear, because he might return *non liquet*—"it is not clear," if he wished to avoid the responsibility of deciding a doubtful cause.

The function of the *judex* and the influence which it had on the development of the civil law, are eminently worthy of consideration. A judgment may be described as a conclusion from a legal syllogism. The question, Are such cases as that alleged entitled to redress? involves the major premise; Is this case such? the minor; and if both inquiries are answered

[1] Amos, Hist. and Princ. of the Civil Law, p. 188.

[2] Maynz, i. No. 101, pp. 193, 195.

[3] Gaius, c. iv. § 52; Poste, p. 441.

affirmatively, the judgment follows as a necessary inference. Both questions may be determined by the same person, or the former submitted to a judge learned in the law, and the latter to a popularly constituted tribunal, so that each shall operate as a check on the other, and no judgment can be pronounced unless both concur. Such was the method of the civil law, and it also prevails in England and the United States, where as at Rome, the verdict of the citizen is not less essential than the sanction of the court.

It results from what has been said that the formulary system and trial by jury have a common principle, although differently applied. The Roman method was probably better suited to the attainment of the ends of justice in each particular case than our own. The *judex* was ordinarily of senatorial or equestrian rank, presumably impartial as chosen by the parties, and from his education and intelligence more competent than the average juror to disentangle a complicated web of evidence, and view the facts in the light of principles. On the other hand, he did not come from the body of the county, or answer to the requirement of Magna Charta — that every man shall be tried by his peers; and a trial before an individual, however wise or learned, was less calculated to foster the sentiment of freedom than when twelve men are taken from the people to maintain the order which is essential to all, and be at the same time the guardians of private right.

The Roman institutions were nowhere more defective than in the inadequacy of the tribunals for the investigation and punishment of crime. The nice and complex mechanism which proved so effectual in civil cases, was inapplicable to the *judices* who sat for the trial of public wrongs with an uncontrolled dominion as regarded both the facts and the law, and if they did not, like the Athenian dicasts, condemn without sufficient cause, were too often members of a political ring and prepared to condone offences by which they profited. It was here that the want of a stable judiciary was painfully evident, and hastened the downfall of the republic. A strong and upright presiding judge may be unable to keep a venal or partial jury in the straight path, but he can so present the case in his charge as to render the unrighteousness of the verdict manifest, and awaken a public sentiment that will prevent a repetition of the offence. Rome was not, even in the declining years of the republic, wanting in men competent for the discharge of such an office; and in Horace's *justum et tenacem propositi virum*, we have an ideal portrait of a magistrate that may have been present to Papinian when meeting death at the hands of Caracalla rather than justify the emperor's murder of his brother; but political science was not sufficiently advanced to develop the idea that the judicial function should be kept distinct, and confided to men who are so placed as to be beyond the reach of intimidation and undue influence.

There are two extremes in the administration of justice: one to leave it to the popular voice, as expressed in an assembly of the citizens, or by persons taken from the community at large; the other, to place it in the hands of magistrates appointed by and representing the state.

If the former method is adopted, the law is fluctuating and uncertain, or bends to the prejudices or passions of the hour, while the judiciary may under the latter become instruments in the hands of the government, and sanction acts that endanger liberty or private rights. The true mean is to admit the citizen to such a share in application of legal principles as will afford an appeal to the common-sense and practical experience of every-day life.

Both extremes were experienced at Athens, where the decision of civil and criminal causes was at first exclusively intrusted to magistrates who, according to Mr. Grote, were not infrequently corrupt, arbitrary, or oppressive; and then to merely popular tribunals which construed the law as they thought proper, without being bound by the previous course of decision, and gave less heed to the evidence than to the plausible falsehoods, calumnies, and irrelevant statements of the advocates and parties. Notwithstanding Mr. Grote's able apology for the Athenian dikasteries, both methods would seem to have been equally objectionable, and the Romans were the first among civilized nations to adopt a method which, while giving the magistrate a sufficient measure of authority to maintain the stability of the law, left the duty of applying it to the facts to persons holding a private station, and therefore free from official bias.

The use of such an admixture of the popular element in promoting even-handed justice is attested by the experience of England, where the contest for freedom was maintained from age to age in the House of Commons and the jury-box, and with hardly less risk than when the struggle took place in the field. There are few more moving episodes in forensic history than the trial of Sir Nicholas Throckmorton, before a hostile commission appointed by Queen Mary, as an accomplice in the gallant though ill-fated rising of Wyatt against the Spanish marriage, which was abhorrent to all classes of the English people. Denied the aid of counsel, of witnesses, of books, frowned on and browbeaten by the court, and baited by the attorney-general, Throckmorton made a manly and pathetic appeal to the hearts and consciences of the jurors, which resulted in an acquittal, although they knew that they might be visited by the Star Chamber with fine and imprisonment, as they actually were.[1]

So the London grand jury, in the succeeding century, dismissed the charges against Shaftesbury, who held the place in the popular heart that was subsequently filled by Wilkes, although they were compelled to deliberate before the judges in the hope that they would not venture to ignore the bill in such a presence. The news was received with shouts of joy in the city, but deeply wounded the king, who is said to have exclaimed that he was the last man in his dominions to get law or justice, and it was not until the court procured the election of sheriffs who were devoted to its interest, and could through their means pack the jury-box, that Shaftesbury was forced to seek safety in exile.[2]

[1] 1 State Trials, 870, 901.

[2] Cooke's Life of Shaftesbury, ii. 303, 315; 6 State Trials, 1171.

It is not less noteworthy that although the composition of the jury which in the following reign acquitted the Twelve Bishops was of the first

The State Trials afford frequent and painful proofs of the subserviency of too many of the English judges, and their readiness to favor the crown, at the expense of the accused; and although the Revolution of 1688 produced a marked improvement by giving the judiciary a firm tenure, the evil did not entirely disappear until the close of the last century, and would have been still greater had it been possible to proceed to judgment without a verdict.[1]

In the struggle which, with Wilkes as its pretext, was maintained under George III. against the oligarchical pretensions of the House of Commons and the royal prerogative, the cause of popular rights would have fared ill but for the juries; and it was owing to them, rather than to the courts, that the press became free, and the doors of the House of Commons were thrown open to the reporters. It is not therefore surprising that the English people regarded trial by jury with an almost superstitious reverence, and were intimately convinced that the chief end of the Constitution was to place twelve men in the jury-box.

It was, as we may believe, owing to a like distribution of the judicial function at Rome that magistrates chosen for a single year by a popular vote not only administered justice during successive centuries with wisdom and impartiality, but contributed largely to the growth of scientific jurisprudence. The prætor might dismiss the complaint, on the ground that even if the plaintiff's allegations were true he was not entitled to redress, or he might prescribe the issue which should be laid before the *judex;* but here his function ceased, and he neither heard the evidence nor determined whether it sustained the case. Moreover, his rejection of the demand resembled a non-suit in not being final, and did not forbid a renewed application to his successor in office. Little could ordinarily be gained by corrupting such a judge, and he was

importance to the designs of James, the only man who was in favor of conviction was the Court brewer, who is said to have complained that if he acquitted the bishops he should brew no more for the king, if he found them guilty the king would be his only customer.

[1] See the preface to the second edition of the State Trials.

more likely to win than to forfeit popular favor by a faithful discharge of his trust.

A system which tended to limit the power of the magistrate by referring the decision of both criminal and civil causes to a private judgment, was naturally obnoxious to a despotic government which sought to bring everything within its control, and could not be advantageously administered unless the community contained a sufficient number of men competent to act as *judices*.

When the empire declined, this condition could no longer be fulfilled, and at the close of the third century the provincial magistrates were directed by Diocletian to consider and determine all causes without referring them to a *judex*. Constantine made a like alteration in the course of procedure in Italy and at Rome, and the ancient method was entirely abrogated before Justinian assumed the purple.

The inquiry is an interesting one, as teaching that every system should be considered as a whole, and depends for success on the adjustment and combination of its parts. No sound thinker would argue from the results obtained at Rome, that election by a popular vote for a brief term of judicial office should be substituted for the appointment during good behavior as practised by our forefathers, and which is still the rule in the courts of the United States. The prætorship lay in the path of political preferment, and was sought for, not as the crown of a life devoted to the profession of the law, but as a stepping-stone to the consulship; and we should now be loath to confide our lives and fortunes to magistrates chosen for a year, and who accepted a place on the bench with a view to an ulterior object. No feature of the Roman system is more remote than this from the ideas of the present day, and there is none which seems so irreconcilable with the stable and impartial administration of justice.[1]

[1] The ill consequences that might have been anticipated followed during the last days of the republic, and the relaxation of public and private virtue, due to the extension of the Roman dominion. Politics when corrupt infect even the judgment-seat, and Verres, and men like him,

Various causes contributed to correct the ill effects that might have been anticipated from such a method, and render it on the whole conducive to good. Among these may be enumerated the training of the class from which the Roman magistrates were generally taken, and their honorable ambition to achieve distinction in the service of the state.

Rome, like England, presents the spectacle of an aristocracy resting upon a popular basis, and if the means by which power was attained were sometimes violent or corrupt, they were yet as a whole calculated to discipline the mind, and evoke the qualities that are essential in public life. It was a marked feature of the Roman system to unite functions which are now regarded as incompatible, and are intrusted to different hands. If the head of a patrician house was a soldier he was also a jurist, and sat with open doors at sunrise to receive those who sought his advice; and as his responses were not paid for or given solely in the interest of the client, they had a judicial weight which seldom belongs to the opinions of a lawyer in modern times.[1] A Roman who did not understand the laws of his country was disqualified for public life, and the same man was not infrequently distinguished both as a jurist and a commander. Trebatius passed from the practice of his profession to take a command under Cæsar in the Gallic war, while Cicero became the governor of a province and divided his official year between a campaign against the revolted mountain tribes and the administration of justice. So Cæsar found time, in the midst of the hazards and preoccupation of the struggle which ended in the subjugation of Gaul, to recross the Alps to Cisalpine Gaul and take his place in the tribunal; and seems to have

could not only pervert the prætorship to the basest uses, but might make their edicts retroactive, for the purpose of employing them as a means of extortion and illicit gain. Cicero in Verrem, Act. II. 41–46. In Cicero's oration for Quintius, the prætor is charged with having wrested the law to the prejudice of the defendant, and the *judex* warned against yielding to undue influence in terms that would hardly be tolerated in a modern tribunal.

[1] Accarias, i. No. 21.

been not less capable as an administrator and judge than as a general.

Such a training was eminently calculated to develop the sentiment that justice should be dispensed according to fixed principles. In entering office the prætor published a summary or exposition of the rules which he proposed to follow. This self-imposed restraint was known as the *edictum perpetuum*, in contradistinction to *edicta prout res incidit*,—or orders made with a view to a specific case. The phrase did not signify that the edict was unalterable or binding on his successors, but simply that it was a standing order like our rules of court. In theory, an entirely new edict might be issued every year; but the practice was different, because each magistrate naturally built on the ordinances of his predecessors with such emendations as experience suggested.

The practice seems to have originated with the prætor peregrinus, but was followed by the urban prætor, and wherever justice was administered by a Roman governor or magistrate with prætorian powers, and we can readily conceive how largely the effort to harmonize the rules and customs of the various provinces must have contributed to generate or strengthen the conception of a natural law common to all nations, and constituting the true basis of jurisprudence.[1]

The prætor was thus subject to two important checks,—one, that he had to look for principles to the ordinance which he had promulgated at the commencement of his term of office; the other, that he was obliged to refer the facts to a *judex* chosen by the parties, and whom he could not control. A venal and rapacious magistrate might disregard these restraints; and the accusation against Verres was twofold,—that his edict was so drawn as to facilitate extortion, and that it had been disregarded whenever it stood in his way.[2] It should, however, be remembered that Verres held office during a period of transition, while the republic was passing away and the empire had not yet arrived; and we cannot

[1] Arnold's Roman Provincial Administration, pp. 48, 50.

[2] Cicero in Verrem, Act. II. 41–46.

justly infer from his misconduct that the administration of justice was generally corrupt at Rome. Most nations have seasons that for good or evil are exceptional, and produce men of abnormal growth. No English judge save Jeffries even in the worst times left such a reputation as Verres, but we may find a parallel to his enormities in Sicily, in the invective of Burke and of Macaulay against Warren Hastings, although no two men would be more unlike in character and motives than the Englishman and the Roman.

It may however, be conceded that the strain during the last years of the republic was too much for human rectitude. In depriving Rome of the liberty which she denied to the provinces, Cæsar simply hastened a revolution that had become inevitable, and which temporarily ameliorated the condition of mankind as it certainly favored the development of jurisprudence. The energy which freedom had generated survived the fall of the republic, and found an ample field in the administration of the vast and varied empire,—which, stretching in every direction from the Mediterranean as a centre, embraced the entire civilized world and numerous semi-barbarous tribes. The men who have been reared under a free government are the same after a Cæsar has taken the place of a chief magistrate as they were previously, and may transmit their liberal sentiments to their offspring. It is in the third or fourth, rather than in the first generation that we must look for the fruits of a despotic change. Despite the havoc, the confiscations, and the wholesale assassination of the century that followed the outbreak of the Social War, the lettered classes at Rome held fast to philosophy and the cultivation of the law; and the restoration of order brought with it, in the necessity for reducing the various races of the empire to a common system, an opportunity for the practical application of such studies, which had never been known before, and will probably not occur again. It is not therefore surprising that although society felt the benumbing influence that attends absolute power, even when exercised for wise ends, the lamp of jurisprudence should have burned with a steady lustre until in the general decadence it was no longer fed. The law then ceased to be a living science, and the ancient world had during the residue of its allotted span, to depend on the accumulated labors of the past with little capacity to add to the store, and with a lessening ability to apply or fully comprehend.

If the formulary method had many advantages it was not free from serious defects which operated unfavorably on the development of jurisprudence. While the civil resembled the common law in calling the citizen to aid in the administration of justice, and making the result depend on his verdict, it did not provide that the trial should take place in the presence and under the supervision of a judge empowered to decide legal questions incident to the determination of the facts. The *judex* was not necessarily a jurist, but might yet have to determine questions of the first importance, and involving recondite legal principles that lay outside of the established rules of law, and were not to be found in any treatise.[1]

Fraud is eminently a question of law as well as fact; and yet if the controversy was whether a stipulation or conveyance had been obtained fraudulently, the prætor submitted the issue broadly, without defining what would be such a misrepresentation or artifice as would justify the equitable abrogation of a right that had been acquired in accordance with legal forms.[2] It is not surprising that the *judex* should, when thus left to his own resources, and without, as it would seem the power of appealing to the prætor for instructions, have hesitated as to the proper course; and his embarrassment would be the greater because he might be made personally answerable for rendering a judgment contrary to law, and could not rely on his good faith or ignorance as a defence.[3]

Litigants so placed would naturally seek to strengthen their cause by obtaining the opinions of some of the noted jurisconsults, who held a higher place at Rome than has ever been accorded to the legal profession in any other age or country; and if a Scævola or Sulpicius declared that the plaintiff's case

[1] Poste, p. 437.
[2] Gaius, c. iv. § 47; Maynz, i. No. 126, p. 227, note 27.
[3] Gaius, c. iv. § 52; Poste, p. 441.

was defective in fact or law, or that there was such fraud or failure of consideration as would constitute a defence, and no opinion of equal weight was thrown into the opposite scale, the judge would ordinarily incline to the side which was sustained by the greater weight of character, intellect, or learning. Such seems to have been the origin of the *responsa prudentum*, which had so large a share in moulding or developing the Roman law. Their influence was the greater because, as I have already intimated, there was little in the course of procedure at Rome, save it may be the imperial rescripts or decisions, that could be regarded as answering to the reasoned judgments of the English and American bench. No such opinions could well be delivered by the prætor, whose function ordinarily consisted in framing the issue for the judge, nor by the judge, who was not a magistrate or always learned in the law. The result was an almost entire inversion of what we now regard as the true relation between the administration and the practice of the law. There was no body of men at Rome set apart to hold the scales of justice and having the requisite stability of tenure for the discharge of the judicial function, and the effect was to give the opinions of the bar a large part of the weight we now assign to what falls from the bench. If the jurisconsult took part in framing the edict that was to guide the prætor during his year of office, and gave his advice when the case transcended the ordinary rules, and must be dismissed or a new formula invented, his opportunity was still greater when the suit came before the *judex*.[1] The high character, learning, and ability of an advocate will sometimes obtain a verdict in England or the United States that is not in accordance with legal principles, notwithstanding the efforts of the presiding judge; and the influence of such qualities must have been greater under the system which prevailed at Rome.

The jurisconsult might give his response in a writing addressed to the judge or transmit it orally through the client, or he might appear and plead the cause in person;[2] but as

[1] Gaius, c. iv. § 45; Poste, p. 437.

[2] Poste, p. 437.

time wore on the first named method seems to have been generally adopted as carrying greater weight.

It is not surprising that the emperors should have desired to give a class which possessed no inconsiderable share of legislative and judicial power, a semi-official character and bring it under their control. Augustus designated certain jurisconsults as entitled to give responses with his sanction; and although the right was not denied to others, the persons so appointed had greater weight and might be consulted by the judges when advice was needed. Adrian took another step in the same direction by enacting that the opinions of the privileged class should be conclusive when unanimous, but if they differed the judge might follow whichever he deemed preferable.[1] Opinions from such a source, embodying the fruits of so much labor and experience, were naturally handed down and cited in analogous cases and became the basis of systematic treatises. Many works of the kind were composed during the republic,[2] and they became still more numerous under the empire, and presented such conflicting views, that while developing the law as a science they were yet a hindrance to the effectual administration of justice by men, who as I have already intimated, were accustomed to receive rather than give the rule, and when Papinian and Ulpian differed, hardly ventured to have an opinion of their own. This marks the second stage in the process by which jurisprudence was first elucidated, and then obscured. If the opinion of a great lawyer might justly influence the judicial mind, although asked for and perchance indirectly remunerated by a client, and having an excusable leaning

[1] Gaius, c. i. § 7; Poste, p. 22; Warnkönig, § 33, p. 124; Maynz, i. No. 189, p. 289.

[2] The part ascribed to Portia in the "Merchant of Venice" is as consonant with that filled by the Roman jurisconsult as it is foreign to the ideas and practice of the present time, and it would be interesting to know whether the conception was traditional in Italy or derived from books.

Aufidius Namusa is said to have written or compiled one hundred and forty legal essays, and a still greater number were ascribed to his instructor Sulpicius. Warnkönig, § 37, p. 137; Maynz, i. No. 140, p. 240.

to his side, equal weight could hardly be denied to the principles which he enunciated when free from bias, in a work carefully prepared for the guidance of the courts and the profession.

The change was, nevertheless, great, and might not be beneficial. Instead of answers to questions put in a case actually in hand, and with a view to a practical result that would test their truth, the courts had now to depend on treatises composed by a multitude of writers, who were not always equal to their self-appointed task, and whose divergencies might perplex a well-trained mind or afford an excuse for a partial or corrupt decision. In addition to their original works, Ulpian and Paul wrote commentaries on Papinian, and so obscured their author or confused the judges as to draw forth an indignant criticism from Constantine, and induce him to decree that their notes should be suppressed.[1] A subsequent constitution of the same emperor enacted that the works of Paul should be viewed with respect, and universally accepted. A century later Theodosius II. confirmed the writings of Gaius, Papinian, Ulpian, Paul, and Modestinus, and provided that they, and the jurists whom they cited, should alone be referred to or relied on in the tribunals. When they differed, the majority should prevail, or if the opinions were equally divided, that of Papinian should preponderate; if he had expressed none, the *judex* might decide.

If the lawgiver may lay down rules, it belongs to the judge to apply what he has prescribed, and in so doing to invoke the aid of reason wherever found; and when the field of research is circumscribed arbitrarily by a statute, the law is curtailed as a science and jurisprudence must necessarily decline. Beyond all doubt the writings of the classical age of Roman jurisprudence were superior to any that could be produced when Rome was no longer the seat of empire, and the theological controversies of Augustine and Pelagius, of Athanasius and Arius, engaged the energies that were formerly devoted to politics or the law.

If treatises were, or could be made effectual as statutes, no

[1] Maynz, i. No. 234, p. 345.

better course could be pursued at any time than that which gave the writings of Gaius and Papinian the force of positive law; but I need hardly say that they are so essentially different, that much which constitutes the peculiar merit of a treatise would be a defect, or out of place in a statute.

Had the authority of the writers to whom men then looked for the doctrine of the civil law, depended on the imperial will, and not on their reputation for learning and legal judgment, the injunctions of Theodosius might have been obeyed, and there would have been little need for a further codification or abridgment. It seems, however, to have been disregarded; and the complaint that amidst the multitude of teachers it was impossible to discern legal truth, was reiterated as persistently as before, and the jurist who sought to advise his client, or to uphold his cause in court, might be obliged to consult two thousand treatises, containing not less than three millions of lines and expressing divergent views; or if he turned to what we now call the statute law, would find himself confronted by a multitude of ordinances that had been accumulating for centuries, and were not infrequently contradictory or inapplicable through the lapse of time. Had the law been a living science, and society on the advance, the evil would have been at least partially remedied by the composition of works that would have superseded the writings of a former age; and if the five great jurists, who by general consent stood in the front rank, had been occasionally cited, as we now refer to Littleton or Coke, the host of inferior writers would have been overlooked, or left to the research of the legal antiquarian. Such a result could not be looked for in an effete age, when men had learned to fold their arms and look to government for aid; and the remedy finally came through the commissions appointed by Justinian, which resulted in the compilation of the Code, the Digest, and the Institutes.

The first named of these useful works, for such they proved, was simply intended to supply a need which must be experienced in every age where legislation is complex. Two jurists, Gregorian and Hermoginian, had collected the constitutions in force under Constantine, in works known by their names; and those promulgated subsequently were published by Theodosius the Younger, A.D. 438, in a compilation known as the Theodosian code. As new edicts were issued in each succeeding reign these compilations became inadequate, and in the year 528, Justinian appointed a commission of ten jurists, among whom Tribonian was conspicuous for industry and learning, with authority to review the ordinances contained in the Gregorian, Hermoginian, and Theodosian codes; to correct what was erroneous or contradictory; to omit what had become obsolete; and form a collection that would be adapted to the existing state of things, and facilitate the administration of justice. This compilation, which is distinctively known as the Code, was commenced in the first year of Justinian's reign, completed in the short space of fourteen months, and published solemnly by an edict that forbade the citation of any statute which it did not contain.

The Code may be likened to the Revised Statutes of the United States or of New York; and if Tribonian and his colleagues escaped the criticism which has been levelled at those compilations, of having caused more doubts than they removed, it may have been in consequence of the superior merit of their work, or because the subjects of a despotic prince did not venture on the freedom of speech that may be practised with impunity in a republic.

Encouraged by the success of the Code, Justinian directed the commissioners to enter on a more extensive task, which was however more questionable both as regarded the plan and the method of carrying it into effect. It was nothing less than to gather from the entire body of writers on the civil law, such passages as were sound in principle, and suited to the existing state of things, and mould the fragments into a new work, not arranged according to a scientific method, but following the order of the perpetual edict as that which was best known, and would facilitate reference. As extracts from so many different sources might not readily coalesce, the commissioners were not only authorized to omit all that was obsolete or superfluous, but to make such additions or emendations as might be requisite to correct what appeared irreconcilable or erroneous.[1] It is not easy to determine the number or extent of the variations in an abridgment where the original is for the greater part lost, and the commentators differ as to how far Tribonian and his colleagues availed themselves of the license given by Justinian; but it is certain that they did not hesitate to make such changes and interpolations as they thought requisite for uniformity and clearness.

These falsifications, or as they have been termed, *emblemata* or embroideries of Tribonian, were sometimes trivial, as when "tradition" was substituted for the mancipation which had been abolished; but in other instances they materially varied the sense of the original.[2] Such a method might have been unobjectionable, had the alterations been specified or noted, but as actually employed tended to give an incorrect idea of the former law, that might render its actual condition less clear. The general opinion, however seems to be that the changes were, on the whole so slight that we may infer that jurisprudence underwent less alteration in the three centuries that had elapsed since the reign of Severus, than the last fifty years have produced in England.

The commission proceeded with so much diligence under the eye of a master who could both punish and reward, that in the short space of three years, the two thousand treatises and three millions of lines to which I have already referred, were reduced to one twentieth of their original bulk, without so far as appears, omitting anything that was essential to the end in view, although much was no doubt laid aside or expunged that would be deemed inestimable at the present day.

While the Digest was in the course of preparation, Justinian directed Tribonian and two other jurists to prepare a treatise containing the first elements of legal knowledge, and that might serve as an introduction to the study of the law. They consequently had an opportunity of showing that they

[1] Constitutio, Deo auctore de conceptione Digestorum, §§ 4–9; Mackeldey, § 71.

[2] Gibbon, ch. 44.

were not merely compilers, and could take a comprehensive and scientific view of legal principles; but they prudently declined the test, and preferred to mould their Institutes on a work by Gaius bearing the same title, and written more than three centuries before, adding some passages from other jurists, and altering what required a change. This treatise was given to the world on the 23rd of November, A. D. 533, and the publication of the Digest followed on the 16th of December, although neither work was to take effect as law until the last day of the year.

It were invidious to inquire whether Justinian's share of the praise due to the *corpus juris civilis* is greater than that which belongs to the conception of a useful thought carried into execution through the labors and abilities of others; but it is generally conceded that the workmanship of the Digest is inferior to the materials, which did not gain by the manner in which they were employed. It may be likened to a mosaic, or a building of the middle ages where fragments taken from the edifices of a former age and higher style of art are used to build the walls or adorn the superstructure.

Writings of a period separated by a greater gulf, as regarded manners and faith, than that which divides us from the England of Queen Elizabeth, were scanned for passages that might when collated form a code, not only for the subjects of the Eastern Empire but for generations yet unborn and the entire civilized world; and when these fragments had been arranged in the order of the prætorian edict, as promulgated in the reign of Hadrian, Justinian waved the wand of absolute power over the completed work, and not only declared it law but the only source from which the law should be deduced. When it is considered that the latest of the authors whose works were thus employed flourished three hundred years before Justinian, we may be surprised that such a method should have been measurably successful, rather than that it should have fallen short of the clearness, accuracy, and fulness which the imperial legislator contemplated.[1]

Notwithstanding the care taken to harmonize the somewhat

[1] Maynz, i. No. 246, p. 355, note 24.

heterogeneous elements of the Digest, it is said by those who have made it the subject of a critical study to be disfigured by antinomies and contradictions, which were presumably as perplexing to the tribunals of that age as they have since proved to commentators, and like most attempts at codification, gave rise to doubts hardly less grave than those which it was intended to dispel.[1]

Some conception may be formed of the process and its results by supposing Parliament to enact that extracts from the writings and decisions of Coke, of Chief Baron Gilbert, of Blackstone, Mansfield, Eldon, and perchance of Kent and Story, should be the only authorities cited at the bar or followed by the courts. Such a plan might, if wisely employed, and restricted within proper limits, have some obvious advantages. Justinian did not, like ordinary codifiers, endeavor to frame rules covering the entire field of jurisprudence, that may be erroneous, and must prove inapplicable to cases which the legislature does not anticipate or thoroughly comprehend, but adopted the safer policy of recurring to principles that had been deduced by former jurists in considering the cases that were submitted for their opinion, and selecting such as had stood the test of time and were suited to the needs of a society which had necessarily undergone many changes during the intervening centuries. Had this been all, his course would have been practically wise as affording an effectual aid to magistrates who, in a degenerate age, had lost the capacity for original thought. In enacting that the various paragraphs or fragments which compose the Digest should have the effect of laws, he disregarded the line which separates principles from rules and gave precedents the force of statutes. The true function of a precedent is to guide the judicial mind, by indicating the path which has been trodden on like occasions, and may presumably be followed with safety. It is not, therefore, obligatory, but simply a reason why a particular course should be adopted, unless some sufficient reason can be adduced for proceeding in a different direction. To erect the opinion of a jurist or of a judge into a law is, therefore, to

[1] Maynz, i. No. 246, p. 355, note 25.

convert the stepping-stones that should facilitate the advance of jurisprudence into barriers that cannot be overpassed even for the sake of attaining a truth that lies beyond.[1]

The Institutes are, if possible, still more remote than the Digest from what would now be regarded as the proper method of codification. Congress might conceivably authorize Mr. Bristow or some other well-known jurist to condense the law books of the preceding centuries into a code; but it is not conceivable that they should authorize him to write an elementary treatise on jurisprudence and then declare it law, even if he took the precaution of making the work a reproduction of Kent's Commentaries. Such a plan was not inconceivable at Rome, where, as I have elsewhere shown, the writings of the jurisconsults were converted by a natural process from evidence of the law into laws; and an emperor who had taken the books of a bygone age to form a code might well desire to complete the edifice with a treatise which, though not proceeding from his pen, was written by a delegate, and might therefore, according to imperial ethics, be regarded as his own.

The edicts which confirmed and promulgated the Institutes and Digest are verbose and egotistical, and speak the language of oriental despotism, rather than of the dignified simplicity of classic Rome. The Code, Digest, and Institutes were to be reverenced and observed as laws by the senate and mankind, all the more ancient sources being closed. "Let no one" — so ran the decree — "dare to compare them with what existed previously, or inquire whether either is in any respect dissonant, because all that they contain is alone and solely to be obeyed;" and it was further declared that every one who ventured to cite or produce in court or on any occasion when there was need of law, aught from any books save those which the emperor had prepared and promulgated, should be regarded as a counterfeiter, and, with the judge who shared his fault, be visited with the penalties appropriate to such an offence.[2]

[1] Fremery, Études de Droit Commercial, p. 5.

[2] Constitutio de confirmatione Digestorum, § 19.

The plan which was thus carried into effect had been not less pompously announced in a prior edict, which declared that absolute authority would be conferred on the Digest by the imperial command, and that no one, however skilled in jurisprudence, would be allowed to write a commentary upon it, or obscure its clearness by his verbosity, as had happened in former times, when the entire law was confused by the conflicting opinions of its interpreters.[1]

This language disclosed an ignorance that there are limits even to an imperial will, that would have been natural to one born in the purple, but was inexcusable in the Illyrian adventurer, whose abilities had raised him to what was still the foremost place in the world. It was not Justinian who conferred authority on the compilations that have given celebrity to his name, but the principles which he borrowed from the great masters of jurisprudence lent authority to him. Had the Digest and Institutes derived their claim to obedience from no higher source than his command, they might have been grudgingly accepted during his life and within the limits of the Eastern Empire, but would assuredly have had no wider or more enduring sway. It was because of their intrinsic merit, and not of his decree, that these works were received by subsequent generations and throughout the civilized world, as convincing proof that the Roman was not less fitted for legislation than for success in arms.

In the edicts above referred to, Justinian expressed a confident hope and laid a peremptory injunction, and if one has been signally fulfilled and the other as signally disregarded, both results may be ascribed to the same cause.

The injunction was that no one should venture to criticise or even to comment on his work; the wish, that it should endure throughout all succeeding time.[2] No book, not Shakspeare, Dante, nor even the Bible, has been the theme of more persistent, able, and copious commentary than the *corpus juris civilis*. The acutest minds have been engaged for wellnigh

1 Constitutio Deo auctore de conceptione Digestorum, §§ 6, 12.

2 Constitutio Deo auctore de conceptione Digestorum, § 12; Constitutio de confirmatione Digestorum, §§ 3, 23.

seven hundred years in expounding its doctrines and reconciling whatever seemed contradictory or obscure, and it is still regarded throughout a large part of the civilized world as the fountain head of jurisprudence. A work which thus engages the attention of mankind is fitted to endure, and it is because of the merit which induced the disregard of Justinian's prohibition that his wish has been fulfilled.

CHAPTER IV.

DEVELOPMENT OF OBLIGATIONS AT ROMAN LAW.

Definition and Classification of Obligations. — The Primitive Contracts: Sale, Loan, Betrothal. — Mancipation or *nexus*. — Tradition. — Usucapion. — *In jure cessio.* — Final Development of the Law. — The Contracts *re: mutuum, commodatum, pignus, depositum.* — The Contract *verbis* or *stipulatio.* — The Contract *literis.*

According to the definition given in the Institutes, an obligation is the chain of the law by whose compulsion we are constrained to do or render something according to the laws of our country. *Obligatio est juris vinculum quo necessitate astringimur alicujus solvendæ rei secundum nostræ civitatis jura.*[1] The *jura* are the commandments of the law, and the obligation results from the procedure through which they are enforced.

Obligations are therefore essentially personal, binding one man to render some thing or service to another; or in the language of Paulus, as cited by Pellat:[2] *Obligationum substantia non in eo consistit, ut aliquod corpus nostrum aut servitutem nostram faciat, sed ut alium nobis obstringat ad dandum aliquid, vel faciendum, vel præstandum.*

The theory of the Roman law on this head is clearly given in the following citation from the Institutes: —

"The principal division of obligations is into two kinds, civil and prætorian. Civil obligations are those constituted by the laws, or at least recognized by the civil law. Prætorian obligations are those which the prætor has established by his own authority; they are also called honorary.

"A further division separates them into four kinds, for they arise *ex contractu* or *quasi ex contractu*, *ex maleficio* or *quasi ex*

[1] Institutes, 3. 13. [2] Pellat, Manuale Juris Synopticum, p. 432.

maleficio. Let us first treat of those which arise from a contract, which again are divided into four kinds, according as they are formed by the thing, by word of mouth, by writing, or by consent."[1]

Torts and contracts are thus ranged under the same head, as giving rise to liabilities or duties which may be enforced by suit, — a classification which seems logical rather than natural, and ill suited to facilitate the scientific study of the law. Whether a man committed theft, or made default in the repayment of a loan, it was equally his duty to compensate or indemnify the injured party, and the law disregarded the difference of the source in view of the similarity of the result. A liability arising from any source and constituting a cause of action, is consequently an obligation in the sense in which the term was used by the Roman jurists.

It results from the above definition that the obligation of a contract depends upon the remedy by which the fulfilment of the contract may be enforced or redress obtained for the breach, and hence whatever impairs the remedy necessarily impairs the obligation. Such is the interpretation given by the Supreme Court of the United States to the constitutional provision that the states shall not impair the obligations of contracts.

Agreeably to Mommsen, the contracts of sale, of loan, and of betrothal, were the only ones recognized by the earlier Roman law as affording a cause of action, and all others were relegated to the forum of conscience, without other sanction than the shame and loss of reputation arising from a violation of good faith.[2] It was essential that the contract should be made in the customary and symbolical form, and consent did not suffice if given in any other way.

Property might be acquired or transferred at Rome by occupation, adjudication, operation of law, mancipation, tradition, usucapion, or *in jure cessio*. Among these we need only consider the last four.

Mancipation was, in the first instance a real, but subsequently became a formal or symbolical sale, effected through

[1] Institutes, 3. 13. 1, 2. [2] Mommsen, i. 207.

the delivery and acceptance of the thing to be conveyed, attended with the weighing out of the bronze coins or ingots which constituted the price in a balance held by a scaleholder, and in the presence of five other witnesses, who were required to be of full age and Roman citizens.[1] This was the only means, save usucapion or adverse possession, and the *in jure cessio*, by which the title to land, houses, cattle, — in short, the larger part of whatever is most useful or valuable in the earlier stages of social life, — could pass from man to man; and if they were duly employed the purchaser became the owner, and a failure to comply on either side with the contemporaneous stipulations was regarded as a criminal breach of trust.[2]

Such a transfer was termed indifferently *nexus* or *mancipatio*, — *nexus*, because the effect was to bind or knit the right of property to the purchaser; *mancipatio*, because he took manual possession of the thing sold as the owner, so far as its nature and the circumstance would permit.[3] The transfer was in form absolute, but its operation depended on the contemporaneous declarations, which might convert the sale into a pledge, a devise, or a trust.[4] So the vendor might give a warranty or enter into other collateral stipulations, that would impose an obligation from which he could not recede. The form was thus adapted to the requirements of the times, and the XII. Tables sanctioned a change which necessity had introduced, by providing *cum nexum faciet mancipiumque, uti lingua nuncupassit ita jus esto.*

The Roman law made no distinction as regarded title or the means of acquisition or conveyance between real and personal estate. Property was divided into *res mancipi* and *res nec mancipi.* Land, houses, cattle, rustic servitudes or easements, were ranged under the former head, while the latter included gold, silver, household furniture, wearing apparel, pictures, — in short, the multitude of things which advancing civilization brings with it. *Res mancipi* could not be

[1] Gaius, c. i. § 119.
[2] Maynz, i. § 97, p. 702; Mommsen, i. 208.
[3] Maynz, i. § 97, p. 705.
[4] Gaius, c. ii. §§ 102-104; Poste, pp. 76, 183.

transferred by delivery, and *res nec mancipi* were according to the generally received opinion insusceptible of mancipation, though Mommsen holds that mancipation was applicable to all corporeal property, the difference being that some things did not require its aid, and were therefore designated as *nec mancipi*.[1]

It was essential that movables should be present and grasped by the purchaser, while a turf or tile might be symbolically substituted in the case of a house or farm, and mancipation differed in this regard from the feudal livery of seisin, which could only take place on the land.[2] In the progress of time, and when writing came into general use, such transfers were usually, as in the case of a feoffment, attested by a written instrument, which did not pass the title and was merely evidence that it had been conveyed.

A loan was negotiated in like manner by weighing out the amount lent, but with this difference, — that the mancipation was of the borrower's person, which thus became a pledge or security for the debt.[3] Such at least is the account given by Maynz, who says:[4] "In exchange for the sum of money which the creditor counted out to the debtor by means of the balance, the latter mancipated his person to the creditor, and was thenceforth bound or enchained to the latter;" and the transaction thus came to be known under the generic name *nexus*, which was applied alike to loans and sales. If the borrower made default he was adjudged to the creditor, by whom he might be imprisoned or sold into slavery beyond the Tiber.[5] If there were several creditors, each was entitled to his share of the pledge, and the debtor might, according to the letter of the law as laid down in the XII. Tables, be cut into morsels and distributed among the claimants; a rigor which will appear less extraordinary if we reflect that a Roman had a power, as regarded his wife, children, and slaves, — in short, over every one who was under his hand,

[1] Poste, pp. 143, 144; Mommsen, i. 208, note.

[2] Gaius, c. i. § 121.

[3] Maynz, i. § 33; ii. §§ 245, 246, 249.

[4] Maynz, ii. § 345, p. 346.

[5] Dominguet, § 81, note; Maynz, i. § 43, p. 496.

—limited only by his will, and extending to the infliction of death.

The balance was originally used to ascertain the weight of the coin or bullion, but subsequently became symbolical. The scales and scale-bearer were still requisite, but the money might be paid at some other time or place, and the purchaser simply struck the scale with a coin, and claimed the property as his, according to the quirital law. Moreover, the transfer, while in form a sale, might be gratuitous and confer a benefaction on the grantee, or create a trust for the fulfilment of the testamentary wishes of the grantor as perpetuated by the testimony of the witnesses, or declared in a writing authenticated by their seals. An analogue may be found in the feoffment with livery of seisin, which according to the intention declared at the time or manifested in the accompanying deed, might be in fee, for life, or subject to a condition of re-entry, that would render it a charity or mortgage. The *nexus* finally became obsolete, or was superseded by contracts deriving their obligation from assent, signified generally or in some form which usage sanctioned.

There can be little doubt that mancipation originally took place before the assembled people, with a view to publicity and the security of title, and that five witnesses were afterwards substituted as representatives of the classes into which the Romans were divided by the Servian reform. From whatever source the usage was derived, it might continue to exist as tending to insure the presence of a sufficient number of persons to perpetuate the memory of the transaction, and sustain it by their testimony if assailed. This reason gradually lost its force as writing came into general use, and contracts and conveyances were attested by memoranda or *cautiones;* but the *mancipatio* was still used when Gaius wrote,[1] and did not become obsolete until the age of Justinian. This result may be ascribed to the tenacity with which the Romans clung to their traditions, because the distinction between things *mancipi* and *nec mancipi* had long become purely technical, and complicated the administration of justice by making it requi-

[1] Gaius, c. i. § 119; c. ii. §§ 102–105.

site for a purchaser who took by delivery to rely on a real or fictitious usucapion.

Accarias regards it as inconceivable that there could ever have been a period when the scales and ingot were essential to the formation of a contract;[1] but it would be more strange had the *mancipatio* been coeval with the consensual contracts, and sales been made symbolically when the end could have been attained by a few simple words.

The successive development of the Roman contracts is not less obvious than the order of nature in the spring. The question in all ages, and even at the present day, is not merely, Did the parties so agree; but Was the contract duly made, and are there any recognized means of proof? The law of evidence is therefore part of the law of contracts, and that which cannot be legally proved does not, for legal purposes, exist. A contract of sale was not obligatory among the Anglo-Saxons unless it was made in the presence of witnesses who were appointed in each township for such purposes; nor, when Bracton wrote, if not reduced to writing or attended with the payment of earnest money; and a borrower might defeat the claim of the lender by swearing that he was not indebted, and calling his neighbors to attest his credibility.[2] We can, therefore, readily understand that the Romans should at a period anterior to the use of writing have required the transfer of goods or land, or a loan that would expose the borrower to the extreme penalties incident to debt, to be made in a form that would from its publicity and the number of witnesses present put the fact beyond dispute.[3] The *nexus* may, moreover, have been required to give the creditor the hold on the debtor's person, and right of arrest that would not otherwise have existed at the period when the *sacramentum* originated, and consent seems to have been requisite to jurisdiction.

The employment of the *mancipatio* for the creation of a testamentary trust which was finally converted into a will, is

[1] Accarias, ii. No. 494, note 1.

[2] Essays in Anglo-Saxon Law, pp. 167, 187–189, 216, 227.

[3] Maynz, § 222.

succinctly described by Gaius.[1] Wills were originally made before the *comitia calata* or assembly of the *populus* for the transaction of such business as concerned individuals as well as the community; but as it was inconvenient to wait for a meeting which only took place twice a year, a man who wished to provide for the disposition of his property after his death, might mancipate it to some one in whom he confided, and who was known as the *familiæ emptor*, with a stipulation that it should be appropriated in accordance with the terms of the request.

The fictitious purchaser promised formally to comply, and struck the scales with a bronze ingot in token that the transfer was complete. The trust was at first declared orally, but subsequently set forth in an instrument which remained in the testator's keeping, and might be cancelled or altered if he thought proper.[2] The transformation was completed by the prætor, who provided that a writing attested by the seals of seven persons, who stood for the *familiæ emptor*, the scaleholder, and the five witnesses, should operate as a will without the ceremony of mancipation. The law was still further modified by imperial constitutions, which required that the will should be subscribed by the testator in the presence of seven witnesses convened for the purpose, who severally affixed their seals and signatures, in his and each other's presence,—so that the whole should be one transaction.[3] The provision of the English statute of frauds with regard to the execution of a devise seems to have been taken from this source.

Possession taken or acquired in good faith and without notice by virtue of an equitable right or *bona fide* purchase, was known as *usucapio*, and when held for two years in the case of land, or for one in that of chattels, conferred a legal or quiritary title. The transfer of *res mancipi* by delivery vested the beneficial ownership in the grantee, but left the quiritary title in the grantor until the usucapion was com-

[1] Gaius, c. ii. §§ 24, 25.

[2] Institutes 2. 10. 1; Sandars' Justinian, 236; Poste, p. 183.

[3] Institutes 2. 10. 3; Accarias, i. No. 321.

plete; when both met in the grantee, and the property became his absolutely by operation of law. So a purchase from one who had no right to sell, followed by usucapion, might confer a legal title if the buyer believed the vendor to be the owner, and the acquired property had not been obtained violently or by theft.[1] Usucapion may be likened to the "adverse possession" of the common law, but is more nearly analogous to the "*bona fide* purchase" of the Court of Chancery, in requiring good faith on the part of the grantee, although the right of such a purchaser becomes valid as soon as the price is paid and the deed delivered.

The *in jure cessio*, like the fine or common recovery, was an amicable or simulated action, and while applicable to every form of property, was the only means by which things incorporeal, save as it would seem rustic servitudes, could be created, surrendered or transferred.[2] Both parties appeared before the magistrate, the grantor admitted the grantee's title, and it was so adjudged.[3] All these modes of alienation seem to have had a common origin, — namely, the need for a public and notorious means of transfer, that would presumably be challenged if wrongful, and susceptible of proof when just. Land seems to have been originally so far common property among the Latin, as in the case of the Germanic tribes, that it could not be acquired or alienated without the sanction of the state. Mancipation presumably took place in the first instance before the *comitia*, and with their assent, and the five witnesses were members or representatives of the various classes of the people as organized under the Servian reform.[4]

The Institutes and Digest do not give a definition of a contract.[5] A *pact* is indeed described as being the consent of two or more persons in a common purpose; but although such an agreement might operate as an *exceptio*, or defence, it did not impose a legal obligation, unless it was made in the form

[1] Gaius, c. ii. §§ 41, 50; Institutes, 2. 6. 2.

[2] Gaius, c. ii. §§ 28–37; Accarias, i. No. 223.

[3] Maynz, i. § 97, p. 704.

[4] Mommsen, vol. i. ch. 11, 208, note; Maynz, i. § 97, p. 704.

[5] Accarias, ii. No. 493.

prescribed by the law, or had some cause which that recognized.[1] The following extract from Pothier shows this with greater clearness: — "That kind of agreement, the object of which is the formation of an engagement, is called a contract. The principles of the Roman law respecting the different kinds of agreements, and the distinction between contracts and simple agreements not being founded on the law of nature, and being, indeed, remote from its simplicity, are not admitted into our law. Hence it follows that in our law we should not define a contract as it was defined by the interpreters of the Roman law, *conventio nomen habens a jure civili vel causam;* but that it should be defined 'An agreement by which two parties reciprocally promise and engage, or one of them singly promises and engages to the other, to give some particular thing or to do or abstain from doing some particular act.'"[2]

Contracts were ranged by the Roman law as finally developed under the following heads: *re*, *verbis*, *literis*, *consensus;* and none that did not come within this classification could, speaking generally, be prosecuted to judgment.

The contract *re*, as finally developed, would seem to have included the numerous instances in which the execution of an agreement by delivery or payment imposed an obligation, although the agreement itself, as originally made,[3] was a *nudum pactum;* but was confined in its ordinary acceptation to cases where one received property from another under circumstances which rendered it his duty to return it, or a thing of a like kind.[4] The cause of the obligation, or, in other words, that which rendered it susceptible of being enforced by an action, was the delivery and acceptance; but its extent and operation depended on the intention of the parties, as manifested by their acts and language, or where the transaction was a loan on the nature of the property given and received.[5] Thus the delivery of goods or money to a borrower gave rise to an implied promise of repayment; and one

[1] Accarias, ii. No. 493; Maynz, ii. §§ 207, 249.

[2] Andrews' Pothier on Obligations, Part I. ch. i. art. 1.

[3] Maynz, ii. §§ 232, 243, pp. 298, 335.

[4] Sandars' Justinian, 405.

[5] Maynz, ii. § 232.

who receives a pledge is obviously under an obligation to return it on the extinguishment of the debt. So the duty of a borrower to return the thing lent, or another of a like kind, may depend on whether it can be put to its appropriate use without being consumed.

The transfer was originally formal, *per æs et libram*, or mancipation, and a lender could not make the borrower his debtor by simply putting the money in his hands; but it finally came to be considered that the mode of delivery was immaterial, and that the acceptance of property for a specific purpose imposed an obligation to carry it into effect.[1]

Contracts *re* were divided by the Roman jurists into the *mutuum*, the *commodatum*, the *pignus*, and the *depositum*, i. e. the loan for consumption, the loan for use, the pledge, and the bailment for safe keeping; but delivery might give rise to an obligation in numerous instances that did not come under these heads, and which were known as innominate, or unclassed.[2]

A loan for consumption is said in the Institutes to have been termed *mutuum*, because what is mine becomes yours (*ex meo tuum fit*) when lent for such a purpose; and although this definition is purely fanciful, it indicates a truth.[3] Things which are estimated by weight, number, or measure, and cannot be used without being consumed, become the property of the borrower, subject to the obligation of returning a like amount identical in kind though not in substance. For as the loan must under these circumstances remain idle, or be employed in a way that precludes the possibility of its being returned in specie, the parties may fairly be presumed to have contemplated the latter alternative. It needs no argument to prove that if I lend my neighbor a hundred dollars, they are as much his as if they were given absolutely; and the resulting duty is not to return the very coins or bank-notes, but as many dollars as will make up the sum.[4]

It is therefore essential to the validity of a *mutuum* that the things lent should be of such a nature that the return of

[1] Maynz, ii. § 232.
[2] Maynz, ii. §§ 232, 243.
[3] Institutes, 3. 14.
[4] Maynz, ii. § 233; Sandars' Justinian, 406.

a like quantity will presumably be an equivalent; because the contract would otherwise be an exchange instead of a loan.[1] Money is obviously within this category; and it also includes corn, wine, oil, and other articles which are ordinarily sold by count, weight, or measure. But the criterion is not conclusive; and the loan of a book will not be regarded as a *mutuum*, in the absence of an agreement to that effect, although one copy of the edition may be as valuable as any other,—because it may be read and returned in the same condition.

It seems that a loan effected with the ceremony of mancipation gave rise to an implied liability for interest at the rate of ten per cent per annum; and one to whom wheat, oil, or other fungible goods were delivered for consumption might bind himself by a promise to return a larger quantity; but the obligation of a pecuniary loan was limited to the repayment of what had been received, and could not be carried further by a promise unless it was put in the form of a stipulation.[2] The contract was therefore *prima facie* gratuitous, although the lender might entitle himself to compensation by exacting a solemn engagement from the borrower.

The remaining branch of the contract of loan, or *commodatum*, differed from the *mutuum* in some important particulars. It was necessarily gratuitous; for if the lender stipulated for a compensation, the agreement changed its character and became one of letting and hiring. The goods remained the property of the lender; and although it was the borrower's duty to keep them safely and return them in the same condition, still, if they were destroyed or perished through the operation of causes which could not be obviated or controlled by the exercise of due care and diligence, all liability on his part ceased, and the lender was not entitled to damages. The destruction of a *mutuum*, on the other hand, by a *vis major*, or inevitable accident, did not discharge the borrower, although he was entirely free from fault and had derived no benefit from the loan. The rule depended in both instances on the maxim, *res perit domino*, which cast the loss in

[1] Mommsen, i. 213. [2] Maynz, ii. § 234.

the one case upon the borrower and in the other on the lender.[1]

The lender of a *mutuum* or *commodatum* was entitled to terminate the loan at any moment by a demand of payment or restitution, but might be bound by a promise not to exercise this right before a given period, even when, as in the case of a loan for use, the contract was purely gratuitous and the promise would fail for want of consideration if the question arose at common law.[2]

The distinction between the *mutuum* and *commodatum* grew out of the nature of things, and is not, like some of the doctrines of the Roman law, merely logical or formal. It is accordingly recognized by every system of jurisprudence, and not less observed in modern times than in the age of Justinian.

The *depositum* was a contract strictly *in re*, arising from the acceptance of another's property for safe keeping. It could not be constituted simply by consent without delivery, and lost its identity if a different or greater obligation was substituted for that implied by law. A man who promised to take charge of his neighbor's goods or house might be bound as a mandatary or by a stipulation to that effect; but he did not become liable as a depositary until the *res* was actually placed in his hands, or with some one whom he authorized to receive it. As the Roman lawyers made no distinction between real and personal estate, it was immaterial whether the subject-matter was a house or chattel. The obligation arising from the acceptance of such a charge was simply to use ordinary care for the preservation of the property, and keep it as the bailee did his own; and if the bailee undertook to repair the dwelling, to carry the goods elsewhere, to convert them into a different form, or to expend money or labor in any other way for the bailor's benefit, he became a mandatary if the engagement was gratuitous, or a *conductor operis* where he was actuated by a promise of reward.[3] Such an undertaking was moreover, as it would seem, invalid as the rule originally stood, unless put in the form of a stipulation;

[1] Maynz, ii. §§ 234, 237; Poste, p. 300; Institutes, 3. 14. 2.

[2] Maynz, ii. § 237 B, p. 312, note 10.

[3] Maynz, ii. § 239, p. 319.

although as time wore on, mandate and letting and hiring were recognized as consensual contracts depending on mutual assent and valid if that appeared.

While these contracts were ranged under the general head of *re*, or in other words of an obligation arising as an inference from the facts, their nature depended on the intention of the parties and the object they had in view, as gathered from their language as well as from their acts. If a depositary asked and obtained the privilege of using the thing left with him for safe keeping, it became a *commodatum*, which he was bound to guard with jealous care, or a *mutuum* which must be returned in kind at all events.[1] So, where a depositary promised to keep the goods safely, or they were left with him at his own request, and not as a favor to the depositor, the contract partook of the nature of a mandate, and he was answerable for every fault.[2] Such as I have elsewhere stated is also the doctrine of the common law.[3]

In determining the responsibility arising from a bailment, the civil law had regard to whether it was made in the interest of the bailor or the bailee, or for an end that was beneficial to both. One who conferred a favor on another by receiving his goods gratuitously for safe keeping, was not answerable for any injury which they might sustain while under his care, unless he was so grossly negligent as to indicate that he wilfully exposed the property to danger, or was culpably indifferent to its safety. A lender for use, on the other hand stood in the light of a benefactor, and was entitled to require the exact diligence from the borrower which a good father would exercise where the interests of his family were concerned.[4] Such was also the rule where, as in the case of a pledge, the bailment was for the benefit of both parties, because each was as much bound to care for the interests of the other as if his own were not involved.[5]

[1] Maynz, ii. § 239, pp. 317, 320.

[2] Maynz, ii. § 239, pp. 317, 320; Sandars' Justinian, 409.

[3] Coggs *v.* Bernard, 2 Lord Raymond, 909.

[4] Maynz, ii. § 242; Poste, pp. 395–397; Sandars' Justinian, 403; Institutes, 3. 14. 2; Tompkins *v.* Saltmarsh, 14 S. & R. 279.

[5] Maynz, ii. § 242; Poste, pp. 395–397.

A mandate was an exception to this rule, because the obligation was not deduced from the law, but arose from the express or implied undertaking of the mandatary to do all that was requisite and practicable for the fulfilment of the trust; and he was consequently answerable for any loss or failure that might have been averted by due care, or such skill as might reasonably be expected from a man of his training or profession.[1] One who engaged to carry the goods of another to a given point, or to expend labor or skill upon them for the benefit of the owner, was therefore answerable for exact diligence, and could not rely on the gratuitous nature of the undertaking as an excuse for a loss that might have been foreseen and avoided.[2] The rule, as laid down in Coggs *v.* Bernard,[3] and French *v.* Reed,[4] is nearly to the same effect, although the American courts have inclined in other instances to assimilate the obligation of a mandatary to that of a depositary or unpaid bailee, and make him answerable only for such neglect as can be fairly described as gross.[5] In Tompkins *v.* Saltmarsh,[6] which was a suit to recover compensation for the loss of a letter containing money, which the defendant gratuitously undertook to deliver, the court held that he was only liable for the gross negligence, or misfeasance which is *dolo proximus*, or next door to fraud, and a like rule was laid down in Beardslee *v.* Richardson,[7] and Stanton *v.* Bell.[8]

I may add that agreeably to Accarias, a mandatary was in the first instance answerable only for gross negligence, as having no personal interest in the fulfilment of a trust which he undertook solely for the benefit of the principal, and although a more stringent rule was advocated by Ulpian it was through an edict of Diocletian that it acquired the force of law.[9] Maynz relies on Cicero's oration *pro Roscio*

[1] Maynz, ii. § 221, p. 259; Sandars' Justinian, 458.

[2] Fellowes *v.* Gordon, 8 B. Monroe, 415.

[3] 2 Lord Raymond, 909.

[4] 6 Binn. 308.

[5] Eldridge *v.* Hill, 97 U. S. 92; Tracy *v.* Wood, 3 Mason, 132.

[6] 14 S. & R. 275.

[7] 11 Wend. 25.

[8] 2 Hawks, 145.

[9] Accarias, ii. No. 634.

Amerino, as sustaining the opposite view, but says that the point is one about which the jurisconsults differ.[1]

The *obligatio verbis* seems to have sprung from the *mancipatio*, which, as I have already stated, might be shaped to almost any end which the parties desired to effect. Though in form a sale, it became if the vendor so declared his purpose and the vendee assented, a loan, or pledge; and might even be made to operate as a will.[2] So the parties might enter into collateral engagements, which derived a force from the solemnity of the occasion and the presence of the witnesses, that would otherwise have been wanting.[3]

The contract *verbis*, or *stipulatio*, thus came into being as an adjunct to the *nexus* or *mancipatio*, but was subsequently detached from its root, and took the place in jurisprudence as a solemn and customary obligation, which it retained for more than a thousand years and through all the changes of creeds and institutions which marked the rise and decadence of Rome.[4] The form was peculiar, but admirably adapted to the end in view, which was to draw the line between the negotiations which ordinarily precede a contract, and the engagement itself, and define so far as the imperfection of language will permit, the nature of that for which one party stipulated and the other became bound. The stipulator asked, Do you bind yourself? *Spondes?* The person to whom the question was addressed replied, *Spondeo;* and the obligation was complete.[5] So the interrogation and response might be, *Dabis? Dabo. Fide jubes?*—"Dost thou bid me to rely on thy word?" *Fide jubeo.* It was essential that the answer should follow the wording of the question, so as to leave no doubt that both minds had met in a common purpose. We might infer from this peculiarity, were there no other proof, that the stipulation originated at a period when writing was little known or used, and it was necessary to adopt a formula that would leave no doubt as to the intention of the parties, and which the witnesses could not readily forget.[6]

[1] Maynz, ii. § 221, p. 257, note 11.

[2] Gaius, c. iii. § 102; Poste, p. 184; Maynz, ii. § 245.

[3] Maynz, ii. § 245.

[4] Poste, p. 297.

[5] Gaius, c. iii. § 92.

[6] Fremery, ch. iii. p. 25.

In the language of Modestinus, as cited by Pellat, *obligamur . . . verbis, cum precedit interrogatio et sequitur congruens responsio.*[1] The question was the *stipulatio*, and the one who asked, the stipulator, and it was by putting a part for the whole[2] that such contracts came to be known as stipulations.[3] Originally none but Roman citizens could enter into this form of obligation, and they only by the verb *spondeo*, but other modes of expression were gradually recognized as of equal validity. This latitude seems to have been conceded in the first instance to aliens, who were allowed to substitute corresponding words of their own language for those in use at Rome, but subsequently if a Roman asked, *Dabis?* and the person interrogated answered *Dabo*, it was a binding contract; and so of a formal request to another to become a surety, or incur an obligation of any other kind.

It may be inferred from the language of Gaius, who flourished under the Antonines, that the term *spondeo* could not be legally used by an alien, so that while a Roman might contract in Greek, a foreigner who was asked *spondes?* and replied affirmatively was not bound.[4] It was subsequently enacted by the Emperor Leo during the fifth century, that if the parties understood each other and agreed, nothing more should be requisite.[5] This statute dispensed with the use of technical language, but did not abrogate the customary rule which made interrogation and response essential to the validity of an oral contract.

It was essential to the validity of a stipulation that both parties should be present and have the use of speech, and the obligation could not be contracted in writing, or through an agent, nor by a deaf mute.[6] A written offer followed by acceptance, was not valid as a stipulation although it might constitute a sale. So a stipulation by an agent bound him and not his principal, although it was incumbent on the principal to indemnify the agent.

1 Manuale Juris Synopticum, p. 434.

2 Sandars' Justinian, 411.

3 Maynz, ii. § 245, 348.

4 Sandars' Justinian, 412; Maynz, ii. § 245; Gaius, c. iii. § 93.

5 Institutes, 3. 15. 1.

6 Gaius, c. iii. § 105.

A stipulation, like other oral contracts, necessarily depended on the testimony of the persons who were present, or called in as witnesses, and it was usual to guard against their death or forgetfulness by a memorandum of what had occurred. But the instrument was merely evidence, and not the contract, and might be invalidated by proof that the parties did not meet or being present failed to use the customary formula. Fraudulent and litigious persons were thus, as we are informed in the Institutes, enabled to evade their obligations on technical grounds, and there was a great and growing tendency to counteract such attempts by holding the parties to what the writing set forth and they had authenticated by their signatures. Agreeably to Ulpian as cited in Sandars' Justinian from the Digest,[1] "When at the end of the instrument of an agreement, the words usually added were found, namely, *rogavit Titius, spopondit Mœvius*, the agreement was taken to be a stipulation, unless it was expressly shown to be a mere pact." So we are told in the Institutes that if it is written in an instrument that a person has promised, the promise is considered to have been given in answer to a precedent interrogation.[2] And Justinian finally enacted that when the writing declared that the parties were present, no proof should be admissible to the contrary,[3] which did not establish that one or both were in some other place during the entire day.[4] But the recital did not operate as an estoppel, or as it would at common law, preclude evidence in opposition to its terms.

It is a striking proof of the light in which the contract *verbis* was regarded by the Roman jurists, that if a promise made in due form by a question and response was reduced to writing, the document was merely evidence and the suit must be brought on the *stipulatio*, contrary to the English rule which treats the writing as conclusive and discards all that it does not contain.[5]

[1] D. II. 14. 7. 12; Sandars' Justinian, 429.

[2] Institutes, 3. 19. 17.

[3] Institutes, 3. 19. 12.

[4] Maynz, ii. § 245, p. 352.

[5] Institutes, 3. 21; Sandars' Justinian, 439.

The stipulation was, like the common law bond essentially a unilateral contract which only bound the promisor, although it might be conditioned for the performance of an act by the promisee, and fail if he made default. If, however, the parties wished to enter into a reciprocal agreement, as, for instance, an exchange or wager, each might bind himself by a stipulation to that effect, and thus give rise to a contract that would be mutually obligatory.[1]

A promise to give like other pacts, was invalid unless perfected by delivery, or put in the form of a stipulation, and the *lex Cincia* set a limit to injudicious liberality by providing that no gift should exceed a certain maximum. It was subsequently enacted that donations should be reduced to writing and registered; and Justinian finally decreed that a simple promise to give might be enforced by action though not reduced to writing, if the value did not exceed two hundred *solidi*, but that registration should be requisite for all beyond that sum.[2]

It might have been supposed that when the Emperor Leo dispensed with the *solemnitas verborum*, which had been deemed essential to the validity of stipulations, and provided that *sensus et consonans intellectus ab utraque parte* should suffice, the exception which had been made in favor of the four consensual contracts would have become the rule, and that it would have been conceded that when the parties came to a mutual understanding and agreement, form was immaterial except as a means of proof, or for the sake of guarding against fraud.

This result was not attained until long years after the downfall of Rome, and if the Romans are entitled to the merit of having enunciated a principle which is recognized as generally applicable by the European nations which follow the maxims of the civil law, they restricted it within bounds that were much too narrow for the business of life.

The line was so closely drawn that an agreement to part

[1] Maynz, ii. § 246, pp. 352–356, notes 1, 25, 26.

[2] Institutes, 2. 7. 2; Sandars' Justinian, 221; Maynz, ii. § 253, pp. 392, 397.

with property for an equivalent was not binding, unless the consideration was to be paid in money; the reason assigned being that an exchange was not a sale, and therefore did not rank among the contracts which derived their obligation from consent. So there were a multitude of other contracts in which the element of consent was present, but that were not recognized or enforced by the law, unless the party who brought the action had by carrying them into effect acquired the right to insist on performance on the other side. The most plausible explanation of this incongruity is to refer it to the conservative temper engendered by the study of the law, which, though of incalculable value under a popular government, may deserve the reproach of adhering to antiquated rules and confounding forms with principles.[1]

The contract *literis* or *nominibus*, was so called from the manner in which it was formed, and the nature of the evidence adduced for its support. The creditor entered the debtor's name in his books as owing a sum certain for money advanced to him, or laid out for his use, or owing for some antecedent transaction of his own or another's, which he was willing to be answerable for, or assume; and it was incumbent on the debtor to make a corresponding entry charging himself with the amount. If the debtor's book when produced corroborated the creditor's, there was no need of further proof. If it did not, the creditor might still give his book in evidence, and establish the correctness of the entry by showing that it was made with the debtor's assent, or that he had actually received the loan.[2] An obligation so constituted by mutual entries, or by an entry made by one party with the other's sanction, was conclusive on the debtor, who could not agreeably to the strict rule of the civil law show that there was no consideration, and it was not until the age of Cicero that a defence could be made on equitable grounds.[3] The imperial legislation went still further during the third century, by throwing the burden of proof throughout on the

1 Institutes, 3. 15. 1.

2 Sandars' Justinian, 438; Maynz, § 247; Poste, pp. 328, 329.

3 Accarias, ii. No. 581; ii. No. 837, note 2; Cicero de Officiis, iii. 14.

creditor, and requiring him to establish not merely that the defendant had promised, but that the amount which was charged as having been lent to him or laid out for his use was justly due.[1]

The entry which gave rise to this form of obligation was not conclusive, or even admissible in evidence, without proof that it was made with the debtor's assent,[2] which might be established by showing that the defendant was present when the charge was made in the creditor's books; that there was a corresponding memorandum in his own; or presumably, by his failure to produce his books in response to a notice to that effect; and so, no doubt, the creditor might adduce a letter or order from the debtor, authorizing him to make the entry. If the debtor was shown to have agreed to or sanctioned the entry, he was, as the law originally stood, conclusively bound; but he was subsequently permitted to prove that his assent was given in the expectation of a loan or service which was fraudulently withheld.[3]

According to Dominguet it was essential that the debtor's assent should be given in writing, because, as he contends, the obligation would otherwise have been ranked among the consensual contracts. But this view is entirely foreign to the simplicity of the period at which the contract *literis* arose, which would seem to have been anterior to the doctrine that mutual consent might supply the want of form. The Romans, even when not engaged in trade, noted the debits and credits of each day in *adversaria* or tablets answering to the journal or diary of our own times, and these entries were transferred at the end of the month to the *codex* or ledger. A sale or loan would therefore, when the ordinary course of business was pursued, be entered by both parties and not infrequently in each other's presence, and when such was the case the mere production of the books would afford sufficient proof. If the debtor failed to enter the transaction, his assent might

[1] Maynz, ii. § 247, p. 366.

[2] Dominguet, § 185, note, pp. 328, 329; Poste, p. 330; Maynz. ii, § 247, p. 365, note 17.

[3] Maynz, ii. § 248.

be proved *aliunde*, and the entry in the creditor's book would then be conclusive of the obligation.[1]

This form of contract became obsolete before the reign of Justinian, or was superseded by a writing signed by the debtor, and admitting, like the modern due-bill, that he owed a sum certain for money lent, or on some other account.[2] There was this peculiarity, that while one who had given such an instrument might come into court and require that it should be cancelled or surrendered on the ground of fraud, or because the loan had not been made, such a proceeding could not be instituted after the lapse of five years, which Justinian reduced to two. This rule was the reverse of the English law, under which delay precludes the creditor, and not the debtor.[3]

The consideration, though no doubt originally a sum due by the party charged, need not be an advance to him, but might consist in a transaction with a third person which he was willing to have set down as so much money paid, laid out, or expended for his benefit; and became a ready means of assuming another's debt,[4] and as it would seem, if so designed discharging him. Like the stipulation, it was governed by the strict rule of the civil law, and confined to Roman citizens; although aliens might give a written memorandum or acknowledgment of debt, which had the same effect, and finally supplanted the original contract *literis*.[5]

1 Poste, p. 329.

2 Institutes, 3. 21.

3 Accarias, ii. No. 582.

4 Sandars' Justinian, 439; Accarias, ii. No. 578; Moyle's Justinian, i. 478.

5 Gaius, c. iii. § 134 ; Accarias, ii. No. 580, note 6.

CHAPTER V.

THE CONSENSUAL CONTRACTS.

Distinction between the Consensual Contracts of the Roman Law and Contracts on Mutual Promises. — *Emptio Venditio.* — *Locatio Conductio.* — *Societas.* — *Mandatum.* — *Hypotheca.* — *Constitutum.* — Innominate Contracts. — Obligations *quasi ex contractu.*

THE *nexus* might suffice while the Roman territory was limited to a corner of the Campagna, inhabited by frugal and laborious burghers and yeomen; but even supplemented by the *stipulatio* and contracts *re*, it became inadequate when trade increased, and success in arms brought Rome in contact with opulent and populous communities whose wealth lay at her command. The want was supplied by the growth of contracts which derived their obligation from consent, and covered so much ground that little more was needed for the ordinary transactions of life and business.

It was not essential to the validity of a consensual contract that the parties should meet, but simply that there should be a meeting of their minds, and while assent might be communicated through an agent he could not assent for his principal. A man was not therefore bound by a purchase of which he was ignorant, although he had duly authorized the buyer to act in his behalf. He might buy through a broker, but must be informed of and agree to the terms before the seller changed his mind. It followed that one who was clothed with a discretionary power to act for another must contract in his own name, and the obligation bound him and not his principal.[1]

The stringency of this doctrine was relaxed by an exception which was scarcely consistent with the rule. A manager or superintendent was not infrequently appointed to conduct a

[1] Accarias, ii. No. 636.

shop or farm, or act as the master or supercargo of a vessel. In that capacity he bought, sold, and made other contracts which inured to the use of his principal. As the latter reaped the benefit he could not equitably refuse to bear the burden, and the obligation was enforced through actions known as *exercitoria* and *institoria*.[1]

There was the more need for such a modification because the great proprietors and capitalists frequently intrusted the conduct of their affairs to slaves, who could not be made personally responsible in any form of suit, and those who dealt with them would have been remediless, had not the prætor brought the obligation home to the party on whose behalf it was incurred. From this point, which may be regarded as the source of the modern doctrine of agency, there was but a step to holding that the principal was bound by and might proceed on the contracts of the agent; but the change was made hesitatingly, and does not seem to have been accomplished until after the close of the classic period of Roman jurisprudence.[2]

Contracts on mutual promises resemble, but should not be confounded with the consensual contracts of the Roman law, which, as the decisions under the head of mandate show, have no place in English jurisprudence.[3] The validity of a contract of sale or of letting and hiring depends under our system not on the meeting of both minds in a common purpose, but on the promise on either side which constitutes a consideration for the obligation on the other. Hence both parties are entitled to insist on performance, although it has been rendered impossible through some intervening cause; and the loss of the subject-matter of an executory contract for the sale of a specific chattel by death or other inevitable accident, not only discharges the purchaser, but leaves the vendor answerable in damages, unless there is an implied condition that

[1] Accarias, ii. No. 636; Institutes, 4. 7. 2; Amos, Hist. and Princ. of the Civil Law, p. 261; Maynz, § 323.

[2] Accarias, ii. No. 636; Maynz, ii. § 223; Amos, Hist. and Princ. of the Civil Law, p. 261.

[3] Thorne *v.* Deas, 4 Johns. 84.

such a contingency shall annul the contract or operate as a defence;[1] contrary to the doctrine of the Roman law, that the loss is the buyer's and he must pay the price.[2] Such must necessarily be the result when the obligation depends on the consideration and ceases when it fails; but the rule was the direct opposite at Rome where the doctrine of consideration did not prevail; and it was a good answer to a suit for breach of contract that performance was prevented by causes which the defendant could not control, and that he was consequently free from blame.[3] Accordingly, where the execution of a contract for the letting and hiring of work or services became impossible through *vis major*, or other event for which the contractor was not responsible, he was not only exempt from liability, but might exact full compensation for the work which he had been engaged to perform.[4] The rule that advocates need not return their fees if they are unavoidably prevented from appearing in court, seems to have sprung from a principle which should be duly appreciated by members of the bar. The seeming hardship and injustice of the doctrine was modified in practice by an arbitrary presumption that if the fulfilment of a contract to build or manufacture failed before the work was or ought to have been accepted or approved, the fault was the contractor's, unless he showed that it lay in the materials furnished by the *locator* or in the nature of the soil, which rendered it impossible to obtain a secure foundation.[5]

The consensual contracts, or contracts deriving their obligations from agreement without regard to form, were as generally enumerated, *emptio venditio*, bargain and sale, *locatio conductio*, letting and hiring, *societas* or partnership, and *mandatum* or agency. Such contracts were obligatory as soon as the parties agreed on the terms, although nothing had been done or paid on either side, and there was no writ-

[1] Kein *v.* Tupper, 52 N. Y. 550; Dexter *v.* Norton, 47 id. 62.

[2] Maynz, ii. §§ 173–177.

[3] Maynz, ii. §§ 173, 177.

[4] Amos, Hist. and Princ. of the Civil Law, p. 234; Maynz, ii. § 218, p. 249, note 15.

[5] Maynz, ii. § 218, pp. 249, 250, notes 17, 18, 19.

ten evidence. Thus when the subject-matter was determined and the price fixed under a contract of sale, the thing sold was thenceforth at the risk of the purchaser, who would gain if it increased in value and lose if it deteriorated.

Agreeably to the natural view, which seems also to have been the view of the Roman law, whether a contract of sale be for the conveyance of a particular thing or of a thing of a certain kind, it is executory until fulfilled by the delivery of that which the vendor agrees to part with and the vendee to buy.[1] The right of property consequently remained in the vendor until delivery, and if the maxim *res perit domino* had been strictly followed, he would have been answerable if the property was injured or destroyed during the interval. This consequence was avoided by holding that the vendor was only bound to hand over the article in the condition in which it was when the price was paid and the vendee became entitled to possession. Hence, if the subject-matter was a house, and it was injured by fire, or swept away by a flood before the purchaser went into possession, he was still answerable for the price, unless there had been a want of due care on the part of the vendor; and so if the property rose in value the purchaser reaped the benefit.[2]

Contracts for the delivery of things of a certain kind obeyed a different rule; for as the obligation on both sides was *in genere*, neither could rely on impossibility as an excuse, and the vendor's inability to procure the goods was no more a defence for a failure to deliver, than was the purchaser's poverty to an action for the price.[3]

Agreeably to the common law the passage of the title depends on the intention of the parties as manifested by their acts and language. If they agree on the terms, and the subject-matter is set apart or defined, it becomes the property of the buyer, and he must pay the purchase-money although the thing sold perishes before delivery. Where, on the other

[1] Maynz, ii. § 256, p. 407. See Sergeant Manning's note to Bailey *v.* Culverwell, 2 Manning and Ryland, 564.

[2] Maynz, ii. § 210, p. 206; Institutes, 3. 23. 3; Sandars' Justinian, 446.

[3] Accarias, ii. No. 612, note.

hand, the contract is not so far perfected as to pass the title, the buyer will be discharged by the seller's failure to deliver, whether it arises from his fault or an unavoidable accident.[1] A full performance is essential; and if it does not take place the seller cannot recover even for what the purchaser actually received, although the delivery commenced, and its completion was prevented by the destruction of the residue of the goods by fire.[1]

Payment was not less essential to the completion of the contract than delivery, and the right of property remained in the vendor until both requisites were satisfied, unless the sale was on credit, which might be inferred from the vendor's handing the property over without asking for the money.[2]

This was a logical deduction from the doctrine that a contract of sale is executory, and does not pass the title until fulfilled. The common law, on the other hand, holds with a wise regard to the needs of business, that delivery is a waiver of the vendor's right of lien, and leaves him nothing but an action for the purchase-money, unless the purchaser acquires possession by artifice or fraud, when the vendor may retake the goods or maintain replevin.

It must be remembered that, as regarded *res mancipi*, delivery and payment did not pass the legal title, and simply conferred an equitable right that might, if acquired in good faith without notice of a better claim, be perfected through an unbroken possession of two years in the case of land, and one in that of chattels.[3] Such was the rule during the republic, and under the empire, until mancipation was abolished by Justinian.[4] The distinction between *res mancipi* and *nec mancipi* fell with it, and tradition became the sole and customary mode of conveying movable or immovable property.

The Roman jurists finally arrived at the conclusion, though not until after much debate, that the consideration for a sale must be payable in money, and could not consist of value in

[1] Kein *v.* Tupper, 52 N. Y. 550. [2] Maynz, ii. § 210, p. 207.
[3] Maynz, i. § 92, p. 688; Gaius, c. ii. §§ 15, 22; Poste, pp. 143, 530.
[4] Sandars' Justinian, 157.

any other form.[1] It followed as a necessary consequence that an exchange of lands or chattels did not rank among the consensual contracts, and was invalid unless put in the form of a *stipulatio*, or executed by the party who sought to enforce it.[2]

As the validity of a contract of sale depended on the *aggregatio mentium*, or *consensus*, and not on the consideration, so a promise to sell if the buyer signifies his intention to purchase within a certain period, or in other words to give him time for deliberation, is obligatory under the civil law though void under the law of England; [3] and its acceptance by the vendee completes the contract, though it is subject to a condition which suspends its operation,[4] and will defeat it if the vendee does not make his election before the time expires.

We are told by Maynz that the contract of letting and hiring exists when one undertakes to procure for another the use of a thing, or to render him a service in consideration of a payment to be made by the lessee. The lease of a thing is *locatio rei;* that of services, *locatio operarum;* and he who engaged to pay the price was the *conductor*, while the other party was known as the *locator*.[5]

The contract had three requisites; a definite subject-matter, a price or rent, and consent. It was ordinarily essential that the rent should be paid in money; but where the property was productive, as for instance a farm or flock of sheep, the lessor might stipulate for a share of the fruits or increase. Such is the ordinary form of lease at the present day in northern Italy, and it is not infrequent in the United States. It is said by Mommsen, that "the payment must necessarily consist in money; in consequence of which the produce lease among the Romans comes under the contingencies occurring in practical life, though not falling within the theory of jurispru-

[1] Institutes, 3. 23; Boston & M. R. R. Co. *v.* Bartlett, 3 Cush. 224.
[2] Maynz, ii. § 244.
[3] See Boston & M. R. R. Co. *v.* Bartlett, 3 Cush. 224.
[4] Institutes, 3. 23. 1.
[5] Pothier, Contrat de Louage, Partie i. ch. i.

dence;" but this view is at variance with that taken by other commentators.[1]

When one engages the services of another as bailiff, gardener, foreman, or book-keeper, the relation of master and servant arises, and the contract may properly be called a *locatio operarum*, and the person to whom the service is rendered, the conductor. Whether the man himself is hired, his ox, or his services, the case is analogous in principle and comes under the same general head. An agreement to build a house, or a vessel, or do any other specific piece of work, at the contractor's cost and charges, and look to the price for compensation, is so far different that the control and responsibility devolve on the contractor, who proceeds on his own account, although the work when done will inure to the benefit of the employer. Such is the familiar case of an agreement to erect a building on the land of another. The builder stands in an independent position, and may insist on adhering to the contract notwithstanding any orders given by the owner, who cannot refuse to allow the work to proceed in accordance with the terms agreed on, without rendering himself liable in damages.

Such a contract is not therefore a letting of the contractor's services to the employer, but of the right to do the work to the contractor, who becomes the conductor, while the contract is called *locatio operis faciendi*.[2]

The distinction between this form of letting and the *locatio operarum* is attended with this important difference, that while one who hires the services of another is bound to see to the way in which they are performed, and will be answerable for injuries resulting from his negligence, no such consequence follows from a contract for the performance of work, because the contractor is not under the control or supervision of the person for whom the work is done.

The letting of land or chattels imposed a personal obligation on the lessor, without conferring a right of property on

[1] Mommsen, ii. 432; Maynz, ii. § 215.

[2] Sandars' Justinian, 448; Maynz, ii. § 218; Pothier, Contrat de Louage, Partie vii. ch. i.

the lessee, or even the *possessio*, in the technical sense in which the term was used by the Roman lawyers. The lessor continued to be the possessor, not only as regarded third persons, but as between himself and the lessee, his duty being not *rem præstare licere habere*, but *re frui licere*, i. e. that that lessee should enjoy, and not that he should possess. It followed that although the sale or devise of the property to a third person, who was a stranger to the contract, did not terminate the lease, he might still eject the tenant without being answerable in damages, and the tenant was thus compelled to seek redress through an action against the lessor for a breach of the implied undertaking for quiet enjoyment.[1]

Such a doctrine was the natural result of a social condition where the property holders were alone considered, and where the poorer class had little voice or influence in the promulgation or administration of the laws. In like manner, during the infancy of English jurisprudence, a lease was a mere contract which conferred no vested right on the tenant, who held the land at the will of the lessor, and might be ejected at his pleasure.[2] The action of covenant real seems to have been devised as a remedy for this evil, and as the judgment was in the nature of a decree for specific performance, gave an effectual remedy as between the original parties, but being *ex contractu* could not be maintained against a stranger, or even against an assignee of the reversion,[3] and consequently fell into disuse and was superseded by the writ of *ejectione firmæ*, which though originally intended to afford compensation for the loss of the term, finally supplanted the real actions of the earlier law, and became a convenient and effectual remedy for the vindication of the right to land, whether arising from a grant in fee, or a lease for a term of years. Tenancies for years were thus converted from a precarious occupancy into an assured possession of the soil, which, though limited in duration, was attended with the same safeguards as estates of freehold.

[1] Sandars' Justinian, 451; Pothier, Contrat de Louage, Partie ii. ch. i. § 11; Maynz, ii. § 217, p. 245.

[2] 2 Bl. Com. 140, 142.

[3] 3 Bl. Com. 156.

A mandate is, agreeably to the commentators on the Roman law, a contract by which one person agrees to act for another generally in the administration of his property or with regard to some matter which the latter intrusts to his care.[1] It was originally a trust or confidence reposed in the good faith of a friend or relative, that might be violated with impunity, but to which the prætor afterwards gave a legal sanction by compelling the mandatary to render a strict account to his principal, and the latter to bear or reimburse all the costs and charges incurred by the mandatary.[2] Like some other branches of the civil law, it affords a striking proof of the high sense of duty which regulated many of the relations of life at Rome, and formed the ground-work of a system of jurisprudence, which is alike admirable for its logical precision and moral tone.

The mandate continued to be so far a trust throughout the whole period of Roman jurisprudence, that the mandatary was obliged to act in his own name, and that the legal right was in him; and it was by slow degrees, and not without much ingenious manipulation, that the *mandans*, or principal, came to be regarded as the real party to the contract, and was enabled to enforce it through an *actio utilis*, instituted without the intervention of the mandatary.[3]

The mandate was thus brought nearer to the agency of modern jurisprudence, but retained some distinctive features, which, though modified in obedience to the requirements of an advancing civilization, were never entirely obliterated, — one, that it must be gratuitous; another, that the undertakings of the mandatary bound him, and were not binding on the principal. If the mandatary acted with a view to compensation, he became a *locator operis*, and his liability was tested by different rules.[4]

The second feature above mentioned resulted from the inflexible canon of the Roman law that contracts are only oper-

1 Maynz, ii. § 220; Accarias, ii. No. 636.

2 Sandars' Justinian, 45, 81.

3 Sandars' Justinian, 458; Maynz, ii. § 222; Accarias, ii. No. 637.

4 Pothier, Traité des Obligations, Partie i. ch. i. § 1.

ative as between the parties, and can neither confer rights nor impose obligations on third persons.[1] It followed that the *mandans* or principal could neither sue nor be sued on the contracts of the mandatary, although the latter was bound to enforce them for his benefit and might look to him for indemnity; but the impediment was, we have already intimated, surmounted by subrogating the party with whom the contract was made to the action of the mandatary against the principal, and allowing the principal to proceed directly on the contract.[2]

It was a logical consequence of the above principles that the contract was not less binding on the mandatary because made after his authority had ceased through an express revocation, or the death of the principal, and as he was entitled to an indemnity if he had acted without notice and in good faith, the creditor might be substituted in his place.[3]

Such is still the rule of the civil law as administered in modern Europe, although the distinction on which it was founded is no longer recognized, and the agent not only acts for but represents and binds the principal.[4]

On the other hand, agreeably to the theory of representation, as applied at common law, the obligation is the principal's and not the agent's, and therefore cannot arise from a contract made after his death, although the parties are ignorant of the fact.[5] Logical as this rule may be, it may obviously lead to inequitable results. Some of the American courts accordingly hold that the agency subsists, as regards third persons until they are informed that it has ceased.[6]

Whatever the common-law rule may be, where the revocation results from the death of the principal, he cannot by revoking the agency during his lifetime, prejudice persons

[1] Maynz, ii. § 222; Sandars' Justinian, 457.

[2] Sandars' Justinian, 458; Maynz, ii. § 222, p. 261.

[3] Institutes, 3. 26. 10; Accarias, ii. No. 638; Gaius, c. iii. § 160.

[4] Delsol, livre III. tit. xiii. ch. i. iv. pp. 391, 404.

[5] Michigan State Bank *v.* Leavenworth, 2 Williams, 209; 1 Am. Leading Cases, 5 ed. 711.

[6] Ish *v.* Crane, 8 Ohio, N. S. 520, 13 Ohio, 574; Cassiday *v.* McKenzie, 4 W. & S. 282; Dick *v.* Page, 17 Mo. 234.

who act in the belief that it still exists, although the revocation is known to the agent, and he proceeds in fraud of the principal.[1]

The rule was at all events in the first instance the reverse at Rome, because the mandatary was not under these circumstances entitled to an indemnity from the mandant, and the prætor could not consistently give third persons a greater right; and it is not clear that the objection was ever set aside however loudly the case might call for a redress.[2]

While a mandate to buy continued in force until the mandatary had notice that it was recalled, an offer to buy might be revoked by a countermand dispatched before the offer reached the seller or was accepted by him, although the revocation did not arrive until the seller had forwarded the goods;[3] the reason being that in the latter case, the minds of the parties did not meet and there was no sale, while the contract bound the mandatary in the former and through him the principal. Mr. Benjamin regards these results as incongruous;[4] but they seem to be the logical consequences of a system when representation was unknown, and the validity of contracts depended on consent, and not on what one party did or promised on the faith of the promise given by the other.

The mandate like the *mancipatio* was ingeniously used for purposes foreign to its original design, and a direction to advance money or give credit to a third person operated as a guaranty, by binding the mandant to indemnify the lender, although the authority so given might be recalled at any time before it was acted on.[5] Such an adaptation was the more requisite because a guaranty did not rank as a consensual contract, and could not be made directly as to non-existing liabilities save in the form of a stipulation.

The mandate, and the stringency of the obligation which it imposed, will be more readily understood if we reflect that

[1] 1 Am. Leading Cases, 5 Am. ed. 711.
[2] See Accarias, ii. No. 638.
[3] Pothier, Contrat de Vente, No. 32.
[4] Benjamin on Sales, §§ 72, 73.
[5] Poste, p. 350; Accarias, ii. No. 638.

Rome was continually at war, and her citizens liable to be called on brief notice to the field for a campaign which might last for months or years. A man so placed would naturally turn to some friend in whom he could confide, and request him to take charge of his patrimony during his absence, and use the care and diligence which he would exercise if present. The confidence thus reposed would appear sacred in the eyes of a community where every one might, in the course of events, feel the need or be asked to assume the responsibility. To neglect it would be culpable, to betray it infamous; and the mandatary might be held to a stricter account than if he were acting for a reward.[1] It was from this source that the English Court of Chancery derived the exalted conception of a trust, which is a distinctive feature of that tribunal, and serves as an antidote to the commercial immorality engendered by the strain of modern civilization. The mandate, like the relation between patron and client, and the laws that forbade a jurisconsult or advocate to stipulate for or accept compen-

[1] Accarias, ii. No. 634, note 1. The sanctity of such a trust, and the disgrace incident to a failure to fulfil it, are stated in Cicero's oration *pro Roscio Amerino*, in terms that may excite our admiration for a people who set so high a value on good faith.

"In privatis rebus si qui rem mandatam non modo malitiosius gessisset, sui quæstus aut commodi causa, verum etiam negligentius, eum majores summum admisisse dedecus existimabant. Itaque mandati constitutum est judicium, non minus turpe, quam furti; credo propterea quod, quibus in rebus ipsi interesse non possumus, in his, operæ nostræ vicaria, fides amicorum supponitur; quam qui lædit, oppugnat omnium commune præsidium, et, quantum in ipso est, disturbat vitæ societatem. Non enim possumus omnia per nos agere: alius in alia est re magis utilis. Idcirco amicitiæ comparantur, ut commune commodum mutuis officiis gubernetur.

. . . .

"Ergo idcirco turpis hæc culpa est, quod duas res sanctissimas violat, amicitiam et fidem: nam neque mandat quisquam fere, nisi amico; neque credit, nisi ei, quem fidelem putat. Perditissimi est igitur hominis, simul et amicitiam dissolvere, et fallere eum, qui læsus non esset, nisi credidisset." Cicero pro Roscio Am. xxxviii.

This passage, with another in the same oration touching the relation of counsel and client, should be read attentively by every student of the law as containing principles that should be kept in view throughout his professional and private life. Pro Roscio Am. xi.

sation, is a refutation of the idea that the Romans were not only frugal but avaricious, and governed in all their dealings by the hope of gain.[1]

The trust of the English is analogous to the mandate of the Roman law in various particulars, and among others because the trustee, like the mandatary, is not only bound to render his services gratuitously, but cannot after the relation is once established stipulate for compensation, unless the circumstances are such that the cestui que trust is free to choose, and may procure some competent person to fill the place.[2]

The contract of *societas*, or partnership, was, in many of its principal features, the same at Rome as it is now in Europe and the United States, and from the nature of things the remark presumably would apply to China and every other country where men agree to cast their property and services into a common fund with a view to profit; but there are, as might have been anticipated, points where the lines of thought have diverged during the lapse of years, and the obligation has undergone a corresponding change. A partnership might be dissolved under the Roman law at the will of any member, contrary to the general rule that the consent of all the parties is essential to rescission; and such is also the law at the present day when no time is prescribed for the duration of the contract.[3]

The Romans carried the principle to its logical conclusion by holding that the right of dissolution was not precluded by a stipulation that the partnership should continue for a definite period.[4] This view seems with proper limitations to be altogether sound, because a trader should not be compelled to leave his property at the mercy of associates whom he doubts, and may have grounds for distrust that do not admit of legal proof.

[1] See Maynz, ii. § 207; Accarias, ii. No. 494, note 1.

[2] Robinson *v.* Pett, 3 P. Wms. 249; 2 Leading Cases in Equity, 4 Am. ed. 512, 538; Ayliffe *v.* Murray, 2 Atk. 58.

[3] Fletcher *v.* Reed, 131 Mass. 312.

[4] Institutes, 3. 25. 4; Accarias, ii. No. 628, note; Amos, Hist. and Princ. of the Civil Law, p. 241.

The French Code (article 1869), nevertheless, provides that the dissolution of the partnership by the will of one of the associates only "applies to partnerships where duration is unlimited." Some of the English and American authorities take a similar view,[1] while others incline to the Roman law; and Lord Eldon favors, while Kent and Story controvert the idea that the right of withdrawal can be restrained by agreement.[2]

The controversy is to some extent one of terms. All the authorities seemingly agree that a partner may be liable in damages for withdrawing before the appointed time without sufficient cause,[3] and that the assets are, notwithstanding any such renunciation, affected with a trust for the payment of debts and the protection of the remaining partners;[4] and there are perhaps none that would specifically decree the retiring partner to render his time or services, or hold him bound by subsequent contracts with third persons whom he has duly notified.

The characteristic feature of the relation of partnership, as now interpreted, is that the parties not only agree, but are empowered to represent each other in all that concerns the business of the firm, and are at once principals and agents, mandants and mandataries. The contracts made by one are consequently binding on all, notwithstanding any stipulation to the contrary that is not known to the persons with whom they deal, and may not only be prosecuted against them jointly, but enforced by an execution levied for the whole amount on the property of each. The rule was essentially different at Rome, where a partner was not bound by a contract in which he did not unite, unless he had given a mandate to that effect or reaped the profits, and was even then not answerable *in solido* for the whole, but only for his share.[5]

1 Story on Partnership, § 273.

2 3 Kent's Com. 54; Marquaud *v.* New York Manuf. Co., 17 Johns. 525; Skinner *v.* Dayton, 19 Johns. 513.

3 Reiter *v.* Morton, 96 Pa. 229; Story, Equity Jurisprudence, 8, 668.

4 Ambler *v.* Whipple, 20 Wallace, 516.

5 Maynz, ii. § 227; Accarias, ii. No. 627; Sandars' Justinian, 454.

This doctrine was based on two dogmas of the civil law that are hardly consonant with reason: one, that contracts are not obligatory on third persons, although made on their behalf and authorized by them; the other, that a joint promise to do or render a divisible thing, does not bind the parties severally to see that the whole is performed. These still govern the contracts of partnership on the continent of Europe, where the English doctrine that a dormant partner is personally bound by and answerable for the obligations of the firm, is unknown; and indicates, according to Fremery that *et penitus toto divisos orbe Britannos* is applicable to the English law.[1]

Another contract, which, though binding the property rather than the person, depended for its validity on consent, was the *hypotheca*, or, as we now term it, mortgage. Mortgages were originally effected at Rome, as they are with us, by a conveyance of the thing subject to a trust or condition that it should only be used as a means of security and satisfaction. The debtor mancipated the property to the creditor, who engaged to make restitution when paid. A contract which left the title in the debtor while conferring a qualified right of property on the creditor, was finally substituted for mancipation, and took effect immediately on its completion without the delivery of possession, which was essential in the case of a pledge or sale. The mortgagor continued to be the owner, as he does at the present day, but the mortgagee also had an ownership as between the parties and against all the world; and could not only turn the land or goods into money for the payment of the debt, with a preference over intervening purchasers or incumbrances, but maintain an action against any one by whom the property was taken or detained.[2]

Contracts of mortgage thus had the effect, which was denied to contracts of sale, of conferring a right of property without delivery, contrary to the English rule that such agreements, though binding the parties, are not valid against purchasers for value without notice.

[1] Fremery, Études de Droit Commercial, ch. vi. p. 39.

[2] Accarias, i. Nos. 284, 285, 286; Poste, p. 303.

The consensual contracts might from their nature be invalidated by the proof of any fact which showed that they could not be enforced consistently with good faith.[1] Such a defence might, nevertheless, as the law originally stood, be precluded by a charge made with the debtor's consent, or his response to a stipulation which imposed an absolute obligation that could not be controverted on the ground of fraud or failure of consideration.[2] Such an estoppel, like the conclusive effect of a bond or covenant at common law, might be beneficial, as tending to prevent controversy or induce caution in entering into agreements, but at the same time rendered it possible to set toils from which there was no escape. An action for purchase money was *bonæ fidei*, and could not be enforced by a vendor who was chargeable with bad faith; but he might by inducing the purchaser to merge the original agreement in a stipulation or contract *literis*, preclude inquiry into the fraud.[3] Cicero relates an amusing anecdote of a Roman knight, who, having been tricked into buying the Syracusan villa where he was dining, by an operatic scene got up for the purpose by his host, caused the transaction to be entered as a debt in his book and that of the vendor, and found himself as helpless as an Englishman who gave his bond in the reign of Queen Elizabeth would have been but for the Court of Chancery.[4]

That the law should have stood on this basis for centuries without consequences that would have led to a change, may be regarded as evidence of the pristine good faith of the Romans, and it was not until the relaxation of morals in the latter years of the republic, that Cicero's colleague in the prætorship, Aquilius, devised the formula *de dolo* as a remedy for fraud whether it occurred in a consensual or formal contract.[5]

The *constitutum*, or promise to pay an existing debt — one's own or another's — at a certain day, was also so far a consensual contract as to be binding solely by the force of

[1] Accarias, ii. No. 837.
[2] Accarias, ii. No. 581; Poste, p. 330.
[3] Accarias, ii. No. 837, note 2.
[4] Cicero de Officiis, iii. 14.
[5] Cicero de Officiis, iii. 14; Accarias, ii. No. 837, note 2.

the agreement without regard to form, although it was not ordinarily mutual, and did not preclude the creditor from enforcing the original obligation. It afforded a ready mode of guaranteeing antecedent debts, and was frequently so used at Rome, but did not apply to future obligations or credits that had not been already given.[1]

The Roman law did not recognize or enforce contracts depending solely on agreement, save exceptionally, nor until the growth of wealth and population rendered the change essential. The consensual contracts gradually became obligatory; but outside these limits, contracts that were not valid by reason of the facts or the form, were nude pacts, and would not sustain an action.

The effect was to leave numerous agreements that concerned life and business beyond the pale of the law, and dependent on a good faith that might be wanting. If a buyer and seller agreed on the thing and the price, the sale was complete; but consent alone did not give validity to a contract of exchange, nor to a promise by one man to be answerable for such goods as might subsequently be sold to another.[2]

The chasm was partially bridged by the aid of the prætorian legislation, which was so often employed to supplement the deficiencies of the civil law. Although a contract that did not fall under the heads that have been enumerated in this chapter was invalid, it obviously ought not to be used as a means of fraud, and if either party lay by until it was so far performed by the other that he could not equitably refuse to do his share, an innominate obligation arose and might be enforced through an action *præscriptis verbis*.[3] The doctrine was among the last fruits of the formulary system which did so much for jurisprudence;[4] and the pacts which admitted of its application were classified as follows: *do ut des; do ut facias; facio ut des; facio ut facias*, — a generalization which may be simplified by saying that an act done or payment made

[1] Institutes, 4. 6. 8, 9; Accarias, ii. Nos. 720, 721, 722.

[2] Maynz, ii. § 247, p. 342; Accarias, ii. Nos. 603, 654.

[3] Accarias, ii. Nos. 648, 649. [4] Accarias, ii. Nos. 648, 650.

on the faith of a promise, may give rise to an obligation, though the promise was not obligatory.

The innovation was made hesitatingly and by slow degrees; and the commentators differ as to the extent and nature of the remedy. One who parts with his goods or money in reliance on an undertaking which is not performed, is obviously entitled to restitution; and we may believe that this was the first step, and that the prætor did not award a specific performance or compensation in damages until afterwards.

Hugo observes that innominate contracts are not mentioned by Gaius or in the Institutes, and after stating that in Richelon's opinion there were but two species of innominate contracts, — *do ut des* and *do ut facias*, — cites the following extract from the Digest: *Quod si faciam ut des, et postea quam feci cessas dare, nulla erit civilis actio et ideo de dolo dabitur.* In other words, as in the analogous instance of the development of the action of assumpsit from the action on the case, a remedy was found for a breach of contract by treating it as a tort.[1]

The true inference seems to be that an innominate obligation, like the debt or simple contract of the common law, originally arose where value was received as well as parted with; but that it subsequently came to be considered that one who changed his position for the worse on the faith of a promise of compensation, ought to be paid although the transaction was not beneficial to the promisor. Thus, if two persons agreed that a slave belonging to one of them should be freed in consideration of a pecuniary recompense, the agreement was not binding on either side; but if the owner carried it into effect by manumitting the slave, he might maintain an action for the money.[2]

Although performance by either party would render an innominate contract obligatory on the other, the party who did the act might choose whether he would compel the opposite party to fulfil the contract, or rescind it and recover back

[1] Accarias, ii. No. 649.

[2] Maynz, ii. § 243, p. 235, note 25; Accarias, ii. No. 652.

what he had paid or given.[1] This may appear inconsistent with the rule that both parties must be bound, or neither; but was a natural consequence of the doctrine that the obligation of such contracts arises from what is done under them, and not from the agreement itself.

Obligations having a lawful source other than agreement were designated by the Roman jurists as *quasi ex contractu*, as springing neither from a contract nor delict, and yet making a nearer approach to the former character than the latter.[2]

Such an obligation might arise from the unauthorized payment of another's debt.[3] For as such a payment discharged the debtor, it became his duty to reimburse the person by whom it was made, unless the latter acted against his will or with an intention to give.[4] A like consequence followed from acts done on the behalf of a person who from absence could not attend to his own affairs.[5] It was immaterial that the act was done without his knowledge or consent, and repudiated as soon as he was informed, because to the extent of the benefit which it conferred he was bound to bear the burden.[6]

The theory of the English law is, on the contrary, that a benefit conferred without consent is so far from imposing an obligation, that it will not serve as a consideration for a subsequent express promise unless the case admits of ratification.[7] A man cannot satisfy my debt, much less render me his debtor, by an unauthorized payment;[8] nor will the expenditure of money on my land, or other benefit gratuitously conferred impose an obligation.[9] As the rule was stated

[1] Maynz, ii. § 243.

[2] Institutes, 3. 27. 1; Accarias, ii. No. 655.

[3] Institutes, 3. 29; Accarias, ii. No. 690.

[4] Institutes, 3. 29; Accarias, ii. No. 690.

[5] Institutes, 3. 27. 1.

[6] Institutes, 3. 27. 1; Accarias, ii. Nos. 656, 599.

[7] Eastwood *v.* Kenyon, 11 A. & E. 438; Lampleigh *v.* Brathwait, Hobart, 105 *b.*; 1 Sm. L. C. 8 Am. ed. 269.

[8] 1 Sm. L. C. 8 Am. ed. 641, 644, 676; Jones *v.* Broadhurst, 9 C. B. 173; James *v.* Isaacs, 12 id. 791; Sevens *v.* Wilkinson, H. & N. 420; Kennedy *v.* Carpenter, 2 Wharton, 344.

[9] Eastwood *v.* Kenyon, 11 A. & E. 438; Lampleigh *v.* Brathwait, Hobart, 105*b*.

broadly in Eastwood *v.* Kenyon, — a voluntary courtesy or past benefit conferred without a request is neither a source of obligation nor a consideration to uphold an assumpsit.

The common and Roman law nevertheless agree, that the delivery of a chattel under a mistaken belief that it is due imposes a duty of restitution,[1] which may be enforced by an action of detinue, or, after a demand has been refused, of trover and conversion. Assumpsit will not lie because there is no contract, and redress must be sought by other means. When, however, such a payment has been made in money, the appropriate remedy is assumpsit for money had and received.[2] Trover cannot be maintained because money has no earmark, and as debt might have been defeated by the defendant's waging his law, the law feigned a promise contrary to the fact, in order to prevent a failure of justice.

The marked difference between the modern doctrine of contracts, and that which prevailed at Rome, is the power now ascribed to written instruments of merging or superseding all that has gone before, and of being not merely the evidence, but the source of obligations that cannot be controverted save for mistake or fraud. The Anglo-Norman covenant was and is binding by its intrinsic force, and the deeds by which land is conveyed or leased, and men bind themselves to make, to build, or sell, are not less obligatory. Such contracts were unknown to the classic age of Roman jurisprudence, which employed writing to perpetuate the memory of what had been done or agreed on by other means. The *mancipatio* and contract *verbis* were customarily recited or set forth for greater security in writings known as *tabulæ* or *cautiones;* but these documents, like the deed of feoffment of the feudal law, were simply evidence and might be annulled on proof that the transfer or agreement which they professed to record had not been duly made.[3] The contract *literis* was an entry in the creditor's book of money laid out

[1] Institutes, 3. 14. 1; 27. 6; Accarias, ii. No. 659.

[2] See 2 Sm. L. C. 8 Am. ed. 452.

[3] Maynz, ii. § 245, p. 352; Gaius, c. iii. § 134.

or advanced for the debtor, which estopped the latter, and can hardly be deemed an exception to the rule.

In the course of time the use of written instruments became habitual, and they gradually displaced the verbal and customary obligations of the original civil law. Writing was customarily employed in making a consensual contract; and it was finally enacted that if either party to a sale stipulated that it should be reduced to writing, the contract should not be complete until the provision was complied with.[1] A due bill or written promise to pay was substituted for the ancient contract *literis*, and Constantine made instruments of gift obligatory.[2] The *stipulatio* was still purely verbal; and if a memorandum or *cautio* was drawn up, reciting that the parties came together and exchanged the formal question and response, it might be falsified by proof that no such meeting took place, or that the customary forms were not observed.[3] The *cautio*, nevertheless, afforded a presumption that the technical requirements had been fulfilled; and Justinian finally enacted that to invalidate such a document on the ground of absence, it must be shown conclusively that one of the parties was in some other place during the entire day.[4] The point was now reached at which, owing to the growth of new forms, men seek to evade rather than to comply with the old; and during the transitional period which followed the overthrow of Rome, written instruments became what they still are, — the source of obligations as well as the proof.[5]

I may add that the contracts *literis* and *verbis* were distinctively Roman, and aliens employed written instruments known as *syngraphæ* and *chirographæ*, which, as their names import, were of Grecian origin, and binding not merely as evidence but directly.[6] These, when the Latin race decayed and Roman citizenship ceased to exist even in name, came with the *cautiones* from their convenience and certainty, to take the place of the traditional contracts of the civil law, and

[1] Institutes, 3. 23; Amos, Hist. and Princ. of the Civil Law, p. 223.

[2] Sandars' Justinian, 221.

[3] Maynz, ii. § 245, pp. 351, 352.

[4] Institutes, 3. 19. 12; Accarias, ii. No. 499.

[5] Maynz, ii. § 245, p. 352.

[6] Gaius, c. iii. § 134; Poste, pp. 331, 333.

gave rise to the forms which prevail in modern Europe. To this source we may refer the documents which in England, among the Anglo-Saxons, and subsequently to the Conquest, operated in some instances as contracts or conveyances, and were in others memoranda of what was done or agreed upon by other means.[1]

[1] Essays in Anglo-Saxon Law, p. 231; Spence, Eq. Jurisd.

CHAPTER VI.

MODERN APPLICATION OF THE ROMAN LAW.

Law the Exponent of Relations which vary with Time and Circumstances. — Influence of Justinian's Legislation on Jurisprudence. — Title did not pass at Rome by Sale without Delivery. — Reason as given by Fremery. — May pass in England. — Rule under the French Code. — Joint Contract at Common Law for Divisible Performance binds each party for the Whole. — Bound under the Civil Law only for their respective Shares. — Distinction according to Fremery technical.

THE law is the exponent of relations which vary in every age and country. Its main object in regulating the dealings of individuals should be to give effect to the intention of the parties, when that does not endanger the welfare of society; and as the wants and wishes of mankind change with the advance of civilization, and the introduction of new forms of property and government, the law cannot consistently remain the same. This has been urged as a reproach to jurisprudence, but is really a proof of its superiority as a moral science, concerned not with the unalterable course of nature, but with the will and conscience of an intellectual being, who can control or modify the course of events or adapt himself to them.

The effect of contracts, as for instance when the right of property should pass by a sale, and whether two or more persons who promise to pay or render to another should each be answerable for the whole, or only for an aliquot share, should therefore depend not on rules imposed arbitrarily by the legislator or handed down traditionally from antiquity, but on the object which the parties have in view, and the means taken for its attainment.

Beneficial as was the influence of the civil law in reducing to order the chaos which succeeded the downfall of the Roman Empire, and giving the conquerors a standard which, if not the perfection of reason, was higher than any which they could then have established for themselves, it yet tended to retard the progress of jurisprudence by setting limits which few were bold enough to transcend. When once it appeared that the case was covered by the Institutes or Digest, or that they laid down a principle by which it could be ruled, further inquiry was deemed superfluous. I refer to the countries which adopted the civil as their common law; but even where, as in northern France, the customary law prevailed, the question was not as to the merits of either system, or whether doctrines which had originated a thousand years back were applicable to the existing state of things; but did the custom preclude the application of a rule that would otherwise be conclusive.

The fallacy of regulating the effect of agreements made in modern times by rules evolved or promulgated in a society so remote in time, and unlike in organization, as that which existed at Rome, is ably shown in Fremery's Études de Droit Commercial.[1] Contracts are, as he points out, what the agreement of the parties makes them, as declared in terms or deduced from the usages prevailing at the time, and the effect of a contract of sale under Augustus or the Antonines might differ widely from that which it had when the Digest and Institutes were promulgated, and be still more unlike that ascribed to it by the custom of trade and the general understanding of mankind at the present day.

Why a sale bound the parties at Rome, and not the title, is, agreeably to the same author, because the seller undertook, as the contract was then customarily formulated, *præstare emptori rem licere habere*, — terms less wide in their import than *rem dare*, and which did not, agreeably to the decisions of the jurisconsults, import an obligation to confer ownership. Justinian inserted these decisions in the Digest, and made them law, so that, deriving their authority from legislation, they became applicable to every contract of sale, however much it might differ in language or circumstances from that to which they originally referred. When, therefore, the vendor uses the words *rem dare*, instead of *rem habere licere*, and the question arises in a country where the Digest has not the force of positive law, it can no longer consistently be held

[1] Ch. i. p. 5.

that he is not bound to transfer the ownership. And when, instead of using either locution, he simply says, "I sell," and leaves the interpretation to usage, what conclusion should be reached, if all who employ these words understand them as signifying that the vendor binds himself to transfer the ownership?[1]

This exposition renders it clear that the effect of a contract of sale in transferring the right of property, depends not on a fixed or inherent rule, but on the circumstances and the words employed; and as they vary the interpretation should undergo a corresponding change.

The question is, therefore, unless considerations of policy intervene, for the judge, and not for the legislator; and no law can be made that will hold good in every age, and under different social conditions. In holding that title would not pass by a sale without delivery and payment, Gaius or Papinian presumably did not mean to lay down a rule for all time, and irrespective of design, but simply that such was the operation of the contract as then promulgated, and when read in the light of the customs and principles by which the transfer of property was traditionally regulated, Justinian's legislation was an adaptation of the laws and usages of Rome to the existing state of things at Constantinople, by men who did not always understand the true bearing of the decisions which they erected into rules,[2] and should be followed so far only as it is based on scientific and fundamental principles. If the Institutes are still applicable to the relations of partners, and of bailor and bailee, it is from their essential truth, and not because they were written at the command of the imperial codifier. The rule that a partnership may be dissolved at the will of any member when no period is fixed for its duration, is as well established under the existing commercial law as it was at Rome;[3] but we have discarded the doctrine that the contracts of one partner do not bind the others unless authorized by them, or they have shared the benefit; because the

[1] Fremery, ch. i. p. 5; Benjamin on Sales, § 412.

[2] Fremery, ch. i. pp. 4–8.

[3] Institutes, 3. 25. 4; Accarias, ii. No. 628, note 4.

latter rule is technical, and not founded on the nature of things.

It is, as Fremery maintains, owing to a neglect of these obvious considerations that the doctrine that the right of property remains in the seller, however clearly he manifests his intention that it shall vest forthwith in the buyer, until he does some act to carry the purpose into effect, has been treated by commentators and some scientific writers on jurisprudence as of general application, and one which not merely is independent of intention, but cannot be abrogated by a legislative enactment consistently with cardinal principles.[1]

Such a conclusion necessarily rests upon one of two postulates,—that selling does not indicate an intention to bind the thing, or that there is some paramount reason why the law should not carry such a purpose into effect. The former assumption raises a question of fact that does not admit of a fixed or arbitrary rule, and fails when the contract denotes an opposite design, and the latter depends on considerations of policy that may vary with circumstances, and which each nation must determine for itself.

Conceding that the appropriate function of a contract is to bind the parties, there is no reason why they should not by one and the same instrument prescribe what is to be done, and carry it into effect; or, in other words, so formulate the agreement that it shall operate as a conveyance.[2] The *mancipatio* was such an instance, when it no longer took place on the land, and the title passed by the symbolical sale;[3] and another may be found in the English "bargain and sale." So incorporeal hereditaments are insusceptible of delivery, and were classified by the common law as lying in grant; that is, transferable, by the agreement of the grantor to give and the grantee to receive, signified by the handing over of the deed. In like manner the civil-law *hypotheca*, though depending merely on consent unattended with a transfer of possession, conferred a right in the nature of property on the creditor,

[1] Fremery, ch. i. p. 4; Benjamin on Sales, § 412, p. 387.
[2] See Austin's Jurisprudence, i. 385–389.
[3] Accarias, i. No. 222, note 2.

by entitling him to sell the goods or land and apply the proceeds to the payment of the debt, to the exclusion of intervening incumbrancers and purchasers who were strangers to the transaction, and could not be bound by it if viewed merely as a contract.[1]

If the contract can bind the property in the case of an hypothecation, it may be equally effectual in that of a sale; and the question whether it shall so operate in either instance is not one of principle, but of usage or legislation. It is not therefore surprising that while the Roman rule was followed until recently on the continent of Europe, and, as it would seem, in England during the transitional period which succeeded the Norman Conquest, the English courts finally reached the conclusion, that since the parties are principally concerned in the question whether title shall pass on the completion of the contract, or await the further action of the seller, they may regulate it as they think proper unless the consequences are injurious to third persons. While such was the result as to chattels, delivery was more essential in the case of land than formerly at Rome, and an estate of freehold could not be transferred without a formal transfer of possession by livery of seisin on the premises to the feoffee, or some one duly authorized as his agent. The first step towards placing both kinds of property on the same footing was taken by the Court of Chancery, which held that a bargain and sale of land for value, or a covenant to stand seised in consideration of blood or marriage, vested the beneficial ownership in the grantee, or at all events conferred an equitable right of property which the Chancellor would enforce; and when the Statute of Uses was passed in the reign of Henry VIII., this doctrine acquired the force of law.

It was not requisite that the premises should be actually or symbolically handed over to the purchaser; he became constructively possessed as well as entitled, immediately on the completion of the contract, which, but for the nearly contemporaneous Statute of Enrolments, need not have been written

[1] Accarias, i. Nos. 284, 285, 286; Poste, p. 303; *ante*.

or under seal.[1] The necessity for enrolment was obviated subsequently through a lease by bargain and sale, followed by a release of the reversion, — the lease conferring an estate for years which the release enlarged to a fee. All that is requisite for the transfer of the title to land in England and the United States, consequently, is that the vendor should reduce the contract to writing, and authenticate it by a seal, and the right of property will then vest in the purchaser attended constructively with possession. True, the instrument must be delivered, but that is simply as a proof that the contract has been executed, and would not be a substitute for actual delivery if that were requisite.

On turning to the French Code we find the following provision, article 1583. "It [the sale] is complete as between the parties, and the purchaser becomes the owner relatively to the seller by force of law, as soon as the thing and the price are agreed on, although the thing has not been delivered nor the price paid." Nothing is here said about intention, and the passage of the title would seem to be a legal consequence of the completion of the contract. If such be the true interpretation, the Code transcends the rule of the common law, which is, that as the object of a sale is to vest the right of ownership in the purchaser, there is a natural presumption that the parties intend that this result shall ensue forthwith; which ought not to be disregarded unless their language or the circumstances indicate a different purpose, which is a question of fact and must be submitted as such to the jury. It is an inherent defect of codification to lay down rules that do not afford an adequate solution of problems, which though nominally the same, may yet vary with the circumstances of each particular case.

The function of the judge, as the term jurisdiction indicates, is to declare as well as to apply the law; and not only to carry recognized principles to their legitimate results, but to solve new problems analogically where there is no fixed

[1] See Chibborne's Case, Dyer, 229; Busher *v.* Thompson, 4 C. B. 48, 60; 2 Institutes, 671, 675; Jones *v.* Morley, 1 Lord Raymond, 287; 2 Sm. L. C. 8 Am. ed. 541.

rule. The process may be likened to the scientific observation of natural phenomena, which affords data for the verification of what has already been ascertained, or for the discovery of fresh truths. Such were the means employed at Rome, and that are still in use in England and the United States; without them the law would cease to be a living science. The duty of the Legislature, on the other hand, is to care for the safety and government of the state, and the good order and welfare of society, by forbidding what is harmful and enjoining what policy requires. A statute regulating the interpretation and effect of contracts falling under a particular head, as, for instance, the contract of sale, is, unless dictated by considerations of public policy, prejudicial or superfluous; prejudicial if it contravenes the intention of the parties, superfluous if it does not, because the courts would presumably arrive at the same result.

Codification is, moreover, liable to err by erecting principles into rules, and stating specific truths as if they were universal. Had the French code provided that the right of property should pass on the completion of a contract of sale, when such is the design, it would have answered a useful purpose by removing the restraint which grew out of Justinian's codification, but as actually worded, it substitutes one arbitrary rule for another. So the provision of the same code that ambiguous expressions in a contract of sale shall be taken most strongly against the vendor is entirely just as regards an offer made by him and accepted by the buyer, but cannot be applied when the offer comes from the purchaser, consistently with maxim *fortius contra proferentem*, which it was intended to enforce.[1]

How difficult it is for the legislator to anticipate the decision of the judge, and prescribe the conclusion to be drawn before the case arises, appears from the statute of frauds, which though drafted by able lawyers for a beneficial object, would have given occasion for the fraud which it was intended to prevent, had not the Chancellor modified its operation to an extent which in some particulars operated as a repeal, —

[1] Fremery, ch. i. p. 7.

as for instance, by decreeing that suffering the vendee to take possession may supply the want of the writing which the statute required. Such a course of decision has sometimes been described as judicial legislation, but is really the exercise of a power which is essential to the administration of justice, and cannot legitimately be arrogated by the other departments of the government. *Legem dicere* and *legem facere* are so diverse that the legislature can never properly adjudicate; but there are occasions where the judge, in order to prevent a failure of justice, may be obliged not only to supply what the lawgiver has overlooked, but correct what he has enacted. Such was the prætorian jurisdiction as defined by Ulpian, and a like power is exercised by the English and American courts, with results not less beneficial than those attained at Rome.[1]

Justinian seems to have hindered the development of jurisprudence in another particular, by erecting a local custom into a rule which, though founded solely on authority and tending to frustrate intention, is generally regarded as an integral part of the civil law. Agreeably to the English law, persons who enter into a joint engagement are as much bound for its entire fulfilment as if the obligation were several. The suit and judgment should regularly be joint, although this is not essential in the absence of a plea in abatement, but the goods of each co-contractor may be taken in execution for the whole debt, and he must obtain contribution from the others as best he may. The rule of the civil law is the direct opposite, — that an agreement by two or more persons to pay a sum of money or do any other act which is not indivisible in its nature, shall be so apportioned or distributed among the contractors that each shall bear his share, and cannot be made answerable for any greater amount.[2]

If A and B agree to pay $100, A is liable for $50 and B for a like sum, and the creditor cannot call upon either of them for more. In other words, whether the instrument is "We promise to pay $100," and is signed by both, or con-

1 See Accarias, i. No. 20, note 2.

2 Maynz, ii. §§ 186, 192; Fremery, ch. iii. p. 22.

tains two several promises to pay $50 signed by each, the legal effect will be the same, notwithstanding the manifest difference in the terms.[1] The grounds for this conclusion were, according to Fremery, technical, and deduced from the peculiar nature of the stipulation as it existed two thousand years since at Rome, that a single request could give birth to but one action, however numerous the parties who united in the reply, and that the court should consequently in proceeding to judgment, charge each defendant with an amount which would in the aggregate make up the whole.[2] The rule was subsequently extended through a misconception of Tribonian to the consensual contracts and written obligations for the payment of money, and accepted generally in the middle ages by the doctors of the civil law with unquestioning faith as the dictate of a reason that could not err, and finally incorporated with the French Code, which declares[3] that "solidarity," or, in other words, the obligation of each to respond for all, is not to be presumed; it must be expressly stipulated.

While such is the rule as regards persons who are not engaged in trade, the law merchant is, and has been, from the middle ages down to our own time, in accordance with the English law, that the obligation of a promise is identical whether the promisors are one or many, and renders it the

[1] After remarking that the custom of trade is the reverse, and renders each of the parties answerable for the fulfilment of the whole, Fremery observes: —

"Pour justifier la coutume commerciale, on est frappé d'une raison qui parait bien décisive: on ne peut pas admettre que deux modes d'obligation tout-à-fait différens contiennent la même intention et produisent le même résultat. Or, ce mode d'obligation: 'Je promets de payer 50 à Félix,' signé 'Paul'; et 'Je promets de payer 50 à Félix,' signé 'Louis;' est bien différent de celui-ci: 'Nous promettons de payer 100 à Félix,' signé 'Paul'; signé 'Louis.' En analysant rigoureusement cette dernière locution, certes, on y trouvera que Paul promet, et que Louis promet; et que de plus, l'objet de la promesse est 100. Or, ces élémens constituent bien l'obligation solidaire de payer 100 à Félix." Fremery, ch. iii. p. 24.

[2] Fremery, ch. iii. pp. 25, 27.

[3] Article, 120.

duty of each of them to do or render that to which all agreed.[1] As the meaning of words does not vary because the parties are engaged in trade, both propositions cannot be true, and there can be little doubt that if the doctrine of the civil law was logical at Rome, as applied to the stipulation, it is at variance with the common use of language and the interpretation that would be put on a joint undertaking by an unbiased mind.

[1] Fremery, ch. iii. p. 25.

CHAPTER VII.

ASSUMPSIT.

The Anglo-Norman Law of Contracts. — Statute of Westminster II. — Growth of Actions on the Case. — Origin of Assumpsit and the Doctrine of Consideration.

THE civil law, as it was ultimately developed and is now administered on the continent of Europe, agrees with the natural law in deriving the obligation of a contract from the union of two minds in a common purpose to which both are mutually bound, or which one of them is entitled to insist that the other shall fulfil. It is the expectation that is created in the breast of the person to whom the promise is addressed that renders the violation of the agreement wrongful. If I say that I will give my neighbor a horse and he does not assent, I am free to act as I please in the matter; but if he accepts I am morally, and agreeably to the civil law legally bound, if the contract is made in due form. In the earlier ages of the republic, while Rome was yet a petty town contending for existence or dominion with its Etruscan or Samnite neighbors, the forms requisite to the obligation of an agreement were prescribed by usage, and varied with the subject-matter. If they were not complied with the contract was invalid, and it does not appear that the rigor of the rule was mitigated by equitable considerations. As the Roman dominion extended in an ever-widening circle until it reached from the Euphrates to the Northern Ocean, and contracts made on the banks of the Nile or the Seine came to be adjudicated at the Tiber, technical rules were necessarily merged in the conception of general principles, and it would have been difficult for the most careless or indifferent judge not to perceive that the obligation of a contract has a sanction which is independent of the form. The one is but the evidence; the other depends on principles which are inherent in the nature of things, and cannot be disregarded without injustice.

While all that is requisite to a contract, under the civil law as now interpreted, is consent, — that one party should agree to render and the other to receive; the requisites at common law are a promise and a consideration. Consent is essential, but it is given or implied in the consideration, and unless under seal or entered of record, will not be sufficient in any other form. What constitutes a consideration cannot readily be defined; but it may be said in general to be some act or undertaking stipulated for by the promisor and performed or entered into by the promisee on the faith of the engagement which he is seeking to enforce. It may be detrimental to the plaintiff, or beneficial to the defendant, but it must move from the plaintiff. Although the rule is peculiar to the common law it will erelong be extended by the growth of the English race through the larger part of the civilized world, and should be attentively considered by every one who desires to understand our system of jurisprudence.

The distinction may be illustrated by an example. Posting the acceptance of an offer after the offerer has mailed a retraction, does not agreeably to the civil law complete the contract, because one party dissents before the other agrees, and their minds do not meet; but is obligatory under the common law, although the letter never reaches its destination, as varying the position of the offeree, who can no longer dispose of the goods or land to a third person without the risk of a suit.

According to Lord Justice Bramwell, the same result might follow from firing a cannon or hanging out a flag, if stipulated for by the offerer; but this is more questionable because such an act would neither be beneficial to him nor detrimental to the person to whom the offer is addressed.[1] So a promise to pay the debt of a third person, or by a debtor to pay what he owes before or after it falls due, was known at Rome as a *constitutum*, and became obligatory on being accepted by the

[1] Household Insurance Co. *v.* Grant, L. R. 4 Ex. Div. 216.

creditor, whether the original demand was or was not extinguished,[1] but is invalid under the English law in the absence of an agreement for forbearance or other new and valuable consideration.

The doctrine of consideration was as little known to the earlier English as to the civil law, and can no more be found in the pages of Bracton than in the Institutes. Both systems afforded a remedy when the performance of an act on one side gave rise to a definite obligation on the other; but if this was the germ, centuries elapsed before the fruit matured.[2] The Anglo-Saxons followed the rule which is common to most nations in the earlier stages of their growth, that agreements whether mutual or unilateral are not binding unless clothed with some customary or legal form, or so far carried into effect on one side as to be obligatory on the other. The consensual contracts of the civil law had accordingly as little force in England in the reign of Alfred, or as late as the middle of the thirteenth century, as they originally possessed at Rome, and it was essential to the validity of a sale that the price or earnest money should be paid, the thing delivered, or that the agreement should be entered into before the persons who were appointed in each burgh or hundred to serve as witnesses of such transactions.[3] Documentary proof gradually took the place of testimony, and written instruments became, not merely evidence but a conclusive proof of the existence of the agreements which they set forth, or rather gave them the validity which consent alone did not confer.[4] The usage survived the Conquest, and was adopted by the Normans, or coincided with that which they brought from the Continent, and the Anglo-Norman resembled the civil law in holding that a promise made in due form and followed by assent constituted an obligation,— the difference being that writing

1 Institutes, 4. 6. 9; Accarias, ii. Nos. 720–723.

2 Essays in Anglo-Saxon Law, p. 189.

3 Essays in Anglo-Saxon Law, pp. 187, 189, 216; Güterbock, Bracton, pp. 138, 144; Bracton, i. 131 (f. 16 b).

4 Güterbock, Bracton, pp. 139, 144; Essays in Anglo-Saxon Law, pp. 188, 231.

took the place of the formal questions and response.[1] A written undertaking, sealed and delivered by the promisor, and accepted by the promisee, was not only valid without the aid of a consideration, but had the force which belonged in the first instance to the *stipulatio* and contract *literis* and precluded question or dispute, although the chancellor subsequently, as did the prætor, allowed a defence on the ground of fraud or the failure of the cause which lay at the foundation of the contract.[2] Such an instrument is in technical language a covenant, and has the same force now as in the days of Edward I. The seal and writing do not constitute the contract, although they operate as an estoppel and preclude the obligor from denying that it was made.[3] An unsealed promise or agreement was not valid; a custom having the force of law made it essential that the contract should be in writing and authenticated in the manner in common use at the time, that is, with a seal; or, as the rule was stated by Bracton in a maxim borrowed from the civil law, — *ex nuda promissione non oritur actio*.[4]

Whence the usage came we are not definitely informed, but it seems to have sprung from the written instruments which were long employed at Rome to perpetuate the memory of the formal question and response, through which alone save exceptionally a promise could be obligatory, and subsequently as evidence of executed sales or gifts. Such documents known as *cautiones syngraphæ* and *chirographa* were in constant use during the decline of the Roman empire, and after it fell supplanted the *stipulatio* and contract *literis* of an earlier period.[5]

[1] Güterbock, Bracton, p. 139; Bracton, ii. 111 (f. 99 b), 117 (f. 100), 119 (f. 100 b).

[2] Güterbock, Bracton, pp. 139, 144; Sharington *v.* Strotton, Plow. 298.

[3] See Sharington *v.* Strotton, Plow. 298; Bracton, ii. 117 (f. 100), 119 (f. 100 b).

[4] Bracton, i. 129 (f. 16), 298 (f. 38); Güterbock, Bracton, p. 139; Watton *v.* Brinth, 2 Henry IV. 3, pl. 9.

[5] Maynz, ii. §§ 245, 248; Güterbock, Bracton, p. 139; Sandars' Justinian, 439.

This explanation is the more probable, because a written promise for the payment of money had, under the legislation of Justinian, the conclusive effect of the Anglo-Norman covenant, unless set aside within two years on proof that it had been procured fraudulently and that the debt was not due.[1] The seal was of later growth, and was substituted in an illiterate age for the signature which few knew how to write.[2]

Such was the rule with regard to unsealed or parol agreements, so long as they remained executory and nothing was done on either side that rendered them binding on the other. Bracton, who wrote in the reign of Henry III., follows the Institutes and throws little light on contracts as regulated by the English law; but he is careful to note that a sale was not valid unless the property was delivered by the seller, the purchase-money paid, or earnest given by the buyer, or the contract reduced to writing. If all these requisites were wanting, the parties might recede at pleasure, although they had agreed on the thing and the price, and would have been bound agreeably to the Roman law.[3] When, however, a contract to do or render was so far performed as to confer a right to a sum certain, which the debtor refused to pay, or pass the title to a chattel which was withheld by the vendor, redress

[1] Institutes, 3. 1.

[2] Among the Anglo-Saxons the grantor signed the covenant or instrument, or if unable to write, signified his assent by setting a mark or cross to a signature written by another hand, and seals did not come into general use until after the Norman Conquest. 2 Blackstone, Com. 305; Holmes on the Common Law, p. 272. There seems to have been an undefined period during which either method of authentication might suffice, and a writing under the hand of the grantor would presumably have been evidence of the delivery which was the only mode of conveying chattels, and not less necessary in the case of land when there was no particular estate outstanding and it did not technically lie in grant. See Bracton. If such an instrument was admissible to prove livery of seisin, or whether the delivery of a chattel was by way of sale or bailment, it could not under the Anglo-Norman law operate as a contract or impose an executory obligation.

[3] Bracton, i. 488 (f. 61 b.), London, 1878; Güterbock, Bracton, pp. 139, 145.

might be had in detinue in the latter case, or through an action of debt in the former. These remedies were nevertheless inapplicable in many instances, and subject to a serious drawback in all. It was essential to a recovery in debt that the contract should not only be executed by the passage of the consideration, but that it should have moved to the defendant; or, as the principle was sometimes stated, that he should have received a *quid pro quo*.[1] Redress could not, therefore, be had for the breach of an executory agreement, nor where the plaintiff had sold goods or rendered services to a third person on the faith of the defendant's promise that he should be paid.[2] A carpenter who built a house might recover the stipulated price in debt, but the employer could not maintain that or any other form of action for the builder's failure to perform the contract, unless it was under seal.[3]

So a contractor who had entered into an oral agreement for the performance of work, was remediless for a refusal to allow him to proceed, although he had provided the materials and kept himself disengaged in order that he might fulfil the agreement. Moreover, if A sold goods to B, and C promised to pay for them if B did not, or entered into a collateral engagement of any other kind, no debt arose as between A and C, and there was no writ in the register through which A could enforce the promise or obtain compensation for the breach.[4]

This was not all. The action of debt on simple contract was not only confined within these limits, but was subject to a condition which left the plaintiff at the mercy of the defendant, and might be so used as to frustrate a just demand.[5] Even when there was a definite pecuniary obligation substantiated by proof, the defendant might discharge himself by waging his law, that is, by swearing that he had paid it, and

[1] See the cases in the notes to Hunt *v.* Bate, Vaillant's Dyer, 272.

[2] Gilbert on the Action of Debt, p. 365.

[3] Watton *v.* Brinth, 2 Henry IV. 3, pl. 9; 11 Henry IV. 33, pl. 60.

[4] Gilbert on the Action of Debt, p. 364; Reeves, Hist. of the Eng. Law, iii. 404; Jordan's Case, 27 Henry VIII. 24.

[5] Gilbert on the Action of Debt, p. 364.

bringing eleven persons to accredit his oath and swear that they believed that which he said was true.[1]

Such was the law of England with regard to parol contracts during the thirteenth century. A new remedy, however, came into being, which, though framed in tort might yet be used as a means of redress when the wrong consisted not in a refusal to perform the contract, but in proceeding under it and doing the work amiss. The appropriate form of action for a forcible invasion of another's rights was trespass *vi et armis*, and relief obviously could not be obtained by such means where the plaintiff had sanctioned the act for which he sued. One who lamed a horse by pricking his foot was *prima facie* a trespasser, and might be made answerable on due allegation and proof; but it was a sufficient answer to such a complaint, that the defendant was shoeing the horse at the plaintiff's request and drove the nail while so engaged.

Such a plea was not a justification on general principles, because it implied that the injury was occasioned by a want of care or skill; but it was a good technical defence, because it negatived the existence of force, which was an essential ingredient in the right to sue. Recourse was therefore had to the Statute of Westminster II. c. 24, which provided in effect that where there was a wrong which, though analogous, did not fall within the scope of the writs in common use, the clerks in Chancery might frame a like writ *in consimili casu*, adapted to the circumstances. Such was the origin of the action on the case, which proved a plant of rapid growth and not only afforded a remedy for the injurious application of force in pursuance of a request that would have been a defence had the work been properly done, but for numerous other wrongs for which there was no remedy, — or none that afforded adequate relief.

It was accordingly determined as far back as the reign of Edward III., though not without some misgivings, that if a man entered on the performance of a promise without conforming to its terms, or using due care and skill, and thereby injured another's house or chattel damages might be recovered

[1] Gilbert on the Action of Debt, p. 363.

in trespass on the case, and the defendant could neither allege that the contract was parol and invalid, nor rely on it as a justification, because he had not followed the authority which it gave, and the suit was not *ex contractu*, but in tort.[1]

The new action of trespass differed in two material particulars from the old. The wrongful act was not averred to have been done *vi et armis*, and it was averred, or appeared by a necessary inference, to have been done in such wise as to inflict an injury which ought to be redressed. The misfeasance might have occurred in the execution of a promise or it might not, and the promise, if set forth, was material chiefly as showing why the plaintiff did not proceed in trespass *vi et armis*, or as throwing light on the extent and nature of the obligation arising from the transaction as a whole. Whether the smith, in the case already put, gave his services gratuitously or was paid, and whether the agreement, if such existed, was by parol or under seal, he could not rely on the authority which it conferred as an excuse for inflicting an injury that might have been avoided by proper care.

The principle was obviously susceptible of an extended application to wrongs that lay on the border line between tort and contract. One who put a horse on board an overladen ferryboat, and thus caused his death, could not be held in trespass *de bonis asportatis* if the animal had been delivered to him for transportation, but might well be liable in trespass on the case, not because he had broken an express or implied agreement to carry the horse safely across the stream, but because the bailment did not excuse the negligence, although it would have been a good answer to an allegation that the injury had been inflicted forcibly.[2] So where a horse died of malpractice, the farrier would have been answerable in trespass had he treated the animal without the owner's leave, but inasmuch as he had been employed to cure the disease, and the gravamen was negligence, the remedy lay in case.[3] In the case last cited as in that of the ferryman, the writ alleged an undertaking on the defendant's part, and the objection that the action should

[1] 46 Edward III. 19, pl. 19.

[2] 22 Assizes, 94, pl. 41.

[3] 43 Edward III. 33, pl. 38.

be covenant was met by the reply that covenant could not be maintained without a deed, and that the suit was for negligence, and not for a breach of contract.

These decisions were among the first of a long train of cases which led by slow degrees to the transformation of case into assumpsit; but they were, nevertheless, as generally happens in such beginnings, made without any distinct perception of their drift, or the end to which they would ultimately conduce, and the ground taken was, not that the defendant was bound in the first instance or *ex contractu*, but that he had chosen to act, and was consequently answerable for doing that negligently, which, if done, should have been performed with due care.

The question was curiously considered in 46 Edward III. 19, pl. 19, which was trespass against a smith for laming a horse. The writ alleged that the defendant had driven a nail into the horse's foot in such a place that the plaintiff had lost the use of his horse for a long time. Percy objected for the defence that the plaintiff had brought trespass and did not allege force and arms. Finchden replied that the writ was in case, and good. Percy then said the writ should be either *vi et armis* or *maliciose fixit*, and it is neither; and as it does not allege that he gave us the horse to shoe, the presumption is that if any trespass was done it was against the peace. The objection was overruled and the defendant took issue on the facts.

In this instance the pleader did not aver malice, negligence, or contract, and relied on the single ground that as the defendant's conduct was injurious and a cause of loss he was liable in damages, unless he had a defence or justification: and this view was sustained by the court.

It is, nevertheless, obvious that the failure to set forth how the defendant obtained possession of the horse, and that he acted with the plaintiff's consent, gave color to the argument that for all that appeared the injury was forcible, and the action should have been trespass *vi et armis*. The right to compensation for an act done at the plaintiff's request, but in a way to be prejudicial, depends moreover on whether the defendant is responsible for his want of skill. It must always be an answer to an accusation of negligence, that the party charged did as well as he knew how, unless it was his duty to have been better informed.[1]

To warrant a recovery for malpractice it must consequently appear not only that the defendant's treatment of the case was unscientific and injurious, but that he held himself out as a physician, or induced the plaintiff to employ him by an assurance that he possessed the requisite skill and would take proper measures to effect a cure. So a man who, when asked to shoe a traveller's horse, declares that it is not his trade but that he will do his best, is not answerable for any injury that may ensue without proof that it was due to negligence as distinguished from the ignorance which he avows. In Shiells *v.* Blackburne,[2] a mandatary was held excusable on this ground for an erroneous entry at the Custom House which led to the seizure of the goods, although a man who was conversant with such business as a clerk or broker, would have been answerable for the loss. In Dartnall *v.* Howard,[3] the allegation was that in consideration the plaintiff would employ the defendants to lay out £1400 in purchasing an annuity, the defendants promised to perform their duty in that regard, which they did not do, but on the contrary invested the money on the personal security of an insolvent; and the judgment was arrested after verdict because the only duty arising from such an employment is to act faithfully and honestly, and not to be guilty of any gross or culpable neglect.

In determining whether case will lie for an act done at the plaintiff's request, regard should therefore be had to what is said, as well as to what is done. The contemporaneous declarations may enlarge or may lessen the responsibility of a bailee or agent, and while proof that the service was rendered gratuitously will not excuse negligence, evidence that the defendant was hired may conduce to show that he represented himself as competent and cannot plead want of skill as a defence.

[1] 43 Edward III. 33, pl. 38; 48 Edward III. 6, pl. 11.
[2] 1 H. Bl. 158. [3] 4 B. & C. 345.

Agreeably to the civil law, a bailee or depositary without reward, is not answerable save for such misconduct or gross neglect as implies a culpable indifference to the safety of the property committed to his care, and such would also appear to be the English rule; but an undertaking on his part to keep the goods safely, or that he will make good any loss that may occur, varies the case under both systems by imposing the duty of exact diligence incident to a mandate.[1] This is not on the ground of contract; for if it were, the defendant would be bound to fulfil the promise at all events, and could not rely on an inevitable accident, or the tortious act of a third person as an excuse; but depends on the trust arising from the delivery of the goods in reliance on his word. In Coggs *v.* Bernard,[2] the undertaking was to take certain casks of brandy safely and securely out of a certain cellar, and lay them down safely and securely elsewhere; and yet, as Lord Holt observed, if a drunken man had come by while the cart was passing through the streets, and pierced the casks, the plaintiff would not have been entitled to a verdict, because the defendant was to have nothing for his pains. One who seeks to recover against a mandatary or bailee on the ground of negligence, must consequently describe the entire transaction with sufficient clearness to show the relation between himself and the defendant, and the nature of the duty which it was incumbent on the latter to fulfil;[3] and if the case depends in any material particular on a promise, it must be set forth in the declaration,—not because it is obligatory as a contract or when standing alone, but as showing the extent and nature of the trust which the defendant has accepted, and is consequently bound to perform.[4]

The cases in the Year Books are accordingly distinct that a promise may be essential to a recovery in case for negligence, and mark the growth of the common-law doctrine that

[1] Maynz, ii, § 239, notes 12, 27, pp. 317, 319.

[2] 2 Lord Raymond, 909; 1 Sm. L. C. 8 Am. ed. 369.

[3] Judin *v.* Samuel, 1 B. & P. 43; Powell *v.* Layton, 2 id. 365.

[4] See Mast *v.* Goodson, 3 Wilson, 348; Ireland *v.* Johnson, 1 Bing. N. C. 162; Bretherton *v.* Wood, 3 Brod. & Bing. 54.

although a naked undertaking will not impose a liability it may do so when clothed with facts. It followed that the promise must be pleaded with such certainty of time and place as to show where the venue should be laid and the jury summoned, if it were put at issue by a traverse. In the 48 Edward III. 6, pl. 11 the suit was against a surgeon for malpractice in treating the plaintiff's hand, and the writ was adjudged bad for not setting forth where the undertaking to cure the hand was made.

A like question arose in 19 Henry VI. 49, pl. 5, where the declaration averred that the defendant undertook in London to treat the plaintiff's horse for a certain malady, and administered the medicine so negligently that the animal died. The defendant pleaded that the undertaking was made at Oxford, and not at London. Markham contended that the plea was bad, because the suit was brought for the negligence and not on the assumption. The reply was that the defendant was not alleged to be a farrier by profession, and if there was no undertaking and he acted gratuitously the action could not be maintained. This view was sustained by the Court, and Newton added that if the defendant did not promise, the negligence went for nothing. "If," said he, "my hand is diseased, and one applies the remedies to my heel, by which negligence my hand is maimed, I shall have no action unless he undertook to work a cure."

In Coggs *v.* Bernard, Powell, J., said, that in the instance above cited the action was held to lie upon the undertaking, without which it would not have lain; and therefore the undertaking was held to be the matter traversable, and the writ quashed for the want of laying the place where it was made. The just inference is not that the obligation of a bailee is *ex contractu*, but that the possession or acceptance of another's goods may, when coupled with a promise, give rise to a liability that would not follow if either stood alone. The trust has its inception in the promise, but is not obligatory until the goods come to the bailee's hands, or he does some act to carry it into effect.

Accordingly, the same learned judge went on to observe

that a ferryman who overloads his boat will be answerable without any undertaking, because it is his own wrong. The duty arises, under such circumstances, from the public nature of the employment; but every one who receives property for transportation is *ipso facto* under an obligation to be careful, whether he does so as a favor, or in the course of his business or occupation. In Southcote's Case,[1] the bare receipt of a chattel as a deposit was held to imply an undertaking to keep it safely, and return it at all events unless the agreement is special to keep the goods as the bailee would his own.

The rule is now held the other way, — that a depositary is not answerable where there is no fault on his part; but the judgment does not less clearly show that what the law regards in such cases is the obligation arising from the transaction as a whole, including the language held on either side.

The doctrine that a promise may be material and traversable in an action *ex delicto*, although it was not obligatory as a contract, is not less clear under the modern decisions than from the books; although the question is now raised on the general issue, without resorting to a special plea.[2]

In Coggs *v.* Bernard,[3] the action was case against an unpaid bailee and mandatary for negligence in the transportation of certain casks which he had promised to remove safely and securely. Lord Holt pointed out that the confidence reposed by the plaintiff in the defendant's promise gave rise to a trust, but did not constitute a contract. The defendant was not bound to proceed with the execution of the promise, and might have left the casks where they lay; but when he took them in charge it became his duty to use every necessary precaution, and he was answerable for the loss occasioned by his neglect.

The difference between such a trust and a contract properly so called is that the obligation of the latter depends on intention, and may be as much or as little as the parties please, while in the former it is implied by the law, which will not

[1] 4 Rep. 83 b.

[2] See Elsee *v.* Gatward, 5 T. R. 143; Mast *v.* Goodson, 3 Wilson, 348.

[3] 2 Lord Raymond, 909.

suffer it to be made less or greater than justice and good faith require. Accordingly, an unpaid agent or bailee can neither stipulate for immunity from gross negligence or misfeasance, nor be bound by an agreement to insure the property confided to his care, or what comes to the same thing, to make compensation for losses arising from events which he cannot control. It was said on this ground, by an old writer, that if a carrier should refuse to carry the stuff unless a promise were made to him that he should not be charged for any misdemeanor that should be in him, the promise would be void as being against reason and good manners;[1] and such are the best considered decisions of modern times.[2] The public nature of the carrier's employment enters into the account; but the principle is the same whenever the effect of lessening responsibility will be to increase temptation, and open the way for fraud. Conversely, as the remarks of Lord Holt indicate, a depositary or other unpaid bailee will not be bound by a promise to be answerable at all events, or for anything more than the faithful administration of the trust reposed by the bailor. The law was so held in Hatchell *v.* Odom,[3] and the judgment of the Exchequer Chambers in Riches *v.* Briggs,[4] is to the same effect.

It results from what has been said, that the decisions which established that a recovery might be had for misfeasance in the execution of a parol undertaking, were entirely consistent with the rule that it was not binding unless reduced to writing and under seal. The defendant might have given an express promise, or the duty might be implied from his relation as an agent or bailee, but the gist of the action in either instance was not the breach of contract, but negligence in the fulfilment of a trust or duty which should either have been declined

[1] St. Germain, Doctor and Student, Dialogue ii. ch. 38; Noy's Maxims, 43, 92.

[2] Lyon *v.* Mells, 5 East, 428; New Jersey Steam Navigation Co. *v.* Bank, 6 How. 344; Railroad Co. *v.* Manufacturing Co. 16 Wallace, 318; Camden & Amboy R. R. Co. *v.* Burke, 13 Wend. 611; Cole *v.* Goodwin, 19 Wend. 251; Beckman *v.* Shouse, 5 Rawle, 179; Graham *v.* Davis, 4 Ohio St. 381; Camden & Amboy R. R. Co. *v.* Baldauf, 16 Pen. 67.

[3] 2 Dev. & Bat. 302.

[4] Yelv. 4.

or performed with due care. Accordingly, when an attempt was made to extend the remedy to cases where the defendant had done nothing, and the wrong consisted in a failure to perform, the judges stood fast in the ancient ways, and refused to hold him answerable, although the breach of faith on his part was evident and the plaintiff's loss no less clear.[1] As trade increased and business became more complex, the inconvenience was keenly felt, and drove men into Chancery; which led the way to a reform of the law, as has often happened in the history of English jurisprudence. In the reign of Edward IV. the counsel for the defendant in a bill in equity, argued that it was the complainant's folly not to have had a deed, and that if the bill was sustained one who was aggrieved by the breach of an engagement to build a house might have a *subpœna* in equity. The Chancellor replied curtly, "So he may," and added that if the argument was valid a man who made a feoffment to his own use could have no redress, because it was his folly to have selected a feoffee who would not fulfil the trust. By a natural sequence, which was often paralleled in after times, the common-law judges sought, as the remarks of Fairfax in 21 Edward IV. 23, pl. 6, indicate, to vie with the Court of Chancery and retain their suitors, by favoring a remedy which was free from the technicalities that embarrassed the methods of procedure in common use; and the result was, as might have been anticipated where interest and the demands of justice pointed in the same direction, an enlargement of the action on the case to meet the growing requirements of the times. The bare fact that a promise had been made and broken might concern the moralist, but did not from the practical point of view of the English bench justify the intervention of a court of justice; but redress was obviously due where the defendant, having promised to perform or render something if the plaintiff would do or forbear, refused to comply with the agreement, after the plaintiff

[1] Watton *v.* Brinth, 2 Henry IV. 3, pl. 9; 11 Henry IV. 33, pl. 60; Watkins' Case, 3 Henry VI. 36, pl. 33; Elsee *v.* Gatward, 5 T. R. 143; Thorne *v.* Deas, 4 Johns. 84.

had changed his position for the worse on the faith of the promise, and could not recede.[1]

Case, as applied under such circumstances, was a hybrid between tort and contract, and needed but little change to become purely contractual. The cause of action was no longer the defendant's misfeasance in the execution of a promise by which he was not bound, but that he had induced the plaintiff to act by an undertaking which remained unfulfilled. It consequently belonged to the category of deceit or fraud, and could not logically be classed as a trespass, save in the sense in which that term includes every wrong for which men owe reparation or forgiveness. Near as the action of trespass on the case came to contract in some of the above instances, the lines did not meet, and the source of the action on the case on promises, or assumpsit, must therefore presumably be sought in another offshoot from the Statute of Westminster II., which though prompted by the desire to afford a remedy against an assignee for maintaining a nuisance, was yet broad enough to include numerous injuries that could not be adequately redressed by the methods in common use.[2] Case might consequently be employed not only to supplement trespass, but the common-law writs of covenant and deceit; or in other words, as a remedy for injuries growing out of a fraud committed in the making or performance of an agreement, or resulting consequentially from its non-fulfilment, as well as for those occasioned by an abuse of the authority which it conferred.[3] If, for instance, a sale was effected by warranting the goods, and they subsequently proved to be unsound, the purchaser might at his election obtain compensation through a writ of deceit, or an action on the case in which the warranty was averred to have been fraudulent.[4]

In like manner where a sealed agreement was performed literally, though broken to the sense, or the breach was at-

[1] Somerton's Case, 11 Henry VI. 18, pl. 10; 14 Henry VI. 18, pl. 58.

[2] 3 Bl. Com. 51.

[3] Reeves, History of the English Law, ii. 606; 16 Edward IV. 9, pl. 7.

[4] Fitzherbert, Natura Brevium, 94, E.; 2 Chitty's Pleadings, 680.

tended with a consequential damage, covenant, as the law was then held, might fail or prove inadequate, and a writ framed in deceit meet with technical objections, and recourse was had to an action on the case.[1] In 14 Henry VI. 18, pl. 58, the plaintiff declared in case that the defendant had sold him land for a certain sum, and covenanted that a third person should execute a release, which he had not done. It was objected that as in the case of a promise to build a house, if the contract was by deed the remedy lay in covenant, if it was not the suit should be dismissed. The court nevertheless held that the action was well brought, apparently because the grievance was not so much the non-fulfilment of the covenant, as that the plaintiff had been induced to make the purchase by an undertaking which the defendant had failed to keep. So Paston, J., declared in 14 Henry VI. 18, pl. 58, and Juyn, C. J., concurred, that if a smith covenants with me at my inn to shoe my horse, and does not do it, and I proceed on my journey, and the horse is lamed for want of a shoe, I shall have a remedy in case; and so where through the absence of counsel who has been retained to plead my cause, the suit is lost. It was remarked *arguendo* in 20 Henry VI. 34, pl. 4, that a vendor might maintain debt for the price of land; but there was no corresponding remedy for the purchaser, who could not bring detinue as in the case of a chattel, and would be remediless unless he could have an action of deceit or on the case.

No case could well fall more directly within this line of argument than where a sale was made on the faith of a parol guaranty. For as debt could not be maintained against one who had not received an equivalent and was chargeable only by virtue of the promise, and covenant was inapplicable for the want of a seal, there was no remedy save by treating the breach of contract as a tort, and bringing an action of deceit or on the case.

In 12 Henry VIII. 11, pl. 3, which was an action on the case against executors, the plaintiff declared that one J. N. came to his house to purchase goods in company with the

[1] Reeves, History of the English Law, ii. 607.

defendant's testator, and when the plaintiff expressed doubt about the payments, the testator said, "If he does not pay you, I will;" and the goods were thereupon delivered. All the justices were of opinion that the writ was well framed, because there was no other remedy, and as the testator had left sufficient assets there was no reason why his soul should be in jeopardy for the breach of an engagement which the executor had it in his power to fulfil. In like manner the keeper of a gaol was held to be entitled to compensation, on proof that he had liberated a man who was confined for debt in consequence of the defendant's promise to be answerable for the amount. The efficient cause of action in both instances was not the promise, but what had been done in the belief that it would be performed. From this point the transition was easy to holding that compensation was due whenever the plaintiff was misled by an undertaking made with a view of inducing him to act, and broken after he had complied with its terms. The declaration, as finally reduced to form and method, averred that the defendant promised to do or render something in consideration of an act to be done or payment made by the plaintiff; that the plaintiff confiding in the promise did as he was desired; but that the defendant fraudulently intending to deceive and injure the plaintiff did not, nor would keep his promise.[1] The action was not founded in contract, but in tort. It did not rely on the promise as obligatory but on the deceit, through which the injured party had been deprived of his time or property without compensation; and the measure of damages seems, in the first instance at least, to have been not what the defendant promised to give, but the value of that which the plaintiff had parted with in reliance on the promise. The former is, however, necessarily persuasive evidence of the latter, and the *prima facies* soon became conclusive. If I induce a man to sell me a chattel by promising to give him $1,000, it is only just that the value of the chattel should be measured by the price.

Such was the origin of the action on the case on promises,

[1] See Gilbert, Hist. of the Common Bench, p. 65; Tewkesbury *v.* Diston, 6 East, 438, 443.

now commonly known as the action of assumpsit. It had its source in the deceit of some one who, after inducing the plaintiff to act by promise of reward, refused to fulfil it on the plea that it was not authenticated by a seal. Under these circumstances it was obviously equitable that he should make compensation for the loss occasioned by his breach of faith. The right grew out of the consideration, not the promise, and the latter was material only as the means by which the plaintiff had been induced to render his goods or services. As time wore on, this view yielded to a more liberal interpretation, and the action was regarded as being what it really is, *ex contractu*. The inference followed, which has sometimes been too broadly stated, that a consideration is essential to the validity of a contract at common law. Strictly speaking the rule is, as we have seen, the other way, — that if two men agree together, and attest their purpose by a writing under seal, the contract is valid without more. It is only when this form is not complied with, and the agreement is by parol, or in other words not sealed, that one who seeks to enforce it must show that he did or promised something on the faith of the promise made by the other party. But although the necessity for a consideration was exceptional in the first instance, the exception has, as regards the ordinary course of business, become the rule. It was moreover, and still is essential that the act which constituted the consideration should be something for which the defendant stipulated, and not merely something which the plaintiff did in reliance on the defendant's word.[1] A promise to give another $1000 is not less a *nudum pactum* because the promisee buys a house in the belief that the money will be forthcoming, but a promise to give $1000 if the plaintiff will make such a purchase, becomes obligatory as soon as the condition is fulfilled.

It is enough, as the law is now held, to aver that the plaintiff promised to do something on the faith of the defendant's promise. This marks another stage in the growth of the action of assumpsit. A recovery could not, as I suppose, have been had in England before the close of the fifteenth century,

[1] Kirkpatrick *v.* Muirhead, 4 Harris, 117.

unless the plaintiff had acted in reliance on the promise which he sought to enforce; but it soon became obvious that a man may sustain a real loss from the breach of an agreement which has not been carried into effect on either side. A promise to sell and deliver goods or render services, followed by a readiness and willingness to perform, and, when requisite, by an actual tender, came to be considered as a sufficient consideration for a corresponding obligation on the other side.[1]

Parol contracts were consequently ranged under two heads,—promises in consideration of promises, and promises in consideration of performance. In the one case it is performance, in the other the promise to perform, that gives force and validity to the obligation.[2] The distinction is in some respects fundamental; although a plaintiff cannot ordinarily recover on a contract in consideration of mutual promises, without averring performance on his part, or that he was prevented by a refusal or breach on the part of the defendant.

The action on the case on promises, or in other words of assumpsit, thus took its place as the appropriate remedy for a breach of contract, whether the default consisted in a failure to perform or a misfeasance; but it was contended that the new remedy should be confined to cases where the demand was for damages, because the effect of allowing an action, which like assumpsit implied or alleged fraud, to be substituted for debt, would be to preclude the defendant from waging his law, and thus avoid the necessity of pleading issuably and appearing before a jury.[3]

The question was the more important, because it involved the right to maintain indebitatus assumpsit for work done, or on a contract of sale which has been so far executed as to vest the right of property in the purchaser, and entitle the vendor to the price. It remained open until the close of the sixteenth century, and was set at rest by Slade's Case, in the last years of Queen Elizabeth.[4] That was an action of assump-

[1] Strangborough and Warner's Case, 4 Leonard, 3; Gower *v.* Capper, Croke Eliz. 543.

[2] Lampleigh *v.* Brathwait, Hobart, 105.

[3] Gilbert on the Action of Debt, p. 423.

[4] 4 Reports, 94 b.

sit for the price of standing corn which had been bought by the defendant, but for which he, as the declaration averred, "craftily and subtily refused to pay, with intent to defraud the plaintiff." It was objected by Doddington, of counsel for the defence, that the plaintiff might have the ordinary remedy by action of debt, which is an action formed in the Register, and therefore he should not have an action on the case, which is an extraordinary action, and not limited within any certain form in the Register.

Another objection was that "the maintenance of this action takes away the defendant's benefit of wager of law, and so bereaves him of the benefit which the law gives him, which is his birthright. For, peradventure, the defendant has paid or satisfied the plaintiff in private, betwixt them, of which payment or satisfaction he has no witness, and therefore it would be mischievous if he should not wage his law in such case."

The Common Pleas and Queen's Bench differed, and "for the honor of the Law, and for the quiet of the subject, in the appeasing of such diversity of opinions," the case was twice argued before all the Justices of England, and Barons of the Exchequer, first by the Queen's Attorney-General, Sir Edward Coke, for the plaintiff, and John Doddington for the defendant, and again by Coke for the plaintiff, and Francis Bacon for the defendant; and after many conferences between the Justices and Barons, it was resolved in favor of the plaintiff, "in respect of infinite precedents," and because of the manifest inconveniences of the action of debt, which, when money was payable in instalments, could not be brought until the last was due, and left the plaintiff at the mercy of the defendant's oath. The report of the case concludes in these words: "Also it is good in these days in as many cases as may be done by the law, to oust the defendant of his law, and to try it by the country, for otherwise it would be occasion of much perjury."

Such is an outline of the result, and of the steps by which it was attained; but they cannot be traced with the accuracy and precision which the importance of the subject requires. The Year Books give a vivid picture of the daily course of events in court, but want method and completeness, and are not so much reports in the sense in which we now understand the term, as notes from which reports might be compiled. The proceeding opens with an oral declaration of the cause and nature of the action; an earnest discussion follows, in which the arguments of counsel and the *dicta* from the bench are so curiously interwoven as not to be easily distinguishable. There is, perchance, a plea or demurrer; and the debate not infrequently ends in an adjournment without our learning the result or whether the case ever went to judgment. Moreover, the judges did not in pronouncing judgment give the formal explanation of their reasons which became usual at a later period, and the grounds of the decision must consequently be gathered from the views expressed during the argument.

A history of the development of English law from such materials would require a more comprehensive and thorough analysis than has yet been made; and while assumpsit unquestionably sprang from the authority conferred by the Statute of Westminster II., we may not be so sure of the exact line of descent. Case was in the first instance simply a means of adapting the established forms of the common law to novel and unforeseen exigencies. The facts were set forth in the original writ, without regard to form, as in the Roman formula, *præscriptis verbis*, or modern case stated; and if they were analogous in principle to the causes of action which had been recognized as giving a right to redress, the court might proceed to judgment whether the wrong complained of was a tort or breach of contract. Thus, Fineux, C. J., is said to have declared [1] that if one covenants to build a house for me and does not do it, I shall have my action on the case for the non-feasance as well as if he had built it ill; and so, if one makes a bargain with me for £20 that he will grant me an estate, if I pay him £20 and he will not make the grant, I shall have my action on the case, and there is no need for a subpœna in Chancery.

The former proposition sounds strangely in the ears of a lawyer of the present day; but it seems then to have been

[1] 21 Henry VII. 41, pl. 66.

generally conceded that case or a writ of deceit would lie for an injury occasioned by a breach of faith, although the contract was under seal.[1] Such a result was, as the long and curious discussion in the 20 Henry VI. 34, pl. 4, indicates, natural at a period when a literal performance satisfied the requirements of the law, however widely it might deviate from the spirit of the agreement. Thus, it was said in the case last cited, that if a carpenter covenants to build me a house so long, so wide and so high, which he does, but is in default by misjoining it or by other defect of workmanship which is dehors the covenants, the action of covenant fails because all the covenants are fulfilled; and yet I shall have an action on the case, because he has been guilty of misfeasance.[2]

"If," said Babbington, in the 11 Henry VI. 18, pl. 10, "I retain one to purchase a manor for me and he does not do it, I shall have no action against him without a deed; but if he becomes counsel for another in the same matter, I may have an action on the case for the deceit;" and added, that a matter which lies wholly in covenant may, by what happens *ex post facto*, be converted into a deceit, and will then support an action on the case. So in 3 Henry VI. 36, pl. 33, the same judge met the argument of counsel that the remedy for nonperformance is covenant, with the reply that if a carpenter covenants to roof my house before a certain time and the work is not done, so that for want of roof the house is spoiled by the rain, I may have a remedy in case. It was declared in like manner on another occasion that if one covenant to enfeoff me and enfeoffs a third person, it is a great mis-

[1] See Fitzherbert, Natura Brevium, 98 E.

[2] A like question arose under the Roman law, where a stipulation for delivery did not render the promisor answerable for injuries to the thing resulting from his negligence or even misfeasance, which did not preclude the technical fulfilment of the contract; and a promise to deliver a slave might be performed by handing the man over at the appointed time, after administering a dose of poison from which he died. The injured party was finally allowed to recover for the fraud in an action *ex dolo*, on grounds similar to those which in England were held to sustain a recovery in case. Accarias, ii, No. 664.

feasance; the reason apparently being, that such a course would preclude the specific performance that might have been enforced through a writ of covenant real, or a bill in equity, had the land remained in the hands of the covenantor.[1]

Notwithstanding the seeming inconsistency of the language held in the above instances they yet established that while a recovery could not be had for the non-fulfilment of a promise, unless it was under seal and the writ framed in covenant, the case was widely different where the promise was used to mislead, or the defendant acted negligently in carrying it into effect. In the latter instance, the suit came under the general head of trespass, in the former of deceit, although both were classified as case. As time wore on, the incongruity of ranking intentional falsehood with a simple breach of promise became apparent; and assumpsit took its place as a distinct form of action, though still bearing the marks of its origin in the necessity for the averment and proof of a consideration.

A student who follows the line of decision to the point where case was moulded into an action *ex contractu* will naturally expect to find the writ framed in trespass on the case, when the cause of action is the defendant's negligence or want of skill in the execution of the promise, and in deceit on the case where compensation is sought for what the plaintiff was led to do or forbear through a misplaced reliance on the defendant's word. Such was the method in some instances,[2] but the distinction was generally ignored, and trespass on the case brought whether the wrong complained of was misfeasance or deceit. The explanation is that the jurisdiction of the King's Bench was confined to injuries that were not merely hurtful to individuals, but concerned the Crown, as tending to a disturbance of the peace, and it would have lost fees and suitors had the new and growing remedy for breaches of promise been contractual in form as it was in fact.

If the innovation was illogical and dictated by interested motives, it promoted the administration of justice by surmounting a technical objection that did not affect the merits,[3]

[1] 2 Bl. Com. 157, 200.

[2] 16 Edward IV. 9, pl. 7.

[3] Spence's Eq. Jurisd. i. 240, 242.

and might, moreover, be defended on the ground that if a breach of faith was not a breach of the peace, it still tended to disturb the good order of society, which it was the peculiar duty of the king's court to preserve.

The growth of the action of assumpsit is the more explicable because the doctrine that the breach of a promise by which another has been induced to pursue a course that will prove injurious unless the promise is fulfilled, may operate as a fraud, was familiar to the legal mind, and had been applied from an early period through the instrumentality of the writ of deceit.[1] Fraud was as infinite in its variety then as it is now, and the ingenuity of the clerks in Chancery was taxed to adapt this writ to the various forms in which covin might be used as a means of injury.

An oral contract of sale was not valid while executory, and an action would not lie for the vendor's refusal to deliver the goods, or the failure of the purchaser to accept and pay,[2] but the vendor might well be made answerable in an action of deceit, on proof that he had induced the purchaser to take the goods by warranting them without averring that he knew of the defect, or gave the warranty with a fraudulent intent.[3] The remedy was nevertheless circumscribed in its operation, and did not apply in many cases of undoubted wrong. If a vendor performed the contract literally, but broke it in effect, as by delivering unsound wares under a sale with warranty, or granting a rent charge out of the land which he had agreed to convey before making livery of seisin, compensation might be had through a writ of deceit; but the judges had more difficulty, where the defendant simply failed to fulfil his contract, and there was no misfeasance.[4] As this objection did not apply with as much force when the action was on the case, it was employed concurrently with the writ of deceit,

[1] Fitzherbert, Natura Brevium, 95 E. *et seq.*

[2] Bracton, i. 489 (f. 61 b).

[3] Fitzherbert, Natura Brevium, 98 E.; 11 Edward IV. 6, pl. 10; 21 Henry VII. 41, pl. 66.

[4] Reeves, History of the English Law, ii. 606; 20 Henry VI. 34, pl. 4.

and finally took its place, and assumpsit followed as a natural outgrowth.[1]

The line of demarcation between case and assumpsit was nevertheless drawn gradually, and can hardly be said to be well defined even now. It was long customary even when the declaration was professedly *ex contractu*, and *non assumpsit* the appropriate plea, to aver not merely that the defendant promised and failed to perform, but that he had acted fraudulently with an intent to deceive, and the omission of such an allegation would presumably have afforded ground for a demurrer in the time of Coke, and it may be at a later period. An action on the case was still the remedy in common use for a breach of warranty in the sale of chattels, at the close of the last century; and although it was finally established that the purchaser might maintain assumpsit, a recovery may still be had in case without averring that the vendor knew that the goods were unsound; contrary to the general rule that to render a man liable for an erroneous statement it must appear to have been consciously false, or uttered with the reckless disregard of truth which is equivalent to falsehood.[2]

The growth of the doctrine of consideration may be elucidated by the following extract from Reeves's History of the Common Law: —[3]

"It (trespass on the case) was in its conception so near of kin to the action of trespass that it required no small degree of sagacity to perceive the instances in which the old form failed, and it was necessary to make a special writ. The cases in the reign of Edward III. which we have hitherto considered, are founded upon malfeasances, or such instances of neglect as were in the nature of a malfeasance, both of which were so much in the like case (according to the requisition of the Statute of Westminster) with the old writ of trespass,

[1] Reeves, History of the English Law, ii. 606; Fitzherbert, Natura Brevium, 94 C.; Comyns's Digest, Action on the case for Deceit, A. 5.

[2] Stuart *v.* Wilkins, Douglas, 18; Williamson *v.* Allison, 2 East, 446; 1 Sm. L. C. 8 Am. ed.

[3] Vol. ii. pp. 508–510.

that the admitting of them to be objects of this special writ of trespass was obvious and easy. But the action upon the case was found so convenient a remedy that it was wished to extend it still further. They wanted to apply it to cases of non-performance of promises; but these did not so kindly fall within the analogy of former instances. It was thought somewhat harsh to give the name of trespass to a thing which was never done; it took, therefore, some time, and needed the concurrent force of some strong motives to induce the courts to admit these new writs. The present state of the remedies in use, where contracts were not performed, operated very probably towards gaining a support for these new actions upon the case. If a man performed not his covenant, an action of covenant lay; but it had been long held that an action of covenant must be founded on a specialty; so that where the parties had not so bound themselves, that remedy failed. If a man did not pay money which he owed, the remedy was by action of debt, in which the defendant might discharge himself by wager of law, unless the demand was founded upon a specialty; the same in detinue, which indeed was only another form of the action of debt. To obviate these and the like defects, and to legitimate an action of a more effectual nature in matters of contract, was worth the attempt. Several actions of this kind were brought into court before they were allowed and authenticated by a judicial decision in their favor.

"The first case of this kind upon record was in 2 Henry IV. It was an action against a carpenter: *Quare cum*, etc., *assumpsisset*, etc., to build a house within a certain time, he had not done it. It was objected that this was in covenant, and as no writing was shown the action must fail. This was supported also by Brian, who, at the same time, conceded that perhaps if the writ had said that the work had been begun, and had afterwards through negligence been stopped, it might be otherwise; thereby adhering to former determinations respecting malfeasances and cases of negligence. He pronounced, however, this remedy inadequate when the contract was executory, and where the only complaint against the defendant would be for his non-feasance or non-performance. The cause was dismissed on the above objection.[1] In the 11th of the same King, there was exactly the same case before the court; the same objections were raised, the same concession was made, but in plainer terms, and the cause was dismissed on the same grounds as the former.[2] Thus the court seemed to have determined against the very conception of this kind of action. It is remarked upon this case by an author of later times,[3] that in these cases there was no consideration alleged; that it was *nudum pactum*, and therefore the action could not lie; which it cannot be denied may be an additional objection, but it was not taken at the time, and the cause appears by the report to have been dismissed both times upon the same defects, namely, the want of a written covenant, and the prevailing opinion which confined these actions to instances of malfeasance and negligence where the defendant had really done something.

"It must be observed of these determinations that they left all persons who had made agreements without deed (for, if a mere writing, it could not be declared on in covenant), and where nothing had been done to execute the contract, entirely without redress. It is not improbable that the repeated decision of this point might have driven parties so circumstanced into Chancery, where they could have these agreements decreed to be specifically performed. This, perhaps, as well as other considerations, might incline the courts to review this grand point, and try if they could accommodate the notions of law as then understood to the exigency of the occasion, and thereby not only draw back into its proper channel the current of decision from the Chancery to the courts of common law, but, by rendering this action more general, put the nation in possession of what was then much wanted, — a more effectual common-law redress in matter of contract. This was not accomplished till some years after."

So far Mr. Reeves is very clear; but the gradual solution of the problem by the growth of the doctrine of consideration is not stated with equal distinctness either here or in the sub-

[1] 2 Henry IV. 3, pl. 9.

[2] 11 Henry IV. 33, pl. 60.

[3] Bro. Act. sur Case, 40.

sequent pages of his treatise. In the cases cited from the Year Books, the objection to the maintenance of the action seems to have been twofold, — that if there was an obligation the remedy lay in covenant, and not in trespass; if there was none, the defendant could not be made liable in any form of action for remaining merely passive. If, indeed, he acted under a covenant or without one, and the plaintiff suffered through his want of skill or his negligence, an action of trespass on the case might be brought for the misfeasance, but a man could not commit a trespass by standing still.

There were, nevertheless, many wrongs that must go unredressed if the objection was allowed to prevail; and it was partially obviated by extending the writ of deceit to frauds committed in the making or execution of parol agreements, as by selling unsound goods with a warranty of soundness. This form of action, like many of the other proceedings of the earlier common law, was hampered by technicalities, which were obviated by setting forth the facts under the authority conferred by the Statute of Westminster, and leaving the court to draw the inference. Case thus became a remedy for injuries resulting from a breach of faith, although occurring in the course of an agreement that could not have been enforced by suit. If this was conceded, no form of deception could well be more mischievous or call more loudly for relief than where a defendant refused to fulfil a promise for which he had received an equivalent, on the ground that it was not made in the form required by law. Such a non-feasance is more than the breach of a moral obligation; it is the last of a series of steps by which an injury is inflicted that may well be presumed to have been designed from the outset. The writ was accordingly modified to meet the exigency, and it came to be established law that a recovery might be had on showing either that the defendant had injured the plaintiff by acting amiss, or that he had induced the plaintiff to act by a promise that was not fulfilled.

The injury might obviously be as great in one case as in the other; and a remedy was given by moulding the action on the case into an action of assumpsit. Instead of relying on the mere non-fulfilment of a parol promise, which standing alone was not a cause of action, the declaration averred that the defendant promised to remunerate the plaintiff if he would adopt a certain line of conduct; that this course was pursued; but that the defendant, craftily intending to deceive and injure the plaintiff, withheld the stipulated compensation. From this point the transition was, as I have already said, easy to cases where the contract was executory on both sides, and the injury to the plaintiff consisted in the loss of the profit that would have accrued if the contract had been fulfilled.

To have termed the new writ covenant on the case would not, as Mr. Spence seems to suppose, have been logical, because it would have implied that the action was brought for the non-fulfilment of the promise as distinguished from the injurious effect in misleading the plaintiff, and, moreover, have provoked the objection that there was no seal. The choice consequently lay between deceit and trespass, and although the former would have been more consistent with the allegation that the defendant acted with a fraudulent intent, and was customarily used in declaring for a breach of warranty, the latter might be employed without an abuse of terms, and had the advantage of bringing the cause within the jurisdiction of the King's Bench.

It results, from what has been said, that the common law recognizes two types of contracts,—the parol contract, and the agreement under seal or covenant; the latter deriving its validity from the sealing and delivery, which like the formal question and response of the Roman law, imply deliberation and assent, while the obligation depends in the former case on what is done or promised on the faith of the assurance held out by the promisor. The covenant originated at an age when men looked chiefly to form, while the parol contract had its growth at a later period, when substance was more regarded and they had begun to feel that no wrong should be remediless, no injury go unredressed.

An apparent anomaly may be explained on the principles above stated. It was a well established rule of the common law that the right of action lay not with him to whom the promise was made, and who would have been benefited if it had been kept, but with the party from whom the consideration moved on the faith of the promise.[1] If, for instance, A promised to pay B £1,000 if C would go to Rome, and C took the journey, he and not B was regarded as entitled to the reward, and to compel the payment of it by suit. For as the action was, as already stated, brought not to enforce the contract specifically, but to recover compensation for the injury occasioned by the breach of faith, the person who had parted with his property or rendered the stipulated service, was obviously the one who should be compensated in damages. In Thomas *v.* Thomas,[2] Pattison, J., said: "Consideration means something which is of some value in the eye of the law, moving from the plaintiff. It may be some benefit to the defendant, or some detriment to the plaintiff, but at all events it must be moving from the plaintiff." This statement may be accepted as a definition, if we add that the consideration must not only move from the plaintiff, but be something for which the defendant stipulated as the equivalent for the undertaking which the plaintiff seeks to enforce.

The rule may be traced in the reports from the origin of the action of assumpsit down to our own times, although it is not infrequently modified or superseded by principles which the common law has derived from Equity. In Bourne *v.* Mason,[3] one Parry was indebted to the plaintiff and to the defendants in two several sums of money, and a third person was indebted to Parry, and it was agreed between Parry, the plaintiff, and the defendants, that if Parry would permit them to sue for in his name, and recover the amount due him, they would pay what he owed the plaintiff. The defendants brought the suit and recovered, but would not pay the plaintiff. The court held that the plaintiff could not maintain the action, because he was a stranger to the consideration which moved from Parry, who was the actual sufferer by the default.

[1] Thomas *v.* Thomas, 2 Q. B. 851, 859.

[2] 2 Q. B. 851, 859.

[3] 1 Ventris 6.

The principle was applied conversely in a case cited in the report of the above decision. A conversation took place between two fathers, in which one promised that if the other would give his daughter in marriage to his son, he would settle certain lands on the young couple. The marriage took place, but the settlement was not made, and the court held that the husband might maintain an action for the default, because he did the meritorious act. This decision was obviously just. The promise was made to the bride's father, but it was the husband who assumed the burden of a wife in the belief that the defendant would keep his word. The American authorities are to the same effect. In Edmundson *v.* Penny,[1] Edmundson gave Penny a written promise to pay him $25 in one year, for the services which McCandless was to render as a preacher during the interval. It appeared from the evidence that McCandless officiated, and that Edmundson was a member of the congregation. Gibson, C. J., said that a parol promise to one man for the benefit of another, could only support an action by him from whom the consideration moved. The plaintiff must unite in his own person both the promise and the consideration for it, and the promise might be drawn to the consideration for the attainment of this end, but not the consideration to the promise. It followed that the right of action lay not in Penny, to whom the promise was made, and who was to have received the money, but in McCandless, who rendered the services which were the consideration for the promise.

The doctrine was also recognized in Warren *v.* Batchelder,[2] although the court finally concluded that the circumstances did not admit of its application. There A was indebted to B, and B to C, and it was agreed between A and B that the amount owed by A should be paid by him to C on account of the debt due by B. C called on A for the money, which was withheld and he thereupon brought suit. The judges were clearly of opinion that C could not enforce the promise unless he had agreed to forego or cancel his claim against B, or in other words to accept A's promise in satisfaction of B's lia-

[1] 1 Pa. 234. [2] 15 N. H. 129; 16 id. 580.

bility, but they held that such an inference might be drawn from the acceptance implied in the demand on B.

These decisions mark the difference between the civil and common law with a distinctness which cannot be misunderstood. If the obligation of a contract is founded on consent the right must obviously reside in the promisee. If on the other hand it grows out of the consideration, he should sue from whom the consideration moves.

CHAPTER VIII.

TRESPASS ON THE CASE.

Classification of Rights of Action *ex contractu* and *ex delicto*. — Distinction between Assumpsit and Case. — Remedies for tortious Breach of Contract. — Remedy for Injury resulting from Non-fulfilment of a gratuitous Promise.

BROADLY stated, case is a remedy for torts, assumpsit for breaches of contract; but the rule is not universal, and may mislead. Real as is the distinction between tort and contract, it is frequently laid down arbitrarily, and does not readily admit of a precise or scientific classification.

To understand the English law of contracts as contrasted with the Roman law, we must survey the ground covered by the action on the case as well as that which belongs exclusively to assumpsit.

A breach of promise may be as wrongful as fraud or negligence, and fraud is not infrequently practised in entering into a contract or carrying it into effect.[1] A man who receives his neighbor's property as a deposit, or on whose premises it is left for safe keeping while he is away, does not contract in the sense of the common law, and although the obligation was regarded as contractual at Rome, it really springs from a duty which the law implies, and that would be binding though nothing were said on either side.

This is the more obvious because the liability of a finder is the same as that of a bailee, that is, to take ordinary care of the property, and return it when demanded.[2] In like manner while a gratuitous promise to act for another, or to transport

[1] See Kinlyside *v.* Thornton, 2 Wm. Bl. 1111; Shippen *v.* Tankersley, 4 McCrary C. Ct. 259.

[2] Isaack *v.* Clark, 2 Bulstrode, 306; St. Germain, Doctor and Student, Dialogue ii, ch. 38.

his goods, was regarded as a consensual contract by the Roman jurists, it is not obligatory under our system, and if a recovery is had it must be on the ground of misfeasance. It is not therefore surprising that the action on the case originally covered both grounds, and was a remedy alike for deceit, negligence, misfeasance, and a fraudulent breach of promise.

Assumpsit was, as we have seen, finally segregated, and became the appropriate means of redress for the non-fulfilment of a contract; but various obligations which had been classed by the civil law as contractual were still regarded by the English courts as *ex delicto*, and enforced through a writ in case. These were, as they still are, mainly causes of action arising from a breach of duty as distinguished from a breach of promise, although the promise might be one of the circumstances out of which the duty arose. The contracts *re* of the Roman law, namely, the *depositum* or gratuitous bailment for safe keeping, the *commodatum* or loan for use, and the *pignus* or pledge, belong to this category; under which we may also range the mandate and cases where possession is acquired by finding.[1] Under these circumstances the liability arises out of the duty of every one who has charge of another's property to use due care, and if injured through neglect or misfeasance the remedy is not *ex contractu* but in tort. Such also is the rule where a loss is occasioned by misfeasance in the execution of a mandate, or promise to act for another's benefit without compensation, and generally wherever there is no promise or no consideration, and hence no contract, and the obligation grows out of the facts.

There are, moreover, instances where case may be maintained, although a promise is essential to the right of action, and whether it is or is not obligatory as a contract; or, to state the proposition somewhat differently, where the defendant would be answerable though the promise were gratuitous, the plaintiff may choose between case and assumpsit, notwithstanding the existence of a consideration. Either action may consequently be brought against a carrier for hire, or, as it would seem, against an innkeeper; although the remedy would be

[1] Isaack *v.* Clark, 2 Bulstrode, 306; Jones on Bailments, p. 52, note 22.

exclusively in case if the defendant were acting without compensation, because he has the goods and should use due care whether he is or is not paid.[1] So a loan for use not only gives rise to a trust from the confidence reposed, but is a valuable consideration for any undertaking the borrower may think fit to make; and he may consequently be held answerable in case for fraud or negligence, or in assumpsit on an express or implied promise to take care of the goods and return them in the same condition, unless prevented by some insuperable cause, or even to be absolutely responsible for their safety as an insurer.

A loan for consumption stands on a different footing, because the property becomes the borrower's and there is no trust. He cannot therefore be made answerable on the ground of negligence, or rely on unavoidable loss as a defence, and the remedy is *ex contractu* for the non-fulfilment of the obligation to return a like amount. A request for a loan is in effect a promise to repay, and if the loan is pecuniary creates a debt which may be recovered in an action for money had and received.

It is not less well settled that where a tort is also a breach of contract the plaintiff need not proceed *ex contractu*, but may declare in case, although he may equally well maintain assumpsit; or as the principle is stated in Chitty's Pleading,[2] although there be an express contract, yet if a common-law duty grows out of the relation which it creates, a recovery may be had in case for the non-fulfilment of the duty, although it is also a violation of the contract.[3]

A shepherd who sets a dog upon the sheep which he has been hired to tend may be charged upon the contract or as a wrongdoer, and so where the master of a vessel or a common carrier is negligent in keeping the goods which are intrusted to him for carriage.[4]

[1] Baltimore Railway Co. *v.* Kemp, 61 Md. 619, 623, 625; Stanley *v.* Bircher, 78 Mo. 245.

[2] p. 135.

[3] Stanley *v.* Bircher, 78 Mo. 245.

[4] Dickson *v.* Clifton, 2 Wilson, 319; Burnett *v.* Lynch, 5 B. & C. 589; Mast *v.* Goodson, 3 Wilson, 348; Bretherton *v.* Wood, 3 Brod. & Bing. 54.

An averment that the defendant agreed to deliver certain bonds to the plaintiff, and in lieu thereof delivered forged and worthless instruments having the semblance of such bonds, is a valid complaint in tort, although the plaintiff might have maintained assumpsit; and it has been said that when a delict grows out of and is dependent on a contract, the action may either be *ex contractu* for the breach of promise, or *ex delicto* for the wrong done under the pretence of carrying the contract into effect.[1] In like manner case will lie for the non-fulfilment of a common-law duty, although the law implies a promise for its fulfilment, and one who takes an assignment of a lease under and subject to the covenants may consequently be liable to the assignor either in case or assumpsit, if they are not performed.[2]

These decisions are not obsolete even in the states where the common-law forms of action have been abolished, because the distinction between tort and contract is fundamental and constantly recurs in the administration of justice.[3]

It is established, in accordance with these principles, that a promise which, from the want of a consideration, is not obligatory as a contract, may yet lay the foundation for a recovery in case, as defining the relation which the defendant holds to the plaintiff, and the amount of diligence, time, and attention it was incumbent on him to bestow.[4] Such an averment does not change the character of the action; the appropriate plea is still "not guilty;" and merely introduces a new ingredient which modifies the obligation that would have arisen from the facts if standing alone. All that is necessarily implied in evidence that a horse was left in the defendant's keeping is that he is a simple bailee or depositary, and answerable for gross negligence; but what is said at the time may show that he is a mandatary, a borrower, a hirer, or a contractor, and bound to exact diligence or more than ordi-

1 Shippen *v.* Tankersley, 4 McCrary C. Ct. 259, 262; Addison on Torts, § 27.

2 Burnett *v.* Lynch, 5 B. & C. 589.

3 Gudger *v.* The R. R., 21 Federal Rep. 81.

4 See Maynz, ii. § 239, pp. 317, 319, notes 12, 27.

nary care. These obligations were regarded by the Roman law as *ex contractu;* but their classification at common law depends not on the presence or absence of a promise, but on whether they are gratuitous or for a reward;[1] and the appropriate remedy in the former hypothesis is case, in the latter assumpsit, although either form of action may not infrequently be employed at the will of the pleader.[2]

The allegation of a promise is therefore no more conclusive of the nature of a cause of action at the present day than it was in the Year Books, and the test is, Does the declaration show a breach of trust, or simply a breach of promise?[3] A criterion may now be found in the general issue, which is "not guilty" in case, and in assumpsit that the defendant "did not promise;" but it was originally permissible to traverse any material allegation, and *non assumpsit* might well be a good plea to an action of tort.

There are accordingly numerous instances where a right of action *ex delicto* grows out of a promise, and could not be maintained had it not been made. The obligation of an unpaid agent or bailee does not, as I have elsewhere shown, ordinarily extend beyond doing as well as he knows how, and he may plead ignorance or want of skill as an excuse; but the case is widely different when he holds himself out as competent and well-informed, or promises to use proper means for the attainment of the end.[4]

In 19 Henry VI. 49, pl. 5, Newton is said to have declared that "if my hand is diseased and one applies the remedy to my heel, I shall have no action unless he undertook to work a cure." This language seemingly goes beyond the mark. The bare fact of acting on behalf of another may not render the agent liable for a want of skill, but it is still his duty to

[1] Coggs *v.* Bernard, 2 Lord Raymond, 909, 917.

[2] Burnett *v.* Lynch, 5 B. & C. 589; Corbett *v.* Packington, 6 B. & C. 268.

[3] Mast *v.* Goodson, 3 Wilson, 348; Corbett *v.* Packington, 6 B. & C. 268.

[4] 48 Edward, III. 6, pl. 11; 19 Henry VI. 49, pl. 5; Shiells *v.* Blackburne, 1 H. Bl. 158, *ante.*

proceed with care; and if he is wanting in this regard and loss ensues, he must respond in damages. Conceding that the mistaken application of a counter-irritant to one part of the person to alleviate pain in another, is not necessarily or even presumably malpractice on the part of one who does not profess to be a physician; still if harm ensues a recovery may be had on proof that the defendant took charge of the case recklessly, without disclosing his want of knowledge, or was so remiss and inattentive as to show that he was careless of the result.

Whatever the rule may be where there is no promise, it is clear that where a man is induced to place his person, child, or goods under the care of another, by an assurance that the duty shall be well and effectually performed, the trust will be co-extensive with the words in which it is declared, and a recovery may be had in case, whether the breach is due to incompetency or neglect.

Attorneys, surgeons, farriers, inn-keepers, common carriers, and other persons exercising a public trade or occupation, are within this principle, because they impliedly hold themselves out as skilled in the performance of their respective callings, and ready and willing to serve all who may apply;[1] and they may also be answerable for declining to act without sufficient cause, because not doing has under such circumstances the effect of a misfeasance.[2] Such is the position of a common carrier who arbitrarily rejects the goods which are tendered to him for transportation, or of an inn-keeper who turns a traveller from his door.

It is not therefore a justification for a physician that he mistook the case or the remedy, if the truth would have been plain to any man who knew the rudiments of his profession, nor for a farrier that he was ignorant of the proper method of shoeing a horse. There is, however, no contract, in the absence of an express or implied agreement for compensation, and the remedy lies in case for the breach of trust.

[1] 3 Bl. Com. 164; Capel's Case, 1 Rep. 54 a.

[2] 3 Bl. Com. 164; Anonymous, 1 Ventris, 336; Lane *v.* Cotton, 1 Lord Raymond, 646, 654.

The doctrine has sometimes been stated too broadly, as if it were true of every man whose trade or occupation is to furnish board or lodging, but it only applies to persons who, by advertising or hanging out a sign, convey the impression that they keep a public house, and are prepared to receive all comers; and there is nothing to preclude a man from announcing that he has opened a house of entertainment which is designed exclusively for families, or that he will not receive bachelors or children, or persons of a particular race, sect, or color.[1]

Paid agents and contractors impliedly undertake that they have the requisite skill and knowledge, or rather that the contract shall be fulfilled at all events, and may be made answerable in assumpsit for a default, whether it is occasioned by a want of skill or negligence. It results from what has been said that although a gratuitous undertaking is not obligatory it may yet modify or enlarge the obligation growing out of a given state of facts, or more accurately may be one of several circumstances which together make it incumbent on the promisor to do or render something to or on behalf of the promisee. The obligation arising from the deposit of a promissory note or other chattel is simply to use ordinary care for its safe keeping; but if the bailee promises to take charge of such an instrument and present it on the last day of grace to the maker, he must either return it to the bailor within such a reasonable time as will enable him to find another messenger, or execute the commission, and will be answerable for any loss arising from a want of punctuality and diligence.[2] There is no consideration, for although the bailor parts with the possession of the note on the faith of the bailee's promise, it is for a purpose of his own, and the benefit is conferred by and not on the bailee. The difference between such a case and a contract for hire is, that in the former the undertaking is obligatory from the outset, while it is a *nudum pactum* in the latter until some act is done or step taken by the promisor

[1] See Calye's Case, 8 Rep. 32 a; 1 Sm. L. C. 8 Am. ed. 249; Rex *v.* Llewellyn, 4 M. & S. 306; Queen *v.* Rymer, L. R. 2 Q. B. Div. 136.

[2] Fellowes *v.* Gordon, 8 B. Monroe, 415; French *v.* Reed, 6 Binn. 308.

to carry it into effect; or to state the proposition somewhat differently, while the act which renders a promise obligatory as a contract must proceed from the promisee, a mandate derives its obligation from the course adopted by the promisor. The question was carefully considered in the leading case of Coggs *v.* Bernard,[1] which gave stability to a rule that had previously been fluctuating and ill-defined. The action was on the case, and the plaintiff declared that the defendant had undertaken to take up several casks of brandy safely from a certain cellar, and lay them safely down elsewhere, but performed the work so negligently that one of the casks was staved and the brandy spilt. After "not guilty" pleaded, and a verdict for the plaintiff, it was moved in arrest of judgment that the defendant was not alleged to be a common porter, or that he was to have anything for his pains. Lord Holt held, in delivering judgment, that the defendant might have removed the brandies or refrained, and if he had chosen to adopt the latter course nobody could have compelled him to proceed; but that when he entered on the performance of the task, it became a trust, and he was answerable for the miscarriage occasioned by his default. "In such a case," said he (that is, when the bailee promises to use due care), "neglect is a deceit to the bailor. For when he intrusts the bailee upon his undertaking to be careful, he has put a fraud upon the plaintiff by being negligent, his pretence of care being the persuasion that induced the plaintiff to trust him. And a breach of a trust undertaken voluntarily will be a good ground for an action.[2] There the case was an action against a man, who had undertaken to keep a hundred sheep, for letting them be drowned by his default. And the reason of the judgment is given, because when the party has taken upon him to keep the sheep, and after suffers them to perish in his default; inasmuch as he has taken and executed his bargain, and has them in his custody, if after he does not look to them an action lies. For here is his own act, viz., his agreement and promise, and that after broke of his side, that shall give a sufficient cause of action.

[1] 2 Lord Raymond, 909.

[2] 1 Rolle Abr. 10; 2 Henry VII. 11.

"But, secondly, it is objected that there is no consideration to ground this promise upon, and therefore the undertaking is but *nudum pactum*. But to this I answer that the owner's trusting him with the goods is a sufficient consideration to oblige him to a careful management. Indeed, if the agreement had been executory, to carry these brandies from one place to another on such a day, the defendant had not been bound to carry them. But this is a different case, for assumpit does not only signify a future agreement, but, in such a case as this, it signifies an actual entry upon the thing and taking the trust upon himself. And if a man will do that and miscarries in the performance of his trust, an action will lie against him for that, though nobody could have compelled him to do the thing."

The line is here distinctly drawn; there is no contract, but there is a trust arising from the delivery and acceptance of the goods which the bailee may renounce, but is obligatory so long as it endures.

A mandate, though springing from mutual promises on one side to act and on the other to indemnify, is yet wanting in mutuality of consideration, because the whole is for the benefit of the mandant, who simply undertakes to keep the mandatary harmless. It is therefore under our system a *nudum pactum*, that will not give rise to a trust until some act is done to carry it into effect, and falls under the head of promises, which, though not obligatory and made with no ill intent, may yet lay the foundation for an obligation *ex delicto*.

The question when a mandate or gratuitous promise to act on behalf of another becomes so far obligatory that a failure to carry it into effect will constitute a wrong that may be redressed by suit, was elaborately considered in Thorne *v.* Deas,[1] which deserves attentive consideration, as not only elucidating the early law, but showing that the doctrine of consideration has undergone no material change since the fifteenth century. The plaintiffs were joint owners of one moiety of a brig, and the defendant was sole owner of the other moiety. The brig sailed on a voyage to the West Indies,

[1] 4 Johns. 84.

with Thorne, one of the plaintiffs on board; and on the day of her departure a conversation took place between him and the defendant, in which Thorne requested the defendant to insure the vessel, and the latter replied that it should be done at once. Some ten days afterwards, the other co-plaintiff, Daniel Thorne, was told by the defendant that the insurance had not been effected. He expressed his dissatisfaction, and said that if the defendant did not take out a policy he would do so himself. The defendant replied that Thorne might make himself easy, the insurance should be effected on that very day. In point of fact, however, this promise was not fulfilled, and the vessel having been lost, the plaintiffs brought an action on the case to recover damages for the injury occasioned by the breach. A verdict was taken for them at the trial, subject to the question whether there was any consideration to support the promise. In delivering the opinion of the court, Kent, C. J., said that the defendant's promise to effect an insurance was merely voluntary. If one who made such an agreement entered upon the execution of the business, and did it amiss from a want of care, an action would lie for the misfeasance. But the weight of authority clearly was that the non-performance of a voluntary contract could not be made the ground of a recovery in damages. The opposite view was indeed taken in the treatise of Sir William Jones, on the Law of Bailments, but the learned author had not produced a single adjudged case in support of his opinion, which could only be sustained on a doctrine of the civil law that had not been incorporated with the law of England. The rule, as stated in the Institutes, was that any one might refuse to accept a commission; but that if he agreed to execute the mandate, it must be fulfilled, or the person who gave it notified in time to enable him to look for another agent, or transact the business in person. The equity of this principle was as obvious as the injury that might result where a man, in reliance on the good faith of another who had promised to perform a service, omitted to take measures for his own protection. There were, however, many obligations which the law did not enforce, but left to the forum of the individual conscience.

One of the earliest cases on the subject was Watton *v.* Brinth,[1] where the declaration averred that the defendant promised to repair certain houses for the plaintiff, and neglected to do it, — to his damage. The plaintiff was nonsuited because the promise was not under seal; but it was said that if the plaintiff had declared that the work had been commenced, and afterwards by negligence nothing done, the result would have been different. The distinction between nonfeasance and misfeasance was made the ground of the decision. No consideration was stated, and the court held that a covenant was necessary to bind the defendant.

In a subsequent case,[2] an action was brought against a carpenter, setting forth that he had undertaken to build a house for the plaintiff, within a certain time, and had not done it. The plaintiff was nonsuited because the undertaking was not binding without a specialty; but it was conceded that if he had begun to build the house, and had done it ill or negligently, an action would have lain without deed. Brooke, in commenting on this case, remarks that it seems to be good law to this day; wherefore the action upon the case which shall be brought upon an assumption, must state that it was for a sum of money to be paid to the plaintiff, for if nothing is to be paid the promise is *nudum pactum.*

The general question whether assumpsit would lie for a non-feasance agitated the courts down to the time of Henry VIII. There was no dispute or doubt that an action on the case lay for a misfeasance, or the breach of a trust undertaken voluntarily. The point in controversy was whether an action upon the case could be maintained for a non-feasance, or, as it is now called, the non-performance of a naked promise; and whether there was any remedy where the party had not secured himself under seal. But none of these cases went so far as to say that assumpsit would lie for the non-fulfilment of a promise without alleging a consideration, and when at last an action on the case for the non-performance of an undertaking came to be established, the necessity of showing a consideration was explicitly avowed.

[1] 2 Henry IV. 3, pl. 9.

[2] 11 Henry IV. 33, pl. 60.

There was, therefore, no just reason to infer from the ancient authorities that such a promise as the one before the court was good without a consideration. The whole current of the decisions ran the other way, and from the time of Henry VII. to the present the rule had been uniformly the same.

The doctrine of Sir William Jones, in the Essay on Bailments, was true in reference to the civil law, but totally unfounded under the law of England; and those who attentively examined the head of "Mandate," in that treatise would agree that it had been hastily and loosely written.

The counsel for the plaintiff had contended that if the general rule of the common law was against the right to maintain an action under such circumstances, the question under consideration was a commercial one, and governed by a different principle. The case of Wilkinson *v.* Coverdale,[1] was upon a promise to cause a house to be insured, and Lord Kenyon held the defendant liable because he had proceeded to execute the commission and had done it negligently. An examination of the decisions which had been cited on behalf of the plaintiff would show that they all rested on this principle. The defendant was consequently upon the whole case entitled to judgment.

This decision is in accordance with the current of authority in England in modern times, and notwithstanding the seeming failure of justice, may be practically wise, as preventing the litigation that would ensue if a gratuitous promise could be made the foundation of a suit. The case in 3 Henry VI. 36, pl. 33, on which Sir William Jones principally relied as an authority for the position that a mandate is obligatory at common law, would seem to have been misunderstood by him, and certainly does not warrant the inference. The suit was against a millwright, and Strange declared on the plaintiff's behalf that the defendant undertook to make a mill and raise it by Christmas, at which time the work was not done, to the plaintiff's wrong and damage, ten marks. Rolf for the defendant prayed judgment of the writ, because it stated that

[1] 1 Esp. 75.

the defendant was to make the mill without setting forth how much he was to have for doing it.

Three questions were discussed at the bar and on the bench. — Did a parol agreement require a consideration? Ought the court to infer that the defendant was to be compensated for his work, although it was not expressly stated? Could a recovery be had in trespass where nothing had been done, and the wrong consisted in a mere failure to comply with the terms of an agreement? A majority of the judges were with the plaintiff on the third point, and against him on the second, but they all seem to have agreed that unless the defendant was to be paid he was under no legal obligation, and could not be made answerable for the default. The discussion was cut short by the Chief Justice, who observed, "All that we say is vain, for they have not yet demurred; therefore plead or demur, and it can be considered at leisure." Rolf thereupon pleaded that the mill was made, and the plaintiff notified; who replied that he did not want the mill, and relied on this as a discharge, and the case then went over to another day. Although the court did not give judgment, the report justifies the conclusion deduced by Brooke, that "if it be not expressed what he is to have for his work, it is a nude pact *unde non oritur actio*."[1]

The case of Elsee *v.* Gatward[2] is closely analogous to Thorne *v.* Deas. The declaration set forth that the plaintiff retained the defendant, who was a carpenter, to repair a house before a given day, and that the defendant accepted the retainer but did not perform the work within the time; *per quod*, the walls of the plaintiff's house were damaged. Lord Kenyon said that if the suit had been in assumpsit, it could not have been sustained for want of a consideration. The declaration stated that the defendant was retained to build and repair certain houses; but it was not stated that he was to receive any consideration, or that he entered upon the work. No consideration resulted from his calling as a carpenter, nor from the undertaking; and the amount of the whole was that he had deceived the plaintiff and broken his promise, and for this no

[1] Brooke, Tit. Action sur le Case, pl. 7.

[2] 5 T. R. 143.

action could be maintained. In Coggs *v.* Bernard,[1] Lord Holt had cited and recognized the case in 11 Henry IV. 33, pl. 60, where an action was brought against a carpenter for that he had undertaken to build a barn for the plaintiff, and had not done it; and it was adjudged that the action would not lie. And this opinion was conclusive, because the justice of the case did not depend on the form of the action; and if assumpsit could not be maintained under such circumstances, a recovery could not be had by bringing the action in tort.

The subject was reviewed in Balfe *v.* West,[2] where the defendant, who had gratuitously accepted the office of steward of a horse-race, was held not to be responsible for a loss arising from his failure to take the necessary measures to determine by whom the race was won, although the result might have been different if he had entered on the performance of the trust.

It is not less well established that one who enters on the performance of a mandate, or gratuitous undertaking to act on behalf of another, is responsible not only for what he does, but for what he leaves unfulfilled; and cannot rely on the want of a consideration as an excuse for the omission of any step that is requisite for the protection of the interests intrusted to his care.

In French *v.* Reed,[3] the plaintiff wrote requesting the defendants to effect an insurance from Philadelphia to two ports in the Island of St. Domingo. The defendants obtained an insurance to one port only, and the vessel was captured on her voyage from the first port (where she had arrived in safety) to the second. There had been intimacy and business dealings between the plaintiff and the defendants some time previously; but when the plaintiff gave the order the balance of accounts was in the defendants' favor, and there was no circumstance which rendered it obligatory on them to render, or entitled the plaintiff to demand such a service. The jury were instructed that although the defendants were not bound to accede to the plaintiff's request, yet when they agreed to do as he desired and did it ill, they became liable

[1] 2 Lord Raymond, 909. [2] 13 C. B. 466. [3] 6 Binn. 308.

for the consequences; and a verdict was accordingly rendered against them for the full amount. It was held in like manner in Gill *v.* Middleton,[1] that a promise on the part of a landlord to make repairs which are not stipulated for in the lease is without consideration, and may consequently be repudiated or performed at his option; but that if he sees fit to perform it he will be answerable for the manner in which the work is done.

The practical difference between the Roman and English law, therefore, is as to the period when the obligation begins, which, according to the former system, is when the defendant undertakes, and under the latter when he enters on the performance of the work. There is no consideration in either case: none before the work is begun, because until then the mandant may recall the request, and with it the implied promise of indemnity; and none afterwards, because beginning to render a gratuitous service to another is obviously not a consideration for a promise to complete the task. There would consequently be no obligation, were it not that when the mandatary begins to act, and thus not only gives undeniable evidence that he considers himself bound, but may induce the mandant to refrain from acting for himself, a trust arises, not *ex contractu*, but from the facts, which may be enforced by suit. It may be asked: How can such a result be reconciled with the principles of the common law? Does one who agrees gratuitously to build a house bind himself irrevocably by laying the foundation? or can a recovery be had for a failure to fulfil a naked promise to repair a watch, on proof that it was delivered to and accepted by the defendant? If such be the law, what becomes of the doctrine of consideration? The subject is an intricate one; but the objection would appear to admit of the following answers: 1st. No recovery can be had in such cases for the mere breach of promise, or without proof of special damage. An action will not lie against a carpenter for beginning to roof a house and leaving it unfinished, in the absence of a consideration, unless the plaintiff shows that the goods or furniture it contained were injured by the want of

[1] 105 Mass. 477.

covering, and consequent exposure to the elements. 2d. If no loss has arisen, and subject to the duty of making compensation if it has, a gratuitous undertaking may be rescinded, although the mandatary has entered on the performance of the work, on notice to the mandant and an opportunity given to him to engage some other person to complete what is left unfulfilled. If I promise to mail a letter for a friend, and find that I have not time, I may return it without incurring any liability, unless there is an opportunity to send it through another channel, and he suffers from the delay.

What is such a commencement of performance as will render a mandatary answerable for not completing the work or executing it negligently, has not been accurately defined, and may give rise to questions that cannot easily be solved. Had the plaintiff in Thorne *v.* Deas placed a written acceptance of an offer to insure the brig in the defendant's hands, on the faith of an assurance that it should be given to the underwriter, would an omission to deliver the letter within a reasonable time have been a misfeasance, rendering him answerable in damages? — and if this inquiry should be answered affirmatively, what is the difference between such a case and one where the message is sent orally, through an intermediary, who promises to give it, but fails?

It may also be observed that although the cases cited from the Year Books in Elsee *v.* Gatward and Thorne *v.* Deas show that a mandate is not obligatory as a contract, they do not cover the entire ground, because the plaintiff did not there aver a consequential injury arising from the defendant's breach of faith; and it was explicitly declared that where the non-feasance operates as a deceit a remedy might be had in tort and, as it would seem, whether there was or was not a consideration for the promise.[1] The smith who omitted to shoe the traveller's horse, the carpenter who failed to roof the house at the appointed time, are seemingly instances in point; for although the undertaking was spoken of as a covenant, it can hardly be supposed that a promise to fit a shoe would be reduced to writing and authenticated by a seal.

[1] 3 Henry VI. 36, pl. 33; 11 Henry VI. 18, pl. 10.

The distinction between misfeasance and non-feasance has no place in the law of contracts properly so called, and does not apply in covenant or assumpsit. If a man enters into a valid agreement to build a house, which he does not fulfil, the plaintiff may recover, whether the breach consists in an absolute refusal to perform the agreement, or in the negligent and unskilful manner in which the work is done. But if there is no contract, or none which is valid, he cannot be made answerable unless he enters upon the performance of the duty and does it ill, and the remedy must then be sought in case as distinguished from assumpsit. The point will appear in a clearer light, if it is regarded as springing from the law of trusts and not of contracts. What is said must no doubt be taken into view in determining the extent and nature of the obligation, as well as what is done; but this is true of every declaration of trust. A contract cannot exist without a consideration, and a consideration must be something moving from the plaintiff and detrimental to him, or beneficial to the defendant. Such a definition obviously excludes a gratuitous bailment, which imposes a burden on the bailee for the bailor's benefit. In Pickas *v.* Guile,[1] the declaration alleged that the defendant, in consideration that the plaintiff had then and there delivered certain broadcloths and packs of wool to him at his request, promised to deliver the same to the plaintiff when requested; and Yelverton showed in arrest of judgment that there was no consideration laid in the declaration to draw a promise from the defendant, for the defendant had no benefit from the cloths but *nudam custodiam*, which is rather a charge than a benefit, for the defendant could not use them. *Quod fuit concessum per totam curiam*, and *nil capiat per billam* entered. The law was held the same way by the Exchequer Chamber in Riches *v.* Briggs,[2] reversing the court below, which had given judgment for the plaintiff.

It was decided conversely in Corbett *v.* Packington,[3] that there is no legal duty to redeliver arising from the acceptance of goods for safe keeping, on which a recovery can be had in case; and that if damages are given on such grounds it must

[1] Yelv. 128. [2] Yelv. 4. [3] 6 B. & C. 268.

be in assumpsit and for the breach of an express promise. The proper course is to make a demand, and bring trover if the property is withheld.

It was notwithstanding determined in Wheatley *v.* Low,[1] conformably to Ostrand *v.* Crossing,[2] and Starkey *v.* Milne,[3] that parting with money and intrusting it to an unpaid bailee or mandatary will uphold an undertaking on his part to pay it over to a third person to whom the bailee is indebted; and in Whitehead *v.* Greetham,[4] the court held that a recovery might be had in assumpsit for the breach of a promise to use due care in investing a sum of money for the plaintiff, although it was not averred that the defendant was to be paid for his time and trouble.

If this view is just, the delivery of a chattel for a purpose which concerns the bailor, and is not in any sense beneficial to the bailee, is a consideration for any contract that the parties may think fit to make relatively to the matter in hand. The bailor may stipulate that the bailee shall be answerable for the event, and not merely for the want of care, and a recovery had against one who gratuitously receives a package of money or a bale of merchandise for transportation, on a promise that it shall arrive in safety, or even to compensate the owner for intrusting it to his care.

Moreover, an obligation may, as we have seen, arise without a transfer of possession; and a mandatary, who promises to effect an insurance and enters on the execution of the trust, is bound to do all in his power to bring it to a successful termination, whether the vessel is or is not delivered to him.[5] So the liability of one who undertakes to make an investment for another, arises from the confidence reposed in his judgment and discretion, and may exist although the money does not pass through his hands, and is paid directly to the borrower.

The true theory seems to be that the acceptance of another's goods gives rise to a trust, which is coextensive with the purpose for which they are delivered and received, and that will

[1] Croke Jac. 668.

[2] Rolle Abr. § 11, pl. 7.

[3] Id. § 32, pl. 13.

[4] 1 McClel. & Y. 205.

[5] French *v.* Reed, 5 Binn. 308, *ante*.

be obligatory so long as it endures, although it may be determined on reasonable notice to the bailor. The obligation is ordinarily to keep safely and surrender on demand; but the bailee may equally be bound to carry elsewhere or deliver to a third person. The declaration should nevertheless be in case, because the allegation of a contract implies that the defendant has bound himself irrevocably and cannot recede.[1] In Wheatley *v.* Low,[2] which is designated by the reporter as an action on the case, the plaintiff averred that he was indebted to one J. S., and gave £10 to the defendant with the intent that he should deliver it to J. S. in part payment, which the defendant promised to do, and assigned as a breach that the payment had not been made. A verdict having been found for the plaintiff on a plea of nonassumpsit, it was moved in arrest of judgment that the acceptance of money to be paid over to another cannot be a consideration to uphold a promise. This argument was overruled, and judgment entered for the plaintiff, on the ground that the acceptance of the money and a promise to deliver it was a good consideration to charge the defendant.

There can be no doubt that the bailment and acceptance of goods or money are a sufficient consideration, or more accurately cause, to render it incumbent on the bailee to surrender what has been intrusted to his care, or even to hand it over to a third person, if such was his undertaking to the bailor; and what Wheatley *v.* Low really determines is in accordance with Coggs *v.* Bernard, that one who enters on the performance of a gratuitous undertaking or mandate may be made answerable in case for a want of diligence or good faith. The declaration set forth a promise, but this does not show that the suit was *ex contractu*, because, as Lord Holt pointed out, it is the bailment and undertaking which together constitute the trust.

The same explanation applies to Whitehead *v.* Greetham,

[1] See The American Jurist, xvi. 253, 276; Coggs *v.* Bernard, 2 Lord Raymond, 909, 920; Dickson *v.* Clifton, 2 Wilson, 319; Brown *v.* Dixon, 1 T. R. 274; Elsee *v.* Gatward, 5 id. 143.

[2] Croke Jac. 668.

where, as Best, C. J., observed, the delivery and acceptance of the money rendered the defendant answerable for its application in the manner designated by the plaintiff, and tacitly or expressly agreed to by him. What these decisions indicate is, that a recovery may be had in such instances either in assumpsit or case, or rather that the difference is merely formal and both remedies substantially the same. A reference to the precedents will accordingly show that, whichever form is adopted, the declaration equally avers an undertaking by one party, and a delivery by the other, — the only difference being that compensation is sought in the one case for the disregard of the duty arising from the transaction regarded as a whole, and in the other the breach of an implied promise that the duty shall be fulfilled.[1]

It results from what has been said that the question is one of pleading, and not as to the right. The books agree that the bailment of goods or money may give rise to a trust in favor of the bailor or a third person, depending for its nature and extent on what is said and done on either side; and the doubt is as to the means by which the obligation should be enforced, and whether assumpsit can be used concurrently with case or as a substitute for a bill in equity.

[1] 2 Chitty's Pleadings, 334, 370; 1 Sm. L. C. 7 Am. ed. 447; Garland *v.* Davis, 4 How. 131, 143; Memphis & Charleston R. R. Co. *v.* Reeves, 10 Wallace, 176; Dixon *v.* Barclay, 22 Ala. 370.

CHAPTER IX.

ROMAN AND COMMON LAW CONTRASTED.

Source of Obligation. — Promise to give Refusal. — Guaranty. — Agency or Mandate. — Contracts for the benefit of, or performance by, Third Persons. — Acceptance of Offer. — Consideration. — Cause. — Parties.

THE obligation of a contract is, as I have elsewhere shown, derived by the civil law as finally developed, from the confidence reposed by either party in the good faith of the other, and the wrong of disappointing an expectation that has been deliberately excited. It arises at common law, in the case of the parol or unsealed agreements through which the business of life is for the most part carried on, from the passage of the consideration; or, in other words, from the loss incurred, value given, or obligation contracted on the faith of the promise. The two methods are in this respect contrasted, a consideration adding nothing to the validity of the contract in the one, and being essential to its obligation in the other. It follows that while assent may give validity to a promise under the civil law, although the contract is unilateral, there will be no obligation at common law unless something is done or promised on the other side. Hence, where one gives another the refusal of that which he desires to sell; or in other words, agrees not to dispose of the property without first offering it to him, or that he shall have a certain time within which to determine whether he will accept, the compact is invalid under the latter system from the want of a consideration; but has, agreeably to the former, a sufficient cause in the hope that the offeree will consider the proposal favorably and be induced to purchase.[1] So a promise to be answerable for the good con-

[1] Boston & M. R. R. Co. *v.* Bartlett, 3 Cush. 325; Fisher *v.* Seltzer, 11 Harris, 308; Payne *v.* Cave, 3 T. R. 144.

duct of a third person, or for such sums as may be lent to him during the ensuing year, becomes irrevocable under the civil law when assented to by the promisee, but is not binding at common law unless under seal, or until credit is actually given in reliance on the promise.[1]

These are not the only instances of a diversity, which is so far radical that some care is needed in reasoning from the civil to the common law, and an attempt to harmonize both doctrines may lead to results that are not compatible with either. The Roman jurists held, in conformity with the principle that contractual obligations result from consent, that a third person could neither take advantage of nor be bound by a contract.[2] So far the rule is logical, and recognized by every system of jurisprudence. But the doctrine that the acts and contracts of one who is authorized to act for or represent another are the acts and contracts of the principal, did not prevail at Rome. A mandate, which in our eyes is a power or authority, was regarded by them as a contract, which bound the principal to the mandatary, but established no direct relation between the principal and the persons with whom the mandatary contracted for his benefit.[3] If a mandatary entered into an agreement which the principal refused to fulfil, the agent, and not the principal was liable; and so if the opposite party made default, the mandatary alone could sue.[4]

The rule was inflexible and never abrogated,[5] although it was evaded by the aid of one of those ingenious fictions which have been used in all ages to supplement the law.[6] A mandatary or agent who contracted with a third person had a remedy against him on the contract, and against his principal for indemnity, which it was his duty to use for the protection of the parties beneficially interested. And as the prætor consid-

[1] Offord *v.* Davies, 12 C. B. N. S. 748; Calvert *v.* Gordon, 3 M. & R. 124; Gordon *v.* Calvert, 2 Simon, 253, 4 Russell, 581.

[2] Pothier, Traité des Obligations, Partie i. ch. i. art. 5, § 54; Maynz, ii. § 206; Poste, p. 314.

[3] Maynz, ii. § 222, p. 259.

[4] Maynz, ii. §§ 206, 222; Delsol, livre III. tit. xiii. ch. i.

[5] Maynz, ii. § 206, p. 188.

[6] Maynz, ii. § 222, p. 263.

ered that which ought to be done as actually done, they were finally allowed to proceed directly on the contract, not as having been made by them, but as one made for their use. If, for instance, one sold or leased, or entered into an engagement of any other kind through an agent, the party with whom the agent contracted might proceed in his right against the principal, while the latter was in his turn subrogated to the agent's remedy to compel the fulfilment of the contract.[1] This did not exonerate the mandatary, who continued to be personally liable, and might be a loser through the insolvency or bad faith of the principal; but it seems that during or perhaps before the time of Justinian, he was relieved from responsibility unless he had exceeded his instructions or made the agreement in his own name without disclosing his principal.[2] Such is now the rule of the modern civil law as administered on the European continent, or the reverse of what it originally was at Rome.

It is proper to add that as the consensual contracts derived their obligation from the meeting of the minds on either side; so the parties need not be present, and might signify their assent by a letter, or through an agent or messenger. But an agent could not contract for his principal, or bind him to a third person by agreeing to terms which he did not specifically authorize or approve.

The steps by which the Roman law was freed from the rule that a principal is not bound by the contracts of his agent were gradual and the work of centuries;[3] and we may be surprised that it did not sooner occur to jurists of so much practical good sense and acuteness, that he who acts through another whom he has duly authorized is in the same position as if he acted personally. No such question can arise under a system which derives the obligation from the relation between the promisor and the person from whom the consideration

[1] Accarias, ii. Nos. 636, 637.

[2] Poste, pp. 353, 355; Delsol, livre III. tit. xiii, ch. i, § 162; Pothier, Traité du Contrat de Mandat, ch. iii. § 2, No. 87; Traité des Obligations, Partie ii. ch. vi. art. 2, § 2.

[3] Poste, p. 355.

moves; and hence at common law a parol contract binds the principal, and not the agent, unless it is made on the agent's credit, when both are ordinarily answerable. So one who parts with value, or enters into an obligation on the faith of an assurance from another, is equally entitled to compensation whether the promisor prescribes the terms on which he is willing to be bound, or leaves them to the discretion of a third person, whom he employs or authorizes.

Agreements under seal follow a different rule, and are not obligatory on third persons although made on their behalf, and by one whom they have authorized; and hence a principal cannot sue or be sued on a covenant by or with his agent, although a court of equity will compel the agent to place the remedy at his disposal, or he may proceed in the agent's name,[1] and rely on the covenant as his warrant. The question, nevertheless, depends on the letter of the contract, or more accurately on the intention which it discloses; and if the agreement purports to be made by the principal he will be bound, although he does not put his hand to the instrument and the seal is affixed by the agent.[2]

We are indebted to the technicality of the Roman law of mandate, and the efforts made to shape it in this and some other particulars to the ends of justice, for a principle which has been adopted by the courts of equity, and serves to mitigate the rigor of the common law. I refer to the doctrine that one may be compelled to use his legal remedies for the benefit of the party beneficially interested; and in a way to throw the burden on the person on whom it should ultimately devolve.[3] It is on this ground that a surety who pays the debt is subrogated to the remedies of the creditor; and that a creditor who, having two funds open to him while another creditor has access to but one, exhausts the latter fund, may be compelled to cede the former to the party whom he has prejudiced by his act. Such is now the rule in the United

[1] See 1 Am. Leading Cases, 5 ed. 728; Evans *v.* Wells, 22 Wend. 324, 325; Townsend *v.* Hubbard, 4 Hill, 351; Bellas *v.* Hays, 5 S. & R. 427.

[2] Wilks *v.* Black, 2 East, 142; Mussey *v.* Scott, 7 Cush. 217.

[3] Maynz, ii. §§ 188, 206, 222, pp. 84, 190, 261.

States, although it was confined at Rome and subsequently in the English Court of Chancery to cases where the surety stipulated that the payment should operate as a purchase, as distinguished from an extinguishment of the debt.[1]

Agreeably to the civil law, the object of a contract, or in other words what the debtor agrees to do or render, must be certain, must be possible, and must be useful to the creditor, — that is, something in which he is interested, and for which he will be entitled to compensation if the contract be not fulfilled.[2]

The first of these requisites results from the nature of things. Until the parties agree what one is bound to perform and the other entitled to demand, there can be no obligation, because their minds do not meet in a common purpose, and because there is nothing to guide the tribunals in assessing damages or enforcing a specific performance. What, how much, where, and when, must consequently be defined with a clearness that leaves no doubt that cannot be resolved; although in this as in most other cases, that is certain which may be reduced to certainty, and a contract is not necessarily invalid because what is to be given and received is left to the determination of a third person, or even to one of the parties interested.[3]

Performance must be possible, or, more accurately, what is contracted for must not be such that from its own nature it cannot be done or rendered; for if it is a thing which might be done, it is immaterial that it is one which the debtor is unable to do. A promise to put a girdle round the earth in forty minutes; to make a payment to one's self; to bring a roc's egg from Mount Caucasus; to sell a freeman into slavery; or convey a public building, — as, for instance, the Houses of Parliament, or the Capitol at Washington, — is absurd, and therefore destitute of obligation;[4] and such, if taken literally, would also be the rule with regard to a promise that it shall not rain to-morrow, or that a house or vessel shall not be

[1] See Maynz, ii. § 188, p. 86.
[2] Maynz, ii. §§ 199, 206; Delsol, livre III. tit. iii. ch. ii. § 3.
[3] Maynz, ii. § 199.
[4] Delsol, vol. ii. 413, livre III. tit. iii. ch. ii.; Maynz, ii. § 199.

wrecked, or consumed. But such promises may be liberally interpreted as undertakings to be answerable for the loss or damage that will result if they are not fulfilled, and will then take effect as contracts of guaranty or insurance.[1]

What is promised must also be useful or beneficial to the promisee, because the law will not, agreeably to the same authorities, sanction an obligation that can answer no good purpose, or award damages where there is no loss.[2]

It follows, according to the Roman jurists, from the second and third of the above rules, that one can neither promise that a third person shall perform, nor stipulate for a performance that will be exclusively beneficial to a third person; in the former case because the object is impossible, since no man can compel another to act; in the latter, because the promisee has no interest in the fulfilment of the contract.[3] Both rules were technical, and gave rise to numerous distinctions by which they were practically evaded. A man could not undertake that another should withhold or render, but might undertake to cause him to fulfil the contract, or to be answerable if he did not. Thus it is said in the Institutes,[4] that one cannot promise that Titius shall give five gold pieces, but if he promises to cause Titius to give them he will be bound; and if the words admitted of it, such was the interpretation put on the contract in obedience to the principle that agreements shall, if possible, be so construed as to take effect.[5] So an undertaking that another shall perform, or to pay a sum certain if he does not, may be obligatory on the promisor.[6] According to Pothier, a promise to pay the damages occasioned by another's act or default is also binding, and such is the reasonable interpretation which the common law puts on all promises to be answerable for a third person, whether they are worded absolutely or as guarantees.

[1] See Jones *v.* How, 9 C. B. 1, 9.

[2] Pardessus, No. 177; Maynz, ii. § 199; Delsol, livre III. tit. iii. ch. ii.

[3] Poste, p. 314; Maynz, ii. § 206; Pardessus, No. 190; Pothier, Traité des Obligations, Partie i. ch. i. art. 5, Nos. 53, 54, 56.

[4] 3. 19. 19.

[5] Maynz, ii. § 206, note 5.

[6] Maynz, ii. § 206, note 5; Pothier, Traité des Obligations, Partie i. ch. i. art. 5, No. 56.

The rule that a man could not stipulate for a benefit to a third person in which he himself had no concern, might in like manner be virtually annulled by a turn of phrase; and we are told by Pothier that while "I cannot stipulate that you shall present the Thesaurus of Meerman to Jacques, because that would be to stipulate for another, and for a thing in which I have no interest, I may stipulate that if in a given time you do not make the present, you shall give me twenty pistoles, because the gift is then simply a condition which suspends the obligation, and the object of the contract is a payment in which I have an interest."

The doctrine that the creditor must have an interest in the performance of the contract, and the doctrine that he must not stipulate for what it is impossible to perform, have little or no place in a system which bases the obligation on the consideration, and not the promise; for as the right of action in assumpsit grows out of the wrong done the plaintiff by inducing him to change his position for the worse by an assurance that something which he desires shall be done in return, it is not necessarily an answer that the promisor undertook more than could be performed, or that the plaintiff would not have been a gainer had the promise been fulfilled.

The weight of English and American authority is on the contrary that a man who promises, impliedly guarantees that the promise can be performed, and cannot rely on absolute or relative impossibility as a defence.[1] As Lord Holt observes in Thornborow *v.* Whitacre,[2] the impossibility of the thing and the impossibility of doing it are all one, and come to this, that the defendant could not perform his agreement; which is not a defence.

If a promise which from the nature of things cannot be performed,—as, for instance, to touch the stars with one's finger or provide a perpetual motion,—is void, it is because the parties cannot be supposed to have seriously intended or relied on

[1] See Wild *v.* Harris, 7 C. B. 1005; Millward *v.* Littlewood, 5 Ex. 775; Jones *v.* The College, L. R. 6 Q. B. 124; Clifford *v.* Watts, L. R. 5 C. P. 577, 585; Scully *v.* Kirkpatrick, 29 P. F. S. 331.

[2] 2 Lord Raymond, 1164.

that which it is obviously beyond the power of man to fulfil. Still less is it an excuse for a wilful breach of faith on the part of the defendant, in failing to perform an undertaking which it is within his power to fulfil, that the money is to be paid or the service rendered to a third person whom the plaintiff desires to benefit, and that he is not a loser by the default.

The rule is the same where the agreement is under seal, although for a different reason. A covenant by A with B to pay a sum certain to C is obligatory on A, and B may recover the whole amount in damages if it is not fulfilled. Such is the effect of a bond conditioned for a payment to be made or service rendered to a third person, and a covenant is simply a less artistic way of arriving at the same result.[1]

Another instance where the civil and common law are too diverse to be easily reconcilable, may grow out of an offer made through the mail and accepted by a letter which does not arrive until after the offer has been recalled. Agreeably to the Roman jurists, it was essential that the recipient of an offer should not only signify his acceptance, but that it should be communicated to the offerer. Such mutual knowledge was inevitable where, as in the case of a stipulation, it was requisite that both parties should stand face to face, and although presence was not necessary in the case of a consensual contract, still the obligation grew out of reciprocal engagements which were not binding until interchanged. It was therefore, according to the commentators, indispensable that the parties should not only be of one mind, but that each should be informed of the other's purpose,[2] or, as the rule was stated by the chancellor, in Mactier *v.* Frith: "To make a valid contract it is not only essential that the minds of the contracting parties should meet on the subject of the contract, but they must communicate that fact to each other, so that both may know that their minds do meet." It follows, according to Pothier, with whom Pardessus agrees, that if Paul writes to Pierre offering goods at a certain price, and then posts another

[1] Loosemore *v.* Radford, 9 M. & W. 657.

[2] Mactier *v.* Frith, 6 Wend. 103; see Thomson *v.* James, 18 Dunlop, 1.

letter announcing that he has changed his mind, Pierre's subsequent acceptance will be invalid although signified before the second letter arrives.[1]

It is a corollary to this proposition, about which the commentators do not, however, entirely agree, that the contract remains open until the acceptance is communicated or made known to the offerer, and that either party may consequently retract at any time before the letter conveying the intelligence is delivered; because, though both may be of the same mind, there is no actual meeting or concourse of their wills.[2] Such also, as we have seen, was the opinion of the chancellor in Mactier *v.* Frith, although his decree was reversed by the Court of Errors.

The civil-law rule was applied by the Supreme Court of Massachusetts in McCulloch *v.* The Eagle Ins. Co.[3] The defendants offered to insure the plaintiff's vessel by a letter written on the first of January. It was received on the third, and the plaintiff posted his acceptance the same day; but the defendants had in the mean time mailed another letter retracting the first, and announcing their determination not to take the risk. The letters crossed each other on the way, so that the case was analogous to that cited from Pothier. The vessel was lost afterwards at sea. The court held that the contract was not complete, and gave judgment for the defendants. Shaw, C. J., said: "The offer did not bind the plaintiff until it was accepted, and it could not be accepted to the knowledge of the defendants until the letter announcing the acceptance was received, or at most, until the regular time of its arrival by mail had elapsed."

Such is not the rule of the common law, where the obligation of a contract depends on the fulfilment of the terms prescribed by the promisor, and the requirement of an offer made through the mail is satisfied by posting the acceptance, although

[1] Pothier, Contrat de Vente, No. 32; Pardessus, Nos. 360, 373, 374.

[2] Maynz, ii. § 200, note 11; Toullier, Droit Civil, liv. iii. tit. iii. ch. v. No. 324, note 3; Merlin, Répertoire de Jurisprudence, Tit. vente, § 1, art. 3, No. 11.

[3] 1 Pick. 278.

it is never delivered. In other words, the party who makes such an offer impliedly agrees that if the person to whom it is addressed signifies his assent through the same channel, he will risk the loss of the letter and hold himself bound, although it is lost or delayed, and he parts with the goods in the belief that the offer is declined.[1]

In Tayloe *v.* The Merchants' Ins. Co.,[2] the court held that the rule that mutual knowledge is essential to the completion of a contract, or, in other words, that each party must know that the other has agreed, is inapplicable to parties at a distance, because it would preclude a binding contract through the post-office, by leaving an opening for retraction while the offer was on the way, and until the acceptance arrived.

The question is, for what did the promisor expressly or impliedly stipulate; because if that can be ascertained and is complied with, he cannot allege its insufficiency as a reason why he should not be bound, unless the request is too entirely frivolous to take effect as a consideration. The test is not mutual assent or knowledge, but—Did the defendant fulfil what the plaintiff required? An offer is an undertaking to be bound if the opposite party will enter into a reciprocal engagement, which must ordinarily be delivered to the offerer or his agent in order to be valid.[3] When, however, the proposal is made through the mail, the case is so far altered that it is altogether reasonable to suppose that what the offerer intends is that the offeree shall bind himself by posting his acceptance, and if this requirement is fulfilled the contract is complete, and cannot be invalidated by the subsequent loss of the letter, nor by a retraction of which the offeree is ignorant at the time of the acceptance. The performance of the act for which the promisor stipulated as the condition on which he is willing to be bound renders it obligatory at common law, whether he does or does not know that the condition has been fulfilled; and hence, as Bramwell, L. J., observed in Household Ins. Co. *v.*

[1] Tayloe *v.* The Merchants' Ins. Co., 9 How. 390; Vassar *v.* Camp, 1 Kernan, 441; Dunlop *v.* Higgins, 1 H. L. C. 381. Household Ins. Co. *v.* Grant, L. R. 4 Ex. Div. 216.

[2] 9 How. 390. [3] Hebb's Case, L. R. 4 Eq. 9.

Grant,[1] a man who writes offering to sell on certain terms, provided the person to whom the letter is addressed will signify his assent by firing a cannon, hanging out a flag or posting an acceptance, cannot recede after the condition has been complied with, although he does not hear the report, see the signal, or receive the answer. There is under the circumstances a consideration which, in the case of the posting of the acceptance, cannot be pronounced inadequate; and moreover inadequacy is not a defence.

The doctrine that an act done in pursuance of a request may complete a contract without a previous or explicit notification of the intention to comply, and although the opposite party is not informed till afterwards, is not unknown to the civil law, but it occupies a much less considerable place than in our jurisprudence.[2]

In reading some of the decisions on this much controverted question, and notably the judgment in Mactier *v.* Frith, one cannot but perceive that the court labored under the difficulty of reasoning from the principles of the civil law to conclusions which could only be sustained on the basis of English jurisprudence. It was by the same misleading light that the Supreme Court of the United States held that a guaranty, of such advances as the party to whom it is addressed may think fit to make to a third person, will not sustain an action unless the creditor transmits or notifies his acceptance within a reasonable time.[3] This conclusion would be entirely just under the civil law, where such a guaranty becomes binding on acceptance, but is not well founded in the common law, where the undertaking may be recalled at any time before the advances are actually made, notwithstanding an explicit promise that it shall continue in force for twelve months, or some other definite period, on which the party to whom and the

[1] L. R. 4 Ex. Div. 216.

[2] Pardessus, No. 249; 2 Am. Leading Cases, 5 ed. 112.

[3] Wildes *v.* Savage, 1 Story, 22; Douglass *v.* Reynolds, 7 Peters, 113; Lee *v.* Dick, 10 id. 482; Adams *v.* Jones, 12 id. 207; Davis *v.* Wells, 104 U. S. 166; Davis Sewing Machine Co. *v.* Richards, 115 id. 537; 2 Am. Leading Cases, 5 ed. 76; White *v.* Reed, 15 Conn. 457.

party in whose behalf the guaranty was given have relied in making their engagements.[1] It is accordingly contrary to the English precedents, and disregarded by many tribunals on this side of the Atlantic,[2] although followed in others and in the court where it was originally enunciated.[3]

Contracts are divided by the civil lawyers into synallagmatic or bilateral, and unilateral, that is, contracts which bind only one of the parties, and contracts which bind both.[4] This classification is less applicable at common law, where parol contracts derive their force from the consideration, and no one can exact the fulfilment of a promise unless he did or promised something in return. An undertaking to be answerable for such advances as may be made to a third person during the ensuing year, is, agreeably to the civil law, a unilateral contract and irrevocable immediately on acceptance, although subject to a condition which suspends its operation;[5] but the common law regards such a guaranty as a mere offer or pollicitation, which may be recalled notwithstanding an express stipulation to the contrary, and does not become obligatory until the advances are actually made, when both sides are charged and the contract is in effect bilateral.[6]

If, however, the guarantor covenants instead of giving a parol promise, he will be irrevocably bound in spite of the want of mutuality, because sealed agreements follow the rule of the civil law that an undertaking followed by assent constitutes a unilateral contract, although nothing is done or

[1] Offord *v.* Davies, 12 C. B. N. S. 748.

[2] Douglass *v.* Howland, 24 Wend. 35; Union Bank *v.* Coster, 3 N. Y. 203; City Bank *v.* Phelps, 86 id. 484; Noble *v.* Koontz, 17 Md. 283; Mitchell *v.* M'Cleary, 42 id. 374; Powers *v.* Bumcratz, 12 Ohio St. 273; Carman *v.* Ellidge, 40 Ia. 409; Case *v.* Howard, 41 id. 479; Wilcox *v.* Draper, 12 Neb. 138; Wadsworth *v.* Allen, 8 Grattan, 174.

[3] See Douglass *v.* Howland, 24 Wend. 35; Smith *v.* Dann, 6 Hill, 543; Caton *v.* Shaw, 2 Harris & Gill, 13; Powers *v.* Bumcratz, 12 Ohio St. 273, 286.

[4] Code Napoleon, Art. 1102, 1103; Delsol, livre III. tit. iii. ch. i.; Pardessus, No. 138.

[5] Maynz, ii. § 205.

[6] Offord *v.* Davies, 12 C. B. N. S. 748; 12 East, 227.

promised on the other side. It follows that one who wishes to give a prospective guaranty that will be binding from the outset without a mutual engagement, in London as well as in Paris, must affix his seal, because the form, though immaterial under the French law, will supply the want of a consideration in England.[1]

Contracts are also classified by the French writers on the civil law, relatively to the end in view, as *contrats de bienfaisance*, and *contrats intéressés* or *à titre onéreux*. In contracts of beneficence, the object of the person who makes the promise is to confer a benefit on the promisee. In contracts *à titre onéreux*, the promise is made in consideration of the advantage to be derived from the obligation assumed or act done by the opposite party. A promise to assist a friend is obviously a contract of beneficence, and so is a gratuitous promise to guaranty the pre-existing debt of a third person; while a guaranty of a contemporaneous or prospective sale or loan has a mixed character, and is at once beneficent as it regards the debtor, and onerous relatively to the creditor.[2] *Contrats intéressés* or *à titre onéreux*, consist, agreeably to Pardessus, of mutual promises each depending on the other, or of a promise conditioned for the performance of some act on the other side, so that what is cause for one party is obligation relatively to the other.[3]

We have seen that parol contracts do not admit of this classification, and are nothing if not *à titre onéreux;* and that to render a *contrat de bienfaisance* valid, it must be made with the opportunity for deliberation implied in sealing and delivery. Here the common law would seem to be both right and wise. Agreeably to the Roman law, which the Code Napoleon follows,[4] a gift may be recalled for the ingratitude of the donee or his ill treatment of his benefactor; and one who seeks to enforce a promise to give by legal process is harsh, if not ungrateful, and should at least be prepared to

[1] Calvert *v.* Gordon, 7 B. & C. 809; 3 M. & R. 124; Gordon *v.* Calvert, 2 Simons, 253, 4 Russell, 581.

[2] Delsol, livre III. tit. iii. ch. i.

[3] Pardessus, No. 176; Delsol, livre III. tit. iii. ch. iii. § 4.

[4] Art. 955.

show that there is no doubt as to the donor's purpose, and that he went so far towards carrying it into effect that he cannot justly change his mind.[1]

It is obvious that if every unguarded utterance, or the expression of a casual purpose, could be enforced as a contract there would be an opening for mistake or fraud. The Code Napoleon guards against this danger by providing that where the subject matter exceeds one hundred and fifty francs in value, the contract must be in writing or established by written evidence; and the Roman law imposed a like restraint on donations and promises to give.[2] As this rule would unduly fetter trade, commercial contracts are exempted from its operation, and may be made by word of mouth. A legislation so essentially arbitrary has given rise to numerous distinctions.[3] A purchase made with a view to the profit to be derived from a resale is, according to Pardessus, an act of commerce, although the buyer is not a shopkeeper or merchant, and it is an isolated transaction not falling within the ordinary scope of his business.[4] Still, a farmer does not become a merchant by buying a yoke of oxen for the plough, although he intends to fatten the animals and send them to market when they are no longer fit for work.[5] The purchase of cattle by a drover or other person habitually engaged in trade, will on the other hand be none the less a commercial transaction, because they are incidentally used for farming purposes during the interval. The effect is to complicate the question with an artificial rule, and make the validity of the contract depend, not simply on what is said or done, but on the status of the parties and the object which they have in view.

We may congratulate ourselves that these refinements are unknown to our jurisprudence. They are wholly unsuited to the genius of a system which appeals to the common sense of mankind through the jury box. Instead of inquiring whether

[1] Delsol, livre III. tit. iii. ch. iv. § 2; Maynz, i. § 253, pp. 403, 404.

[2] Code Napoleon, Art. 1344; Pardessus, No. 262; Maynz, ii. § 253, p. 397.

[3] Pardessus, Nos. 77, 78, 79.

[4] Pardessus, No. 5.

[5] Pardessus, No. 12.

the defendant is a merchant, or curiously investigating the motive which induced him to buy, the practical question of the common lawyer is: "Has the alleged promise a consideration, or is it authenticated by a seal?" In the latter case the engagement is formally, and the presumption is deliberately, made. In the former the plaintiff must prove the consideration as well as the promise, or, in other words, that he changed his position for the worse on the faith of what was said or written by the defendant, thus affording a test of the reasonableness of the contract and the credibility of the witnesses.

The doctrine of consideration is of modern and English growth, but an approximation to it may be found in the rule that the execution of an innominate contract, that is, of a contract not recognized by the civil law, might impose the obligation which did not arise from the contract itself;[1] and the development of both doctrines was so closely analogous as to show that they resulted from like causes, although there is no reason to suppose that the common law was derived in this regard from that of Rome. The law everywhere begins with technical and customary rules, which as society advances are moulded in accordance with principles, or altered to meet the requirements of the times. If the Roman jurists ascended to the height of the principle which was laid down by the commentators of a later period, that the meeting of two minds in a common purpose, or in other words a promise given and accepted, constitutes a contract, they did not make it a general rule.[2]

Outside of the four consensual contracts, — sale, hiring,

[1] *Ante.*

[2] It is said by Pothier that the principles of Roman jurisprudence as to the different kinds of pacts, and as to the distinction between contracts and simple pacts, not being founded on the natural law, and being foreign to its simplicity, were not adopted by the French law (Traité des Obligations, ch. i. art. 1); and Delsol observes that the rule in France that contracts save exceptionally are consensual, was the exception at Rome (Delsol, livre III. tit. iii. ch. i.). It is nevertheless true that but for the philosophical spirit which evolved the principle, the exception might not have become the rule. *Ante.*

partnership, and mandate, — which rested on special grounds, it was essential that the parties should, if there was no pre-existing debt or demand, stand face to face and go through the formal question and reply known as a *stipulatio*, or that something should have been delivered and received under circumstances which gave rise to an obligation; and the form was so much of the substance, that a writing setting forth that all the legal requisites had been observed, might, even as late as the reign of Justinian, be set aside by proof that the promisee was not actually present when the obligatory words were pronounced, or that they were not uttered in response to a request from him.[1]

During the Empire, although the precise date is unknown, a writing signed by the debtor became *prima facie* evidence of the debt which it set forth or undertook to pay. This method came into general use as between lender and borrower, and may well have been the origin of the promissory note of the commercial, and the covenant of the common law. The contract *literis* of an earlier period was an entry in the books of the creditor, with the debtor's consent, that a certain amount was due from or had been laid out for him, which, though originally conclusive, might in the process of time be set aside, on proof that no such payment had been made or charge incurred.[2] Like our books of original entry, it presupposed a certain amount of good faith and might easily be abused, and perhaps on this account became obsolete before the reign of Justinian, and was replaced by a written acknowledgment, which like the modern due-bill might be invalidated by proof of a want or failure of consideration; although it was enacted that if the debtor did not within five years, which Justinian reduced to two, contest the debt, he should be precluded from doing so at any future period.[3]

[1] The *constitutum*, or day set for payment, might appear to be an exception, but was limited to agreements to satisfy some antecedent debt or obligation, — the promisor's or another's. Maynz, ii. § 251, pp. 386, 390. *Ante.*

[2] Poste, p. 330, *ante.*

[3] Maynz, ii. §§ 247, 248, pp. 365, 370; Institutes, 3. 21.

Contracts which did not come within the foregoing categories were designated as innominate or unclassed, and would not sustain an action. Hence, as business increased and became more complex, there were numerous agreements which the law did not recognize, and that might be violated with impunity. If the parties were at a distance, and contracted by letter, or met and omitted to ask and answer, and the agreement was not a partnership, a sale, a hiring and letting, an hypothecation, or a mandate, or founded on some antecedent obligation, it was invalid. The ingenuity of the Roman lawyers was taxed to obviate an inconvenience which, though partially overcome by holding that a mandatary might contract for his principal, would have been intolerable had not the consensual contracts covered so much ground, and they finally reached the conclusion that if an innominate contract might be repudiated while executory, good faith forbade such a defence as against one who had acted in the belief that it would be fulfilled. Redress seems to have been confined, in the first instance, to enabling one who had performed his part of the agreement to recover back what he had given, but as such relief was inadequate and might be impracticable, it was subsequently determined that if the defendant in such an action had been benefited, he might be compelled to render the stipulated equivalent; and from this there was but a step to holding that if the plaintiff had fulfilled the contract, the defendant was answerable although the service was rendered to a third person.[1] Thus an agreement to manumit a slave in consideration of a sum of money, was not binding under the civil law unless sanctioned by a stipulation; but if the master freed the slave, he might recover the compensation.[2] Here however, the Roman jurists paused, and never reached the point attained by the common law, that mutual promises followed by a readiness to perform may be a ground of recovery, although nothing has actually been done by the plaintiff and they were not exchanged in the way prescribed by the law. There was the less necessity for such a course, because the

1 Maynz, ii. §§ 243, 244, pp. 330–346.
2 Maynz, ii. § 243, notes 25, 26, pp. 335, 336.

consensual contracts derived their force from agreement, and embraced the transactions which most concern mankind and occur in the ordinary course of life and business.

I may now advert to the doctrine of cause, which fills a large place in the civil law and is not unknown to our own jurisprudence.[1] The Roman jurist held that every contract must have a cause, and that the failure of the cause would be fatal to the validity of the contract; or, as the principle is stated in Toule and D'Anvillier's Commentary on the French Codes, there can be no effect without a cause, and obligations are not an exception to the rule. If there was no cause but a bare agreement, the pact was nude and would not sustain an action against a Roman citizen; but when a cause was present it imposed an obligation and gave birth to an action.[2] The cause of an obligation *ex contractu* is that which renders the contract valid, and may be the form or nature of the contract, or some fact on which it depends, or arising out of what is done or promised on either side.[3] In the case of a stipulation, the cause was the formal question and reply; in the contract *literis*, the entry in the books of the creditor with the debtor's consent; in the consensual contracts, the mutual agreement; in contracts *re*, the delivery of the thing lent, pledged, or deposited. And turning to the common law, we find the cause of a covenant in the sealing and delivery of the deed; of the obligation to pay a creditor, in the debt; and of a parol contract, in the thing given or promised in return. As thus viewed, cause is a generic term which may coincide but is not synonymous with consideration.

Such was the doctrine in its original form, when men looked to the letter of the contract, and had little regard to the equitable considerations which arose at a later period. It was subsequently held that every contract should have some inducement which the tribunals could recognize as constituting a basis for the obligation which they were asked to enforce.

[1] Thomas *v.* Thomas, 2 Q. B. 851; Sharington *v.* Strotton, Plow. 309, note.

[2] Maynz, ii. § 207, p. 191; note to Sharington *v.* Strotton, Plow. 309.

[3] Maynz, ii. §§ 207, 243, pp. 191, 330.

The cause is accordingly defined in Delsol's Treatise on the Code Napoleon,[1] as the *motif immédiat*, which determines the party to contract; and, if that is insufficient which seems to be a mixed question of law and fact, the contract fails. *Motif* here means moving force or power, and must not be confounded with the motives which actuate the party, — as, for instance, his need of money, or the expectation of making an advantageous bargain.[2] We are informed by the same author that in the contract of sale the vendor's obligation has for its cause that of the buyer to pay the price; and the buyer's, that of the vendor to deliver the thing sold. But he also says that the cause of a contract of gift is the intention to confer a benefit on the donee, while the obligation of a borrower arises from the receipt of the loan. In like manner we are told by Pardessus,[3] that although the cause of a commercial contract is ordinarily some equivalent, so that what is cause for one party is obligation for the other, it may equally well exist where nothing is to be given in return, as where one gratuitously guarantees the debt of a third person, or promises to fulfil a contract which has not been duly executed and cannot be enforced. These instances can hardly be reduced to the same category. If friendship for the donee is the cause of a gift, that of an agreement to buy should by a parity of reasoning be the desire of the purchaser to become the owner of the thing sold.

Agreeably to Pothier, every contract should have a just cause, and if the cause is false or contrary to justice, good faith, or morals, the contract will be void; and such substantially are the provisions of the Code Napoleon.[4] If, for instance, an heir promises to satisfy a legacy which has been charged on the estate by the will of the ancestor, without knowing that the bequest has been revoked by a subsequent codicil, the cause is false and the promise fails.[5] Here the cause is unreal, or exists only in the mind of the promisor;

[1] Vol. ii. livre III. tit. iii. ch. ii. p. 315.

[2] Thomas *v.* Thomas, 2 Q. B. 851, 861.

[3] No. 176.

[4] Art. 1131.

[5] Pothier, Traité des Obligations, Partie i. ch. i. § 6, Nos. 42, 43.

but the effect is the same where there is a failure of cause, and the death of an artist who has been promised a sum certain for a portrait, will invalidate the contract by frustrating the expectation which is its cause.[1]

The cause must not, according to the same authorities, be unlawful or the result of an arbitrary or unjust demand ; and hence a promise by a creditor to whom the debtor's estate has been adjudged in satisfaction of the amount due, to compensate him for surrendering the title deeds, may be obligatory if made from motives of beneficence or liberality, but not if extorted by a refusal to give up the deeds.[2]

It is said by Delsol, that a want of cause cannot be distinguished from the falseness of the cause, because no one but a fool or madman will bind himself without a motive; but the question seems to be whether a motiveless contract, or, what comes to the same thing, one for which no sufficient motive can be assigned, is obligatory on a man of sound mind. We may believe that in the first instance the tribunals simply looked to see whether the cause satisfied the technical requirements of the law, or in other words, whether the contract was duly executed; but that in process of time, it came to be considered that they ought not to enforce a contract for which no reasonable cause could be assigned; as, for instance, a promise made by a man of moderate means from whim or caprice, to bestow the greater part of his fortune on one much richer than himself, and who has no claim on his bounty or regard.[3] We are accordingly told by Pardessus, that the cause of a commercial contract must not only exist, but be grave or serious, and will not have that character if the promised equivalent is entirely out of proportion to the object of the obligation; or in other words, if what the defendant is to receive is grossly inadequate to that which he agrees to

[1] Delsol, livre III. tit. iii. § 4, p. 417.

[2] Pothier, Traité des Obligations, Partie i. ch. i. § 6, No. 42.

[3] It was accordingly declared in the Digest, 44. 40. 2, 3, as cited in Poste's Elements of Roman Law, p. 216, that one who sought to enforce a stipulation which had been made without cause, might be met with a plea of fraud, although his intention was not originally fraudulent.

give. Hence, agreeably to the Roman law, the price must not be so insignificant relatively to the value of the thing sold that it cannot be considered as real, and if it did not amount to half, the vendor might agreeably to an edict of Diocletian rescind the sale;[1] a rule not easily reconcilable with the theory of consideration but consistent with that of cause. If such is the rule of the civil, it is not recognized by the common law, nor in equity, where in the absence of fraud and mistake it would be a sufficient answer to such a defence on the part of a man of sound mind, that it was his folly to enter into the engagement without considering whether there was a sufficient cause.[2]

It results from what has been said that while what is known as the consideration of a contract at common law may also be its cause, the latter term has a much wider signification. Thus the pre-existing debt of a third person is a sufficient cause for a covenant, but will not sustain a parol promise. Still, both systems have this in common, that although a consideration is not essential to the validity of a sealed instrument, the failure of the consideration, or more accurately of the cause, may be a defence. In the case already put, of a covenant that another will pay what he owes, there is no consideration; but if it appears that the debt was not due or had been satisfied, the covenant will be set aside by a chancellor, as a *stipulatio* would have been under like circumstances by the prætor in ancient Rome, and we may believe that the doctrine was transmitted through the ecclesiastics who held the great seal under the Norman and Angevin kings.[3]

The distinction may be further exemplified by a covenant to stand seised, which needed no consideration if the suit were for damages, but would not be enforced by a chancellor, or give rise to a use, unless based on some sufficient cause, such as consanguinity or marriage, although before the statute of Henry VIII. clothing uses with possession, the former would have been of no moment in a court of common law, and the latter inadequate unless contracted on the faith of the covenant.

[1] Maynz, ii, §§ 209, 214, pp. 202, 234.

[2] 2 Leading Cases in Equity, 12, 373.

[3] Poste, p. 316.

The authorities which have been referred to, show that if the consideration of the common, answers to the cause of the civil law, it is something more.[1] Thus the forms of declaration in assumpsit aver that in consideration that the plaintiff would do or promise, the defendant promised, that the plaintiff complied, but that the defendant did not keep his promise. Here the expectation that the plaintiff will comply with the implied request is the cause of the defendant's promise; but it is the fulfilment of the request which renders the promise obligatory.

What is a good cause for a contract is to some extent a matter of opinion, and may vary from age to age, or with the advance of civilization. In the last century a wager which of two drops of rainwater would first reach the bottom of a pane, or whether the plaintiff's father would outlive the defendant's, was not unworthy of the attentive consideration of a court of justice, and it was from such a case that Lord Mansfield deduced a principle of no small moment to the law of insurance, — that an agreement to assume a past risk may be valid if the event be unknown.[2] All wagers are now regarded in the United States as frivolous and demoralizing, or in other words, as having no sufficient cause, and will consequently be dismissed by the tribunals, even when made in the form or under cover of a simulated sale of stocks or merchandise.[3]

If the doctrine of cause is wanting in definiteness and precision, it may still be a useful check on the folly or extravagance which incurs obligations that are entirely disproportioned to the object in view. It is of comparatively little moment in our jurisprudence, where if anything has been received or parted with that can operate as a consideration, the courts ordinarily inquire no further;[4] but the consideration and the promise should still be related as cause and effect, and if either is

[1] Thomas *v.* Thomas, 2 Q. B. 851, 857, 858.

[2] The Earl of March *v.* Pigot, 5 Burrow, 2802; 2 Am. Leading Cases, 5 ed. 848.

[3] Brua's Appeal, 5 P. F. S. 294; Bigelow *v.* Benedict, 70 N. Y. 202; Harris *v.* Tumbridge, 83 N. Y. 92.

[4] Burr *v.* Wilcox, 13 Allen, 269; Paynter *v.* Chamberlyn, 1 Rolle Abr. 22, pl. 21; Dutton *v.* Poole, 1 Ventris, 318; Hardesty *v.* Smith, 3 Ind. 41.

frivolous or incongruous there is no sufficient ground for damages.[1]

The doctrine that a consideration is essential to the validity of a parol promise, meets with a seeming exception in the case of a promissory note.[2] An absolute written promise to pay a sum certain imposes an obligation by virtue of the Law Merchant and the Statute of Anne, and may be enforced on proof of defendant's signature without evidence of a consideration;[3] — contrary to the general rule that he who promises must stipulate for something to be done or promised in return, and that if he does not the promise will be void.[4] The exception is however apparent rather than real. A promissory note is presumed to be on some sufficient consideration for the furtherance of trade, and to obviate the difficulties that might arise if it were necessary to call witnesses to show that the instrument was subject to a condition which has been fulfilled, but the presumption may be rebutted by evidence that the promise was in fact unconditional, and the note will then be invalid as in other cases where contracts are made without consideration.[5] In Baker *v.* Walker,[6] a note which had been made payable at a future day, in consideration of a judgment against the maker, was held valid only because the obligation of the judgment was suspended until the note fell due. Accordingly, in Crofts *v.* Beale,[7] a suit on a promissory note payable on demand was held to be sufficiently answered by a plea that the instrument was made as collateral security for a debt due from a third person to the plaintiff, which the defendant was not at the time of executing the note, or ever, bound to pay or secure, and that there was no value or consideration for the note save as aforesaid. The note being due at once, negatived rather than implied an agreement for forbearance; and although time had in fact been given, the case was governed by the general principle that doing or refraining will not be a

[1] Schnell *v.* Nell, 17 Ind. 29; Shepard *v.* Rhodes, 7 R. I. 470.

[2] Powers *v.* Fowler, 4 El. & Bl. 511.

[3] Hartman *v.* Shaffer, 21 P. F. S. 312.

[4] Ibid.

[5] Swain *v.* Ettling, 8 Casey, 486.

[6] 14 M. & W. 465.

[7] 11 C. B. 172.

consideration, unless the party who acts or abstains does so in accordance with some express or implied request constituting the condition on which the promisor agreed to be bound. This decision shows with great clearness that where there is no consideration for a promise, the contract cannot be rendered valid by putting it in the form of a promissory note.[1]

We have seen that where a promise is made to one man for a consideration moving from another, the right of suit resides at common law in the latter, and not in the former.[2] It is equally well settled, on a principle common to every system of jurisprudence, that the obligation of a contract is under ordinary circumstances confined to the parties, and cannot be enforced by third persons.[3] The explanation of the seeming inconsistency is, as I have elsewhere stated, that the action of assumpsit had its origin in tort, and that he who suffers from the wrong ought to recover, although he was a stranger to the promise and became entitled by acting on the inducement which it held forth. Subject to this principle, which does not apply to sealed instruments, the common agrees with the civil law in holding that they who make the agreement are the persons by whom it must be enforced.[4]

There are, notwithstanding, exceptions to both the above rules. One of them may arise when money is delivered by one man to another, to be handed over to a third. Under these circumstances, it might appear that no action could be maintained by the latter. He is not a party to the consideration or the contract, and cannot be said to have given value or changed his position for the worse on the faith of the undertaking of the bailee; and such is undoubtedly the only admissible conclusion, if the case is regarded as one of contract and not of property or title. The question may, however, be regarded in a different aspect. If a plaintiff cannot enforce a contract to which he is a stranger, a defendant cannot withhold the property of the plaintiff merely because he received it from

[1] Bingham *v.* Kimball, 17 Ind. 396. [2] *Ante.*

[3] Guthrie *v.* Kerr, 4 Norris, 303.

[4] McGunigal *v.* Mong, 5 Barr, 269; Pollock *v.* Chapman, 8 Weekly Notes of Cases, 433; Mississippi Cent. R. R. Co. *v.* Southern R. R. Ass'n., 8 Phila. 107.

a third person. This is too plain for argument, where the title was originally in the party who brings the suit, and equally true where the transaction confers a title. If, for instance, a horse were left for me at a livery stable as a present, or in payment of a debt, the keeper could not contest my right on the ground that I was a stranger to the contract of bailment; and the case is not materially different where money is placed to my credit with a banker, or in the hands of one who agrees to receive and hold it as my agent. The proper remedy in the former case is trover or replevin; and although a recovery may be had in debt or assumpsit in the latter, the action is founded not on the express contract, but on the obligation arising from the transfer, and the promise which the law implies when money is withheld or misappropriated in fraud of the rightful owner.[1] The principle, as stated by Chief Baron Gilbert, is as follows: "If A bails money to B, to be delivered to C, on demand, C may have an action of debt against B for the money, because by the delivery of A, B took it as the property of C, and thereby made himself his debtor." [2]

The question when a delivery to one man for the use of another will confer a right on the latter is, nevertheless, one of the most difficult and doubtful known to the law. It arose as far back as the case of Brand *v.* Lisley,[3] where the plaintiff declared that one W was indebted to him in £100, and had delivered to the defendant certain goods to satisfy the debt, and that the defendant subsequently, in consideration that the plaintiff would forbear to demand the goods, promised to pay the debt. A motion was made in arrest of judgment on the ground that there was no consideration for the promise, or none on which a suit could be maintained by the plaintiff, but the court held that by the delivery of the goods to the defendant to satisfy the plaintiff's claim the plaintiff acquired a right of property, and his forbearing to assert it was a sufficient consideration for the promise.[4] This decision shows that if a re-

[1] Lilly *v.* Hays, 5 A. & E. 549; 1 Sm. L. C. 8 Am. ed. 271.

[2] Gilbert on the Action of Debt, p. 362.

[3] Yelv. 164.

[4] 2 Leading Cases in Equity, 3 Am. ed. 1657; Winkley *v.* Foye, 2 Fogg, 171; Beans *v.* Bullitt, 7 P. F. S. 221.

mittance is made by A to B, with directions to pay the amount to C, or hold it for his use, the transfer may be as effectual as if it were made to C in person. Two things are, however, essential to such a result. In the first place, A must intend to relinquish all control over the fund and vest it absolutely in C; and next, B must accept it as his agent. In the absence of proof, the presumption is that the person who receives the money is answerable to him who makes the remittance, and not to him to whom the payment is to be made.[1]

If a debtor sends me a sum of money, with instructions to pay it over to his creditor if the latter will accept it in satisfaction of the debt, I may return the money, or write declining the commission and inquiring what shall be done with the remittance. In either event the fund will remain the debtor's property, and may be attached as such by any one who holds a judgment against him. The result will be the same if I communicate the offer to the creditor, and the attachment is laid before he accepts. A more difficult question would arise if I were directed to pay the debt unconditionally, without asking for a receipt in full. Under these circumstances, it might be contended that the right of the creditor became absolute as soon as the money was received by me. The weight of authority, however, would seem to be that more is requisite, and that the property will not pass until the creditor is informed of what has been done, and signifies his assent. An assignment for the benefit of creditors is, notwithstanding, valid under the decisions in the United States, unless they dissent, on the principle that assent should be presumed to an act done for their benefit.[2] The point has, notwithstanding, been ruled differently in England, on the ground that such a transfer is voluntary, and may be set aside by the assignor until it is communicated to the creditors and accepted by them.[3]

[1] 2 Leading Cases in Equity, 3 Am. ed. 1659.

[2] Brooks *v.* Marbury, 11 Wheaton, 78; Wilt *v.* Franklin, 1 Binn. 502; Read *v.* Robinson, 6 W. & S. 329.

[3] Ellison *v.* Ellison, 6 Ves. 656; Wallwyn *v.* Coutts, 3 Meriv. 707; 3 Simons, 14; Garrard *v.* Lord Lauderdale, 3 Simons, 1; 1 Leading Cases in Equity, 3 Am. ed. 390, 424.

It is held in Pennsylvania, in conformity with the above principle, that a third person may enforce a parol contract which is made exclusively for his benefit or gives rise to a trust for him.[1] Sealed instruments do not admit of this exception, and the covenantee alone can sue, although the party equitably entitled may proceed in his name and file the instrument as his warrant of attorney.[2]

The question arose and was critically considered in Miss. Cent. R. R. *v.* Southern R. R. Association.[3] It was there agreed, under seal, by and between the plaintiff and defendant, that the defendant should, in consideration of a lease of the plaintiff's franchises, pay certain mortgage bonds which had been executed by the plaintiffs, and were outstanding in the hands of third persons. The holders of the bonds brought an action in the name of the Miss. Cent. R. R. Co., to enforce the agreement without any express authority to that effect, on the ground that they were the parties beneficially interested, and as such impliedly authorized. The court held that the Miss. Cent. R. R. Co. was also interested in the fulfilment of the agreement as a means of paying its debts, and consequently entitled to recover for their use. Had the contract been by parol, the bondholders could not have maintained assumpsit, and it followed that they could not bring covenant in the name of the Railroad Company without their consent. The rule which had been granted to stay the proceedings was consequently made absolute. Sharswood, J., said, in delivering judgment:—

"In Blymire *v.* Boistle,[4] Mr. Justice Sergeant examines the authorities with his usual accuracy and discrimination, and states that, although they are not all reconcilable with each other, they seem to warrant this distinction, that if one pay money to another for the use of a third person, or, having money belonging to another, agrees with that other party to pay

[1] Hind *v.* Holdship, 2 Watts, 104; Torrens *v.* Campbell, 24 P. F. S. 476; Townsend *v.* Long, 27 id. 143; Justice *v.* Tallman, 5 Norris, 147; see also Merriman *v.* Moore, 9 id. 78.

[2] Miss. Cent. R. R. Co. *v.* The South. R. R. Ass'n., 8 Phila. 107; Ardesco Oil Co. *v.* North Amer. Oil & Min. Co., 16 P. F. S. 375.

[3] 8 Phila. 107.

[4] 6 Watts, 182.

it to a third, an action lies by the person beneficially interested. But when the contract is for the benefit of the contracting party, and the third party is a stranger to the contract and consideration, the action must be by the promisee. In further illustration of this distinction, he adds, where one person contracts with another to pay money to a third, or to deliver over some valuable thing, and such third party is thus the only party interested, he ought to possess the right to release the demand or recover it by action. But where a debt already exists from one person to another, a promise by a third person to pay such debt being for the benefit of the original debtor, and to relieve him from the payment of it, he ought to have a right of action against the promisor for his own indemnity, and if the promisor were also liable to the original creditor he would be subject to two separate actions at the same time for the same debt, which would be inconvenient, and lead to injustice."

I may here observe that if two or more persons agree that a certain thing shall be done or forborne, in furtherance of a common purpose, the contract will not be less mutual because the engagement is formally made to a third person whom they design to benefit, or who is to act as a trustee in carrying it into execution. It is on this ground that compositions among creditors to discharge the debtor on receiving a part payment of the debt, depend for their validity, contrary to the general rule that a smaller sum cannot be a satisfaction for greater.

In like manner, where several persons subscribe to a church, hospital, or railroad, the promise of each will be a sufficient consideration for those of the others, and no one can recede without the consent of all.[1] The contract may be and generally is in terms, with the treasurer, trustees, or other representatives of the association or body corporate which is to receive or disburse the fund, but the law will give effect to the intention which is to create a mutual and binding obligation.

A different view prevails in New York and Massachusetts, under which such a subscription cannot be enforced, unless

[1] Gittings *v.* Mayhew, 6 Md. 113; Troy Academy *v.* Nelson, 24 Vt. 189; Caul *v.* Gibson, 3 Barr, 416; Chambers *v.* Calhoun, 6 Harris, 13.

money is laid out or labor performed on the faith of the promise, and before it is recalled.[1] It is nevertheless conceded that if work is done, or liabilities assumed before the contract is rescinded, the subscribers will be bound;[2] and in The Wayne Institute *v.* Smith, the Court said that if such promises were gratuitous in the first instance, they became binding if any loss, expense, or legal obligation was incurred in the belief that the subscription would be paid.

The question arose in Helfenstein's Estate,[3] where Sharswood, J., observed, in delivering the judgment: —

"Had the decedent united with others as a subscriber to the fund for the increase of the Library of the Theological Seminary, the note upon which the appellant made his claim might have been sustained under the case of Caul *v.* Gibson.[4] Or if the note had been accepted by the trustees before the death of the promisor, it would have stood on the footing of the principle applied in Chambers *v.* Calhoun;[5] for in such case, if the trustees assumed the duty imposed upon them by the terms or conditions of the note, it would have been a sufficient consideration to sustain the promise. But when the decedent died, the trustees had not accepted the note, and his death was a countermand in law of the offer, for such it must be considered until accepted. In Phipps *v.* Jones,[6] where there was a subscription with others for the benefit of a proposed association to build a church, the court held that it was a mere proposal, revocable until the association was formed and the promise accepted, and that the death of the subscriber was such a revocation. The promise, therefore, was *nudum pactum.* Nor can it be sustained as a declaration of trust."

[1] Farmington Academy *v.* Allen, 14 Mass. 172; Bridgewater Academy *v.* Gilbert, 2 Pick. 579; The Church *v.* Kendall, 121 Mass. 528; Stewart *v.* The Trustees, 2 Den. 403; The Orphans' Home *v.* Sharp, 6 Missouri Appeals, 150.

[2] The Trustees *v.* Robinson, 21 N. Y. 234; Wayne Institute *v.* Smith, 36 Barb. 576; McDonald *v.* Gray, 11 Ia. 508; Pryor *v.* Cain, 25 Ill. 292; Pitt *v.* Gentle, 49 Mo. 74; Workman *v.* Campbell, 46 id. 305.

[3] 27 P. F. S, 331.

[4] 3 Barr, 416.

[5] 6 Harris, 13.

[6] 8 Harris, 260.

CHAPTER X.

CONSIDERATION.

Adequacy of Consideration. — Forbearance. — Marriage. — Performance to which one is already bound. — Dissolution or Alteration of Executory Parol Contracts. — Consideration must be the Result of Agreement.

If the requisites to a contract exist, or in other words, if the plaintiff does an act or incurs a liability on the faith of the promise made by the defendant, the law will not inquire whether the consideration is in a just proportion to the compensation claimed; for as the plaintiff is necessarily entitled under these circumstances to some damages, the price agreed upon will be taken as the measure of the amount.[1] In the words of Tindal, C. J., in Hitchcock *v.* Coker,[2] "It is enough that there is actually a consideration, that such consideration is legal, and that it has some value." Gross inadequacy may, in connection with other circumstances, be evidence of fraud or undue influence; but if a man, who is not shown to be *non compos* or wanting in ordinary capacity, agrees with his eyes open to give more for a thing than it is worth, he must submit to the loss arising from his own want of care or judgment. This rule may sometimes operate to sustain a hard and unconscionable bargain, but is in the long run beneficial to the community by diminishing the amount of litigation, and compelling men to reflect beforehand on the consequences of their engagements. If there be any consideration, the court will not weigh the extent or value of it,[3] and forbearance for a

[1] Worth *v.* Case, 42 N. Y. 362; Hitchcock *v.* Coker, 6 A. & E. 438; Skeate *v.* Beale, 11 id. 983.

[2] 6 A. & E. 438.

[3] Hind *v.* Holdship, 2 Watts, 104; Phillipps *v.* Bateman, 16 East, 356, 372; Payne *v.* Wilson, 7 B. & C. 423; Callisher *v.* Bischoffsheim, L. R. 5 Q. B. 449; Hesser *v.* Steiner, 5 W. & S. 476; Silvis *v.* Ely, 3 id. 420; Downing *v.* Funk, 5 Rawle, 69.

single day may support a promise by a third person to pay a debt of many thousand pounds. "There is no case," said Rogers, J., in Hind *v.* Holdship,[1] "where mere inadequacy of price, independent of other circumstances, has been held sufficient to set aside a contract between parties standing on equal ground, and dealing with each other without any imposition or oppression.[2] And the inequality, says Chancellor Kent, in Osgood *v.* Franklin,[3] amounting to fraud, must be so strong and manifest as to shock the conscience and confound the judgment of any man of common sense. Many motives may be assigned for Holdship, who was a creditor of the firm and desirous of being an assignee, coming under the obligation to pay certain specified creditors. Whether the contract is advantageous or not, is not the question. It is sufficient that he made the promise under the idea that it would be beneficial. The assignment was an act done by a third person, which was a good consideration for a promise to pay."

In Neal *v.* Gilmore,[4] a promise by a husband and his wife that if a child of tender years would stay with them until he was of age, they would raise and care for him as if he was their own, and at their death give him all they had, was held to be on a sufficient consideration, although the material benefit was conferred on and not by the promisee, because the promisors received an equivalent in the society and companionship of the child. So, in Frank's Appeal,[5] a note executed and delivered by David Frank to the plaintiff, Babetta Frank, in case she would marry his son Henry, was held to be valid not only between the parties but against the creditors of the maker, although he was insolvent at the time, and a gratuitous transfer would have been set aside as fraudulent. "Marriage," said Sharswood, J., "is a valuable consideration, and in the absence of fraud prevails against creditors. In the words of Lord Coke, there is no consideration respected in law as the consideration of marriage in respect of alliance and posterity." In like manner, where a father promised

1 2 Watts, 104.
2 2 Leading Cases in Equity, 4 Am. ed. 1237.
3 2 Johns. Ch. 23.
4 29 P. F. S. 421.
5 9 P. F. S. 190.

orally to give certain lands to a son as an inducement to marriage, and put him and his wife in possession, the contract was specifically enforced against the donor and another son to whom he subsequently conveyed the premises by deed.[1]

In Hardesty *v.* Smith,[2] a plea that the patent right which constituted the consideration of the contract on which the plaintiff sued, could not be applied to any useful purpose, and was of no value to the defendant, was held not to constitute a good defence. The court said that parties who were of sufficient mental capacity for the transaction of business had a right to make their own bargains. The owner of a chattel was entitled to fix the price which he would take, and the buyer's judgment was the best guide to the amount which it was worth his while to give. So, parting with any right which was a man's own was a sufficient consideration for any promise that might be made on the other side. The consideration agreed upon might largely exceed any benefit that could be derived, and yet the bargain stand. The purchaser got the thing for which he had stipulated, and in the absence of fraud, warranty and mistake of fact, if it did not answer his expectations it must still be presumed to be worth what he agreed to give. The same rule was laid down in Nash *v.* Lull,[3] and Howe *v.* Richards.[4] So, though a promise to pay a debt which is not due, in consideration of forbearance, is invalid,[5] it may, agreeably to some of the authorities, be obligatory, if the creditor has instituted legal proceedings in the belief that he has a good cause of action, and discontinues them in reliance on the promise. When, however, inadequacy appears on the face of the transaction, from computation or by a necessary legal inference, the contract will be invalid altogether or for the excess.[6] An agreement to accept a smaller sum in payment

[1] Whitehill *v.* Lousey, 2 Yeates, 109.

[2] 3 Ind. 41.

[3] 102 Mass. 60.

[4] 102 Mass. 64.

[5] Hamaker *v.* Eberley, 2 Binn. 509; Wade *v.* Simeon, 2 C. B. 548; Forth *v.* Stanton, 1 Wms. Saund. 210; Jones *v.* Ashburnham, 4 East, 455.

[6] Forth *v.* Stanton, 1 Wms. Saund. 210; Jones *v.* Ashburnham, 4 East, 455; Wade *v.* Simeon, 2 C. B. 548; Schroeder *v.* Fink, 60 Md. 436.

of a larger is not binding as an accord, and will not operate as satisfaction if performed,[1] and this is equally true of a promise to give time for the payment of a debt in consideration of a promise to pay it in full with interest when the delay expires, unless there is an express or implied stipulation that the debt shall not be paid until the period fixed by the agreement arrives.[2]

A contract by which the debtor agrees to pay interest at a future day, in consideration of a promise by the creditor to forbear until then, is, however, as it would seem, binding on both sides,[3] and there is no doubt that the payment of interest in advance is a good consideration for a promise of forbearance.[4]

In Kellogg *v.* Olmstead,[5] a promise by a debtor not to discharge a debt until a future period, and to pay it then with interest, was, notwithstanding, held insufficient to uphold a promise by the creditor to extend the time of payment until the day arrived; and the same point was decided in Gahn *v.* Niemcewicz.[6]

It is, on the other hand, equally well settled that where the consideration is something new, or different from that to which the creditor was already entitled, the law will not pause to examine whether the right which he acquires is more or less valuable than that which he relinquishes. A horse or the note of a third person may, for instance, be a good satisfaction of a demand for a much greater amount or value; and it will be no answer to allege that the maker of the note is insol-

[1] Smith *v.* Bartholomew, 5 Met. 276; Harriman *v.* Harriman, 12 Gray, 341; Smith *v.* Phillips, 77 Va. 548; Mechanics' Bank *v.* Huston, 11 Weekly Notes of Cases, 389; Foakes *v.* Beer, L. R. 9 App. Cases, 605; 1 Sm. L. C. 8 Am. ed. 648.

[2] Van Allen *v.* Jones, 10 Bosw. 369; Bailey *v.* Adams, 10 N. H. 162; Russell *v.* Buck, 11 Vt. 166; Wheeler *v.* Washburn, 24 id. 293; 2 Am. Leading Cases, 5 ed. 469.

[3] Bailey *v.* Adams, 10 N. H. 162; Fowler *v.* Brooks, 13 id. 240; Chute *v.* Pattee, 37 Me. 102.

[4] Grafton Bank *v.* Woodward, 5 N. H. 99; New Hampshire Savings Bank *v.* Ela, 11 id. 335; 2 Am. Leading Cases, 5 ed. 468.

[5] 25 N. Y. 189. [6] 11 Wend. 312.

vent or the horse unsound. In 1 Smith's Leading Cases, 640,[1] it is said on the authority of Pinnel's Case,[2] that a peppercorn may be a satisfaction for a debt of £1000; and it is now held, contrary to the rule formerly laid down in Cumber *v.* Wane,[3] that the note or check of a debtor, or of one of two or more joint debtors, is a good consideration for an agreement to waive the original demand, and rely solely on the note.[4]

In Curlewis *v.* Clark,[5] Parke, B., said that the plea was in substance that the plaintiff had taken the acceptance of a third person for £25, with the name of the drawer in blank, in satisfaction of £60 4*s.* 6*d.* of the amount sued for, if the acceptance was paid; but if not, that the debt should be satisfied on the payment of £10. This afforded a good answer to the action. The acceptance being for a less sum than the amount due, the plaintiff might possibly have made a bad bargain; but inasmuch as the plaintiff might have accepted a diamond or a chattel of any kind in satisfaction, there was no reason why he might not take an "acceptance." In Pinnel's Case,[6] it was resolved by the whole court that payment of a lesser sum in satisfaction of a greater cannot be a satisfaction for the whole, because it appears to the judges that by no possibility a lesser sum can be satisfaction of a greater; but the gift of a horse, hawk, or robe in satisfaction is good, because it shall be intended that the thing which the plaintiff has agreed to take will be more beneficial to him than the money in respect of some circumstance, or otherwise he would not have so agreed. The principle was clear that the court could not enter into the value of the consideration.

[1] 8th Am. ed.

[2] 5 Rep. 117; Dyer, 76; Singleton *v.* Thomas, 73 Ala. 205; Earl *v.* Peck, 64 N. Y. 506.

[3] 1 Strange, 426; 1 Sm. L. C. 8th Am. ed. 633.

[4] Sibree *v.* Tripp, 15 M. & W. 23; Thompson *v.* Percival, 5 B. & Ad. 925; Sheehy *v.* Mandeville, 6 Cranch, 253; Mechanics' Bank *v.* Huston, 11 Weekly Notes of Cases, 389; Goddard *v.* O'Brien, L. R. 9 Q. B. Div. 37.

[5] 3 Ex. 375; Lyth *v.* Ault, 7 Ex. 669; 1 Sm. L. C. 8 Am. ed. 638, 640, notes to Cumber *v.* Wane.

[6] 5 Rep. 117 a.

In New York, however, the courts still follow Cumber *v.* Wane, and taking the note of the debtor or of one of several debtors, may suspend the right of action, but will not preclude the creditor from enforcing the original demand if the instrument is not paid when due.[1]

As a smaller sum cannot be a satisfaction for a larger, so an agreement to pay a larger sum in consideration of the receipt of a smaller, will be invalid unless the payment is to be made at a future day, or there is some other ingredient which prevents the defect from appearing on the face of the contract by a necessary inference.[2] It was accordingly declared in Shepard *v.* Rhodes that an agreement for the exchange of unequal sums of money at the same time, or at different times, unless time was a material element, was not binding, and that the courts might and should under such circumstances inquire into the equality of the agreement, because the subject-matter on either side not only had a fixed value, but was the standard by which all other values were measured.[3] The same point was decided in Schnell *v.* Nell.[4]

A promise not to prosecute or enforce a demand which has no foundation in law or fact, is not a consideration, because such an undertaking is neither a harm to the promisor, nor a benefit to the promisee; and hence proof that there was no debt is a sufficient answer to a declaration on a promise in consideration of forbearance.[5] In the case last cited, Lord Ellenborough said that, notwithstanding the opinion imputed to Chief Justice Hyde, a promise by a mother to pay the debt of her son if the plaintiff would refrain from taking his dead body in execution, did not constitute a cause of action. It might as well be pretended that a promise in consideration that one would withdraw the pistol which he had levelled at the breast of a third person, could be enforced against the

[1] Rawley *v.* Foote, 19 Wend. 516; Cole *v.* Sackett, 5 Hall, 516.

[2] Downing *v.* Funk, 5 Rawle, 69; Calkins *v.* Chandler, 36 Mich. 320; Clark *v.* Russel, 3 Watts, 213.

[3] Shepard *v.* Rhodes, 7 R. I. 470.

[4] 17 Ind. 29.

[5] Forth *v.* Stanton, 1 Wms. Saund. 210; Hamaker *v.* Eberley, 2 Binn. 509; Jones *v.* Ashburnham, 4 East, 455.

party who had been coerced into making it, by such an unlawful display of force.

A compromise of a disputed claim, or the discontinuance of a suit already brought, may nevertheless uphold a promise, although the demand was unfounded and the plaintiff could not have recovered if he had gone to trial.[1] It is, however, essential that the party who seeks to enforce such a contract should have acted with a sincere belief that the suit which he compromised or withdrew was valid, and proof that he knew he had no cause of action will be a defence.[2] "It is," said Tindal, C. J., "almost *contra bonos mores*, and certainly contrary to principles of natural justice, that a man should institute legal proceedings when he is conscious that he has no good cause of action;" and it was held that a promise extorted by such means was necessarily invalid.[3]

The consideration must not be so indefinite that the court or a jury cannot ascertain whether it has been fulfilled. It is a part of the contract, and should, like that, be certain or capable of being reduced to a certainty. Such a question may arise where one promises that if fresh advances are made to a third person he will be answerable for the whole account, including what the debtor already owes,—or that if the creditor will forbear he will pay the debt, without specifying the amount to be lent in the former instance, or how much time is to be given in the latter.[4] It has accordingly been held that forbearance, in pursuance of a request to that effect, will not constitute a consideration, unless there is something in the language used or the circumstances, to indicate how long the creditor is to refrain, or what will be a reasonable delay.[5] That interpretation should nevertheless be pre-

[1] Cook *v.* Wright, 1 B. & S. 559; Longridge *v.* Dorville, 5 B. & Ald. 117; Callisher *v.* Bischoffsheim, L. R. 5 Q. B. 449; Payne *v.* Bennet, 2 Watts, 427; Rice *v.* Bixler, 1 W. & S. 445; Worrall's Accounts, 5 id. 111; Jones *v.* Rittenhouse, 87 Ind. 348.

[2] Wade *v.* Simeon, 2 C. B. 548; Davisson *v.* Ford, 23 W. Va. 6, 17.

[3] 2 Leading Cases in Equity, 4 Am. ed. 1703, 1712.

[4] See Oldershaw *v.* King, 2 H. & N. 517.

[5] Sidwell *v.* Evans, 1 P. & W. 383; Lonsdale *v.* Brown, 4 W. C. C. 148; Semple *v.* Pink, 1 Ex. 74.

ferred which will sustain the contract, and the court will be slow to allow one who has induced another to refrain or act, to withhold the stipulated compensation on the ground that the request was indefinite as to amount or time.[1] This is very clear when the benefit is received or accepted by the defendant, and may be true where it is conferred on a third person in consequence of what he has said. For as the error, if such exists, grows out of the vagueness and uncertainty of his language, and would not have existed had he been more precise, so the loss should be borne by him. The law was so held in Oldershaw *v.* King, where Erle, J., said: "Looking at the whole letter and the circumstances under which it was written, and considering the importance of further advances, I come to the conclusion that the consideration contemplated was that further advances should be made and time given by the creditor before he would press for the payment of the existing debt. Though the contract did not bind the creditor to make further advances, or to give time, unless he chose to do so, it is clear that if he did make the advances and did give time, that which was contingent at the time when the instrument was written became an absolute and binding contract. I am also of opinion that although the amount of further advances and of the time to be given be not defined, still if time is given and advances are made, it is enough. These undefined terms should be construed with reference to the facts given in evidence; *ut res magis valeat quam pereat.* The guarantor has obtained what he bargained for, and we must hold him to his promise." The undertaking in this case was "in consideration of your forbearing to press for the immediate payment of the debt now due by my uncles, I hereby engage to guarantee the payment of any sum they may be indebted to you during the next six years, not exceeding £1000;" and the case can hardly be reconciled with Semple *v.* Pink, where a promise to pay the note of a third person if the creditor "would hold it over," without stating for how long, was held

[1] Oldershaw *v.* King, 2 H. & N. 517; Hamaker *v.* Eberley, 2 Binn. 509; Caldwell *v.* Heitshu, 9 W. & S. 51; Calkins *v.* Chandler, 36 Mich. 320; Downing *v.* Funk, 5 Rawle, 69; Payne *v.* Wilson, 7 B. & C. 423.

to be too vague and indefinite to sustain an action. The better opinion is in accordance with the decision in Oldershaw *v.* King, that the question in such cases is one of fact, — whether the creditor gave a reasonable time for payment, and that if this is answered in the affirmative the guarantor will not be less answerable because he did not specify how long the delay was to continue.[1]

It has been seen that a promise will not be less binding because it is prompted by motives of kindness and no equivalent is expected or received by the promisor, if the language employed is that of obligation and there is a sufficient consideration moving from the promisee. For although the common does not agree with the civil law in holding that the desire to confer a benefit may sustain a contract where there is no other cause, still a man cannot withhold the compensation which he has promised for the performance of an act, on the ground that it is not a benefit to him.[2]

It is accordingly established that a detriment to the plaintiff may be a valuable consideration, although no advantage accrues to the defendant.[3] The obligation of a surety rests upon this basis; and forbearance, although but for a single day, to proceed against a debtor may sustain a promise by a third person to be answerable for the payment of the amount due, though that may prove to be many thousand pounds, because the delay may result in the loss of the debt, and the law having no standard by which to measure the compensation, allows it to be fixed by the agreement of the parties. So one who promises to be answerable for the expenses incurred in resisting a disputed claim must make his promise good, although he was not interested in the result.[4] It has been held repeatedly, for like reasons, that a promise to pay another a sum in gross or annually if he will take a wife, is

[1] Downing *v.* Funk, 5 Rawle, 69; Calkins *v.* Chandler, 36 Mich. 320; Clark *v.* Russel, 3 Watts, 213.

[2] Van Rensselaer *v.* Akin, 44 Barb. 547.

[3] Dorwin *v.* Smith, 35 Vt. 69; Smith *v.* Rogers, 35 id. 140; Carr *v.* Card, 34 Mo. 513; Castner *v.* Slater, 50 Me. 212; Bunn *v.* Guy, 4 East, 190; White *v.* Baxter, 71 N. Y. 254; Addison on Contracts, p. 9.

[4] White *v.* Baxter, 71 N. Y. 254.

binding, and may be enforced if the condition is fulfilled.[1] Agreements of this kind were of such constant occurrence, and gave rise to so much litigation at an earlier period, that the statute of frauds provided that no recovery should be had upon them unless they were reduced to writing.[2]

Although one may be bound by a promise made on behalf of another, and from which he can receive no benefit, such a meaning should not readily be ascribed to language which admits of another and not less reasonable interpretation. Hence it has been said that in an action on a guaranty the proof of the promise must be so clear, explicit and certain, as to leave no doubt of the intention to become answerable for the debt. Still no one will be permitted to use loose and ambiguous expressions, calculated to create an expectation in the mind of the person to whom they are addressed, and then escape from liability under cover of the doubt arising from his own want of accuracy and precision. The question under these circumstances is not so much what he meant, as what meaning his words would naturally convey:[3] and, if they are calculated to mislead the other party it is immaterial that there was no such design;[4] and it was held to follow, in Lawrence *v.* McCalmont, that when the words of a guaranty admit of two interpretations, and the creditor has lent his money on the faith of that which is most favorable to him, it should be adopted when the instrument comes to receive a legal construction.[5]

Whether a man means to bind himself irrevocably, or only to declare a purpose which may be recalled, is, however, a question depending on a just construction of his words taken in connection with all the material circumstances, and that may be reasonably viewed with a greater inclination in his

[1] Saver *v.* Fielder, 32 Beav. 1; Frank's App. 9 P. F. S. 190.

[2] Tweddle *v.* Atkinson, 1 Best & Smith, 393, 399; Montacute *v.* Maxwell, 1 P. Wms. 618, 620; Caton *v.* Caton, L. R. 1 Ch. App. Cases, 137, 2 H. L. 127.

[3] Mason *v.* Pritchard, 12 East, 227.

[4] Mason *v.* Pritchard, 12 East, 227; Bell *v.* Bruen, 1 How. 169, 186; Lawrence *v.* McCalmont, 2 id. 426, 450.

[5] Douglass *v.* Reynolds, 7 Peters, 113; 2 Am. Leading Cases, 5 ed. 39.

favor when the promise is gratuitous, than when it is in consideration of a benefit received.[1] One who promises to indemnify another for loss incurred in assisting a hostile claim, cannot refuse to fulfil his engagement on the ground that he was not interested in the result;[2] but his want of interest may be taken into view in determining the meaning which should be attached to his words;[3] and so when one promises to assist another in a business in which he is not concerned.[4]

In Shadwell *v.* Shadwell,[5] an uncle wrote the following letter to his nephew: —

> "MY DEAR LANCEY, — I am glad to hear of your intended marriage with Ellen Nicholl, and, as I promised to assist you at starting, I am happy to tell you that I will pay to you £150 yearly during my life, and until your annual income derived from your profession of a chancery barrister shall amount to six hundred guineas, of which your own admission will be the only evidence that I shall receive or require.
>
> Your ever affectionate uncle,
>
> CHARLES SHADWELL."

The plaintiff married Ellen Nicholl, shortly after receiving this letter, and now sued for arrears of the annuity which was withheld. The defendant pleaded that the marriage had been agreed upon between the plaintiff and the said Ellen Nicholl before the letter was written, and that there was no consideration for the promise other than that which the writing expressed. It was contended, under these circumstances, that the promise was invalid because the plaintiff was under a previous moral and legal obligation to take Ellen Nicholl as his wife, and had contracted the marriage in pursuance of that obligation and not of the inducement held out by the defendant, and that the terms of the letter indicated that it was a mere expression of a kind and affectionate purpose, and not intended as a binding contract. A majority of the judges were however, of the opinion that there was a sufficient con-

1 Hartman's Appeal, 3 Grant, 271; Beaumont *v.* Carter, 32 Beav. 586; Richards *v.* Richards, 10 Wr. 78; Lloyd *v.* McNamara, 7 Harris, 130.

2 Belknap *v.* Bender, 75 N. Y. 451.

3 Lloyd *v.* McNamara, 7 Harris, 130.

4 Richards *v.* Richards, 10 Wr. 78.

5 9 C. B. N. S. 159.

sideration of detriment to the plaintiff and benefit to the defendant to support the promise: of detriment to the plaintiff, because he had incurred a liability which he might not be able to meet from his own resources; of benefit to the defendant, because his wishes were gratified by the settlement of his nephew in life. The more formidable objection that the plaintiff was already bound to contract the marriage, though not noticed in the opinion of the court, was dwelt on with much emphasis by Mr. Justice Byles, who likened the case to a promise to pay a man £500 for breaking his leg. The defendant had not expressly or impliedly requested the plaintiff to contract the marriage; and if he had, the plaintiff was already engaged, and did not act in consequence of the request. The letter was, therefore, one of mere kindness, and imposed no legal obligation.

On all the points involved we may regard the judgment as well founded. A promise to remunerate a man for performing an obligation which he has already incurred may be binding, if the obligation is one from which he could withdraw, or which he might legitimately refrain from executing. In Carroll *v.* Nixon,[1] a promise to indemnify the plaintiff against any loss that might arise from a bond which he had executed eight days previously as surety for an administrator, was held valid because the plaintiff might otherwise have applied to the court to be exonerated from the bond; and a similar decision was made in Drury *v.* Fay.[2] So the plaintiff in Shadwell *v.* Shadwell might but for the defendant's letter have agreed with his intended wife to postpone the fulfilment of his engagement, or break it off altogether. Such considerations are known as "continuing," and various instances are given in Chitty on Contracts.[3] Moreover, the plaintiff was only bound to marry within a reasonable time, which might depend on his ability to support a wife, and his marrying sooner than he would otherwise have done in reliance on the promise was a sufficient consideration. On one point, however, the defendant might well have been successful if the case had gone to a jury instead of being argued as one of law. To constitute a consideration the

[1] 4 W. & S. 517. [2] 14 Pick. 326. [3] 6th ed. p. 59.

act must not only be one which the defendant has expressly or impliedly requested, but the doing of it must be in consequence of the request. When, therefore, the plaintiff does not enter into a reciprocal engagement, and the inference is drawn from his acts, the question is one of fact to be determined in view of the circumstances. A promise to pay another $100 annually so long as the promisee continues to reside in his own house, would probably fail as a cause of action, from the natural presumption that the plaintiff would have remained where he was if the defendant had not promised. Still, if it appeared that the house was beyond the plaintiff's means, and that the promise was designed to induce him to incur the expense and had presumably influenced his decision, it would be the duty of the jury to find for the plaintiff.

Chief Justice Gibson said, in Clark *v.* Russel,[1] that it was not enough that the defendant had promised to pay the debt, if the plaintiff would forbear, and that the latter had refrained from suing, unless the request was the moving cause of the forbearance. It might be that the plaintiff would have remained quiescent from other motives, if nothing had been said by the defendant. The question should, therefore, have been left to the jury, and not treated as one of law by the court.

We have seen that to render a parol contract binding at common law, some act must be performed, or obligation assumed, on the faith of the assurance given by the promisor. It is the wrong done in inducing the promisee to give value or incur a liability, and then refusing the stipulated compensation, that confers the right of action.

The connection between the promise and the injury must consequently be averred with certainty in the declaration, and established by proof. It is not enough that one party has adopted a course in reliance on the assurances of the other from which he cannot recede without loss, unless it also appears that the latter specifically induced the act by the promise of a recompense which is withheld. To maintain assumpsit the consideration must consequently not only result from the promise, but be designated as the condition on which the

[1] 3 Watts, 213.

promisor is willing to be bound.[1] If A promises to give B $10,000, and the latter thereupon goes to Europe, takes a wife, or incurs liabilities of any other kind, in the confident expectation of receiving the promised aid, no right of action will accrue if the gift is withheld.[2] But a promise to give B $10,000 if he will go to Europe or contract a marriage, is a different thing, and B may recover on showing that the condition has been fulfilled.[3] So, taking a promissory note as collateral security for an antecedent debt, will not render the creditor a purchaser for value although followed by forbearance, unless there is an express or implied agreement to that effect, or it is the condition on which the instrument is given.[4] To constitute a contract, the parties must be dealing with an expressed or implied understanding that one or both of them is to be bound, and advising a friend or neighbor to make a purchase is not, even when coupled with an assurance of pecuniary aid, a sufficient ground on which to sustain an action.[5]

To render a consideration valid, it must therefore be the express or implied condition on which the obligation of the promise depends. An absolute parol promise is not binding at common law; to render the undertaking valid it must be under seal, or must stipulate for some act or agreement on the other side. A contract of sale may, for instance, be resolved into a promise to sell if the purchaser will buy, and a promise to buy if the purchaser will sell. In the language of Pardessus, the promise of one party is the cause for the obligation of the other, and so reciprocally. Under these circumstances the promises are mutual; but the agreement will be equally valid when the promise is conditioned for an act which the promisee need not perform, unless he thinks proper, as in the common case

1 Kirkpatrick *v.* Muirhead, 4 Harris, 117, 126; Muirhead *v.* Kirkpatrick, 9 Harris, 237; Fenouile *v.* Hamilton, 35 Ala. 319.

2 Dashwood *v.* Jermyn, L. R. 12 Ch. Div. 776.

3 Shadwell *v.* Shadwell, 9 C. B. N. S. 159.

4 See Kirkpatrick *v.* Muirhead, 4 Harris, 117; Fenouile *v.* Hamilton, 35 Ala. 319; Oates *v.* The National Bank, 10 Otto, 239, 245.

5 Richards *v.* Richards, 10 Wr. 78.

where A agrees to be answerable for such goods as may subsequently be sold to B.

"A consideration," said Bell, J., in Kirkpatrick *v.* Muirhead,[1] "must be the result of agreement. The parties must understand and be influenced to the performance of the particular act by something of value, of convenience or inconvenience, recognized by all of them as the moving cause. That which is a mere fortuitous result, flowing incidentally from an arrangement but in no degree prompting the actors to it, is not to be esteemed a legal consideration." In other words, unless the consideration is inherent in the promise when originally made the contract will be void, and the deficiency cannot be supplied by a gratuitous or voluntary act done by the promisee, although occasioned by and a natural result of the confidence reposed in the good faith and diligence of the promisor.

Forbearance is a good consideration when induced by the request of the party who makes the promise. But a promise to pay the debt of a third person will not be binding because the creditor omits to sue, or proceeds to execution in the belief that the promise will be fulfilled; and it will make no difference in the application of the principle that the debtor becomes insolvent during the interval.[2] The injury sustained under these circumstances may be real, but it is not one for which the promisor is responsible. Proof that A gave C an oral or written undertaking that a bond from B to C should be paid within the year, and that C forbore in reliance on the promise until the debt was lost, will not therefore without more, support an action by C against A. To render such a guaranty obligatory it must appear that the forbearance was the condition on which the guarantor agreed to be bound, and that the creditor gave time on the faith of the agreement. The remarks of Chief Justice Gibson on this subject in Clark *v.* Russel,[3] are profound and well worthy of the attention of the student.

In like manner, although marriage is a valuable consideration, proof that the defendant relied on a promise of pecuniary

[1] 4 Harris, 117, 126. [2] Bixler *v.* Ream, 3 P. & W. 282.
[3] 3 Watts, 213.

assistance in entering into a matrimonial engagement, will not suffice unless it is also shown that the defendant requested the plaintiff to contract the marriage, or promised specifically to make a settlement upon him if he did; and no recovery can be had on a gratuitous promise to build a house or effect an insurance for the plaintiff, even when the latter sustains special damage from his reliance on the word of the defendant, and a consequent failure to take measures for his own protection.[1]

Such an undertaking was obligatory as a mandate under the Roman law, but is not recognized by the law of England. The law was so held in Thorne *v.* Deas, although the plaintiff had omitted to insure his vessel, in reliance on the defendant's promise to see that a policy was taken out, and thus sustained a total loss.

It results from the same principle that a promise to pay money on the happening of a contingency not depending on or governed by the will of the promisee, or of some one in privity with him, is a *nudum pactum* which cannot be rendered binding by proof that the event occurred on which it was conditioned; as for instance, that the defendant will give a certain amount of money towards the erection of a church or hospital if others will contribute as much, and that the sum thus named was actually subscribed.[2] And the rule that damages cannot be recovered for a breach of contract unless something has been done or a loss incurred by the plaintiff at the defendant's instance, or on the faith of a promise made by him, goes so far that when a promise is made to one man in consideration of an act to be performed by another, the right of suit lies with the latter, as the person who has complied with the terms prescribed and will be the real loser if the promise be not fulfilled.[3]

The case of Thorne *v.* Deas might perhaps have been decided differently had the declaration averred that the defendant promised to insure the vessel if the plaintiff would refrain

[1] Thorne *v.* Deas, 4 Johns. 84; Elsee *v.* Gatward, 5 T. R. 143; Balfe *v.* West, 13 C. B. 466.

[2] Stewart *v.* The Trustees, 2 Den. 403, 417.

[3] *Ante*, Edmundson *v.* Penny, 1 Barr, 334.

from effecting an insurance, and that the plaintiff forbore in consequence of the request. For although the consideration must consist of some act done or avoided by one party at the instance of the other, the concession made by the former need not be in any respect beneficial to the latter;[1] and in Watkins *v.* James,[2] a promise by the defendant to procure a draft from A, who was indebted to the plaintiff, and credit it in an account on which the plaintiff was indebted to the defendant, was held to give a valid right of action on proof that the plaintiff had forborne to proceed against A, who became insolvent during the interval. The court said that the plaintiff had trusted to the defendant's promise, and but for it would have attended to the business himself. He was therefore entitled to be indemnified for the loss occasioned by the breach. This case comes so near Thorne *v.* Deas that the judgments cannot easily be reconciled. If the promise of the defendant to collect the amount due by A operated as an express or implied request to the plaintiff not to take measures for that end, there was a sufficient consideration to support the promise; but the mere fact that the plaintiff remained quiescent, in reliance on the good faith of the defendant, obviously could not render that a contract which was not such in the first instance.

It results from what has been said that to give a right of action on a parol contract at common law, there must first be an express or implied promise, coupled with and depending on a condition to be fulfilled by the promisee, and constituting the agreement properly so called, and, next, such a compliance with the condition as will render the promise absolute and legally valid.

The rule as stated in 1 Smith's Leading Cases, 266, is "that whenever the consideration of a promise is executory, there must, *ex necessitate rei*, have been a request on the part of the person promising. For if A promise to remunerate B, in consideration that B will perform something specified, that

[1] Fuller's Case, Godb. 94; Haines *v.* Haines, 6 Md. 435, 438; Kenedy *v.* Cotton, 28 Barb. 59; Brown *v.* Ray, 10 Ired. 72; Watkins *v.* James, 5 Jones (N. C.), 105.

[2] 5 Jones (N. C.), 105.

amounts to a request to B to perform the act for which he is to be remunerated." The more philosophical statement of the proposition, however, is that there must be a promise operating as a request, or in other words, specifying some act on the fulfilment of which the obligation of the promise depends.[1] The request which lies at the bottom of most implied contracts is accordingly interpreted by the law as a conditional promise that if the thing required is done, as much shall be given in return as it is worth.

It is well settled agreeably to these principles, that while a promise to bestow or settle a sum certain on another will not be rendered binding by proof that the latter made a purchase from which he would have refrained if the promise had not been given, a recovery may be had on a promise to provide the means of payment if another will buy, because the liability incurred by the promisee is a sufficient consideration.[2]

For like reasons it is not enough to show that the defendant promised to reward the plaintiff for doing or forbearing, and that the plaintiff complied, unless it also appears that he was induced by the promise, or in other words, that it was a present and actuating motive. Where the promises are mutual, this is a natural and, as it would seem, inevitable inference; but there may be more room for doubt when the promise is conditioned for performance without exacting a reciprocal engagement, as when one promises to be answerable for the debt of a third person, if the creditor will give time for payment, and leaves him free to choose, and it may then be a question whether his subsequent indulgence was induced by the promise, or had some other cause.[3]

It has been said to follow from the above principle that doing that to which one is already bound is not a consideration, because it does not sufficiently appear whether the plaintiff was actuated by the original engagement or that subsequently

[1] King *v.* Sears, 2 C. M. & R. 48, 53.

[2] Chitty on Contracts, 52, 6th ed.; Pierce *v.* Woodward, 6 Pick. 206; Crosbie *v.* M'Doual, 13 Ves. Jr. 148, 160.

[3] Clark *v.* Russel, 3 Watts, 213.

made.[1] Such an inference is questionable, because what the law requires is not that the promise shall be the only motive for the contract, but that it shall be an actuating or inducing cause.[2]

If the defendant stipulates for an act which the plaintiff performs, there is a presumption that the relation is one of cause and effect, which can only be rebutted by proof that the request did not reach the plaintiff, or that he did not fulfil it within a reasonable time.[3] The better opinion would seem to be that the defect is not one of consideration but of cause.[4] If a man could make a refusal to perform or render what he owes the means of extorting a reward from the injured party, there would obviously be a temptation to commit such defaults in the hope of profiting by the wrong. It has accordingly been held that as it is the duty of a creditor to surrender the securities in his hands immediately on receiving the amount due, so a promise to compensate him for fulfilling this obligation is invalid;[5] or, as the principle was stated in Crosby *v.* Wood,[6] the surrender of a paper which is unlawfully withheld and which a court of equity would order to be delivered up or cancelled, will not support an executory contract. In like manner no recovery can be had on an undertaking to pay a witness a larger sum for the loss of time incident to his attendance in court than the law prescribes;[7] and an undertaking to reward a constable or police officer for serving a writ or arresting a criminal, or a sailor for proceeding with the vessel until the completion of the voyage, is in the same category.[8] In Robb *v.* Mason,[9] the court held, in accordance with this

[1] Shadwell *v.* Shadwell, 9 C. B. N. S. 159; Burr *v.* Wilcox, 13 Allen, 269; Herring *v.* Dorell, 8 Dowl. 604.

[2] Williams *v.* Carwardine, 4 B. & Ad. 621; Thomas *v.* Thomas, 2 Q. B. 851; Loring *v.* Boston, 7 Met. 409; Shadwell *v.* Shadwell, 9 C. B. N. S. 159.

[3] Loring *v.* Boston, 7 Met. 409.

[4] Pothier, Traité des Obligations, Partie i, ch. i, § 6, No. 43.

[5] Cowper *v.* Green, 7 M. & W. 633.

[6] 2 Seld. 369.

[7] Collins *v.* Godfrey, 1 B. & Ad. 950; Wimer *v.* Worth, 104 Pa. 317; 1 Wharton, Contracts, §§ 489, 500.

[8] Harris *v.* Carter, 5 E. & Bl. 559; Smith *v.* Whildin, 10 Barr, 39.

[9] 11 Pa. 300.

principle, that the payment of the purchase money by the vendee will not uphold a promise by the vendor to make compensation for an injury to the land resulting from the acts of a third person since the sale, because a refusal to pay would be a wrong, and a man cannot justly make the breach of an obligation a means of gain. A promise to do that to which the party is already bound neither adds to nor takes from the original obligation, and being a nullity is not a consideration for any undertaking that may be given in return.[1]

A promise to pay an additional sum for the completion of work which the plaintiff has agreed to do, but threatens to leave unfinished, has notwithstanding been held valid in Massachusetts, although he might have been sued for the default, because he is entitled to choose between that risk and the certainty of loss from going on at the price originally named.[2]

The judgment in Munroe *v.* Perkins was as follows: "It is contended that the parol promise was without consideration. This depends entirely on the question whether the first contract was waived. The plaintiff having refused to perform that contract, as he might do, subjecting himself to such damages as the other parties might show they were entitled to recover, he afterwards went on upon the faith of the new promise, and finished the work. This was a sufficient consideration. If defendants were willing to accept his relinquishment of the old contract, and proceed on a new agreement, the law, we think, would not prevent it." The same view was taken in Lattimore *v.* Harsen, and in Wilgus *v.* Whitehead, cited and relied on in Munroe *v.* Perkins, though the point actually determined was that a landlord who agrees orally that the rent shall be paid at a later period than that named in the lease, cannot distrain for the failure to pay at the day, whether the instrument is or is not under seal.

In these instances the original contract was by deed; but the court held that although it could not have been varied by an executory parol agreement, the case was different where

[1] Wimer *v.* Worth, 104 Pa. 317, 320.

[2] Munroe *v.* Perkins, 9 Pick. 298, 305; Lattimore *v.* Harsen, 14 Johns. 331.

the plaintiff went on to do the work on the faith of an assurance that he should receive the amount for which he sued.

It has been held in like manner that the delivery of a machine to one by whom it has been ordered and in part paid for, may be a consideration for his waiving the right to damages for the manufacturer's failure to have it ready at the appointed time.[1]

Agreeably to the view taken in England, a promise to pay for the completion of a contract with a third person may be valid, although it would be void if the promisor were a party to the contract, and entitled to enforce it by suit.[2] In Scotson *v.* Pegg, Wilde, B., said, in delivering judgment: "Why is there no consideration? Is it because the plaintiffs, in delivering the coals, are only performing that which they were already bound to do? But to say that there is no consideration, is to say that it is not possible for one man to have an interest in the performance of a contract made by another. But if a person chooses to pay a certain sum of money in order to induce another to perform that which he has already contracted with a third person to do, I confess I cannot see why such a promise should not be binding. Here, the defendant, who was a stranger to the original contract, induced the plaintiffs to part with the cargo, which they might not otherwise have been willing to do, and the delivery of it to the defendant was a benefit to him. I accede to the proposition that if a person contracts with another to do a certain thing, he cannot make the performance of it a consideration for a new promise to the same individual. But there is no authority for the proposition that where there has been a promise to one person to do a certain thing, it is not possible to make a valid promise to another to do the same thing. Therefore, deciding this matter on principle, it is plain to my mind that the delivery of the coals to the defendant was a good consideration for his promise, although the plaintiffs had made a previous contract to deliver them to the order of other persons." The soundness of this distinction is questionable, because the wrong of a breach of contract and the mischief of allowing it to be a source of

[1] Moore *v.* The Detroit Works, 14 Mich. 266.
[2] See Scotson *v.* Pegg, 6 H. & N. 295, 298.

profit, are the same whether the person on whom the stress is put is a party to the contract, or merely beneficially interested in its performance.

It is held in England, and would seem to be conceded by some tribunals in the United States, that an executory parol contract may be dissolved or varied before breach by an agreement to that effect without any new consideration, which involves the proposition that if one who has entered into a contract declares that he will not fulfil it as it stands, nor unless his demands are acceded to and the other party assents, the new agreement will supersede the old.[1]

In Holmes *v.* Doane the defendant agreed to carry the plaintiff in his vessel to California, if the plaintiff would work as a carpenter in preparing her for sea and during the voyage; but before sailing the defendant changed his mind and refused to take the plaintiff on board, unless he would sign the shipping papers and pay $25. The plaintiff agreed and signed the papers, but being unable to pay the money was left on the wharf. The plaintiff brought suit, but was held to have waived his right under the original agreement by consenting to the new. Dewey, J., said, in delivering judgment: "The defendant might show that at a period prior to the sailing of the vessel he gave notice to the plaintiff that he would not comply with the original agreement, and would hold himself responsible for all damages, by reason of such breach of contract, and that the plaintiff thereupon elected not to avail himself of his right to recover damages therefor, but chose to make a new contract giving the defendant more advantageous terms, in consequence of which the defendant agreed to carry the plaintiff to California. Such new contract would be a valid contract between the parties, and no new consideration further than that arising in the case supposed was necessary to give effect to the agreement, and make it the basis of future liability between the parties."[2]

[1] Wilgus *v.* Whitehead, 6 W. N. C. 537; Foster *v.* Dawber, 6 Ex. 839; Holmes *v.* Doane, 9 Cush. 135.

[2] Munroe *v.* Perkins, 9 Pick. 298, 305; Lattimore *v.* Harsen, 14 Johns. 331; Blood *v.* Enos, 12 Vt. 625.

No case could more clearly exemplify the mischief of such a rule. If the master of a vessel can wait until a passenger is ready to embark, and then demand a higher price than that originally named, he obviously has the upper hand, and may exact any sum which he thinks fit to ask.[1]

There can be no doubt that where, as in countries governed by the civil law, the obligation arises from consent, it may be dissolved in the same manner; but the better opinion would seem to be that as a consideration is essential to the formation of a contract at common law, so it should be requisite for its dissolution;[2] and it is generally conceded that contracts under seal, and simple contracts after breach, or that have been executed by the passage of a consideration, cannot be varied by parol, unless the new agreement has been so far acted on or carried into effect that it would be inequitable to enforce that originally made.[3]

We have seen that the consideration must be the result of agreement, or in other words that the promise must be made with a view to the act or undertaking which constitutes the consideration, and the consideration be induced by the promise. The parties need not meet together or correspond, but the plaintiff must know of the promise and be influenced by it in rendering the service; and hence a reward for the apprehension of a criminal cannot be claimed by one who did not know that it had been offered,[4] — although, if he had such knowledge, it need not have been his only motive for giving the information which led to the arrest. For like reasons a promise by a creditor to extend the debt if the debtor will give security, is not a consideration for an agreement by a third person to be answerable as a guarantor, unless the

[1] See Robb *v.* Mann, 11 Pa. 300; Wimer *v.* Worth, 104 id. 317, 320; McCarty *v.* Hampton Building Association, 61 Ia. 287.

[2] Thurston *v.* Ludwig, 6 Ohio St. 1; 1 Sm. L. C. 8 Am. ed. 663, 667; Taylor *v.* Winters, 6 Phila. 126; McCalla *v.* Ely, 14 P. F. S. 254.

[3] Adams *v.* Nichols, 19 Pick. 275; Thurston *v.* Ludwig, 6 Ohio St. 1; 1 Sm. L. C. 8 Am. ed. 663; McCalla *v.* Ely, 14 P. F. S. 254; Spangler *v.* Springer, 10 Harris, 454.

[4] Fitch *v.* Snedaker, 38 N. Y. 248.

promise is communicated to him, and he pledges his credit as a means of carrying it into effect.[1]

In Ellis *v.* Clark, the plaintiff sold the wood growing on his land and took the purchaser's note for the price, but refused to allow him to remove the timber after it had been cut, without security. They then called on the defendant, who put his name on the back of the note at their joint request, to accommodate the purchaser, but without knowing the circumstances or why he was asked to affix his signature, and the court held that the defendant was not answerable, because a past act cannot be a consideration, and none resulted from the agreement to permit the removal of the timber, which was not brought to his knowledge. Gray, C. J., said the minds of the parties must meet and agree upon the whole contract, including the promise on the one side and the consideration for it on the other, and an agreement between a debtor and creditor for forbearance will not be a consideration for a promise by a third person to pay the debt, unless it is made at his request. The same doctrine may be found in Kirkpatrick *v.* Muirhead,[2] and it was recognized in the Supreme Court of the United States, in the recent case of Oates *v.* The National Bank.[3]

The weak point of the judgment in Ellis *v.* Clark seemingly is that signing or endorsing a promissory note for the accommodation of another, impliedly authorizes him to pledge the writer's credit to any one who will give value on the faith of the assurance so held forth, and may be likened to a letter of credit or guaranty addressed to all the world, and undertaking to be answerable for any debt which the holder may contract to an amount not exceeding the sum named in the instrument. For when the nature and value of the consideration are left to the choice of a third person, his determination is obligatory on the promisor, who cannot complain though it be unwisely exercised.

It follows logically from the above principles that when a statute requires that the agreement shall be in writing, the consideration must be set forth as well as the promise. For

[1] Ellis *v.* Clark, 110 Mass. 389.

[2] 4 Harris, 117, 126.

[3] 10 Otto, 239, 245.

as a parol contract is not valid unless some act is done or obligation assumed in pursuance of an express or implied request from the promisor, the consideration is an integral part of the contract without which it is necessarily incomplete. It is because of this principle that a plaintiff cannot rest his case on proof of a parol contract without showing the consideration for which it was made. In Wain *v.* Warlters,[1] the defendant gave a written promise guaranteeing the payment of a draft which had been accepted by a third person. If the question had arisen under the civil law, as finally developed, the contract would have been binding on proof that the guaranty had been delivered to the creditor, and accepted by him, and it was contended on behalf of the plaintiff that such was also the rule under the law of England. But the court held that inasmuch as a consideration is not only essential to the validity of a contract, but must result from some express or implied condition attached to the promise, the failure to set the consideration forth in the writing which the statute required, was a fatal defect rendering the agreement void.

It results conversely from the same principle that although the memorandum of a guaranty must disclose all the requisites to a contract, it need not set forth the assent of the creditor, or that he agreed to the terms proposed by the guarantor.[2]

In Powers *v.* Fowler the action was brought on a written promise that the contract of a third person should be performed within three months, if the plaintiff would agree to forbear till then, and the objection taken by the defence was that it did not appear by any written evidence that the plaintiff had accepted the proposition, or agreed to wait until the six months had expired. On the other hand, it was said that in all the cases in which the creditor had failed from the insufficiency of the memorandum, the promise as set forth was absolute, and that if the writing disclosed a promise on a condition to be fulfilled by the promisee, the requirements of

[1] 5 East, 10.

[2] Stadt *v.* Lill, 9 East, 348; Moore *v.* Campbell, 10 Ex. 323; Powers *v.* Fowler, 4 E. & B. 511.

the statute were satisfied, and the performance of the condition might be shown *dehors* the writing by any legitimate means of proof. Lord Campbell said, in delivering judgment, that if it appears from the express words of the writing, or is a necessary inference from them, that the defendant's promise was upon the terms of the plaintiff's performing some condition, the performance of which would be a benefit to the defendant or a detriment to the plaintiff, it will then sufficiently appear that there is a condition on the performance of which the plaintiff may sue. The cases cited for the defendant were cases where the writing showed an absolute promise to pay, subject to no condition. In the case before the court there was an express condition that the plaintiffs should accept the offer. Their acceptance was averred in the replication, and happened to be in writing, but would, under a long train of cases, beginning with Stadt *v.* Lill, have been as effectual if it had been given orally.

The point determined in these instances has ceased to be material in England, under the Statute 19 and 20, Vict., c. 97, which provides that the consideration for a promise to assume the debt or default of another need not appear in writing, and the courts of this country have in general refused to follow the case of Wain *v.* Warlters, for reasons which it is unnecessary to discuss. But the light thrown by that case and Powers *v.* Fowler is valuable to every one who would form a just conception of the different aspect in which a contract is viewed under the Roman and English law.[1]

It has been said that the consideration must be something detrimental to the plaintiff or advantageous to the defendant, but it is more accurate to say that the declaration taken as a whole must show a ground for compensation other than the mere breach of promise.[2]

In Shadwell *v.* Shadwell,[3] Byles, J., was of opinion that a promise to make the plaintiff an allowance if he married, failed

[1] Shively *v.* Black, 9 Wr. 345; Holmes *v.* Mitchell, 7 C. B. N. S. 361; Statute 19 & 20 Vict. ch. xcvii. § 3.

[2] Paynter *v.* Chamberlyn, 1 Rolle Abr. 22, pl. 21.

[3] 9 C. B. N. S. 159.

for want of a consideration; and he somewhat irreverently likened such a contract to an undertaking to pay a man for breaking his leg. Had the comparison been just the inference would have been undeniable, because the law will not enforce a frivolous or immoral contract. What must be proved to sustain an action of assumpsit is not that what the plaintiff did on the faith of the defendants' promise was prejudicial in itself or its immediate consequences, but that he was led thereby to adopt a different course from that which he would have pursued had the promise not been made.[1] One who marries on the faith of a promise to provide the means to support his family is clearly within this rule, and if a recovery cannot be had for an injury inflicted on one's self for a stipulated reward, it is because the consideration is immoral, and not because it is insufficient.

A promise in consideration that the plaintiff would refrain from marriage would no doubt be invalid under both systems of jurisprudence, not for want of a consideration, but as contrary to legal policy and lacking a sufficient cause. It is not so easy to determine whether a promise to reward one for taking a temperance pledge, or discontinuing the use of intoxicating liquors, though clearly good under the civil, would have a sufficient consideration at common law; and in the analogous case of Binnington *v.* Wallis,[2] an agreement with a mistress that no further immoral connection should take place between the parties, and to pay her an annuity so long as she should continue to lead a good and virtuous life, was held to be a nude pact and as such invalid.

I have endeavored to show, in treating of the law of mandate, that if parting with the possession of a chattel and placing it in the hands of a bailee imposes a duty on him which may be enforced through an action on the case, it will not render a promise to keep the chattel safely, to carry it elsewhere, or to expend money or labor in any other way, irrevocable, or uphold it as a contract, because if the alleged consideration moves from the promisee, it is not in any just sense detrimental to

[1] Fuller's Case, Godb. 94; Moss *v.* Printing Co., 64 Ind. 125.

[2] 4 B. & Ald. 650.

him or beneficial to the promisor; and in Hatchell *v.* Odom,[1] a promise that if the plaintiff would send back a slave which he had purchased from the defendant, the latter would either cure the man or refund the price, was accordingly held invalid. The court said there was no detriment to the plaintiff or benefit to the defendant that could support the contract. The only promise that could be implied under the circumstances was for the exercise of proper skill and diligence. If such a contract could be enforced, a lawyer might be bound by a promise to pay for the privilege of taking the case of a client into court, or a physician compelled to make compensation for an opportunity of displaying his skill in curing a patient.

[1] 2 Dev. & Bat. 302.

CHAPTER XI.

IMPLIED PROMISES.

Promise implied in Request. — Presumptions from the Relations of Parties. — Voluntary Services. — Implied Request. — Payment of another's Debt. — Payment by Mistake. — Effect of express Agreement on implied Promise.

In general where an act is done or service rendered in pursuance of a request, the law will imply a promise to pay what it is worth. This rule does not apply unless it appears from the nature of the act, from what was said at the time, or by some other sufficient means of proof, that the parties were dealing on the basis of contract and not of charity, friendship, or benevolence. Where goods are ordered in a shop or market, or a man is requested to render a service in the way of his trade or profession, the question does not admit of a reasonable doubt, and it may be said in general that he who asks for and receives a benefit ought to pay for it, unless he can show some circumstance taking the case out of the general rule. Services are ordinarily rendered in the expectation of an equivalent, and an act done on request will not be presumed to have been gratuitous, in the absence of proof. Had the request to insure in Thorne *v.* Deas, been addressed to a broker instead of being made to a part-owner, the law would have implied an undertaking to pay a reasonable compensation, and the plaintiff might have recovered for the non-feasance.[1] In Kidder *v.* The Boom Co.,[2] the jury were told that "all that the law requires to constitute a contract is a benefit conferred by one party and accepted by the other in the course of business and not as a gratuity, and with an agreement or understanding that the latter is to incur a debt or obligation and the former be entitled to make a charge. When such is the case, it is not

[1] Miller *v.* Wilson, 12 Harris, 114.

[2] 12 Harris, 193.

necessary that the price should be fixed, because the law will imply that he who performs the service shall receive as much as he reasonably deserves to have." These instructions were affirmed on a bill of exceptions to the charge by the court above. Or, as the rule is stated in Addison on Contracts:[1] "If a man does work on the order of another under such circumstances that it must be presumed that he looks to be paid as a matter of right, then a contract will be implied by that person." And in determining whether such an implied promise exists, the law does not so much consider the intention of the person who receives the benefit, as what the person by whom it is conferred is reasonably entitled to expect. If, for instance, a husband abandons or expels his wife without cause, and she is supplied with necessaries by a third person, the law will imply a promise of compensation, although the evidence may clearly indicate that the service was rendered without the request and against the will of the husband. A man may on this ground be liable for the funeral expenses of his wife, if he fails from absence or other cause to take proper measures for her interment.[2] And where the defendant took his trunk with him on an excursion train with full knowledge that the company did not carry luggage gratuitously on such trains, he was held liable on a contract to pay what the carriage of the trunk was worth, contrary to the intention with which he acted.[3]

The presumption that the service for which the plaintiff seeks to recover compensation was rendered under an implied agreement for remuneration, may be repelled by evidence that the relation between the parties was such as to exclude the inference that they were dealing on the footing of contract.[4]

A woman resides in the house of another person for months or years. No contract is proved on either side; but she cooks, washes, and takes care of the children, or acts as the

[1] Addison on Contracts, p. 23.

[2] Jenkins *v.* Tucker, 1 H. Bl. 90, 94; Bradshaw *v.* Beard, 12 C. B. N. S. 344.

[3] Rumsey *v.* R. R. Co., 14 C. B. N. S. 641.

[4] Potter *v.* Carpenter, 76 N. Y. 157.

nurse of some member of the family who is ill. Under these circumstances, a claim is not infrequently advanced by one party for wages, and by the other for board. Such controversies are often exceedingly difficult to decide. If the parties are strangers in blood, and it is not shown that the act was one of hospitality or friendship, it may be reasonably supposed to have been done with the expectation of receiving a reward. But it is well settled that when such a case arises between parent and child, the law will not imply a promise when none is proved to have been made expressly. Hence, the jury should be told that no recovery can be had for board on one side, or for wages on the other, unless the parties so agreed;[1] and it is immaterial in this regard that the child was of full age, because the filial relation will be presumed to have continued unless the contrary is proved. The rule does not apply as one of law to more distant relatives: and where a niece resides with her uncle, or one sister is an inmate of the household of another, the question whether the relation is that of guest or servant is one of fact, depending on the intention of the parties as deduced from all the circumstances.[2] When, however, it appears in evidence that the plaintiff considered himself as a member of the family, and was so regarded by those around him, the presumption is that what he received was as an equivalent for what he gave. This is true even in the case of a stranger, and applies *a fortiori* to that of a relative.[3] The rule was broadly stated in Updike *v.* Titus, in the following terms: "The law implies no promise to pay for services rendered by members of a family to each other, whether by children, parents, grand-parents, brothers, step-children, or other relatives. No action can be maintained for such services in the absence of an express contract or engagement to pay for them. The rule rests on the simple reason that such services are not performed in the expectation of receiving a remuneration for the benefit conferred." It is proper to add that although an express promise for compensation is not less

[1] Updike *v.* Titus, 2 Beas. 151; Hertzog *v.* Hertzog, 5 Casey, 465; Candor's Appeal, 5 W. & S. 515; Leidig *v.* Coover, 11 Wr. 534.

[2] Neal *v.* Gilmore, 29 P. F. S. 421, 427.

[3] Ibid.

binding because the parties are father and child,[1] language that would ordinarily import an obligation, may when uttered by a parent be interpreted as a mere expression of an intention, which is not binding and may be changed at pleasure.

The case of Swain *v.* Ettling,[2] affords another illustration of the principle that the law will not imply a promise where the inference that the services were rendered with a view to remuneration is negatived by the relation between the parties. The suit was on a promissory note, and the evidence at the trial showed that the plaintiff lived with the defendant's intestate as his mistress, and that subsequently to the execution of the note he gave her money, and paid various debts which she had contracted. The court was requested to charge the jury that "even if A. H. Simmons was indebted to the plaintiff on said notes, and he afterwards paid to her, or at her request, or with her consent expended or invested money for her use, such payments, expenditures, or investments are presumed to have been made in discharge of the indebtedness, and not as gifts." The request was refused, and the jury were instructed "that such a presumption arises when the relation between the parties is of a business character, or where there is nothing to explain the relation between them. When, however, it is not that of business, as where money is paid by a father for a son, or by a man for his mistress, other presumptions arise. In the present instance, it is for the jury to decide whether these payments were loans or gratuities, as a question of fact upon the evidence, and upon all the probabilities of the case as presented by the evidence." The charge was sustained on a writ of error to the court above. It was held on like grounds, in Potter *v.* Carpenter,[3] that in services interchanged between friends and neighbors as a matter of mutual accommodation, a promise to pay will not be implied, although the benefit to one of the parties is much in excess of that received by the other. Even where the request is coupled with a promise, it may still be apparent from the circumstances that the defendant was simply expressing an intention, and neither meant to

1 Neal *v.* Gilmore, 29 P. F. S. 421, 427.

2 8 Casey, 486.

3 76 N. Y. 157.

incur an obligation nor was so understood. "We have," said Lowry, J., in Richards *v.* Richards,[1] "nothing but the testator's 'advice' to the plaintiff to buy the farm and not move West, accompanied with an assurance that he would furnish him with the balance of the purchase-money. But this does not make a legal contract. Assurances of assistance accompanying kind advice are never intended as contracts, and conformance to advice is never intended as a legal consideration for the kind assurances that accompany the advice, though it is a motive for their fulfilment. It would be exceedingly hurtful to the freedom of social intercourse to create even a suspicion in the public mind that those kind offers of advice and assistance which take place among friends and kindred could be converted into contracts which the law would enforce." So when a new promise is relied on to take the case out of the statute of limitations, the question whether the defendant spoke in jest or earnest, should, if there is reasonable doubt, be submitted to the jury, or may even be withdrawn from them if the occasion or manner was such as to indicate that he did not intend to revive the debt.[2]

The request need not be express, but may be implied where one incurs a liability at another's instance and for his benefit, although the plaintiff is the only person bound, and no direct obligation rests on the defendant. It is, for instance, the auctioneer and not the owner of the goods left with him for sale, who is answerable for the payment of duties imposed by the act of Parliament on such transactions, but the auctioneer may notwithstanding recover the amount so paid from the owner, as being a necessary consequence of or incidental to the end for which he was employed, and it is immaterial that the owner did not know of the payment or wish to have it made.[3] In Brittain *v.* Lloyd, the rule was laid down in the following terms in delivering judgment: "If one ask another

[1] 10 Wr. 78, 82.

[2] Moore *v.* Bank of Columbia, 6 Peters, 86; Wainman *v.* Kynman, 1 Ex. 118.

[3] Brittain *v.* Lloyd, 14 M. & W. 762; Brown *v.* Hodgson, 4 Taunt. 189; Hassinger *v.* Solms, 5 S. & R. 4.

instead of paying money for him to lend him his acceptance for his accommodation, and the acceptor is obliged to pay it, the amount is paid for the borrower, although the borrower be no party to the bill nor in any way liable to the person who ultimately receives the amount. The borrower, by requesting the acceptor to assume that character which ultimately obliges him to pay, impliedly requests him to pay, and is as much liable to repay as he would be on a direct request to pay money for him with a promise to repay it. In every case, therefore, in which there has been a payment of money by the plaintiff to a third party, at the request of the defendant, express or implied, to repay the amount, this action is maintainable.[1]

The authorities are in conformity with the above principle,— that asking another to be surety, indorser or guarantor, or entering into a joint obligation with him, is an implied request that he will discharge the debt, which will sustain an action of indebitatus assumpsit on proof that it has been fulfilled, although the guaranty is invalid, or the payment is not made till both parties are protected by the bar of the statute of limitations.

In Alexander *v.* Vane,[2] goods were sold to A and B on the faith of A's declaration that if B did not pay for them he would; and it was held that A was thereby impliedly authorized to discharge the debt in the event of B's default, and might consequently maintain an action against him on proof that the condition had been fulfilled, although the guaranty was merely oral, unless B had notified him to rely on the statute of frauds as a defence, or revoked his authority in some other way. "The plaintiff," said Parke, B., "is bound to prove that he paid the money with the authority of the defendant. If the engagement had been made in the absence of the defendant, it would have given no authority to the plaintiff to pay the money, and the payment would have been made without any authority, express or implied. But it being made in the presence of the defendant, there was an implied con-

[1] 14 M. & W. 762.

[2] 1 M. & W. 511; Brittain *v.* Lloyd, 14 M. & W. 762; Ford *v.* Keith, 1 Mass. 139.

tract that, if the plaintiff paid the money, the defendant would repay it. It is precisely the same as if the defendant had requested the plaintiff to pay the money. Then, has that authority been countermanded? If not, there is no doubt that it was a payment for the defendant's use, and at his request."

In many of the cases above cited there was an intention to contract, although it was not explicitly declared; but a contract may be implied for the furtherance of justice in opposition to the truth. Money paid under a mistake of fact, as for instance to satisfy a debt which does not exist, may consequently be recovered back in an action of indebitatus assumpsit, although the defendant never promised, and steadfastly maintained that the debt was due and that he was entitled to keep what he had received.[1]

None of the elements of a contract are present, and the real basis of the action is the existence of a right which cannot be enforced by any other means. For as trover or replevin will not lie for money unless the plaintiff can show that he is entitled to specific coins or notes, the law feigns a promise in order to prevent an entire failure of remedy. No such fiction was requisite under the Roman law, where the only point to be considered was whether the facts gave rise to an obligation which it was incumbent on the defendant to fulfil.[2] In the language of Gaius, "He who gives with the intention of paying means to discharge rather than to contract an obligation." The liability was accordingly regarded as arising not *ex contractu*, but as if a contract had been made. The case is still more marked where a man takes his neighbor's chattel, claiming it as his own, and converts it into money. Here the cause of action is manifestly *ex delicto*, and the sale simply an aggravation of the original wrong. It is nevertheless established that the owner may waive the tort and recover the proceeds in an action for money had and received, because the defendant owes reparation, and if the plaintiff is willing to

[1] Mechanics' Bank *v.* Earp, 4 Rawle, 384; Mowatt *v.* Wright, 1 Wend. 385; Milnes *v.* Duncan, 6 B. & C. 671; Thomas *v.* Brady, 10 Barr, 164, 179; 2 Sm. L. C. Am. ed. 408.

[2] Gaius, c. iii, § 9; Institutes, 3. 14. 1.

receive it in that form a promise is implied contrary to the fact.[1]

It is equally well settled that when one pays money, or does any other act in fulfilment of an obligation which, though binding his person or estate, ought as to the whole or in part to be discharged by another, the law will imply a promise of indemnity or compensation which may be enforced by suit;[2] or as the rule was stated by Strong, J., in Taylor *v.* Gould, a count for money paid and expended may be supported by proof of any payment not merely voluntary, made for the defendant's use, or that relieves him from a burden. It is immaterial that the defendant did not request or desire the payment, and would have resisted it if he could, because he will be presumed to have given a consent that could not rightfully be withheld. Hence a surety who has paid the debt may maintain indebitatus assumpsit against the principal, and a like remedy may be had when the arrears of a paramount ground-rent or of taxes are discharged by a tenant.[3]

The payment must not be merely voluntary.[4] In the language of Mr. Justice Kennedy, a stranger cannot make the debtor of another his debtor, by paying the debt for him to the creditor without the debtor's consent.[5] But the plaintiff need not be personally liable; it is enough that the obligation is a lien on his personal or real estate. When, therefore, a lessor for years fails to pay a paramount rent-charge or ground-rent, and the goods of the lessee are liable to be distrained for the arrears, he may anticipate the danger by payment, and recover the amount from the lessor on a count for money laid out and expended, or set it off in a suit brought for the rent reserved in the lease.[6] So if A leaves his goods on B's premises at

[1] 1 Sm. L. C. 8 Am. ed. 272, 282.

[2] Hassinger *v.* Solms, 5 S. & R. 4; Taylor *v.* Gould, 7 P. F. S. 152, 157.

[3] Notes to Lampleigh *v.* Brathwait, 1 Sm. L. C. 7 Am. ed. 287; Caldwell *v.* Moore, 11 Pa. 58.

[4] England *v.* Marsden, L. R. 1 C. P. 529; Wallace's Estate, 9 P. F. S. 401; 1 Sm. L. C.

[5] See Kennedy *v.* Carpenter, 2 Wharton, 344, 364.

[6] 1 Sm. L. C. 7 Am. ed. 292.

his request, or in pursuance of an express or implied contract with him, and they are distrained for B's rent, A may pay the landlord and recover the amount from B;[1] although it has been held that the action will not lie when the goods are left on sufferance, without any authority or request.[2]

The principle is the same where one to whom real or personal property has been sold or leased, is compelled to pay a lien or charge created by the grantor;[3] and hence a tenant holding under a lease executed by a mortgagor subsequently to the mortgage, may set off a payment made to the mortgagee in order to avoid an eviction, against the mortgagor's claim for the rent.[4] For as the mortgagee is entitled to the rents and profits, and may eject the tenant if they are withheld, so the mortgagor cannot claim that as owing which has already gone to satisfy the amount due on the mortgage, under the stress of a necessity arising from his default. So when the purchaser of land which has been mortgaged fails to pay the taxes, and the mortgagee is compelled to discharge them in order to save his lien, he may recover the amount from the purchaser as money expended for his use.[5]

It has been held in some instances that where there is an express agreement it will be presumed to cover the whole ground, and preclude the right to imply anything that it does not set forth.[6] In Kennedy *v.* Carpenter, the plaintiff paid a note, which he had endorsed for the defendant's accommodation some years previously, and sought to obtain reimbursement through a suit for money laid out and expended, which was brought within six years of the payment, but after the note had been barred by the statute of limitations. Kennedy, J., said that the surety's right to an indemnity could not be enforced at law prior to the time of Lord Mansfield, and was

1 Exall *v.* Partridge, 8 T. R. 308.

2 England *v.* Marsden, L. R. 1 C. P. 529.

3 Hogg *v.* Longstreth, 10 W. N. C. 95.

4 Doe *v.* Barton, 11 A. & E. 307, 314; Johnson *v.* Jones, 9 id. 809.

5 Parker's App. 8 W. & S. 449.

6 Kennedy *v.* Carpenter, 2 Wharton, 344; Spencer *v.* Parry, 3 A. & E. 331.

one of the many remedies borrowed from the Court of Chancery, and that when he took a security from the principal or received a direct undertaking from him to pay the debt, he could not apply to a chancellor for the remedy which might be had at law, or maintain an action on the implied promise which was the legal substitute for a bill in equity. It was said to follow that as an indorser has a right of action against the maker if the latter makes default, he must pursue it, and the law will not imply a promise of indemnity, or uphold a suit for money laid out and expended, even when the note was endorsed for the maker's accommodation, and the parties stand in the relation of principal and surety. Judgment was accordingly rendered for the defendant, on the ground that the statute of limitations runs in such cases from the maturity of the instrument, and not from the time when it is paid, and that the plaintiff's right to an indemnity had been lost by the delay.

This decision is contrary to the main current of authority in England and the United States, and was virtually overruled in Taylor *v.* Gould,[1] which establishes that an express agreement by a principal debtor to indemnify the surety, will not preclude the latter from recovering, on an implied promise to repay whatever he is compelled to disburse on account of the debt. In this instance the bank at which a promissory note had been discounted, obtained a judgment against the makers (Scoffin & Gould), who paid the amount to the indorsers (Taylor & Co.), and took a written agreement from them, as follows: —

> "We agree to have the judgment entered in this cause satisfied, we having been paid the full amount of said debt, the original note having been originally given to us; and to save the said Scoffin & Gould from any liability on the same, they repaying the costs up to this date, said judgment shall be satisfied within sixty days on the record.
>
> "February 17th, 1858. D. B. Taylor & Co."

The indorsers did not satisfy the judgment, and Gould's property was taken and sold for the debt. Gould thereupon

[1] 7 P. F. S. 152.

brought indebitatus assumpsit against Taylor & Co., and it was insisted for the defence, first, that the agreement being express, negatived any implied promise; and next, that as it was with both indorsers both should have been joined. These points were overruled in the court below, and a writ of error taken to the Supreme Court.

Strong, J., said: "If this suit were founded directly and solely upon the agreement of Feb. 17th, 1858, referred to in the first and second counts of the declaration, it might be that it could not be maintained, brought as it is by John H. Gould alone. That agreement was made with Scoffin & Gould; the promise, so far as there was any, was made to them both, and both of them had a legal interest in its performance. It matters not that each may have had a several interest in the benefit to be derived from it. If their interest in the contract itself was joint, they could only sue upon it jointly. The nonjoinder of Scoffin might, however, probably have been cured by amendment in the court below. Whether such an amendment could be allowed after a writ of error sued out, we need not now inquire. The action is not founded exclusively upon that agreement. There is a count for money paid, laid out and expended. It may be admitted that to support each of the counts, even that for money paid, the agreement is necessary, but the general count does not rest upon any promise contained in it, and may be supported by proof of any payment not voluntary, made for the use of the defendants or in their relief, by Gould, the plaintiff. The use of the agreement was to show that the payments made by the plaintiffs, averred in the narration to have been made on the 6th day of January, 1861, were for the benefit of the defendants and in their relief, and that they were not voluntary. The situation of the parties is very material to be considered. Scoffin & Gould had given their note to the defendants, which the defendants had indorsed to the Farmers' Bank of Bucks County. It was therefore the right of the bank to call upon the makers or the indorsers for payment. Suit was brought, and judgment was recovered against Scoffin & Gould, the makers. Then the makers paid the amount of the judgment, not to the bank, but to the defendants who had indorsed the note to the bank, and the defendants agreed to have the judgment satisfied within sixty days. They also agreed to save Scoffin & Gould from any liability on the same. The agreement was made on the 17th day of February, 1858. They did not, however, cause the judgment to be satisfied, nor did they save Scoffin & Gould from liability in consequence of it.

"On the contrary, Gould, the plaintiff, was compelled to pay it in 1861. Now what was the effect of all this? Obviously this: By the payment of the money to the defendants the duty was cast upon them to pay it to the bank, and thus relieve both Scoffin and Gould. As between the parties to the agreement the paramount obligation was cast upon Taylor & Co. True, both parties were liable to be called upon to pay the bank, but as between themselves, Scoffin & Gould were no more than sureties of the defendants. When, therefore, Gould, one of those sureties, paid the debt, the law immediately raised a promise of the defendants to reimburse to him what he had paid. That promise sustains the third count in the declaration. Most of the assignments of error have been made without regard to this view of the case. They treat the agreement of February 17, 1858, as a simple promise to pay a sum of money within sixty days, and a promise made to Scoffin & Gould. If such were all the effect of that agreement, the statute of limitations would be a bar to this action, and moreover, the action could not be sustained in the name of Gould alone. But it is also an engagement to indemnify, and that engagement was not broken until Scoffin & Gould were harmed by the judgment, which was in 1861, within six years of the commencement of the suit. The agreement is yet more. It made the debt to the bank, as between the parties to it, the debt of the defendants, throwing upon them the primary obligation to pay it, and therefore as an instrument of evidence it tended to prove that the money paid by Gould in 1861 was paid for them and for their relief."

CHAPTER XII.

ANTECEDENT CONSIDERATION.

Warranty after Sale. — Husband's Promise to pay Wife's ante-nuptial Debt. — Executor's Promise to pay Testator's Debt. — Promise to pay joint Debt apportioned by Statute of Limitations. — Promise to pay Debt to or for a third person. — Promise may be Evidence of antecedent Obligation. — Or reduce such Obligation to Certainty. — Implied Promise to pay for Service rendered on Request. — The Common Counts proceed on such a Promise. — Non-Assumpsit, *infra sex annos*. — Account stated, and What will support It.

THE authorities which have been cited show that the obligation of a contract depends at common law on what is done or promised on the faith of the assurance held out by the promisee. It follows that a past act cannot serve as the consideration for a promise. If the nature of the transaction is such as to give rise to an obligation, the law will imply a promise to fulfil it; if it is not, a subsequent promise will not create the liability which was wanting in the first instance. It is immaterial as regards the application of this principle, that the plaintiff parted with value which came to the hands of the defendant, or that the latter was benefited in some other way: the question remains, — Did the defendant enter into an express or implied engagement at the time? And if the reply is in the negative, he cannot bind himself afterwards, save on some new consideration, or through an instrument under seal.[1]

In Hayes *v.* Warren the case was brought into the King's Bench on a writ of error to the Common Pleas, where judgment had been rendered by default for the plaintiff, and it was objected that, as the fourth count was for work done for

[1] Hayes *v.* Warren, 2 Strange, 933; 2 Barn. 55, 71, 140; Docket *v.* Voyel, Croke Eliz. 885; Jeremy *v.* Goochman, id. 442; Hunt *v.* Bate, Dyer, 272 b.

the defendant, in consideration whereof he subsequently promised to pay, without alleging that the work was done at his request, there was no consideration to raise an assumpsit. The Chief Justice and Page, J., said that had the question arisen after verdict, the allegation that the work was done for the defendant might have been taken as implying that it was done at his request, but that such an inference could not be drawn in aid of a judgment by default. The case was less favorable than if it had been for goods bargained and sold, because the acceptance of the goods would have been a virtual agreement to pay for them, but work might be done for another without his privity or assent.

In like manner, where the allegation was that in consideration that the plaintiff had sold and conveyed a farm and lot of ground to the defendant, the latter undertook and promised to pay for it, judgment was arrested after a verdict.[1] The court held that if it had been averred that the defendant had accepted or entered into possession of the land conveyed, his assent might have been considered equivalent to a request, but that such a request could not be inferred from the facts alleged by the plaintiff.

So in Mills *v.* Wyman,[2] where a son of full age fell sick among strangers and was supported by them until he died at their expense, the father was said not to be bound by a promise of repayment which he had given on hearing of the circumstances after the death of his son. So also a recovery was refused in Dearborn *v.* Bowman,[3] on a promise to make compensation for past services rendered by the plaintiff in circulating political documents to promote the election of the defendant, but without his assent or knowledge. "The rule of the law," said Shaw, C. J., "seems now well established, although it may formerly have been left in doubt, that the past performance of services constitutes no consideration even for an express promise, unless they were performed under the express or implied request of the defendant, or unless they were done in performance of some duty resting

[1] Comstock *v.* Smith, 7 Johns. 87.

[2] 3 Pick. 207.

[3] 3 Met. 155.

on him.[1] As the services were not done at the request of the defendant, as they were not done in the discharge of any obligation which it was his duty to fulfil, there was no consideration to convert the alleged promise into an obligation."[2]

It is established in accordance with these decisions, that a service rendered voluntarily without a request is not a consideration for a subsequent promise, unless the promisor accepts the benefit under circumstances which leave him free to refuse. The use of goods that have been left at a man's door without orders to that effect is evidence of an acceptance that may supply the want of a request, but the case is obviously different where one constructs a building on the land of another without his knowledge or assent, or erects a structure differing materially from that specified in the agreement under which the work was done.[3]

For like reasons the obligation arising from an antecedent act or agreement, cannot be varied by an undertaking to that effect, or, as the rule is sometimes stated, when the plaintiff relies on a subsequent promise it must be co-extensive with the consideration, and such as to time, manner and amount as the law would imply had no express promise been given, and if the defect appears on the face of the pleadings, the declaration will be bad on demurrer, or judgment may be arrested after verdict.[4]

It follows that a warranty given after the sale is not binding on the vendor, and that he may recover the price in full, notwithstanding a promise to make a deduction for the unsoundness of the thing sold. The principle was applied in

[1] Mills *v.* Wyman, 3 Pick. 207; Loomis *v.* Newhall, 15 id. 159; Dodge *v.* Adams, 19 id. 429.

[2] Balcom *v.* Craggin, 5 Pick. 295; Shepherd *v.* Young, 8 Gray, 152; Bartholomew *v.* Jackson, 20 Johns. 28; Carson *v.* Clark, 1 Mo. 113; Snevily *v.* Reed, 9 Watts, 396; Geer *v.* Archer, 2 Barb. 420; Ingraham *v.* Gilbert, 20 id. 151.

[3] Bryant *v.* Stilwell, 24 Pa. 319; Shaw *v.* The Turnpike, 3 Penrose & Watts, 445; Munroe *v.* Butt, 8 E. & B. 738; Smith *v.* Brady, 17 N. Y. 173; The Trustees *v.* Bennett, 3 Dutch. 512.

[4] Hopkins *v.* Logan, 5 M. & W. 241; Roscorla *v.* Thomas, 3 Q. B. 234; Jackson *v.* Cobbin, 8 M. & W. 790.

Roscorla *v.* Thomas.[1] The plaintiff there obtained a verdict on a declaration alleging a warranty of a horse in consideration of an antecedent sale, and a motion was made in arrest of judgment on the ground that the consideration did not support the promise. In delivering the opinion of the court, Lord Denman said that it was a general rule, subject to exceptions which did not apply in the present instance, that the consideration must be co-extensive with the promise. In the case before the court the only promise that would result from and be co-extensive with the consideration, was a promise to deliver the horse upon request. The preceding sale being without a warranty, imposed no duty or obligation on the vendor.

It was clear therefore that the consideration would not raise an implied promise that the horse was sound or free from vice. But the promise alleged in the declaration must be taken to be, as in fact it was, express. It was therefore necessary to determine whether that fact warranted the extension of the promise beyond the limits within which it would be implied by the law, and whether the consideration, though insufficient to raise an implied promise, would nevertheless support an express one; and the court was clearly of opinion that it would not. The cases in which it has been held that an express promise might be valid where the circumstances would not give rise to an implied obligation, were collected and reviewed in the note to Wennall *v.* Adney,[2] and in Eastwood *v.* Kenyon.[3] They were cases of voidable contracts subsequently ratified, of debts barred by operation of law subsequently revived, and of equitable and moral obligations, which, but for some legal rule, would have been of themselves sufficient to have raised an implied promise. All these cases were distinguishable from and inapplicable to the case under consideration, which fell within the general rule that a consideration past and executed would support no other promise than such as would have been implied by the law.

This decision is sustained by a long train of cases coming down from a remote period, which establish that no liability

[1] 3 Q. B. 234. [2] 3 Bos. & P. 247. [3] 11 A. & E. 438.

will be imposed by a promise based on an antecedent consideration where none existed previously; and as a corollary to that proposition, that a naked promise to vary or extinguish an obligation growing out of a past contract or transaction, is not less ineffectual.[1]

The doctrine was applied in another form in Vandakin *v.* Soper.[2] The declaration averred that the defendant was indebted to the plaintiff, to one Enos Soper, and to Uriah Arnold in the sum of $81.07 for land before that time sold and conveyed to him at his request, and that the defendant afterwards assumed and faithfully promised to pay the plaintiff his share, or one third part of the amount so due, — namely, the sum of $27.14. A verdict was taken for the plaintiff at the trial, and the question arose on a writ of error to reverse the judgment. Skinner, C. J., said that the consideration on which the plaintiff averred the promise to have been made, was a pre-existing debt due from the defendant to the plaintiff and to other persons jointly. There was nothing in the record by which it could be determined whether the plaintiff relied upon an expressed or implied promise, and in the view taken by the court it was immaterial which, because the facts alleged were not sufficient to charge the defendant upon an undertaking express or implied. It was not a promise in consideration of forbearance, nor was it a promise in consideration of the joint demand or any part thereof. There were no averments in the declaration that could constitute a defence to a joint action on the original demand, and if a recovery could be had in such a proceeding the plaintiff could not succeed in this. The ground principally relied on in his behalf was that the defect was cured by the verdict. Defects merely formal would be aided by a verdict, and the omission of that which must necessarily be presumed to have been proved at the trial would not be a ground for arresting the judgment, but such a presumption could not be in-

[1] Hunt *v.* Bate, Dyer, 272 b.; Jeremy *v.* Goochman, Croke Eliz. 442; Thornton *v.* Jenyns, 1 M. & G. 166; Kaye *v.* Dutton, 7 id. 807; Comstock *v.* Smith, 7 Johns. 87; Ehle *v.* Judson, 25 Wend. 97; Snevily *v.* Reed, 9 Watts, 396.

[2] 1 Aiken, 287.

dulged with regard to anything which was not set forth in the declaration, or that did not appear by a necessary inference from the averments which it contained. It did not follow because proof was given of the promise, that a consideration was also proved, or that any other consideration existed than that which the plaintiff had averred. The judgment was therefore erroneous and must be reversed.

For like reasons a promise by a husband to pay an antenuptial debt of his wife's will not make the debt his own, or render him personally liable after her death;[1] and a promise by an executor to pay a debt due by the testator is invalid, and does not impose a personal obligation.[2] The declaration in Rann *v.* Hughes averred that the defendant's intestate was indebted to the plaintiff in the sum of £983, and died possessed of assets sufficient to pay that amount, and that letters of administration were granted to the defendant "by reason of which he became liable to pay the same, and being so liable undertook and promised to pay." The case was taken to the House of Lords, and the judgment which had been rendered for the plaintiff in the court below reversed on the ground, as stated by Chief Baron Skinner, that "if I promise generally to pay on request what I was liable to pay upon request in another right, I derive no advantage or convenience from the promise, and therefore there is no sufficient consideration for it."

A joint debt may nevertheless be apportioned through the operation of the statute of limitations, followed by a promise on the part of one of the debtors to pay the whole, or so much thereof as properly devolves on him, and the promise may then be enforced in a suit against the promisor.[3]

The consequences of this decision are important where, as in Pennsylvania, a promise by one joint-contractor will not revive the debt as against the rest. It shows, first, that the party making the promise will be bound; and, next, that the appropriate mode of enforcing his liability is by a declaration setting forth the joint contract, the intervention of the statu-

[1] Cole *v.* Shurtleff, 41 Vt. 311. [2] Rann *v.* Hughes, 7 T. R. 350 n.

[3] Lechmere *v.* Fletcher, 1 C. & M. 623.

tory bar, and the subsequent undertaking by the defendant which renders the debt severally binding on him.

It follows from the above principles that a promise by a debtor to pay the debt to a third person, or by a third person to pay the debt, is invalid unless sustained by a seal, or a consideration other than the debt itself. Here the common law again differs from the law of Rome, where an undertaking by one who was indebted, or by another for him, to pay the amount to the creditor, or with his assent to a third person, was binding, though not put in the form of a stipulation, and depending for its obligation solely on the duty of keeping faith. A debt may nevertheless be the subject of a dealing or negotiation, that will give rise to a consideration and impose a new liability. A promise to pay the debt at a future day with interest if the creditor will wait till then, is valid on this ground, which will also support an undertaking by a third person to guaranty the amount due.

The rule applies in pleading as well as in evidence; and where the promise is declared upon as subsequent, it must be such as the law would imply from the consideration, and if it does not conform to this rule the plaintiff cannot recover by aid of an express promise. Or, as the principle is sometimes stated, the consideration must be co-extensive with, and support each and every part of the promise. When, for instance, it is averred that the defendant was indebted to the plaintiff for goods sold and delivered, or for money lent, a recovery may be had on the allegation of a promise to pay on request without proving that such promise was made in point of fact; but if the declaration were, after reciting the sale or loan, to aver a promise to pay in goods, or at a future day, it would be bad on demurrer or on a motion in arrest of judgment;[1] and it would be no answer to the objection to say that the defendant made the promise, for whether he did or not, it is without foundation, and invalid. In Hopkins *v.* Logan[2] the plaintiff averred that the defendant was indebted to the plaintiff on an account stated, and had in consideration thereof promised to pay at a future day, and the court held the defect

[1] Hopkins *v.* Logan, 5 M. & W. 241.

[2] 5 M. & W. 241.

fatal. For like reasons a count alleging a promise to pay a pre-existing debt to a third person, or to pay one of three joint creditors his proportion of the debt, is defective on its face, and will not uphold a judgment.[1]

It is an obvious consequence of the same principle, that in declaring on an express promise, or to speak more accurately, on one which imposes an obligation other than that which the law would imply, the consideration must be averred as contemporaneous with the promise, or as having been done or rendered at the defendant's request; and if it is set forth as antecedent, the declaration will be invalid.[2]

Although a subsequent promise will not alter the contract, it may be material evidence of what the contract is. If, for instance, a suit is brought for the price of a chattel, and the defendant proves that a conversation took place after the sale, in which the plaintiff admitted that the chattel was unsound and promised to make an abatement from the price, the jury should be told that the promise is not binding as such, but that it is notwithstanding ground for an inference that the sale was subject to a warranty or condition that has not been fulfilled. The customary fee of a broker in Philadelphia for effecting a sale of real estate is one per cent, and a subsequent promise will not entitle him to recover a larger sum. But inasmuch as mankind seldom agree to give what they do not owe, such a promise may be evidence that the original agreement was for two, three, or four per cent on the price. This is, however, only true when the terms of the contract are subject to a reasonable doubt; for when they are reduced to writing, or established by the testimony of witnesses, the obligation cannot be varied by a subsequent promise which is not sustained by a new and adequate consideration. In Pitts *v.* Pitts,[3] where the action was brought on a note which had been given to the plaintiff by her father during her residence in his family, the jury were instructed that if the plaintiff

[1] Vandakin *v.* Soper, 1 Aiken, 287.

[2] Comstock *v.* Smith, 7 Johns. 87; Jeremy *v.* Goochman, Croke Eliz. 442; Hayes *v.* Warren, 2 Strange, 933.

[3] 21 Ind. 309.

continued to live with her father after her majority as she had done previously, with no duties or responsibilities, and was provided with necessaries as one of the family, she was not entitled to recover for her services, unless there was an express understanding between them before the services were rendered that she should receive such compensation, and if the note was given for such past services and there was no such understanding, it was invalid. But if the note was given for such past services, the fact that it was given gave rise to a presumption that there had been a previous understanding that such compensation should be made; and unless such presumption was overcome by evidence that no such understanding existed, the verdict should be for the plaintiff.

When an act is done at the request of another, and the parties fail to fix the price, the law will imply a promise to pay what the service is reasonably worth; but it has been held that a subsequent promise to give a specific sum may be as binding as if it had been made in the first instance.[1] The promise does not, however, constitute the contract; it operates by reducing that to certainty which the parties have left vague and undetermined. In Lampleigh *v.* Brathwait,[2] the declaration averred that whereas the defendant had previously slain one Patrick Mahune, and after the said felony done, instantly required the plaintiff to labor and do his endeavor to obtain a pardon from the king, whereupon the plaintiff, in pursuance of the request, did by all means he could, during many days labor and do his endeavor to obtain the king's pardon for the said felony, to wit, in riding and journeying at his own charges from London to Boston where the king then was, and to London back, and so to and from New Market, to obtain the pardon of the defendant; and afterwards the defendant in consideration of the premises promised the plaintiff £100, which he had not paid. A verdict was found for the plaintiff, when it was moved in arrest of judgment that the consideration was passed, and that it did not appear that the plaintiff

[1] Riggs *v.* Bullingham, Croke Eliz. 715; Bosden *v.* Thinne, Yelv. 40.
[2] Hobart, 105.

had obtained the pardon, or that his efforts were in any way beneficial to the defendant. But the court held that although a voluntary courtesy will not uphold an assumpsit, the case is different where the act is done at the request of the party who makes the promise; for then the promise though subsequent relates back to the request. And they were equally clear that inasmuch as the plaintiff was neither required, nor promised to obtain the pardon, but only to do his endeavor to that end, he had fulfilled the agreement, and was entitled to the compensation which he asked.

Two things appear from this decision; one, that where the consideration moves from the plaintiff, and is a detriment or loss to him, it will be sufficient although no benefit accrues to the defendant; the other, that when an act is induced by a request and the compensation is left uncertain, the deficiency may be supplied by a subsequent promise.[1] It has accordingly been held in various instances that a promise to pay a sum certain in consideration of an antecedent marriage contracted at the defendant's request, will relate back to the request, and impose an obligation which may be enforced by an action of assumpsit.[2] Here from the uncertain value of the consideration no recovery could be had without the promise, because a man obviously cannot maintain a *quantum meruit* for marrying his wife, there being under these circumstances no exact measure of the damages.[3] In Moorhouse *v.* Colvin,[4] a promise to a man before marriage to "notice his wife" in the will of the promisor, but "to what amount I cannot say," was accordingly held void for uncertainty, but might no doubt have been rendered binding by a subsequent undertaking to pay a sum certain.

The case of Lampleigh *v.* Brathwait may be thought to err by treating an inference of fact as one of law. It is obvious that when the parties have not fixed the price, a subsequent

[1] Elderton *v.* Emmens, 4 C. B. 479; Townsend *v.* Hunt, Croke Car. 408; Riggs *v.* Bullingham, Croke Eliz. 715; Sidenham and Worlington's Case, 2 Leonard, 224.

[2] Hunt *v.* Bate, Dyer, 272 b; Marsh *v.* Kavenford, Croke Eliz. 59.

[3] Waters *v.* Howard, 8 Gill, 262.

[4] 9 Eng. L. & E. 136.

promise on the part of the defendant is *prima facie* evidence of what the service is reasonably worth. Viewed in this aspect, the promise would not be conclusive, and the defendant might still show the real value of the service. The true explanation of the case seems to be that when the price is not fixed, and it cannot be known what compensation a jury would award, the parties are entitled to liquidate the damages by agreement. If the defendant, under these circumstances, promises to pay a sum certain, which is agreed to by the plaintiff, a new contract will arise binding on both. It is the assent of the plaintiff which gives validity to the promise, and if he is free to claim more, the defendant will not be bound to pay this much.[1]

It has been said, in some instances, that an act done in pursuance of a request, which does not imply a promise, may acquire the force of a contract through a subsequent promise.[2] In Bosden *v.* Thinne, the plaintiff, who had become a surety for a third person at the defendant's request, was obliged to pay the debt, and a promise to compensate him was held binding although not given till after payment. A like decision was made in Sidenham and Worlington's Case;[3] and it appears to have been held in divers instances that a marriage contracted at the defendant's request is a valuable consideration for a subsequent promise to pay a definite amount.[4]

These decisions may perhaps be supported on the ground that the subsequent undertaking shows that the request was in the nature of a promise; but if so the inference is one of fact, and not necessarily conclusive. It is universally conceded that a recommendation of a friend or correspondent as solvent and deserving to be trusted, or even a request that a sale or advance may be made to him, does not imply a promise to be answera-

[1] Wimer *v.* Worth, 104 Pa. 320.

[2] Kaye *v.* Dutton, 7 M. & G. 807; Hunt *v.* Bate, Dyer, 272 b.; Bosden *v.* Thinne, Yelv. 40; Paul *v.* Stackhouse, 2 Wr. 302, 304.

[3] 2 Leonard, 224.

[4] Sidenham and Worlington's Case, 2 Leonard, 224; Hunt *v.* Bate, Dyer, 272 b.

ble for the debt, because the natural inference is that the vendor is to get his money from the buyer.[1] But a subsequent promise to be answerable for or assume the debt may, agreeably to some authorities, be enforced by suit.[2] In the cases where the question has actually arisen, the request was, however, such as to imply a promise which the subsequent express promise reduced to certainty, or else there was some act done, or promise made on behalf of the defendant which he subsequently ratified. Thus, in Paul *v.* Stackhouse,[3] the loan was made on the faith of the borrower's assurance that the defendant would give his note as security, and when the latter subsequently executed the instrument, the contract became his own. An act done at the request of another will not be a consideration, unless the intention was to charge him, or his credit was the inducement to the act. A letter stating that a charitable institution was in need of funds, and asking the person to whom it was addressed to give the requisite amount, obviously would not be a sufficient foundation for a subsequent undertaking to refund the sum so paid. And this is equally true of a request that goods shall be sold to a third person, unless it is so worded as to be in effect a guaranty of the debt.[4] When the relation between the parties is one of charity or beneficence, it cannot be made legally obligatory by the most express promise.[5] A subsequent engagement may, however, be convincing as an admission, where it would fail as a contract; and when it is doubtful whether the defendant intervened as a friend or neighbor, or as a guarantor, his promise to pay the debt may properly be allowed to turn the scale.[6]

A subsequent promise may, therefore, have a twofold operation; first, as tending to show that the parties were mutually

[1] Bushnell *v.* Bishop Hill Colony, 28 Ill. 204; Russell *v.* Clark, 7 Cranch, 69; Barker *v.* Halifax, Croke Eliz. 741.

[2] Bosden *v.* Thinne, Yelv. 40; Paul *v.* Stackhouse, 2 Wr. 302.

[3] 2 Wr. 302.

[4] Barker *v.* Halifax, Croke Eliz. 741; Russell *v.* Clark, 7 Cranch, 69.

[5] Hamor *v.* Moore, 8 Ohio St. 239.

[6] Bosden *v.* Thinne, Yelv. 40.

bound, and so understood it from the outset;[1] and next, when this is proved or conceded, by reducing the agreement to order and certainty, and affording a measure of the damages. But an act done voluntarily, without a request, or in response to a request which, like an application for charity, does not operate as a promise, is not a consideration, even when it results in a benefit to the defendant, or relieves him from a burden which he might otherwise have to bear.

The doctrine that a promise may relate back to a request, and impose an obligation which might not otherwise exist, was recognized in Paul *v.* Stackhouse.[2] There Paul told Sprogle that if Stackhouse would lend him (Sprogle) $300, he (Paul) would be security for that amount. This assurance was communicated to Stackhouse, who made the loan and took Sprogle's note, which was subsequently signed by Paul. A suit was brought on the note against Paul, which went to judgment, and he took the case to the court above. It was contended on his behalf that the only consideration was the pre-existing debt of a third person, which could not sustain a promise even when put in the form of a promissory note. Woodward, J., said: "Taking the evidence contained in the first and second specifications of error, it may, without undue license, be treated as Paul's request to Miss Stackhouse to lend Sprogle the money in question. He promised Sprogle he would go his security, and this was an authority to the latter to say so to the creditor. Sprogle communicated it to Miss Stackhouse, and she let Sprogle have the money on the faith of Paul's promise thus sent to her. What was this but saying, 'Let Sprogle have the money, and I will be his security for the repayment?' The money was loaned and a note taken at a year, signed only by Sprogle. Three days after the year was up Paul signed it. There was his contract fully completed, but completed, it is said, on a consideration that was past and executed. It is true, as a general rule, that the consideration which binds a surety must be executory, but where the thing

[1] Gale *v.* Golsbury, Dyer, 272 b. (in notes); Hatch *v.* Purcell, 1 Foster, 544; Wilson *v.* Edmonds, 4 id. 517.

[2] 2 Wr. 302.

was done at the instance or request of the surety, a past consideration binds him. Pitman, in his excellent little treatise on Principal and Surety,[1] states the rule in regard to past considerations by the instance of the old case of Hunt *v.* Bate.[2] A's servant was arrested in London for a trespass, and J. S., who was well acquainted with the master, bailed the servant, and afterward A, for his friendship, promised to save him harmless; J. S. was compelled to pay the condemnation money, and it was held that an action did not lie upon A's promise, because the bailing which was the consideration was past and executed before. 'A consideration, therefore,' says the writer, 'which is executed is not sufficient to support a subsequent promise, unless indeed the act was done at the request of the party promising, for then the promise is not a naked one, but couples itself with the precedent request, and is, therefore, founded on a good consideration.' Some of the cases which he cites in support of the latter branch of the rule do not sustain the proposition, but others do. It was said by Mr. Justice Wilmot, in 1765, in Pillans *v.* Van Mierop,[3] that it was well settled that where the act is done at the request of the person promising, it will be a sufficient foundation to graft the promise upon."

This judgment may be sustained on either of two grounds; one, that Paul's declaration to Sprogle was a virtual request to Stackhouse to lend the money on his (Paul's) credit, which took effect as a promise of repayment when Stackhouse made the advance; the other, that when the borrower, Sprogle, declared that Paul would be his surety, and Paul ratified the undertaking by executing the promissory note, it became as much his as if it had been made by him in the first instance. All that the judgment can fairly be regarded as establishing is, that when it is doubtful whether a request was so made and understood as to operate as a promise, a subsequent express promise may be conclusive that the relation was one of contract and binding as such on the promisor. It was also said in this instance, that an agreement by a married woman to be answerable for work done for a third person operates as a request,

[1] Law Library, vol. xl, p. 57. [2] Dyer, 272 b. [3] 3 Burr. 1671.

which, though not imposing an obligation at the time, may become obligatory through an undertaking to that effect after the death of the husband.

A promise to pay for materials which had been furnished for the erection of a building on the defendant's land, although without a request from him, was nevertheless held valid in Landis *v.* Royer,[1] on the authority of Cunningham *v.* Garvin.[2] Sharswood, J., said: "The jury were instructed that if the lumber was originally furnished on the credit of the defendant's building, his subsequent promise to pay would be on a sufficient consideration. This ruling, we think, is fully sustained by the decision of this court in Cunningham *v.* Garvin. It was there held that a past consideration flowing from a benefit conferred, would support an express promise; in other words, that a benefit derived from the unsolicited services of another creates a moral obligation to compensate that other, and though not enough without a previous request to give rise to an implied, is sufficient to sustain an express assumption. A considerable part of the value of the defendant's house was derived from materials furnished by the plaintiff on the credit of it, and with the expectation of being paid for them. Unless there was some other equitable consideration, which is not presented, to vary the case in the points put to the judge, surely there can be no question that it would have been immoral and unjust for the defendants to enjoy the plaintiff's property without paying him for it."

In Cornell *v.* Vanartsdalen,[3] repairs made by a tenant with the knowledge and consent of the landlord, were in like manner said to create a moral obligation to reimburse the tenant, which would uphold a subsequent express promise to that effect. These decisions seem to be vestiges of the doctrine that a moral obligation may become legally binding through an express promise, which, though generally received at one period in England and in the United States, is now as generally repudiated.[4]

The rule that a past transaction will not sustain any promise

[1] 9 P. F. S. 95. [2] 10 Barr, 366. [3] 4 Barr, 364.

[4] Roscorla *v.* Thomas, 3 Q. B. 234; Paul *v.* Stackhouse, 2 Wr. 302.

which the law would not imply, cannot be evaded by the introduction of a nominal consideration, or of a consideration which is inadequate to the promise.[1] In Shepard *v.* Rhodes, a declaration averring that the plaintiff had released the defendant, and agreed to look solely to the assignee to whom the defendant had conveyed his property for the benefit of his creditors, and that the defendant subsequently in consideration thereof and of one dollar, promised to pay the debt, was accordingly held bad on demurrer as not disclosing a sufficient consideration; and the same view was taken in Schnell *v.* Nell, of a promise by a husband to pay a legacy left by his wife, in consideration of one cent, of natural love and affection, and of the services she had rendered to him during her life.

An enumeration of the instances in which a subsequent express promise may be obligatory, would be incomplete without adding that if a man who is under an equitable obligation promises to fulfil it, the contract may in some instances be enforced by suit.[2] Accordingly, if the principal debtor promises the surety to discharge the debt when due, the latter may sue at once if the promise is not fulfilled, instead of waiting as he otherwise would have been compelled to do until he had satisfied the obligation out of his own funds, and then bringing an action for money paid, laid out and expended.[3] In like manner an assignee of a chose in action who receives a promise of payment from the debtor, may enforce it by a suit in his own name, because the promise operates as a ratification of the equitable duty resulting from the assignment.[4] Equitable in this sense is not synonymous with just or equal, and denotes the existence of some right or obligation which a chancellor would enforce by a decree.

[1] Shepard *v.* Rhodes, 7 R. I. 470; Schnell *v.* Nell, 17 Ind. 29.

[2] Geer *v.* Archer, 2 Barb. 420; Stewart *v.* Eden, 2 Caines, 150; Hudson *v.* Critcher, 8 Jones (N. C.), 485; La Touche *v.* La Touche, 3 H. & C. 576.

[3] Keller *v.* Rhoads, 3 Wr. 513; Stewart *v.* Eden, 2 Caines, 150; Swift *v.* Crocker, 21 Pick. 241; Haseltine *v.* Guild, 11 N. H. 390.

[4] Crocker *v.* Whitney, 10 Mass. 316; Cromelien *v.* Manger, 5 Harris, 169; Tiernan *v.* Jackson, 5 Peters, 580.

The doctrine above stated may seem singularly at variance with the forms of pleading in common use, which set forth the consideration as antecedent to the promise. But the seeming anomaly is due to another well-established principle, that when a contract of any kind results in a definite pecuniary obligation, the law will imply a promise to fulfil it. An anonymous case in Godbolt's Reports,[1] is said to have determined as early as the 24th Elizabeth, that when the declaration avers that the defendant being indebted promised to pay, that is a consideration and will uphold the promise. Instead of declaring specially on the contract, the pleader accordingly sets forth so much of the transaction as is necessary to show the existence of the debt or duty on which the suit is founded, and then avers a promise of payment or performance which, though not made in fact, results by a necessary implication from the premises. This method of pleading was long regarded by the sticklers for precedent as an innovation; and Lord Holt is said to have remarked that he was a bold man who first ventured on it, but as it was at once briefer and less technical, it grew into favor and became established under the name of the common counts.[2]

The law is often censured for prolixity, but these forms compress as much into a brief compass as is easily possible to human ingenuity. A contract may be long and intricate to build a house in a way minutely described in the accompanying specifications, but if these have been complied with, and the time for payment has arrived, the whole may be summed up in a brief recital that the defendant was indebted to the plaintiff for work done and materials furnished by the latter at his request, and being so indebted promised to pay on request, but hath not fulfilled his promise to the damage of the plaintiff. This obviates the necessity for spreading the contract at length upon the record, with a careful and elaborate averment of the performance of every stipulation or proviso which

[1] p. 13.

[2] Field *v.* Dale, 1 Rolle Abr. 11, pl. 8; Hodge *v.* Vavisor, 1 Rolle R. 413; Oliverson *v.* Wood, 3 Lev. 366; Hayes *v.* Warren, 2 Strange, 933; 2 Sm. L. C. 8 Am. ed. 833.

is from any cause a condition precedent to the right of action. In like manner a recital that the defendant was indebted to the plaintiff for goods sold and delivered at his request, and promised payment, took the place of the more formal count upon mutual promises, or upon a promise to pay if the plaintiff would sell and deliver, which was in use at an earlier period.

The advantages of this method of pleading caused it to be employed in cases where it might at first sight seem to be inapplicable. In declaring on a promissory note, for instance, we do not count upon the promise which was actually made, but upon another which really has no existence. The declaration avers that the defendant executed a written promise to pay the plaintiff a sum certain; that by force thereof and of the statute in such case made and provided he became liable to pay so much, and being liable promised to make the payment. Here the concluding averment would appear to an unlearned eye a superfluous repetition of what has been already alleged. If, however, we now suppose the statute of limitations to be pleaded as a defence, the convenience of this mode of declaring will become apparent. Had the plaintiff declared exclusively on the instrument or, in other words, on the express written promise made originally by the defendant, the new promise or acknowledgment which it is now necessary to rely on could not have been replied or given in evidence, without a variance or departure that would have been fatal to the right of action. But inasmuch as the declaration proceeds upon an implied promise which is not tied down to circumstances of time or place, it is enough if the defendant was liable to pay the note from any cause when the writ issued. The allegation that the defendant did not promise within six years in manner and form as the plaintiff has averred, may consequently be met by an averment that he did, and the issue sustained by any proof that will show an implied promise within that time. And as an unqualified acknowledgment of the debt satisfies this condition, it may be given in evidence without a variance from the declaration.[1]

[1] Haymaker *v.* Haymaker, 4 Ohio St. 272; Leaper *v.* Talton, 16 East, 420; Griffith *v.* Roxbrough, 2 M. & W. 734; Stericker *v.* Barker, 9 id. 321.

The rule applies even when the promise is conditioned to pay when able, or if the debtor cannot find a receipt; it being well settled that a conditional promise which has become absolute through the fulfilment of the condition, may be given in evidence under a declaration alleging an unconditional implied promise to discharge the liability incurred by the defendant.[1]

To maintain an issue joined on a plea of non assumpsit *infra sex annos*, the plaintiff must nevertheless prove an acknowledgment conformable to the promise set forth in the declaration, to wit: either an unconditional acknowledgment from which a promise to pay will be inferred, or a conditional acknowledgment which, having become absolute through the fulfilment of the condition, may be given in evidence without a variance from the declaration.[2] In Irving *v.* Veitch,[3] it was accordingly held that a conditional promise might be given in evidence under an issue joined on a plea of the statute to a suit on a promissory note, notwithstanding the objection that it was inconsistent with the demand set forth in the declaration, and that there could be no recovery under such circumstances without a special count. The same point was decided in Humphreys *v.* Jones.[4]

A more difficult question is presented where a demand is barred by the statute of limitations or a discharge in bankruptcy, and a new promise given differing from that which the law would have implied before the bar attached. Such a case may arise where the defendant promises to pay the debt in goods, or to satisfy a contract for the delivery of goods by the payment of money. It has been held under these circumstances that a recovery cannot be had either on the promise or the original cause of action. The promise does not operate to revive the debt, because it purports to create a new and different liability, and is invalid as a contract for want of a consideration. If the plaintiff declares on the agreement as

[1] Hill *v.* Kendall, 25 Vt. 528; Guy *v.* Tams, 6 Gill, 82; Stone *v.* Rogers, 2 M. & W. 443; Hart *v.* Prendergast, 14 id. 741, 746.

[2] Hart *v.* Prendergast, 14 M. & W. 741.

[3] 3 M. & W. 90.

[4] 14 M. & W. 1.

originally made, he will fail at the trial from the variance between the pleadings and the proof, and a declaration on the new promise will be bad even after verdict, unless it sets forth some new and adequate consideration.[1] In Reeves *v.* Hearne,[2] the plaintiff relied on a promise to make and deliver clothing in payment of a debt barred by the statute of limitations. Parke, B., said the case was substantially the same as if the promise had been made before the bar of the statute attached, when it would simply have been an accord without satisfaction, and as such, invalid. The question arose in Earle *v.* Oliver,[3] on a demurrer to a declaration averring a promise by the defendant before his discharge in bankruptcy, that if the plaintiff should be compelled to pay the sum of £250, for which he was answerable under a guaranty which he had executed for defendant's benefit, the defendant would repay the amount with interest if he had the means. Parke, B., said that two objections had been urged for the defence: first, that a debt or liability in a course of being barred by a certificate, cannot be a consideration for a promise which a debt or liability not barred by a certificate would not support; and that agreeably to the course of the modern decisions, beginning with the case of Hopkins *v.* Logan,[4] and ending with Roscorla *v.* Thomas,[5] a debt was not a consideration for any promise which the law would not imply from it; and that a promise to pay when the party was able could not be so implied; second, that a promise to pay interest could not be supported by such a consideration, and was as objectionable as if the promise had been to do any collateral thing. The court was of opinion that these objections ought not to prevail. Lord Mansfield had, no doubt, deviated from the strict rule of the common law, in Hawkes *v.* Saunders,[6] and Atkins *v.* Hill;[7] but the point actually presented in those instances was that where the consideration is beneficial and would give rise to an implied promise, if the defendant were not protected from lia-

[1] Reeves *v.* Hearne, 1 M. & W. 323; Earle *v.* Oliver, 2 Ex. 71; Short *v.* McCarthy, 3 B. & Ald. 626; Titus *v.* Ash, 4 Foster, 319.

[2] 1 M. & W. 323.

[3] 2 Ex. 71.

[4] 5 M. & W. 241.

[5] 3 Q. B. 234.

[6] Cowper, 290.

[7] Cowper, 284.

bility by some provision of the statute or common law meant for his advantage, he might renounce the benefit of that law, and if he promised to pay the debt, which was only what an honest man ought to do, the law would compel performance. There was a very able note to the case of Wennall *v.* Adney,[1] explaining this at length. The instances given to illustrate the principle were, among others, the case of a debt barred by a certificate or by the statute of limitations; and the rule laid down in these instances had been so constantly followed, that it must be considered as the established law. A debt so barred was unquestionably a sufficient consideration for a promise to pay it whether absolute or unqualified, qualified or conditional. Promises to pay such a debt simply, or by instalments, or whenever the party had the means, were all equally supported by the past consideration, and when the debt had become payable *instanter*, might be given in evidence under the ordinary declaration in indebitatus assumpsit.

So where the debt was not already barred by the statute, a promise to pay the creditor would make it a new debt, and a promise to an executor to pay a debt due to the testator created a new debt to him. But it did not follow that, though the promise revived the debt in such cases, such a debt would be a sufficient consideration for a promise to do a collateral thing, as to supply goods or perform work and labor, and the cases were decisive that such a promise was but an accord unexecuted, and that no action would lie for not executing it.[2] The result was, that as a conditional promise to pay the debt supported by the original consideration would have been valid, so a conditional promise which when absolute would only be a renewal of the original liability, and to the same extent, might be equally good and rest on the same basis. The remaining objection related to the promise to pay interest, which, in the opinion of the court, was supported by the same consideration as the undertaking for the payment of the principal. The promise was to pay the debt conditionally, and if the debt was not paid that the defendant would pay interest as a compensation for the delay.

[1] 3 Bos. & P. 247, 252.

[2] Reeves *v.* Hearne, 1 M. & W. 323.

I may, in this connection, advert to one of the common counts which is constantly employed and of great practical importance. The pleader avers that the defendant was indebted to the plaintiff upon an account stated between them, and being so indebted promised to pay. It is said in Addison on Contracts,[1] that the promise is implied in respect of the statement of the account; but it is more accurate to say that it is implied from the existence of the debt, which again is presumed from the express and deliberate acknowledgment made by the accountant. It is probable that this method of pleading was originally applied where a settlement was had between merchants, and a balance struck which might be the result of long and complicated dealings on either side. It is now, however, well settled that any express or unqualified admission that a sum certain is due to the plaintiff, whether oral or in writing, is an account stated in the sense in which the term is used in pleading.[2] If, for instance, the defendant gives an I O U, or on the presentation of a bill admits that it is due, a recovery may be had without further proof, as on an account stated.[3] Such evidence is, however, merely *prima facie*, resting on the natural presumption that the defendant would not have made an admission contrary to his interest unless it was true, and may, as in the analogous case of a promissory note, be rebutted by proof that no consideration moved at any time from the plaintiff, and that nothing is in point of fact due to him.[4]

When the suit is on implied promise, non assumpsit not only puts the promise at issue but the consideration from which it is deduced. When, for instance, the declaration avers that the defendant was indebted to the plaintiff for goods sold and delivered, and being so indebted promised to pay, a denial of the promise is in effect a denial that the goods were sold, because if such a sale was made the price is due and the prom-

[1] p. 38.

[2] Buck *v.* Hurst, L. R. 1 C. P. 297; Purdon *v.* Purdon, 10 M. & W. 562; Porter *v.* Cooper, 1 C. M. & R. 386, 394; Perry *v.* Slade, 8 Q. B. 115.

[3] Fesenmayer *v.* Adcock, 16 M. & W. 450; Payne *v.* Jenkins, 4 C. & P. 324.

[4] Lemere *v.* Elliott, 6 H. & N. 656.

ise to pay it follows as a legal inference. This remark does not, however, apply when the declaration is on an express promise in consideration of some act done or promise made on the other side, and the effect of non assumpsit in putting all the averments of such a count at issue, can only be ascribed to a practice which convenience introduced and custom has now made inveterate.

CHAPTER XIII.

MORAL OBLIGATION.

Moral Obligation as the Consideration for an express Promise. — Distinction between Legal Consideration barred by Statute, etc., and Moral Obligation. — Rule in Pennsylvania.

It was held at one period that if one who was bound in morals clothed the obligation with an express promise, the contract was valid and might be enforced by suit.[1] The doctrine seems to have originated with Lord Mansfield, who inclined to the rule of the civil law that a promise deliberately made should be obligatory, unless it is unlawful or immoral. "If," said he, in Hawkes *v.* Saunders, "a party is under a moral obligation which no court of law or equity can enforce, the honesty and rectitude of the thing are the consideration." This dictum, which was not necessary to the determination of the case in hand, where the antecedent obligation might have been enforced by a bill in equity, passed into the current of decision and was generally accepted as law.[2]

It was declared in like manner in Hemphill *v.* McClimans,[3] that an existing moral duty not enforceable by law is a sufficient consideration for an express promise; and in Cunningham *v.* Garvin, Bell, J., said that a benefit derived from the unsolicited services of another, creates a moral obligation of sufficient potency to sustain an express promise to make

[1] Hawkes *v.* Saunders, Cowp. 290; Atkins *v.* Banwell, 2 East, 505; Cooper *v.* Martin, 4 East, 76; Wing *v.* Mill, 1 B. & Ald. 104; Lee *v.* Muggeridge, 5 Taunt. 36; Doty *v.* Wilson, 14 Johns. 378; Willing *v.* Peters, 12 S. & R. 177.

[2] Trumbull *v.* Tilton, 1 Foster, 128; Cunningham *v.* Garvin, 10 Barr, 366, 368; Greeves *v.* McAllister, 2 Binn. 591; Montgomery *v.* Lampton, 3 Met. (Ky.) 519; Stewart *v.* Eden, 2 Caines, 150; Doty *v.* Wilson, 14 Johns. 378; Bently *v.* Morse, id. 468; Glass *v.* Beach, 5 Vt. 172.

[3] 12 Harris, 367.

compensation. So in Greeves *v.* McAllister,[1] the plaintiff and defendant were bail for the same person, although in different suits, and the court held that the act of the former in pursuing and arresting the principal debtor who had made his escape, was a sufficient consideration for a promise by the latter to bear half the expense, although it appeared from the evidence that the plaintiff had acted for himself in making the arrest without communicating his intention to the defendant.

This doctrine was applied under a great variety of circumstances on both sides of the Atlantic.

A father was under a moral obligation to maintain his child, and ought to compensate those who fulfilled the duty in his default.[2] The sheriff incurred a liability through the escape of the defendant in an execution; it was the duty of the latter to indemnify the sheriff.[3] A debtor who received a release in full in consideration of a partial payment, was morally bound to pay the residue when able.[4] A married woman to whom money was advanced to meet a pressing need, ought to refund it after the death of her husband, if she had the means.[5] And if the parties who were under obligations of this or a like kind chose to ratify them by an express promise, it would be legally binding, and might be made the foundation of a recovery in damages.

The question arose in Lee *v.* Muggeridge,[6] on a promise by a widow to repay money which had been advanced at her request to her deceased husband during his life. It was contended on behalf of the defendant that as the contract was void when originally made it could not be a consideration. Mansfield, C. J., however, said that where a person is bound morally and conscientiously to pay a debt, a subsequent promise will give a right of action. There could be no stronger

[1] 2 Binn. 591.

[2] Atkins *v.* Banwell, 2 East, 505; Cooper *v.* Martin, 4 id. 76.

[3] Doty *v.* Wilson, 14 Johns. 378.

[4] Willing *v.* Peters, 12 S. & R. 177; Trumbull *v.* Tilton, 1 Foster, 128.

[5] Lee *v.* Muggeridge, 5 Taunt. 36; Vance *v.* Wells, 8 Ala. 399; Hemphill *v.* McClimans, 12 Harris, 367.

[6] 5 Taunt. 36.

moral obligation than that set forth on the record. The case was not legally distinguishable from that of Barnes *v.* Hedley[1] where it had been held that a promise to repay the amount originally advanced under a contract void for usury, was binding on the debtor and might be enforced by suit. The rule for a new trial was accordingly discharged.

The merit of correcting the fallacy belongs to the writer of the learned note to Wennall *v.* Adney.[2] It was there shown that the cases where a past consideration had been upheld on the ground of moral obligation, really hung on a very different principle. They were all cases of a precedent consideration, which would have given rise to an implied promise but for the intervention of some positive rule of law which might be waived by the party for whose benefit it was introduced. An express promise might revive a good or valuable consideration, which had been barred by a statute or the lapse of time, but it would not give validity to a moral obligation when there was no consideration from which an obligation could legally arise. This view was adopted in Mills *v.* Wyman.[3] It appeared at the trial that the defendant's son was ill and in distress away from home, and had been relieved by the plaintiff, who procured a nurse and physician and supplied his wants until he died, and a letter from the defendant promising to repay the expense which had been incurred was declared to be a *nudum pactum*.

It was held in like manner in Hatchell *v.* Odom,[4] that if a duty is sufficiently clear and definite to be a subject of legal cognizance, it will be enforced through the fiction of an implied promise; if it is not, an express promise will not bring it within the reach of the law. This was the only practical criterion; because there are a multitude of moral obligations which must be left to the interior forum, as being too refined and delicate to be investigated judicially, or made the ground of a recovery in damages. Gaston, J., said that the declaration contained two counts. The verdict was a general one, and so was the judgment; if, therefore, either count was bad the judgment

[1] 2 Taunt. 184. [2] 3 Bos. & P. 247, 249. [3] 3 Pick. 207.
[4] 2 Dev. & Bat. 302.

must be reversed. The first count alleged that the defendant had sold the plaintiff a certain slave as sound which was unsound and of no value; that the unsoundness afterward came to the plaintiff's knowledge; and that thereupon in consideration of the premises and that the plaintiff would return the slave to the defendant, the latter undertook to cure the slave or pay back the price; and that the slave was accordingly returned, but that he was not cured or the price repaid. The point mainly relied on for the plaintiff was that the defendant was morally bound to reimburse the plaintiff, and that this obligation constituted a sufficient consideration to make the promise binding in law. It was not contended that he was under a legal obligation to make reimbursement, because, the sale having been without warranty and without fraud, the vendee was bound to bear the loss arising from the defects of a thing which he had made his own. But it was insisted that no man could keep with a safe conscience the price of an article sold as valuable and afterward found to be worthless; and that although the performance of the duty to make restitution could not be compelled while the obligation rested only in conscience, yet the law would gladly seize on a promise to perform it and uphold it as binding. It was always gratifying in the administration of the law to enforce the precepts of natural justice, but the law could not successfully compel the performance of all the moral duties even by those who had expressly assumed to fulfil them.

There were many duties to our fellow-men which an enlightened conscience recognized, that were either too refined to be discerned, too indefinite to be prescribed, or too imperfect to be enforced by human institutions, or which were regulated by a standard of morals too high to be applied as an ordinary instrument for measuring legal obligation. Those duties which were plain, definite and positive, and which could be practically enforced in the business of life, were recognized as legal obligations, and an undertaking to perform them was raised through the fiction of an implied promise.

There was however a class of cases where, although the obligation might be plain and perfect, and ordinarily a proper subject of legal cognizance, yet its performance could not be compelled because of some rule of public policy, and where therefore the law would not imply a promise. If, however, in these cases a promise was made after the interdict had been removed, and when holding it valid would not conflict with the rule, there was no longer a reason why the promise should not be enforced. There was a clear moral obligation to return money which has been borrowed, and the law in general required that the duty should be performed. From principles of public policy, however, it would not enforce such an obligation against a *feme covert* or an infant, because it denied to the one the legal capacity to contract and allowed it to the other only to a very limited extent. But if after the *feme covert* became a widow, and the infant attained full age, they distinctly and unequivocally promised to pay what they would have been bound to pay but for the protecting and disabling rule of law, the promise would be as binding as it would have been had there been no such rule. So if a certificated bankrupt promised to pay his former creditor, or a debtor assumed to pay a debt which had been barred by the statute of limitations, the law would enforce the promise because the original obligation had been reassumed at a time when no legal rule stood in the way. But a promise however express must be regarded as a nude pact if founded solely on a consideration which the law held insufficient to create a legal obligation, and from which no implied promise could be inferred as it regarded any one.

If the supposed moral obligation of the defendant to remunerate the plaintiff for the loss arising from the sale was dismissed as not constituting a sufficient consideration, there was no other consideration that could support the promise. No benefit could accrue to the defendant from being permitted to incur the expense and trouble of endeavoring to cure the slave, nor had any loss been occasioned to the plaintiff. It was not averred that the slave had been injured, but only that he had not been cured. Whatever, therefore, might be the obligation of the promise *in foro conscientiæ*, in law it was without consideration and void.

The question arose not long afterwards in England in the

case of Eastwood *v.* Kenyon,[1] where a declaration alleging the expenditure of money by a guardian improving the real estate of his infant ward; a ratification by her on coming of age; her subsequent marriage to the defendant whereby he was benefited to the full extent of the amount so laid out; and a promise of repayment on his part, — was held bad after verdict as not disclosing a consideration. The doctrine of Lee *v.* Muggeridge[2] that a moral obligation will support a promise, was condemned by Lord Denman as having no place in English law; and he pointedly observed that if it were true every promise would be legally binding, because every promise carries with it a moral obligation.

It is generally held in accordance with these decisions that to render a subsequent undertaking valid, some act must have been done or service rendered on the faith of an express or implied request, and that when this element is wanting it will not be enough to show that the defendant was morally bound to remunerate the plaintiff and ratified the obligation by an express promise.[3] Hence a promise by a child to maintain an aged parent, or by a parent to compensate the care and services that have been bestowed on a sick or helpless child, cannot be enforced on the ground of morals where there is no legal liability aside from the promise.[4] So if a vendor who has sold without warranty is morally bound to indemnify the purchaser for a defect which frustrates the object for which he bought, the duty is not one which the law will enforce, even when fortified by an express promise.[5] And although

1 11 A. & E. 438.

2 5 Taunt. 36.

3 Hamor *v.* Moore, 8 Ohio St. 239; Updike *v.* Titus, 2 Beas. 151; Nightingale *v.* Barney, 4 Greene (Ia.), 106; Paul *v.* Stackhouse, 2 Wr. 302; Geer *v.* Archer, 2 Barb. 420, 424; Dearborn *v.* Bowman, 3 Met. 155; Wiggins *v.* Keizer, 6 Ind. 252; Eakin *v.* Fenton, 15 id. 59; Ingraham *v.* Gilbert, 20 Barb. 151; Thorne *v.* Deas, 4 Johns. 84; Watkins *v.* Halstead, 2 Sandf. 311; Cook *v.* Bradley, 7 Conn. 57; Loomis *v.* Newhall, 15 Pick. 159; Dodge *v.* Adams, 19 id. 429; Bates *v.* Watson, 1 Sneed, 376; Holt *v.* Robinson, 21 Ala. 106.

4 Mills *v.* Wyman, 3 Pick. 207; Cook *v.* Bradley, 7 Conn. 57.

5 Roscorla *v.* Thomas, 3 Q. B. 234; Geer *v.* Archer, 2 Barb. 420; Williams *v.* Hathaway, 19 Pick. 337.

the breach of a promise to repay a benefactor who stands in need may be justly condemned as a mark of ingratitude and bad faith, it cannot be made the foundation of a recovery in assumpsit.[1]

It was held at one period that an insolvent debtor who has been discharged or released in consideration of a partial payment, is under a moral obligation that will uphold a subsequent promise to pay the residue.[2] But these cases are now overruled by others which establish that when a debt is extinguished by a release, or through an accord and satisfaction, it ceases to exist for all purposes and cannot be made the basis of a contract.[3] The rule applies even when the satisfaction is nominal or illusory, by the arrest of the debtor under a *capias ad satisfaciendum* from which he is discharged,[4] or the note of a third person which is not paid.[5] It was indeed said in Trumbull *v.* Tilton, that whether the bar arises under a certificate in bankruptcy or a release, it is equally within the control of the debtor and may be waived by him, but there is an obvious distinction between the extinguishment of a debt voluntarily and by the act of the law.[6]

The result will be the same whether the consideration relied on to sustain the promise is an obligation to indemnify the plaintiff for a wrong, or to make compensation for a benefit conferred or service rendered. In Beaumont *v.* Reeve,[7] the declaration averred that the defendant had seduced the plaintiff and induced her to cohabit with him, whereby she was injured in her character and deprived of the means of gaining an honest livelihood; that they agreed to discontinue the immoral connection and live asunder; and that the defendant as

1 Hamor *v.* Moore, 8 Ohio St. 239.

2 Willing *v.* Peters, 12 S. & R. 177; Trumbull *v.* Tilton, 1 Foster, 128.

3 Snevily *v.* Reed, 9 Watts, 396; Valentine *v.* Foster, 1 Met. 520; Stafford *v.* Bacon, 1 Hill, 532; Shepard *v.* Rhodes, 7 R. I. 470; Warren *v.* Whitney, 24 Me. 561; Montgomery *v.* Lampton, 3 Met. (Ky.) 519; Wright *v.* Clark, 34 Miss. 116.

4 Wright *v.* Clark, 34 Miss. 116.

5 Snevily *v.* Reed, 9 Watts, 396.

6 Shepard *v.* Rhodes, 7 R. I. 470; Montgomery *v.* Lampton, 3 Met. (Ky.) 519.

7 8 Q. B. 483.

a compensation for the injury and in consideration of the premises undertook to pay the plaintiff a certain sum annually towards her maintenance, which he had not done. The circumstances might be thought to appeal strongly to the discretion of the court, but it was held that they did not constitute an exception to the general rule.

The argument may be summed up in the language of Lord Denman in Beaumont *v.* Reeve:[1] "The moral consideration which alone appears cannot support assumpsit. That principle has been lately acted upon by this court in Eastwood *v.* Kenyon,[2] where we adopted the doctrine laid down in the note to Wennall *v.* Adney.[3] The result is that an express promise cannot be supported by a consideration from which the law could not imply a promise, except where the express promise does away with a legal suspension or bar of a right of action which, but for such suspension or bar, would be valid. This result we arrived at after much deliberation, and we now adhere to it."

If there were no other reason for acquiescing in this conclusion it would be enough that there are no certain means of ascertaining which among the multitude of moral obligations will uphold an express promise. Men owe much to their kinsmen, their friends, and their neighbors that cannot be withheld without a violation of the moral law; and it would be equally difficult to maintain that this is a sufficient consideration for an assumpsit in every such instance, and to distinguish the cases where an action will lie from those which should be left to the decision of the individual conscience.[4]

The doctrine that a moral obligation may uphold a promise was assigned in Pennsylvania as the *ratio decidendi* as far down as Hemphill *v.* McClimans,[5] and, judging from the language in the somewhat recent case of Landis *v.* Royer,[6] has not been definitively abandoned. It was nevertheless gravely questioned in Paul *v.* Stackhouse,[7] and declared to be inappli-

[1] 8 Q. B. 483. [2] 11 A. & E. 438. [3] 3 Bos. & P. 247.

[4] Farnham *v.* O'Brien, 22 Me. 475; Hatchell *v.* Odom, 2 Dev. & Bat. 302, 306.

[5] 12 Harris, 367. [6] 9 P. F. S. 95. [7] 2 Wr. 302.

cable where, as in the case of a surety, the consideration does not move to or benefit the promisor. Woodward, C. J., said, in delivering judgment: "The contract of suretyship rests necessarily upon a consideration that is valuable. The consideration may be in the form of an inconvenience to the party promised or of an advantage to be gained by either the principal debtor or the surety, and it may be ever so slight; but in the one form or the other, a consideration which the law denominates valuable must be proved, or a surety cannot be made legally liable. What is called a moral obligation is insufficient to support the promise of a surety. It is often said in the books, as was laid down by Gibbs, J., in Lee *v.* Muggeridge,[1] that, wherever there is moral obligation to pay a debt or perform a duty, a promise to perform that duty or pay that debt will be supported by the previous moral obligation; but it is believed that in all cases which may be cited in support of the rule there was an original consideration beneficial to the party promising, and which might have been enforced on an implied promise, had it not been for some statute provision or some positive rule of law which, with a view to the general good, exempted the party from legal liability in the particular instance."[2] In the case before the court the money was loaned to Sprogle at the instance and request of Paul, which was a sufficient consideration for his subsequent promise. Such was the true ground for the judgment in Hemphill *v.* McClimans,[3] where the defendant was held answerable on a promise made after the death of her husband for work done at her request during his life for their son. A majority of the court, however, insisted on resting her legal liability on her moral obligation, and thus made the case a mischievous precedent. There was no doubt a moral obligation to pay for labor which she had induced others to expend for the benefit of her son, but like most other moral obligations it

[1] 5 Taunt. 36.

[2] See the cases cited in notes to Edwards *v.* Davis, 16 Johns. 281, 284. See also Mills *v.* Wyman, 3 Pick. 207, Smith *v.* Ware, 13 Johns. 257, and C. J. Gibson's observations in Kennedy *v.* Ware, 1 Barr, 445.

[3] 12 Harris, 367.

was enforceable *in foro conscientiæ* rather than in a court of law.

The theory that a man may be legally bound by a promise to fulfil a moral obligation was reiterated in Landis *v.* Royer,[1] and a man who supplies a contractor with the materials for a house which he has agreed to build, with a lien on the premises conferred by statute for the price, was said to have a claim in morals on the owner of the land, which will support a subsequent promise on his part to pay the amount due.

It is, nevertheless, generally conceded that the promise must be founded on a moral obligation which is so clear and unequivocal as to leave no room for doubt, and which the law would enforce if the circumstances did not constitute an exception to the general rule. However honorable the sentiment which prompts a woman to assume the burden of her deceased husband's debts, or a father to discharge the liabilities contracted by his son, there is nothing in either case that will uphold a promise, and it is immaterial that the demand is for necessaries furnished at the request of the wife and for family use, because the law will presume that she was acting for her husband, and that the debt was his, unless it be shown that the services were rendered, or the goods supplied specifically on the credit of her separate estate.[2]

Applying this test to the relations growing out of a contract for the erection of a house, it will appear that the owner fulfils his entire duty by paying the contractor, and is under no moral or legal obligation to the person whom the builder employs, that can sustain a promise, save where, as seems to have been the case in Royer *v.* Landis, the builder has not been paid, and the owner is equitably bound to appropriate the amount due him to the material-men and the mechanics who suffer through his default.

[1] 9 P. F. S. 95.

[2] Ehle *v.* Judson, 25 Wend. 97; Goulding *v.* Davidson, 26 N. Y. 604, 610, 615; Littlefield *v.* Shed, 2 B. & Ad. 811; Meyer *v.* Haworth, 8 A. & E. 467; La Touche *v.* La Touche, 3 H. & C. 576.

CHAPTER XIV.

RATIFICATION AND WAIVER.

Ratification by subsequent Promise. — May be implied by Silence. — What Acts may be Ratified. — Ratification of an Agent's Tort. — Ratification of unauthorized Payment. — Ratification of Forgery. — Waiver of Defence by subsequent Promise. — Waiver of Statute of Limitations. — Waiver of Discharge in Bankruptcy. — Waiver of Coverture as a Defence. — Waiver where Contract is Illegal or Fraudulent.

WE have seen that a promise will not impose an obligation where none exists, or render that a debt which was not such originally. There are, nevertheless, two grounds on which a contract which failed in the first instance, or became invalid subsequently, may be confirmed by a promise. One of these is waiver, the other ratification. Ratification is an adoption of a contract made on our behalf by some one whom we did not authorize, which relates back to the execution of the contract and renders it obligatory from the outset. Waiver is a renunciation of some rule which invalidates the contract, but which, having been introduced for the benefit of the contracting party, may be dispensed with at his pleasure. It is a familiar maxim that a ratification relates back and is equivalent to a command.

An act done or contract made officiously by a self-constituted agent is consequently as valid when ratified by the principal as if he had authorized it in the first instance.[1]

So the right of an agent to indemnity is the same whether he was employed beforehand or his acts adopted afterwards.[2]

The chief requisite to a ratification is that the party for whom the act is done or contract made, shall deliberately

[1] Tooker *v.* Sloan, 30 N. J. Eq. 394; Waterson *v.* Rodgers, 21 Kan. 529.

[2] Doty *v.* Wilson, 14 Johns. 378; Ingraham *v.* Gilbert, 20 Barb. 151; Kenan *v.* Holloway, 16 Ala. 533.

adopt it as one for which he is willing to be answerable, with a knowledge of the circumstances; and any unequivocal manifestation of such a purpose will be as effectual as an express promise or formal declaration.

One who recognizes an unauthorized subscription for stock as valid by an express declaration to that effect, or by an equally expressive silence, is as much bound as if he had assented at the time.[1] In like manner an insurance effected without authority may, when ratified, render the insured liable for the premium and the insurers for the loss,[2] although the ratification does not take place until after the goods or vessel have perished,[3] and the institution of the suit is the only evidence of the intention of the plaintiff to enforce the contract made on his behalf.[4] So a promise to reimburse another for money paid to discharge a debt due by the promisor is legally equivalent to a prior request.[5]

In Doty *v.* Wilson the court held that where the sheriff had been compelled to pay a debt in consequence of the escape of the debtor from custody under an execution, the act was done on behalf of the latter, and he was bound by a subsequent promise of repayment. "When a man," said Thompson, C. J., "pays money for me without my request, and I afterwards agree to his act, this is equivalent to a previous request." The benefit to the defendant coupled with his express promise amounts to a previous request, and renders the payment one made on his behalf, and for which he is willing to be answerable.

In Smith *v.* Plummer,[6] a contract made for the benefit of the defendants was held in like manner to have been ratified by their giving it in evidence as a defence to a suit brought contrary to its terms.

In Hassinger *v.* Solms,[7] an agent who had taken up a note indorsed by his principal contrary to the express orders of the

[1] Phila. W. & B. R. R. Co. *v.* Cowell, 4 Casey, 329.

[2] Lucena *v.* Craufurd, 1 Taunt. 325; Stirling *v.* Vaughan, 11 East, 619; Flemming *v.* Ins. Co., 4 Whart. 59.

[3] Hagedorn *v.* Oliverson, 2 M. & S. 485.

[4] Flemming *v.* Ins. Co., 4 Whart. 59; 2 Am. Leading Cases, 844.

[5] Doty *v.* Wilson, 14 Johns. 378.

[6] 5 Whart. 89.

[7] 5 S. & R. 4, 8.

latter, by giving a new note in his own name was held entitled to enforce a subsequent promise of indemnity, which was said to operate as a ratification of the act of the agent. And while the unauthorized payment of a debt will not place the debtor under an obligation to the person by whom the payment was made, he cannot set it up as a defence to a suit brought by the creditor without incurring a liability for money laid out and expended for his use.[1]

The ratification need not be express, but may be implied from facts or circumstances, or even from the failure of the person for whose benefit the act was done to dissent, when duly notified.[2] Silence, it is said, may give consent, and a man who does not speak when the occasion requires it will not be allowed to object subsequently.[3] This is universally conceded when the defect consists in an excess and not in an entire want of power,[4] and may be equally true when a stranger intervenes from motives of friendship or benevolence. The question arose in Phila. W. & B. R. R. Co. *v.* Cowell, under the following circumstances: The plaintiff, who resided in England, brought suit in Philadelphia against the railroad company for the dividends accruing on his stock, and the defence was that they had been applied in payment of other stock which had been subscribed for by Mr. Charles H. Fisher in the plaintiff's name. It appeared that Mr. Fisher was not the plaintiff's agent, and had no business connection with him, but made the subscription in the belief that it would be equally beneficial to him and to the railroad company. Mr. Fisher wrote immediately to inform the plaintiff of what had been done, but received no reply, and the plaintiff finally after the lapse of seven years claimed the dividends on the stock which he originally held. It was contended on his behalf that inasmuch as Mr. Fisher's intervention was gratuitous, he might stand aloof

1 Accarias ii. No. 690, p. 692; Carter *v.* Black, 4 Dev. & Bat. 425; Jones *v.* Broadhurst, 9 C. B. 173; Belshaw *v.* Bush, 11 id. 191; James *v.* Isaacs, 12 C. B. 791; 2 Leading Cases in Equity, 3 Am. ed. 231.

2 Breed *v.* The Bank, 4 Col. 481; Brigham *v.* Peters, 1 Gray, 139, 141.

3 Phila. W. & B. R. R. Co. *v.* Cowell, 4 Casey, 329.

4 Kentucky Bank *v.* Combs, 7 Barr, 543; Brigham *v.* Peters, 1 Gray, 139.

and allow the act to pass in silence. The court, however, was of opinion that although this might vary the aspect of the case, and weaken the inference to be drawn from the plaintiff's silence, it was still evidence from which the jury might infer that he had ratified the subscription. "The prior relations of the parties," said Woodward, J., in delivering judgment, "may lend an importance to the fact of silence, but it is a mistake to make the competency of the fact depend on those relations. I am aware that Livermore[1] cites with approbation the opinion of civil-law writers that when a volunteer has officiously interfered in the affairs of another person, and made a contract for him without any color of authority, such other person is not bound to answer a letter from the intermeddler informing him of the contract made in his name, nor is his silence to be construed into ratification. But it is to be remembered that such writers are not laying down a rule of evidence to govern trial by jury, but are declaring rather the effect upon the judicial mind of the party's silence. It is one thing to say that the law will not imply a ratification from silence, and a very different thing to say that silence is not a circumstance from which with others a jury might imply it."

A body corporate may equally with an individual be bound by acquiescence in the acts of an unauthorized agent; and it has been held in Pennsylvania that such a ratification may be presumed from the failure of the directors of a bank to object to a contract made by one of their members, and on which the plaintiff has acted, although while the directors were personally cognizant of what occurred, they had no notice of it while sitting as a board.[2]

In the case last cited Williams, J., observed: "The law is well settled that a principal who neglects promptly to disavow an act of his agent by which the latter has transcended his authority, makes the act his own,[3] and the maxim which makes ratification equivalent to a precedent authority is as

[1] 1 Livermore on Agency, 50.

[2] Bank of Pennsylvania *v.* Reed, 1 W. & S. 101; Kelsey *v.* The Bank, 19 P. F. S. 426.

[3] Bredin *v.* Dubarry, 14 S. & R. 27, 30.

much predicable of ratification by a corporation as it is of ratification by any other principal; and it is equally to be presumed from the absence of dissent.[1] It was accordingly held in The Bank of Pennsylvania *v.* Reed,[2] that though the authority of a cashier does not extend so far as to justify him in altering the nature of the debts due the bank, or in changing the relation of the bank from that of a creditor to that of an agent of its debtor, yet a subsequent acquiescence of the bank in such an exercise of power would be conclusive upon it. In delivering the opinion of the court Rogers, J., said: 'It is a very clear and salutary rule in relation to agencies, that when the principal with a knowledge of all the facts adopts or acquiesces in the acts done under an assumed agency, he cannot be heard afterwards to impeach them under the pretence that they were done without authority, or even contrary to instructions: *omnis ratihabitio mandato æquiparatur.* When the principal has been informed of what has been done, he must dissent and give notice of it in a reasonable time; and if he does not, his assent and ratification will be presumed.' If, then, the directors of the bank were informed that the cashier had offered the reward, it was their duty promptly to disavow the act if they did not intend that the bank should be bound by it. If they had notice of the offer, and did not dissent from it, their assent and ratification must be presumed. Nor was it necessary, in order to bind the bank by their acquiescence, that notice should have been given to the directors when sitting in their official capacity as a board. If they were personally cognisant of the offer made by the cashier, it was their duty to call a meeting of the board, and disavow the act, if they were unwilling that the bank should be bound by it. It would be unjust to permit the plaintiff to spend his time and money for the detection of the thief on the faith of the promised reward, and then to repudiate the offer as unauthorized when he had succeeded in apprehending the thief and restoring to the bank the stolen securities found on his person."

To make a ratification effectual it must be of some act done

[1] Gordon *v.* Preston, 1 Watts, 385.

[2] 1 W. & S. 101.

or engagement made for or on behalf of the person whom it is alleged to bind.[1] A plaintiff in an execution will not therefore render himself answerable for a levy on the goods of a third person by accepting the proceeds with a knowledge of the mistake, because the sheriff does not act on his behalf, but as a public agent.[2]

It follows that an act done by another in his own behalf does not admit of ratification, unless it was ordered or requested by some one professing to represent the person whom it is sought to bind. A ratification will not supply the want of a request unless the plaintiff claims as an agent, and not as a contractor. Hence a carpenter who makes repairs under a contract with the tenant, cannot rely on a subsequent promise by the landlord, as a ground for charging him; and so of the unauthorized erection of a building on another's land. For like reasons a payment by a third person under a mistaken impression that the debt is his, cannot be ratified or set up as a defence by the debtor.[3]

In Cummings *v.* Klapp, the court said: "The rule that a ratification is equivalent to a command is exclusively applicable to acts done in the principal's name, otherwise an act confessedly tortious might be ratified by obtaining the sanction of him who has the right." This view does not conflict with what would seem to be the prevailing opinion, that one who distrains avowedly as the agent or bailiff of another may justify under a subsequent command or ratification, although he had no such authority when the distress was made.[4]

[1] See Watson *v.* Swann, 11 C. B. N. S. 756; Buron *v.* Denman, 2 Ex. 167; Wilson *v.* Tummon, 6 Scott, 894, 6 M. & G. 236; De Bolle *v.* The Ins. Co., 4 Whart. 68; Whitehead *v.* Peck, 1 Kelly, 140; James *v.* Isaacs, 12 C. B. 791; Pittsburg & S. R. R. Co. *v.* Gazzam, 8 Casey, 340; Ehle *v.* Judson, 25 Wend. 97; Cummings *v.* Klapp, 5 W. & S. 511; 1 Sm. L. C. 8 Am. ed. 683.

[2] Wilson *v.* Tummon, 6 M. & G. 236.

[3] Merryman *v.* The State, 5 Har. & Johns. 428; Lucas *v.* Wilkinson, 1 H. & N. 420; Kemp *v.* Ball, 10 Ex. 307; Accarias, ii. No. 690, p. 692.

[4] Lamb *v.* Mills, 4 Mod. 377; Trevillian *v.* Pine, 11 Mod. 112; Buron *v.* Denman, 2 Ex. 167, 188.

The question was considered in an anonymous case in Godbolt's Reports, 109, which reads as follows: "In trespass the defendant did justify as bailiff unto another. The plaintiff replied that he took the cattle of his own wrong without that he was bailiff. Anderson, J.: 'If one have cause to distrain my goods, and a stranger of his own wrong without any warrant or authority given him by the other, take my goods not as bailiff or servant to the other, and I bring an action of trespass against him, can he excuse himself by saying that he did it as my bailiff or servant? Can he so father his misdemeanors upon another? He cannot; for once he was a trespasser and his intent was manifest. But if one distrain as bailiff, although in truth he is not bailiff, if after he in whose right he doth it doth assent, he shall not be punished as a trespasser; for that assent shall have a relation unto the time of the distress taken, and so is the book of 7 Henry IV.'"

It might be inferred from the language used in this instance, that an act is not susceptible of ratification unless it is done professedly for and on behalf of the person by whom it is adopted or confirmed. Such a rule must, however, be taken with some qualifications.[1] The distinction seems to be between acts done adversely and contracts.

A ratification cannot operate retroactively to defeat or vary an existing right or remedy, nor will it be allowed to make an act which was tortious when done, lawful.[2] Hence, a wrongful act will not cease to be such on being adopted by a third person, although he is one by whom it might rightfully have been performed, unless the doer was not only acting in his behalf but so declared at the time. There is no such reason why a contract should not be ratified by an undisclosed principal, because the effect is to bind him without discharging the agent. There can be no doubt under the authorities that if one buys or sells for me I may enforce the contract, although made by him in his own name, and without disclosing that he is an agent; and the principle is the same whether I authorize

[1] See Watson *v.* Swann, 11 C. B. N. S. 756.

[2] Buron *v.* Denman, 2 Ex. 167; Bird *v.* Brown, 4 id. 786; 1 Sm. L. C. 7 Am. ed. 292.

him in the first instance or ratify what he does subsequently.[1] The material question is not, Was the agent known to be such? but, Did he intend that the principal should be bound by and entitled to the benefit of the contract?[2]

The line was clearly drawn as follows in Bird *v.* Brown:[3]—

The doctrine, *omnis ratihabitio retrotrahitur et mandato æquiparatur*, is one intelligible in principle, and easy in its application when applied to cases of contract. If A. B., unauthorized by me, makes a contract on my behalf with J. S., which I afterward recognize and adopt, there is no difficulty in dealing with it as having been originally made by my authority. J. S. entered into the contract on the understanding that he was dealing with me, and when I afterwards agreed to admit that such was the case, J. S. is precisely in the condition in which he meant to be; or, if he did not believe A. B. to be acting for me, his condition is not altered by my adoption of the agency, for he may sue A. B. as principal, at his option, and has the same equities against me, if I sue, which he would have had against A. B.

In cases of tort, there is more difficulty. If A. B., professing to act by my authority, does that which *prima facie* amounts to a trespass, and I afterward assent to and adopt his act, there he is treated as having from the beginning acted by my authority, and I become a trespasser, unless I can justify the act, which is to be deemed as having been done by my previous sanction. So far there is no difficulty in applying the doctrine of ratification even in cases of tort. The party ratifying becomes as it were a trepasser by estoppel, he cannot complain that he is deemed to have authorized that which he admits himself to have authorized.

But the authorities go much further, and show that in some cases where an act which, if unauthorized, would amount to a trespass, has been done in the name and on behalf of another

[1] Bird *v.* Brown, 4 Ex. 786, 798.

[2] See Ford *v.* Williams, 21 How. 287; George *v.* Claggett, 7 T. R. 359; Ford *v.* Williams, 21 How. 287; Thomson *v.* Davenport, 9 B. & C. 78; Peterson *v.* Ayre, 13 C. B. 353.

[3] 4 Ex. 798.

but without previous authority, the subsequent ratification may enable the party on whose behalf the act was done to take advantage of it and to treat it as having been done by his direction. But this doctrine must be taken with the qualification, that the act of ratification must take place at a time and under circumstances when the ratifying party might himself have lawfully done the act which he ratifies. Thus, in Lord Audeley's case,[1] a fine with proclamation was levied of certain land, and a stranger within five years afterwards, in the name of him who had right, entered to avoid the fine. After the five years, and not before, the party who had the right to the land ratified and confirmed the act of the stranger. This was held to be inoperative; though such ratification within the five years would probably have been good. Now, the principle of this case, which is reported in many books, and is cited with approbation by Lord Coke, in Margaret Podger's case,[2] appears to us to govern the present. There the entry, to be good, must have been made within the five years; it was made within that time, but till ratified it was merely the act of a stranger, and so had no operation against the fine. By the ratification it became the act of the party in whose name it was made; but that was not till after the five years. He could not be deemed to have made an entry till he ratified the previous entry, and he did not ratify until it was too late to do so. In the present case the stoppage could only be made during the transitus. During that period the defendants without authority from the consignor, Illius, made the stoppage. After the transitus was ended, Illius ratified what the defendants had done. From that time, the stoppage was the act of Illius, but it was then too late for him to stop. The goods had already become the property of the plaintiffs free from all right of stoppage.

It follows that since a stoppage *in transitu* must, as the name implies, take place while the goods are on the way, it cannot be ratified after they have been delivered to the consignee or an agent who receives them on his behalf, nor will the

[1] Croke Eliz. 561, Moore, 457, Poph. 176, nom. Lord Audeley's Case.
[2] 9 Rep. 104 a.

ratification invalidate an intermediate indorsement or delivery of the bill of lading to a *bona fide* purchaser.[1]

In like manner an unauthorized notice to quit cannot be ratified by the landlord subsequently to the period at which the notice would have been valid if coming directly from him,[2] but the objection does not apply when the purpose is to vindicate or enforce the right of a third person, who adopts that which he might equally well perform.

Whatever doubt may exist on this point, the authorities concur that the contract must have been in fact made on behalf of him who adopts or seeks to enforce it as his own; or, as the rule was stated in Watson *v.* Swann,[3] he must be one who could have been ascertained at the time as the person intended to be benefited by the contract.[4] It follows that one cannot ratify or enforce a policy of insurance without showing that it was intended to cover and protect his interest in the property at risk.[5] The contract need not be made by the agent as such. He may contract as a principal, and then prove that he was acting on behalf of another who has since ratified the contract; but one who performs an act that would be tortious if done in his own right without naming his principal, cannot escape liability by fathering the act on a third person who has the right. A man who distrains as my bailiff need not have authority from me at the time, but he must profess to be acting for me or the distress will be insusceptible of ratification, and no subsequent adoption of the act on my part will protect him from liability as a trespasser.[6]

The contract must moreover be such that it may inure to the use of the party by whom it is adopted. A contract to indemnify A cannot be ratified or enforced by B, although he is the only party interested, and A was in fact acting on B's behalf or made the contract for his benefit. Hence an insur-

[1] Bird *v.* Brown, 4 Ex. 786, 798.

[2] Right *v.* Cathall, 5 East, 491; Doe *v.* Walter, 10 B. & C. 626.

[3] C. B. N. S. 756.

[4] 1 Sm. L. C. 684.

[5] De Bolle *v.* The Ins. Co., 4 Whart. 68; Steele *v.* The Ins. Co., 5 Harris, 296; 2 Am. Leading Cases, 845.

[6] Anon. Godb. 109; Buron *v.* Denman, 2 Ex. 167. See 2 Am. Leading Cases, 845.

ance cannot avail for the protection of one who is not named in the policy, unless it contains the words "for whom it may concern," although such was the intention of the person by whom the insurance was effected.[1]

It is obvious from what has been said that the question whether an act admits of ratification is one which may easily give rise to controversy. Goods are furnished or money lent to a child or wife, and the father or husband promises indemnity or compensation: is such a case within the rule that ratification may supply the want of a request? The answer should, as it seems, depend on whether the contract was made or order given in the name of the defendant, or with an assurance that he would assume the debt or be answerable for its payment. If it was, the ratification will relate back and may be enforced by suit.

In Hassinger *v.* Solms,[2] the plaintiff had guaranteed a note of a third person at the defendant's request, and the latter said that if the note was renewed the plaintiff must not look to him for reimbursement. Such a renewal was, however, effected with the plaintiff's guaranty and an additional indorser, but without the defendant's knowledge, and the latter when told what had been done said that it made no matter; the indorser was as good as the bank, and he would save the plaintiff harmless. The plaintiff was finally compelled to take up the note, and sued the defendant for money laid out at his request. Tilghman, C. J., said, in delivering judgment, that it had been contended that the defendant was a mere stranger to the plaintiff's act in effecting the renewal, and that it was not done on his behalf. This conclusion was not warranted by the evidence. The renewal of the note with an additional security might be advantageous to the defendant, or might occasion the loss of the debt. Whether beneficial or injurious, it was contrary to his instructions and might have been disavowed. He had, however, chosen to affirm it by a deliberate promise, and the ratification operated as a request. It was immaterial that the renewal was effected in the plaintiff's name if the act was in truth done on behalf of and for the benefit of

[1] Finney *v.* The Ins. Co., 8 Met. 348.

[2] 5 S. & R. 4.

the defendant. Gibson, J., dissented from the opinion of the court, on the ground that there was no evidence that the plaintiff had renewed the note as the defendant's agent. An act done as another's agent might be ratified, but the rule did not apply where the doer was acting for himself. If the verdict was allowed to stand, a jury might presume a previous request in every instance where an act apparently beneficial became the foundation of a subsequent promise.

The conclusion reached by the majority seems to be correct. Duly considered the question comes to this: Does a surety forfeit the right to indemnity by giving time without the assent, or contrary to the instructions of the principal? and there can be little doubt as to the reply unless the principal is prejudiced by the delay. In Doty *v.* Wilson,[1] the payment by the sheriff of a debt for which he had become answerable through the escape of the defendant, was in like manner held to be susceptible of ratification by the party whose obligation was discharged, notwithstanding the objection that the payment was not made in his name, or designed to benefit him. The court said that the case was clearly one where a subsequent promise might supply the want of an authority or request. This decision should, however, apparently be referred to the familiar principle that when a man is compelled to assume a burden through the default of another for which the latter is primarily liable, the law will imply a promise of indemnification. In this aspect, however, the express promise was unnecessary, and a recovery might have been had without it.

Ratification cannot be effectual unless the contract is so far complete as to bind the agent, or at the least render him answerable to the party with whom he deals, should it not be adopted by the principal. A man who effects an insurance on my behalf without an authority from me is liable for the premium, and the insurers are not prejudiced by my adoption of the contract, which gives them an additional remedy without varying their position relatively to the agent;[2] but no such liability results from an unauthorized payment on a contract

[1] 14 Johns. 378.

[2] Bird *v.* Brown, 4 Ex. 798.

which neither binds me nor the person who assumes to be my agent. He who pays does not intend to contract, but simply to give effect to a contract which he ignorantly supposes to exist, and as there is no mutual obligation the insurers are also free.[1] In the case first cited a man became extremely ill while he was negotiating for an insurance on his life, and a friend paid the premium without his knowledge or informing the insurers that he was at the point of death. The court held the concealment fraudulent, and that the policy could not be enforced by his executors.

Miller, J., said that down to the time of the payment there had been nothing more than negotiations, and there was no meeting of the minds. The amount and time of payment were still under consideration. To hold that when he was *in extremis* an hour or two before he breathed his last, a friend could pay this small sum to an agent of the company, without the agent or the company having any idea of the condition of the dying man, and thus secure an obligation to pay his administrator $5000 within sixty or ninety days, is to affirm that one party to a negotiation can delay his assent to the terms of the contract until the changes of fortune enable him to reap all the benefits, and throw all the losses on the other side, and then, for the first time, do what was necessary on his part to make the contract obligatory.

The case of Whiting *v.* The Massachusetts Insurance Company is not so clear. An application for a life insurance was accepted and the policy delivered early in May, with a request that the insured would send the premium. The policy was conditioned not to take effect "unless the advance premium was paid during the lifetime of the insured." The request for payment was renewed by letter on the 21st of May; but the insured had in the mean time been taken dangerously ill, and his sister made the payment with his money without informing him. He died on the 27th, and his executors brought a suit on the policy, which was dismissed on the following grounds: Had he made the first annual payment, the second

[1] Piedmont Life Ins. Co. *v.* Ewing, 92 U. S. 377; Whiting *v.* Mass. Ins. Co., 129 Mass. 240.

might have been paid by a stranger on his behalf; but as the case stood there was no contract, and therefore nothing that was susceptible of ratification. Moreover, the payment came too late. A man was not entitled to wait until he was *in extremis* before determining whether he would take advantage of an insurance, and what he could not do or authorize he could not ratify.

It is not easy to coincide with this result. The contract was seemingly complete on the acceptance of the application and delivery of the policy; and if the insurers might have treated a failure to pay the premium as a breach of condition, they might also waive the default and recover the money from the insured. There was therefore seemingly an existing demand against him, and a ground on which a friend or relative might humanely intervene to save a forfeiture. The circumstances repelled instead of warranting the idea that the insured acted fraudulently or with a design to play fast and loose, and when his sister paid the premium his assent might be presumed as to an act done for his benefit, or a ratification by his executors take the place of a command.

It results from what has been said that a forgery does not admit of ratification. One who commits such a crime acts not on behalf of, but against the person whose handwriting he counterfeits, and does not profess to represent or to have been authorized by him, but to affix his very signature and be in fact himself.[1] The subsequent adoption of such an instrument cannot, therefore, supply the authority which the forger did not profess to have. A forged bond or note obviously wants the essentials of a contract, because the intention is not to bring the minds of the obligor and obligee together, but to practise a fraud on both.

In Shisler *v.* Vandike, Gordon, J., said: "The distinction between the cases seems to be this: when the fraud is of such a character as to involve a crime, the ratification of the act from which it springs is opposed to public policy, and hence cannot be permitted; but where the transaction is contrary

[1] McHugh *v.* Schuylkill Co., 17 P. F. S. 391; Shisler *v.* Vandike, 11 Norris, 447.

only to good faith and fair dealing, where it affects individual interests and nothing else, ratification is allowable. It is, indeed, conceded in Pearsoll *v.* Chapin [1] and Negley *v.* Lindsay,[2] that if the original contract be illegal or void for want of consideration, no subsequent ratification will help it. If, however, the indorsement under consideration was forged, it was not only void for want of authority, but it was also illegal, and so comes under the condemnation of all authority." [3]

A like view was taken in the case of Brook *v.* Hook.[4] The defendant's name was forged by one Richard Jones to a joint and several promissory note, purporting to be made in favor of the plaintiff by the defendant and Jones. While the note was current the defendant signed the following memorandum in order to prevent the prosecution of the forger, at the same time denying that the signature to the note was his, or written by his authority: "I hold myself responsible for a bill dated the 7th of November, 1869, for £20, bearing my signature and Richard Jones's, in favor of Mr. Brook." The majority of the court were of opinion (Martin, B., dissenting), that there was no ratification. Kelly, C. B., said: "In all the cases cited for the plaintiff the ratification was of an act pretended to have been done for or under the authority of the party sought to be charged, and such would have been the case here if one had pretended to have been authorized by the defendant to put his name to the note, and that he had signed the note for the defendant accordingly, and had thus induced the plaintiff to take it. In that case, although there had been no previous authority, it would have been competent to the defendant to ratify the act, and the maxim before mentioned would have applied. But here Jones had forged the name of the defendant to the note, and pretended that the signature was the defendant's signature; and there is no instance to be found in the books of such an act being held to have been ratified by a subsequent recognition or statement. Again, in the cases cited, the act done, though unauthorized at the time, was a civil act, and capable of being made good by a subse-

[1] 8 Wr. 9. [2] 17 P. F. S. 217. [3] 11 Norris, 447.
[4] L. R. 6 Ex. 89.

quent recognition or declaration; but no authority is to be found that an act which is itself a criminal offence is capable of ratification."

It has, notwithstanding, been declared in the United States in various instances, that the adoption or recognition of a forged instrument may bind the party whose signature was simulated, and render the obligation as much his as if he had authorized or executed it.[1] Some of these decisions may be referred to the ground of equitable estoppel,—that the defendant had by recognizing the contract as valid, misled the plaintiff, and induced him to relax his efforts for the conviction of the offender or the recovery of the amount due;[2] while in others, the plaintiff had received the proceeds of the forgery, or been benefited in some other way.[3] In The Greenfield Bank *v.* Crafts, however, the Supreme Court of Massachusetts went to the extent of holding that a man who adopts a forged note or bond, or treats it as one by which he is willing to be bound, cannot question it subsequently, although none of the elements of an equitable estoppel are present, and the plaintiff would have no case but for the doctrine of ratification.

It seems that a deed or contract may be susceptible of ratification although executed by one who while professedly acting on behalf of the alleged principal is really practising a fraud on him and intends to convert the proceeds to his own use.

In Garrett *v.* Gonter,[4] the court held, in conformity to this principle, that a mortgage executed under a forged power of attorney during the absence of the mortgagor, might be ratified by her, although she could not have confirmed the power of attorney. "It is," said Strong, J., "hardly accurate to speak of ratifying a forged instrument. It may be adopted, but adoption does not relate back and validate prior acts. If the letter of attorney was forged in 1854 no act of Mrs. Gonter

[1] Fitzpatrick *v.* The Commissioners, 7 Humph. 224; Greenfield Bank *v.* Crafts, 4 Allen, 447.

[2] Forsyth *v.* Day, 46 Me. 176.

[3] Livings *v.* Wiler, 32 Ill. 387; Union Bank *v.* Middlebrook, 33 Conn. 95.

[4] 6 Wright, 143.

in 1859, after her return from Europe, could make it efficient from its date. But she could confirm the mortgage, for that was executed in her name by a professed agent acting under a real or pretended authority. To ratify that required no new consideration from the mortgagee. And if the evidence satisfied the jury that she had ratified it, the plaintiff was entitled to recover even though she had never signed the power of attorney, and though that was forged. It requires no formality to ratify what one has done in another's name under a professed agency; consent to the act, approval of it, are all that is essential." The distinction made in this instance between the forgery of the power of attorney, and the acts done under it and therefore on behalf of the alleged principal, was approved in Shisler *v.* Vandike, but would seem to be logical rather than just. A mortgage executed under cover of a forged authority is itself a forgery, although the agent signed as such, and did not counterfeit the handwriting of the alleged principal. Moreover, the whole is an entire transaction, and no part of it is less essential than the rest or more susceptible of enforcement.

In fictione juris semper existit æquitas. In other words, legal fictions are introduced in furtherance of justice and not to defeat her ends. The principal's confirmation of the act may accordingly be deemed equivalent to a request for the purpose of entitling him under the contract, but will not impose an additional burden on the defendant, or deprive him of any remedy to which he is justly entitled, without substituting an equivalent.[1] An unauthorized entry for the breach of a condition in a lease, or a notice to quit, is therefore insusceptible of ratification, because the landlord might otherwise arbitrarily hold the tenant as such, or treat him as a trespasser.[2] It might seem at first sight as if the ratification of a policy of insurance after the loss was within this principle, but it must be remembered that one who deals with an agent without verifying his authority, trusts solely to his credit, and cannot complain because the contract is enforced by a third person who

[1] Pollock *v.* Cohen, 32 Ohio St. 514.
[2] See Buron *v.* Denman, 2 Ex. 167, 188.

was not originally answerable for the consideration, and would perhaps have declined to pay it had the event been adverse.

The ratification of a tortious act may charge the principal, but will not ordinarily exonerate the agent from any liability that may have resulted from his wrong. In Buron *v.* Denman it was notwithstanding held that a ratification by the Crown of an act done by an individual, may remove the liability from his shoulders and transfer it to the government. The plaintiff was a Portuguese slave-trader, the defendant a captain in the English navy, and the alleged trespass consisted in the destruction of buildings on the coast of Africa in which the plaintiff kept his human merchandise. The controversy lay between an alien seeking redress in the English courts and a commander whose act had been adopted by the government, and consequently depended not merely on the municipal law, but on the law of nations. The case does not therefore justify the inference, that the king's command or ratification will render an act done contrary to the laws of England rightful, or preclude redress for an injury inflicted on an English subject. Such a doctrine would be contrary to the fundamental doctrine that, although the king can do no wrong, his ministers are responsible and cannot rely on his authority as a justification. Parliament may in its omnipotence deprive one who has suffered from a tortious act of the right to compensation in damages, because the statute, even when worded retroactively, operates not on the irrevocable past but on its consequences; but such a ratification is not possible to Congress unless the act is one which they might have authorized consistently with the Constitution of the United States. Such is the rule as between our government and its citizens; but if the United States were to ratify an injury inflicted on a subject of a foreign power, and which if done *flagrante bello* would have been justified by the laws of war, the doer would be exonerated from responsibility, and the sufferer remitted to his own government, which might seek redress through negotiation or an appeal to arms.[1]

[1] See People *v.* McLeod, 25 Wend. 482.

An act of Congress approved March 2, 1857, provides "That all acts,

We have seen that ratification is a confirmation of a contract by giving the assent which was wanting in the first instance, as where one promises to pay a bond or note made in his name by an unauthorized agent.[1] An undertaking to be bound by or answerable under a contract which, though duly made or authorized, has failed in con-

proclamations and orders of the President of the United States, or acts done by his authority or approval after the fourth day of March, Anno Domini eighteen hundred and sixty-one, and before the first day of July, Anno Domini eighteen hundred and sixty-six, respecting martial law, military trials by court-martial, or military commissions, or the arrest, imprisonment, and trial of persons charged with participation in the late rebellion against the United States, or as aidors or abettors thereof, or of any violation of the laws or usages of war, or of affording aid and comfort to rebels against the authority of the United States, and all proceedings and acts done or had by courts-martial, or military commissions, or arrests or imprisonment made in the premises by any person by the authority of the orders or proclamations of the President, made as aforesaid, or in aid thereof, are hereby approved in all respects, legalized, and made valid to the same extent and with the same effect as if said orders and proclamations had been issued and made, and said arrests, imprisonments, proceedings, and acts had been done under the previous express authority and direction of the Congress of the United States, and in pursuance of a law thereof previously enacted and expressly authorizing and directing the same to be done. And no civil court of the United States, or of any State, or of the District of Columbia, or of any district or territory of the United States, shall have or take jurisdiction of, or in any manner reverse any of the proceedings had or acts done as aforesaid, nor shall any person be held to answer in any of said courts for any act done or omitted to be done in pursuance or in aid of any of said proclamations or orders, or by authority or with the approval of the President within the period aforesaid, and respecting any of the matters aforesaid; and all officers and other persons in the service of the United States, or who acted in aid thereof, acting in the premises shall be held *prima facie* to have been authorized by the President." — 14 U. S. Stat. at Large, 432.

The doctrine that a ratification is equivalent to command has never been carried further than in this instance. If the statute is constitutional, Congress is as all powerful as Parliament, and may put the military power above the civil not only where war actually exists, and at places occupied by the hostile or contending forces, but throughout the country, and in districts where the courts are open and the ordinary course of life undisturbed.

[1] Day *v.* McAllister, 15 Gray, 433; Garrett *v.* Gonter, 6 Wr. 143.

sequence of the disability of one or more of the parties, or through some positive rule of law, rests on a different principle, — that every one may forego a right introduced for his own benefit, and that can be relinquished without prejudice to the community at large.[1] A subsequent promise may, accordingly, operate as a waiver of a defence that would otherwise be valid. There must, nevertheless, in every such case, be a foundation on which to build. One cannot render a contract without consideration valid by promising not to take advantage of the want of consideration:[2] and so of a contract which is contrary to the policy of the law.[3] When, however, a consideration moves from the plaintiff under circumstances which would render the defendant liable but for some positive rule of law, he may affirm the contract by a subsequent promise. Accordingly where a statute gives a defence to a contract without extinguishing the debt, the liability may be revived by a new promise. The debtor is under these circumstances the judge in his own case, and if he thinks fit to waive the protection given by the law, by an unqualified acknowledgment of liability, he cannot change his mind subsequently, to the injury of the creditor. The promise does not, however, impose a new obligation, it merely revives that arising out of the original contract between the parties. Such is the well-known case of a promise to pay a debt barred by the statute of limitation,[4] or a discharge in bankruptcy.[5] The promise may fall short of the original obligation, and be qualified where that was absolute, but it cannot impose a new or a different liability. A promise by a bankrupt to pay when able is accordingly binding if he has the means; but a pecuniary demand

[1] Yaw *v.* Kerr, 11 Wr. 333. [2] Belknap *v.* Bender, 75 N. Y. 451.

[3] Shisler *v.* Vandike, 11 Norris, 447.

[4] Wennall *v.* Adney, 3 Bos. & P. 247; Kingston *v.* Wharton, 2 S. & R. 208; Maxim *v.* Morse, 8 Mass. 127; Yates *v.* Hollingsworth, 5 Har. & J. 216; Walbridge *v.* Harroon, 18 Vt. 448; Farmers' and Mechanics' Bank *v.* Flint, 17 id. 508; Johnson *v.* Evans, 8 Gill, 155; Ross *v.* Ross, 20 Ala. 105; Phelps *v.* Williamson, 26 Vt. 230; 1 Sm. L. C. 8 Am. ed. 988; Turner *v.* Chrisman, 20 Ohio, 332.

[5] Trueman *v.* Fenton, Cowp. 544; Field's Estate, 2 Rawle, 351; Bolton *v.* King, 105 Pa. 78; 1 Sm. L. C. 8 Am. ed. 1462.

will not be revived by a promise to pay in goods or services.[1] The principle was accurately stated by Woodward, C. J., in Yaw *v.* Kerr:[2] "With us the action is always brought on the original undertaking, and when the statute is pleaded, the new promise is proved, not to raise a cause of action, but to show that the legal objection to the old promise has been waived. The plea of the statute is addressed not to the contract but to the remedy. 'I admit the promise and contract,' is its language in effect; 'but you delayed your suit so long that you cannot maintain it after six years.' The reply in substance is, 'True, there is such a rule of law, but you waived it by renewing your promise within six years, and therefore it cannot avail you to defeat my action.' In this manner the action is withdrawn from the operation of the statute. But the action on what? Obviously and always, the action on the original undertaking. Thus we avoid all tanglements about the consideration of the new promise. It needs no consideration, for it is not sued upon." The rule is now established on this basis in England, and generally in the United States.[3]

It has, notwithstanding, been decided in Pennsylvania that the doctrine of waiver is inapplicable to demands that have been barred by a discharge in bankruptcy.[4] In the opinion of the court the original obligation is, under these circumstances, entirely gone, and all that remains is a moral obligation to satisfy a creditor who has not received his due, which may acquire legal force from an express promise to fulfil it. The suit must, consequently, be brought on the new contract, and a declaration on the former cause of action will fail at the trial, on the ground of variance. For like reasons a promise will not revive an agreement under seal, or entitle it to rank as a specialty, and the suit must be brought in assumpsit and not in covenant.[5]

A certificate in bankruptcy would, nevertheless, appear to be as much within the rule that every one may waive a privi-

[1] Reeves *v.* Hearne, 1 M. & W. 323; Earle *v.* Oliver, 2 Ex. 71; 1 Sm. L. C. 7 Am. ed. 962, 998; Kaye *v.* Dutton, 7 M. & G. 807.

[2] 11 Wr. 333.

[3] Yaw *v.* Kerr, 11 Wr. 333.

[4] Bolton *v.* King, 105 Pa. 78.

[5] Fields' Estate, 2 Rawle, 351.

lege given for his benefit, as the bar of the statute of limitations. Both statutes confer legal exemptions from demands which subsist in morals, and will if the defence be not duly interposed, be enforced by the courts. If the party entitled to avail himself of the exemption waives it expressly by a promise, or tacitly by omitting to put it on record by a plea, the effect is the same as regards the matter in controversy as if the certificate of discharge had not been granted, or the six years had not elapsed. The statute operates not on the right, but on the remedy, or rather leaves the question to the debtor's conscience, and if that decides that the right subsists, and the judgment is unequivocally declared by a promise, the right stands as it did in the first instance, and the law will give it effect. It is immaterial that the agreement originally made was in writing and under seal, or was a promissory note, and the subsequent promise oral, because the promise does not vary the cause of action and simply shuts out the defence. We may, therefore, believe with the court below in Field's Estate,[1] that upon a promise after bankruptcy to pay a bond-debt, and where the only consideration for the promise is the old debt, the promisee must recover upon his bond, or he cannot recover at all.

It has been held on like grounds that a contract for the sale and delivery of goods, or to do any other specific act, cannot be taken out of the statute by an undertaking to that effect, because the declaration in such cases is necessarily special on the promise originally made, and the new promise cannot be given in evidence without a variance.[2] Such, undoubtedly, is the true inference if the new promise is viewed as a contract, but not if it should be regarded as a waiver of the right to rely on the lapse of time as a defence.[3]

There is no substantial difference as regards principle where the plaintiff has sustained a detriment, or conferred a benefit on the defendant at the request of the latter, but under circumstances which do not give rise to an implied promise, or

[1] 2 Rawle, 351, 353. [2] Suter *v.* Sheeler, 10 Harris, 308, 310.

[3] Whitehead *v.* Howard, 2 Brod. & Bing. 372; Boydell *v.* Drummond, 2 Campb. 157; Wetzell *v.* Bussard, 11 Wheat. 309; Titus *v.* Ash, 4 Foster, 319.

more accurately where such a promise does not arise in consequence of some legal rule or disability;[1] and the defendant may consequently bind himself by an express promise after the circumstances have undergone a change, or the disability which prevented the obligation from arising has ceased.[2] A promise by one who has been restored to reason to pay for services rendered while he was insane, is within this principle; and so is a promise by a woman after the death of her husband, to make compensation for work done, or money lent at her request during coverture.[3] For where the law would imply a promise if the party were able to contract, he may bind himself by an express agreement on becoming *sui juris*. This would seem to be the true foundation of the doctrine and not that of the moral obligation on which it is sometimes based.[4] A woman who has regained her freedom of action is obviously entitled to waive the disability imposed for her protection during coverture, and may be precluded from setting aside a lease or conveyance made by her husband by ratifying or benefiting by it after his death.[5] The danger incident to oral evidence does not affect the principle, and the legislature may guard against it by requiring the promise to be in writing. It is not material in this aspect of the question whether the consideration moves to the *feme covert*, or to some one else whom she desires to benefit; and a woman may consequently be bound by a promise to pay a note given as a security for money advanced to her husband.[6] In this instance, however, the wife had a separate estate which would have been liable in equity,[7] and she might, therefore, with more reason be made personally answerable at law.

The courts originally held that a contract by a married

[1] Yaw *v.* Kerr, 11 Wr. 333.

[2] Flight *v.* Reed, 1 H. & C. 703.

[3] Lee *v.* Muggeridge, 5 Taunt. 36; Hemphill *v.* McClimans, 12 Harris, 367; Brown *v.* Bennett, 25 P. F. S. 420; Trout *v.* McDonald, 2 Norris, 144; Wilson *v.* Burr, 25 Wend. 386; Goulding *v.* Davidson, 26 N. Y. 604.

[4] Paul *v.* Stackhouse, 2 Wr. 302; Hatchell *v.* Odom, 2 Dev. & Bat. 302.

[5] Brown *v.* Bennett, Cowp. 201; Trueman *v.* Fenton, id. 544.

[6] Vance *v.* Wells, 8 Ala. 399.

[7] Forrest *v.* Robinson, 4 Porter, 44; Sadler *v.* Houston, id. 208; 1 Leading Cases in Equity, 5 Am. ed. 742.

woman was merely void, and could not be rendered obligatory by a promise made after the termination of the coverture.[1] This view still prevails in North Carolina and other states.[2] And as the theory of a moral consideration has been discarded, it seems doubtful whether Lee *v.* Muggeridge would now be followed in England.[3] The better opinion nevertheless, seems to be that as all the elements of a valid contract would be present, but for the disability resulting from the defendant's coverture, if she chooses to cure the defect after she has become *sui juris*, there is no reason why the obligation should not be enforced.[4] In La Touche *v.* La Touche,[5] a promissory note given by a married woman for advances made to her husband, was said to be a good consideration for another note made after his death, because her separate estate was bound, and the equitable liability upheld the promise.

A promise by a drawer or indorser to pay a bill or note from which he has been discharged by a failure to present the instrument in due season, or to give notice of dishonor, will preclude the promisor from taking advantage of the *laches* of the holder.[6] To render such a waiver valid it should, however, appear inferentially or by direct proof that the defendant was aware of the facts constituting the defence;[7] it being well settled that a waiver or ratification by one who is ignorant of any material fact or circumstance is nugatory, and leaves the parties precisely where they were before.[8]

Although a man may waive a defence given for his benefit, he is not entitled to vary the settled policy of the law, or set aside a rule which has been established for the protection of the community at large, and a ratification of an illegal con-

[1] Lloyd *v.* Lee, 1 Strange, 94; Goulding *v.* Davidson, 26 N. Y. 604.

[2] Jones *v.* Reed, 9 N. C. 269; Hazard *v.* Barker, 52 Vt. 429; Howe *v.* Wildes, 34 Me. 566.

[3] Eastwood *v.* Kenyon, 11 A. & E. 438.

[4] Paul *v.* Stackhouse, 2 Wr. 302, 306.

[5] 3 H. & C. 576.

[6] Tebbetts *v.* Dowd, 23 Wend. 379; Long *v.* Crawford, 18 Md. 220; Hughes *v.* Bowen, 15 Ia. 446.

[7] Arnold *v.* Dresser, 8 Allen, 435; Hughes *v.* Bowen, 15 Ia. 446.

[8] 1 Am. Leading Cases, 5 ed. 720.

tract is tainted with the vice of the original transaction, and is invalid. A promise to pay a gaming debt, or for value received under a contract in fraud of the revenue, is within this principle, and so of an attempted confirmation of a contract made and carried into effect on Sunday contrary to a statute.[1]

Agreeably to the view taken in England and generally in the United States, a usurious contract is in like manner not merely voidable but so entirely void that it cannot be confirmed by the most formal promise or an agreement under seal. This is simply because the parties are bound by the legislative prohibition, and have no more right to set it aside subsequently than to disregard it at the time. If, however, the debtor and creditor come together and rescind the usurious agreement, the statute is no longer applicable, and a promise to return the amount actually received may be valid.[2] This has been said to depend on the moral obligation of the borrower to reimburse the lender, but properly falls under the rule that an express promise may revive a precedent good consideration, which might have been enforced through an implied promise but for the intervention of some positive rule of law. The disability arising from a prohibitory statute may in like manner be repealed, and the contract then become susceptible of confirmation though illegal when first made. In Flight *v.* Reed,[3] a bill of exchange given after the repeal of the statutes against usury, in renewal of a usurious note executed when the prohibition was in force, was accordingly held to be a valid cause of action, notwithstanding the objection that as the original security was void, it could not be a consideration for a subsequent promise. The court said: "Such a consideration has sometimes been called a moral consideration, and we think unfortunately so; for the term used as a definition tends to include too wide a range of subjects. And there are many conjunctures in which a man may feel himself morally bound

[1] Haydock *v.* Tracy, 3 W. & S. 507; Foreman *v.* Ahl, 5 P. F. S. 325.

[2] Barnes *v.* Hedly, 2 Taunt. 184; Goulding *v.* Davidson, 26 N. Y. 604, 606; Hammond *v.* Hopping, 13 Wend. 505; Miller *v.* Hull, 4 Den. 104; see Flight *v.* Reed, 1 H. & C. 703, 718.

[3] 1 H. & C. 703.

to pay, and to promise to do so, which the law would not recognize as a good consideration. But a loan of money is a very different thing. The very name of a loan imports that it was the understanding and intention of both parties that the money should be repaid. And though at the time of the advance, the law, for reasons of public policy, forbids any liability and incapacitates the parties from making a binding contract, there is no reason why a binding contract should not be made afterwards if the legal prohibition be removed. And the consideration, which would have been sufficient to support the promise if the law had not forbidden the promise to be made originally, does not cease to be sufficient when the legal restriction is abrogated. There is, therefore, it seems to us, reasonable ground for this qualified proposition, namely, that a man by express promise may render himself liable to pay back money which he has received as a loan, through some positive rule of law or statute intervened at the time to prevent the transaction from constituting a legal debt."

When, however, a prohibitory law is still in force and invalidates the contract as originally made, the defect cannot be cured by a subsequent promise or ratification. The question arose in Day *v.* McAllister.[1] The plaintiff sued on a promissory note; and the defence was that it was made on the Lord's Day and therefore void. At the trial in the Common Pleas, Bishop, J., declined to instruct the jury that, although the note was made on the Lord's Day, the action might still be maintained if the defendant had by any subsequent promise or act on a week-day ratified the note; and that if the defendant retained the property for which the note was given, treated it as his own, or disposed of it, or of part of it and received the money therefor, it was evidence tending to show such ratification. A verdict was returned for the defendant, and the plaintiff alleged exceptions. Hoar, J., said the contract on which the plaintiff declares being an illegal contract, expressly prohibited by statute, will not support an action.[2]

[1] 15 Gray, 433.

[2] Bayley *v.* Taber, 6 Mass. 451; Pattee *v.* Greely, 13 Met. 284; Merriam *v.* Stearns, 10 Cush. 257.

It has no legal force or obligation. No repudiation by a formal act was necessary to render it inoperative. It had no partial validity such as would make it capable of a subsequent completion. The statute which prohibited it was not designed merely for the protection of the defendant, giving him a personal privilege which he might waive, but rested on the grounds of broad public policy.

The defendant could not ratify the illegal contract, because its want of validity did not depend in any degree on his choice. The law annulled it, and there was no subject of ratification. He might make a new one; but any arrangement or agreement between the parties on any subsequent day, whether direct and express or implied from their dealings with each other's property, would be a new and independent transaction. It was not quite accurate to speak of the ratification by a party of something which the law forbade, and which was made void, not for want of full consent, but in spite of it.[1] The distinction was observed in Williams *v.* Paul,[2] and in the decision of the recent case of Stebbins *v.* Peck.[3] In the latter case the word "ratification" was used, but it was in connection with the word "adoption," and was not intended, as the context showed, to give any countenance to the idea that the contract could be made valid, *ab initio*, by any subsequent agreement between the parties.

A contract prohibited by statute may nevertheless be ratified at a time or under circumstances to which the statute does not apply; or to speak more accurately, the parties may enter into a new contract which, though relating to the same subject matter, is free from the vice of the original transaction.[4] Such, apparently, is the principle of the cases which establish that the parties to a usurious loan may agree that the creditor shall relinquish his claim to the illegal interest, and the debtor repay the principal. So an executory agreement made on Sunday is void, and cannot be enforced by either party. If, however, it is subsequently carried into execution by the pay-

[1] Bayley *v.* Taber, 6 Mass. 451; Pattee *v.* Greely, 13 Met. 284; Merriam *v.* Stearns, 10 Cush. 257.

[2] 6 Bing. 653.

[3] 8 Gray, 553.

[4] 20 American Jurist, 255.

ment of the price or the delivery of the goods, an implied contract will arise, which, in the absence of proof, will be presumed to be in accordance with the terms originally prescribed.[1] The act of the creditor in receiving part-payment of the debt before maturity, in pursuance of an agreement to give time to the principal, was accordingly held in Uhler *v.* Applegate[2] to discharge the surety, although the agreement itself was inoperative and void as having been made on Sunday.

The court said that when the plaintiff took the money subsequently, a new contract arose by which he was bound, and it seems to have been held that the original agreement might be given in evidence to show what the understanding was. So where the defendant entered on the plaintiff's land, and occupied it under a lease made on the Lord's Day, such subsequent entry and user gave birth to a contract where none existed previously, and the plaintiff was allowed to recover in assumpsit for use and occupation, although he must have failed in a suit brought specifically on the lease.[3]

It results from these decisions that if goods are sold on Sunday, and delivered on a succeeding day, the law will imply a promise to pay a reasonable price, which unless the contrary is shown, will be that originally named. The delivery and acceptance operate as a new contract, which in the absence of proof will be presumed to be like that originally made. In other words, an alleged sale of a chattel on Sunday will not preclude the parties from selling it again for the same price on a week-day; and such an agreement may be presumed from the delivery of the chattel, although nothing is said at the time.[4] In Foreman *v.* Ahl,[5] fifteen mules were sold on Sunday for $160 each. Thirteen were delivered forthwith, and the remaining two on the following day; and the court held that the jury might properly award compensation for these, but not for those which had been handed over and

[1] Williams *v.* Paul, 6 Bing. 653; Stebbins *v.* Peck, 8 Gray, 553.

[2] 2 Casey, 140.

[3] Adams *v.* Gay, 19 Vt. 358; Dodson *v.* Harris, 10 Ala. 566; Uhler *v.* Applegate, 2 Casey, 140.

[4] Stebbins *v.* Peck, 8 Gray, 553.

[5] 5 P. F. S. 325.

accepted on the Lord's Day, contrary to law. Woodward, C. J., said: "The better view is that, though the contract was entire in the first instance, the parties severed it in the performance, and made it not the purchase of fifteen mules *in solido* as one round and complete transaction, but the purchase of fifteen mules *per capita* at $160 per mule. In this view it is clear that while the plaintiff cannot steer clear of the Sunday law as to thirteen of the mules, he may as to the two delivered on Monday; for as to them, though the bargain was begun on Sunday, it was not consummated until Monday."

It has been already stated that when a contract made on Sunday is carried into effect on an ensuing week-day, the presumption is that the minds of the parties remain unchanged; and the original agreement will consequently be evidence of the final intent, which, though not conclusive, should not be disregarded without sufficient cause. If, for instance, a horse is sold with warranty on Sunday and delivered the next day, the jury may and ought to hold the vendor answerable if the animal proves to be unsound. Such is virtually the doctrine of Uhler *v.* Applegate, already cited, and it is the only one consistent with the ends of justice. It was, notwithstanding, held, in Bradley *v.* Rea,[1] that although where goods which have been sold on Sunday are delivered and accepted by the purchaser on Monday, the vendor may maintain an action to recover the value of the goods upon an implied assumpsit, the price fixed by the contract will not be binding on either party, nor will the vendor be bound by a warranty given at the time of the sale. Hoar, J., said: "The instruction was that though the pigs were selected and marked on Sunday, and the price to be paid for them fixed on Sunday, yet if the pigs were to be weighed and delivered on Monday, the contract of sale would be valid. This was right if it conveyed the idea that the contract made by the delivery on Monday would not be void. But if the jury understood it to mean that the whole contract, including the agreement made on Sunday, would become valid and operative in law by reason of the weighing and delivery

[1] Foreman *v.* Ahl, 5 P. F. S. 325; Chestnut *v.* Harbaugh, 28 id. 473; Shuman *v.* Shuman, 3 Casey, 90.

on Monday, they would be led to a wrong result. The recent cases of Day *v.* McAllister,[1] and Ladd *v.* Rogers,[2] are decisions upon the point. In those cases it was held that a contract which is illegal because made on Sunday is wholly nugatory and void, and incapable of ratification; and that the rights of the parties depend exclusively on their agreement on the day when it is lawful for them to perform secular business. If all that took place on Monday, therefore, was the weighing and delivering of the pigs by the plaintiff and the acceptance of them by the defendants, the price fixed on Sunday would not be binding on either party, nor could the defendants avail themselves of any warranty which was made on Sunday. The plaintiff could only recover upon an implied assumpsit for a *quantum valebat*."

Contracts vitiated by fraud were held at one period by the Supreme Court of Pennsylvania to be merely void, and as such insusceptible of confirmation by a subsequent promise.[3] But these decisions are clearly against the weight of authority, which establishes that the right to avoid a contract on the ground of fraud is a privilege conferred for the protection of the injured party, and may be waived by him if he finds it preferable to affirm the transaction and seek a remedy in damages for the deceit.[4] When, for instance, the vendor wilfully misleads the purchaser as to the quality of the goods, the latter may either rescind the sale, or retain the goods and claim a deduction from the price corresponding to the injury inflicted by the fraud;[5] but he must elect which of these courses he will adopt and cannot recede from his choice when once made.[6] The contract must, however, be dealt with as a

1 15 Gray, 433.

2 11 Allen, 209.

3 Duncan *v.* McCullough, 4 S. & R. 483; Chamberlain *v.* McClurg, 8 W. & S. 31; Jackson *v.* Summerville, 1 Harris, 359.

4 Selway *v.* Fogg, 5 M. & W. 83.

5 Adler *v.* Fenton, 24 How. 407; Downer *v.* Smith, 32 Vt. 1; Stevens *v.* Hyde, 32 Barb. 171; Barton *v.* Simmons, 14 Ind. 49.

6 Croft *v.* Wilbar, 7 Allen, 248; Addison on Contracts, 229, 7th ed.; Bassett *v.* Brown, 105 Mass. 351; Allaire *v.* Whitney, 1 Hill, 484; 4 Den. 154; Leaming *v.* Wise, 23 P. F. S. 173.

whole, and if any part of the consideration is accepted with a knowledge of the fraud, it will be no longer possible to reject the residue.[1] "The plaintiff," said Crompton, J., in Clarke *v.* Dickson, "must rescind the contract *in toto* or not at all; he cannot both keep the shares and recover the whole price. That is founded on the plainest principles of justice. If he cannot return the article he must keep it, and sue for his real damage in an action for deceit." This just and reasonable doctrine is now recognized in Pennsylvania,[2] where the recent decisions may be considered as virtually overruling Duncan *v.* McCullough and Chamberlain *v.* McClurg, notwithstanding the distinctions taken by Sharswood, J., in Negley *v.* Lindsay.

No new consideration is requisite for such a confirmation other than the right to hold the opposite party to the contract, which would be lost if it were rescinded; but it will not preclude the right to damages or compensation for the injury occasioned by the fraud, which cannot be extinguished without a release, or an accord and satisfaction.[3]

The question has ordinarily arisen out of the buyer's retention of the goods, or his election to deal with them as his own, with a knowledge that the sale was fraudulent on the part of the vendor; but the rule is stated in Addison on Contracts,[4] as applicable alike to executed and executory agreements, and whether the ratification is by acts or words. It is well settled in accordance with this principle that he who sues for damages for the fraud, or who knowingly accepts or retains any benefit under it,[5] or who uses the property as his own after the fraud has been discovered, thereby affirms the validity of the contract, and cannot subsequently exercise the right of

[1] Clarke *v.* Dickson, 12 Bl. & E. 148.

[2] Pearsoll *v.* Chapin, 8 Wr. 9; Negley *v.* Lindsay, 17 P. F. S. 217; Leaming *v.* Wise, 23 id. 173; Shisler *v.* Vandike, 11 Norris, 447.

[3] 1 Leading Cases in Equity, 4 Am. ed. 832; Heastings *v.* McGee, 16 P. F. S. 384; Whitney *v.* Allaire, 4 Den. 554.

[4] pp. 230–298.

[5] Share *v.* Anderson, 7 S. & R. 63; Wilson *v.* Bigger, 7 W. & S. 125.

rescission.[1] A recognition or admission of the validity of the contract in the course of conversation with a third person, will not, however, operate as a confirmation, which can only arise from some act done under the contract, or a communication made to the opposite party or some one acting in his behalf.

[1] Heastings *v.* McGee, 16 P. F. S. 384; Pearsoll *v.* Chapin, 8 Wr. 9.

CHAPTER XV.

UNILATERAL CONTRACTS.

Promises in consideration of Performance. — Time of Performance. — May be retracted before Performance. — Unless under Seal. — Guaranty of Advances at the Option of the Promisee.

WHAT is a sufficient consideration for a promise depends on the terms prescribed by the promisor, and may be as various as the human mind, but it must in general be some act done or refrained from, or some engagement made at his request, and beneficial to him or detrimental to the promisee. When the request is that the promisee shall do a particular thing, performance is the one thing needful for the completion of the contract.[1] When, on the other hand, the promisor requires that the promisee shall enter into a mutual engagement, the condition must be fulfilled and performance will not suffice without a promise to perform.

Parol agreements may consequently be ranged under the two heads of promises in consideration of promises, and promises in consideration of performance.[2] In contracts of the latter description compliance is the sufficient and indispensable evidence of the promisee's assent, and a recovery may be had on proof that the act was done in the way prescribed, without showing that the plaintiff declared his intention to accept or act under the promise.[3] This results from the obvious truth

[1] Cottage Street Church *v.* Kendall, 121 Mass. 528; Train *v.* Gold, 5 Pick. 380; Powers *v.* Bumcratz, 12 Ohio St. 273; White *v.* Baxter, 71 N. Y. 254; Langdell, Summary of the Law of Contracts, § 12.

[2] Clark *v.* Russel, 3 Watts, 213, 217; Lampleigh *v.* Brathwait, Hobart, 105.

[3] Weaver *v.* Wood, 9 Barr, 220; Brogden *v.* The R. R. Co., 2 App. Cases, 666, 691.

that one who enters into an engagement is entitled to prescribe the terms on which he is willing to be bound, and if these are complied with cannot justly ask for more. "There is," said Maule, J., in The Fishmongers' Company *v.* Robertson,[1] "a large class of cases mentioned by Pothier, where A promises to do something if another party, B, will do something also. This contract is not binding on B, but if he does the act it becomes binding on A." "So," Patteson, J., observed in Morton *v.* Burn,[2] "if I say that if you will furnish goods to a third person I will guaranty the payment, you are not bound to furnish them, but if you do furnish them in pursuance of the contract you may sue me on the guaranty." It is established, in accordance with these principles, that one who promises to reward another for doing an act or rendering a service, cannot withhold the stipulated compensation on the ground that the promisee did not give the reciprocal promise, which was not asked for, and remained free to do as he thought proper.[3] This is entirely consistent with the rule that both parties must be bound or neither, because such a promise is in the nature of a continuing offer, and may be recalled at any time before the person to whom it is made, does, renders, or refrains. In Patton's Executors *v.* Hassinger,[4] a man of full age became ill while working for the plaintiff, and was nursed and taken care of by him. His father on learning what had occurred declared, although not in the plaintiff's presence, that whoever took care of his son should be well paid. These words were related to the plaintiff, who continued to provide for the son till he died, and subsequently called on the father for compensation, when the latter admitted his liability and said he would pay as soon as he had the means. A suit having been brought against the father, it was held that as the plaintiff had rendered the stipulated service he was entitled to recover, although he had not announced his intention to the defendant,

[1] 5 M. & G. 131, 171. [2] 7 A. & E. 19.

[3] Patton *v.* Hassinger, 19 P. F. S. 311; Loring *v.* Boston, 7 Met. 409; Powers *v.* Fowler, 4 E. & B. 511; Oldershaw *v.* King, 2 H. & N. 517; Wadsworth *v.* Allen, 8 Gat. 174; Goward *v.* Waters, 98 Mass. 596.

[4] 19 P. F. S. 311.

or declared his willingness to accept and act under the promise. Thompson, C. J., observed that compliance with a proposition is the most significant proof of acceptance, and that as the promise was not to pay the son's debt, but an independent undertaking, it did not come within the statute of frauds, or require to be in writing.

The rule was accurately stated in Lent *v.* Padelford,[1] where Jackson, J., said that one of the reasons in arrest of judgment was that no sufficient consideration was set forth in the declaration. The declaration stated that in consideration that the plaintiff would delay the service of an execution against a third person, the defendant promised, and it was then averred that the plaintiff did delay the service accordingly. This appeared to the court sufficient, and was the usual mode of declaring in such cases in the books of entries. This manner of stating the consideration and the contract was not confined to cases of forbearance. It was not uncommon in actions for goods sold, to declare that in consideration that the plaintiff would sell and deliver to the defendant certain goods, the latter promised to pay the price, and then to aver that he did sell and deliver accordingly. So, in consideration the plaintiff would do any other specific thing, and then aver the performance without alleging that the plaintiff had promised to do it. Under such circumstances mutual promises were not requisite to give validity to the contract.

The point was decided the same way in Duval *v.* Trask,[2] and again in Train *v.* Gold,[3] where a promise that a third person should indemnify the plaintiff if he executed a writ which had been placed in his hands as sheriff, was held to bind the promisor on proof that the levy had been made and returned, although the plaintiff did not signify his intention to accept or act under the promise, and the only manifestation of his assent was doing the act required, and although the whole evidence of the contract lay in a letter written by the defendant to which no answer was returned by the plaintiff, so that the case was like in principle to a letter of credit or prospective guaranty. "If," said Wilde, J., in delivering the opinion

[1] 10 Mass. 230. [2] 12 Mass. 154. [3] 5 Pick. 380.

of the court: "A promises B to pay him a sum of money if he will do a particular act, and B does it, the promise thereupon becomes binding, although B at the time of the promise does not engage to do the act. In the intermediate time the obligation is inert or the promise suspended, and until the performance of the condition there is no consideration and the promise is *nudum pactum;* but on the performance of the condition by the promisee it is clothed with a valid consideration which relates back to the promise, and it then becomes obligatory. So if a reward be offered for the apprehension of a culprit or for the doing of any other lawful act, the promise when made is *nudum pactum;* but when any one relying upon the promised reward performs the condition, this is a good consideration for the previous promise and it thereupon becomes binding on the promisor." In Morse *v.* Bellows,[1] the defendant was in like manner held liable on a promise to repay the plaintiff the amount which he might expend in the purchase of certain bonds, although the latter had made the purchase in question without giving notice of his assent to the contract or of his intention to act in accordance with its terms. And in Barnes *v.* Perine,[2] the court said that a promise in consideration of the future performance of an act indicated by the promisor becomes binding as soon as the act is done, although the promisee may not have bound himself to do it.

The same ground was taken in Kennaway *v.* Treleavan.[3] The action was brought on the following instrument: "I hereby guarantee to you, Messrs. Kennaway & Co., the sum of £250, in case that Mr. Paddon should default in his capacity of agent and traveller to you." Baron Parke observed, it had been said and truly, that there was no binding contract on the plaintiffs, and that notwithstanding the guaranty they were not bound to employ Paddon. There were, however, many contracts not binding on both sides at the time when made, and where the whole duty rested with one of the contracting parties. A guaranty fell under that class, when a person said: "In case you choose to employ this man as your agent for a week, I will be responsible for all such sums as he

[1] 7 N. H. 549. [2] 9 Barb. 202. [3] 5 M. & W. 498.

shall receive during that time and neglect to pay over to you." The party indemnified was not bound to employ the person designated, but if he did employ him, the guaranty took effect and became binding on the party who gave it. It was, therefore, no objection in the case before the court to say that the plaintiffs were not obliged to take Paddon into their service, but having done so the guaranty attached and the defendants became responsible for the default.

In like manner one who mails a written order for goods may be bound to accept and pay for them, although he receives no reply, and the first intimation that the vendor intends to comply with the request is the arrival of the goods. The question depends on the wording of the order, and if that is a positive direction to send the goods, it will be enough for the person to whom it is addressed to do as he is bid, without entering into an engagement to that effect.[1] Such an interpretation should not, however, be adopted unless the meaning is clear, and the natural inference is that the writer expects a reply. In the case last cited, Cooper wrote to Altimus inquring if he had staves to sell, and Altimus answered: "If you would let me know how much you would give, I could get four thousand at $50 per thousand." Cooper replied on the 18th of October: "If they are rift staves and good, I will give you $35 per thousand delivered at the station." Altimus sent the staves without answering, but they were rejected by Cooper on the ground that his letter of the 18th was an offer which should have been accepted in order to complete the contract. The court held that the letter was an order which did not call for a reply, and became obligatory on him when the staves were tendered in accordance with its terms. The judgment is obviously sound; but the case may also be resolved into an offer on the plaintiff's part to procure staves for the defendant at such prices as he should think fit to indicate, and an acceptance of it by the plaintiff with a statement of the sum which he was willing to give.

To make a promise in consideration of performance valid, the act must be done before the expiration of the period named

[1] Cooper *v.* Altimus, 12 P. F. S. 486.

by the promisor, or where no time is prescribed, within a reasonable time.[1] In the case first cited the defendant wrote on the 8th of October requesting an allotment of fifty shares in a joint stock company. The allotment was not made until the 23d of November, and the court gave judgment for the defendant on the ground that there had been an unreasonable delay. So in Loring *v.* Boston, the arrest of a criminal three years and eight months after a reward had been offered for his apprehension, was held to be too late to satisfy the requirements of the promise.

The act which contributes the consideration and completes the contract need not however be done in the promisor's lifetime, unless there is an express or implied condition to that effect, and the executors of one who has agreed with another to be answerable for the amount that may become due to him by a third person on the balance of accounts, may be compelled to pay for goods sold to the principal debtor after the guarantor's death, but before it was communicated or became known to the creditor.[2]

It has been already stated that a promise is not obligatory at common law unless the promisee has varied his position in consequence of the inducement held out by the promisor. Until some act is done or engagement made on the faith of the promise it is *nudum pactum*, and may be recalled at pleasure. Or to state the rule more accurately, a promise in consideration of performance operates as a request, and if the person to whom it is addressed proceeds after notice has been given to him to desist, he is not entitled to compensation.

The observation of Chief Justice Gibson, in Weaver *v.* Wood,[3] that when the consideration is executory the promise may be retracted at any time before performance, is entirely just where the promisee has neither done nor agreed to do what the promisor desired. If, for instance, I promise another $100 if he will cut down a tree at any time in the course of the coming year, without asking for or receiving a reciprocal

[1] Ramsgate Hotel Co. *v.* Montefiore, L. R. 1 Ex. 109; Loring *v.* Boston, 7 Met. 409.

[2] Bradbury *v.* Morgan, 1 H. & C. 249.

[3] 9 Barr, 220.

engagement, I may countermand my request at any time before the work is actually begun, and if he insists on proceeding it will be at his peril. In like manner a promise to be answerable for such money as may be advanced to a third person within a certain period may be recalled even when the engagement is that the guaranty shall endure until the time expires. In Offord *v.* Davies,[1] the defendants jointly and severally guaranteed for the space of twelve calendar months the due payment of all such bills of exchange as the plaintiff might discount for the benefit of a third person whom the defendants desired to befriend. The defence was that after the making of the guaranty, and before the plaintiff had discounted such bills of exchange or advanced any money, the defendants countermanded the guaranty, and requested the plaintiff not to give credit under it to the principal. Earle, C. J., said, in delivering judgment, that "the promise by itself created no obligation, and was in effect conditioned to be binding if the plaintiff acted upon it either to the benefit of the defendants or to his own detriment. But until the condition had been at least in part fulfilled, the defendants were entitled to revoke the promise. In the case of a guaranty in the ordinary form, the right of revocation before the credit had been given was not denied; and this right was not affected by the promise being expressed to be for twelve months, or the fact that some discounts had been made before the notice of revocation, and repaid." Judgment was accordingly entered for the defendants.

The difference between contracts which become valid on assent, and those which derive their obligation from the passage of a consideration, is marked by this decision with great distinctness. A covenant to be answerable for such defaults as may be committed by a third person during his continuance in the employment of the covenantee, cannot be annulled by the covenantor without the consent of the other party to the obligation. In Calvert *v.* Gordon,[2] the bond sued on was conditioned for the fidelity of one Edwards as collecting clerk of the plaintiffs while he should continue in their service. The

[1] 12 C. B. N. S. 748.

[2] 3 M. & R. 124.

obligor died after the execution of the bond, and the defendant, as his executrix, thereupon gave notice that she would no longer be responsible for the good conduct of Edwards, and that if the plaintiffs continued to employ him they must take the risk. The only difference between this case and Offord *v.* Davies arose from the seal. The court held that the guarantor might have stipulated that he should be entitled to withdraw on notice. He had not done so, and had, on the contrary, covenanted to be answerable during an indefinite period. Such engagement was obligatory, and must be observed. An application was subsequently made for relief in equity without success.[1]

The result of the authorities, therefore, is that inasmuch as a guaranty under seal is binding immediately upon delivery and acceptance, it cannot be recalled by the covenantor, even when conditioned for the performance of some act by the covenantee which constitutes its consideration, or more properly cause, and which the latter may omit or fulfil at pleasure. An unsealed guaranty, on the other hand, does not become obligatory until a consideration moves from the creditor, and a revocation will consequently be in time down to the last moment before he gives or agrees to give the credit required by the guarantor.

The Roman was in these, and some other respects, more analogous to the English law than is the civil law as administered in Europe at the present day. The stipulation became obligatory and precluded retraction as soon as the question met with a formal response, whether it was, or was not, subject to a condition. An informal unilateral promise, on the other hand, was *nudum pactum*, and might, even when made in consideration of an act to be done by the promisee, be recalled before he complied, although performance on his part might give rise to an innominate obligation.

An offer or pollicitation was not obligatory until the person to whom it was addressed agreed to comply, and it made no difference that the offerer promised to allow the offeree time to make up his mind, and not to retract during the interval.

[1] Gordon *v.* Calvert, 2 Simons, 253; 4 Russell, 581.

A Roman could not, therefore, any more than can an Englishman, bind himself informally to give the refusal of a house or chattel, or that another should have a day or week to decide whether he would do an act or render a service with a view to remuneration, because mutuality was essential to a consensual contract, and the only effectual means of making a unilateral promise was a stipulation, as it now is a covenant. A naked guaranty like that given in Offord *v.* Davies, and Bradbury *v.* Morgan would have been as revocable at Rome as it is in England at the present day, even if an obligation might have arisen from an advance made or credit given while it was still standing and unrecalled.

On the downfall of the Roman Empire the customary form, which had been so long observed became obsolete, and if the intention on one side to promise, and on the other to assent, was clearly expressed it mattered not by what words. The promise might be absolute or conditional; but the obligation arose in either case from the engagement made on one side and the assent given on the other, and not from the performance of the terms prescribed by the promisor, although it might fail if they remained unfulfilled. While such was the result on the continent of Europe, the Anglo-Norman jurists adhered to the doctrine of the Roman law, — that a naked pact will not sustain an action.[1] If the promise was made by deed, the sealing, delivery and acceptance of the instrument were conclusive evidence that both minds had met in a common purpose; but a parol undertaking was invalid. It was at length established that a promise and a consideration, or in other words, an act done, or liability incurred by one party in pursuance of an assurance given by the other, are not only, equally with delivery and acceptance, or the Roman question and response, proofs of agreement, but impose an obligation that cannot be violated consistently with good faith. The civil and common law thus diverged, and are now separated by a greater interval than divides either from the Roman law.

It has been held in some instances, and taken for granted in others, that although the promisee need not bind himself to

[1] *Ante*, p. 16.

do the act which constitutes the consideration for the promise, he must still signify his assent or acceptance forthwith, or within a reasonable time; and if this requisite is not complied with cannot recover on proof that the act was done. If such is the rule of the civil, it does not prevail at common law, where the fulfilment of that which the promisor requests or stipulates for has always been deemed the best and sufficient proof of assent, and notice need not be given unless the circumstances are such that the defendant cannot inform himself by inquiry.[1] In Yard *v.* Eland the plaintiff declared that forasmuch as the defendant was indebted to the plaintiff's wife as executrix of J. S. for arrears of rent incurred in the lifetime of J. S., the defendant assumed to the plaintiff that in consideration that the plaintiff at the special instance and request of the defendant would forbear to sue the defendant until Michaelmas next following, he would pay the money to the plaintiff, etc., and that the plaintiff *assumptioni fidem adhibens* forbore to sue, etc., until Michaelmas, etc., and averred that his wife was alive, and that the defendant had not paid the money. And upon *non assumpsit* pleaded, and a verdict rendered for the plaintiff, Gould moved in arrest of judgment that it was not averred that when the defendant desired a day of payment the plaintiff consented to give it to him; but it was only said *quod assumptioni fidem adhibens* he forbore, so that the defendant might remain in fear all the time; and so the consideration failed. But to this it was answered by the court that it was averred that the plaintiff forbore, etc., which was sufficient consent, and judgment was rendered for the plaintiff. Although the point that the defendant ought to have declared his assent whether he did, or did not, bind himself to comply, was not made by counsel or adjudged by the court, it still is one that would hardly have passed *sub silentio* in this and numerous other instances had it been deemed tenable.

The principle is the same whether the consideration consists in doing or refraining, and a request for time followed by

[1] See Powers *v.* Bumcratz, 12 Ohio St. 372; Douglass *v.* Howland, 24 Wend. 35; Yard *v.* Eland, 1 Lord Raymond, 368; 2 Am. Leading Cases, 5 ed. 94-106; Langdell, Summary of the Law of Contracts, §§ 2, 4, 6, 12.

forbearance will uphold a promise by a third person to pay the debt, although the creditor does not bind himself by a promise, or the guarantor name the period during which the delay is to continue, because he may be presumed to have intended a reasonable time, and the question whether it has been accorded is one of fact for the jury.[1] The courts are slow to permit a defendant to withhold compensation on the plea that his language was too vague to constitute a contract, and might have been taken in a different sense from that in which it was understood, and acted upon.[2]

In Clark *v.* Russel,[3] the question was answered by one who thoroughly understood the principles and practice of the common law. "It is not essential," said Chief Justice Gibson, "that the plaintiff should have bound himself to forbear or stay proceedings on the original security so as to give an action for a breach of promise. Such an agreement would undoubtedly be a valid consideration, and might be so laid according to the precedents in cases of mutual promises which are reciprocally the consideration of each other, and which must therefore be simultaneous, concurrent and equally obligatory; but where the consideration is not promise for promise, less than a positive engagement to do an act which when done is to be the meritorious cause of the promise, may be a sufficient consideration for it. A positive act is more evincive of the distinction than a negative one. If I promise to compensate my neighbor if he will do a specific act of service for me, and he does it in consequence, he may maintain an action, though he had not bound himself to do it. The consideration of such a promise belongs to the class called executory, the promise itself being in its nature conditional. . . . Now the condition of forbearance belongs to the executory class, being usually so stated in the precedents; and it differs in no particular from the instance put, except that the act is of a negative instead of an affirmative nature; and it is this negative

[1] Downing *v.* Funk, 5 Rawle, 69; Clark *v.* Russel, 3 Watts, 213; Yard *v.* Eland, 1 Lord Raymond, 368; 2 Am. Leading Cases, 5 Am. ed. 104.

[2] Giles *v.* Ackles, 9 Barr, 147; Caldwell *v.* Heitshu, 9 W. & S. 51.

[3] 3 Watts, 213.

nature, rendering as it does the motive of the act equivocal, that induces the mind to hesitate. It might be supposed from an expression of the judge who delivered the judgment in Bixler *v.* Ream,[1] that a positive engagement to forbear was thought indispensable in all cases; but it is intimated in the succeeding sentences that actual forbearance at the instance of the defendant may also be sufficient, on the principle that a single spark of benefit received on the foot of the promise is a valid consideration."

A different view prevails in Massachusetts where it has been decided on grounds that are by no means clear, that forbearance in pursuance of a request is not a consideration unless the creditor binds himself to give time.[2]

A guaranty of such advances as the creditor may think fit to make, is obviously within the rule that a promise to be answerable in consideration of an act to be done at a future period, may be binding without other evidence of assent than that resulting from the doing of the act by the promisee; and hence it is not necessary in declaring on such an instrument to aver that it was accepted, or in other words, that the guarantor was informed that the creditor had received and would entertain his proposition, which is all that such a request calls for until the time arrives for granting or withholding what it asks. If the latter gives the credit or makes the stipulated advance, the obligation is complete, and no further evidence of assent is requisite.[3] In Bradbury *v.* Morgan a declaration setting forth that the defendant's testator requested the plaintiffs to give credit to a third person, and promised to guaranty the running balance of his account, was accordingly held good on demurrer, although it did not aver that the plaintiffs accepted the guaranty or signified their assent otherwise than by a compliance with the request, which did not take place until after the guarantor's death.

[1] 3 P. & W. 282, 285.

[2] Mecorney *v.* Stanley, 8 Cush. 85; Manter *v.* Churchill, 127 Mass. 31. See Boyd *v.* Freize, 5 Gray, 553.

[3] Johnston *v.* Nicholls, 1 C. B. 251; Chapman *v.* Sutton, 2 id. 634; Boyd *v.* Moyle, id. 643.

This rule prevails in New York, Maryland, Michigan, Ohio, and Tennessee, and is the only one consistent with the doctrine of pleading and the principles of the common law.[1]

When, however, the offerer merely declares his willingness to be bound if it is agreeable to the creditor, and may induce him to give better terms to the principal debtor, there will be no contract unless he gives notice of his assent,[2] and a guaranty is thereupon given in an unqualified form. A declaration that a man does not object to make a promise obviously is not an agreement, but a mere expression of his readiness to enter into an engagement.[3] In Mozley *v.* Tinkler,[4] the defendant wrote as follows: "Mr. France informs me that you are about publishing an arithmetic for him and another person, and I have no objection to being answerable as far as £50. For my reference apply to Messrs. Brook & Co., of this place." The court said that it was not necessary in contracts of this nature that both the parties should be bound. It was sufficient if the party sued was shown to be liable. In the present instance it was, however, clear that the defendant only meant to be bound, in case on inquiry the plaintiffs should be satisfied in regard to his solvency. And as this was a matter peculiarly within the knowledge of the plaintiffs, they ought to have given notice of it to the defendant before proceeding under the guaranty. The same point was determined in Morten *v.* Marshall.[5] In McIver *v.* Richardson,[6] the question arose on the following letter written by the defendants to the plaintiff: —

"GENTLEMEN, — As I understand Messrs. David Anderson & Co., of Quebec, have given you an order for rigging, etc., which will amount to about £4,000, I can assure you from what I know of their honor

[1] Douglass *v.* Howland, 24 Wend. 35; Smith *v.* Dann, 6 Hill, 543; Union Bank *v.* Coster, 3 N. Y. 203, 205; Caton *v.* Shaw, 2 Harris & Gill, 13; Powers *v.* Bumcratz, 12 Ohio St. 273; Bright *v.* McKnight, 1 Sneed, 158; Farmers' & Mechanics' Bank *v.* Kercheval, 2 Mich. 504; Clark *v.* Russel, 3 Watts, 213; Yard *v.* Eland, 1 Lord Raymond, 368; Bradbury *v.* Morgan, 1 H. & C. 249; 2 Am. Leading Cases, 5 ed. 107; Marshall *v.* M'Cleary, 42 Md. 374.

[2] Gaunt *v.* Hill, 2 Stark. 9, 18.

[3] Symmons *v.* Want, 2 Stark. 370.

[4] 1 C. M. & R. 692.

[5] 2 H. & C. 305.

[6] 1 M. & S. 557.

and probity, you will be perfectly safe in crediting them to that amount; indeed I have no objection to guarantee you against any loss from giving them this credit."

This paper was communicated by Anderson to the plaintiffs, who were not satisfied but required an additional security, which was given, and the rigging thereupon sold and delivered. Anderson & Co. subsequently made default, and suit was brought against the guarantor. Lord Ellenborough said that the question to be determined was whether the letter should be viewed as a perfected and conclusive guaranty, or merely as a proposition tending to a guaranty. It was regarded by the court in the latter aspect. What the language of the writer implied was that if applied to he would guaranty, but no such application had been made. On the contrary, it appeared that other security had been demanded and obtained. It was not until some time afterwards, and when the purchaser had failed, that the defendants learned that their proposition had been communicated to the plaintiffs. The letter must therefore be regarded as a mere overture and not as a promise. If the defendant had been notified that it was entertained, and had thereupon signified his consent, it would have been converted into a contract. As the matter stood there was nothing by which he could be bound.

The main ground of the judgment seems to have been that it did not sufficiently appear that the plaintiffs gave the credit on the faith of the promise. It is not enough that the promisee pursues the course indicated by the promisor, the promise must be the inducement to the act.[1] If he is influenced by motives which are foreign to the promise, and it is not a proximate or operative cause, the obligation does not attach. There is, nevertheless, a manifest distinction between a readiness to contract and an actual promise. One who says he is willing to be answerable, if it is desired, is not answerable unless he is notified and enters into the engagement. The expression of a purpose or design which the party does not pledge himself to carry into effect is not a promise. If A writes to B that if it is satisfactory to him A will guaranty any loan

[1] *Ante;* Clark *v.* Russel, 3 Watts, 213.

that B may make to C, and B does not reply or signify his assent in some other way, A cannot know whether B requires security, nor whether he deems A's security adequate, nor that he is willing to have any business relations with A. Under these circumstances there are two conditions, — one that B shall communicate his willingness, the other that the advance shall be made; and there is no contract unless both are fulfilled. But this interpretation should not be adopted unless the sense requires it, because ambiguous language should always be taken most strongly against the person by whom it is employed.

On the basis of these decisions the Supreme Court of the United States and some of the State courts have raised a superstructure extending much beyond the foundation. Every promise however positive and unequivocal, to be answerable for such sales or advances as may be made to a third person, is treated as an overture or proposal requiring acceptance. It is not enough that the principal debtor obtains the credit asked for; the guaranty must be accepted or the intention to act under it communicated to the guarantor, and he must be informed of the extent and nature of the advances within a reasonable time after they are made. Some decisions go still further by requiring a demand on the principal, and that his default shall be made known to the guarantor. This curious and elaborate system has generally been referred to Russell *v.* Clark.[1] The doctrine of Chief Justice Marshall in that instance is however, substantially the same as that of Lord Ellenborough in McIver *v.* Richardson, that the paper in evidence was not a promise, but an overture which unaccepted did not constitute a contract. The common law was not left behind until Douglass *v.* Reynolds.[2] Suit was there brought on a letter addressed by the defendants to the plaintiffs in the following words: —

"GENTLEMEN, — Our friend, Mr. Chester Haring, to assist him in business, may require your aid from time to time, either by acceptance or indorsement of his paper, or advances in cash. In order to save you from harm in so doing, we do hereby bind ourselves severally

[1] 7 Cranch, 69.

[2] 7 Peters, 113.

and jointly to be responsible to you at any time for a sum not exceeding $8,000, should the said Chester Haring fail to do so."

On the trial of the case the court was asked to instruct the jury: "1st. That to entitle plaintiffs to recover, they must prove that notice was given within a reasonable time of the receipt of the said letter of guaranty that the same had been accepted. 2d. That the plaintiffs must prove that, in a reasonable time after the making of the advances, acceptances and endorsements for the said Haring, on the faith of the said guaranty, they notified the defendants of the amount and extent thereof. 3d. That to entitle the plaintiffs to recover they must also prove that payment was demanded from the principal, and that notice of such demand and non-payment was given in a reasonable time to the defendants." These instructions were refused by the court below, and the question brought on error before the Supreme Court of the United States. Story, J., held, in delivering judgment, that the first proposition ought to have been affirmed. A party giving a letter of gnaranty had a right to know whether it was accepted, and whether the person to whom it was addressed meant to give credit on the footing of it or not. It might regulate in a great measure his course of conduct and his exercise of vigilance in regard to the party in whose favor the guaranty was given. Especially was it important in the case of a continuing guaranty, since it might guide his judgment in recalling it or suspending it. The second proposition was said to be correct in principle but not applicable to the case in hand. If the guaranty had been limited to a single transaction it would clearly have been the duty of the plaintiffs to have given notice of the advances, acceptances and indorsements made to Haring within a reasonable time after they were made. The case under consideration was that of a continuing guaranty in which the parties contemplated a series of transactions; and as the defendants must, in receiving notice of the acceptance, necessarily have understood that there might be successive advances, acceptances and endorsements, which would be renewed and discharged from time to time, there was no ground of principle or policy on which to rest the doctrine that notice of each successive transaction as it arose should be given. All that could be required was that when all the transactions between the plaintiffs and Haring under the guaranty were closed, the guarantors should have notice within a reasonable time, of the amount for which they were responsible. And if the instruction had asked nothing more than this, it would have been directly within the authority of Russell *v.* Clark,[1] and could not properly have been withheld from the jury.[2] The third proposition was said to be clearly just. "By the very terms of this guaranty, as well as by the general principles of law, the guarantors were only collaterally liable upon the failure of the principal debtor to pay the debt. A demand upon him and a failure on his part to perform his engagement were indispensable to constitute a *casus fœderis.* The creditors were not bound to institute any legal proceedings against the debtor, but they were required to use reasonable diligence to make demand and give notice of non-payment." When, however, the case came again before the court[3] it was held that the failure to make demand on the principal and give notice of his default, was not a defence unless it resulted in injury to the guarantor, and would consequently be excused by proof that he was insolvent when the debt matured.

It has been held in numerous instances, in accordance with the doctrine of Douglass *v.* Reynolds, that a guaranty is not binding unless the assent of the person to whom it is addressed is communicated to the guarantor, or the circumstances are such as to excuse the want of notice by showing that he knew the intention of the creditor to accept and act under the guaranty.[4]

[1] 7 Cranch, 69; and Edmondston *v.* Drake, 5 Peters, 624.

[2] Oxley *v.* Young, 2 H. Bl. 613; Peel *v.* Tatlock, 1 Bos. & P. 419.

[3] See 12 Peters, 497.

[4] Lee *v.* Dick, 10 Peters, 482; Adams *v.* Jones, 12 id. 207; Mussey *v.* Rayner, 22 Pick. 223; Lawrence *v.* McCalmont, 2 How. 426; White *v.* Reed, 15 Conn. 457; Kay *v.* Allen, 9 Barr, 320; Lowe *v.* Beckwith, 14 B. Mon. 184; Oaks *v.* Weller, 13 Vt. 106; 16 id. 63; Lowry *v.* Adams, 22 id. 160; Emerson *v.* Graff, 5 Casey, 358; Kellogg *v.* Stockton, id. 460; King *v.* Batterson, 13 R. I. 117; Thompson *v.* Glover, 78 Ky. 193, Davis Sewing Machine Co. *v.* Jones, 61 Mo. 409; Davis Sewing Machine Co. *v.* Richards, 115 U. S. 524. See Cooke *v.* Orne, 37 Ill. 186.

Notwithstanding the high authority of the court by which this rule was first laid down, it would seem to have no foundation in the common law. All that is requisite to the validity of a promise in consideration of performance is that the thing stipulated for shall be done, and assent need not be given beforehand, because the intention is that the promisee shall be free to act as he thinks proper when the time arrives. He is not asked to promise, but to perform, and until the time of performance comes, assent is a useless ceremony, which leaves the parties where they were before. The source of the decision must, consequently, be sought in the civil law where the obligation of a promise depends on the assent of the promisee, and the terms prescribed by the promisor are regarded not in the light of a consideration, but as conditions which suspend and may avoid the obligation.[1] Agreeably to this doctrine, an undertaking to repay such loans or advances as may be made to a third person, becomes obligatory immediately on acceptance, although it cannot be enforced until the money is actually advanced or credit given. Such obligations are designated by Pothier as *conditionelles potestatives*, and bind the debtor while leaving the creditor at large; but they notwithstanding follow the general rule that assent must not only be given but announced, which applies whether the engagement is absolute or conditional, gratuitous or for a stipulated reward. If I promise my neighbor $50 if within a year he will cut down a tree that darkens my windows, and he accedes, I am bound while he has twelve months in which to make up his mind, and if I prevent him from felling the tree, he will be as much entitled to the money as if he had actually done the work.

It is, in like manner, entirely competent under the same law for one who desires to sell or purchase, to give a promise that the opposite party shall have time for consideration, which will be obligatory immediately on receiving the assent of the promisee, although he does not enter into a reciprocal engagement, but will fail if he does not agree to the terms proposed before the delay expires. The condition is not,

[1] Pothier, Traité des Obligations, Partie ii. ch. iii. art. 1, §§ 1, 2, 3. Nos. 198–214; Maynz, i. § 38, ii., § 205.

therefore, as in the case of an ordinary offer, precedent, but subsequent to the obligation.[1]

A promise may, nevertheless, be subject to a condition precedent, which is essential to the obligation, and must be fulfilled before that can come into being. The question depends on the intention of the parties, as gathered from their language or the nature of the transaction. If I say that I will give $500 for a horse, the undertaking depends necessarily for its effect on the willingness of the owner to part with the animal, and is not obligatory until he accepts. Such a promise is known as a pollicitation, or offer, and operates both as a promise and a request; a request that the offeree will agree to sell, and a promise that if he does the offerer will buy; and consent, though signified only by an inclination of the head, operates as a reciprocal engagement which completes the contract.

The rule is stated in M'Douall's Institutes,[2] as cited in Dunlop *v.* Higgins:[3] "Conditional obligations properly so termed are presently binding and irrevocable, and only the effect is suspended; but sometimes the obligation is only to be contracted upon a condition which affects the very substance of it. Thus an offer has an implied condition of acceptance, whereby alone the consent of the other party accedes and converts the offer into a contract, so that it is not binding but ambulatory or revocable till it is accepted, and, therefore, either revocation by the offerer, or the death of either party before acceptance, voids it. The same rule holds in mutual contracts; the one party subscribing is not bound till the other subscribe likewise."

The doctrine that a promise may become obligatory on performance, although the promisor is ignorant of the promisee's assent at the time, and until he is informed that the work is done, is so far recognized by the civil law as now administered in France, that the acceptance of a mandate may be tacit and result from its execution by the mandatary;[4] and we may infer

[1] Langdell, Summary of the Law of Contract, §§ 2, 4, 6, 12.

[2] Title 4, p. 98.

[3] 1 H. L. C. 381.

[4] Code Napoleon, Art. 1985.

from the language held by Pardessus that such is also the rule when a merchant executes an order from his correspondent under circumstances which do not admit of a previous notification or reply.[1]

On turning from parol promises to contracts under seal, we shall find that the common law and civil law agree that the obligation of a covenant dates from delivery and acceptance, even when it is conditioned for the performance of some act by the covenantee, and the latter is free to choose whether he will or will not comply.

The subject was carefully examined by Cowen, J., in Douglass *v.* Howland,[2] and the doctrine that a promise in consideration of performance cannot be enforced on proof that the service was rendered or work done, unless it also appears that the promisee signified his assent or acceptance, shown to be at variance with an unbroken line of precedents in the English books, and some authoritative decisions in our own. "There is," said he, "a class of cases which hold that under a contract guaranteeing a debt yet to be made by another, the guarantor is not liable to a suit without notice that the guaranty has been accepted and acted upon. Indeed they go farther; if notice of accepting the guaranty be not given within a reasonable time no debt whatever arises.[3] I will only say that these cases have no foundation in English jurisprudence, where the adjudications are numerous and clear the other way.[4] In Comyns's Digest[5] it is said on a promise to pay on the performance of an act by the promisee to a third person, the promisee need not give any notice, for the promisor takes it on himself to get notice at his peril; and a great many cases are cited to that effect.[6] All the cases requiring mere guarantors to be treated as indorsers rest on *dicta* of two distinguished American judges in cases of a mixed character, where the defence, it was agreed, would be complete independently of

[1] Pardessus, Partie ii. tit. iii. ch. v. No. 251; Benjamin on Sales, § 73.

[2] 24 Wend. 35.

[3] Babcock *v.* Bryant, 12 Pick. 133.

[4] Harris *v.* Ferrand, Hard. 36, 42.

[5] Tit. Plead., C. 75.

[6] And see as to a guaranty of a debt already due Warrington *v.* Furbor, 8 East, 242; Swinyard *v.* Bowes, 5 M. & S. 62.

any such ground;[1] the counsel cited no English books, and all the learned court found there was one case, in which, as they remarked, Eyre, C. J., seemed to have been of opinion that in guaranties for good behavior notice of any embezzlement ought to be given in a reasonable time.[2] The decision was finally rested on the dictum of Chief Justice Marshall, and was very strong in favor of the guarantor. It was on a guaranty to pay for goods deliverable to another on such terms as the creditee and the principal should agree on, if the principal did not pay; and though strictly followed by a sale and delivery to the principal and a default on his part to pay, yet it was held that no action would lie, — at least till notice of the circumstances had been given by the plaintiff to the surety. Other cases hold guaranties of this character to almost the same degree of strictness in giving notice to guarantors as the law merchant has introduced between indorsees and indorsers.[3] In Norton *v.* Eastman, a like principle was imputed to a decision of this court in Stafford *v.* Low.[4] The latter, however, merely holds that a declaration made to another of a willingness to become a guarantor if required, would not render the declarant liable as a guarantor without a compliance with the express condition, which meant giving notice; in short, that the letter on which the plaintiff based his claim did not amount to a guaranty.[5] McIver *v.* Richardson[6] was then cited as a case of similar character. Beekman *v.* Hale[7] puts both the former cases on that footing, and acts upon them, adding that there must be notice or a subsequent consent to become a guaranty. Such cases are exceptions to the general rule, that notice is not required. They are cases of express condition, like Birks *v.* Trippet, already cited from Saunders.[8] It is proper to say that

[1] Marshall, C. J., in Russell *v.* Clark, 7 Cranch, 69, 92; Story, J., in Cremer *v.* Higginson, 1 Mason, 338, 340; Russell *v.* Perkins, id. 368, 371; Rapelye *v.* Bailey, 3 Conn. 438.

[2] Peel *v* Tatlock, 1 Bos. & P. 419.

[3] Greene *v.* Dodge, 2 Ham. 430, 439, 440; Norton *v.* Eastman, 4 Greenl. R. 521.

[4] 16 Johns. 67.

[5] 16 Johns. 69, 70.

[6] 1 M. & S. 557.

[7] 17 Johns. 134.

[8] 1 Wms. Saund. 32; and see 1 Wms. Saund. 33, Note (2); Com. Dig. Plead. Ch. 69.

this place in Comyns's Digest is cited by Putnam, J., in Babcock *v.* Bryant. But the cases cited in Comyns are like those in the note to 1 Saund. 33, where the request or notice is expressly required. 'There,' says Serjeant Williams, 'the request is parcel of the contract.' All the cases cited by him are of collateral matters, to be done on request by the very words of the contract, and even these cases do not extend to a proper debt or duty of the party promising. There though he by words make the request or notice a condition, yet the bringing of the action is a sufficient notice, and such is the very first case cited in the note.[1] I forbear to search farther for the English law after the admission implied by Douglass *v.* Reynolds.[2] The question was there examined by Mr. Justice Story; the only cases cited by him are Oxley *v.* Young,[3] and Peel *v.* Tatlock, the latter being also noticed, as mentioned before, by the Supreme Court of Connecticut. In Oxley *v.* Young the surety was holden liable, and I do not find any countenance given to the idea that notice was necessary by way of condition. The defendant ordered goods for another, and guaranteed that he should pay for them. They were accordingly shipped to him by the plaintiff, the guarantee.

"It is true that notice of the shipment was given to the defendant, and he sought to raise a defence on the subsequent neglect of the vendor. Eyre, C. J., said the right to sue on the guaranty attached when the order was put in a train for execution, subject to its being actually executed, and the right could not be divested even by the wilful neglect of the vendor. As to Peel *v.* Tatlock, it has been impossible for me to perceive that even an intimation was intended of notice being essential. The difficulty felt by Eyre, C. J., seems to have been whether the creditor had not defrauded the guarantor by industrious concealments. I may then, I think, repeat with great confidence that all the cases requiring notice are American, and depart from the rule of the common law. Douglass *v.* Reynolds, as Mr. Justice Story observes, may be sustained by the dictum of Chief Justice Marshall, and indeed

[1] Yelv., 66, see Com. Dig. Plead. Ch. 70.

[2] 7 Peters, 113, 125.

[3] 2 H. Bl. 613.

by Edmondston *v.* Drake,[1] where the court, with that learned Chief Justice at its head, carried the dictum into a direct adjudication. No English case is claimed by Mr. Justice Story in any of his decisions as sustaining the doctrine in the least. Chief Justice Marshall does not cite even one in his opinions.

"The short answer which English cases, decided long before our Revolution, furnish is that the guarantor by inquiring of his principal, with whom he is presumed to be on intimate terms, may inform himself perfectly whether the guaranty was accepted, the conditions fulfilled and the payment made. Where that can be done the cases all hold that notice is not necessary even as preliminary to the bringing of an action, much less to found a right of action. The only exception is the well known one of collateral parties to bills of exchange or promissory notes."[2]

"The law is established on this basis in New York, Maryland, Michigan, and some of the other States.[3] In Powers *v.* Bumcratz, Gholson, J., said: "It would be unjust to the courts which have held notice of the acceptance of a guaranty of future advances or credit to be necessary, to suppose that they intend to deny as a general proposition that if a promise be made by one man to pay if another will perform, a silent performance will not give a right to payment, or the existence of obligations which acquire their validity from future action and not from immediate assent.[4] The tenor of these decisions appears to be that in guaranties of future credits or advances, there is to be implied a condition that notice of acceptance shall be given, or that from the indefinite character of such guaranties a rule of construction must be applied (and that without reference to the language used), by which they are to be held as mere offers or propositions to guaranty, and

[1] 5 Peters, 624.

[2] Philips *v.* Astling, 2 Taunt. 206.

[3] Union Bank *v.* Coster, 3 N. Y. 203; City Bank *v.* Phelps, 86 id. 484; Caton *v.* Shaw, 2 Harris & Gill, 13; Bright *v.* McKnight, 1 Sneed, 158; Farmers' & Mech. Bank *v.* Kercheval, 2 Mich. 504; Crittenden *v.* Fiske, 46 id. 70; Powers *v.* Bumcratz, 12 Ohio St. 273; Davis *v.* Ellidge, 40 Ia. 109; Case *v.* Howard, 41 id. 479; Wilcox *v.* Draper, 12 Neb. 138; Noble *v.* Koontz, 17 Md. 283; Kline *v.* Raymond, 70 Ind. 271.

[4] 2 Am. Leading Cases, 5 ed. 104, 105.

therefore requiring assent; and the latter is the ground now generally assumed. It certainly is not supported by the English decisions which have been noticed; and the English precedents and decisions in cases where the point might have been presented, and various remarks of the English judges, go so far to sustain the statement that the English authorities present no trace of such a doctrine." [1]

In Caton *v.* Shaw,[2] the line was in like manner drawn between a proposition or overture and a positive engagement, and a guaranty of the latter kind held to be binding without notice of acceptance.[3] So in Jackson *v.* Yandes,[4] the court said that a proposition for a guaranty must like every other offer be accepted, but that an absolute promise to pay for such advances as another shall make needs no acceptance, and will be binding as soon as credit is given on the faith of the promise; and such clearly is the rule of the common law.[5] It is proper to observe that the question cannot arise when, as in Douglass *v.* Howland, the contract is under seal, because delivery is essential, and as that implies acceptance no other proof or notification of assent is requisite. Agreeably however to some recent decisions a covenant to guarantee or indemnify against the consequences of a future act does not become obligatory on delivery, in the absence of notice of acceptance, unless the nature of the act is such as to confer a benefit directly on the covenantor.[6]

The subject was elaborately reviewed in two recent judgments, which qualify and sustain the doctrine of Douglass *v.* Reynolds.[7] In the case first above cited the guaranty was as follows: "For and in consideration of one dollar, to us in

[1] 2 Am. Leading Cases, 5 ed. 104.

[2] 2 Harris & Gill, 13.

[3] 2 Am. Leading Cases, 4 ed. 96, 97.

[4] 7 Blackf. 526.

[5] Morton *v.* Burn, 7 A. & E. 19; Powers *v.* Fowler, 4 E. & B. 511; Johnston *v.* Nicholls, 1 C. B. 251; Chapman *v.* Sutton, 2 id. 634; Douglass *v.* Howland, 24 Wend. 35; Smith *v.* Dann, 6 Hill, 543; Union Bank *v.* Coster, 3 N. Y. 203.

[6] Davis *v.* Wells, 104 U. S. 159; Davis Sewing Machine Co. *v.* Richards, 115 id. 524.

[7] Davis *v.* Wells, 104 U. S. 159; Davis Sewing Machine Co. *v.* Richards, 115 id. 524.

hand paid by Wells, Fargo, & Co. (the receipt of which is hereby acknowledged), we hereby guarantee unto them, the said Wells, Fargo, & Co., unconditionally, at all times, any indebtedness of Gordon & Co., a firm now doing business at Salt Lake City, Territory of Utah, to the extent of, and not exceeding, the sum of ten thousand dollars ($10,000) for any over-drafts now made, or that may hereafter be made at the bank of said Wells, Fargo, & Co."

The instrument was signed and sealed by the defendants, delivered to Gordon & Co., and by them to the plaintiffs, who gave the stipulated credit, and finally sued for the sum of $6,200 due for over-drafts. We may infer, notwithstanding the recital, that value was not actually received by the guarantors in any form, and that the plaintiffs did not give or notify their assent save by receiving the instrument and acting on the assurance which it held forth. The case, therefore, turned in the opinion of the court on an estoppel growing out of the receipt, and that seemingly would have arisen independently of an admission which was the thinnest possible pretence. Davis *v.* Wells is, I believe, the first instance in the history of the common law in which the recital or existence of a consideration has been deemed requisite to the validity of a bond or covenant.[1] Sealed instruments do not need such support, and the delivery which is essential to their obligation necessarily implies acceptance.

The court held that a consideration passing directly between the parties to a guaranty implies the assent without which a promise is not binding in law or morals. A guaranty of an existing debt, and a guaranty of subsequent advances were equally within this principle. Such also is the case when the proposal comes from the guarantor and is accepted by the creditor, or from the creditor and is accepted by the guarantor, and also where the instrument is in the form of a bilateral contract, which binds the creditor to make the contemplated advances, or creates by its recitals a privity between him and the guarantor, because in each of these cases assent is either expressed or necessarily implied. The instrument sued on

[1] Livingston *v.* Tremper, 4 Johns. 416.

was not a mere unaccepted proposal, but carried on its face conclusive evidence that it had been accepted by Wells, Fargo, & Co., and that it was understood and intended to be, on delivery to them, a complete and perfect obligation of guaranty. That evidence lay in the words "for and in consideration of one dollar to us paid by Wells, Fargo, & Co., we hereby guarantee," etc. It mattered not that the consideration thus set forth was nominal. The point was made in Lawrence *v.* McCalmont,[1] and overruled by Mr. Justice Story, who said: "The guarantor acknowledged the receipt of one dollar, and is now estopped to deny it. A valuable consideration, however small or nominal, given or stipulated for in good faith, is, in the absence of fraud, sufficient to support an action on any parol contract; and this is as true of contracts of guaranty as of other contracts."[2]

It did not affect this conclusion that the present guaranty was for future advances as well as for an existing debt. The recital of a consideration showed a completed contract based on mutual assent, and if it was a contract for one purpose it was a contract for all. If notice of the advances made under the guaranty would have been requisite, it was waived by the words "unconditionally and at all times," which excluded any conditions that might otherwise have been implied, and rendered the undertaking absolute.

In the Davis Sewing Machine Co. *v.* Richards,[3] the question arose on an instrument so nearly analogous to that considered in Davis *v.* Wells, that the result must have been the same, but for a slight difference in phraseology which was presumably intended to convey the same idea. The words were these: "For value received, we hereby guarantee to the Davis Sewing Machine Company, of Watertown, N. Y., the full performance of the foregoing contract on the part of John W. Poler, and the payment by said John W. Poler of all indebtedness, by account, note, indorsement of notes (including renewals and extensions) or otherwise, to the said Davis Sewing Machine Company, for property sold to said John W. Poler, under

[1] 2 How. 426, 452.
[2] Dutchman *v.* Tooth, 5 Bing. N. C. 577.
[3] 115 U. S. 524.

this contract, to the amount of three thousand ($3,000) dollars."

This writing was on the same paper with another, which purported to be an agreement by the plaintiffs to deliver, and by Poler to accept and pay for, sewing-machines on the terms therein specified. The instruments were signed respectively by the defendants and by Poler, and sent by Poler to the plaintiffs, who executed the contract without notifying the defendants, or informing them that they accepted the guaranty. The plaintiffs subsequently sold machines to Poler, which he did not pay for, and the suit was brought for the default.

There can be little doubt as to the true import of the undertaking in this instance. It was a promise by the defendants that if the plaintiffs would enter into an agreement with Poler it should be faithfully performed by him, and when the stipulation was fulfilled the guaranty became absolute. It was not requisite, agreeably to the authorities, to notify the defendants, because they could obtain the necessary information from the principal debtor, and as the liability might eventually fall on them, it was their duty and interest to keep themselves informed of his proceedings and liability under the contract.[1]

The defendants were, notwithstanding, held to be entitled to judgment under the rules stated in Davis *v.* Wells, which were summed up as follows: —

"A contract of guaranty, like every other contract, can only be made by the mutual assent of the parties. If the guaranty is signed by the guarantor at the request of the other party, or if the latter's agreement to accept is contemporaneous with the guaranty, or if the receipt from him of a valuable consideration however small is acknowledged in the guaranty, the mutual assent is proved, and the delivery of the guaranty to him or for his use completes the contract. But if the guar-

[1] Haverleigh *v.* Leighton, Jenkins' Centuries, 311; Powle *v.* Haggar, Croke Jac. 492; Cutler *v.* Southern, 1 Wms. Saund. 116; Vyse *v.* Wakefield, 6 M. & W. 442, 452; Douglass *v.* Howland, 24 Wend. 35; Lent *v.* Padelford, 10 Mass. 230.

anty is signed by the guarantor without any previous request of the other party, and in his absence, for no consideration moving between them except future advances to be made to the principal debtor, the guaranty is in legal effect an offer or proposal on the part of the guarantor needing an acceptance by the other party to complete the contract."

The case at bar belonged to the latter class. There was no evidence of any request from the plaintiff to the guarantors, or of any consideration moving from him and received and acknowledged by them. A general recital "of value received," without stating from whom, was quite consistent with a consideration received from the principal debtor only. It was not until some days after the signature and delivery of the guaranty that the plaintiffs entered into the contract with Poler, and the defendants were not informed of this, or that the guaranty was accepted before the demand made on them for payment.

The difference between the recital which was the turning point of this decision, and that considered in Davis *v.* Wells, is slight, and to an ordinary eye might appear trivial. A promise to be answerable for value received from Paul, and a promise to be answerable to him for value received, are so analogous that both should seemingly be interpreted in the same way — *ut res magis valeat*, and in obedience to the rule that unilateral contracts are to be taken most strongly against the covenantor.[1] The object in either case is to preclude controversy by an admission that all has been done which is requisite to render the contract valid, and as the writing will naturally be so understood by the person to whom it is delivered, the intention should not be frustrated by refined distinctions.[2]

It is not easy to fix the meaning of "acceptance," as employed in the above judgments. As defined by Professor Langdell, and generally applied, it signifies the promise to

[1] Beeson *v.* Patterson, 12 Casey, 24; Gates *v.* McKee, 13 N. Y. 232, 236; 2 Sm. L. C., notes to Roe *v.* Tranmarr, 7 Am. ed. 470.

[2] Lawrence *v.* McCalmont, 2 How. 426, 450; Mason *v.* Pritchard, 12 East, 227; 2 Am. Leading Cases, 5 Am. ed. 139.

comply which converts an offer into a contract. So understood, it is not predicable of a guaranty or other unilateral contract.[1] On the other hand, if by acceptance we are to understand the assent which is essential to the obligation of every promise, it cannot be more unequivocally manifested than by fulfilling the condition on which the promisor agrees to be bound.[2] When it is that there shall be promise for promise, the promisee must not only enter into a reciprocal engagement but transmit it to the promisor, although, agreeably to the recent decisions, it need not reach or be received by him.[3] When on the other hand, what the promisor stipulates for is performance, the contract is complete as soon as the act is done, whether it be or be not known or communicated to the promisor.[4] If the circumstances are such that he cannot inform himself by inquiry, it may be requisite to give him notice; but this is a condition subsequent that will

[1] Langdell, Summary of the Law of Contracts, § 12.

[2] Watson *v.* McLaren, 19 Wend. 557; 26 id. 425; Russell *v.* Wiggins, 2 Story, 213; Hamilton *v.* The Lycoming Ins. Co., 5 Barr, 339; Lent *v.* Padelford, 10 Mass. 230; Loring *v.* The City of Boston, 7 Met. 409; Langdell, Summary of the Law of Contracts, §§ 2, 4, 6. "There are other important particulars in which a bilateral contract differs from one that is unilateral in respect to the acceptance of an offer; while in the latter the acceptance is merged and lost sight of in the performance of the consideration, in the former the giving of the consideration is merged and lost sight of in the acceptance; while in the latter the performance of the consideration necessarily implies an acceptance of the offer, in the former the acceptance of the offer necessarily implies the giving of the consideration. Therefore a mere offer in terms and an acceptance in terms are sufficient to form a bilateral contract, but not a unilateral contract. So an acceptance in terms is a *sine qua non* in a bilateral contract, while in a unilateral contract an acceptance in terms may be, and commonly is, dispensed with. Again, in a unilateral contract the offer becomes a contract in consequence of what the offeree does, in a bilateral contract in consequence of what he says. The reason why an acceptance in terms is necessary, and why it also suffices in a bilateral contract, is that what is called an acceptance is in that connection also and chiefly a counter-promise." Langdell, Summary of the Law of Contracts, § 12.

[3] Household Ins. Co. *v.* Grant, L. R. 4 Ex. Div. 216; White *v.* Corlies, 46 N. Y. 467.

[4] *Ante*, p. 315; Langdell, Summary of the Law of Contracts, § 6.

annul the contract if unfulfilled, and not a step that must be taken to call it into being.[1] It is immaterial, as regards the operation of the principle, whether the promisor's object is to benefit another or to benefit himself, because the obligation depends upon what the promisee does or parts with on the faith of the promise, and not on what the promisor receives. When therefore, A writes that he will be answerable for such advances as C may require and B see fit to make, and sends the letter by C or through the mail, B need not reply, because he is left free to choose, and all that he can say is that he will take the matter into consideration, which conveys no information and leaves the guarantor as much in the dark as he was previously.[2] Such a guaranty is a standing offer or request which may be retracted any time before acceptance, or accepted at any time before retraction.[3]

The utmost therefore that can be required of the creditor is, that he shall inform the guarantor when the advance is made or credit given, and an earlier notification will be premature and futile.[4] This seems to be universally conceded where the writing is under seal, and cannot take effect without the delivery which involves acceptance; and would seem to be true of every instrument intended for the benefit or protection of the promisee, and sent or given to and retained by him.[5] It matters not that weeks and months elapse before the guarantor learns that his request has been complied with, if he intentionally gave the creditor time to consider whether he would do the act or enter into the agreement, and is notified as soon as there is anything definite to annunciate.[6] It was conceded in Davis *v.* Wells, that notice of acceptance need not be given when the consideration moves to the guar-

[1] Langdell, Summary of the Law of Contracts, §§ 2, 4, 6.

[2] Langdell, Summary of the Law of Contracts, § 6.

[3] See Church *v.* Brown, 21 N. Y. 315, 325, 329; Offord *v.* Davies, 12 C. B. N. S. 748; Loring *v.* The City of Boston, 7 Met. 409; Freeman *v.* The City of Boston, 5 id. 56.

[4] *Ante*, p. 313; Langdell, Summary of the Law of Contracts, §§ 4, 6.

[5] Langdell, Summary of the Law of Contracts, § 2; Douglass *v.* Howland, 24 Wend. 35.

[6] Boston & M. Railroad Co. *v.* Bartlett, 3 Cush. 224.

antor, and is of a nature to afford the requisite information; and the case is substantially the same where the consideration, though moving to a third person, is attended with notice.

"Though," says Professor Langdell, in his Summary of the Law of Contracts,[1] "the acceptance of an offer and the performance of the consideration are different things, and though the former does not imply the latter, yet the latter does necessarily imply the former; and as the want of either is fatal to the promise, the question whether an offer has been accepted can never in strictness become material in those cases in which a consideration is necessary; and for all practical purposes it may be said that the offer is accepted in such cases by giving or performing the consideration."

This passage is relied on in Davis *v.* Wells[2] as sanctioning the position that performance will not operate as an acceptance, unless the consideration moves to the promisor; which is not what it indicates or the author intends. No argument is necessary to show that doing what the promisor stipulates for or requires, is equally a manifestation of assent, whether the act is beneficial to him or to a third person whom he desires to aid. An order to paint or repair a house renders the person who gives it answerable for the price, although he is not notified or informed until after the work is done, and whether the house belongs to him or another. There is a marked difference in this regard between consensual contracts, and contracts where all that is needed is that one party shall agree to confer, and the other be willing to receive. In the former case there must be acceptance, that is, a counter-promise which implies that the offeree is to signify his consent by some means calculated to inform the offerer. In the former it may be implied from the delivery and retention of an instrument made for the benefit of the covenantee, and operating as of security or payment.[3] It is accordingly established under the English cases and well-considered decisions in the United States, that in declaring on a guaranty or promise to indemnify, it is enough to say that the promise was made and

[1] § 2. [2] 104 U. S. 159, 166.

[3] Langdell, Summary of the Law of Contracts, §§ 2, 12, 13, 14.

that the plaintiff acted or forbore on the faith of the promise, without averring that it was accepted, or that the defendant was informed of the intention of the plaintiff to comply.[1] In like manner, while it was indispensable that the writing required by the statute of frauds should disclose all the essentials to the contract, it was enough if the consideration was set forth without averring the assent of the promisee, except in so far as it was involved in the consideration; and the rule applied whether the consideration moved between the parties or to a third person.[2]

Agreeably to the view taken in Missouri, Kentucky, and some other States, "the reason for requiring an acceptance of the offer of guaranty, and a notice expressed or implied of such acceptance, is that the guarantor may have an opportunity of arranging his relation with the party for whose benefit the guaranty is given; and the rule will not be pressed beyond the reason." In other words, acceptance and notice are requisite not to complete the contract, but to enable the guarantor to protect himself and obtain an indemnity from the principal debtor.[3] This ground has been discarded by the Supreme Court of the United States,[4] but was originally taken by Chief Justice Marshall in Russell *v.* Clark, and subsequently by Story, and would seem to be the only one on which Douglass *v.* Reynolds can be defended.[5]

[1] Yard *v.* Eland, 1 Lord Raymond, 368; Powers *v.* Fowler, 4 E. & B. 511; Lent *v.* Padelford, 10 Mass. 230; Duval *v.* Trask, 12 id. 154; Train *v.* Gold, 5 Pick. 380; 2 Am. Leading Cases, 33, 95; Morton *v.* Burn, 7 A. & E. 19; Powers *v.* Bumcratz, 12 Ohio St. 275, 290; Beeson *v.* Patterson, 12 Casey, 24; *ante*, p. 306.

[2] Wain *v.* Warlters, 5 East, 10; Powers *v.* Fowler, 4 E. & B. 511; Kennaway *v.* Treleavan, 5 M. & W. 498; City Bank *v.* Phelps, 86 N. Y. 484; Young *v.* Brown, 53 Wis. 333.

[3] Thompson *v.* Glover, 78 Ky. 193, 195; Central Savings Bank *v.* Shine, 48 Mo. 456; Montgomery *v.* Kellogg, 43 Mass. 486, 493; Beebee *v.* Dudley, 30 N. H. 249, 253.

[4] See Davis *v.* Wells, 104 U. S. 166; The Louisville M. Co. *v.* Wilson, 10 How. 461, 475.

[5] *Ante*, p. 319.

CHAPTER XVI.

BILATERAL CONTRACTS.

Promises in consideration of Promises. — Offer. — Bid at Auction. — Time and Mode of Acceptance of Offer. — Contracts by Mail. — Contracts by Telegraph. — Conditional or qualified Acceptance invalid. — Retraction of Offer. — Death of Offerer or Principal.

A CONTRACTING party may, nevertheless, instead of agreeing to pay if the opposite party will perform, and leaving the latter free to act as he thinks proper, require an immediate and reciprocal engagement and decline to be bound if it is not given. Such contracts are well known in pleading as contracts on mutual promises, as distinguished from contracts in consideration of performance. Mutuality is essential in both instances, because neither party can be bound while the other is at large.[1] The difference grows out of the terms prescribed by the promisor, which are in the one case that the promisee shall agree, and in the other that he shall do or refrain; and as a promise is not a substitute for performance in the latter case, so performance is insufficient in the former without a promise to perform.[2] If I promise to give my neighbor $10 if he will mow my lawn, it is enough if he does the act when the time arrives, without binding himself by an engagement, but if I offer him a price for his corn, he must agree to sell the corn at that price if he means to hold me to the contract, and in default of such a promise on his part I may refuse the grain when tendered. Or, as the rule is sometimes stated, a subsequent voluntary compliance will not suffice when the

[1] Johnston *v.* Fessler, 7 Watts, 48; Head *v.* Diggon, 3 M. & R. 97; Fisher *v.* Seltzer, 11 Harris, 308; Werden *v.* Woodruff, 38 Mich. 130; Quick *v.* Wheeler, 78 N. Y. 300.

[2] Langdell, Summary of the Law of Contracts, § 12.

promisor requires the promisee to bind himself by an engagement from which he cannot recede.[1] But for this rule there would be no certainty on the part of buyers or sellers, or indeed in any transaction where it is essential that each party should know what he may expect from the other.

It follows that when the promise is what is commonly termed an offer, or in other words, an undertaking to be answerable if the person to whom it is made will enter into a reciprocal engagement, the contract is not obligatory unless the promisee signifies his assent to the terms proposed. If, for instance, A promises to pay the debt of a third person if B will agree not to proceed against the debtor, actual forbearance will not be enough without the agreement which A requires.[2] And so when the guarantor promises to be answerable for subsequent advances, if the creditor will bind himself to give time for the payment of a past account, the latter must enter into the obligation if he means to enforce the guaranty.[3]

In Fellows *v.* Prentiss, Chancellor Walworth observed, in delivering his opinion in the Court of Errors, that it was obvious that the defendant did not intend to be answerable for any future sales to his nephew, unless the plaintiff should on receipt of his letter send an answer agreeing to the terms proposed. Such a reply was, therefore, at once the consideration and condition on which he was willing to be answerable for the debt. It was an offer to guaranty new advances if the plaintiff would agree to give time on the antecedent debt, and as the plaintiff had not bound himself to do so, the contract failed of effect. The same doctrine may be found in Beekman *v.* Hale,[4] and has been applied in numerous instances in England and the United States.[5]

[1] Johnston *v.* Fessler, 7 Watts, 48. See Beckwith *v.* Cheever, 21 N. H. 41; Eggleston *v.* Wagner, 46 Mich. 618.

[2] Cobb *v.* Page, 5 Harris, 469; Johnston *v.* Fessler, 7 Watts, 48.

[3] Beekman *v.* Hale, 17 Johns. 134; Fellows *v.* Prentiss, 3 Den. 512; Cope *v.* Albinson, 8 Ex. 185.

[4] 17 Johns. 134.

[5] Johnston *v.* Fessler, 7 Watts, 48; Payne *v.* Ives, 3 Dow. & R. 664.

It results from what has been said that if A offers to sell to B and names the price, the contract is not binding until B agrees to buy, and the rule applies although the vendor requests the purchaser to take the matter into consideration, or promises him the refusal of the goods until a certain time. Such an engagement may be obligatory in morals, but is in law an offer unaccepted, and that may consequently be recalled.[1] This is not because assent is requisite as in the civil law, but for a different reason,—that until the purchaser is bound there is no consideration for the promise. Which party spoke first, the offeree to accept or the offerer to retract, and whether the words employed amount to an acceptance or revocation, is, when the grant does not depend on the interpretation of a writing, a question of fact for the jury.[2]

In Cooke *v.* Oxley,[3] the declaration was that the defendant proposed to sell and deliver 266 hogsheads of tobacco to the plaintiff at a certain price, whereupon the plaintiff desired the defendant to give him time to agree to or dissent from the proposal till the hour of four in the afternoon of that day, to which the defendant agreed, and thereupon promised the plaintiff to sell and deliver the tobacco upon the terms aforesaid, if the plaintiff would agree to purchase the same and give notice to the defendant before four in the afternoon of that day. The plaintiff then averred that he agreed to purchase the tobacco and gave notice thereof to the defendant before the hour of four arrived, and offered to pay the price, but that the defendant refused to comply with his promise. A verdict having been rendered for the plaintiff, the judgment was arrested on the ground that the pleadings did not disclose a consideration.

This case is obviously analogous to Offord *v.* Davies.[4] The promisor agreed in both instances to be bound until a certain

[1] Head *v.* Diggon, 3 M. & R. 97; The School Directors *v.* Trefethren, 60 Ill. App. 127; Eskridge *v.* Glover, 5 St. & P. 264; Burton *v.* Shotwell, 13 Bush, 271; Beckwith *v.* Cheever, 21 N. H. 41; Dickinson *v.* Dodds, L. R. 2 Ch. Div. 463.

[2] Quick *v.* Wheeler, 78 N. Y. 300.

[3] 3 T. R. 653.

[4] 12 C. B. N. S. 748.

time, and was, notwithstanding, held entitled to revoke the promise before the time arrived on the ground that there was no consideration moving from the promisee. The principle consequently was the same, although applied under different circumstances, and like decisions may be found in Tucker *v.* Woods [1] and Beckwith *v.* Cheever.[2]

In like manner a bid at an auction or sheriff's sale may be retracted at any time before the hammer falls.[3] It was contended in Payne *v.* Cave, that if an offer made under such circumstances could be withdrawn after prior bidders had been discharged there would be manifest injustice. The court was, notwithstanding, clearly of opinion that, mutuality being essential to the obligation of contracts, the purchaser could not be bound until the vendor's assent was made known through the hammer of the auctioneer, which did not fall in the case under consideration until after the withdrawal of the bid.

In Payne *v.* Cave, Buller, J., said: "An auction is not inaptly called a *locus penitentiæ.*" Every bidding is nothing more than an offer on one side, which is not binding on either side till it is assented to; but according to what is now contended for, one party would be bound by the offer and the other not, which can never be allowed. The law was held the same way in Fisher *v.* Seltzer, although it was one of the conditions of the sale that no one should withdraw his bid.

In these instances the promise was recalled before acceptance. It is equally well settled that when no time is prescribed, the person to whom the offer is addressed must accept at once, or within a reasonable time. If he delays, the promise falls by its own weight.[4] The person who makes the offer is presumed to act in view of existing circumstances, and the person to whom it is addressed obviously ought not to lie by until these have changed. He must therefore decide forthwith, or before the delay accorded by the other party to the contract has expired. Otherwise an offer might be accepted after the lapse of months or years, and when the state

[1] 12 Johns. 190.
[2] 21 N. H. 41.
[3] Fisher *v.* Seltzer, 11 Harris, 308; Payne *v.* Cave, 3 T. R. 148.
[4] Eliason *v.* Henshaw, 4 Wheat. 225.

of things was no longer the same. If an article is exposed for sale to-day at a certain price, and the buyer does not agree, a larger sum may be asked to-morrow when he returns prepared to buy. In like manner, an offer to sell sent through the mail must, agreeably to commercial usage, be accepted by the first post which leaves during business hours of the following day; and if it be not, the vendor may dispose of the goods as he thinks proper.[1] In Maclay *v.* Harvey an acceptance, mailed on the fourth day after the receipt of the offer, was held to be out of time, although the letter was sent at once to the post-office by a messenger, and the delay was due to his neglect.

The rule that acceptance must be prompt unless the circumstances or language of the offer justify delay, applies *a fortiori* when the negotiation is conducted through the telegraph and time is presumably essential to the end in view.[2] The court held that, in view of the channel through which the negotiation was conducted, and the fluctuating price of the commodity which the purchaser proposed to buy, the response should have been immediate and with no more delay than was required for deliberation; and that a message sent over the wires on the following day came too late to complete the contract. The rule in regard to the length of the time an offer will continue and when an acceptance completes the contract, is laid down in Parsons on Contracts.[3] "Whether an offer be made for a time certain or not, the intention or understanding of the parties is to govern. . . . If no definite time is stated, then the inquiry as to a reasonable time resolves itself into an inquiry as to what time it is rational to suppose the parties contemplated; and the law will decide this to be that time which as rational men they ought to have understood each other to have had in mind." Applying this rule, it seemed clear that the intention of the plaintiff in making

[1] Averill *v.* Hedge, 12 Conn. 424; Minnesota Oil Co. *v.* Lead Co., 4 Dill. 431; Dunlop *v.* Higgins, 1 H. L. C. 381; Taylor *v.* Rennie, 35 Barb. 272; Maclay *v.* Harvey, 90 Ill. 525.

[2] Minnesota Oil Co. *v.* Lead Co., 4 Dill. 434.

[3] Vol. i, p. 482.

the offer by telegraph to sell an article which fluctuated so much in price, must have been upon the understanding that the acceptance, if at all, should be immediate, and as soon after the receipt of the offer as would give a fair opportunity for consideration. The delay therefore was too long, and manifestly unjust to the plaintiff, for it afforded the defendant an opportunity to take advantage of a change in the market and accept or refuse the offer as would best subserve his interests.

All that the rule requires is that the offer should be accepted while it is still standing and in force, that is to say, within a reasonable time, or before the time fixed by the party who makes the offer has expired.[1] As in the parallel case of a promise in consideration of performance, if the consideration arises subsequently before the promise is revoked, it need not exist at the time.

The case of Cooke *v.* Oxley has sometimes been regarded as determining that a subsequent acceptance is necessarily invalid. The decision there, however, turned on a point of pleading, and might have been different if the question had arisen on the evidence. The contract as declared on, that the defendant would give the plaintiff time to decide, was manifestly invalid, and although it appeared at the trial that the acceptance took place before the offer was withdrawn, this was not set forth with sufficient distinctness in the declaration. If the offer and acceptance co-exist they need not occur simultaneously. To render the contract binding the purchaser must ordinarily accept at once; but this results from the presumed intention of the parties, and not from an inflexible rule of law. If the vendor gives the purchaser twenty-four hours for deliberation and the latter declares his assent within the appointed time and before the vendor recalls the offer, the contract is complete, and it will then be too late for the vendor to say that he has changed his mind. If both parties meet, one prepared to accept, the other to retract, whichever speaks first will have the law on his side. Such in effect is

[1] Stone *v.* Harmon, 31 Minn. 512; Bernstein *v.* Lans, 104 Mass. 216; Goward *v.* Waters, 98 id. 596.

the usual course at a sale by auction where acceptance is declared by the hammer of the auctioneer, and a bid cannot be recalled after that has fallen although there is no appreciable interval.

This question arose in Boston and Maine Railroad Company *v.* Bartlett,[1] where the defendant gave the complainant thirty days for consideration and the offer was accepted before the time went by. The court said that the promise when originally made was without consideration, and did not constitute a contract. It was a mere offer, and might as such have been withdrawn at any time before acceptance. When, however, the defendants assented, the minds of the parties met, and it was too late for either to recede without the consent of the other. The acceptance then related back to the offer, and the case became in all respects such as it would have been if both had occurred simultaneously. If a different doctrine was laid down in Cooke *v.* Oxley, it was erroneous and should be disregarded. In France, Scotland, Holland, and the other countries which followed the civil law, a man who gave another until a future day to decide whether he would accept an offer, could not withdraw it before the day arrived. Much might be said in favor of this rule and to show that the party who was injured by the breach of such an engagement should have redress. In England and the United States, however, a consideration was indispensable, and where none existed the contract was invalid. A promise to sell might be withdrawn notwithstanding an assurance that it should remain open for consideration. If, however, it was accepted before being revoked, the contract was as obligatory as if both promises were simultaneous.

For like reasons an offer sent by post cannot be retracted after the acceptance has been mailed, although the letter is delayed in passing through the post-office and does not reach the person to whom it is addressed for weeks or months. In Adams *v.* Lindsell,[2] the defendants wrote offering to sell at a fixed price, the answer to be sent forthwith. The letter was misdirected and did not reach its destination for several days,

[1] 3 Cush. 224. [2] 1 B. & Ald. 681.

and the defendants not hearing from the plaintiff as soon as they anticipated, parted with the goods. The plaintiff had in the mean time, and immediately after the receipt of the offer, written and despatched an acceptance which was delivered in due course of mail. Under these circumstances it was contended that the minds of the parties had never met, and there could be no valid contract. Before the plaintiffs agreed to accept, the defendants had irrevocably changed their minds. The court was, however, clearly of opinion that the sale was complete and bound the defendant. If the argument which had been made on their behalf prevailed, no contract could ever be made through the post-office. For if the vendor was not bound until the answer of the purchaser was received, the same *locus penitentiæ* would exist on the other side until the purchaser was informed that his reply had reached the vendor, and was assented to by him. In this way the transaction would be spun out indefinitely without ever reaching a termination. The offer must consequently be regarded as continuing or renewed during each instant that the letter was travelling through the post, and when it finally reached the vendor and was accepted, the minds of the parties met, and there was no further room for retraction on either side.

As one who makes an offer may enlarge so he may limit the period for acceptance, or provide that it shall be sent to a certain place, or by a particular mode of conveyance; and if his directions are not followed, it will not be enough to allege that the letter was delivered to him elsewhere.[1] In this instance, the defendants sent an offer for flour from his mill near Harper's Ferry, by a teamster in his employ, with a request that the plaintiffs would reply by return of wagon. Instead of complying literally, the plaintiffs forwarded their acceptance of the offer to the defendants' residence at Georgetown, by the first regular mail, which left five days later. The court held that a purchaser has the right to dictate the terms on which he will buy, and unless these are complied with he is not bound. All his arrangements may be made with a

[1] Eliason *v.* Henshaw, 4 Wheat. 225.

view to the circumstance of place, and he is the only judge of its importance.

In thus entering on the consideration of contracts made by persons at a distance from each other through the post-office or by letters interchanged in any other way, new points arise, and it becomes necessary to consider when such an agreement is complete, and whether it is essential that the person who mailed the offer should know that it has been accepted. An acceptance is virtually a promise to comply with the terms of the offer, and therefore can only arise from something said or written to the offerer. It is implied in the definition of an agreement that it shall be between the parties, and the most formal declaration of intention to a third person will not constitute a contract. Obviously I am not bound to keep a promise made to one who does not wish it to be fulfilled, nor unless he manifests his willingness in a way to convey the information to me. A written like an oral acceptance must therefore be communicated to the party who made the offer, or to some one whom he has expressly or impliedly authorized, and this requirement is not fulfilled by giving it to the writer's agent or messenger, with orders to deliver it to the offerer.[1] In Hebbs' Case, Hebbs wrote asking that certain shares in a newly formed company might be allotted to him. The directors instructed their agent through the mail that such an allotment should be made, and the shares were registered as Hebbs', and it was held that this did not complete the contract, or render it obligatory on him to take and pay for the shares. Lord Romilly said: "If A writes to B a letter offering to buy land of B for a certain sum of money, and B accepts the offer and sends his servant with a letter containing his acceptance, I apprehend that until A receives the letter A may withdraw his offer, and B may stop his servant on the road and alter the terms of his acceptance, or withdraw it altogether; he is not bound by communicating the acceptance to his own agent. Dunlop *v.* Higgins decides that the posting

[1] Hebbs' Case, L. R. 4 Eq. 9; British & Am. Telegraph Co. *v.* Colson, L. R. 6 Ex. Div. 108, 117.

of a letter accepting an offer constitutes a binding contract, but the reason of that is that the post-office is the common agent of both parties. In the present case, if Mr. Hebbs had authorized the agent of the company to accept the allotment on his behalf there would have been a binding contract, but he gave no such authority, and as he had withdrawn his original offer before he received the letter of the directors, the position of the parties was changed, and that letter became an offer which required the acceptance of Mr. Hebbs to constitute a binding contract."

The same person may nevertheless be an agent for both parties, and when such is the case the mailing of a letter to him by either of them may have the same effect as if it were addressed to the other.[1] In Hallock *v.* Insurance Co., the plaintiff applied for an insurance to the agent of the company, Breck, and the latter forwarded the application to the company, who executed the policy and sent it by mail to the agent. The train was detained for two days by a heavy fall of snow, and during the interval the plaintiff's house was destroyed by fire, and the insurance company thereupon sent a telegram to the agent declining the risk, which reached him in advance of the mail and before he received the policy. The court held that when the policy was sent by mail to Breck he took in trust for the insured, and not for the insurers. It was a delivery to Breck to deliver to the plaintiff, and therefore a good delivery to the plaintiff. The act by which one signifies his acceptance of an offer need not be known to the offerer.

It has also been said, and is no doubt true in general, that a promise must be made by some means which not only may but do convey the meaning to the promisee, while he must be equally explicit in his reply. As Merlin ingeniously suggests, an oral offer to a deaf man is not binding, nor will he be bound by a promise of acceptance signified with his fingers to one who does not understand the language of signs. The commentators on the civil law accordingly hold that to convert an offer or pollicitation into a contract, the party to whom it is addressed must not only assent, but his acceptance must

[1] Hallock *v.* Ins. Co., 2 Dutch. 268.

be communicated to the party from whom the offer came.[1] This is generally conceded where the parties contract orally and face to face, and Merlin contends that the principle is the same when they are at a distance from each other, and writing is substituted for speech. *Epistola non contrahit sed nuntiat dominum contrahere.* It is not the letter but the intelligence which it conveys that constitutes the contract. Hence when the negotiation is conducted through the mail the contract is not complete, agreeably to this view of the law, until the acceptance is received, nor unless it is so expressed that it can be understood, nor if the writer despatches a second letter which overtakes the first and both are delivered at the same instant.[2]

It may be said with regard to this observation that written language is not on the same footing as spoken. Words are fugitive, but writing remains and is susceptible of delivery. A promise made in English to one who only understood Russian, would be analogous to the case of the deaf man supposed by Merlin, but it may be contended that if the Englishman were to reduce the acceptance to writing and send it through the mail, the contract would be complete immediately on the receipt of the letter, although the persons present could not read it and it was necessary to look for an interpreter. Still I apprehend that the acceptance would not be obligatory in such a case if an interpreter could not be found within a reasonable time and with due diligence. The doctrine of the French jurists accordingly seems to be that posting an acceptance does not complete the contract, which will on the contrary be revocable while the letter is passing through the mail, and fail if it be not delivered.

It follows that if one who has mailed a letter of acceptance signifies his dissent by a second letter, which overtakes the first, and both are delivered at the same time, there is no contract.[3]

[1] Maynz, ii. § 201, note 11.

[2] Merlin, Répertoire de Jurisprudence, Title vente, § 1, art. 3, No. 11, Pardessus, Droit Commercial, No. 250; see Thomson *v.* James, 18 Dunlop, 1.

[3] Merlin, Répertoire de Jurisprudence, Title vente, art. 3, No. 11. See Dunmore *v.* Alexander, 9 Sh. & D. 190. The civil law rule on

Such would also seem to have been the opinion which originally prevailed in England, although it is now superseded by one more in conformity with the common-law doctrine that the contract is complete on compliance with the terms prescribed.

In Kennedy *v.* Lee,[1] Lord Eldon said: "I have always understood the law of the court to be with reference to this sort of contract that if a person communicates his acceptance of an offer within a reasonable time after the offer being made, and if within a reasonable time of the acceptance being communicated no variation has been made by either party in the terms of the offer as made and accepted, the acceptance must be taken as simultaneous with the offer, and both together as constituting such an agreement as the court will execute."

While this language shows that the offer, and the acceptance need not be simultaneous, it would seem to indicate that

this head seems to be accurately given in the following extract from the argument for the defence in Thomson *v.* James, 18 Dunlop, 1. "The rule of law, as given in the Digest, *De Pactis*, in the words of Ulpianus, is that the meeting of the acts of the will must take place, like the meeting of two physical bodies, in one place. There must be *duorum pluriumvæ in idem placitum consensus.* To satisfy this definition, the concourse of the wills of both or all the contracting parties must be simultaneous. When both parties are in the same place, *inter præsentes*, the application of the rule is easy. In such a case, in order to complete the contract, the act of the will of each must be made known to the other. If, therefore, acceptance of the offer be made by a sign which is not understood by the offerer, there is no contract. So if the offer be made in writing, and the party to whom it is made writes an acceptance, and does not deliver it, there is no contract because there is no *concursus* of wills. *Inter præsentes*, therefore, there is no contract until the act of the will of each is known to the other. From the same definition it may be further deduced that consent may be given *inter absentes per nuntium*, or *per epistolam.* And this is quite consistent, provided you have an equivalent to what the law requires *inter præsentes.* This is well stated by a French civilian, Pardessus, who says: 'There is required not only that the offer be known to the party to whom it is made, and the acceptance to the offerer, but that up to the moment of the acceptance being made known, when the concourse of will takes place, the will of the offerer shall have continued. Nothing farther is necessary then. No notification of receipt of the acceptance is required.'"

[1] 3 Meriv. 440.

the minds of both parties must be unchanged until the intention to accept the offer is communicated to the person who made it, and that there may even then be a *locus pœnitentiæ* or change of purpose.

It was accordingly decided in McCulloch *v.* Insurance Co.,[1] that to render an acceptance valid it must be communicated to the offerer, and that the defendants were consequently at liberty to recall their proposal to insure the plaintiff's vessel after he had mailed his acceptance, and until the letter actually came to hand. It is a necessary inference that a negotiation for an insurance through the post-office is subject to the contingencies which may arise between the sending of the letter and the receipt of the reply, and that if the loss of the vessel becomes known during the interval both parties will be discharged. This decision may be consistent with the principles of the civil law, but is at variance with the common-law rule that the obligation of a contract depends on the consideration, or in other words, on the fulfilment of the conditions prescribed by the promisor. If this leaves him in the dark the fault is his own, and he cannot demand more, or complain of the want of information for which he did not stipulate. Such is the case when an offer is sent through the post-office, because the offerer may reasonably be supposed to intend that the contract shall be complete as soon as the answer is deposited in the letter-box, and to take the risk incident to that mode of communication. The judgment in McCulloch *v.* Insurance Co.,[2] has accordingly been overruled by the subsequent course of decision, which coincides, on both sides of the Atlantic, with Adams *v.* Lindsell.[3] In Hamilton *v.* Insurance Co.,[4] the defendants agreed to insure the premises if the trustees who held the legal title would give their consent in writing, and an earthen flue was substituted for a sheet-iron one.

[1] 1 Pick. 278.

[2] 1 Pick. 278.

[3] See Dunlop *v.* Higgins, 1 H. L. C. 381; Duncan *v.* Topham, 8 C. B. 225; Hamilton *v.* Ins. Co., 5 Barr, 339; Tayloe *v.* Ins. Co., 9 How. 390; Boston & Maine R. R. Co. *v.* Bartlett, 3 Cush. 224; Abbott *v.* Shepard, 48 N. H. 14; Stockham *v.* Stockham, 32 Md. 196.

[4] 5 Barr, 339.

These conditions were complied with, and the premium paid to the agent of the insurance company, who was asked to call and ascertain that the alteration had been made. He did not attend to this request, and the buildings having subsequently been destroyed by fire, the defendants refused to pay the loss on the ground that the contract was not complete, and that no policy had been executed. Gibson, C. J., said that to render the insurers liable the terms of the contract must have been determined on either side, so that nothing remained but the execution and delivery of the policy. In McCulloch *v.* Insurance Co.,[1] the plaintiff wrote to learn the terms on which the defendants would be willing to insure his vessel, and was answered that they would do so at 2½ per cent. He immediately sent an order for insurance on the terms proposed; but before it was mailed the defendants despatched another letter declining to take the risk, and it was held that at no instant had there been a simultaneous expression of assent. On a principle somewhat analogous stood Cooke *v.* Oxley,[2] where it appeared by the declaration that the defendant had offered the plaintiff a commodity at a certain price provided the latter would give notice of his acceptance before four o'clock in the afternoon, that the notice was given within the time, but that the article was not delivered, and judgment was arrested because the plaintiff had not laid a cause of action. This case was resolvable into the principle that either party may retract his offer while the matter is pending, just as a bid at auction may be retracted before the hammer is down. Such, too, was the principle of Routledge *v.* Grant,[3] and it was a very practicable one, where the negotiation was not carried on through the post-office. The last decision on the point was irreconcilable with McCulloch *v.* Insurance Co. In Adams *v.* Lindsell,[4] the defendants offered to sell the plaintiffs a parcel of wool on terms expressed in their letter: "receiving an answer in course of post." The letter being misdirected did not go by course of post, but the plaintiffs wrote as soon as it was received that they would take the wool at the price

[1] 1 Pick. 278. [2] 3 T. R. 653. [3] 3 C. & P. 267.
[4] 1 B. & Ald. 681.

proposed. The defendants, however, not having received an answer when they expected it, sold the wool to another person. The court said that if a bargain could not be closed by letter before the answer was received, no contract could be completed through the medium of the post-office. That if the defendants' offer did not become obligatory when the letter of acceptance was posted, the plaintiffs by a parity of reasoning would not be bound till they were notified that the defendants had received the answer and assented to it, and so it might go on *ad infinitum*. That the defendants must be considered in law as making a continuing offer during every instant their letter was travelling through the mail; that the contract was completed by the posting of the letter of acceptance; and that, as the delay arose from the mistake of the defendants themselves, the case stood relatively to them as if the answer had arrived in due course. The learned reporter of McCulloch *v.* Insurance Co., had attempted to distinguish it from Adams *v.* Lindsell, principally on the ground that a treaty respecting insurance is necessarily subject to contingencies while it is in the process of formation. This observation was undoubtedly just. But the question remained: When is it entirely formed? Had the ship in the former case returned before the plaintiffs answered, the negotiation would have ended, but it did not follow that they could have retracted their acceptance after it had been mailed. The two cases were irreconcilable, and the only just conclusion was that an actual concurrence of assent was the ruling circumstance, and the time at which it was communicated or made known comparatively immaterial. Applying this principle to the case in hand, it stood as follows: the insurance company had offered to effect an insurance for a certain premium on the performance by the plaintiff of two conditions, which were fulfilled and the company notified. There was no supineness on the part of the plaintiff, at least none which had not been induced by the agent, while the company, on the other hand, was chargeable with positive negligence. A promise to reward a man if he will do a service was binding if he did it, though he did not engage to render the service. The nature of a conditional promise resting on an executory consideration, was explained in Clark *v.* Russel,[1] and what was there said showed that the plaintiff, having actually performed what he had been requested to do, might justly claim the benefit of the insurance. The contract was completed when the company had notice that its conditions were performed; and from that moment they became answerable for the risk incurred.

The notice referred to in the above opinion as completing the obligation, is not the acceptance of the civil law, but the notification which the common law requires when the defendant's liability depends on a fact which lies beyond his ken and within the plaintiff's. Thus a tenant who wishes to enforce a covenant to repair must inform his landlord that the premises are out of order and need repairing.[2]

A similar decision was made in Tayloe *v.* Insurance Co.[3] The defendants wrote offering to insure the plaintiff's house on certain terms, and the contract was held to be complete as soon as the acceptance of the proposition was mailed. The court said that when a person to whom an offer is made through the post-office writes an answer giving his consent and puts it in the letter-box, there is a binding contract whether the letter does or does not reach its destination. It was erroneous to suppose that an acceptance was not binding until it became known to the other party, and it was on the contrary well settled that the contract was perfected by the meeting of both minds in a common purpose, although one of the parties might be ignorant that the other had given his assent.

The view taken in Hamilton *v.* Insurance Co.,[4] by Chief Justice Gibson is borne out by the decision in Harris' Case.[5] There one who had applied for shares in a joint-stock company posted a letter in Dublin withdrawing his application after an allotment had been put in the London post-office. The letters crossed each other on the way, and it was held

1 3 Watts, 213, 217.

2 Vyse *v.* Wakefield, 6 M. & W. 442; 7 id. 126; 2 Am. Leading Cases, 5 ed. 68.

3 9 How. 390.

4 5 Barr, 339.

5 L. R. 7 Ch. 587.

that he must take and pay for the shares. The Chancellor said that the contract had been completed exactly in the way that the applicant desired. He gave his address in Dublin, and the company, according to the ordinary usage of mankind in such matters, sent their answer to that address through the post. It did not signify at what hour either letter arrived or which was first delivered, because the obligation became irrevocable when the company posted the letter of allotment.

It is said in Parsons on Contracts,[1] on the authority of these decisions and of Hutcheson *v.* Blakeman,[2] that an offer made by mail cannot be withdrawn by a notification which does not reach the other party before the answer containing his acceptance is mailed. "If, for instance, A writes on the 1st of January from Boston to B in Baltimore, making an offer, and this letter reaches Baltimore on the 3d, and B forthwith answers the letter, accepting the offer, putting the letter into the mail that day; and on the 2d of January A writes withdrawing the offer, and his letter of withdrawal reaches B on the 4th, there is nevertheless a contract made between the parties. If the offer was to sell goods, B on tendering the price may claim the goods; if the offer was to insure B's ship, B may tender the premium and demand the policy, and hold A as an insurer of his ship; and so of any other offer or proposition."

It is a corollary to this rule that a delay in the transmission of the acceptance, or its entire miscarriage through the default of the post-office or the condition of the roads, will not invalidate the assent which has been already given, or excuse a refusal to perform the contract, although the effect is to mislead the opposite party and induce him to suppose that his offer has been declined, and he in consequence disposes of the goods to a third person, or takes some other step which renders it impracticable to carry out the terms proposed. For as the obligation is complete immediately on the posting the acceptance, it ought not to be defeated by a default for which the writer is not responsible, and which may with more pro-

1 * 484.

2 3 Met. (Ky.) 80.

priety be set down to the account of the opposite party. A vendor who sends an offer through the mail accepts the risk incident to that mode of conveyance, and if a loss results it should be borne by him and not by the purchaser. The case is analogous to that which would arise if a proposal were sent by a servant, with instructions to wait for an answer which was lost through the negligence of the messenger.[1] In Dunlop *v.* Higgins,[2] Dunlop & Co. wrote from Glasgow to Higgins & Co., at Liverpool, offering to sell them two thousand tons of pig iron. This letter was received by the Messrs. Higgins on the 30th of January, and on the same day though not by the next succeeding post of that day, they despatched an answer in these terms: "We will take the two thousand tons pigs you offer us." Although this letter was written and sent on the 30th of January, it bore date on the 31st, and one point in the case was that the error might have contributed to mislead Dunlop & Co. Owing to a severe frost and heavy fall of snow the acceptance was not delivered to Dunlop & Co. until the 1st of February, when they made the following reply: —

"GLASGOW, 1st February, 1845.

"We have your letter of yesterday, but are sorry that we cannot enter the two thousand tons pig iron, our offer of the 28th not having been accepted in course."

The Messrs. Higgins answered on the 2d of February that they had erroneously dated their letter on the 31st of January, but that, as the post-mark showed, it was really mailed on the 30th. The iron was not furnished, and having risen rapidly in price, the question whether the contract had been completed was raised by a suit.

The case ultimately came before the House of Lords. The Chancellor said the exception was that the jury were directed that if the plaintiffs posted their acceptance in due time according to the usage of trade, they were not responsible for any casualties in the post-office. This raised the question whether the letter being delayed, not by the act of the

[1] See Vassar *v.* Camp, 1 Kernan, 441.

[2] 1 H. L. C. 381.

writer but by an accident connected with the post, should deprive him of the right which would have existed if the letter had arrived in due course. He could not conceive that the point was at all doubtful. If a man did all he could, more should not be required. If the usage of trade was to forward the answer to such an offer by means of the post, and the party mailed his acceptance on the proper day, did he not do everything that he was bound to do, and could he be made responsible for that over which he had no control?

If such be the principle, it must hold good when the letter is destroyed or stolen in passing through the post-office, and never reaches the person to whom it is addressed. It was accordingly declared in Duncan *v.* Topham,[1] on the authority of Dunlop *v.* Higgins, that the contract is complete on the posting by one party of a letter addressed to the opposite party and accepting the terms which he has offered, although the letter of acceptance is not delivered, or the fact made known to him in any other way; and the same rule was applied in Vassar *v.* Camp.[2] In the case last cited the defendants wrote by mail, proposing to sell the plaintiffs ten thousand bushels of first quality Jefferson county barley at sixty-seven cents per bushel, on or before the 20th of October next, and the plaintiffs accepted the offer by a letter posted in due season, but which, owing to some unexplained default in the post-office, was not delivered. They wrote not long afterward asking why the barley did not arrive, and were then informed of the miscarriage of the letter of acceptance. The defendants, in consequence of not hearing from the plaintiffs, omitted to procure the barley, and before the cause of the delay was discovered grain had risen to such a price that the contract could not be carried into effect without a loss. The court held the excuse insufficient, and that the defendants must bear the loss, which amounted to $2,000.

The court said that the defendants had, it was true, stated in the course of the correspondence which led to the formation of the contract, that as soon as the plaintiff's answer "was received they would send amongst the farmers and secure the

[1] 8 C. B. 225. [2] 1 Kernan, 441.

first lots, even at an extra price," and that "if the offer was accepted they must have immediate notice;" but this did not materially affect the case, because the notice thus stipulated for was presumably a notice by the mail, through which the whole negotiation was no doubt expected to be, and was in fact conducted. When notice was to be given by mail it was sufficient, in most if not in all cases, to deposit it in the post-office. The party could then do nothing more to insure its safe delivery, and was not responsible for its miscarriage. It followed that the contract was perfected on the fourth of September when the plaintiffs signed the writing which had been forwarded to them for acceptance, and deposited it in the post-office addressed to the defendants.

The language held in Trevor *v.* Wood,[1] is to the same effect, although the acceptance was telegraphed and the question grew out of a delay in the transmission of the message, which led the defendant to believe that his offer was declined.

These judgments and that pronounced in Dunlop *v.* Higgins may be considered as outweighing British & American Telegraph Co. *v.* Colson,[2] where the court took a distinction between the case where the letter, though delayed by a storm, the state of the roads or other accidental causes, is delivered as soon as circumstances will permit, and that in which it is lost or destroyed and never reaches the person to whom it is addressed, and held that in the latter case there is no binding contract. Baron Bramwell said that if the acceptance was intrusted to a messenger who took the best and quickest mode of conveyance, but was kept back by frost or snow, and did not arrive until hours or days after he was expected, the contract would be complete notwithstanding the delay, and that the principle was the same when a delay occurred in transmission through the mail; but it was fallacious to reason from such a state of things to that where the letter was never delivered or received. The answer to this argument is that since, as Bramwell conceded, the obligation of the contract dates from the period at which the acceptance is mailed, it cannot be avoided by the happening of a subsequent event, in the absence

[1] 36 N. Y. 307.

[2] L. R. 6 Ex. 108.

of an express condition to that effect, or, as the argument was put in Harris' Case,[1] if the contract after the letter has arrived in time is to be treated as having been made from the time the letter was posted, the reason is that the contract was actually made at that time. There is nevertheless the practical objection that when the letter is delayed by an accident to the mail, or a break in the telegraph wires, the person to whom it is addressed may ascertain the cause by inquiring at the proper office, and should wait until communication is restored; but that when the trains are running regularly and there is no obstacle to the transmission of a telegram, there is nothing to put him on his guard, and he may reasonably infer that the reason why he does not receive a reply is that none was sent, and that the offer has fallen through the lapse of time.

The effect of this course of decision is to compel one who makes an offer through the post-office, to take the risk of the casualties incident to that mode of communication, whether they occur during the transmission of his letter or of the reply. Hence, if I write by mail offering to sell, and the response does not arrive in due course, I must find out as best I may whether the delay is due to the negligence of my correspondent in not answering, or the failure of the post-office to deliver his reply, and cannot safely part with the goods until I have ascertained the truth. The inconvenience is less since the introduction of the telegraph, which affords a ready mode of inquiring whether the offer was received and has been accepted or delivered.

The controversy is now presumably closed in England by the recent case of Household Insurance Co. *v.* Grant.[2] The defendant there applied by a letter written and mailed on the 30th of September for one hundred shares in a joint-stock company, and on the 20th of the succeeding month a letter was duly addressed and posted assenting to his request, but which from some unexplained cause never reached the defendant. The judicial committee of the Privy Council held that the contract was complete immediately on the posting of the

[1] L. R. 7 Ch. 587, 596. [2] 41 L. T. N. S. 298.

letter, and that the defendant was liable to pay the calls made on the shares. The judgment of Thesiger, L. J., was substantially to the following effect: Whatever might be said in the abstract of the notion that the minds of the parties must meet at the one and the same moment, that notion practically lay at the foundation of the English law on the formation of contracts, and it was not less well established that both must be brought together by mutual communications. Where the negotiation took place through the mail, the best mode of harmonizing these elements was to treat the post-office as the agent of both parties. If that theory was adopted, it followed that as soon as the letter of acceptance was mailed the contract was as binding as if the acceptor had put his letter into the hands of a messenger sent by the offerer to deliver the offer and receive the answer. The implication that the contract became absolute as soon as the acceptance was posted might sometimes be attended with injurious consequences, but it was impossible so to adjust the conflicting rights of parties residing at a distance from each other and negotiating through the post-office, that the mistakes of the mutual agent should fall equally on both. The question was relative; and in cases like that before the court the balance of convenience inclined to the rule that where the offer contained nothing to the contrary, neither party could retract after the acceptance had been mailed. This did not preclude the offerer from stipulating that he should not be bound unless the answer was actually received.

Bramwell, L. J., dissented *totis viribus*, on the following grounds: The rule was that the acceptance must be communicated in order to constitute the contract, which implied that the letter or message must reach the person who made the offer. The rule was clear, and had been authoritatively stated by Brian, C. J., in the Year Book 17 Edw. IV., 1.[1] If the rule did not hold good when the acceptance was in reply to an offer through the mail, it must be by virtue of some general principle which applied whenever the post-office was used as the means of communication (a doctrine that would lead to great

[1] Cited in Blackburn on Sales, p. 190.

inconvenience), or else because one who sends a letter by post must be presumed to agree not only that the reply may be transmitted through the same channel, but that he will be bound although the letter never comes to hand. A man might no doubt enter into such an agreement, as he might agree that his offer should be conclusively accepted by hanging out a flag, firing a cannon, or depositing a letter in a certain place; but the question was, — Should such an agreement be implied? Why should mailing the acceptance have any greater effect than giving it to a messenger? It was alleged that the acceptance would be revocable in one case, and not in the other; but this was begging the question, for although the post-office would not give back the letter, its arrival might be anticipated by a message sent by hand, or by a telegram. It was an alarming inference that a letter written under the influence of an honest misapprehension was necessarily conclusive, although the person addressed was informed of the mistake before the delivery of the letter. When a letter sent by mail arrived, the contract was complete from the posting of this letter. So of a letter sent by hand; but if the letter did not come there was no contract. If Chief Justice Brian were there to decide the question, he would say that the law should be the same since the establishment of the post-office as it was before, namely, "that a communication, to affect a man, must be a communication, that is, must not only be sent but delivered."

It may be observed with regard to this conflict of opinion, that the difference between the majority and minority of the court was one of fact rather than of principle. It was conceded by the minority that if the terms of the offer were that posting should be a sufficient communication nothing more was requisite, and the contract would be complete although the letter did not arrive. On the other hand, the majority of the court were equally ready to admit that if the offerer said, "If I do not hear from you by return of post I will not be bound," the acceptance must not only be posted, but reach its destination. What the court had to determine, therefore, was what the parties should be presumed to have intended where their meaning was not expressed in terms, a question obviously not so much of law as of commercial usage.

We have seen that Thesiger, L. J., said, in delivering judgment, that to effect a valid contract "the minds of the parties must be brought together at one and the same moment," and that this lay at the foundation of the English law upon the subject. If such were really the rule of the common law, as it is of the civil, it should be attended with the same consequences under both systems of jurisprudence. Agreeably to the civil law, as interpreted in France, and generally by the Continental jurists, it is essential not only that the offer should be known to the party to whom it is made and the acceptance to the offerer, but that the acceptance should be delivered or communicated to the offerer before he has unequivocally changed his purpose.[1] Conversely, the retraction of an offer will take effect as soon as it is posted, although it does not reach the opposite party until after he has signified his assent. The English law is, as already stated, the direct opposite,—that a retraction is not effectual until it is made known, while an acceptance takes effect at once and although it never reaches the person who made the offer. We have, therefore, the singular spectacle of a court professing to be governed by a rule derived from the law of another age and country, and yet rejecting the conclusions of the commentators who have made that law a life-long study. The true explanation of the divergence is, as the chancellor indicated in Dunlop *v.* Higgins, that the obligation of a contract arises at common law not from a mere concurrence of wills or purposes, but from the fulfilment of the terms prescribed by the promisor, in good faith and without notice that he has changed his mind. If A writes to B that he will give him one thousand dollars for thirty bales of cotton, if B will post a letter declaring his acceptance of the offer, and B writes such a letter and puts it in the mail,

[1] Merlin, Répertoire de Jurisprudence, Tit. vente, No. 11; Touillier, Droit Civil, liv. iii. ch. v. No. 321, cited in Thomson *v.* James, 18 Dunlop, 1; Mactier *v.* Frith, 6 Wend. 103. See Maynz, ii. § 201, note 11; Pardessus, Traité du Droit Commercial, No. 250. See Wharton on Contracts, § 18.

A is bound although he has despatched another letter stating that he will not buy, because the posting of the letter is a consideration moving from B at A's request, and which renders the promise irrevocable. In other words, the validity of an acceptance is tested under the civil law by the rules applicable to promises, while the question is regarded at common law as one of performance.

An acceptance sent by mail cannot be effectual as a promise until it reaches the offerer, nor will it bring both minds together if they have diverged during the interval; but it is an act done at his request and constituting a consideration which completes the contract. Thus, in the case already put, of a correspondence between a Russian and an Englishman, the understanding being that each should write in his own language, the receipt of a letter of acceptance from the Englishman would not, as I infer, complete the contract agreeably to the civil law if the Russian did not understand English and could not procure an interpreter, but would be obligatory at common law as affording all that he had asked for, and in the way prescribed. What the English authorities really establish, therefore, is, to use the language of Blackburn, that when one "makes an offer through the mail, and expressly or impliedly says, 'if you accept, send the answer by the post,' then as soon as the person to whom the offer is made puts the acceptance beyond his control by depositing it in the letter-box, there is an extraneous act which clinches the offer, and the contract is therefore complete."[1]

It does not appear that the dicta of Brian, C. J., in the case cited from the Year-Book 17 Edw. IV., are contrary to this position, or can be relied on to sustain the opinion of Lord Justice Bramwell. The report, as translated in Blackburn on the Contract of Sale, shows that the question arose on a plea to an action of trespass for breaking and entering the plaintiff's close, and taking away the growing crops, that the parties had agreed that the defendant should go to the place where the aforesaid standing wheat and oats were, and if they pleased him that he should then take the same, paying therefor 3*s*. 4*d*.

[1] See Brogden *v*. Metropolitan R. R. Co., L. R. 2 App. Cases, 666, 692.

per acre. It was further averred that the defendant went to the place, saw the crops, was well content and took them; which was the trespass complained of. The plea was demurred to and held insufficient by Brian and the other judges on the following grounds, as stated by him: 1st. That it could not have been intended that the defendant should take the corn without paying for it, although the case would have been different in this regard if the plaintiff had said "Take, and pay when you will," or named a future day for payment. 2d. The plea was defective in not showing that the defendant had certified the plaintiff that he was satisfied, "for it is trite learning that the thought of man is not triable, for the devil himself knows not the thought of man." Had the agreement been that "if the bargain pleased him he should show it to such a one, then he need not have done more, for that is a matter of fact." The fair inference from this language seemingly is not that the acceptance need be communicated to the person who makes the offer, but that it must be declared overtly by some means stipulated for by the offerer, and tend to make the acceptance known to him, whether that effect be or be not produced.[1]

Firing a cannon or hanging out a flag might not come within the definition as being too merely trivial; but this cannot be said of posting a letter, because as soon as it is mailed the position of the writer changes, and he can no longer dispose of the goods without exposing himself to an action for damages by the person to whom it is addressed.[2] And as he is necessarily in suspense, and obliged to decline other proposals until he learns whether the letter has or has not been delivered, posting is a sufficient consideration to complete the contract when such is the express or implied condition of the offer.

The doctrine that the contract may be perfected by an ac-

[1] White *v.* Corlies, 46 N. Y. 467, 469; Howard *v.* Daly, 61 id. 362, 366. In Howard *v.* Daly depositing a written acceptance in the defendant's letter-box was held to be within this rule, although he never saw or received the document.

[2] See Holbrook *v.* Insurance Co., 2 Dutch. 268.

ceptance which is not made known or actually communicated to the party who made the offer, is of comparatively recent growth; and time alone can determine its true limits, and whether it was not unduly extended in Vassar *v.* Camp. The hardships incident to holding that one may be bound by that which he does not and cannot know, were forcibly portrayed in the British and American Telegraph Co. *v.* Colson,[1] and may raise a doubt whether a rule which involves such consequences is altogether sound and should be adopted without qualification.

The inclination of the authorities seems to be that contracts made by telegram obey the same rule as contracts through the mail, and are complete as soon as the acceptance is left at the office of the telegraph company for transmission, although the sender withdraws the message immediately afterwards, and before it is forwarded to the party from whom the offer came or the contents have been communicated in any other way.[2]

In Minnesota Oil Co. *v.* Collier Lead Co., Nelson, J., said: "It is well settled by the authorities in this country, and sustained by the later English decisions, that there is no difference in the rules governing the negotiation of contracts by correspondence through the post-office and by telegraph, and that a contract is concluded when an acceptance of a proposition is deposited in the telegraph office for transmission. This rule was not strenuously dissented from on the argument, and it was substantially admitted that the acceptance of an offer by letter or by telegraph completes the contract when such acceptance is put in the proper and usual way of being communicated by the agency employed to carry it; and that when an offer is made by telegraph, an acceptance by telegraph takes effect when the despatch containing the acceptance is deposited for transmission in the telegraph office, and not when it is received by the other party."[3]

[1] *Ante*, p. 147.

[2] Trevor *v.* Wood, 36 N. Y. 307; Minnesota Oil Co. *v.* Collier Lead Co., 4 Dill. 434.

[3] See an article entitled "The Law applicable to the Negotiation of Contracts by Telegraph," Am. Law Reg. vol. xiv. No. 7, 401.

This language may be thought to be too broad. A written acceptance is not complete until it reaches the person from whom the offer came, or some one who receives it on his behalf, or is under an imperative obligation to deliver it to him; and sending such a paper through a servant or agent will not render it obligatory while it is in the keeping of the messenger, or before delivery to the party to whom it is addressed, because until then it is subject to the control of the writer, and may be altered or destroyed. In like manner a telegraphic message may, as I suppose, be recalled by the sender, not only before it has been sent over the wires, but afterwards, down to the last moment which precedes delivery. A telegraph company is not like the post-office established by the government for public uses, but a private agency, which cannot be made answerable for non-feasance in the absence of a contract express or implied, or to one by whom it has not been employed. If A telegraph to B for goods, or for rooms at a hotel, and the message is not forwarded, both parties may be losers, but the damage to B is *absque injuria* and A is the only person who can maintain a suit. Hence until the order is communicated to B it may be countermanded by A, and the company will be liable in damages for transmitting it contrary to his wishes. So we may believe that one who replies by telegraph to an offer sent by mail, may exercise a like control over the message while it is on the way, and that the person to whom it is addressed cannot recover damages for the failure of the company to forward a communication for which he has not paid. When, however, a proposal made by telegraph is accepted through the same channel, it may plausibly be contended that the parties have selected the company as their common agent, and that the contract is complete as soon as the message is placed in the hands of the operator for transmission. The obligation of a contract arises from the fulfilment of the conditions on which the promisor agreed to be bound, and if these are that the promisee shall signify his assent by a writing sent to a telegraph office or put in the mail, nothing more is requisite.[1] From this point of view

[1] See Brit. & Am. Telegraph Co. *v.* Colson, L. R. 6 Ex. 108, 119.

both parties are entitled to require that the acceptance shall be forwarded without alteration or delay, and it cannot rightfully be withdrawn or cancelled without the consent of both. The test is, can the company surrender the acceptance without being liable to the party who made the offer. If the question must be answered negatively in view of all the circumstances, the contract is complete.

In Trevor *v.* Wood,[1] the appellants, who were dealers in bullion in New York, had agreed with the respondents, who followed the same line of business in New Orleans, to deal with each other in the purchase and sale of dollars, and that all the communications between them in reference to such transactions should be by telegraph. On January 30th the appellants telegraphed from New York to the respondents at New Orleans, asking at what price they would sell one hundred thousand Mexican dollars. On the 31st of the same month the respondents answered by telegram that they would deliver $50,000 at 7¼; and the appellants forthwith telegraphed their acceptance of this offer, and at the same time posted a letter acknowledging the receipt of the respondents' telegram, and enclosing a copy of their own. Owing to some derangement of the wires the appellants' telegram did not reach the respondents till the 4th of the following month, after they had telegraphed, "No answer to our despatch; the dollars are sold." The appellants replied: "Your offer was accepted; the dollars must come, or we will hold you responsible." The case was sent to a referee, who found for the appellants, and the award was sustained in the court of last resort. Scrugham, J., said it had been established in Mactier *v.* Frith[2] that the concurrence of the minds of the parties manifested by an overt act is all that is necessary to complete a contract, and that despatching a letter announcing the writer's consent to a proposal is such a manifestation, and there was nothing either in that case or in Vassar *v.* Camp to indicate that this effect depended on the letter being sent by mail. This was the more obvious, because when the letter in Mactier *v.* Frith was written there was no mail between New York and the Island of St.

[1] 36 N. Y. 307.

[2] 6 Wend. 103.

Domingo, where it was to be delivered. The mailing of a letter declaring the writer's assent to a proposition operated as an acceptance, not from the nature of the agency employed for its transmission, but because it was an unequivocal signification of the writer's purpose to close with the offer. The object of the parties in the case under consideration in agreeing to transact their business by telegraph was manifestly to give their negotiations through that channel the same force and validity that they would have if carried on by mail. It could not be said that the appellants did not communicate their acceptance in the proper way, because they adopted the method of communication on which both parties had previously agreed. It followed that the sending of the telegraphic despatch must be regarded as an acceptance of the respondents' offer, although it did not reach them until after they had sold the dollars. There was no principle on which an agreement to communicate by telegraph could be held to imply a warranty that the communication should be received, and the just inference on the contrary was that the parties respectively assumed the risks incident to the forwarding of the despatch.

The distinctive feature of this case seems to have been the agreement that all the negotiations that might take place between the parties should be by telegraph. But for this stipulation the letter which was posted immediately on the receipt of the defendants' offer of January 31st would have perfected the contract, and precluded a change of purpose. The effect was to supersede the post-office, and put the telegraph in its place as the agency on which both parties relied, and which was to act for and represent both. The judgment can hardly therefore be regarded as establishing that, in the absence of such an agreement, leaving a message at a telegraph office is equivalent to mailing it.

It results from the definition of an acceptance that it must strictly pursue the offer, and be a clear and unqualified assent to the terms which that prescribes, without addition, alteration, or omission. If there be any variance the entire proposal falls, and what remains is a new offer which stands in as much need of acceptance as that originally made; and hence if the offeree does not answer or declines to accede, the negotiation is at an end.[1] If, for instance, the vendor proposes to sell and deliver on April 1st, and the purchaser replies that he will take the goods on March 31st, and nothing more is said on either side, the sale is not complete, and an action will not lie for the non-delivery of the goods or for the price. So if the offer is of a hundred bushels and the person to whom it is made answers that he will take ninety-nine, there is no contract unless the vendor replies agreeing to the change. The principle is clearly stated as follows, in Benjamin on Sales,[2] — The acceptance must be unconditional. If a condition be affixed by the party to whom the offer is made, or any modification or change in the offer be requested, this constitutes in law a rejection of the offer, and a new proposal equally ineffectual to complete the contract until assented to by the first proposer. Thus, if the offer by the intended vendor be answered by a proposal to give a less sum, this amounts to a rejection of the offer, which is at an end, and the party to whom it was made cannot afterwards bind the intended vendor by a simple acceptance of the first offer." [3]

In Hutchison *v.* Bowker,[4] the defendant wrote an offer to sell a cargo of *good* barley. The plaintiff replied: "Such offer we accept, expecting you will give us *fine* barley, and full weight." The defendant wrote back: "You say you expect we shall give you '*fine* barley.' Upon reference to our offer you will find no such expression. As such we must decline shipping the same." It was shown on the trial that *good* barley and *fine* barley were terms well known in the trade, and that *fine* barley was the heavier. The jury, al-

[1] See Potts *v.* Whitehead, 8 C. E. Gr. 512; Smith *v.* Wetherell, 4 Bradwell App. 655; First National Bank of Quincy *v.* Hall, 101 U. S. 43, 54; Baker *v.* Johnson County, 37 Ia. 186; Hoyt *v.* Brown, 19 N. Y. 111; Maclay *v.* Harvey, 90 Ill. 525; Smith *v.* Hughes, L. R. 6 Q. B. 597; Addenell's Case, L. R. 1 Eq. 225; L. R 4 H. L. 305; Baker *v.* Hall, 56 Wis. 100; Merriam *v.* Lapsley, 2 McCrary, C. Ct. 606; Kyle *v.* Kavanagh, 103 Mass. 356; Falls Mfg. Co. *v.* Broderick, 12 Mo. App. 378; Utley *v.* Donaldson, 94 U. S. 48.

[2] 2d ed., pp. 33, 34, 57, 59.

[3] Hyde *v.* Wrench, 3 Beav. 334.

[4] 5 M. & W. 535.

though finding that there was a difference in the meaning of the two terms, found a verdict for the plaintiff. It was held that the meaning of the words was for the jury, but that their effect was for the court, and the plaintiff was non-suited on the ground that he had not given the unqualified assent which is essential to an acceptance.

The question arose in Routledge *v.* Grant.[1] The defendant offered to purchase the lease of a house, possession to be given on the 25th of July, and a definite answer within six weeks. The plaintiff accepted the proposal, offering possession on the 1st of August. The defendant afterwards, and before the six weeks had expired, retracted his offer. The court held that inasmuch as the plaintiff's acceptance of the offer was not within the terms proposed, and there had been no proper acceptance of it before the offer was withdrawn, the minds of the parties did not meet and there was no valid agreement.

It was said in like manner in Eliason *v.* Henshaw [2] to be an undeniable principle, that an offer of a bargain by one person to another imposes no obligation upon the former until it is accepted by the latter according to the terms in which the offer was made. Any qualification of or departure from those terms invalidates the offer unless the same is agreed to by the person who made it. Until the terms of the agreement have received the assent of both parties the negotiation is open, and imposes no obligation on either side.

We have seen that an offer may be withdrawn at any time before the party to whom it is addressed has signified his assent by some means which he cannot recall. When both parties are together the effect depends on which speaks first, the one to retract or the other to accept the offer.[3] When they are at a distance from each other there is this material difference, that the acceptance is obligatory as soon as it is posted, while the retraction can have no effect until it is made known through the mail or in some other way. The question in such cases is not which was first written or first mailed, but whether the retraction was received before the acceptance

[1] 3 C. & P. 267. [2] 4 Wheat. 225. [3] *Ante*, p. 138.

was put in the post-office. If A mails his acceptance of B's offer, the contract is not less complete because B has written to withdraw the offer, and the letter is actually on its way. The law was so held in Adams *v.* Lindsell,[1] which establishes that an offer made by post is renewed in contemplation of law at each instant of time that the letter is travelling through the mail, and until the person to whom the offer is addressed is duly informed that it has been withdrawn.[2]

The authorities are not less clear that the receipt of a letter or telegram announcing that the offerer has changed his mind, may operate as a revocation down to the last moment before the offeree has signified his assent by some act or declaration which he cannot recall, and though he has written or sent an acceptance through the mail to his agent, with instructions to deliver it to the offerer.[3]

The civil law prescribes a different rule, under which both parties must concur in a common purpose at the moment when the contract is completed by acceptance, and an offer cannot be accepted after it has been withdrawn, although the retraction has not been actually communicated or made known.[4]

"The consent," says Pothier, "which is of the essence of the contract of sale may, as we have already said, be given orally by the interchange of promises or by letters missive. . . . In order that consent should exist in the latter case, the purpose of the party who has written to make the offer must be unchanged until his letter reaches the other party, and the latter has declared his assent. Such continuance will be presumed as long as there is nothing to the contrary; but if I have written to a merchant of Leghorn a letter in which I

[1] B. & Ald. 681.

[2] Byrne *v.* Tievenhoven, L. R. 5 C. P. Div. 344; Stevenson *v.* McLean, 5 Q. B. Div. 346; Tayloe *v.* Ins. Co., 9 How. 390; Wheat *v.* Cross, 31 Md. 99, 103; Stockham *v.* Stockham, 32 id. 396; Kentucky M. Ins. Co. *v.* Jenks, 5 Ind. 96; Lungstrass *v.* German Ins. Co. 48 Mo. 201. See Hamilton *v.* Ins. Co., 5 Barr, 339, 343, *ante*, 143; Thomson *v.* James, 18 Dunlop, 1.

[3] *Ante*, p. 138.

[4] Pardessus, Droit Commercial, No. 256; Merlin, Répertoire de Jurisprudence, Tit. vente, § 1, art. 3, No. 11, *ante*.

propose to purchase of him a certain quantity of merchandise at a certain price, and before my letter has reached him I write a second letter withdrawing my proposal, although the merchant of Leghorn, in ignorance of the change of my intentions, answers that he accepts the proposed bargain, yet there is no contract of sale between us; for my intention not having continued until the time at which my letter was received and my proposal accepted, the concurrence of our wills which is essential to a contract of sale did not exist. It must be observed, however, that if my letter causes the merchant to be at any expense in proceeding to execute the contract proposed, or if it occasions him any loss; as, for example, if in the intermediate time between the receipt of my first and that of my second letter the price of the merchandise falls, and my first letter has led him to miss an opportunity to sell it before the fall of the price, — in all these cases I am bound to indemnify him, unless I prefer to agree to the bargain as proposed by my first letter. This obligation results from that rule of equity that no man should suffer for the act of another; *nemo ex alterius facto prægravari debet.* I ought therefore to indemnify him for the expense and loss which I occasion by making him a proposition which I afterwards refuse to execute. For the same reason, if the merchant, on the receipt of my first letter, and before receiving the second, which contains a revocation of it, ships for my account and forwards the merchandise, though in that case there has not properly been a contract of sale between us, yet he will have a right to compel me to execute the proposed contract, not in virtue of any contract of sale, but of my obligation to indemnify him, which results from the rule of equity above mentioned."[1]

This may be a logical inference from the doctrine that both parties must not only signify their intention, but continue to be of the same mind until the completion of the contract, but it approaches very nearly to a *reductio ad absurdum.* We have seen that a promise is not effectual until it is communicated to the promisee; and the reason applies with still more force to an uncommunicated retraction. It is not so much

[1] Pothier, Contrat de Vente, No. 32.

the intention, as what is said or written and the impression which the language is calculated to produce, that should be considered in determining the effect of dealings between man and man. Of what consequence is it to one who has entered into an engagement on the faith of a request or promise from me, that I have changed my mind, if he has not been informed of the change. This is universally conceded when the request is that another shall make a purchase on my account, and there is no difference as regards the principle when I ask him to sell to me. All the authorities concur that a contract made through an agent is not less binding because his authority has been revoked, if he has not been informed and is ignorant of the fact, and as such a contract is in effect with the principal, the same rule should prevail whether the contract is direct or through an intermediary.

Another consequence of the doctrine that one who makes an offer through the post-office may be bound although he does not know that it has been accepted, is that the contract will not be less obligatory because the offerer dies before the acceptance is delivered. If A writes to B that he will sell at a certain price, and B mails a written acceptance of the offer, the goods are his although A's death occurs immediately afterward, and while the letter is still on its way.

Agreeably to the generally received opinion,[1] an unaccepted offer will fail on the death of the offerer, although the other party gives his assent subsequently in ignorance of the fact, not on the ground of revocation, but because a contract cannot be made with a person who has ceased to exist. The recent authorities nevertheless hold, in accordance with the doctrine of the civil law, that the execution of an order given directly or through an agent or mandatary for work or merchandise, in the belief that the person from whom it comes is still living, is a ground for compensation, although he dies before the goods are forwarded, or the services rendered.[2]

[1] Dickinson *v.* Dodds, L. R. 2 Ch. Div. 475; Mactier *v.* Frith, 1 Paige, 434; 6 Wend. 103, 113; Bradbury *v.* Morgan, 1 H. & C. 249.

[2] See Ish *v.* Crane, 8 Ohio St. 520; 13 id. 574; Cassiday *v.* McKenzie, 4 W. & S. 282; Merlin, Répertoire de Jurisprudence, Tit.

The problem admits of a ready solution at common law; for as the right of action in assumpsit grows out of some act

vente, § 1, art. 3. The remarks of the Lord President on this head, in giving judgment in the case of Thomson *v.* James, 18 Dunlop, 1, deserve an attentive consideration. "The argument of the defender upon this branch of the case was rested upon what I cannot help regarding as a strained application of a rule or maxim, sufficiently sound in general application, but which cannot be applied in the most strictly literal sense that the words admit of. It was contended that as the offerer had changed his mind and had posted a letter announcing that change before the offeree had declared his mind by posting his acceptance, the intention or consent to purchase cannot be held continued until the consent to sell was declared, and consequently that at no one moment of time was there *in idem placitum consensus atque consentio,* which is said to be essential to a paction. It was argued upon a rigid application of that definition that the completion of the contract was interrupted by a change of mind, though not yet communicated, just as it would have been by the death or insanity of the offerer, and that all these three events are classed together by some writers as being alike revocations of the offer. Death or insanity may prevent the completion of the contract as effectually as the most complete revocation, but they are not properly revocations of the offer. They are not acts of the will of the offerer, and their effect does not rest upon a supposed change of purpose. They interrupt the completion of the contract, — that is, the making of the contract, because a contract cannot be made directly with a dead man or lunatic. The contract is not made until the offer is accepted; and if the person with whom you merely intend to contract dies or becomes insane before you have contracted with him, you can no longer contract directly with him. You cannot by adhibiting your acceptance to an offer, and addressing it to a dead man or a lunatic, make it binding on him whether his death or insanity be or be not known to you. In such a case there is no revocation in the correct sense of the word, but there is an interruption, an effectual obstacle to the completion of the contract, equivalent in result to a revocation, though operating by very different facts and very different principles. Revocation or recall is an act of the offerer, by which he communicates his purpose to purchase, the offeree is entitled to regard that purpose as unchanged until a change is communicated. He has acquired a right, which he retains until it is withdrawn from him by a communication from the party who conferred it. If he exercises the right by a completed act of acceptance of the offer before notice has reached him, or ought in ordinary course to have reached him, the contract will be binding, although a change of mind on the part of the offerer had taken place, and although he had taken a step towards communicating that change of mind by writing a letter and putting it into the post-office. In a great many cases the maxim that there must be a concurrence of will the moment of com-

done or engagement entered into at the defendant's express or implied request, so his death is immaterial if the plaintiff is ignorant of the fact and proceeds in the belief that he is still alive, and there is no reason why the acceptance of an offer should be an exception to this rule. It is but just that every man should be accountable in person or estate for the natural and probable consequences of what he does or says. One who makes an offer by the mail or through an agent must know that he may die before it reaches the person to whom it is addressed, and that it may be accepted or acted upon in ignorance of his decease; and if such a result ensues his executors should be held to the obligation which the testator virtually incurred during his life. The point arose in Bradbury *v.* Morgan,[1] in an action against executors on the following instrument, which the testator had executed and delivered to the plaintiff: —

"I request that you will give credit in the usual way of your business to Henry Jones Leigh, of Leather Lane, Holborn; and in consideration of your doing so, I hereby engage to guarantee the regular payment of the running balance of his account with you until I give you notice to the contrary, to the extent of one hundred pounds sterling.

(Signed) "J. M. Leigh."

pletion of the contract cannot be rigidly or literally applied. The very opposite may be the fact. Although one cannot by accepting an offer bind a dead or insane person, he may bind an unwilling person, — one who has altogether changed his mind. Such cases are not infrequent. If an offer bears that it is to be binding for a certain number of days or hours, the offerer may repent before the lapse of the given time, and yet at the end of it may find himself unwillingly bound; or if an offerer changes his mind, but does not take the proper steps to have his change of mind conveyed to the offeree, — either writes no letter, or writes a letter which he omits to send or sends it by mistake to a wrong place, he may find himself unwillingly bound. Other cases may be figured. Mere change of mind on the part of the offeree will not prevent an effectual acceptance, — not even although that change of mind should be evinced by having been communicated to a third party or recorded in a formal writing, as for instance in a notarial instrument; in all these cases a binding contract may be made between the parties without that *consensus* or *concursus* which a rigidly literal reading of the maxim or rule would require."

[1] 1 H. & C. 249.

The declaration did not aver that the plaintiffs assented to or accepted the offer, or that they gave notice of their intention to act in accordance with the request, and simply set forth that the plaintiffs, from time to time, credited the said Henry J. Leigh in the usual course of their business, and that the running balance of his account afterwards and before they knew of his death amounted to £100, and was due and unpaid. The defendant pleaded that the said running balance was for credits given and goods sold and delivered after the said J. M. Leigh's death, and not in his lifetime. The court held on demurrer that J. M. Leigh's death did not revoke the request, or preclude a recovery against his executors for goods which the plaintiff had sold and delivered in the belief that he was still living. The writing was not a power or authority, but a promise on a condition which the plaintiff had fulfilled, and was consequently entitled to remuneration. Here the consideration was performance; but the principle is the same when the promise is conditioned for a reciprocal promise, and the acceptance of an offer in ignorance that it has been revoked by death should consequently give rise to an obligation that may be enforced by and against the representatives of the deceased.[1]

Bradbury *v.* Morgan is consonant with the theory of the common law, but obviously irreconcilable with the doctrine that both minds must meet to constitute a contract. Agreeably to Offord *v.* Davies,[2] there was no such meeting in the guarantor's lifetime, and it obviously could not take place after his decease. A Roman tribunal might nevertheless have arrived at a like result, by interpreting the writing as a mandate and holding the mandatary entitled to compensation for advances made without notice that his authority was gone. A sale made by an agent in ignorance of the principal's death should for a like reason entitle him to the stipulated reward; but the point was decided otherwise in Campanari *v.* Woodburn,[3] on the ground that death is an absolute revocation, or rather that as the principal contracts and the agent is a mere

1 See Mactier *v.* Frith, 6 Wend. 103.

2 12 C. B. N. S. 748, *ante*.

3 15 C. B. 400.

intermediary the sale is merely void.[1] This conclusion might be just were not agency, as the Roman jurists viewed it, a contract which imposes a mutual obligation and entitles the agent to indemnity for acts done in carrying it into effect, and that a service rendered in pursuance of a request or mandate, without notice that it has been revoked, is a ground of compensation whether the doer is acting on his own behalf or for the person by whom the request was made. Acts done and contracts made by an agent in ignorance that it has been revoked by death, are accordingly valid under the civil law, and bind the principal's estate in the hands of his heirs and administrators; and such is the inclination of the recent authorities in the United States, although the earlier course of decision was the other way.[2] In Cassiday *v.* McKenzie,[3] the court held, in conformity with a dictum of Lord Lougborough's, in Tate *v.* Hibbert,[4] that the payment of a check after the drawer's death, but before it was known to the holder or drawee, was valid and could not be questioned by the drawer's executors. The draft was in this instance on a particular fund and operated as an equitable assignment, but the judgment went on the general ground above stated; which was also adopted in Ish *v.* Crane.[5] There is no substantial difference between such a case and that where the offer is made directly by the principal and accepted in the belief that he is still alive, and we may believe that both will ultimately be governed by the same rule.

The question is critically examined in the following extract from Benjamin on Sales:[6] "Both the common and the civil law concur in relation to the case where an order for purchase or sale is transmitted by correspondence to an agent of the writer. If A, in Liverpool, order his correspondent, B, in New York, to purchase a cargo of flour for account of A, and B execute the order before receiving a countermand, A

[1] Hunt *v.* Rousmanier, 8 Wheat. 174; 1 Am. Leading Cases, 5 ed. 711.

[2] Ish *v.* Crane, 8 Ohio St. 520; Knapp *v.* Alvord, 10 Paige, 205; Hunt *v.* Rousmanier, 8 Wheat. 174; Campanari *v.* Woodburn, 15 C. B. 400.

[3] 4 W. & S. 282. [4] 2 Ves. Jr. 118. [5] 8 Ohio St. 520.

[6] § 72.

remains bound, even though he may have posted the countermand before the execution of the order. The civil law is expressed on this point: *Si mandassem tibi ut fundum emeres, postea scripsissem ne emeres, tu antequam scias me vetuisse, emuisses, mandati tibi obligatus ero, ne damno afficiatur is qui mandatum suscepit.*[1] The contract here is one of agency, not of sale, and governed by different principles, for in agencies a revocation of authority by the principal cannot take effect till it reaches the agent.[2]

"But although this is a different contract, the analogy is very strong between it and a bargain and sale by correspondence. If A send an agent to B with a proposal for sale, even the civilians admit that A cannot revoke the authority of the agent to make the offer until the revocation reaches him. So that if A despatches C with an order recalling the authority, even before the agent had made the offer, A would still remain bound by a bargain made before C's arrival with the countermand. Why should there be any difference when the proposer sends his proposal by the public post, which he authorizes to deliver it. A, by sending a letter from London addressed to B, in Manchester, really gives to the public post authority to hand to B a written offer, and to receive an answer in behalf of A. Even on the doctrines of the civil law, it would seem to be permissible under such circumstances to hold that A's revocation comes too late, if it only arrives after the completion of the bargain thus authorized to be made in his behalf. In reality the true theory of the case seems to be that an offer sent by mail is an authority to the party to whom it is sent to bind the sender by acceptance, and includes an implied promise that no revocation is to take effect until received by the agent."

It may be observed with regard to the view taken in the above extract, that the civil law might logically hold that death precluded the acceptance of an offer, but did not invalidate a contract between a mandatary and the person with

[1] Dig. 17. 1.

[2] Story on Agency, § 470, 6 ed.; per Bayley, J., in Salte *v.* Field, 5 T. R. 211, 215; Smart *v.* Sanders, 5 C. B. 895, 917.

whom he dealt on behalf of the mandant. In the former case there could be no contract in the strict sense of the term, because there was no one to contract with; in the latter the contract was not with the dead man but the mandatary, and the only question was, whether the latter was entitled to an indemnity for an act done *bona fide* in the fulfilment of his trust. And as his right in this regard was altogether clear, so the prætor had no difficulty in exonerating him by subrogating the opposite party to the remedy against the person who had succeeded to the principal's estate and was responsible for the fulfilment of the obligations which he had incurred while living.[1]

[1] Maynz, ii. p. 211, § 224.

CHAPTER XVII.

MUTUALITY.

Performance instead of Mutual Promise. — Contract wanting in Mutuality may become Binding on Performance. — Oral Acceptance of Written Offer. — Performance by one under Disability to contract. — Signature of Party charged sufficient under Statute of Frauds. — Rule in Pennsylvania.

THE rule that a voluntary compliance will not give a right of action where a positive engagement is required, does not apply when the consideration moves to the defendant, and the benefit is accepted and enjoyed by him. Under these circumstances the law will imply a promise to pay what the service is reasonably worth, and measure the value by the price originally fixed.[1] A more difficult question arises where the defendant has no notice of the benefit conferred, and cannot decline. If one who has rejected an offer to buy, changes his mind and forwards the goods, and they are received and used by the purchaser, the contract is complete without any further proof of assent on either side. If, for instance, A were, after refusing to build a barn at the price named by B, to erect the building in B's presence, or with full knowledge on his part, the latter would be as much bound as if he had agreed in the first instance. The obligation grows out of the strong presumption of assent afforded by the conduct of the parties. If, however, B were at a distance, and knew nothing of what was going on, he might seemingly keep and use the barn without remunerating A.

In the instance above supposed A rejects the proposal made by B; what if he should agree without the forms which the law requires? The point is not altogether clear, but the better opinion would seem to be that B's promise operates under these circumstances as a continuing request, and will become

[1] See Grove *v.* Hodges, 5 P. F. S. 504, where it is said that executed contracts are obligatory without regard to mutuality.

binding on performance. In other words, the promisor is not bound, but may be so if the promise is acted on before it is recalled. The question arose in the Fishmongers' Company *v.* Robertson,[1] where it was contended that as the plaintiffs were a body corporate, and the agreement which they sought to enforce was not under seal, it did not bind them and could not be obligatory on the defendant. Conceding that they had done all that the writing called for, still they had not bound themselves to do it, which was what the terms of the contract required. There was consequently a want of mutuality which discharged the defendant.

Tindal, C. J., said, in delivering judgment, that the argument for the defence was that the company could not sue as plaintiffs on an agreement which could not have been enforced against them as defendants. The court inclined to think that the ratification implied in bringing suit rendered the contract obligatory on the corporation; but aside from this the declaration contained an averment of the performance of every matter which was a condition precedent to the right of action.

The question therefore was reduced to whether in the case of a contract executed before action brought, where it appeared that the defendants had received the whole benefit of the consideration for which they bargained, it was a defence that the plaintiffs were not originally bound, the contract not having been made under their common seal. There was no ground of reason or justice on which such a proposition could be sustained. The defendants had been benefited by the fulfilment of the various covenants which constituted the consideration for their own promise. It could not therefore be regarded as a *nudum pactum*, nor could they justly allege their inability to enforce stipulations which had already been performed, as a reason why they should be exonerated from the obligation which had been assumed by them, on the ground of their inability to sue the plaintiffs. It might possibly be the case that up to the time when the company adopted the contract by complying with its terms, there was a want of mutu-

[1] 5 M. & G. 131.

ality from their not being compellable to perform, and that the defendants might during that interval have been entitled to retract on the ground of a want of consideration. If such a line of defence could have been taken in the first instance, it failed when the company executed the contract by doing that for which the defendants stipulated. The decisions on guaranties, and among others Kennaway *v.* Treleavan,[1] and those which established that a contract signed by the defendant only might be enforced under the statute of frauds, notwithstanding the want of mutuality, tended strongly to support the principle on which the court relied in giving judgment.[2]

The principle is the same where a married woman enters into an executory agreement. Under these circumstances she cannot be compelled to perform the contract; but if she does perform it, the other party is bound to give the promised equivalent. In Walker *v.* Coover,[3] Snyder assigned two bonds to Mrs. Patton in consideration of a promise on her part to pay his debts, which was fulfilled. An attachment execution was then issued against Snyder, and served on the obligor who alleged the assignment as a defence. The court held that although the contract could not have been enforced against Mrs. Patton, she had still acquired a vested right by the payment of the consideration, which was valid as against the assignor and those claiming under him as creditors.

It seems that a court of equity will not, any more than a merely legal tribunal, enforce an executory contract of sale at the instance of a *feme covert;* but this doctrine ceases to be applicable when the contract has so far been executed on her part that it would be a fraud in the vendor to retract. In Vance *v.* Nogle,[4] a *feme covert* went into possession under an agreement for the sale of land, paid part of the purchase-money, and was ready and willing to give a bond and mortgage for the residue in accordance with the terms of the agreement, and it was held that the heirs of the vendor could not dispossess her under the equitable jurisprudence of Pennsylvania, under which the defendant in an ejectment may rely

[1] 5 M. & W. 498.
[2] *Ante.*
[3] 15 P. F. S. 430.
[4] 20 P. F. S. 176.

on any fact or circumstance that would entitle him to a decree of specific performance if he were a complainant.

For like reasons the acceptance by a married woman of an offer for the purchase of goods will not complete the contract or preclude the offerer from declaring that he has changed his mind; but if he makes no such announcement and she forwards the merchandise he cannot refuse to accept and pay. The rule applies conversely, and a married woman who receives a full consideration for an equitable assignment of her interest in a fund, and is unable or declines to reimburse the assignee, will not be allowed to allege her coverture as a reason why a chancellor should not uphold the transfer although it does not pass the legal title.[1]

It results from these decisions that what is essential to a recovery is not that the contract shall be mutually obligatory, but that the plaintiff shall have complied with the terms on which the defendant declared his willingness to be bound.[2] This is generally conceded where the contract is conditioned for performance, and not less true where the defendant stipulates for a reciprocal engagement which, though not in the form required by law, is given and received without objection. A contract by one who, like a married woman is under a personal disability, is so far an exception to this rule, that it will not be enforced unless there has been such a fulfilment on her part that the opposite party cannot equitably withhold the stipulated recompense.[3]

An analogous point to that determined in the Fishmongers' Co. *v.* Robertson, may, as Tindal, C. J., intimated, arise under the fourth and seventeenth sections of the statute of frauds, where the plaintiff does not affix his signature to the contract.

Agreeably to the fourth section as re-enacted in most of the States of this country, no action shall be brought to charge any person on any contract for the sale of lands, tenements, or hereditaments, unless in writing and signed by the party to

1 Fryer *v.* Rishell, 3 Norris, 521.

2 See Grove *v.* Hodges, 5 P. F. S. 504.

3 See Glass *v.* Warwick, 4 Wr. 140; Ramborger *v.* Ingraham, 2 id. 14; Walker *v.* Coover, 15 P. F. S. 430; Vance *v.* Nogle, 20 id. 176.

be charged, or some agent thereto lawfully authorized. This language implies that one who signs may be charged, although the other party to the contract does not affix his signature. It has been contended that such a contract is wanting in mutuality, and does not afford a ground for a decree of specific performance.[1] This objection may be valid where the intention is that the writing shall be executed by both parties, and one omits to sign through mistake or fraud, but it does not apply in favor of one who puts his name to an instrument knowing that it is obligatory on him, and will not bind the other party. The statute of frauds does not avoid the contract, it merely requires that the contract shall be established by a writing signed by the party whom it is sought to charge. Every one is presumed to be cognizant of the legal consequences of his acts, and a vendor who signs the contract without requiring the signature of the vendee, must be supposed to know that it rests with the latter to say whether the sale shall be carried into effect. When therefore, the vendee files a bill for specific performance and tenders the price, the vendor has all that he is entitled to expect.[2] The agreement is thenceforth mutual, and the objection that it was not such in the first instance, comes with an ill grace from one who is endeavoring to evade a moral and legal obligation. The defence rests exclusively on the statute, and the intention of the legislature plainly is that a defendant who has signed shall not allege that the plaintiff did not.

The question in Laythoarp *v.* Bryant[3] was whether the defendant's signature on the back of a paper containing the terms and particulars of a sale at auction of the good-will and lease of certain premises, bound him, although the plaintiff did not sign and could not have been made answerable at law or before a chancellor. Tindal, C. J., said, it had been contended that unless the plaintiff signed there was a want of

[1] See Benedict *v.* Lynch, 1 Johns. Ch. 370; Geiger *v.* Green, 4 Gill, 472; Wilson *v.* Clarke, 1 W. & S. 554; Parrish *v.* Koons, 1 Pars. Eq. 79.

[2] Ives *v.* Hazard, 4 R. I. 14; Perkins *v.* Hadsell, 50 Ill. 216; Estes *v.* Furlong, 59 id. 298.

[3] 2 Bing. N. C. 735.

mutuality. If so, the fault lay at the door of the defendant, who might have required the plaintiff's signature before affixing his own. There was no authority nor any reason for saying that the signature of the parties made the agreement. The agreement on the contrary took place before any signature. It had accordingly never been heard or dreamed of that both parties must sign. Take the case of a letter from an executor promising to pay a debt of the testator. Had it ever been said that in order to charge him there must also be a letter from the party addressed? If the executor's letter contained merely an offer, that offer indeed must be accepted, to make the promise binding, but if it contained a promise on adequate consideration no further signature was necessary for its validity. So in the analogous case of a promise to pay the debt of a third person, it was every day's practice to receive a guaranty in evidence without requiring the signature of the creditor to be shown. It had been decided in like manner that if the vendee signed a note or memorandum for the purchase of goods, he would be bound although the writing was not signed by the vendor.[1] The same principle prevailed in equity where a contract signed by one party for the sale of land would be specifically enforced, although he could not have a corresponding remedy against the opposite party.[2] This doctrine had been questioned by Lord Redesdale and Sir Thomas Plumer, but the current of decision remained unchanged.

The point arose in this instance in a suit for damages, but the preponderance of authority is, that as there is nothing in the language of the act to impair the obligation of the contract as regards a party who signs, so it may be specifically enforced against him, although he would not have had a corresponding remedy if the complainant had not filed the bill. This interpretation was contemporaneous with the statute,[3] and

[1] Emmerson *v.* Heelis, 2 Taunt. 38; Allen *v.* Bennet, id. 169.

[2] Seton *v.* Slade, 7 Ves. 275; 2 Leading Cases in Equity, 4 Am. ed.; Fowle *v.* Freeman, 9 Ves. 351; Bowen *v.* Moris, 2 Taunt. 374.

[3] Hatton *v.* Grey, 5 Vin. Abr. 525; 2 Cases in Ch. 164; Coleman *v.* Upcot, 5 Vin. Abr. 527, pl. 17; 2 Eq. Cases, 45; Buckhouse *v.* Crosbey, 2 Eq. Cas. Abr. 32.

although criticised with much logical acumen by Lord Redesdale and Sir Thomas Plumer,[1] has maintained its ground in England, and is now established in the United States.[2]

In Coleman *v.* Upcot,[3] "the Lord Keeper decreed the defendant to perform the agreement, for that it was directly within the statute of frauds as being an agreement signed by the party to be charged with the same, and there was no need of its being signed by both parties, and the plaintiff by his bill hath submitted to perform what was required of his part to be performed. If one (being in company) offers a bargain and writes it down, and another takes it up and prefers his bill, there is a sufficient agreement."

Such a contract is analogous to a covenant that another shall have the privilege of buying, or for the good behavior of a servant whom he is about to employ. The party who executes the instrument cannot allege that the other is not bound, as a reason for not fulfilling the obligation which he has voluntarily incurred.[4] The duty arises in the one case from the sealing and delivery, and in the other from the manifest intention of the statute that the party who signs shall not be discharged. A contract of sale is not less obligatory at common law because the vendee promises orally and the vendor in writing. It is, therefore, entirely competent for the legislature to set the former free while leaving the latter bound. Such an enactment is not contrary to natural equity, because the vendee cannot enforce the agreement without making the stipulated compensation, and because the vendor contracts in subordination to the enactment and to the rule which it prescribes. In like manner, a contract for the sale of merchandise is obligatory on the vendor under the seventeenth section of the statute, although the vendee does not

[1] See Lawrenson *v.* Butler, 1 Sch. & L. 13.

[2] Shirley *v.* Shirley, 7 Blackford, 452; Wright *v.* King, Harr. Ch. 12; Ives *v.* Hazard, 4 R. I. 14; Penniman *v.* Hartshorn, 13 Mass. 87; Old Colony R. R. *v.* Evans, 6 Gray, 25; Douglass *v.* Spears, 2 N. & McC. 207; McCrea *v.* Purmort, 16 Wend. 460; Davis *v.* Shields, 26 id. 341.

[3] 5 Vin. Abr. 527, pl. 17.

[4] *Ante:* see Calvert *v.* Gordon, 3 M. & R. 124; Gordon *v.* Calvert, 2 Simons, 253.

affix his signature, and could not be compelled to pay the price;[1] and so, conversely, the vendee cannot defend an action for the purchase-money, on the ground that the vendor did not sign the note or memorandum, and might have withheld the goods.[2]

The main current of authority is in accordance with these decisions, that it is not an answer to a bill for a specific performance that the complainant did not sign the contract, and might have violated it with impunity.[3]

This interpretation is sustained by the letter of the enactment, which does not require the signature of both parties, but that the instrument shall be signed by him who is to be charged, and is not less consonant with its purpose, which is to afford a safeguard against fraud and perjury. There can be little danger of false swearing where the plaintiff adopts the contract, and it is established against the defendant by written proof. Under these circumstances, all that the legislature had in view is attained, and it is fallacious to insist on the want of mutuality as a reason for exacting more.

The opposite doctrine — that the writing must be signed by both parties — was, notwithstanding, advanced in Boucher *v.* Van Buskirk,[4] and seems to prevail in Kentucky;[5] and in Duvall *v.* Myers,[6] the court adopted the argument of Lord Redesdale, that a specific performance should not be decreed unless both parties are bound, although the objection was to

[1] Sanborn *v.* Flagler, 9 Allen, 474; Egerton *v.* Mathews, 6 East, 307; Laythoarp *v.* Bryant, 2 Bing. N. C. 735; Russell *v.* Nicoll, 3 Wend. 112; Justice *v.* Lang, 42 N. Y. 493.

[2] Emmerson *v.* Heelis, 2 Taunt. 38; Allen *v.* Bennet, 2 id. 169; Barstow *v.* Gray, 3 Greenl. R. 409, 415.

[3] Justice *v.* Lang, 42 N. Y. 493; Clason *v.* Bailey, 14 Johns. 487, 490; Morin *v.* Martz, 13 Minn. 191; Old Colony R. R. *v.* Evans, 6 Gray, 25; Douglass *v.* Spears, 2 N. & McC. 207; Sams *v.* Fripp, 10 Richardson, Eq. 447; Barstow *v.* Gray, 3 Greenl. R. 409; Getchell *v.* Jewett, 4 id. 350; Rodgers *v.* Saunders, 16 Me. 92; Laning *v.* Cole, 3 Gr. Ch. 229; Esmay *v.* Gorton, 18 Ill. 483; McConnell *v.* Brillhart, 17 id. 354; Ives *v.* Hazard, 4 R. I. 14; Hunter, *ex parte*, 1 Edw. Ch. 1; Woodward *v.* Aspinwall, 3 Sandf. 272; Young *v.* Paul, 2 Stock. 401; Barnard *v.* Lee, 97 Mass. 92.

[4] 2 H. K. Marshall, 345.

[5] Jones *v.* Noble, 3 Bush, 694.

[6] 2 Md. Ch. 401.

the terms of the contract, and not that the complainant was not personally bound.

In the majority of the instances hitherto considered, the contract disclosed by the instrument was mutual, and purported to have been made by both the parties, though signed only by one, or else imposed a unilateral obligation which, though wanting a consideration, was sustained by a seal; but it is equally well settled that an oral acceptance of a written proposal to sell goods or land may constitute an agreement that equity will enforce,[1] and on which a recovery may be had at law.

The principle was clearly stated by the Vice-Chancellor in Warner *v.* Willington: "The other ground of demurrer is that the memorandum was not a memorandum of agreement, but only an offer or proposal which the defendant retracted before it was accepted by the plaintiff. Now there is a clear distinction between a memorandum of offer and a memorandum of agreement. In the case of an offer, no doubt the party signing it may at any time before acceptance retract; but if it be an agreement, though signed by one party alone, he cannot retract at his pleasure, but all he can do is to call upon the other party to sign or rescind the agreement. A memorandum of agreement supposes that the two parties have verbally made an actual contract with each other, and when the terms of such contract are reduced to writing and signed, that is sufficient to bind the parties signing; but if the memorandum is of an offer only, that assumes that there has been no actual contract between the parties.

"Taking this as a memorandum, not of an agreement but of an offer not then finally accepted, the question is whether there has been a sufficient acceptance by the plaintiff before the defendant retracted. What is alleged by the plaintiff as an acceptance was his sending the draft lease. This raises another question: Can acceptance be by parol without writing? And it is singular that I cannot find any case in which

[1] Esmay *v.* Gorton, 18 Ill. 483; Farwell *v.* Lowther, 18 id. 252; Warner *v.* Willington, 3 Drew. 523; Smith *v.* Neale, 2 C. B. N. S. 67; Reuss *v.* Picksley, L. R. 1 Ex. 342; Sanborn *v.* Flagler, 9 Allen, 474.

it is determined that a parol acceptance of a written proposal is sufficient; but I think, upon principle, that a parol acceptance would be sufficient, because when one party has signed a written proposal, and the other expressly accepts it by parol; as, if he says in express terms, 'I accept the proposal,' that reduces it to a case of a parol agreement come to between the parties, and a memorandum of the agreement signed by one; in which case, it is clear that signature of one party is sufficient to bind him, although the other has not signed."

In Sanborn *v.* Flagler,[1] the question arose under the seventeenth section of the statute, on the following memorandum, signed with the initials of both parties: —

"Will deliver to S. R. & Co. best refined iron, 50 tons within 90 days, at 5 cts. per lb., 4 off cash. Plates to be 10 to 16 inches wide, and 9 feet to 11 long. This offer good till 2 o'clock, September 11th, 1862. J. H. F., J. B. R."

The plaintiff testified that the instrument was written by him, and that he and the defendant signed their initials, the plaintiff the initials "J. B. R." and the defendant the initials "J. H. F.," and that before two o'clock on the day named, and before the plaintiff left the defendant's office, he accepted the proposition and so stated to the defendant verbally.

It was contended for the defence that inasmuch as the acceptance was oral and did not bind the plaintiff, the contract failed for want of mutuality. This objection was overruled on the following grounds: "The note or memorandum on which the plaintiffs rely to maintain their action contains all the requisites essential to constitute a binding contract within the statute of frauds. It is not denied by the defendant that a verbal acceptance of a written offer to sell merchandise is sufficient to constitute a complete and obligatory agreement on which to charge the person by whom it is signed. In such case, if the memorandum is otherwise sufficient, when it is assented to by him to whom the proposal has been made, the contract is consummated by the meeting of the minds of the two parties, and the evidence necessary

[1] 9 Allen, 474.

to render it valid and capable of enforcement is supplied by the signature of the party sought to be charged, to the offer to sell. Indeed, the rule being well settled that the signature of the defendant only is necessary to make a binding contract within the provisions of the statute relating to sales of merchandise, it necessarily follows that an offer to sell and an express agreement to sell stand on the same footing, inasmuch as the latter, until it is accepted by the other party, is in effect nothing more than a proposition to sell on the terms indicated. The acceptance of the contract by the party seeking to enforce it may always be proved by evidence *aliunde*."

The necessity for mutuality was nevertheless strenuously asserted in Wilson *v.* Clarke,[1] in a suit brought for the purchase-money on an oral assignment of a lease, and was decided adversely to the plaintiff, on the ground that he was not entitled to enforce the fulfilment of a contract which he was under no obligation to perform. The argument for this interpretation is as follows: —

The fourth section of the statute implies that the agreement shall be obligatory on him who signs, although the other party does not. It is not in force in Pennsylvania, and the question arises under the first three sections. There is consequently no ground for an exception to the general rule that both parties must be bound or neither will be. A contract signed by only one party ought not to be specifically enforced against the other party, because he cannot have a like remedy. Where a contract which is intended to be mutual fails on either side, the whole is invalid. Unless the vendor is under an obligation to convey, the purchaser ought not to be made liable for the price; nor can a purchaser who has not bound himself to pay, justly require the vendor to execute a deed. A chancellor, when uncontrolled by the legislative will, never executes a contract which is not a source of mutual obligation and mutual remedy.

A like view was taken in Parrish *v.* Koons,[2] and again in the case of Meason *v.* Kaine.[3] There Meason, Kaine, and Cope agreed orally to buy land together from Shoaf, but the

[1] 1 W. & S. 554. [2] 1 Pars. Eq. 79, 81. [3] 13 P. F. S. 335.

written contract with the vendor was in the names of Kaine and Cope, and it was held that they could not maintain an action against Meason for his share of the purchase-money. "Unless," said Sharswood, J., "Meason could have recovered in an equitable ejectment, or by a bill in equity compelled a conveyance or assignment of one-third of the equitable interest to him, it would manifestly be unjust and inequitable to oblige him to pay for and take it. That would be altogether a one-sided contract. Had the purchase turned out an advantageous one, Kaine and Cope could have kept it and set Meason at defiance. Equity is part of the law of Pennsylvania. One of the fundamental principles adopted by courts of equity in bills for specific performance is that there must be a mutuality of remedy. Both parties must have a right to a decree; otherwise it would follow that the court would decree a specific performance when the party called upon to perform it might be in this situation, that if the agreement was disadvantageous to him he would be liable to the performance, and yet if advantageous, he could not compel it.[1] Kaine and Cope would be placed in a position to say to Meason, heads we win, tails you lose. This is exactly the case here if, as we have seen, Meason could not have enforced the verbal agreement with Kaine and Cope that he should have an interest of one-third in the purchase. Shoaf certainly could not have compelled him directly to pay the price, how then can he be compelled indirectly in actions for contribution by Kaine and Cope? Had there been any evidence by letter, receipt, or written acknowledgment, the statute of frauds would have been satisfied, but there was nothing but oral testimony to show that he had any connection with the transaction."

The principle may be just, as applied to cases under the statute of frauds as re-enacted in Pennsylvania, but certainly cannot be laid down as a rule. Mutuality is not requisite at common law where the contract is unilateral, or where the consideration is performance and not a promise to perform, and it is not easy to see why it should be regarded as indispensable by a chancellor.[2]

[1] Bodine *v.* Glading, 9 Harris, 50.

[2] *Ante.*

It is accordingly as well settled in Pennsylvania as it is in England that an undertaking to convey or let may be specifically enforced by the promisee, although he does not enter into a reciprocal engagement, and might have refused a lease or deed if tendered.[1]

The law was so held in Kerr *v.* Day,[2] and D'Arras *v.* Keyser;[3] and more recently in Smith's Appeal.[4] There Smith agreed in writing to sell a tract of land to Raydure, and that he "should have the refusal for ten days from date," and Raydure was held to be entitled to a specific performance, although he did not sign the memorandum, and his acceptance was merely verbal. So in Napier *v.* Darlington,[5] a stipulation that the lessee should be entitled to purchase at the end of the term at a given price was enforced at the instance of an assignee, although the exercise of the right was purely optional as regarded both him and the assignor.

The ground of these decisions is that when the complainant declares his intention to take the land, by filing the bill he becomes equitably the owner, and as he is thenceforth unable to retract, the obligation becomes mutual, and a cross bill may be maintained by the defendant for the purchase-money.

The question is affected in Pennsylvania by considerations which are peculiar to that State. The first three sections of the English statute are drawn into one, which provides that estates created orally, and "without a writing signed by the party so creating the same or his agent thereto lawfully authorized in writing," shall have "the force and effect of estates at will only," and there is no provision answering to the clause of the fourth section of the English statute, which enacts "that no action shall be brought . . . to charge any person, . . . upon any contract or sale of lands, tenements, or hereditaments, . . . unless the agreement upon which such action shall be brought, or some memorandum or note thereof, shall be in writing, and signed by the party to be charged."

[1] Ives *v.* Hazard, 4 R. I. 14; Willard *v.* Tayloe, 8 Wallace, 557; 2 Leading Cases in Equity, 3 Am. ed. 1090.

[2] 2 Harris, 112. [3] 2 Casey, 249. [4] 19 P. F. S. 474.

[5] 20 P. F. S. 64.

An oral agreement for the sale of real estate is consequently valid in Pennsylvania and may afford a good cause of action; but the authorities nevertheless establish that the recovery must in the absence of fraud be limited to what the plaintiff has actually paid or expended in endeavoring to carry out the contract, and that the vendor can neither tender a deed and have judgment for the price, nor the vendee obtain damages for the loss of his bargain. This conclusion was adopted by the courts that the statute might not be evaded, and to avoid the inconsistency of giving a contract to sell or lease the effect denied to an actual transfer. It may therefore reasonably be contended that when the vendor's promise is merely oral, and confers no legal or equitable right to or interest in the land, the vendee is not bound to pay the price, although he gives a written undertaking to that effect and authenticates it by his signature.

It may be said, in answer to this view of the law, that although an oral contract of sale is not valid as such, it operates as a continuing offer or request, and if the vendor tenders a deed or files a bill for specific performance within the appointed time, the purchaser has all that he is entitled to require, and the statute, which is only designed to protect the vendor, cannot be invoked in his behalf. The objection for want of mutuality ought not to prevail, because all that a chancellor ordinarily requires is that both parties shall be bound at the time of bill filed or rendering the decree;[1] and unilateral contracts are constantly enforced on this ground against the covenantor, although there was no obligation on the covenantee until he came into equity for relief. The weak point of such an argument is, that as the right of property remains in the seller, the contract is executory, and the vendor is not entitled to the purchase-money and must seek redress in an action for the damages resulting from the breach of the contract.

One point would seem to be entirely clear. If the vendee can be compelled in Pennsylvania to accept and pay for the land

[1] See Green *v.* Richards, 8 C. E. Gr. 32; 2 Leading Cases in Equity. 1000.

when the vendor is not under an obligation to convey, he may equally well be compelled whether he did or did not sign the contract. The vendor's signature is an indispensable requisite, without which he cannot be compelled to convey, but no such rule is prescribed for the purchaser, whose liability depends on the doctrines of the common law and the equitable considerations which govern a chancellor.

It is established under the above enactment that if the vendor affixes his signature the legislative requirement is satisfied, and a bill for specific performance may be maintained on his part or by the purchaser. The vendor is bound by his signature, and the purchaser has an equitable estate or interest, and can no more object to paying the price than if he had received a deed. It does not vary the case that the purchaser's offer or acceptance is merely oral, because the statute does not require him to sign, but simply that no estate or interest shall pass unless the writing is signed by the vendor.[1]

The soundness of this conclusion is amply vindicated in the following extract from the judgment of Strong, J., in Tripp *v.* Bishop: —

"Neither the British statute nor ours requires that the written agreement or memorandum of the sale should be signed by both parties; a receipt for the purchase-money if it describes the lands, has been held sufficient;[2] and even a note or a letter has more than once been held to be a sufficient agreement to take the case out of the statute.[3] This is even more certain under our statute than under that of 29 Charles II. The words of the latter are: 'unless the agreement, or some memorandum thereof, shall be in writing and signed by the party to be charged therewith.' Our act declares that all leases, estates, interests of freehold, etc., shall have the force and effect of leases or estates at will only, unless put in writing, and signed by the parties so making or creating the same, that is, the parties making the leases or creating the

[1] Lowry *v.* Mehaffy, 10 Watts, 387; McFarson's Appeal, 1 Jones (Pa.), 503; Simpson *v.* Breckinridge, 8 Casey, 287; Tripp *v.* Bishop, 6 P. F. S. 424; Smith's Appeal, 19 id. 474; Napier *v.* Darlington, 20 id. 64; *ante.*

[2] 9 Ves. 234, 121, 466.

[3] Sugden on Vend. 45.

estate. It is then only the lessor or grantor who is required to sign the agreement. His contract must be in writing and signed by him; but the statute requires no written evidence of the engagement of the lessee or grantee. The statute of frauds was passed for the protection of land-owners. It was intended to guard them against perjuries in the proof of parol contracts. To secure this protection it prescribed a rule of evidence, by which alone their estate can be divested. This is intimated in Lowry *v.* Mehaffy. There it was ruled that an agreement for the sale of land reduced to writing and signed by the vendor alone, and delivered to the vendee, is all that the statute requires. It is true that in that case it appeared the contract had been partially executed, but not sufficiently to give effect to a parol sale. After all, it was the signature of the agreement by the vendor which alone made the sale effective. The same thing was ruled in McFarson's Appeal.[2] The case of Wilson *v.* Clarke,[3] is not in conflict with these decisions. There the contract rested entirely in parol. The vendor had signed no agreement; he could not therefore have been compelled to make a conveyance, and for this reason he was not allowed to enforce the contract specifically against the other party."

We may infer from the language held in this instance that a specific performance may be decreed not only against but at the instance of a vendor who signs, although the contract is not signed by the purchaser, because there is a consideration moving to the latter, and, in the absence of the fourth section, nothing to make it requisite for him to affix his signature.

It follows conversely from the same premises, that if the vendor does not sign the contract it cannot be specifically enforced by or against the purchaser. The vendor is protected by the express language of the statute, and it would be unjust to make the purchaser pay for what he has not received and the vendor is under no obligation to render.[4] Or, to state the proposition somewhat differently, where the vendor's undertaking is merely oral and does not confer any equitable right

[1] 10 Watts, 387. [2] 1 Jones (Pa.), 503. [3] 1 W. & S. 554.
[4] Meason *v.* Kaine, 13 P. F. S. 335, 340.

or title, there is no consideration that can bind the purchaser to pay the price, or do more than compensate the vendor for any loss that may grow out of a breach of the contract.

It does not vary the rule that the contract is reduced to writing and signed by the vendee, because what the statute provides is not, as in England, that the instrument must be signed by the party to be charged, but that no estate or interest shall pass if it be not signed by the grantor or vendor, and the common law makes no distinction between verbal and written contracts. In neither case can a purchaser have a decree of specific performance against a vendor who has not affixed his signature, and such a remedy will not therefore be afforded against the purchaser.[1]

The intention of the Legislature to protect the owners of real estate from being compelled to part with their property without the certainty of written evidence, is not less clearly manifested in Pennsylvania than in England, and would obviously be frustrated if the value of the land could be recovered in an action for the breach of an oral agreement to sell or lease; and hence although the fourth section of the English statute has not been re-enacted, the damages in such a suit are limited in the absence of fraud to what the purchaser has actually expended in the belief that the contract will be fulfilled. The rule, as stated in Hertzog *v.* Hertzog,[2] is as follows: "The omission from our statute of frauds and perjuries of the fourth section of the British statute, after which ours was modelled, left us free to sue on parol contracts for the sale of lands; but such actions were rare in the early history of our jurisprudence, and when they were brought the measure of damages, though not very distinctly defined in the cases, was so controlled that specific performance of the contract should not be virtually enforced. It is too manifest for debate that if the value of the land may be recovered in an action on the case upon the parol contract, the statute as we have it is as effectually evaded as if the land itself were

[1] See Meason *v.* Kaine, 13 P. F. S. 335; Bowser *v.* Cessna, 12 id. 148; Ellet *v.* Paxson, 2 W. & S. 418.

[2] 5 Casey, 465.

recovered in ejectment. Therefore it was, that while the personal action was sustained because forbidden by nothing in our statute, the damages recovered were measured by other standards than the value of the land at the time of the recovery. In some of the early cases, it would seem, the damages were nominal; in none were they more than compensatory for what had been paid on the footing of the contract."

It results from this decision that the measure of damages in a suit against the vendor on an oral contract, is not the value of the land, which would be equivalent to a decree of specific performance, nor yet the difference between its value and the price, which would come nearly to the same thing, but what the vendee has spent in examining the title or on account of the purchase-money.[1]

The question consequently is not what would the purchaser have gained had the contract been fulfilled, but what did he expend on the faith of the vendor's promise to convey. If the consideration consists of services that have been rendered wholly or in part, the recovery will be limited to what they were reasonably worth, and as the value of the land is immaterial and may tend to mislead the jury, it is inadmissible in evidence.[2]

In Thompson *v.* Sheplar,[3] Williams, J., said: "It is well settled law in this State that an action will lie on a verbal agreement for the sale of land, and in the absence of fraud that the measure of damage for its breach is compensation for the money paid and expenses incurred on the faith of the bargain. If no consideration has been paid, and no expenses incurred, only nominal damages are recoverable; but where there has been fraud in the sale a different rule as to the measure of damages obtains. In such cases it has been uniformly held that damages may also be recovered for the loss or value of the bargain. But if no fraud was meditated or designed in making the contract, the refusal to perform it is

[1] Thompson *v.* Sheplar, 22 P. F. S. 160; Harris *v.* Harris, 20 id. 170.

[2] Hertzog *v.* Hertzog, 5 Casey, 465; Ewing *v.* Thompson, 16 P. F. S. 382.

[3] 22 P. F. S. 160, 165.

not such a fraud as will enable the vendee to recover compensation for the loss or value of the bargain. If damages for such loss were allowed to be recovered for the breach of the contract on the ground that the refusal to perform it was in itself a fraud, it would in most cases of parol sales operate as a virtual repeal of the statute of frauds; for though the vendee might not recover the land for which he bargained, of what avail would be the statute if he could recover its value in money? It is obvious that such a recovery would in almost any case be equivalent to specific performance."

In Bowser *v.* Cessna[1] the purchaser was notwithstanding held liable, on what seems to have been an oral contract, for the difference between his bid and what the premises brought at a resale, or in other words, for the loss of the bargain, although he could not have been adjudged to pay the purchase-money. This decision may be regarded as overruled by the judgment in Harris *v.* Harris.[2]

It is proper to add that, although a purchaser who is put in possession under an oral contract which the vendor subsequently refuses to fulfil, may obtain a decree of specific performance on the ground of fraud, the remedy must be sought before a chancellor, and the recovery will be confined at law to the return of the consideration and a reasonable compensation for the amount laid out in improvements which enhance the value of the land.[3] The purchaser is not entitled to more than compensation for his actual loss, unless the vendor is guilty of fraud in the concoction or execution of the contract, as distinguished from the bad faith implied in inducing the vendee to enter on and improve the land, and then refusing him a deed.

[1] 12 P. F. S. 148.

[2] 20 P. F. S. 170.

[3] 1 Leading Cases in Equity, 3 Am. ed. 1032; McNair *v.* Compton, 11 Casey, 23; McKowen *v.* McDonald, 7 Wr. 441; Harris *v.* Harris, 20 P. F. S. 170.

CHAPTER XVIII.

SALE OF SPECIFIC GOODS.

Executed and Executory Contracts of Sale. — Transfer of Title. — Delivery requisite under Roman Law. — Title may pass at Common Law by Virtue of the Contract. — Goods must be specified, and Price susceptible of being reduced to Certainty. — Mode of Specification. — Sale of an Undivided Part. — Appropriation. — Measure of Damages for Breach of an Executory Contract of Sale. — Vendor's Lien. — Resale. — Retention. — Stoppage *in transitu*. — *Caveat emptor*. — Vendor not answerable at Common Law in the Absence of Fraud and Warranty.

SALE is a generic term which includes cases where the contract vests the right of property in the purchaser and confers a corresponding right to the price on the vendor, and cases where it simply imposes a personal obligation on the vendor to deliver the goods, and on the purchaser to accept and pay for them. In the latter case the contract is said to be executory or unfulfilled; in the former it is executed, that is, carried into effect. Where it is executed the buyer becomes the owner immediately on the completion of the contract, and may maintain trover or replevin if the goods are withheld, while the vendor may sue for and recover the entire purchase-money; but the only remedy for the breach of an executory contract is an action of assumpsit to recover compensation for the difference between the value of the goods and what the purchaser agreed to give, with such consequential damages as the nature of the injury demands.

A sale of specific goods is executed or executory according to the intention of the parties as gathered from its terms or explicitly declared, while a contract for the sale of goods of a certain kind, or answering to a particular description, is necessarily executory until the parties agree as to the very things which the vendor is to deliver and the purchaser to receive.

Strictly speaking a contract cannot be executed until both parties have fulfilled all that they agreed to do, as for instance, in the case of a contract of sale, by the delivery of goods and the payment of the price. Such was the view taken at Rome, but such is not the law of England.[1]

Agreeably to the Roman law a contract of sale did not pass the right of property until the goods were delivered to the purchaser or subject to his dominion and control.[2] It results from this doctrine, as logically applied in Scotland, that merchandise which has been not only sold but paid for may be taken in execution by the vendor's creditors down to the last moment before delivery, and the purchaser left to seek redress in an action to recover back the price, which in the case of an insolvent vendor will generally prove illusory.[3] The common-law rule is the direct opposite, — that where the price is fixed and the subject-matter ascertained with an intent to pass the right of property, the law will carry the purpose into effect although the purchase-money has not been paid or the goods delivered.[4] And as this rule meets the requirements of business life, it has been adopted not only in England and the United States, but in countries which like France and Holland follow the principles of the civil law. Agreeably to the Code Napoleon[5] the sale is complete between the parties, and the property is acquired in law by the purchaser with regard to the seller, as soon as the thing and the price are agreed on, though the thing has not been delivered or payment made.[6]

Delivery seems to have been originally essential to the transfer of the right of property in chattels, as in the shape of livery of seisin it certainly was to give a title to land;[7] but if such was the rule in the time of Bracton, it underwent a change, and was established at an early period as it now stands.[8]

The rule and the reason for it were perspicuously stated by Parke, B., in Dixon *v.* Yates:[9] "By the law of England

[1] *Ante*, pp. 88, 108.
[2] Wait *v.* Baker, 2 Ex. 1.
[3] See Bell, Contract of Sale, pp. 11, 13.
[4] Olyphant *v.* Baker, 5 Den. 379, 382.
[5] Article 1583.
[6] Delsol, Commentary on the Code Napoleon, iii. 174; *ante*, p. 112.
[7] *Ante*, p. 17.
[8] 1 Blackburn on the Contract of Sale, 189.
[9] 5 B. & Ad. 313.

the sale of a specific chattel passes the property in it to the vendee without delivery. . . . Where there is a sale of goods generally no property in them passes till delivery, because until then the very goods sold are not ascertained; but where by the contract itself the vendor appropriates to the vendee a specific chattel, and the latter thereby agrees to take that specific chattel and to pay the stipulated price, the parties are then in the same situation as they would be after a delivery of goods in pursuance of a general contract. The very appropriation of the chattel is equivalent to delivery by the vendor, and the assent of the vendee to take the specified chattel and to pay the price is equivalent to his accepting possession. The effect of the contract, therefore, is to vest the property in the bargainee."

This doctrine has been criticised by some writers, including Mr. Austin, on the ground that a contract only binds the parties, and that a conveyance is requisite to pass the title or confer a right to the thing.[1] The distinction is nominal rather than real, because a conveyance is simply a contract made in a form which, agreeably to the usages of the period, is self-executing and needs no further act to carry it into effect. Though a writing duly authenticated is ordinarily deemed essential to a conveyance, there is nothing in the nature of things that prevents spoken words from being as effectual as written, and if the right of property can be conveyed without delivery by a deed or bill of sale, it may equally well be conveyed by an oral agreement, which according to the

1 "No right to a thing properly speaking is ever given by contract. Where a thing is the subject of a contract the right is not over or in the thing, but a right to an act of transfer or assignment of the thing on the part of the obligor." Austin's Jurisprudence, Lect. 14, p. 388. Hence an argument that delivery is essential to the transfer of ownership, which would have more weight if delivery did not depend for its effect on the accompanying words and circumstances which may render it a conveyance, a loan, a deposit or a trust. Whether a man who hands what belongs to him to another means to give, sell, or to let, and on what terms, must be gathered from his language which, if explicit, and where such is the legal or customary rule, may well operate directly on the thing though it remains in his possession. *Ante*, p. 110.

mutual understanding is to operate directly on the subject-matter and render it the buyer's. What the law regards in either case is the intention, and the form is merely a means of placing the existence of the intention beyond dispute. Such is the established rule as regards chattels; and if a writing is requisite in the case of land, it is owing to the provisions of the statute of enrolments and of the statute of frauds.[1]

It is accordingly well settled that when the vendor appropriates the goods to the buyer, or in other words, signifies his intention that the right of property shall pass forthwith, and the buyer assents, the law will carry the intention into effect, although no act is done on either side.[2] It is immaterial as regards the principle that the goods are to be delivered at a future time or place, or that they are unfinished and that the vendor is by the terms of the agreement to complete them before delivery, or that he is to do some act to render them more valuable or fit for use. Such circumstances may be a reason for supposing that the parties do not mean to pass the title, but will not defeat the intention if it exists. Accordingly, when a boar was sold, as it would seem, in payment of an antecedent debt, with a stipulation that the vendor should castrate the animal and deliver it if it survived the operation, and if it did not, pay the purchaser forty dollars, the court held that the purchaser acquired the title and might transfer it to a third person.[3] So the title may pass, although the goods are to be delivered by the vendor at a time and place designated by the buyer,[4] or though the sale is for cash and the goods have not been delivered or paid for, because the understanding may well be that the vendor is to keep the possession as a security for the price and the purchaser have the

[1] See Busher *v.* Thompson, 4 C. B. 48, 60; 2 Coke's Institutes 671, 675; 2 Sm. L. C. 8 Am. ed. 541; *ante*, pp. 108, 109, 111.

[2] Martin *v.* Adams, 104 Mass. 262; Warden *v.* Marshall, 99 id. 305; Arnold *v.* Delano, 4 Cush. 33; Bigler *v.* Hall, 54 N. Y. 167; Groat *v.* Gile, 51 id. 431; Olyphant *v.* Baker, 5 Den. 382; Sweeney *v.* Owlsley, 14 B. Monroe, 413; Terry *v.* Wheeler, 25 N. Y. 520; Thorndike *v.* Bath, 114 Mass. 116.

[3] Marble *v.* Moore, 102 Mass. 443.

[4] Terry *v.* Wheeler, 25 N. Y. 520, 525.

right of property with the attendant risk.[1] As Lowry, C. J., observed in Winslow *v.* Leonard,[2] "The vesting of the title depends upon the intention of the parties to be derived from the contract and its circumstances; and actual delivery, weighing, and setting aside the goods, are only circumstances from which the intention may be inferred as matter of fact.[3] And this is the principle of numerous cases wherein the title has been held to vest, although there has been no measurement." [4]

The question is nevertheless one of intention as manifested by acts or language, and if that is that the right of property shall remain in the vendor until he forwards the goods or does some act to facilitate their removal, the condition must be fulfilled, and it is not enough that they have been weighed or counted and are ready for delivery in every other particular.[5] In other words, the difference between the Roman and English law is not that the title will vest on the completion of the contract without an overt act on either side, but that it may.[6]

It has accordingly been decided in numerous instances that where the quantity is unknown and the goods are to be measured, weighed, or counted in order to obtain the data for the computation of the price, there is a natural presumption that the purchaser is not to become the owner until the requisite steps have been taken to ascertain how much he is to pay, which will prevail, unless the acts and language of the parties show that their intention is that the title shall pass at once.[7]

In Hanson *v.* Meyer,[8] the sale was of all the starch then on storage in a warehouse at £6 per hundred weight, and the

[1] Tarling *v.* Baxter, 6 B. & C. 360; Martindale *v.* Smith, 1 Q. B. 389.

[2] 12 Harris, 14.

[3] 12 Pick. 76; 20 id. 280; 3 W. & S. 14.

[4] 13 Pick. 175; 5 Met. 452; 5 Johns. 395; 1 East, 192; 2 B. & C. 540; 6 W. & S. 357; 6 Rand. 473; 1 Den. 48; 4 C. B. 864; Joyce *v.* Adams, 4 Selden, 291; Kein *v.* Tupper, 52 N. Y. 550.

[5] See Winslow *v.* Leonard, 12 Harris, 14.

[6] Riddle *v.* Varnum, 20 Pick. 283; Smyth *v.* Craig, 3 W. & S. 14, 20.

[7] Russell *v.* Nicoll, 3 Wend. 112; McDonald *v.* Hewett, 15 Johns. 349; Rapelye *v.* Mackie, 6 Cow. 250, 253; Nicholson *v.* Taylor, 7 Casey, 128; Logan *v.* Le Mesurier, 6 Moore, P. C. C. 116; Hutchinson *v.* The R. R. Co. 59 N. H. 487.

[8] 6 East, 614.

seller gave the buyer an order on the warehouseman for the delivery of "all my starch." The purchaser became bankrupt, and it was held that the right of property remained in the seller, and that he was not bound to surrender the goods to the assignees or liable to them in trover. For like reasons where a stack of bark was sold at £9. 6*s.* per ton, and part weighed and delivered, and the rest carried away by a flood, the loss was thrown on the seller. Had the agreement been that the purchaser should give a gross sum for the stack whether it contained more or less, the bark would have been at his risk, but as he was to pay so much per ton the right of property in that portion of the goods which had not been weighed remained in the vendor.[1]

Much may depend in such cases on whether the goods are to be counted, weighed, or measured by the vendor or the purchaser. If the duty is to be performed by the vendor, the inference is strong if not irresistible that the possession and right of property are to remain with him until it is fulfilled,[2] while an opposite inference may be drawn if the purchaser is to make the count or hold the scales.[3]

In Russell *v.* Nicoll the action was assumpsit for the non-delivery of a quantity of cotton under the following contract:

> "Sold by Daniel Rapelye, for our account, to R. M. & J. Russell, five hundred bales of cotton at sixteen and a half cents per pound. Said cotton was purchased for our account at Huntsville, and is to be delivered on its arrival at this port from New Orleans at any time between the present date and the first day of June next, and the amount to be cash on delivery, to be re-weighed and two per cent tare allowed. New York, Feb. 9, 1825.
>
> (Signed) FRANCIS H. NICOLL & Co."

Eleven bales of cotton belonging to the defendants and forming part of that which they had agreed to sell, arrived at New

[1] Simmons *v.* Swift, 5 B. & C. 855.

[2] Russell *v.* Nicoll, 3 Wend. 112.

[3] Winslow *v.* Leonard, 12 Harris, 14; Scott *v.* Wells, 6 W. & S. 357; O'Keeffe *v.* Kellogg, 15 Ill. 347; Kohl *v.* Lindley, 39 id. 195; Hutchinson *v.* Hunter, 7 id. 140; Hutchinson *v.* The Commonwealth, 82 id. 472, 480.

York before the first of June, and were demanded by the plaintiffs, but the defendants refused to deliver them on the ground that the contract was executory and did not pass the title, and that, as the whole of the five hundred bales did not arrive before the first of June, they were not bound to deliver the part which had actually come to hand. A nonsuit was entered at the trial and a motion to take it off was subsequently argued before the court in banc and dismissed.

Marcy, J., said the main difficulty in the case was to determine the real character of the contract. On the one hand, it was said to be an actual and unconditional sale of the cotton, with a warranty that it should arrive at the port of New York, by the first of June, 1825; on the other, that it is an agreement to sell on condition that it should arrive before that time. It was very clear that if the plaintiffs had brought trover for the cotton they could not have sustained their action.

The cases of McDonald *v.* Hewett,[1] Rapelye *v.* Mackie,[2] and Shepley *v.* Davis,[3] were decisive that the title will not vest in the purchaser so long as any step remains to be taken by the vendor for the purpose of ascertaining the quantity and price. It followed that the contract was executory and not executed. Something was to be done before the title to the cotton passed from the defendants to the plaintiffs. It was to be brought to New York, weighed there, and paid for by the plaintiffs, after making the deductions stipulated in the agreement. The defendants could retain the possession of it even after it arrived in New York, for the purpose of weighing it and until it was paid for by the plaintiffs. The payment and delivery were dependent and simultaneous acts. Applying to this property the test mentioned by Spencer, J., in the case of McDonald *v.* Hewett, who would have been the sufferers if the cotton had been lost on its voyage from New Orleans to New York, or while at the latter place before it had been weighed? Beyond all question, the loss would have fallen on the defendants.

The rule in question is, nevertheless, merely a guide to the interpretation of the contract, which, though valuable as such,

[1] 15 Johns. 349. [2] 6 Cow. 250. [3] 5 Taunt. 617.

will not be allowed to override the intention of the parties when explicitly declared, or resulting by an obvious implication from their language as viewed in the light of the facts and circumstances.[1] As Cockburn, C. J., observed in Martineau *v.* Kitching,[2] "There is nothing in point of principle and common sense to prevent a man passing the property in a thing he proposes to sell and the buyer to purchase, although the price may remain to be ascertained afterwards." Goods which are set apart or designated as the property of the purchaser, or actually or constructively delivered to him, may consequently be his and at his risk although they have not been counted, weighed, or measured, and it is still unascertained what he has to pay.[3]

There can be no sale without a certain price, but *id certum est quod certum reddi potest.* When the parties agree how much is to be paid for each pound or bushel this requisite is fulfilled, and the weight or quantity may be ascertained subsequently by measurement or the scales, and the amount will then be a question of arithmetic, and not less certain than if the computation had been made in the first instance.[4] It is no doubt true that a sale for cash cannot be carried into effect until the price is definitely known; but this does not apply to a sale for credit, and there is nothing to preclude an agreement that the title shall pass at once and the vendor retain possession until the goods can be weighed or measured and the sum computed. Regard should be had in deducing the intention when the contract is in writing, to the instrument as a whole rather than to particular words or phrases; and "I have this day sold" may, in accordance with this canon, be interpreted as an executory contract which leaves the right of property in

[1] Winslow *v.* Leonard, 12 Harris, 14.

[2] L. R. 7 Q. B. 436.

[3] See Dennis *v.* Alexander, 3 Barr, 50; Scott *v.* Wells, 6 W. & S. 357; Winslow *v.* Leonard, 12 Harris, 14; Swanwick *v.* Sothern, 9 A. & E. 895; Turley *v.* Bates, 2 H. & C. 200; O'Keeffe *v.* Kellogg, 15 Ill. 347; Holliday *v.* Burgess, 34 id. 193; Seckel *v.* Scott, 66 id. 106; Riddle *v.* Varnum, 20 Pick. 280; Solomons *v.* McKinstry, 13 Johns. 27; Boswell *v.* Green, 1 Dutch. 390; Nicholson *v.* Taylor, 7 Casey, 128.

[4] Groat *v.* Gile, 51 N. Y. 431.

the vendor; or "I agree to sell" as an actual sale, vesting the title in the purchaser.[1]

It was said in Scott *v.* Wells, and repeated in Dennis *v.* Alexander, that it is only where there is something to be done by the very terms of the contract for the ascertainment of the price, that the sale is incomplete. A more accurate statement of the proposition would seem to be that where the contract provides that the goods shall be measured or finished before delivery or payment, there is ground for an inference that the title is not to pass until the condition is fulfilled.[2] A like inference may be drawn where the contract is silent; but such a stipulation is implied. Price is an essential element without which there can be no sale; and when the agreement is to pay so much per pound or bushel, and the weight or quantity is unknown, there is a plain implication that the goods are to be weighed or measured in order to ascertain how much the purchaser is to pay.

Whether this is to be a condition precedent to the passage of the title depends, as I have already stated, on what was mutually understood or agreed. The just inference seems to be, that where the price is not definitely ascertained, it affords ground for a presumption that the right of property is to remain in the vendor until the computation has been made; which may nevertheless be repelled by proof that the parties meant that it should vest forthwith.

"In the sale of personal property, the general rule of law is, that when, by the terms of the contract, the seller agrees to do anything for the purpose of putting the property into a state in which the buyer is bound to accept it, or into a condition to be delivered, the title will remain in him until he has performed the agreement in this respect. The general rule will not prevail, where, by the terms of the agreement, the title is to vest immediately in the buyer, notwithstanding something remains to be done to the goods by the seller after

[1] See Russell *v.* Nicoll, 3 Wend. 112; McGlynn *v.* Maynz, 104 Mass. 263; Winslow *v.* Leonard, 12 Harris, 14.

[2] See O'Keeffe *v.* Kellogg, 15 Ill. 347; Seekel *v.* Scott, 66 id. 106, 110; Records *v.* Railroad, 9 Phila. 55.

delivery. Thus, in Riddle *v.* Varnum,[1] it was held that the jury, where there was evidence of such intention, might infer a delivery to the buyer sufficient to vest the title, although something remained to be done by the seller, while the general doctrine above stated, in cases where there is no evidence of intention to complete the sale and pass the title, is fully affirmed. And in Farley *v.* Bates,[2] it was said that the court must look to the intention as drawn from the terms of the contract, in order to determine whether title to the property immediately passed.[3] In all cases, however, the intention of the parties as to the time when the title is to pass can be ascertained only from the terms of the agreement, as expressed in the language and conduct of the parties, and as applied to known usage and the subject-matter. It must be manifested at the time the bargain is made. The rights of the parties under the contract cannot be affected by their undisclosed purposes, or by their understanding of its legal effect.

"In the case at bar, it was not in dispute at the trial, that by the contract of April 15, the fish was to be put on flakes and further dried by the plaintiff, and afterward weighed by him for the purpose of ascertaining the quantity and price. This was to be done for the purpose of fitting the goods for delivery. By the general rule, therefore, the property not actually taken away by the defendant remained in the plaintiff, unless there is evidence which would justify the jury in finding that by further agreement, notwithstanding this feature of the contract, the title was to pass immediately to the defendant. We can find no evidence of such agreement in the case stated. All that was said and done on April 15th is consistent with an intention to leave the title in the plaintiff until the fish were fully cured, weighed, and delivered, according to the general rule of law, and there is nothing to vary the application of that rule."[4]

Whatever the rule may be under other circumstances, it is clear on principle and under the authorities that an agreement

[1] 20 Pick. 280.

[2] 2 H. & C. 200.

[3] Young *v.* Matthews, L. R. 2 C. P. 127; Story on Sales, 298 a.

[4] Foster *v.* Ropes, 111 Mass. 15.

to sell goods of a certain kind or answering to a particular description, will not pass the title till the very things which the purchaser is to receive are definitely ascertained, which can only be by mutual consent, as distinguished from an unauthorized appropriation or selection by the vendor. This rule grows out of the nature of things, and will not bend to the intention of the parties. It is immaterial that the goods are in the vendor's possession unless they are not merely pointed out to the purchaser, but what the latter agrees to buy. If the vendor is free to choose whether he will deliver them or other goods of a like kind, the purchaser will have a corresponding right to require that the selection shall not be made without his assent or concurrence, subject to a liability in damages if his approval is wrongfully withheld.[1] The law is clearly stated in the following extract from Benjamin on Sales:[2] "Until the parties are agreed on the specific individual goods, the contract can be no more than a contract to supply goods answering a particular description, and since the vendor would fulfil his part of the contract by furnishing any parcel of goods answering that description, and the purchaser could not object to them if they did answer the description, it is clear there can be no intention to transfer the property in any particular lot of goods more than another till it is ascertained which are the very goods sold. It can make no difference although the goods are so far ascertained that the parties have agreed that they shall be taken from some specified larger stock. In such a case the reason still applies; the parties did not intend to transfer the property in one portion of the stock more than in another, and the law, which only gives effect to their intention, does not transfer the property in any individual portion."[3]

In Rapelye *v.* Mackie,[4] the plaintiffs had ninety-nine bales of

[1] Godts *v.* Rose, 17 C. B. 229; Rapelye *v.* Mackie, 6 Cow. 250; Winslow *v.* Leonard, 12 Harris, 14.

[2] Ch. iv. p. 317.

[3] Woods *v.* McGee, 7 Ohio, 469; Scott *v.* King, 12 Ind. 203; The Bank *v.* Gillette, 90 id. 268; Hutchinson *v.* The Commonwealth, 82 Pa. 472, 480; Golder *v.* Ogden, 15 id. 528; Scudder *v.* Worster, 11 Cush. 573.

[4] 6 Cow. 250.

cotton marked "G. G. & Co.," of which thirty were at Myers & White's warehouse in Brooklyn, and sixty-nine at Van Bokelin's warehouse in the same town, and sold sixty-six bales to the defendants, which were described in the bill of parcels as "containing nineteen thousand eight hundred pounds," at twelve dollars per hundred-weight; but there was no reference to the place of storage, nor did it appear from the evidence that the defendants had the above-mentioned bales in view in making the contract, or intended to purchase any specific goods. The defendants paid $1,800 down, and the cotton at Myers & White's having been destroyed by fire a night or two afterwards, it was contended that the loss should be borne by them. The court held that the contract might have been fulfilled by the delivery of a number of bales answering to that mentioned in the bill of parcels, from any warehouse in New York or Brooklyn, and that even if it was to be regarded as limited to the bales which the plaintiffs actually had in Brooklyn, there was nothing to indicate whether it was to come from Myers & White's warehouse or from Van Bokelin's. It followed that there was no ground on which the defendants could be held answerable for the price of goods, which not only were not delivered, but had never been marked or set apart as theirs. Otherwise the vendor might elect after the event, and throw the loss on the purchaser by treating whichever parcel was destroyed as that which belonged to him. The case had been likened to that of the sale of a certain weight or number out of a larger mass, but such was not the fact as disclosed by the evidence.

An analogous decision was rendered in White *v.* Wilks.[1] The contract there was for twenty tons of linseed oil; and it appeared in evidence that the vendor had a much larger quantity in various cisterns in different warehouses, and the note or memorandum of the transaction did not specify the place where the oil was kept, or what oil was to be delivered, and both particulars were unknown to the purchaser. It was decided that the title remained in the vendor, although the sale

[1] 5 Taunt. 176.

note stated that he "held the oil for the purchaser's accommodation, charging one shilling per ton per week rent."

It is essential, as the rule is generally applied in England and by some tribunals in the United States, that the contract should not only relate to some specific goods or chattel, but that the bales, casks, gallons, or bushels which the purchaser is to have, should be so far marked or segregated that no further steps are requisite to enable him to identify and claim them as his own.[1] If all the grain on board a vessel or in a warehouse is sold at so much per bushel, the understanding being that the purchaser shall take possession and ascertain the quantity by measurement, the question whether the right of property shall vest at once is one of intention, and should be left as such to the jury; but if part only be sold the whole will remain the vendor's property and at his risk until the portion which the purchaser is to take has been ascertained, and it does not vary the case that the whole is of one kind and alike in quality. If A has one thousand bushels of wheat in store, and sells one hundred of them to B without separating them from the mass, B will, if these decisions are sound, not acquire a title to the whole, because such is not the design; nor yet to any part of it, because the contract does not apply to one part more than another; or, as the principle was stated in Gillett *v.* Hill,[2] "Where there is a bargain for a certain quantity out of a greater quantity, and there is a power of selection in the vendor to deliver which he thinks fit, there the right does not pass until the vendor has made his selection, and trover is not maintainable before that is done. If I agree to deliver a certain quantity of oil in tuns out of eighteen tuns, no one can say which part of the whole quantity I have agreed to deliver until the selection is made. There is no individuality until it has been divided."[3] A

[1] See Keeler *v.* Goodwin, 111 Mass. 490; Morrison *v.* Dingley, 63 Me. 553.

[2] 2 C. & M. 530.

[3] The principle has been recognized or applied in numerous instances, —Golder *v.* Ogden, 3 Harris, 528; Hutchinson *v.* Hunter, 7 Barr, 140; Hutchinson *v.* The Commonwealth, 32 P. F. S. 472, 480; The Bank *v.* Gillette, 90 Ind. 268; Scudder *v.* Worster, 11 Cush. 573; Waldo *v.* Belcher,

sale of a given weight or quantity to be separated from a larger mass, as where a merchant sells a thousand bushels of the grain which he has on board a ship or in his granary, will not therefore, agreeably to this principle, pass the right of property; and if the ship is lost, or the granary consumed by fire, the loss will fall on the vendor.[1]

Accordingly, where Duncan agreed to purchase three hundred barrels of oil from Haldeman, and paid for it, and Haldeman pointed out a number of barrels standing on the bank of the river, and requested Duncan to test the quality of the oil, which he did and declared himself satisfied; but the three hundred barrels were not set apart and the whole was subsequently swept away by a flood, it was held that the goods were at the vendor's risk and that the purchaser was entitled to have back what he had paid.[2] This case is the more remarkable because the purchaser paid the price and took a receipt in full, and would certainly have thought it hard had the goods been taken in execution by the vendor's creditors, as they clearly might if the title remained in him.

In Hutchinson *v.* Hunter,[3] one hundred barrels of molasses of unequal contents, part of a specified larger stock, were sold without being designated by marks or numbers, or separated from the rest, and the court held that the contract wanted a feature which was essential to complete it. The goods must be individualized or segregated from the bulk or quantity with which they were blended, or individualized in some other way before the title could pass, and would remain the property of the vendor until that was effectually done, although the contract might be so worded as to indicate an opposite design.

Agreeably to the same principle, the execution and delivery of a warehouse receipt will not pass the title unless there are some specific goods answering to the description given in the instrument, or capable of being identified as that

11 Ired. 609; Ferguson *v.* The Bank, 14 Bush, 555; Waldron *v.* Chase, 37 Me. 414; Kelsea *v.* Haines, 41 N. H. 246; Ockington *v.* Ritchie, 41 id. 275.

[1] See Winslow *v.* Leonard, 12 Harris, 14.

[2] Haldeman *v.* Duncan, 1 P. F. S. 66.

[3] 7 Barr, 140.

which the vendor agreed to part with and the purchaser to acquire. In Ferguson *v.* The Bank,[1] Krauth, Ferguson & Co. gave a receipt to the Bank of Kentucky for 3,600 sugar-cured hams, marked "Krauth, Ferguson & Co., Eclipse," as collateral security for the payment of a note of $5,000. They failed soon afterwards, and their assets passed into the hands of an assignee, who contested the validity of a pledge to the bank. It appeared in evidence that Krauth, Ferguson & Co. had a much larger number of sugar-cured hams than that mentioned in the receipt, which all bore the same marks but were of different qualities and values, and it was contended that they and the assignee claiming under them were estopped from denying the title which they had formally admitted. The court said that, by the statutes of Kentucky, the delivery or pledge of a warehouse receipt was a symbolic delivery, and would be equivalent to actual delivery if the property which it represented was so far segregated or identified that the title could pass as between vendor and purchaser. Such was not the case where as in the present instance, the sale was of a certain quantity to be taken from a greater bulk, and the doctrine advanced in Kimberly *v.* Patchin,[2] that separation is not essential where the mass is identical in kind and like in quality, must be regarded as an innovation on the common law which should not be followed.

This decision is clearly sound so far as it regards the passage of the title, but it may be doubted whether the court was equally right in holding that there was no equitable lien, or ground for the intervention of a chancellor. A court of equity does not ordinarily enforce contracts for the sale or conveyance of chattels, because the presumption is that the injury may be compensated in damages, but this argument does not apply when the object is security for the payment of a debt, and a specific performance may then be decreed not only as between the original parties, but against third persons, who, like an assignee for the benefit of creditors, are not purchasers for value.[3]

[1] 14 Bush, 555. [2] 19 N. Y. 330.

[3] 1 Leading Cases in Equity, 4 Am. ed. 1095, 1108; 2 id. 1628.

Agreeably to the Roman law, the loss occasioned by the destruction of the subject-matter of a sale before delivery fell on the buyer, who was answerable for the purchase-money although he never got the property or became the owner, because the doctrine of consideration was unknown and the inability of a party to a mutual contract to perform his share did not preclude him from enforcing the contract, unless it arose from a want of care or diligence as distinguished from a *vis major* or other uncontrollable force.[1]

No such distinction exists at common law where the obligation results from the consideration and ceases when that fails, and the non-fulfilment of an executory contract from whatever cause discharges the buyer,[2] and would render the seller liable in damages though performance has become impossible through the loss or destruction of the thing sold, but for an implied condition that the subject-matter shall continue to exist.[3]

The mode of specification is immaterial if it is sufficiently precise, and may be by designating a particular lot or parcel, or by describing the barrels or packages which the purchaser is to have by their marks or numbers in the bill of sale or other memorandum of the contract.[4] In Dugan *v.* Nichols,[5] the owner of a quantity of oil in casks pointed out twenty

[1] Institutes, 3, 23, 3, Accarias, Nos. 612, 662; Maynz, §§ 177, 210, 211; *ante*, p. 87. The seller lost the thing, but the buyer was the real loser because he had to pay for it. Institutes, 3. 23, § 3. This result was not in the opinion of the Doctors of the Civil Law contrary to natural justice. The buyer was simply compelled to fulfil his promise and could not ask that the seller should suffer from an accident for which he was not to blame. Pothier, Contrat de Vente, Partie iv.

[2] Kein *v.* Tupper, 52 N. Y. 550.

[3] Taylor *v.* Caldwell, 3 B. & S. 826; The School District *v.* Dauchy, 25 Conn. 530, 535; Dexter *v.* Norton, 47 N. Y. 62. "In contracts where the performance depends on the continued existence of a person or thing, a condition is implied that the impossibility of performance arising from the perishing of the person or thing shall excuse the performance." Taylor *v.* Caldwell, 3 B. & S. 826, 838.

[4] See Dowell *v.* Taylor, 2 Mo. App. 329; Arnold *v.* Delano, 4 Cush. 33; Smyth *v.* Craig, 3 W. & S. 14.

[5] 125 Mass. 43.

casks standing apart from the rest, and named the price, which was paid, and the sale was held to be complete and pass the title although the oil remained in the vendor's possession. In like manner, where a brewer gave a bill of sale for "sufficient barley now in my brewery to make malt enough (which is to be made in the brewery) to pay a note" which he had given to the purchaser, and immediately thereafter went with him to a heap at the south end of the building, and made delivery thereof by saying, "I deliver you this barley in pursuance of the contract," it was held, in view of the end which was security, that the title passed not only as between the parties but against a subsequent purchaser with notice, although the quantity in the heap was not known or ascertained until afterwards, and there was no agreement as to price or value.[1] So if a bill of sale of a given number of barrels of mackerel, which describes them as marked "No. 1," "No. 2," and "No. 3," respectively, covers all that the vendor has on hand of any one of the brands, they will become the property of the buyer although they are intermingled with others and distinguishable from them only by the marks or brands. It is not essential in this or any other case where the intention is to part with all, that the parties should know how much, or have the data for an immediate computation of the price, if the rate is agreed on and the calculation can be made after the number of gallons or bushels have been ascertained by weighing or measurement. On the other hand, if the vendor has one hundred and fifty barrels marked No. 1, 2, or 3, and sells one hundred barrels of that brand, the title will remain in him until they are set apart or delivered.[2] Chapman, J., said that a designation by some visible mark was a sufficient separation, and that it was not essential that the mark should be impressed or made for that end. If the barrels were inspected and marked of different qualities, for example, No. 1, No. 2, and No. 3, and the whole of that marked No. 1 was sold and formally delivered, the property might pass and the delivery be perfect, although the bar-

[1] Wooster *v.* Sherwood, 25 N. Y. 278.

[2] Ropes *v.* Lane, 9 Allen, 502; 11 id. 591.

rels No. 1 remained intermingled with the other barrels which had different marks. So if there were one hundred barrels marked No. 1, and the owner contracted to sell one hundred and fifty barrels, the vendee would acquire a title to the hundred barrels.

Actual delivery is not essential, and the right of property will pass as soon as the goods are measured out or set apart with the purchaser's assent or under an express or implied authority from him, although they remain in the vendor's warehouse or on board his vessel.[1]

In Rugg *v.* Minett the contract was executory, to sell so many hundred weight of turpentine deliverable in casks, and so much of the turpentine as had actually been drawn off into casks and weighed, was held to be at the buyer's risk although the residue remained in bulk. So in Records *v.* Railroad,[2] the court held that the property in six car-loads of lumber — parcel of a larger quantity which had been sold subject to inspection — passed when the inspector finished his count and rendered a certificate to the parties, although the residue had not arrived at the railway station.

In these instances, the right of property was held to pass as to so much of the goods as had been appropriated, although the residue remained in bulk in the vendor's possession and could not be identified or distinguished. The general rule, nevertheless, is that when the contract is entire for a certain weight or quantity, the whole will be at the vendor's risk, although part has been not only weighed or measured out but laden on carts or in barges belonging to the purchaser and sent by him for that purpose.[3] In Rochester & Ohio Oil Co. *v.* Hughey,[4] the purchaser of a given quantity of oil sent two barges, which were to be filled by the vendor; and the ques-

[1] Rhode *v.* Thwaites, 6 B. & C. 388; Aldridge *v.* Johnson, 7 E. & B. 885; Rugg *v.* Minett, 11 East, 210; Scott *v.* Wells, 6 W. & S. 357; Smyth *v.* Craig, 3 id. 14; Hutchinson *v.* The Commonwealth, 82 Pa. 472, 481.

[2] 9 Phila. 55.

[3] See Russell *v.* Nicoll, 3 Wend. 112; Mead *v.* Degogter, 16 id. 632; Berker *v.* Higgins, 21 N. Y. 397; Kein *v.* Tupper, 52 id. 550, 555, *ante.*

[4] 6 P. F. S. 322.

tion was whether the right of property had passed in so much of the oil as was actually put on board one of them, and it was held that he could not be compelled to take a partly filled barge, any more than he could have been compelled to accept half a barrel of oil under a contract for a barrel.

It has been held in some instances, that where the entire mass or bulk is delivered with a view of enabling the purchaser to separate or set apart the number of tons or bushels which he has agreed to purchase, and return the residue to the vendor or hold it subject to his order, the right of property will pass at once, if such is the intention of the parties as deduced from the circumstances.[1] In the case last cited, the sale was of forty-three thousand bricks in a kiln containing a larger quantity. The purchaser went into possession of the brickyard, and it was held that he thereby acquired a title to the forty-three thousand bricks, although they were not counted or separated.

In Kimberly *v.* Patchin,[2] it was justly observed with regard to this decision that if separation was indispensable, the grant of a right or privilege to select would go for nothing until it was exercised. If, on the other hand, it is a mere circumstance, and important as indicating that something more is to be done, it must yield whenever the will of parties clearly is that it shall not be an obstacle to the attainment of the end which they have in view.

The rule that the sale of a part which is not segregated or distinguished from the mass, will not pass the right of property even if so designed, is therefore, agreeably to many authorities, subject to the following qualifications: Where several persons are joint-owners of goods or chattels, each may transfer his interest without a preliminary division to a purchaser, who will stand in the position previously held by the vendor and be entitled to an undivided share. A sale by a sole owner of one-third, one-half, or one-fourth, will produce a like result by rendering the vendor and purchaser tenants

[1] Weld *v.* Cutler, 2 Gray, 195; Crofoot *v.* Bennett, 2 Comst. 258.

[2] 19 N. Y. 330.

in common of their respective shares.[1] It is immaterial as regards the application of this principle whether the property in question is a specific chattel (a horse or a bale of cotton), or consists of things which like wheat and oil are identical in kind and presumably uniform in value. The question is one of fact, depending on whether the intention is to confer a several title to part, or to render the buyer a joint owner of the whole; and it is only in the former case that the specification or separation of the goods can be essential to the effectual operation of the contract.

The case is more complicated where the intention is to confer a several right so far as it can be done without separating or marking what the buyer is to have, and regard must then be had to the nature of the property in hand. If the sale is of a given quantity out of a larger mass, which is so far uniform as to render it immaterial which part the buyer is to have, and the purpose is to vest the title immediately in him, he becomes a tenant in common, though not in the sense in which the term is generally understood.[2] Ordinarily a joint ownership cannot be parted save by consent, or with the aid of a chancellor. Each owner has an interest in the whole, and hence no one of them can dispose specifically of his portion without incurring a liability to the others. The case is widely different where a given number of bushels of wheat are sold out of a larger quantity, and either party may then take as many bushels as justly belong to him without consulting his co-tenant, and hold the latter answerable in trover for a refusal to accede to such a demand.[3]

In Hurff *v.* Hires, one Heritage had four or five hundred bushels of corn in bulk, and sold three hundred bushels to Hurff, who paid the price but stipulated that the corn should be allowed to remain where it was until it hardened suffi-

[1] See Cushing *v.* Breed, 14 Allen, 376; Ferguson *v.* Bank, 14 Bush, 555; Kimberly *v.* Patchin, 19 N. Y. 330.

[2] Cushing *v.* Breed, 14 Allen, 376; Kimberly *v.* Patchin, 19 N. Y. 330.

[3] Hurff *v.* Hires, 39 N. J. L. 4; 40 id. 581; Waldron *v.* Chase, 37 Me. 414; Pleasants *v.* Pendleton, 6 Rand. 473; Chapman *v.* Shepard, 39 Conn. 413; Russell *v.* Carrington, 42 N. Y. 118; Kimberly *v.* Patchin, 19 id. 330; Clark *v.* Griffith, 24 id. 595.

ciently to be merchantable. The entire mass was subsequently taken in execution under a writ against Heritage, and it was held that Hurff might maintain trover against the sheriff notwithstanding the want of separation, because the presumption was that the parties did not intend that the title should remain in the vendor and be liable to be sold for his debts, and if so there was no reason why their purpose should not be carried into effect.

The case of Hutchinson *v.* Hunter[1] can hardly be regarded as at variance with this doctrine, because the court explicitly declared that the impediment was not merely a want of separation, but that the barrels were of unequal quantities and values, and either ground would presumably have been insufficient without the other.

The case is still clearer for the application of such a principle when the vendor of things which are ordinarily estimated by weight or measure, and presumably uniform in value, gives the purchaser an order for a certain number of gallons or bushels on the warehouseman or wharfinger with whom they have been deposited for safe keeping or shipment, which is accepted by the bailee; and the latter will then be precluded from denying that he has that amount of merchandise on hand belonging to the purchaser, and may be liable in trover if it is sold to a third person or not forthcoming when demanded.[2]

The leading case is Whitehouse *v.* Frost.[3] There the owners of forty tuns of oil lying in a cistern, of which they had the key, sold ten tuns of it to Frost and received the price. Frost resold to Townsend and gave him an order for the oil on the original vendors, which the latter accepted; and it was decided, first, that the title had vested in Townsend although the ten tuns had not been measured out or separated, and next, that

[1] 7 Barr, 140.

[2] Cushing *v.* Breed, 14 Allen, 376; Keeler *v.* Goodwin, 111 Mass. 490; Russell *v.* Carrington, 42 N. Y. 118; Whitehouse *v.* Frost, 12 East, 614; Newhall *v.* Langdon, 39 Ohio St. 87; Hutchinson *v.* The Commonwealth, 82 Pa. 472, 481. See Carpenter *v.* Graham, 42 Mich. 191; Gillett *v.* Hill, 2 C. & M. 530.

[3] 12 East, 614.

Frost could not detain or stop the oil for the dishonor of the acceptance which Townsend had given for the purchase-money, because there was a virtual delivery to him. The cases of Gillett *v.* Hill,[1] Woodley *v.* Coventry,[2] and Knights *v.* Wiffen,[3] are to the same effect, save that the exception to the general rule that "until an appropriation from a bulk is made, so that the vendor has said what portion belongs to him and what belongs to the buyer, the goods remain *in solido* and no property passes," was put on the ground that the defendant had by accepting the delivery-order led the plaintiff to alter his position for the worse, and was consequently precluded from denying what he had thus formally admitted. In Woodley *v.* Coventry, the plaintiff paid part of the purchase-money on the faith of the acceptance; but in Knights *v.* Wiffen the price had been already paid, and the court held that the omission to demand it back might reasonably be ascribed to a mistaken confidence in the defendant's word.

The case of Cushing *v.* Breed[4] follows in the same line of decision by holding that where the goods are in the custody of a third person, and the vendor gives an order on him for part, which is accepted, he becomes as much a bailee for the purchaser as if the goods had been handed over to the latter and returned for safe keeping; and no further delivery or appropriation is requisite to pass the title. The case was distinguished by the court from that where the vendor retains the custody of the goods and makes a similar admission, on the ground that under these circumstances there is something further for him to do, — such as weighing, measuring, or marking, and the intention presumably is that the title shall not pass until this is accomplished. The property was in the hands of a bailee, and when he became a custodian for the vendee, his possession was the possession of his principal.

The court also relied on the fact that the grain in controversy was in an elevator, and must, according to the usage of trade, be regarded as held by the respective owners as tenants in common. It followed that each was entitled to such a pro-

[1] 2 C. & M. 530. [2] 2 H. & C. 164. [3] L. R. 5 Q. B. 660.
[4] 14 Allen, 376.

portion as the quantity bore to the entire mass. If one of them sold a certain number of bushels, it was a sale of property owned by him in common, and removal was not essential to complete the transfer; and when the vendor gave the vendee a delivery order which the agents accepted, and agreed to store the property for him, the appropriation was complete, and the vendee thenceforth held the goods as a joint owner.

It was an elementary principle that a tenant in common of personal property in the hands of an agent, might dispose of the whole or any part of his interest by the method above stated, or by any other method which was equivalent. Actual separation or taking away was not essential, because the agent acted for the new principal, and held the property for him. The principle was the same whether the proprietors were numerous, or the vendor and vendee owned the whole; and if the latter resold what he had bought, his vendee might by the same course of dealing also become a tenant in common to the extent of his interest.

It may be inferred from the language held in this instance, that the vendor cannot vest the right of property in the purchaser by a formal declaration or admission that he holds a certain number of bushels or gallons for him, if they in point of fact form part of a larger mass, although the whole is of one kind, and so much alike in quality, that each drop or particle is equivalent to every other, and there is no room for choice. The goods must, according to this doctrine, be set apart or marked, or be in the hands of a third person who agrees to hold them for the purchaser, or at the very least receives an order from the vendor to that effect; and such actually was the judgment in the previous case of Scudder *v.* Worster.[1]

It was decided, for like reasons, in Hutchinson *v.* The Commonwealth,[2] that the holder of an accepted order on a pipe-line oil company is specifically entitled to the quantity of oil which the order calls for, and may maintain trover if it is withheld, although the pipes and reservoirs of the company contain a much larger quantity of oil, and his share is not measured

[1] 11 Cush. 573.

[2] 82 Pa. 472.

out or separated. Such also was the view taken in Hibbard *v.* The Merchants' Bank[1] of a warehouse receipt as giving constructive possession of goods which were not set apart or identified.

Notwithstanding the ground taken in these instances, it does not appear to be material whether the custodian of the goods is the vendor or a third person, if he in fact holds them for the vendee and subject to his order; and the weight of authority in the United States accordingly is that such a relation may grow out of an express or implied agreement in the contract of sale, without the ceremony of handing them over to the purchaser, and receiving them back from him as his.[2]

In Kimberly *v.* Patchin the question was considered on grounds that have largely influenced the subsequent course of decision, and will perhaps ultimately be adopted by the courts which still adhere to a different view. The case grew out of the following circumstances: — Agreeably to the evidence, Shuttleworth, on being shown two piles of wheat belonging to Dickinson, expressed a doubt whether they contained six thousand bushels, which was the quantity that he wished to buy. Dickinson was of opinion that they did, and undertook to make up the amount if it fell short. Shuttleworth then agreed to buy six thousand bushels at seventy cents per bushel, and gave Dickinson a draft for the price, and at the same time took a written memorandum or receipt acknowledging that he had six thousand bushels in store subject to his (Shuttleworth's) order. The wheat was left in the warehouse, and proved, when subsequently measured, to amount to six thousand two hundred and forty-nine bushels. The defendants bought from Shuttleworth, and obtained possession of the quantity mentioned in the memorandum given by Dickinson, but the latter had, as it would seem, previously disposed of the entire contents of both piles to the plaintiffs, who brought trover on the ground that as the six thousand bushels were

[1] 48 Mich. 118.

[2] Hurff *v.* Hires, 40 N. J. L. 581; Kimberly *v.* Patchin, 19 N. Y. 330.

not separated or delivered, the right of property remained in Dickinson, and had been transferred to them; and that the defendants must seek a remedy in an action against Shuttleworth for the breach of contract.

Comstock, J., said: "It is a rule asserted in many legal authorities, but which may be as fitly called a rule of reason and logic as of law, that in order to an executed sale, so as to transfer a title from one party to another, the thing sold must be ascertained. This is a self-evident truth when applied to those subjects of property which are distinguishable by their physical attributes from all other things, and, therefore, are capable of exact identification. No person can be said to own a horse or picture, unless he is able to identify the chattel or specify what horse or what picture it is that belongs to him. It is not only legally but logically impossible to hold property in such things, unless they are ascertained and distinguished from all other things; and this I apprehend is the foundation of the rule that, on a sale of chattels, in order to pass the title the articles must if not delivered be designated, so that possession can be taken by the purchaser without any further act on the part of the seller. But property can be acquired and held in many things which are incapable of such an identification. Articles of this nature are sold, not by a description which refers to and distinguishes the particular thing, but in quantities which are ascertained by weight, measure, or count, the constituent parts which make up the mass being indistinguishable from each other by any physical difference in size, shape, texture, or quality.

"Of this nature are wine, oil, wheat, the other cereal grains, and the flour manufactured from them. These can be identified only in mass or quantities, and in that mode, therefore, they are viewed in the contracts and dealings of men. In respect to such things, the rule above mentioned must be applied according to the nature of the subject. In an executed and perfect sale the things sold, it is true, must be ascertained. But as it is not possible in reason and philosophy to identify each constituent particle composing a quantity; so the law does not require such an identification. Where the quantity and the general mass from which it is to be taken are specified, the subject of the contract is thus ascertained, and it becomes a possible result for the title to pass, if the sale is complete in all its other circumstances.

"An actual delivery cannot be made, unless the whole is transferred to the possession of the purchaser, or unless the particular quantity sold is separated from the residue. But actual delivery is not indispensable in any case in order to pass a title, if the thing to be delivered is ascertained, if the price is paid or a credit given, and if nothing further remains to be done in regard to it. It appears to me that a very simple and elementary inquiry lies at the foundation of the present case. A quantity of wheat being in store, is it possible in reason and in law for one man to own a given portion of it, and for another man to own the residue without a separation of the parts. To bring the inquiry to the facts of the case; in the store of Dickinson there was a quantity not precisely known. In any conceivable circumstances could Shuttleworth become owner of six thousand bushels, and Dickinson of the residue, which turns out to be two hundred and forty-nine bushels, without the portion of either being divided from the other? The answer to this inquiry is plain. Suppose a third person, being the prior owner of the whole, had given to Shuttleworth a bill of sale of six thousand bushels, and one to Dickinson for the residue, more or less, intending to pass to each the title, and expressing that intention in plain words, what would have been the result? The former owner most certainly would have parted with all his title. If, then, the two purchasers did not acquire it no one could own the wheat, and the title would be lost.

"This would be an absurdity. But if the parties thus purchasing could and would be the owners, how would they hold it? Plainly according to this contract. One would be entitled to six thousand bushels, and the other what remained after that quantity was subtracted. Again suppose, Dickinson having in store and owning two hundred and forty-nine bushels, Shuttleworth had deposited with him six thousand bushels for storage merely, both parties agreeing that the quantities might be mixed. This would be a case of confusion of property where neither would lose his title. In the law of bailments it is entirely settled that Shuttleworth, being the bailor of six thousand bushels, would lose nothing by mixture, and it being by consent, it is also clear that the bailee would lose nothing.[1]

"These and other illustrations which might be suggested, demonstrate the possibility of a divided ownership in the six thousand two hundred and forty-nine bushels of wheat. If then, the law admits that the property while in mass could exist under the condition, it was plainly competent for the parties to the sale in question so to deal with each other as to effectuate that result. One of them being the owner of the whole, he could stipulate and agree that the other should thenceforth own six thousand bushels without a separation from the residue. And this, I think, is precisely what was done. The six thousand bushels might have been measured and delivered to the purchaser, and then the same wheat might have been re-delivered to the seller under a contract of bailment. In that case the seller would have given his storehouse receipt in the very terms of the one which he actually gave and he might moreover, have mixed the wheat thus re-delivered with his own, thereby reducing the quantity sold and the quantity unsold again to one common mass. Now the contract of sale and of bailment, both made at the same time, produced this very result. The formalities of measurement and delivery pursuant to the sale and of re-delivery according to the bailment, resulting in the mixture as before, most assuredly were not necessary in order to pass the title, because these formalities would leave the property in the same condition under which it was left, that is to say, in the actual custody of the vendor and blended together in a common mass. Those formal and ceremonial acts were dispensed with by the contract of the parties. They went directly to the result without the performance of any useless ceremonies, and it would be strange indeed, if the law denied their power to do so. . . .

[1] Story on Bailments, § 40; 2 Bl. Com. 405.

"It is unnecessary to decide whether the parties to the original sale became tenants in common. If a tenancy in common arises in such cases, it must be with some peculiar incidents not usually belonging to that species of ownership. I think each party would have the right of severing the tenancy by his own act; that is, the right of taking the portion of the mass which belonged to him, being accountable only if he invaded the quantity which belonged to the other. But, assuming that the case is one of strict tenancy in common, the defendant became the owner of six thousand and the plaintiff of two hundred and forty-nine parts of the whole. As neither could maintain an action against the other for taking possession merely of the whole, more clearly he cannot if the other takes only the quantity which belongs to him."

This argument is open to criticism notwithstanding its apparent force. Beyond doubt, if the owner of six thousand bushels or any other quantity of wheat disposes of an undivided share or interest to one person and then sells the residue to another, the title will pass from him and vest in the purchasers. But the assumption that selling two thousand bushels out of such a mass to the first purchaser, and four thousand to the second, will produce the same result, begs the very point in controversy, which is whether such a sale transfers the title or leaves it in the vendor subject to a liability on his part for damages, in the event of his failure to fulfil the agreement by separating and delivering the respective shares. The latter view is, as we have seen, that taken by the Roman jurists, and generally at the present day in England.

It is more difficult to answer the inference drawn from the rule which is said to prevail where two or more persons blend or mingle goods of a like kind, as in the not uncommon case where parcels of wheat belonging to different owners are thrown into a common receptacle for storage or transportation, and if neither party loses anything by such an intermixture, or ceases to be severally entitled to his share, a like result may, as the Chief Justice intimated, ensue from a sale of a given quantity out of a greater bulk, attended with an agreement that the vendor shall hold the goods as if they had been delivered to the vendee, and re-delivered to him for safe keeping with his own.[1]

The principle of Kimberly *v.* Patchin was applied in Cobdell *v.* Stowell,[2] to an agreement between tenants in common that each should be specifically entitled to his share. "Conceding," said Lott, C. J., "as it is claimed on behalf of the defendant, that the parties were tenants in common of the corn and oats which were raised by the plaintiff on the defendant's farm, and that, as a general rule, one tenant in common cannot maintain trover against his co-tenant without showing a loss, sale or destruction of the property held in common, that concession is not available as a ground for the reversal of the judgment appealed from. It appears, from the evidence given on the trial, that after a portion of the grain had been used and sold by each of the parties, it was mutually agreed between them how the portion remaining undisposed of should be divided. The manifest intention of that agreement was to give the plaintiff a certain specific quantity as his share of both the corn and oats, with a right to take and hold it, without any further interest therein or claim thereto by the defendant. The portion to which he became entitled, although not in fact actually separated from the residue, was undistinguishable therefrom in quality and value, and could be ascertained with as much certainty by measure as if such separation had been made, and the plaintiff had the right to take it and hold it as his own separate property. The effect of that agreement was to vest the quantity so apportioned to the plaintiff in him individually, as effectually as a sale by both parties to a third person of a certain number of bushels either of corn or oats would have vested the title thereto in him as his absolute property. Although it still continued in the possession of the defendant, unseparated from that which was apportioned to himself, he held it all as affected and qualified by that agreement, and subordinate to the rights resulting from and conferred by it. The apportionment operated as a severance of the tenancy in common which had previously existed,

[1] See Marvin *v.* Wallis, 6 E. & B. 726.

[2] 31 N. Y. 73.

and changed the undivided into a divided ownership; the defendant thereafter stood in the relation of a bailee to the plaintiff as to his share."

It is clear, on authority and principle, that an agreement that the vendor shall retain the possession of the goods may render him as effectually the bailee of the vendee, as if they had been delivered and handed back.[1]

The rule in such cases was laid down in Jackson *v.* Anderson.[2] There Fielding, a resident of Buenos Ayres, consigned a barrel containing 4,700 Spanish dollars to Laycock & Co., and at the same time advised the plaintiff that 1,969 of them were intended for him on account of a pre-existing debt, and would be handed over by the consignee. Laycock & Co. pledged the dollars to the defendants, who sold them to the Bank of England, and it was held that they were answerable in trover to the plaintiff for the value of the coins which had been designed for him. Mansfield, C. J., said that the want of separation was not a defence. The defendant had disposed of all the dollars, and consequently of those which belonged to the plaintiff, and as all were of the same value it could not be a question as to what particular dollars were his. It was not like the case of tenants in common who have a right to every part of each particle in the mass or heap. Here one had a right to a certain number, and the others to the rest. So in Gardner *v.* Dutch,[3] one who was entitled to seventy-six bags of coffee forming part of a larger lot, and not in any way separated or distinguished from the rest, was allowed to maintain replevin for his part against the sheriff, who had attached the whole as the property of the person to whom it originally belonged.

The doctrine of Kimberly *v.* Patchin is followed in New York, Maine, Connecticut, New Jersey, Virginia, and some other States, and with some necessary qualifications will perhaps ultimately prevail throughout the Union, as conducive to the dispatch and certainty which are essential to the successful

[1] Beaumont *v.* Brengeri, 5 C. B. 301; Castle *v.* Sworder, 6 H. & N. 828; Hurff *v.* Hires, 40 N. J. L. R. 581, 592.

[2] 4 Taunt. 24.

[3] 9 Mass. 427.

prosecution of commercial operations.[1] In the case last cited the court held, reversing the judgment of the court below, that where the bulk is uniform in kind and quality, and selection would be an empty form, there is no rule which overrides the intention of the parties as expressed in terms or appearing by a necessary implication, or precludes the property from passing immediately on the completion of the sale.[2] In Clark *v.* Griffith,[3] the plaintiffs were in possession of four billiard tables under an agreement with the defendant, which entitled them to one without specifying which. The defendant removed all the tables; and it was held on the authority of Kimberly *v.* Patchin that, as he could not rightfully remove more than three, and when that number was taken the tenancy in common was at an end, the plaintiffs might well maintain trover for the asportation of the fourth.

The doctrine that several rights of ownership may co-exist in an undivided bulk, prevails in Pennsylvania, although it has not yet been applied to the sale of a given quantity out of a larger mass in the hands of the vendor. In Henderson *v.* Lauck,[4] the vendor hauled a quantity of grain which he had sold for cash, to the purchaser's mill, and emptied it on a heap of other grain belonging to him; the understanding being that the price should be paid in full as soon as the last cart-load was delivered. The money was evasively withheld; and it was decided that the vendor might maintain replevin for a number of bushels corresponding to that which he had delivered, although they were intermingled with the purchaser's grain and could not be specifically identified.

[1] Russell *v.* Carrington, 42 N. Y. 118; Chapman *v.* Shepard, 39 Conn. 413; Pleasants *v.* Pendleton, 6 Rand. 473; Newhall *v.* Langdon, 39 Ohio St. 87, 94; Steel Works *v.* Dewey, 37 id. 242; Hurff *v.* Hires, 39 N. J. L. 4; 40 id. 581; Watts *v.* Hendry, 13 Fla. 523; Waldron *v.* Chase, 37 Me. 414; Carpenter *v.* Graham, 42 Mich. 191. See a lucid summary of the authorities in Ralston on Sales of an Undivided Part, Phila. 1885.

[2] See Russell *v.* Carrington, 42 N. Y. 118; Waldron *v.* Chase, 37 Me. 414; Pleasants *v.* Pendleton, 6 Rand. 473; Hurff *v.* Hires, 40 N. J. L. 581.

[3] 24 N. Y. 595.

[4] 9 Harris, 359.

Lowrie, J., said: "Does the fact that on receiving it, the buyer mixed it with other grain of his own of the same kind in one heap, prevent its specific reclamation? The answer of the court below was in the negative, and so is the Roman law;[1] and such is the very point in Inglebright *v.* Hammond,[2] as to grain, and of Ryder *v.* Hathaway,[3] as to cord wood. In all these cases the owner is allowed to take back his own share of the bulk, kind for kind, measure for measure. It does not change the result that the seller saw the mixture take place without objection; for by consenting to such a mixture, the owners acknowledge that each parcel is of like quality, and that each one may take out the proportion that he cast in.[4] It was not the seller that was wrong in allowing the mixture, in reliance on the promise of the buyer; and to permit the buyer to allege the mixture in bar of the right of reclamation is to permit him to gain by his own fault. Indeed, every principle of law is against the buyer, for it was he that did the wrong in mixing the grain, if he was not ready to pay for it; and the usual rule would give the bulk to the seller until the buyer should separate his own. But this does not apply to goods so indistinguishable as grain, if the measure of each one's share be known. On the general subject of confusion of goods and effects, the rule is that he who wrongfully causes it must submit to all the risk and inconvenience of making a clear and well-defined identification and separation.[5] Even debts due to a principal, and mixed up by an agent with his own, may be specifically followed."[6]

It is nevertheless held in Massachusetts and some of the other States, in conformity to what would seem to be the rule in England, that the right of property cannot pass as between vendor and purchaser until that which the purchaser is to have is identified either by actual segregation or by some visible

1 Inst. 2. 1. 38; Dig. 6. 1, 2, 3.

2 19 Ohio St. 337; 11 U. S. Dig. 95.

3 21 Pick. 298.

4 Dig. 41. 1. 7, 8.

5 30 Me. 237, 295, 370; 7 Conn. 275; 20 Vt. 333; 15 Ves. 436; 2 Johns. Ch. R. 108; 2 Blackf. 383; 7 Mass. 127; 8 Pick. 443.

6 2 Pick. 86; 5 id. 7; 3 Mass. 232.

sign or mark, which is not less certain than if the goods had been set apart as his.[1]

In Scudder *v.* Worster,[2] A sold B two hundred and fifty barrels of pork, part of a larger lot all of the same quality, having the same marks and stored in his cellar, but no separation was made. B sold and delivered one hundred barrels of the same to C, and afterwards sold D the remaining hundred and fifty barrels, and gave him an order on A therefor, which being presented to A, he assented to hold the same on storage for D, but nothing was done to distinguish or separate the hundred and fifty barrels from the other pork of the same brand still in A's cellar. While the pork remained so stored, B became insolvent, and A thereupon refused to deliver the hundred and fifty barrels to D; and it was held that they were not so specified or separated from the mass, that D could maintain replevin for them against A.

Dewey, J., observed, in giving judgment: "In the case of Hutchinson *v.* Hunter,[3] which was an action of assumpsit to recover payment for one hundred barrels of molasses sold to the defendant, the same being parcel of one hundred and twenty-five barrels, and the whole destroyed by fire while in storage, and before separation or designation of any particular barrels, it was held that the plaintiff could not recover, the sale never having been consummated, and Rogers, J., said: 'The fundamental rule which applies to this case is, that the parties must be agreed as to the specific goods on which the contract is to attach, before there can be a bargain and sale. The goods must be ascertained, designated, and separated from the stock and quantity with which they are mixed before the property can pass.' So in Golder *v.* Ogden,[4] where a contract was made for the sale of two thousand pieces of wall-paper, the purchaser giving his notes therefor to the vendor and taking away with him one thousand pieces, and it was agreed that the other thousand pieces should remain until called for by

[1] See Scudder *v.* Worster, 11 Cush. 573; Golder *v.* Ogden, 3 Harris, 528; Waldo *v.* Belcher, 11 Ired. 609; Ferguson *v.* The Bank, 14 Bush, 555; Scott *v.* King, 12 Ind. 203; The Bank *v.* Gillette, 90 id. 268.

[2] 11 Cush. 573. [3] 7 Barr, 140. [4] 3 Harris, 528.

the purchaser; upon a question of property in the remaining thousand pieces between the assignees of the vendor and the purchaser, it was held that these thousand pieces not having been selected by the buyer, or separated or set apart for him, but remaining mingled with other paper of the same description, did not become the property of the alleged buyer as against an assignment for the benefit of the creditors of the vendor. The principle advanced in that case seems to be the sound one. — 'That the property cannot pass until there be a specific identification in some way of the particular goods which the party bargains for. The law knows no such thing as a floating right of property, which may attach itself to one parcel or the other, as may be found convenient afterwards.' The case of Waldo *v.* Belcher [1] was the case of a sale of corn by a vendor having in his store three thousand one hundred bushels of corn, and selling two thousand eight hundred bushels of the same; but the two thousand eight hundred bushels were never separated from the three thousand one hundred, and the whole was after the sale destroyed by fire, and it was held that the property in the two thousand eight hundred bushels did not pass to the vendee, though it would have been otherwise had it been a sale of all the corn in the crib. The ground of the decision was that there had been no separation, and that it could not be ascertained which corn was the property of the vendee until it was separated. The purchaser could not bring detinue, because he could not describe the particular thing. This would be equally so as to replevin. The case of Merrill *v.* Hunnewell,[2] bears strongly upon the question before us. It was a sale of nine arches of bricks in a kiln containing a larger number, but not separated from the residue, or specifically designated. After the vendor had by other sales reduced the quantity on hand to less than nine arches, upon a question of property between the vendee and an attaching creditor of the vendor, it was held that the purchaser took no property in the bricks, the sale being of part of a large mass not delivered nor designated. . . .

"In the argument of this case on the part of the plaintiff,

[1] 11 Ired. 609.

[2] 13 Pick. 213.

the case was put as a case of intermixture of goods, and it was argued that such intermixture having taken place the plaintiff might for that cause hold the property as his. But in fact there was no case of intermixture. The entire property was always in the defendants.

"It was also urged that the defendants were estopped to deny that the one hundred and fifty barrels of pork were the property of the plaintiff, having given a bill of sale of the same, and under the circumstances stated in the statement of facts. Had this been an action to recover damages for the value of one hundred and fifty barrels of pork, this position might be tenable, and the defendants estopped to deny the property of the plaintiff in such one hundred and fifty barrels. This would be so if an action had been brought against the defendants as bailees of one hundred and fifty barrels of pork, and for not delivering the same.

"But the distinction between the case of an action for damages for not delivering one hundred and fifty barrels, and that of replevin, commanding the officer to take from the possession of the defendants one hundred and fifty barrels, and deliver the same to plaintiff as his property, is an obvious one. To sustain the former, it is only necessary to show a right to one hundred and fifty barrels generally, and not to any specific one hundred and fifty barrels; but to maintain replevin, the plaintiff must be the owner of some specific one hundred and fifty barrels. If bought, they must be specifically set apart, or designated in some way as his, and not intermingled with a larger mass of like kind owned by the vendor."

The last-mentioned proposition, that what the defendants had admitted was that the plaintiff was entitled to one hundred and fifty barrels out of those in their possession, and not that they possessed one hundred and fifty barrels specifically belonging to the plaintiff, would seem to be just; but so much cannot be said for the argument that the case before the court resulted from a sale and not from an intermixture, because if there is nothing in the nature of things, nor any inflexible rule of law, which precludes the creation of several rights of ownership in a mass or bulk without segregation or division;

such a state of things may as well arise from an express or implied agreement as from the act of one or more of the owners in confusing or mingling the goods by casting all in the same mass.[1]

The point was virtually conceded in Cushing *v.* Breed.[2] For if the agreement implied in sending grain to an elevator can render the parties tenants in common in such sort that each may take the number of bushels to which he is entitled without the concurrence of the others, and maintain trover or replevin if they are withheld, a like result may follow from a stipulation or understanding to that effect between a vendor and purchaser, whether the goods are in the former's keeping or held by a bailee or agent. A like remark applies to Knights *v.* Wiffen,[3] because if the seller can be estopped by what passes between him and a third person, he may equally be estopped by what passes between him and the buyer, if it appears that the latter acted on the faith of an express or implied assurance that the right of property should be in him notwithstanding the failure to separate or remove the goods.

The doctrine of Kimberly *v.* Patchin[4] is obviously inapplicable, unless every part of the mass is so far equivalent to every other, as to make selection superfluous, and entitle each of the persons interested to alien, remove, or otherwise dispose of his proportion without the presence or concurrence of the others; and if there is any inequality or disparity in kind, price, or value, the contract will not pass the title to any particular thing or package which is not designated or set apart, although it may render the purchaser a tenant in common of the whole.[5] An owner may obviously sell one-third or one-half of the wine in his vaults without separating or marking any part of it, although the casks are of various sizes and con-

[1] Aldridge *v.* Johnson, 7 E. & B. 885, 899; Henderson *v.* Lauck, 9 Harris, 359.

[2] 14 Allen, 376, 380; *ante.* [3] L. R. 5 Q. B. 660.

[4] 19 N. Y. 330.

[5] Hurff *v.* Hires, 40 N. J. L. R. 581; Foot *v.* Marsh, 51 N. Y. 288; Hutchinson *v.* Hunter, 7 Barr, 140; Warren *v.* Buckminster, 24 N. H. 336; Smart *v.* Batchelder, 57 id. 140; Newhall *v.* Langdon, 39 Ohio, 87, 94.

tain different vintages; but what the purchaser acquires will be an interest in each cask, and not an exclusive title to any one. But a sale of twenty casks out of a larger lot, of unequal values, must necessarily fail from uncertainty, unless they are so marked or designated as to indicate which the buyer is to have.[1] Such is seemingly the only point determined in Ferguson *v.* The Bank,[2] although the language of the court went much further, and to the full extent of the doctrine that separation or identification is equally essential, whether the mass consists of like or of different things.

"To substitute an arrangement between the parties for a manual delivery of a parcel of property mixed with an ascertained and defined larger quantity, it must be so clearly defined that the purchaser can take it, or, as the assignee of the purchaser did in Kimberly *v.* Patchin, maintain replevin for it. In this case the larger quantity, parcel of which was understood to be contracted to the plaintiffs, consisted of one hundred and fifty barrels containing three different qualities of oil, but sixty-eight of which (forty-seven of the Buffalo and Erie oil, and twenty-one barrels marked 'V. B.') corresponded with the sample by which the hundred barrels were sold. The residue, forty-six barrels of the 'Murray' oil, were superior to the sample, and thirty-six, known as the 'Lemon' oil, were inferior to the sample. The plaintiffs would not have the right to take the 'Murray' or superior oil, and could not be compelled to take the 'Lemon' or inferior oil. And if the sample was, as the witness at one time stated, a poor sample of the most inferior oil, then but thirty-six barrels of that description, containing less than fifteen hundred gallons, could have been selected from the whole quantity; and hence the plaintiffs were without adequate means of redress, unless by action, for failing to deliver the quantity of oil sold conforming to the sample."[3]

The case of Ferguson *v.* The Bank[4] may be sustained on this ground, although it was not taken by the court, because the

[1] Hutchinson *v.* Hunter, 7 Barr, 140; Woods *v.* McGee, 7 Ohio, 467.

[2] 14 Bush, 555.

[3] Foot *v.* Marsh, 31 N. Y. 293.

[4] 14 Bush, 555; *ante.*

hams were of unequal size and value; but the remark does not apply to Golder *v.* Ogden,[1] where all the rolls of paper were alike.

It is obvious, in any aspect of the question, that a sale of an undivided share cannot confer a several right, without such an appropriation as will in contemplation of law be equivalent to separation, and entitle the purchaser to take his portion without the concurrence of the vendor, or any further act on his part; and hence when the goods are outstanding in the hands of a third person, the contract will be executory until he receives a delivery order or other notification of a like kind from the vendor; because he may otherwise ignore the purchaser, and look solely to the person to whom he was accountable before the sale.[2]

In Keeler *v.* Goodwin, part of a quantity of grain in the hands of a warehouseman was sold without being separated from the mass, and it was held that the title would not pass without such notice from the vendor as to render it incumbent on the bailee to hold the goods for the purchaser or deliver them to him; although the court declined to say whether the bailee's assent was requisite to complete the transfer.

It is essential in considering the authorities to remember that when the legal requisites are satisfied, namely, that the goods must be ascertained and the price fixed or ascertainable, the question is, What did the parties intend? — which should be submitted as one of fact to the jury, unless there is an entire want of evidence, or the contract is so far reduced to writing as to bring the case within the rule that the interpretation of written evidence belongs to the court.[3] The title cannot pass until the goods are designated or specified; but it does not follow that it will pass when this condition is fulfilled, because either party may exact more, and the vendor make payment a condition precedent, or the vendee stipulate that the property shall not be at his risk before delivery. So, while payment does not necessarily complete the sale, it may afford ground for an inference that the purchaser would not have

[1] 3 Harris, 528. [2] Keeler *v.* Goodwin, 111 Mass. 490.

[3] See Fuller *v.* Bean, 34 N. H. 290, 305; Kelsea *v.* Haines, 41 id. 246.

parted with the money on the strength of the vendor's word, without receiving a present equivalent.[1] A like inference may be drawn when the goods are sold or transferred as security or in payment of a loan or debt, and the end which the parties have in view requires that the right of property should vest in the purchaser.[2] The argument has not so much weight conversely, because an unpaid vendor has a lien, and consequently runs no risk so long as the goods remain in his possession. Still, the fact that the sale was for cash, and the price was not so far ascertained as to admit of payment, must always have some weight in determining whether the contract was executory or passed the title.[3]

Who is to bear the loss if the goods are destroyed before delivery, has been treated in some instances as the criterion whether the title is in the vendor or the purchaser, but it merely affords ground for an inference, which may be more or less strong, according to circumstances.

In general *res perit domino*, and hence the person who will suffer if a thing be destroyed may be presumed to be the owner; but the rule may obviously be superseded by an agreement that the title shall be in one party and the other take the risk;[4] and when the goods were left with the vendor with a stipulation that they should be at his risk for two months, it was held to be a reasonable inference that any loss that might occur after that period was to be borne by the purchaser, whether the right of property did or did not pass to him.[5]

A contract for the sale of goods which are not specified or selected obviously requires a further agreement for its completion, which, like that originally made, must proceed from consent as distinguished from a manifestation of the individual will. For as the question what goods answer the description

[1] See Hurff *v.* Hires, 39 N. J. 4; 40 id. 581.

[2] Young *v.* Matthews, L. R. 2 C. P. 127; Wooster *v.* Sherwood, 25 N. Y. 278.

[3] Godts *v.* Rose, 17 C. B. 229; Swanwick *v.* Sothern, 9 A. & E. 895; McDonald *v.* Hewett, 15 Johns. 349.

[4] Castle *v.* Playford, L. R. 7 Ex. 98.

[5] Martineau *v.* Kitching, L. R. 7 Q. B. 436.

is one in which both parties are interested, so each has a right to be heard, and neither can impose his choice arbitrarily on the other. The vendor and purchaser must therefore concur in the selection, or if made by one it must be authorized or ratified by the other. As it was said by Holroyd, J., in Rhode *v.* Thwaites,[1] the selection of the goods by one party, and the adoption of that act by the other, converts that which before was a mere agreement to sell into an actual sale, and the property thereby passes; or, as the rule was stated in Warren *v.* Buckminster,[2] the buyer and seller may unite in making the selection, or it may be made by the seller and agreed to by the buyer; the difference being that in the former case the buyer acts directly, while in the other his action is indirect.[3]

It follows that a tender or appropriation by the vendor will not pass the title, unless it is adopted or authorized by the purchaser, even when the goods are in every respect such as he agreed to pay for, and cannot be declined without a liability in damages.[4]

In Campbell *v.* The Mersey Docks,[5] the purchase was of two hundred and fifty bales of cotton out of a cargo of five hundred bales. The cotton was subsequently landed and warehoused, two hundred and fifty bales being entered in the purchaser's name, and the certificate sent to him, and the court held that he could not maintain trover without showing that he had assented to the appropriation. The case of Jenner *v.* Smith,[6] is to the same effect. The authority or assent need not however be express, but may be implied from the terms of the contract, the purchaser's acts and declarations, or the usual course of trade.[7] It is not requisite that the pur-

1 6 B. & C. 388.

2 24 N. H. 336, 343.

3 See Gilman *v.* Hill, 36 N. H. 311; Bailey *v.* Smith, 43 id. 141; Ockington *v.* Ritchie, 41 id. 275.

4 Jenner *v.* Smith, L. R. 4 C. P. 270; Kelsea *v.* Haines, 41 N. H. 246; Wait *v.* Baker, 2 Ex. 1; Messer *v.* Woodman, 22 id. 172; Ockington *v.* Ritchie, 41 N. H. 275.

5 14 C. B. N. S. 412.

6 L. R. 4 C. P. 270.

7 See Aldridge *v.* Johnson, 7 E. & B. 885; Atkinson *v.* Bell, 8 B. & C. 277.

chaser should assent subsequently or concur at the time, if it appears by any sufficient means of proof that the vendor was to act for both.[1] As Willis, J., observed in Campbell *v.* The Mersey Docks,[2] "The assent of the vendee may be given prior to the appropriation by the vendor. It may be either express or implied, and it may be given by an agent of the party,—for instance, by the warehouseman or wharfinger." In Aldridge *v.* Johnson, the contract was for the purchase of one hundred quarters of barley, parcel of a larger quantity which lay in the vendor's granary, and which the vendee had inspected and approved; and it was also stipulated that the vendee should furnish the sacks, and that they should be filled by the vendor and forwarded by rail. The sacks were accordingly sent, and one hundred and fifty of them filled, but the vendor having failed refused to fill the rest or allow the whole or any part of the barley to be delivered under the contract.

The court held that the intention that the vendor should measure out the barley for the buyer, and forward it to him as his, was entirely clear both from the terms of the contract and the act of the purchaser in furnishing the sacks, and that when the vendor acted on the authority thus conferred, the appropriation was complete. This only applied to so much of the barley as had been separated from the heap and put in the sacks, and the right of property in the residue remained in the vendor and passed to his assignees in bankruptcy.

In determining whether the right of appropriation is in the vendor or the purchaser, we must consider which is to do the first act that cannot be effectually performed until the choice is made, because it will then be a natural if not inevitable inference that the privilege of selection rests with him.[3] "When from the terms of an executory agreement to sell unspecified goods, the vendor is to dispatch the goods or to do anything that cannot be done till the goods are appropriated,

[1] Brown *v.* Hare, 3 H. & N. 484; 4 id. 822; Merchants' Bank *v.* Bangs, 102 Mass. 291.

[2] 14 C. B. N. S. 412.

[3] See Blackburn on Sales, 128; Aldridge *v.* Johnson, 7 E. & B. 885, 897, 901; Heyward's Case, 2 Rep. 35.

he has the right to choose which the goods shall be, and the property is transferred the moment the dispatch or other act has commenced, for then by virtue of the power conferred by the agreement the appropriation is made final."[1]

Under these circumstances the purchaser need not be present or agree at the time, because his assent has been given beforehand and in a way which is insusceptible of revocation. Hence when it appears from the wording of the contract, the acts or declarations of the parties, or the settled course of trade, that the vendor is to pack or to set apart the goods, or take some other step which would be futile or ineffectual if they were not to become the purchaser's, the title will pass as soon as the parcels are made up or the goods segregated, although they have not been delivered and are still in the vendor's possession;[2] and the same result will follow for a still stronger reason, when the understanding or agreement is that the vendor is to forward the goods, and he puts them on a car or vessel or delivers them to a common carrier for transportation to the purchaser's residence or place of business.[3]

The cases of Sneathen *v.* Grubbs,[4] and Wenger *v.* Barnhart,[5] might appear to be at variance with this doctrine. In that first cited, the vendors agreed in writing "to load for Sneathen & Nelson and deliver at their landing, two barges of coal from the vendor's mine, near Greenfield, price 4¼ cents per bushel, terms cash when delivered in Pittsburg." The barges were furnished by the purchaser and taken by the vendors to their mines and loaded, but were unable to leave the wharf in consequence of the lowness of the water, and while lying there were taken under a writ of replevin issued by the purchasers.

1 Blackburn on Sales, 128.

2 Rhode *v.* Thwaites, 6 B. & C. 388.

3 Fragano *v.* Long, 4 B. & C. 219; Dutton *v.* Solomonson, 3 B. & P. 582; Morberger *v.* Hackenberg, 13 S. & R. 26; Schmertz *v.* Dwyer, 3 P. F. S. 335; Johnson *v.* Stoddard, 100 Mass. 306; Krulder *v.* Ellison, 47 N. Y. 36; Rodgers *v.* Phillips, 40 id. 519.

4 7 Norris, 147.

5 5 P. F. S. 300. See Goodall *v.* Skelton, 2 H. Bl. 316; Dixon *v.* Yates, 5 B. & Ad. 313; Boulter *v.* Arnott, 1 C. & M. 333.

The court held that the title did not pass and the suit must fail. The case of Wenger *v.* Barnhart is nearly to the same effect, save that the goods had been put into a railway car belonging to the company though standing on the vendor's siding, and entered by his order in the company's manifest book as consigned to the purchaser, when the vendor suddenly changed his mind on learning that the purchaser had failed, and directed that they should be shipped on his own account, and the decision was that the delivery was not complete and the purchaser could not maintain replevin. The real point in both instances seems to have been, not that the contract was unexecuted or that there was not such an appropriation as would pass the title, but that the vendor had not finally parted with the possession, and might consequently insist on his lien for the purchase-money which had not been paid or tendered, or stop the goods as being still on the way. It is not requisite, according to the rule laid down in Blackburn on Sales, that the dispatch or other act which constitutes the appropriation should have been completed, but merely that it should have been commenced, because the vendor's choice or election is thereby unequivocally declared, and cannot be subsequently varied to suit his interests or the course of events;[1] or as the rule has been laid down by the Supreme Court of Massachusetts, when from the nature of the agreement the vendor is to make the appropriation, then as soon as the act is done, and the property identified and set apart, with the intention unconditionally to apply it to the fulfilment of the contract, the title vests and the sale is complete.[2]

In Aldridge *v.* Johnson,[3] the sale was of one hundred quarters of barley out of a much larger quantity, and the vendor filled a number of sacks which were sent for that purpose by the purchaser, but which did not hold much more than fifty quarters, and it was held that the right of property passed sackful by sackful as to so much of the barley as was put in the sacks, although it remained in the vendor's granary, and he

[1] Benjamin on Sales, § 360; Blackburn on Sales, 128.

[2] Merchants' Bank *v.* Bangs, 102 Mass. 291.

[3] 7 E. & B. 885.

subsequently returned it to the heap from which it had been taken. The vendor became a bankrupt; and the court decided that trover might be maintained against his assignees for their refusal to surrender the barley which had been appropriated to the purchaser, because the vendor's wrongful act in blending it with his own property could not defeat the title, which had already vested.

The rule laid down in these instances is entirely consistent with the doctrine also advanced in Blackburn on Sales, that an intention to appropriate specific goods, or preparations however costly for that end, will not pass the title even when they leave no doubt that such was the vendor's purpose.

It is established in Pennsylvania and generally throughout the Union, in accordance with the above principles, that the proper time for making the charge in a shop-book or book of original entries, is when the goods are measured out or set apart in pursuance of the vendee's order, or finished and ready for delivery to him, because the title passes at that moment although they are not sent or called for until some time afterwards and the vendor's lien subsists.[1]

The vendor's purpose and whether he means to appropriate the goods to the purchaser, are questions of fact for the consideration of the jury, even when he is expressly or impliedly authorized to select for the buyer and might vest the title at once in him, because he may still if he thinks fit keep the right of property in himself and make the shipment for his own account; and such an inference will in the absence of contravening proof, be drawn when the bill of lading is taken in his name, or transferred to a third person, with a bill of exchange drawn on the purchaser for the price and to secure its payment.[2]

[1] See Wollenweber *v.* Ketterlinus, 5 Harris, 389, 398; Merchants' Bank *v.* Bangs, 102 Mass. 291.

[2] See Holmes *v.* The Bank, 6 Norris, 525; Holmes *v.* Bailey, 11 id. 57; Wenger *v.* Barnhart, 5 P. F. S. 300; First National Bank *v.* Crocker, 111 Mass. 163; Brown *v.* Hare, 3 H. & N. 484, 494; 4 id. 822, 830; Brandt *v.* Bowlby, 2 B. & Ad. 932; Wait *v.* Baker, 2 Ex. 1.

Such a shipment may nevertheless operate as an appropriation that will vest the right of property in the buyer, on his fulfilling the implied condition, by accepting the accompanying bill of exchange or paying the price, without any further act done on either side.[1] "Under a contract for sale of chattels not specific," said Cotton, L. J., "the property does not pass to the purchaser unless there is afterwards an appropriation of the specific chattels to pass under the contract, that is, unless both parties agree as to the specific chattels in which the property is to pass, and nothing remains to be done in order to pass it. In the case of such a contract the delivery by the vendor to a common carrier, or (unless the effect of the shipment is restricted by the terms of the bill of lading) shipment on board a ship of or chartered for the purchaser, is an appropriation sufficient to pass the property. If however, the vendor when shipping the articles which he intends to deliver under the contract, takes the bill of lading to his own order, and does so not as agent or on behalf of the purchaser but on his own behalf, it is held that he thereby reserves to himself a power of disposing of the property, and that consequently there is no final appropriation, and the property does not on shipment pass to the purchasers. When the vendor on shipment takes the bill of lading to his own order, he has the power of absolutely disposing of the cargo, and may prevent the purchaser from ever asserting any right of property therein; and accordingly in Wait *v.* Baker,[2] Ellershaw *v.* Magniac,[3] and Gabarron *v.* Kreeft[4] (in all of which cases the vendors had dealt with the bills of lading for their own benefit), the decisions were that the purchaser had no property in the goods, though he had offered to accept bills for or had paid the price. So if the vendor deals with or claims to retain the bill of lading in order to secure the contract price, as when he sends forward the bill of lading with a bill of exchange attached, with directions that the bill of lading is not to be delivered to the purchaser till acceptance or payment of the bill of exchange, the appropriation is not absolute, but

[1] Mirabita *v.* The Bank, L. R. 3 Ex. 164, 172.

[2] 2 Ex. 1. [3] 6 Ex. 570. [4] L. R. 10 Ex. 274.

until acceptance of the draft or payment, or tender of the price, is conditional only; and until such acceptance or payment or tender, the property in the goods does not pass to the purchaser; and so it was decided in Turner *v.* Trustees of Liverpool Docks,[1] Shepherd *v.* Harrison,[2] and Ogg *v.* Shuter.[3] But if the bill of lading has been dealt with only to secure the contract price, there is neither principle nor authority for holding that in such a case the goods shipped for the purpose of completing the contract do not, on payment or tender by the purchaser of the contract price, vest in him. When this occurs there is a performance of the condition subject to which the appropriation was made, and everything which according to the intention of the parties is necessary to transfer the property, is done; and, in my opinion, under such circumstances, the property does, on payment or tender of the price, pass to the purchaser."

The just inference from the authorities seems to be that so long as the seller holds or retains the control of the bill of lading, he virtually holds the goods, and may impose any condition that would be valid if they were actually in his hands.[4]

It is said in Addison on the Contract of Sale, that "where the commodity is selected in bulk by the purchaser, the ownership will pass as soon as the quantity sold has been separated from the mass, and tendered to the purchaser or placed at his disposal." This language seemingly implies that an agreement to buy part of a larger quantity, which is seen and approved at the time, authorizes the vendor to make a selection from the mass which will bind the purchaser and vest the right of property in him. What the authorities establish is, that under these circumstances slight evidence may suffice to show that the vendor is authorized to act for and represent the purchaser. When a mass alike in kind and quality has been approved by the purchaser and the price is paid, or the sale is made on credit, and the next step in the usual course of business is the packing, forwarding, or delivery of the goods,

1 6 Ex. 543.
2 L. R. 4 Q. B. 197, 493; 5 H. L. 116.
3 L. R. 10 C. P. 159.
4 Benjamin on Sales, § 399.

it may reasonably be inferred that the vendor is to make the selection as a necessary means for the attainment of the end in view.

It results from the above principles that when the agreement is for the delivery as well as sale of things of a certain kind, and they are tendered at the time and place prescribed, the right of property will pass forthwith and the purchase-money may be recovered in an action for goods sold and delivered, although they were rejected by the purchaser and are still in the vendor's hands.[1] For as delivery cannot be made until the goods are ascertained, he who is to deliver is presumably empowered to select.

In determining whether the contract is executory or for specific goods, regard should be had to every fact which will enable the court to identify the subject-matter, including its situation, kind, and ownership, and oral evidence may be given, although the contract is in writing and within the statute of frauds.[2]

In Macdonald *v.* Longbottom,[3] a written offer of "sixteen shillings per stone for your wool, delivered in Liverpool," was made and accepted through the mail, and testimony that the vendor had told the purchaser sometime previously, that he had a quantity of wool and would like to sell, was held admissible as affording ground for an inference that it was the thing sold. The Chief Justice and Wightman, J., said "that for the purpose of showing what is the subject-matter of a contract, oral evidence may be given of any fact or circumstance within the knowledge of the parties, before and at the time when the contract was made, and there could not be the slightest objection to the admission of the conversation as a means of identifying the wool. But the line was accurately drawn, by holding that a statement in the course of the same conversation as to the weight of the wool, not having been embodied in the writing, did not enter into or form part of

[1] See Hayden *v.* Demets, 53 N. Y. 426; Nichols *v.* Morse, 100 Mass. 523; McLean *v.* Richardson, 127 id. 339.

[2] Pollen *v.* Le Roy, 30 N. Y. 549, 550.

[3] 1 E. & E. 977.

the contract and must be disregarded as a mere expression of opinion.

In Pollen *v.* Le Roy, the bought-and-sold note was as follows: "Sold T. O. Le Roy & Co., for account of Pollen & Colgate, one hundred and fifty tons soft English lead, of Walker, Parker and Walker brand, to arrive per Providence from Newcastle, at 6⅝c. per pound, cash." The lead proved on arrival to be branded "Walker & Parker," and the buyers refused to receive it on that ground, as not being what they had purchased. The weight of the testimony was that there was no such firm as Walker, Parker & Walker, and no lead in the market bearing such a mark. The court held that evidence might be received to show that the lead in controversy was manufactured by the firm of Walker, Parker, Walker & Co., and branded by them "Walker & Parker," and that on such proof the question of identity was for the jury, and had been properly submitted to them. Emott, J., said: "The defendants objected to the admission of evidence offered by the plaintiffs to show the reason why the same lead manufactured by the firm of Walker, Parker, Walker & Co., was sometimes marked with the full name of the firm and sometimes "Walker, Parker & Co.," and that there was no difference in lead with these two different marks. If there had been shown to have been any lead in market of the precise description, or with the brand described in the contract between these parties, this evidence would probably have been immaterial. But the jury have found that there was no such mark or brand of the article known, and at the stage of the case when this evidence was received there was no evidence tending to show the existence of any such brand of lead. There was no firm with these names in the trade besides the firm of Walker, Parker, Walker & Co., in England, from whose members and employees this evidence was obtained. And under these circumstances, the facts to which I have referred were properly received to explain the meaning of the parties, and upon the main issue to which I shall presently refer. Similar considerations will dispose of the objection to the evidence to show how the lead made by this house was ordinarily spoken of in trade and in conversation. This was competent in explanation of the ambiguity which had arisen in respect to the contract, assuming the bought-and-sold note to describe an article which did not exist.

"The defendants' counsel asked one of the defendants, who was a witness, and who negotiated the purchase from the broker, 'What conversation passed on the subject of this sale prior to the actual delivery to these respective parties of the sale note?' This was objected to and excluded. The sale was concluded by a bought-and-sold note in writing, containing all the elements of a contract, the names of the parties, price, description of the article, time of delivery and time of payment. It certainly was not competent to vary this by evidence of what passed in the previous negotiations. Evidence of fraud, or of a warranty, was not admissible under the pleadings in this case. The only issue is the contract, and its performance as to the specific article sold and tendered. It may be that evidence of conversation between the parties as to the article intended might be competent in the state of facts which was developed in that particular, although it is not necessary to concede as much as this. But the difficulty with the question which was excluded in this instance, is that it was too broad. The witness was not asked if anything was said in reference to the brand or description of lead, or what was said upon that subject; but he was asked what conversation passed on the subject of the sale before it was concluded. This was too general an inquiry, and does not present the point discussed on the present argument."

In Winslow *v.* Leonard,[1] Long & Co. gave the plaintiffs the following written memorandum: —

> "We have this day sold to Winslow, Lanier, & Co., four hundred tons of pig metal, now at our landing at Washington Furnace, or that will soon be delivered there, and we hereby direct our clerk to give them possession thereof."

It did not appear that the vendors had any iron at the landing when the above paper was executed, and the controversy

[1] 12 Harris, 14.

was as to eighty-two tons of iron which had been shipped from that point some time previously in barges belonging to one John Brennan. The plaintiffs contended that this was part of the iron which they had purchased, while the contention of the defendants was that the iron in question had been specifically transferred to Brennan during the voyage, by a contract which, though subsequent to that under which the plaintiffs claimed, was yet specific and transferred the right of property, and that they were in possession as his bailees. The court below instructed the jury that the plaintiffs were entitled to the verdict as having the prior title, and a writ of error was taken to the Supreme Court, which reversed the judgment on the following grounds: "The words in the contract 'we have this day sold' would seem to indicate a perfect sale, and not merely a contract to sell, and therefore a vested title to specific metal. But the metal is described as 'now at our landing, or that will soon be delivered there.' This raises a doubt whether any specific metal was sold, and seems to indicate only a contract to sell. It does not as yet appear that there was any iron at the landing, or where it was to come from. For aught that appears any four hundred tons will answer the description. It may be that the vendors had not any or so much on hand. If they had any, and it had been stolen or destroyed an hour after the contract, we have as yet no evidence that would throw the loss on the vendees. We discover no definition of the subject-matter, except as pig metal. The true reading of the contract would therefore seem to be, 'We have bargained with Winslow, Lanier & Co. to deliver to them at our landing four hundred tons of pig metal.' Still we do not say that there can be no evidence that there was a defined lot of metal in the intention of the parties. We see none on this record. And especially we do not see how this metal, which was on its way to Pittsburg, can, without other evidence, be embraced by the contract."

There can be little doubt that the desire to do justice between man and man by inclining the balance to an unpaid vendor, or in favor of a purchaser who has parted with his money and is in danger of losing the goods, has led to the refinements which perplex this branch of jurisprudence, and render the course of decision obscure or contradictory. Such fluctuation has a tendency to defeat the end for which law is so instituted, — to serve as a sure guide in the affairs of life, and lessen the need for advocates and judges.

The measure of damages for the breach of an executory contract is the difference between the market value of the goods and the price,[1] and the rule applies whether the suit is brought by the vendor or the purchaser. For as the goods remain the vendor's property, and may be sold at the current rate if he thinks proper, he need not sustain a greater loss than the amount by which what he was to receive exceeds that which he agreed to give; and this is also true of the purchaser, who having the money in his hands may go into the market and procure what he wants, unless no such goods can be found when he may be entitled to a larger sum on the allegation and proof of special damage.[2]

On the other hand when the contract is so far executed as to pass the title, and there has been no default or *laches* on the part of the seller, he may sue for and recover the entire purchase-money, although the goods are still in his hands and have not been delivered.[3] "When," said Strong, J., in the case last cited, "the subject of the sale is a specific article, and the contract has been so far completed as to vest the right of property in the vendee, the possession being retained only because the price is not paid, there seems to be no good reason why the vendor should not be permitted to recover the agreed value. He has fully complied with all that he was under an obligation to do. He has parted with his property and given the full equivalent for the stipulated price. His

[1] McCombs *v.* McKennan, 2 W. &. S. 216; Griffiths *v.* Perry, 1 E. & E. 680; Haines *v.* Tucker, 50 N. H. 307.

[2] Barron *v.* Arnand, 8 Q. B. 604; Valpy *v.* Oakeley, 16 id. 941; Clement *v.* Messerole, 107 Mass. 362.

[3] Thompson *v.* Alger, 12 Met. 428; Nichols *v.* Morse, 100 Mass. 523; Morse *v.* Sherman, 106 id. 430; Pearson *v.* Mason, 120 id. 53; Ballentine *v.* Robinson, 10 Wr. 177.

title having passed to the vendee, his right to the price would appear to be consummated."

Such is also the rule where one fails or refuses to accept and pay for goods which have been made to his order, or under a contract with him.[1]

It is not essential to such a suit and the recovery of the entire purchase-money, that the goods should be actually tendered or accepted. The vendor is not bound to send or carry the goods, in the absence of a stipulation to that effect, and will fulfil his whole duty in the premises by having them ready for the purchaser and notifying him of the fact.[2] And as the latter may under these circumstances take possession at any moment, he has all that he is entitled to require, and the delivery being in contemplation of law complete, the vendor may maintain an action for goods sold and delivered.

Although the title passes at common law under a sale of a specific chattel without payment or delivery, the vendor may still retain possession as a security for the price unless he has impliedly waived the right by making the sale on credit. This privilege, which is known as the vendor's lien, is simply a right to keep possession so long as the purchaser is in default, and will be waived by the delivery of the goods to the purchaser, or to a carrier for transportation to him, or in short to any one who receives them as his bailee or agent and who owes no duty or obligation to the vendor. It does not vary the case that the delivery is made on the faith of a promise to have the money ready on the next, or on the afternoon of the same day;[3] and the same result will ensue if the purchaser takes the goods with the vendor's assent, or even without it, unless the vendor uses due diligence to regain possession by following the goods, or issuing a writ of replevin,

[1] Ballentine *v.* Robinson, 10 Wr. 177; Shawhan *v.* Van Nest, 25 Ohio St. 490; Gordon *v.* Norris, 49 N. H. 376; Bement *v.* Smith, 15 Wend. 493.

[2] Pollen *v.* Le Roy, 30 N. Y. 549; Benjamin on Sales, § 679.

[3] See Leedom *v.* Philips, 1 Yeates, 527; Harris *v.* Smith, 3 S. & R. 20; Bowen *v.* Burk, 1 Harris, 146; Backentoss *v.* Speicher, 7 Casey, 324; Mackaness *v.* Long, 4 Norris, 158.

because the delay will otherwise give rise to a presumption of acquiescence.[1] "If," said Rogers, J., in Bowen *v.* Burk, "one sells goods for cash and the vendee takes them away without payment, the vendor should immediately reclaim them by pursuing the party and retaking them; and this may be done when necessary even by force. But when he lies by and makes no complaint in a reasonable time, he tacitly consents to the absolute transfer of the title and the sale is consequently complete."

It is not less well settled that when the delivery is the unauthorized act of a clerk or servant,[2] or the purchaser obtains possession by deceit or artifice, or a wilful falsification, the vendor may follow and reclaim the goods wherever they can be found unless they have passed to a *bona fide* purchaser.[3] In Harris *v.* Smith the defendant offered to give his note with one Yerkes as an indorser, to which the plaintiff assented, and sent the goods on the faith of the defendant's promise that he should have the note forthwith. The note did not come, and it appearing that Yerkes had not agreed to indorse for the defendant, the court held that there was such evidence of fraud as would enable the plaintiff to maintain replevin. "Where," said Gibson, C. J., "performance and delivery are understood by the parties to be simultaneous, possession obtained by artifice or deceit will not avail; the fraud vitiates the whole transaction." The sale cannot, however, be set aside or the goods reclaimed, because the securities given for the price and in reliance on which the delivery was made, prove to be worthless, nor although the purchaser is insolvent and conceals the fact from the vendor. To justify such a course there must be conscious falsehood as distinguished from an error resulting from mistake or ignorance.[4]

[1] See Leedom *v.* Philips, 1 Yeates, 527; Bowen *v.* Burk, 1 Harris, 146.

[2] Lelar *v.* Brown, 3 Harris, 215.

[3] See Harris *v.* Smith, 3 S. & R. 20.

[4] Smith *v.* Smith, 9 Harris, 367; Harner *v.* Fisher, 8 P. F. S. 453, 457; Backentoss *v.* Speicher, 7 Casey, 324.

It has been well said that the promise to deliver involved in an agreement of sale, and the promise to pay the purchase-money, are mutually dependent, and neither party is bound to perform without a contemporaneous performance by the other. "Payment of the price is the condition on which alone the purchaser can require the seller to complete the contract by the delivery of the goods."[1] But it is not less true that while both acts are concurrent, one will frequently precede the other. If the vendor is not bound to deliver without payment, the purchaser ought not to be required to part with his money before receiving the goods. The case is therefore one requiring mutual good faith and confidence, and where a pretence of a readiness and willingness which does not exist may operate as a fraud entitling the injured party to treat the entire transaction as null and void. Payment and delivery are so far concurrent that the money should be forthcoming as soon as the purchaser receives the goods, but he is not obliged to pay before delivery, nor until it is complete, although the goods come by parcels and cannot all be brought at once.[2] It follows that goods which have been deposited on the vendee's premises in expectation of an immediate payment may be reclaimed if it is not made, and it will make no difference that part were left days or hours, if the delivery is continuous and there has been no unnecessary delay.[3]

Accordingly, where corn which had been sold for cash was hauled successively to the vendor's mill, and payment demanded as soon as the last load arrived, the court held that the lien had not been waived, and that the corn might be replevied if the price was not paid, although the loads had been emptied on other corn belonging to the vendee, and the writ was executed by taking the quantity to which the vendor was entitled indiscriminately from the heap.[4]

A condition that the title shall not pass until the price is

[1] See Haskins *v.* Warren, 115 Mass. 514.

[2] Mount *v.* Lyon, 49 N. Y. 552; Paul *v.* Reed, 52 N. H. 136; Owens *v.* Weedman, 82 Ill. 409.

[3] Henderson *v.* Lauck, 9 Harris, 359; Paul *v.* Reed, 52 N. H. 136.

[4] *Ante.*

paid may nevertheless be valid as between the parties notwithstanding the delivery of the goods to the purchaser,[1] and perhaps against subsequent purchasers with notice,[2] but not against creditors,[3] notice being inoperative where creditors are in question unless it is anterior to the debt.[4] But a sale or bailment, with a mere right or option on the part of the bailee to buy if he thinks proper, will not pass the title or bring the goods within the reach of his creditors.[5]

It may be observed in this connection that the term "delivery" is used in various senses, which must be distinguished to prevent misapprehension, or rather that there may be three steps in the process by which the goods pass from the vendor to the purchaser, each known as "delivery" in legal or common parlance, but differing in fact and in their bearing on the relations of the parties. A delivery is said to occur when the goods are set apart for the purchaser, and he has notice or knowledge of the fact, because the vendor thereupon becomes a bailee for the purchaser, who is constructively possessed and may remove them at pleasure, although the vendor is also a possessor and does not lose his lien.[6]

The goods are also said to be delivered when they are handed over to a common carrier for transportation to the purchaser, and the vendor thereby waives his lien, although he may still stop them *in transitu* on learning the insolvency of the purchaser, or that the notes given for the price have been dishonored.[7]

Finally, the goods may be tendered to and received by the purchaser, or by some one whose duty it is to hold them sub-

[1] Henry *v.* Patterson, 7 P. F. S. 346; Coggill *v.* The Railroad, 3 Gray, 545; Hotchkiss *v.* Hunt, 48 Me. 213, 218.

[2] See Rowe *v.* Sharp, 1 P. F. S. 26.

[3] Martin *v.* Mathiot, 14 S. & R. 214; Rose *v.* Story, 1 Barr, 190; Jenkins *v.* Eichelberger, 4 Watts, 121; Haak *v.* Linderman, 14 P. F. S. 499.

[4] 2 Leading Cases in Equity, 4 Am. ed. 96.

[5] Chamberlain *v.* Smith, 8 Wr. 431; Myers *v.* Harvey, 2 P. & W. 478; Rowe *v.* Sharp, 1 P. F. S. 26; Enlon *v.* Klein, 29 id. 488; Henry *v.* Patterson, 7 id. 346.

[6] Townley *v.* Crump, 4 A. & E. 58.

[7] Keeler *v.* Goodwin, 111 Mass. 191; *ante.*

ject to his orders, and as such delivery is actual it will preclude the right of reclamation for insolvency, or on any ground short of mistake or fraud.[1]

On the breach of an executory contract by the refusal of the vendee to accept the goods, the vendor may by virtue of his authority as owner proceed to a resale, which, if made publicly with notice to the vendee, or in any other appropriate way, will be *prima facie* evidence of the value of the goods and consequently of the damages. It is nevertheless not conclusive, and the vendee may show that the market rate is higher, or that with due care the goods would have brought more.[2] In Girard *v.* Taggart the jury were instructed that the damages were ordinarily liquidated by a resale, but that they were not bound by that mode of estimation if they could find another more conformable to the truth, and a like view was taken in Andrews *v.* Hoover and McCombs *v.* McKennan.

The vendor's right is not so clear in principle where the contract is executed, and vests the title in the purchaser; for as the goods are his they cannot be resold by the vendor save on the ground of an implied authority analogous to that of a pledgee to dispose of the goods which he holds in pawn. The practice seems to have been dictated by necessity in the case of perishable goods, and became general as avoiding the risk and charges incident to delay, and was declared by Best, C. J., in Maclean *v.* Dunn,[3] to be alike consistent with convenience and law and one which the court was anxious to confirm. The inclination of the English courts is nevertheless, agreeably to Benjamin on Sales,[4] against the vendor's right to dispose of that which has ceased to be his own, although it has not been paid for by the purchaser; but the cases cited by the learned author do not sustain his position, and turned on the well-settled principle that the damages for the breach of an

[1] See Benjamin on Sales, § 675; Jones *v.* Marsh, 22 Vt. 144; Phelps *v.* Hubbard, 51 id. 489.

[2] Girard *v.* Taggart, 5 S. & R. 19; Andrews *v.* Hoover, 8 Watts, 239; McCombs *v.* McKennan, 2 W. & S. 216.

[3] 4 Bing. 722.

[4] § 787.

executory contract will be nominal unless the value exceeds the price.[1]

Whatever the English rule may be, it is established in the United States, that on the breach of an executed contract by a refusal to accept the goods, the vendor may proceed to a resale on the purchaser's account, and if the proceeds are not enough to pay the contract price maintain an action of indebitatus assumpsit for the difference.[2]

"The usage," said Kent, C. J., in Sands *v.* Taylor,[3] "in such cases is to sell the article after due notice to the other party to take it, and that in default of doing so the article will be sold. This usage is convenient and reasonable, and for the best interest of both parties."

In exercising this privilege the vendor acts for the purchaser as well as himself, and must make the sale in the way dictated by usage and best suited to promote their common interest, which may either be publicly at auction or through a broker, according to the circumstances and the course of business.[4]

It has been said that all the law requires in such cases is the good faith and exact diligence which are incumbent on every one who is acting for another in a matter which concerns both.[5] Taken generally, this is no doubt true, but the better opinion would seem to be that as the vendor may choose between selling the goods and keeping them as the purchaser's, he should announce his determination in time to enable the latter to protect himself; and although it was also said in Pollen *v.* Le Roy that the vendee need not be informed of the time and place of sale, such information should obviously be given whenever it is at all practicable, in

[1] See Valpy *v.* Oakeley, 16 Q. B. 941; Griffiths *v.* Perry, 1 E. & E. 680.

[2] Bagley *v.* Findlay, 82 Ill. 524; Sands *v.* Taylor, 5 Johns. 395; Bement *v.* Smith, 15 Wend. 493, 497; Shawhan *v.* Van Nest, 25 Ohio St. 490, 499.

[3] 5 Johns. 395, 410.

[4] Bagley *v.* Findlay, 82 Ill. 524; Sands *v.* Taylor, 5 Johns. 395; Pollen *v.* Le Roy, 30 N. Y. 549; Smith *v.* Pettee, 70 id. 13.

[5] Pollen *v.* Le Roy, 30 N. Y. 549.

order to repel the allegation that the property was sacrificed in his absence.

In Sands *v.* Taylor,[1] the resale was by auction; but the vendor is not bound by an arbitrary and inflexible rule, and should on the contrary adopt the course that will, under the existing circumstances, enable him to dispose of the goods promptly to the greatest advantage.[2]

"Unless the sale is to be public and at auction no notice of the time and place can be given. But in many cases sales by auction are not the usual nor are they a favorable mode of disposing of merchandise. There is nothing in the present case to show that sales by auction are customary in the trade in metal, and there is every reason to infer that such a sale would have resulted much more injuriously to the defendants than the course pursued by the plaintiffs. The ordinary usage of the trade is to effect sales of pig lead through the negotiations of a broker. This usage the plaintiffs were bound to adopt to obtain the full and fair value of the articles."[3]

It has been declared in some instances that in disposing of the goods the vendor acts as the agent of the purchaser, and is held to the same degree of care, judgment, and fidelity that is requisite in an agent to whom goods are sent with instructions to sell them to the best advantage.[4] In the case last cited, Rapallo, J., said: "Immediately after the refusal of the defendants to accept the iron, the plaintiffs notified them of their election to sell it for the account of the defendants, and hold them liable for the difference between the purchase price and the price the iron should realize. The plaintiffs thus promptly took their position, and became agents of the defendants for the sale of the iron, and bound to the exercise of good faith and reasonable diligence to effect the sale at the best price. They would doubtless have been bound to obey

[1] 5 Johns. 395.

[2] Pollen *v.* Le Roy, 30 N. Y. 549; Smith *v.* Pettee, 70 id. 13.

[3] Pollen *v.* Le Roy, 30 N. Y. 549. See Buffington *v.* Quantin, 5 Harris, 310, and Chapman *v.* Morton, 11 M. & W. 534, as to the cognate right of the purchaser when the goods do not answer the terms of the agreement.

[4] Bagley *v.* Findlay, 82 Ill. 524; Smith *v.* Pettee, 70 N. Y. 13.

any instructions which the defendants might have given them as to the time and manner of sale, and which they could follow without sacrificing the lien they had on the iron for the contract price. In the absence of any such instructions they had the right to exercise their discretion within reasonable bounds."

This language is perhaps too broad, and can hardly be reconciled with the dicta in Smith *v.* Pettee. If the vendor acts in the capacity of an agent, one of his first duties must be to keep his principal duly informed of everything that concerns his interest; and he certainly should not omit to give such notice of the time and place of sale as will enable him to be present personally or through an agent. It is, however, obvious that the vendor who is acting for himself as well as the purchaser, stands in the position of a pledgee rather than an agent, and cannot be required to obey the purchaser's instructions unless they are calculated to promote the prompt and advantageous conversion of the property into money as a means of paying the debt.

Where the goods delivered under an existing contract do not answer the terms prescribed, the buyer is not bound to keep them indefinitely; and if the purchaser will not take them away, should seemingly be entitled to dispose of them at auction or at private sale; but the right was denied in Chapman *v.* Morton.[1]

It has been already stated that a resale of goods which have been tendered and rejected under an executory contract, is simply *prima facie* evidence and does not conclude the purchaser, because as the property is not his nor sold on his account, he cannot justly claim the proceeds, although, if they exceed the amount which he agreed to give, it may be inferred that the bargain was disadvantageous to the vendor, and that he was not injured by the default. When, on the other hand, the sale is executed and has passed the title, the purchaser can have no right to a larger sum than the goods have brought, and will be entitled to any surplus that may remain

[1] 11 M. & W. 534, and the case of Buffington *v.* Quantin, 17 Pa. 312, is to the same effect.

after crediting the vendor with the purchase-money. In the former case the resale is a mode of ascertaining the loss, and may show that the vendor is entitled to nominal damages only; in the latter, it may bring the vendor in debt to the purchaser. The distinction is obvious, but has not infrequently been overlooked or disregarded.

It was said in Hayden *v.* Demets,[1] "Upon a valid sale of specific chattels when nothing remains to be done by the vendor except delivery, whether conditioned upon payment or not, the right of property passes to the vendee, at whose risk it is retained by the vendor. The same consequence as to title results from a valid tender upon an executory contract. Upon the refusal of the vendee to accept and pay the price, the vendor may after proper notice, sell and recover the difference between the contract and selling price, or he may retain the property and recover the difference between the contract and actual price, or he may sue for and recover the contract price. If he elects the latter remedy, he holds the property as trustee for the vendee, and is bound to deliver it whenever demanded, upon receiving payment." A like view was taken in Bagley *v.* Findlay.[2]

Notwithstanding these dicta, we may believe that in each of the above supposed cases the remedy is the same, namely by an action of indebitatus assumpsit for the price, the only difference being that when the goods are resold, the vendee must be credited with the proceeds as so much money belonging to him in the hands of the vendor. Nor is there any sufficient ground for the suggestion that the vendor may keep the goods as his own, and sue for the difference between their value and the price. It is a general and well-settled rule, that the failure of one of the parties to an executed contract to perform his part does not set the other free, or defeat the title which has already passed; and hence a default in the payment of the price will not authorize the vendor to rescind the sale, or treat the property as his own, and merely entitles him to choose between storing the goods for the purchaser, and avoiding the

[1] 53 N. Y. 426.

[2] 82 Ill. 524; see Gordon *v.* Norris, 49 N. H. 376.

risk and expense incident to such a course by disposing of them on his account.[1]

A sale on credit is virtually an agreement that the purchaser shall be entitled to possession without payment, and consequently operates as a waiver of the vendor's lien. It nevertheless proceeds on the supposition that the purchaser will be able to pay when the time expires; and hence if anything occurs during the interval to show that this confidence was misplaced, the vendor may retain the goods if they are still in his possession, or stop them on the way to the purchaser, although he cannot retake them after they have been actually delivered to the purchaser, or to one acting for him and subject to his directions. The former right may be designated as that of retention; the latter is known as stoppage *in transitu*, but both are simply a revival or extension of the vendor's lien.

It is accordingly well settled that one who has sold on credit, and learns subsequently that the purchaser was or has become insolvent, or that the bills which he gave for the price have been dishonored, may hold the goods as a security for the price, and if it is not paid proceed to a resale just as in the case of an agreement to sell for cash which is withheld.[2]

In White *v.* Welsh, the defendants sold two hundred and ninety-five hogsheads of sugar then in their warehouse, to the plaintiffs, and took their notes at four months for the purchase-money to be in full when paid, the agreement being that the plaintiffs should be allowed to leave the sugars in the warehouse for one month free of charge with the benefit of the insurance which had been effected by the defendants. The plaintiffs failed before the notes matured, and it was held that the defendants might retain so much of the sugar as remained on hand, although they had delivered part to various persons under orders from the plaintiffs to that effect.

[1] See Blackburn on Sales, 325; Benjamin on Sales, § 782; Martindale *v.* Smith, 1 Q. B. 389.

[2] Bloxam *v.* Sanders, 4 B. & C. 941; Hanson *v.* Meyer, 6 East, 614; Griffiths *v.* Perry, 1 E. & E. 680; Valpy *v.* Oakeley, 16 Q. B. 941; Miles *v.* Gorton, 2 C. & M. 504; White *v.* Welsh, 2 Wr. 396; Wanamaker *v.* Yerkes, 20 P. F. S. 443; *Ex parte* Chalmers, L. R. 8 Ch. Ap. 289.

In White *v.* Welsh,[1] Chief Justice Lowrie said, in delivering the opinion of the court: "Judges do not ordinarily distinguish between the retainer of goods by a vendor, and their stoppage *in transitu* on account of the insolvency of the vendee; because these terms refer to the same right only at different stages of perfection and execution of the contract of sale. If a vendor has a right to stop *in transitu*, *a fortiori* he has a right of retainer before any transit has commenced. It is by the equity of the law that this right is allowed, in order to save an unpaid vendor as late as possible from an irrevocable completion of the contract on his part, when by the unexpected insolvency of the vendee a completion on his part has become improbable. The rule is that so long as the vendor has the actual possession of the goods, or they are in the custody of his agents, and while they are in transit from him to the vendee, he has a right to refuse or countermand the final delivery if the vendee be in failing circumstances."

It has been held in some instances that where the vendor agrees to accept the note or acceptance of a third person in payment, the sale is virtually an exchange, and the insolvency of the maker or acceptor will not justify the rescission of the contract, or a refusal to deliver the goods in compliance with its terms.[2] This conclusion would, however, appear to be logical rather than just; and the weight of authority would seem to be that although such a contract differs from an ordinary credit in substituting the liability of a third person for that of the purchaser, it is still subject to an implied condition that the person who is to make the payment shall not be discredited while the goods are in the vendor's possession or on their way to the purchaser; and hence if the maker or accepter proves to be insolvent during the interval, the vendor may exercise the right of retention or of stoppage *in transitu*.[3]

The path marked out at common law for the vendor of a

[1] 2 Wr. 396.

[2] See Bickall *v.* Waterman, 5 R. I. 43; Wheeler *v.* Schroeder, 4 id. 383; Lightbody *v.* The Bank, 11 Wend. 9.

[3] See 2 Am. Leading Cases, 5 ed. 299–304; Owenson *v.* Morse, 7 T. R. 64; Roget *v.* Merritt, 2 Caines, 117; Benedict *v.* Field, 16 N. Y. 595.

specific chattel was entirely plain,—to abstain from falsehood, and give no assurance that he was not prepared to make good. For the rest, he might express an opinion as to the goodness of his wares, or indulge in mere commendation without being answerable for its truth, unless he went so far as to be justly chargeable with an intention to mislead, and that effect was actually produced.[1] Within these limits he was secure, and it was for the purchaser to take care that the goods were such as he needed, and had no defects that would render them useless or unmerchantable.[2] The purchaser might require a warranty, or put definite questions and insist on exact replies that would, if wilfully false afford ground for setting aside the sale or an action of deceit; but if he omitted these precautions it was his own folly, and he could not look to the law for aid. The whole may be summed up in the maxim *caveat emptor*, which implies that it is for the buyer to inform himself, and not for the seller to inform the buyer, and is still a cornerstone of the contract of sale, as interpreted in England and the United States;[3] and the rule applies although the seller knows that the buyer is laboring under a false impression, if it be one that he has not strengthened or produced.[4] Hence in the absence of warranty and fraud and when the goods answer the terms of the contract, it was, as it still is speaking generally, immaterial that they are worthless to the purchaser, and would bring nothing if exposed for sale, because inadequacy of consideration is not when standing alone a defence.[5]

[1] Tewksbury *v.* Bennett, 31 Ia. 85; Miller *v.* Craig, 36 Ill. 81; Fauntleroy *v.* Wilcox, 8 id. 477; Tuck *v.* Downing, 76 id. 71; Torkelson *v.* Jorgenson, 28 Minn. 483.

[2] Chanter *v.* Hopkins, 4 M. & W. 399; 2 Bl. Com. 451; Lord *v.* Grow, 8 Wr. 88; Borrekins *v.* Bevan, 3 Rawle, 23; Vogel *v.* Knisely, 89 Ill. 598.

[3] Smith *v.* Hughes, L. R. 6 Q. B. 597; Eagan *v.* Call, 10 Casey, 236; Jackson *v.* Wetherill, 7 S. & R. 488; McFarland *v.* Newman, 9 Watts, 35; Whitaker *v.* Eastwick, 25 P. F. S. 229; Waring *v.* Mason, 18 Wend. 434; Hargons *v.* Stone, 1 Selden, 73, 81; Seixas *v.* Wood, 2 Caines, 48; Brewer *v.* Christian, 9 Ill. App. 57; Hight *v.* Bacon, 126 Mass. 10.

[4] Smith *v.* Hughes, L. R. 6 Q. B. 597.

[5] Eagan *v.* Call, 10 Casey, 237; Torkelson *v.* Jorgenson, 28 Minn. 283; Zimmerman *v.* Morrow, id. 367; Brewer *v.* Christian, 9 Ill. App. 57.

The rule and its reason were perspicuously stated in Eagan *v.* Call. "Want of consideration can only be, where the promisee parts with nothing in exchange for the promise. The consideration fails when the promisor does not get that which the promisee agreed to give, as a motive for the promise. But, in the absence of warranty, the soundness or unsoundness of the subject-matter of the sale has nothing to do with the consideration. There is no relation of confidence between the buyer and the seller. In the absence of an agreement by the seller, the purchaser takes at his own risk as to quality. The vendor of a chattel warrants the title, and, in some cases, the species, but nothing more; consequently, when the title passes, the vendee has all that under the contract of sale, the vendor engaged to give him, and therefore the entire consideration for his promise. There is then no failure. The rule of the civil law, that a sound price implies a warranty that the article sold is sound, is not a rule of the common law. I am not now speaking of cases of sale by sample, nor of cases in which the law is said to imply a warranty that the goods sold are the same *in specie* with those mentioned in the contract of sale; Borrekins *v.* Bevan,[1] is one of the latter; though even these cases are, perhaps, rather adjudications of what shall be considered evidence of an express engagement than extensions of the doctrine of implied warranty. There are also to be found decisions, in which it has been held that the law implies in the case of sale of goods by a manufacturer, that they are of a merchantable quality, and other decisions ruling that where goods are sold for a particular use there is an implied warranty that they are fit for that use. But it cannot be generally maintained, that where the buyer has had an opportunity of examining the article, there is any engagement implied in the contract of sale that the seller warrants against latent defects unknown alike to himself and to the purchaser. Certainly, there is no such engagement in the sale of such an article as a horse. The civil-law doctrine would produce endless embarrassments, if applied to the extended operations

[1] 3 Rawle, 37.

of modern trade. It always involves an inquiry into the question, whether the price agreed to be paid was, or was not, a sound price, and, of course, leaves the measure of obligation of the contract to be determined by the jury. But if there be no such engagement by the vendor, then the buyer who has got an unsound or defective article cannot assert that he has failed to obtain all that for which he has contracted to pay. Mere inadequacy of consideration, without warranty or fraud, is no defence to the payment of a bill or note, given for the purchase-money of goods, and the unsoundness or defective quality of the article sold relates only to the adequacy of the consideration." A like doctrine may be found in Misner *v.* Granger [1] and Kohl *v.* Lindley,[2] and it was applied in the case last cited, although the sale was of hay in ricks and the defect was known to the seller and unknown to the purchaser. The civil law, as defined by the XII. Tables, was to the same effect, that the seller's duty was fulfilled by delivery unless he made himself answerable for more, by what he said;[3] and it was not until a later period that he became answerable for defects which he knew and did not disclose, and finally for all undivulged defects whether he was or was not aware of their existence.[4]

The common-law rule is, as the judgment in Eagan *v.* Call indicates, a logical deduction from premises that do not readily admit of any other inference. For as the title passes under such a sale as soon as the parties agree on the thing and the price, all that remains is the payment of the purchase-money and the delivery or setting apart of what the buyer is to receive; and in determining the latter point, little or no regard is paid to the vendor's representations, save in so far as they tended to identify the thing sold. If, for instance, the offer is of a thorough-bred horse in the vendor's stable, which the purchaser sees or may inspect if he thinks proper, he is equally bound whether the horse is or is not a thorough-bred; although if the vendor owns two horses, the term "thorough-bred" may serve to indicate which one the parties have in view.

[1] 4 Gilman, 69.

[2] 39 Ill. 195.

[3] Cicero de Officiis, iii. 116.

[4] Accarias, ii. No. 609.

In the case above supposed the vendor describes or designates the horse as thorough-bred; but the obligation to accept and pay is, according to the generally received opinion, the same, where he warrants the animal's descent or pedigree, instead of simply stating it as a fact, although the purchaser may maintain an action for damages or make a deduction from the price if the warranty proves untrue.

CHAPTER XIX.

SALE BY DESCRIPTION.

Executory Contract for the Sale of Goods of a certain Kind. — Goods must answer Description. — Be sound and merchantable and fit for Use. — Unless Purchaser designates or selects. — Sale by Description of specific Goods. — Title does not pass unless accepted by Purchaser. — Vendor answerable if they differ in Kind or are unmerchantable. — Implied Warranty of Fitness. — Latent Effects. — Effect of Inspection.

SUCH was the established doctrine of the English law when the subject-matter was a specific chattel, and such it remains with some qualifications to be hereafter noted. As society advanced and commerce traced a widening circle, orders were given and contracts made for such goods as the buyer needed, without reference to any particular thing or parcel, and as there was nothing to indicate what the purchaser was to have, save the language held on either side, it was followed in the absence of any other guide.[1] Hence arose a train of consequences. For as it cannot be said under these circumstances, as it may in the instance above supposed of the horse, that whether the thing tendered does or does not correspond with the terms of the contract, it is still that which the purchaser agreed to buy, he may not only refuse to accept or pay, but recover damages for the default. The contract is executory, and does not pass the title until the thing stipulated for is tendered or set apart on one side, and accepted on the other;[2] and hence if the agreement be not fulfilled as regards kind, quality, quantity, or time, it matters not that the difference is slight, and will, in the opinion of the court or jury, have no injurious consequences, because every man

[1] Youghiogheny Iron and Coal Co. *v.* Smith, 16 P. F. S. 340; Dailey *v.* Green, 3 Harris, 118, 125.

[2] *Ante.*

is entitled to judge for himself in such matters and a new contract should not be substituted for that which the parties made.[1]

A day's delay in the shipment or delivery, or sending more or less than the quantity contracted for, though the default be only of a few bales or pounds, or forwarding goods that have been ordered in the same crate or receptacle with others that have not, and thus throwing the burden of selection on the buyer, will therefore as effectually exonerate him, and render the seller as liable as though the goods were behindhand for weeks or months, or there was no resemblance between the thing ordered and the thing sent.[2]

"When" said Woods, J., in Pope *v.* Allis,[3] "the subject-matter of a sale is not in existence, or not ascertained at the time of the contract, an undertaking that it shall, when existing or ascertained, possess certain qualities is not a mere warranty, but a condition, the performance of which is precedent to any obligation upon the vendee under the contract; bcause the existence of those qualities being part of the description of the thing sold becomes essential to its identity, and the vendee cannot be obliged to receive and pay for a thing different from that for which he contracted."

In Rommel *v.* Wingate the plaintiff wrote from New York to the defendant, who resided in Boston, that he had a vessel of 375 tons burthen which he could load with coal on the following Monday. The defendant telegraphed, in reply, "Ship that cargo 375 tons immediately." The plaintiff did not begin to load till nine days afterwards, and then shipped 392 tons: and the court held that the tender was invalidated by the

[1] Bowes *v.* Shand, 2 App. Cases, 455, 465, 480.

[2] Coddington *v.* Paleologo, L. R. 2 Ex. 193; Dixon *v.* Fletcher, 3 M. & W. 145; Cunliffe *v* Harrison, 6 Ex. 906; Levy *v.* Green, 8 E. & B. 575; Bowes *v.* Shand, L. R. 1 Q. B. Div. 470; 2 App. Cases, 455; Roberts *v.* Beatty, 2 Penrose & Watts, 63; Wright *v.* Barnes, 14 Conn. 518; Norrington *v.* Wright, 115 U. S. 188, 204; Marland *v.* Stanwood, 101 Mass. 470; Rommel *v.* Wingate, 103 id. 327; Dailey *v.* Green, 3 Harris, 118, 125; Youghiogheny Iron and Coal Co. *v.* Smith, 16 P. F. S. 340; Woodle *v.* Whitney, 23 Wis. 55.

[3] 115 U. S. 363, 371.

excess as well as by the delay, and that the defendant would not have been bound to accept the coal had it arrived in time.

It is in general enough that the thing tendered under an executory contract should correspond with its terms, and if it does not meet the expectations of the buyer, the fault lies in his own want of precision, and he can no more hold the seller answerable than if he had singled out a horse or carriage, and agreed to the owner's terms without obtaining a warranty that it was sound or fit for use. There is, however, this difference, that while the buyer of a specific thing chooses for himself, one who agrees to purchase or gives an order for things of a certain kind leaves the selection to the vendor, and the latter must consequently take care that the article which he selects or tenders is sound and merchantable, and has no defect that unfits it for the uses to which such things are customarily applied.[1]

"Where," said Cockburn, C. J., in the case last cited, "the buyer purchases a specific article the maxim *caveat emptor* applies, but when the buyer orders goods to be supplied and trusts to the judgment of the seller to select the goods which shall be applicable to the purpose for which they are ordered, there is an implied warranty that they shall be reasonably fit for that purpose."

Such is confessedly the rule where the vendor is also the manufacturer;[2] and the principle is nearly if not quite the same where he expressly or impliedly agrees to furnish or select.[3] The buyer is not entitled to goods of any particular quality or fineness, but has a right to insist that they shall be of medium quality or fineness, and free from such defects as would render

[1] Hart *v.* Wright, 17 Wend. 267; Fish *v.* Roseberry, 22 Ill. 288; Babcock *v.* Trice, 18 id. 420; Doane *v.* Dunham, 65 id. 512, 516; 79 id. 131; Jones *v.* Bright, 5 Bing. 533; Randall *v.* Newson, 2 Q. B. 102; Howard *v.* Hoey, 23 Wend. 350.

[2] Howard *v.* Hoey, 23 Wend. 350; Wright *v.* Barnes, 14 Conn. 518; Kellogg *v.* Denslow, 14 id. 411.

[3] See Gaylord Man. Co. *v.* Allen, 53 N. Y. 515; Beals *v.* Olmstead, 24 Vt. 114; Brown *v.* Sayles, 27 id. 227; Rodgers *v.* Niles, 11 Ohio St. 48; Mann *v.* Everton, 32 Ind. 355; Fish *v.* Roseberry, 22 Ill. 288; Chicago Packing & Pork Co. *v.* Tilton, 87 id. 547, 555.

them unsuited to the use to which such things are customarily put.[1]

Where, for instance, there is nothing in the wording of an order for a threshing or sewing machine, or the circumstances under which it is given, to lessen the vendor's responsibility or indicate which among the multitude of such contrivances he is to procure or make, the purchaser is not bound to accept and pay for a machine which cannot be usefully and practically employed.[2] The rule was so stated by Cowen, J., in Howard *v.* Hoey,[3] and the English law said to be substantially the same, as regards contracts *in genere* for the delivery of things of a certain kind, as that which is administered on the continent of Europe, and formerly prevailed at Rome.

"Agreeably to Bacon's Abridgment[4] a tender of any sort of goods should, unless they are to be delivered according to some sample, be made in a middling kind of goods of the sort." This subject is well considered by Mr. Chipman in his treatise on Contracts,[5] on principles that are universally understood, namely, that where there is a contract to deliver an article (for example, a note for one hundred bushels of wheat), merchantable or marketable quality is always intended by the parties; such as would bring the average market price at least.[6] Suitableness enters into every promise to deliver articles of manufacture. A man orders a garment or a pair of shoes for himself: would any one imagine that because no express warranty of fitness was made, either could not be returned or a recovery resisted after notice to take it back, provided it failed in reasonably fitting the intended wearer? With regard to performing or tendering a thing under executory contracts of this kind, Mr. Chipman very properly refers to what Pothier says of contracts for delivering an indeterminate thing of a particular kind, where, as he says, every

[1] Rodgers *v.* Niles, 11 Ohio St. 48; Story on Contracts, § 386; Broom, Legal Maxims, 614.

[2] Parsons on Contracts, 586; Port Carbon Iron Co. *v.* Groves, 18 P. F. S. 149, 151.

[3] 23 Wend. 352. [4] Tender B. 1. pl. 2. [5] p. 32, *et seq.*

[6] Per Nelson J. in Gallagher *v.* Waring, 9 Wend. 20.

individual comprised in the specified class is *in facultate solutionis*, but must be good, lawful, merchandisable, of suitable quality, good and sufficient in its kind, that is, it should not have any remarkable defect. I use the words found in and illustrated by different parts of Article 283 in Part. 2, ch. 3, § 3, of Pothier on Obligations. For as to this class of contracts, it may be said that the English law, and therefore our own, agrees with the Continental or Roman law, the rule of which in relation to all sales, both executed and executory, is *caveat venditor* not *caveat emptor*.[1] The common law will, I think, be found to have acted universally on the former rule in respect to executory sales, or more properly speaking, agreements to make sales of indeterminate things; though I do not find any case expressly holding the distinction. In short, there is always a warranty or promise implied that the indeterminate thing to be delivered, should at least not have any remarkable defect; though the rule of the common law is clearly otherwise in respect to what is properly denominated a sale."[2]

A different rule has been laid down in Pennsylvania, which puts executed and executory sales on the same footing as regards the duty of the buyer to see that the goods are sound.[3] In Ryan *v.* Ulmer, an order sent by mail for two car-loads of "sweet pickled hams," and which might seemingly have been filled by the delivery of any goods corresponding to its terms, was held not to render it incumbent on the seller to furnish meat that was "sweet, sound, and fit to be used in the trade." The court held that although the parties were at a distance, and there was no inspection or opportunity for inspection, the descriptive words were no part of the contract save as to kind.

It results from this decision, that even when the duty and responsibility of choosing devolve on the vendor, and the thing ordered is provisions, he may procure in the market, or select from his own stores meats that are unsound, forward

[1] Wright *v.* Hart, 18 Wend. 449; Waring *v.* Mason, 18 id. 425, per Walworth, C.

[2] Howard *v.* Hoey, 23 Wend. 350.

[3] Ryan *v.* Ulmer, 16 Weekly Notes of Cases, 121.

them to the purchaser, and demand and recover the full contract price.

The rule, as laid down in Howard *v.* Hoey and generally recognized and applied in England and the United States, is confined to contracts that may be fulfilled by the delivery of any goods of the kind prescribed, but was in the recent case of Doane *v.* Dunham,[1] treated as applicable to the sale of a given quantity or number out of a mass, as where one hundred barrels of flour are standing in a warehouse, and twenty are sold without being specifically designated; or a vendor exhibits a cask of sherry, which the purchaser tastes and approves, and agrees to take five gallons. Under these circumstances the contract is so far executory that the title does not pass until the goods are accepted by the purchaser, or set apart or forwarded in pursuance of an express or implied authority from him; and in the case above cited, it was held to follow that he is entitled to require that they shall be sound and merchantable, and may reject them if they are not. McAllister, J., said: "By the contract in the case at bar, the price was to be paid and sugar delivered in the future. There was, at the time of making it, no selecting or setting apart of any specific barrels from the mass in store so as to pass the property *in presenti*. The contract was therefore executory, and the goods not purchased upon inspection. Under such circumstances, the law will imply that the parties contemplated the sugar should be of a fair and merchantable quality, and will raise a warranty to that effect. It was Dunham's duty to deliver sugar of that kind, which should answer the character and be of the quality contemplated, bringing the average market price. Nothing short of this can be regarded as performance.[2]

"The barrels delivered to the defendant's teamster were of Dunham's selection from the mass in his store. The contract being executory, the law gave the defendants a reasonable time in which to make a fair examination, and see if the sugar answered the character and quality of that called for by the con-

1 65 Ill. 512, 516.

2 Babcock *v.* Trice, 18 Ill. 420; Misner *v.* Granger, 4 Gilm. 69; Howard *v.* Hoey, 23 Wend. 350.

tract. What is such reasonable time is to be determined upon by the jury in view of all the circumstances. If the defendants failed to make the examination within such reasonable time, they will be precluded from the right to offer it back, rescind the contract, and avoid payment on that ground, but would still have the right to rely upon the warranty implied by law in mitigation of damages under the general issue, or, in other words, will be liable upon a *quantum meruit* for the goods. If, on the other hand, they retained the goods only a reasonable time for examination, and immediately upon discovering that they were not of the character or quality called for by the contract, they notified the vendor to take them back, then the contract was rescinded, and no recovery could be had for the price."[1]

The view taken in this instance can hardly be accepted without reservation. The bare fact that the vendor has articles of the kind on hand, and that both parties look to them as a probable and obvious source of supply, will not, as Cowen, J., observed in Howard *v.* Hoey, absolve him from the obligation to deliver merchantable goods, for if his own stock is deficient, he should look elsewhere and select sound and merchantable wares; but the case is widely different when the purchaser agrees to take a certain quantity of a mass which lies open for inspection, and is seen or approved, because the choice is then virtually made and all that remains is to tender or set apart the required number or amount.[2] It is nevertheless an implied condition that the parcels or bales exhibited should be a fair sample of the whole, and a buyer who after examining one of a hundred barrels of flour standing in a warehouse, and finding it good, orders ten, will not be bound to accept them if they prove inferior to that which he saw and approved.

This distinction was disregarded in Selser *v.* Roberts, where a buyer who agreed to take a hundred boxes of canned peaches from a lot shown by the seller, after examining four and finding them sound, was compelled to pay the contract price for the whole, although half proved to be mouldy and unsound.

[1] 2 Kent, Com. Marg. 479, 480.

[2] Selser *v.* Roberts, 105 Pa. 242.

The authorities agree that so far as the purchaser relies on his own judgment he must bear any loss that may arise from his want of skill or knowledge, whether the sale be executory or of a specific thing. A buyer who, instead of using general terms and throwing the burden of selection on the vendor, orders a machine like one which he has seen, or by the name under which machines of a particular make are generally known, may hold the vendor answerable for bad workmanship or materials, but not for a defect arising from the method or principle of construction, which he has virtually designated or prescribed.[1] In Ollivant *v.* Bayley, the defendant saw a machine, and ordered one like it, and the plaintiff agreed in writing to "make a two-color printing machine on my patent principle." The machine was made and delivered, but the defendant refused to pay for it, on the ground that it was practically useless for printing in two colors.

The judge before whom the cause was tried, told the jury that if the defendant ordered a known and ascertained article he was liable, whether it did or did not answer the purpose for which it was bought, but that if it was not so known or ascertained, and the defendant simply ordered and the plaintiff agreed to supply a machine for printing two colors, there could be no recovery unless the instrument was reasonably fit for use. They took the former view and rendered a verdict for the plaintiff, which was upheld.

This decision is obviously near the dividing line, but may be explained on the ground that the words "on my patent principle" were the key to the entire contract, and only rendered the plaintiff answerable for making such a machine as that principle was capable of producing when applied in good faith, with due care as to the workmanship and materials.[2]

[1] Misner *v.* Granger, 4 Gilm. 69; Chanter *v.* Hopkins, 4 M. & W. 399; Ollivant *v.* Bayley, 5 Q. B. 288; Whitmore *v.* South Boston Iron Co., 2 Allen, 58; Tilton Safe Co. *v.* Tisdale, 48 Vt. 83; Walker *v.* Pue, 57 Md. 155; Rice *v.* Forsyth, 41 id. 389; Port Carbon Iron Co. *v.* Groves, 18 P. F. S. 149; Parsons on Contracts, 586.

[2] McGraw *v.* Fletcher, 35 Mich. 104; Robinson *v* Chandler, 56 Ind. 575.

In like manner, where a written offer of a "Mulay curved-slide saw-mill" was accepted by the purchaser, the implied undertaking was said to be that the machine so contracted for would perform such work as that kind of saw-mill ought reasonably to perform, and not that it would answer the purpose of other kinds of saw-mills, nor even of a Mulay saw-mill constructed without a curved slide, and an averment that the machine so sold would not "saw lumber" was held to be insufficient as not disclosing a breach of the contract established by the proofs.

Time brought with it an intermediate case, where the sale is not simply of specific goods, but of the goods as being of a certain quality or kind; and it is now established in the English courts, and generally in our own, that if the goods do not answer the description they may be rejected, and the vendor made answerable for the default.

The contract is still executory and does not pass the right of property without acceptance, but instead of being general for such things as it describes, is for a specific thing of a certain quality, and cannot be satisfied unless the very thing is delivered, nor unless it answers to the words employed. Without some such rule, business could not be securely prosecuted in great commercial centres like New York and London, where the buyer is often unacquainted with the seller, and *caveat emptor* becomes impracticable from the want of time and opportunity to inspect the goods. The purchase of a sack of peas does not, as Lord Abinger pointed out in Chanter *v.* Hopkins,[1] impose any obligation on the buyer, if the contents are in fact beans, although it may render the seller liable in damages unless he is exonerated on the ground of a mistake which renders the contract void, and it will make no difference that the sack was lying in the seller's warehouse and might have been examined by the buyer. For a like reason, one who agrees to buy a cask of wine which is shown to him as sherry, is not bound to accept the wine if it proves to be Marsala, unless it appears that he relied on his own judgment, and agreed to take that very wine, whether it did or did

[1] 4 M. & W. 399.

not answer to the description given by the vendor.[1] So when turnip seed was sold as "Skirving's Swedes," the descriptive words were held to be not a warranty, but an integral part of the contract that would not be satisfied by the delivery of seed of a different kind.[2]

The distinction seems to have been little known to the common law which regarded the descriptive words used by the vendor as either a representation that imposed no liability unless consciously false, or a warranty that might render him answerable in damages, but was not of the essence of the contract and could not be set up as a defence to an action for the price. *Præsentia corporis tollit errorem nominis* was held to be a sufficient answer to a complaint that the purchaser had not got what he asked for and expected to receive; or, as it was sometimes quaintly put, his eyes were his market, and if they were not used to good purpose it was his folly and not the seller's fault. The courts are now governed by the intention of the parties as disclosed by the language held on either side, rather than by set rules and arbitrary presumptions, and if the subject-matter is defined as regards properties or species, the thing tendered or delivered must not only be physically the same as that shown to the purchaser or designated by marks or brands, but be what he stipulated for or agreed to take in other and not less material particulars.

Regard must be had in the application of the principle to the distinction between kind and quality, and an undertaking for kind will not render the seller answerable for defects of quality which do not affect the kind, nor will a stipulation that the quality shall be at the buyer's risk preclude him from insisting on an exact performance as regards kind.[3] In Shepherd *v.* Kain a ship was advertised for sale as copper-fastened, to be taken with all faults without any liability for any defect whatsoever, and a recovery was had against the vendor on proof that some of the fastenings were not copper, because "without faults" signified such faults as were consistent with the ship being as described, to wit, copper-

[1] Borrekins *v.* Bevan, 3 Rawle, 23. [2] Allan *v.* Lake, 18 Q. B. 247.
[3] Shepherd *v.* Kain, 5 B. & Ald. 240; Nichol *v.* Godts, 10 Ex. 191.

fastened. The phrase "without faults" received a like interpretation in Whitney *v.* Boardman.[1]

Whether the seller describes or designates the goods in terms, or refers the buyer to a sample shown at the time, or to the articles delivered to him or to another on a former occasion, the effect is the same, and if intended as an undertaking equally obligatory. In Dayton *v.* Hooglund,[2] the plaintiffs wrote to the defendants, who were manufacturers of nuts and bolts in Cincinnati, that they had sold a lot of Swedish iron to Steers & Potts in Philadelphia, and that if the defendants wished to test the quality of the iron they might buy a ton from Steers & Potts and try it. The defendants purchased as suggested, and finding the iron excellent ordered twenty tons of the same brand from the plaintiffs. The latter manufactured and forwarded the quantity required; but the iron proved to be of inferior quality and unfit for use in the defendants' business, and the court held that the sale was virtually by sample of iron of the quality of that furnished to Steers & Potts, and that as it did not answer that description the defendants might either return it to the plaintiffs, or keep it and recoup the damages arising from the breach.

In Wieler *v.* Schilizzi,[3] the court left it to the jury to say whether an admixture of fifteen per cent of mustard seed destroyed the distinctive character of a commodity, which had been sold as Calcutta linseed *tale quale;* and they found a verdict for the purchaser, which was sustained notwithstanding the words which indicated that the description was not absolute, and that if the quality was like it need not be the same.

It is not essential to the operation of the rule that the description shall be formal or at length, and the designation of that which is offered for sale by a specific name as "opium" is an undertaking which, if the article proves to be spurious or of a different kind, will entitle the vendee to reject it and render the vendor answerable in damages.[4]

The difference need not be entire, and it is enough that

[1] 118 Mass. 242. [2] 39 Ohio St. 671. [3] 17 C. B. 619.

[4] Reggio *v.* Braggiotti, 7 Cush. 166; Hawkins *v.* Pemberton, 51 N. Y. 198.

there is a failure in a distinctive particular which gives character to the whole. A man who buys sherry cannot therefore be compelled to accept madeira, nor a buyer of whiskey, rum, though the bulk of the liquor is in either case water and alcohol, and the difference lies in the essential oils which give flavor to wine and spirits. In like manner, it is a defence to an executory contract for the delivery of coal that it is so mixed with slate or stones as to be unmerchantable or unfit for use;[1] and the rule applies to every adulteration which renders the commodity commercially other than it is designated.[2] So if the order is for sheathing copper and the copper tendered is of a different sort, the contract is as much broken as if the vendor had sent iron or lead.[3]

Oral contracts obey the same rule in this regard as written, and if the goods do not answer to the description, the vendor is answerable and the buyer discharged;[4] although there is this difference, that while the writing will be interpreted by the court in view of all that it contains, and without regard to extrinsic promises or declarations,[5] an oral contract must be left to the jury, and what passes before the parties come to terms is not necessarily excluded from, nor what is said at the time part of the contract.[6]

In Hawkins *v.* Pemberton,[7] the sale took place at auction, and the auctioneer's designation of a commodity as blue vitriol or sulphate of copper, which in truth consisted principally of sulphate of iron, was held to be a constituent element of the contract which must be fulfilled in order to bind the purchaser.

[1] Edwards *v.* Hathaway, 1 Phila. 547.

[2] Jones *v.* Just, L. R. 3 Q. B. 197; Wieler *v.* Schilizzi, 17 C. B. 619; Terry *v.* Bissell, 26 Conn. 23.

[3] Chanter *v.* Hopkins, 4 M. & W. 399, 404; Jones *v.* Bright, 5 Bing. 533.

[4] Wolcott *v.* Mount, 36 N. J. L. 262, 267; 9 id. 496; Bannerman *v.* White, 10 C. B. N. S. 844.

[5] Nichol *v.* Godts, 10 Ex. 191.

[6] Wolcott *v.* Mount, 36 N. J. L. 262; Borrekins *v.* Bevan, 3 Rawle, 23, 39. See Osgood *v.* Lewis, 2 Harris & Gill, 495; Jones *v.* Bright, 5 Bing. 533.

[7] 51 N. Y. 198.

It may be observed in this connection that while the bought-and-sold notes, which are customarily exchanged in England and not infrequently in the United States, embody the contract and cannot be varied orally; this is not true of the invoice or bill of parcels, which is a mere memorandum or recital of what is tendered or delivered for the purpose of carrying the contract into effect, although it may be strong or even conclusive evidence against the vendor from whom it proceeds, or as regards an acquiescent purchaser.[1]

The vendor's liability in cases of this description is not on the ground of warranty, but for a failure to fulfil the agreement by tendering that which he agreed to sell;[2] and as the title will not pass in the absence of a waiver, or a new contract arising from delivery and acceptance, the purchaser cannot maintain trover or replevin, and his right to damages is limited to the difference between the price and the sum which the chattel would have been worth had it been of the kind described.[3] Such at least is the rule *prima facie* and wherever the buyer is entitled to reject the goods, although the question is one of intention, and it may appear that he agreed to take them whether they were or were not as described,[4] and seek compensation in a reduction of the price or a suit for damages, or in other words, that the description was a warranty and not a substantive part of the contract.

It does not necessarily vary the case that the goods are seen and approved, because the contract may still relate to what they are described as being, as well as to what they are.[5] In Josling *v.* Kingsford,[6] oxalic acid, or what passed as such, was

[1] Power *v.* Barham, 4 Ad. & E 473; Wolcott *v.* Mount, 36 N. J. L. 262; Borrekins *v.* Bevan, 3 Rawle, 23, 39; Jones *v.* Bright, 5 Bing. 533.

[2] Haase *v.* Nonemacher, 21 Minn. 486; Cooch *v.* Money, 5 Del. 177, Dayton *v.* Hooglund, 39 Ohio St. 671.

[3] Chanter *v.* Hopkins, 4 M. & W. 399; Mondel *v.* Steel, 8 id. 858.

[4] See Wolcott *v.* Mount, 36 N. J. L. 262.

[5] Borrekins *v.* Bevan, 3 Rawle, 23, 43; Jones *v.* Bright, 5 Bing. 533; Mody *v.* Gregson, L. R. 4 Ex. 49, 54; Tye *v.* Fynmore, 3 Camp. 462; Power *v.* Barham, 4 Ad. & E. 473; Henshaw *v.* Robbins, 9 Met. 83; Wolcott *v.* Mount, 36 N. J. L. 262.

[6] 13 C. B. N. S. 44.

sold without warranty, examined by the purchaser and delivered, but proved though not until the greater part had been used, to have been adulterated with sulphate of magnesia, a defect not visible to the naked eye nor easily discoverable without analysis. The jury were instructed that there was no evidence of a warranty, and the question was whether the article in dispute was oxalic acid in the sense in which the term was used and understood in trade. If it did not come within the meaning of the term, as thus defined, the vendors were answerable, although they had declined to warrant the strength of the acid.

A recovery may, agreeably to the authorities, be had on a specific warranty although the defect would be obvious to an experienced eye, or as appears, even when it is patent and known to the buyer;[1] and the rule applies, although with less force, when specific goods are sold as being of a certain kind.[2] The question then is, What is the subject-matter of the contract,—the thing seen or the thing described? and if the buyer knew that the goods did not answer the description they cannot justly be rejected if there is no other ground.[3] A general warranty may be limited or controlled by proof that the plaintiff was aware of a particular defect,[4] and the reason is stronger where the allegation is that the thing tendered is not that which the purchaser agreed to buy.[5] It has nevertheless been held that a written contract of sale cannot be explained or qualified by proof that the purchaser knew that the commodity was other than that therein described.[6] In Nichol *v.* Godts[7] the bought note was as follows: "Sold this day for Nichol & Sons to U. A. Godts the four under-mentioned parcels of foreign refined rape oil warranted only equal to samples." It appeared in evidence at the trial that

[1] Pinney *v.* Andrus, 41 Vt. 631; House *v.* Fort, 4 Blackf. 296; Scarborough *v.* Reynolds, 13 Rich. 98.

[2] Tye *v.* Fynmore, 3 Camp. 462; Henshaw *v.* Robbins, 9 Met. 83.

[3] Welsh *v.* Carter, 1 Wend. 185.

[4] See Margetson *v.* Wright, 7 Bing. 603; Vendewalker *v.* Osmer, 65 Barb. 556.

[5] See Henshaw *v.* Robbins, 9 Met. 83, 89.

[6] Nichol *v.* Godts, 10 Ex. 191.

[7] 10 Ex. 191.

although the oil was identical in quality with the samples, it was largely adulterated with hemp oil; but witnesses were called on the other side who testified that the buyer was informed that the oil was mixed to some extent with other oils, and that the vendor simply undertook that it should correspond to the samples. The jury were nevertheless instructed that the clause concerning the samples related only to the quality of the article, and that the buyer was entitled under the contract to rape oil, unless the seller could show that agreeably to the settled usage of the oil trade, rape oil was understood to mean a mixture of rape and hemp-seed oil, and that the only question before them was as to the existence of such a custom. They found reluctantly for the buyer, adding that they did so on the legal effect of the contract, and that he well knew what he was buying. The court held in refusing a motion for a new trial, that the interpretation put on the contract was correct, and that testimony was not admissible to vary the effect of the written words. If that sort of evidence was admitted every written document would be at the mercy of witnesses who might be called to swear to anything.

It may be thought that this decision goes too far. In stating that the contract was "only warranted equal to samples," the vendor obviously meant to indicate that he undertook for nothing more, and the writing should seemingly have been construed as a whole. Moreover, the ambiguity was latent, growing out of the application of the contract to the facts. When the parol evidence disclosed that there were no such "parcels" as the contract called for, other evidence of a like kind might well be adduced to show what the parties really had in view. It is a general principle that a cloud raised by the testimony of witnesses may be dissipated in the same way. The maxim *præsentia corporis tollit errorem nominis* may be pushed too far, but should not be lost sight of in determining whether the subject-matter is the thing seen or the thing described.

Whether the purchaser examines the goods or a specimen or sample, the principle is the same and he is equally entitled to show that they do not answer the description given by the vendor. For as all that a sale by sample implies is an undertaking for the identity of the bulk, it will not negative or exclude any express or implied undertaking which relates equally to both,[1] and the law was, as we have seen, so held in Nichol *v.* Godts, notwithstanding an explicit stipulation that the goods were "warranted only equal to sample."[2]

It is immaterial as regards the application of the principle whether the descriptive words are contained in a note or memorandum executed when the contract is concluded or reduced to writing, or in an offer made on one side and accepted on the other; and the description given in an advertisement published by the seller, or the order sent by the purchaser will consequently be binding on both parties unless the sale appears to have been made on a different basis.[3]

In the instances above cited the variance was in kind; but it is not less well settled that the description must be substantially exact as regards quality, and if a commodity which has been advertised before the sale, or is described subsequently in the bill of parcels as sound or chemically pure, proves to be damaged or adulterated it may be rejected and a recovery had in damages.[4]

In Bannerman *v.* White,[5] the seller offered his year's growth of hops. Samples were produced, and before the price was mentioned the buyer inquired had sulphur been used, for if it had been he would not even ask the price. He was told it had not, and the price was then fixed, and the hops sent to his warehouse and weighed in the presence of both parties. He discovered some six weeks afterwards that a small portion of the hops had been sulphured and mixed with the others, and wrote the respondent that the contract was at an end. The seller brought suit for the purchase-money, and the jury found that the affirmation that no sulphur had been used was

1 Mody *v.* Gregson, L. R. 4 Ex. 49; Henshaw *v.* Robbins, 9 Met. 83.

2 *Ante.*

3 Bradford *v.* Manly, 13 Mass. 139; Shepherd *v.* Kain, 5 B. & Ald. 240.

4 Richmond Manuf. Co. *v.* Farquar, 8 Blackf. 89; see Mallan *v.* Radloff, 17 C. B. N. S. 588.

5 10 C. B. N. S. 844.

not wilfully false, but was understood on both sides as a part of the contract and a warranty to that effect. Earle, C. J., said "We avoid the term 'warranty' because it is used in two senses, and the term 'condition' because the question is whether the term is applicable. The effect is that the defendant required and the plaintiff gave an undertaking that no sulphur had been used. This undertaking was a preliminary stipulation, and if it had not been given, the defendant would not have gone on with the treaty which resulted in the sale. In this sense it was the condition upon which the defendant contracted, and it would be contrary to the intention expressed by this stipulation that the contract should remain valid if sulphur had been used. The intention of the parties governs in the making and in the construction of all contracts; and if the parties so intend the sale may be absolute with a warranty superadded, or the sale may be conditional, to be null if the warranty is broken. And upon the statement of facts we think that the intention appears that the contract shall be null if sulphur had been used." It followed that the buyer was entitled to reject the hops and refuse to pay the purchase-money.

Instead of calling the undertaking that "no sulphur had been used" a preliminary stipulation which annulled the contract if unfulfilled, it would seemingly have been more accurate to say that what the plaintiff agreed to sell and the defendant to purchase was not merely the hops which had been grown on the plaintiff's vines, but hops so grown and that had not been sulphured, and as the hops which were delivered did not answer to this description the defendant was no more bound to accept or keep them than he would have been had they, though not sulphured, been grown on other lands. Such contracts are necessarily executory as being not merely for a specific thing, but for a specific thing of a certain kind, and if the thing tendered be not the thing described there is an entire failure of consideration which exonerates the buyer while rendering the seller liable for the breach.

It is established conformably to these decisions in England,

and would seem to be generally held in the United States, that one who sells specific goods "under a certain denomination or description, thereby undertakes as part of his contract that the thing delivered shall be as it is designated or described, and be in effect an article of the kind, species, or quality expressed in the contract of sale."[1]

In Hastings *v.* Lovering[2] the written memorandum was as follows: "sold 2,000 gallons prime quality winter oil," and the court held that the words which designated the quality were as much part of the contract as those which defined the kind, and that the buyer was entitled to damages on proof that the oil contained ingredients which congealed when chilled, and would not have been present had it been strained during winter or without the aid of heat. The judgment in Osgood *v.* Lewis[3] is to the same effect, and may be consulted with advantage as giving a sound and comprehensive view of the law.

The earlier decisions in New York were the other way, — that the name or description by or under which a specific thing is sold is not a warranty or evidence of one, nor does it enter into or form part of the contract, and that a man who sells the jewel on his hand as a diamond may, if he believed it to be such and there is no fraud, recover the contract price although it proves to be a stone of another kind or merely paste.[4]

In one of these instances Peacham wood was sold as Brazil wood; in another the purchaser got a spurious mixture instead of the white lead for which he had inquired; while kelp was delivered in the third, although the sale was of an article

[1] Windsor *v.* Lombard, 18 Pick. 57, 60; Hogins *v.* Plympton, 11 id. 99; Hastings *v.* Lovering, 2 id. 214; Henshaw *v.* Robbins, 9 Met. 83; Osgood *v.* Lewis, 2 Harris & Gill, 495; Wolcott *v.* Mount, 36 N. J. L. 262; 38 id. 496; Whitaker *v.* McCormick, 6 Mo. App. 114; Foss *v.* Sabin, 84 Ill. 564; Morehouse *v.* Comstock, 42 Wis. 626; Merriam *v.* Field, 24 id. 640; 29 id. 592; Beals *v.* Olmstead, 24 Vt. 114; Sparling *v.* Marks, 86 Ill. 125; Haase *v.* Nonemacher, 21 Minn. 486; Bryant *v.* Sears, 49 Ia. 373; McClung *v.* Kelley, 21 id. 568.

[2] 2 Pick. 214.

[3] 2 Harris & Gill, 495.

[4] Seixas *v.* Wood, 2 Caines, 48; Holden *v.* Dakin, 4 Johns. 421; Swett *v.* Colgate, 20 id. 196.

which had been advertised as barilla and was so described in the bill of parcels; and yet it was held in all of them that as there was no intentional misrepresentation or deceit, and the vendor had not expressly warranted the goods, he was not answerable for the misdescription or resulting loss. These decisions seem to have been influenced by a misconception of the judgment in Chandelor *v.* Lopus.[1] The declaration there averred that the defendant being a goldsmith, and having skill in jewels and precious stones, had a stone which he alleged to be a Bezoar stone and sold it for a hundred pounds, *ubi re vera* it was not a Bezoar stone. The plaintiff obtained a verdict, and the court below rendered a judgment in his favor, which was reversed in the Exchequer Chamber for the insufficiency of the declaration. The mistake seems to have been in pleading evidence instead of averring that which it conduced to prove;[2] and the facts set forth might presumably have been laid before a jury under proper averments as they certainly could be now proof of fraud or warranty, or of a contract to deliver an article answering to that designated or described.[3] It is established under the present course of decision, that one who sells an article under a specific name, as for instance "opium," may be held answerable in damages or compelled to refund the consideration if it proves to be spurious or of another kind;[4] and in Sparling *v.* Marks the buyer was allowed on this ground to return a stone which had been exhibited and sold as a diamond; but the complaint or declaration must aver a promise or undertaking, instead of simply narrating facts from which a promise may be inferred and that do not necessarily amount to fraud.[5]

Seixas *v.* Wood and its congeners have been overruled in New York, where the courts now follow the English doctrine

[1] Croke Jac. 4; 1 Sm. L. C. 7 Am. ed. 299, 309.

[2] See Wolcott *v.* Mount, 38 N. J. L. 496, 498.

[3] Hastings *v.* Lovering, 2 Pick. 214; Hawkins *v.* Pemberton, 51 N. Y. 198; Sparling *v.* Marks, 86 Ill. 125.

[4] Reggio *v.* Braggiotti, 7 Cush. 166.

[5] Wolcott *v.* Mount, 38 N. J. L. 496, 498; Carley *v.* Wilkins, 6 Barb. 557; Zimmerman *v.* Morrow, 28 Minn. 367; Power *v.* Barham, 4 Ad. & E. 473.

that the goods must answer to the name or description given by the vendor.[1] Accordingly, where a commodity which had been sold as blue vitriol proved on delivery to be largely mixed with sulphate of iron, the vendor was held answerable for the resulting loss,[2] while in White *v.* Miller[3] damages were awarded to the purchaser on proof that the seed which he had purchased as "Large Bristol Cabbage" was in truth cabbage-seed of a different kind.

The doctrine of the commercial law that a description of the subject-matter of the sale as of a particular kind or quality, is an implied undertaking that it corresponds to the words employed, was adopted in Borrekins *v.* Bevan,[4] and the plaintiff who had purchased an article as "blue paint" after an inspection of a sample, was held entitled to damages on proof that the mass was so largely adulterated as neither to be fit for use as paint, nor to answer to that name in any proper sense of the word. Rogers, J., said there was a class of English cases which bore directly on the question. Among them was Weall *v.* King,[5] which was a sale of "stock sheep," and it was proved they did not answer to the description of stock sheep, that is, sound lambs, but were unsound and afflicted with the rot. Lord Ellenborough held that under such circumstances the purchaser has a right to expect a salable commodity answering the description in the contract. He cannot without a warranty insist that the commodity shall be of any particular quality or fineness, but the intention of both parties must be taken to be that it shall be salable in the market under the denomination mentioned in the contract. The cases of Gardiner *v.* Gray,[6] and Shepherd *v.* Kain[7] were to the same effect, and the principle had been applied in Massachusetts and Maryland.[8] In all sales, therefore, there is an implied warranty that the article corresponds in specie with the

[1] See Wolcott *v.* Mount, 38 N. J. L. 496, 498.

[2] Hawkins *v.* Pemberton, 51 N. Y. 198.

[3] 71 N. Y. 118.

[4] 3 Rawle, 23.

[5] 12 East, 452.

[6] 4 Camp. 144.

[7] 5 B. & Ald. 240.

[8] Bradford *v.* Manly, 13 Mass. 139; Hastings *v.* Lovering, 2 Pick. 214; Osgood *v.* Lewis, 2 Harris & Gill, 495, 518.

31

commodity sold, unless there is some fact or circumstance, of which the jury under the direction of the court are to judge, which clearly shows that the purchaser took on himself the risk of determining not only the quality of the goods but the kind, or that he had waived his right. No such fact existed in the case in hand. The plaintiff had, it was true, like most purchasers, an opportunity for examination, but he did not examine with great minuteness. Of this, however, the jury were to judge under the direction of the court.

This line of decision was subsequently abandoned for that formerly adopted in New York, and it is now held in Pennsylvania that however the thing is called or described, what the purchaser buys is the thing itself, and if that is set apart or delivered he has no further claim in the absence of an express warranty or of fraud.[1] Such, at least, is the rule where the purchaser sees the goods, and it is presumably the same when they might be inspected if he chose to take the time.

In Fraley *v.* Bispham,[2] the purchaser was compelled to pay the full contract price for musty, scentless, and unmerchantable tobacco, although it was described in the bill of sale as "superior sweet-scented Kentucky leaf;" and if this decision may be explained on the ground that the descriptive words were simply a name used in commerce, and had no reference to quality, this can hardly be said of the subsequent decisions.

In Carson *v.* Bailie[3] the court took the further distinction, which was approved in Lord *v.* Grow,[4] that when the purchaser actually sees the goods, there is no standard but identity, and no warranty implied other than that the very goods shall be delivered, and the description in the sold note or bill of parcels will go for nothing as regards both quality and kind. The plaintiff called on the defendants to inquire for lard grease and was shown an article which he agreed to buy, but which though designated by that name in the bill of parcels proved on delivery to be adulterated with rosin and pot-

[1] See Fraley *v.* Bispham, 10 Barr, 320; Carson *v.* Bailie, 7 Harris, 375; Wetherill *v.* Neilson, 8 id. 448.

[2] 10 Barr, 320. [3] 7 Harris, 375. [4] 3 Wr. 88.

ash, and was not according to the testimony of every witness in any proper sense of the term "lard grease." The court below instructed the jury to inquire, Was the thing sold "lard grease"? if it was not, it did not correspond in specie with the bill of sale. They found for the purchaser, but the judgment was reversed on the ground that when goods are sold on inspection the rule *caveat emptor* admits of no exception, and the purchaser must see that what he buys corresponds in kind and quality with the description given by the seller.

In Whitaker *v.* Eastwick [1] the doctrine was applied to a contract for the sale of a cargo of "Wadlinger's coal." The coal was bought on the faith of an assurance that it was good for the purpose of raising steam, but proved on the arrival of the canal-boat to be full of dirt and slate, mixed with other coal, and unmerchantable. Here the contract was executory for the delivery of coal answering to its terms, and as it was the duty of the seller to take care that these were observed, it is not easy to see how the case could fall within the maxim *caveat emptor*, but the court held that the evidence was inadmissible, and the question should not have been left to the jury.

In this diversity of opinion, we may believe that the rule laid down in England, and followed in Massachusetts and New York, is consonant with legal principles, and better suited to promote the cause of morals and the needs of trade. When the contract is embodied in a written instrument, all that the instrument contains is presumably agreed to by both parties, and set forth in the writing for the purpose of defining their respective rights. Hence, much that would be simply a representation were it uttered in the course of a negotiation for a sale, may when recited in the sold note or bill of parcels, justly be regarded as a warranty or an essential term of the contract. Although a representation will not lose its distinctive character or become a substantive part of the contract on being reduced to writing,[2] still the description given in the written

[1] 25 P. F. S. 229.

[2] Behn *v.* Burness, 3 Best & Smith, 751, 754; Myers *v.* Conway, 62 Ind. 474.

evidence of the contract may justly be viewed as indicating what one party is to deliver and the other to receive, and if such is the interpretation of the instrument considered as a whole, the bare fact that the purchaser saw and examined the goods will not justify a countervailing inference.[1] The question is one of construction for the court, which may however consider it in the light of the circumstances as given in evidence or set forth in pleading.[2]

The point was critically considered by Dorsey, J., in Osgood *v.* Lewis, and placed on grounds that cannot easily be assailed. "Whether," said he, the "statement in the bill of parcels that the oil was 'winter pressed' be *per se* a warranty of that fact, is a question of more difficulty. In oral contracts much of the colloquium is never intended or understood by the parties to be an essential component part of the contract; but in written agreements nothing is inserted which is immaterial, no fact stated which is not presumed to be relied on by the parties, and for the truth of which the one does not bind himself to the other. Upon this principle it is that mere recitals in deeds have been held to be covenants; upon this ground must rest the decision that the action of covenant could be supported in Cramer *v.* Bradshaw.[3] There the plaintiff declared on a bill of sale by which the defendant, in consideration of $175, bargained and sold to the plaintiff "a negro woman slave, named Sarah, aged about thirty years, being of sound mind and limb free from all disease." And the defendant in due form in the covenanting part of the instrument (omitting everything as to age or soundness), covenanted only to warrant and defend the slave so sold to the plaintiff, against the defendant and all other persons. The alleged breach was, that the slave was unsound and affected with divers diseases, &c. *Per curiam*, "The words in the bill of sale 'being of sound mind and limb, free from all diseases,' are an averment of a fact and import an agreement to that effect. The words

[1] Borrekins *v.* Bevan, 3 Rawle, 23, 39; Nichol *v.* Godts, 10 Ex. 191; Hastings *v.* Lovering, 2 Pick. 214; Henshaw *v.* Robbins, 9 Met. 83; Osgood *v.* Lewis, 2 Harris & Gill, 495.

[2] Behn *v.* Burness, 3 Best & Smith, 751, 754.

[3] 10 Johns. 484.

were not used as a mere description of the slave, they amount to an express not an implied warranty, to a warranty of the soundness of the slave. The plaintiff is therefore entitled to judgment." The judgment in Nichol *v.* Godts [1] is substantially to the same effect.

The intention that the sale shall be by description may be inferred from any words that do not reasonably admit of a different interpretation, and although the court cannot make a contract for the parties, it may consider what the contract would have been if reduced to writing and set it out in full.[2] One who offers a thing as fit for a particular purpose, or exhibits it as such in response to an inquiry from a buyer, will accordingly be answerable if it be not fit for that purpose,[3] although no such liability will arise from an order for goods of a certain kind merely because the vendor knows or is told the use for which they are designed, or to which they will be put by the purchaser.[4] The rule may be readily applied where the order is in writing, and the buyer does not see or examine the goods before the completion of the contract; but there is more difficulty where he states the object which he has in view, and is shown a specific article which he agrees to buy, and it may then be requisite to determine whether the subject-matter of the contract is the thing which he sees and handles, or a thing answering the descriptive words employed.[5]

In Shepherd *v.* Pybus the bare fact that the plaintiff inspected the barge in question before buying, and while it was

[1] 10 Ex. 191. [2] Randall *v.* Newson, L. R. 2 Q. B. Div. 102.

[3] Brown *v.* Edgington, 2 M. & G. 279; Pacific Iron Works *v.* Newhall, 34 Conn. 67; Dayton *v.* Hooglund, 39 Ohio St. 671; Byers *v.* Chapin, 28 Ohio St. 300; Howard *v.* Hoey, 23 Wend. 350; Hoe *v.* Sanborn, 21 N. Y. 552; Beals *v.* Olmstead, 24 Vt. 114; Whitmore *v.* South Boston Iron Co., 2 Allen, 58; Cunningham *v.* Hall, 4 id. 273; Port Carbon Iron Co. *v.* Groves, 18 P. F. S. 151; Parsons on Contracts, 586.

[4] Dounce *v.* Dow, 64 N. Y. 411; Chanter *v.* Hopkins, 4 M. & W. 399; Ollivant *v.* Bayley, 5 Q. B. 288; Port Carbon Iron Co. *v.* Groves, 18 P. F. S. 151.

[5] Mallan *v.* Radloff, 17 C. B. N. S. 588; Shepherd *v.* Pybus, 3 M. & G. 868; Brown *v.* Edgington, 2 id. 279.

still unfinished in the builder's yard, was held not to preclude him from requiring that it should be reasonably fit for the uses to which such boats are usually applied, while an opposite inference may be drawn, where, as in Ollivant *v.* Bayley, an order is given for a machine like one the purchaser has seen and approved, although the machine so contracted for is not seen before delivery.[1]

The nature of the thing asked for or commanded may nevertheless be such as necessarily to imply the use which the buyer has in view, and the vendor will then be answerable for its fitness for such purposes, although the precise object is not disclosed. An order for a printing-press is an instance of this kind, and another may arise when the subject-matter is a carriage-wheel or pole, or a set of harness.

In Brown *v.* Edgington,[2] the plaintiff sent to the defendant, who was a rope-dealer, for a "crane" rope, and the defendant's foreman, who came to the plaintiff's premises, was told that the rope was wanted for raising pipes of wine. He took the measurement, and the rope was then bought and used, but broke under the strain, and the cask of wine to which it was fastened fell to the ground and was staved. The court held that the defendant had virtually undertaken to furnish a rope fit for the purpose, and was consequently answerable for the loss, although he was not the manufacturer and had bought the rope from a third person, in ignorance of the defect.

In Randall *v.* Newson,[3] the plaintiff bought a carriage with shafts from the defendant who was a carriage-builder, and directed him to furnish a pole, which was sent but broke in consequence of a latent defect, and the horses took fright and were much injured. The jury found that the pole was not reasonably fit for the carriage, but that the defendant had not been guilty of any negligence. It was contended for the defence that if there was any implied undertaking it was simply to use due care, and that the defendant was consequently entitled to judgment on the verdict. This contention was sustained in the court below, and the case taken to the Court

[1] *Ante.* [2] 2 M. & W. 279. [3] L. R. 2 Q. B. Div. 102.

of Appeal, which decided for the plaintiff on the following grounds: "The subject-matter of the contract was not simply a pole, but a pole for the plaintiff's carriage; or to state the proposition in an equivalent form, the thing which would, if the contract were formally drawn up, be described in it as the subject-matter of it, would not be merely a pole generally, but a pole to be purchased for a specific purpose, namely to be used in the plaintiff's carriage." The question was, "What in such a contract is the implied undertaking of the seller as to the efficiency of the pole? Is it an absolute warranty that the pole shall be reasonably fit for the purpose, or is only partially to that effect, limited to defects which might be discovered by care and skill?" The answer lay in the fundamental rule assumed or expressly stated in the authorities, and which comprised all others,—that the article "offered or delivered" "must answer the description of it contained in words in the contract, or which would be so contained if the contract were accurately drawn out." If the subject-matter was merely a commercial article or commodity, the thing tendered or delivered must be that described, that is, that article, and salable or merchantable. If the subject-matter was an article or commodity to be used for a particular purpose, the thing tendered must answer that description, that is, be that article or commodity, and reasonably fit for the purpose. There was consequently no room for the distinction that had been suggested between latent defects and such as were discoverable by examination. If the article did not, in fact, answer the description given of it, the contract was broken whether the defect was patent or latent. The defendant was therefore answerable for all the natural consequences of the defect in the pole, whether he had or had not been negligent.

The sale in this case was executory, for the manufacture or supply of an article not in being, and defined solely by the words employed; but the principle is equally applicable to the sale of a specific existing chattel for a use contemplated by the purchaser and communicated to the seller. It will not, however, be carried further than is requisite for the attainment of the end which the purchaser has in view, and the seller impliedly undertakes to supply, and what the sale of a carriage-pole or of any other article to one who buys with a view to a resale implies, is that the article shall not be so unsound or defective that it cannot fairly be disposed of in the accustomed course of trade. If this criterion is satisfied the purchaser cannot, as it would seem, require more.

For like reasons, a manufacturer who accepts an order for bolt-rods from a person whom he knows to be engaged in the making nuts and bolts, thereby impliedly undertakes to furnish rods that are suitable for such a use, and if they prove to be unfit they may be rejected, or if the buyer so elects, accepted and the damages recouped.[1]

In Gerst *v.* Jones,[2] the plaintiff ordered boxes from a manufacturer of such articles for use in their business as dealers in tobacco. The boxes were received and used, but proved to be made of such green and unseasoned wood that the tobacco which was packed in them became mouldy and unfit for use or sale, and the court held that there was an implied undertaking that the boxes should be reasonably suited to the purpose for which they were ordered, which rendered the defendants answerable for the consequential as well as direct injury resulting from the breach.

It is not always easy to determine whether the sale is executory or executed, generally of such goods as the buyer stipulates for or orders, or specifically of a particular chattel. Where the contract is completed by an order on one side and the acceptance of it on the other without reference to specific goods, the case obviously belongs to the former category; but there is more room for doubt where the declaration of the buyer's want or purpose is followed by the exhibition of an article which he sees and approves; and it may then become requisite to determine whether the selection is made by him or by the vendor, or more accurately, whether the thing is not selected by the vendor as fit for the end in view, and by the buyer as that which meets his requirements as regards appearance, price, and in all particulars save the essential requisite for which the vendor is responsible. In Jones *v.*

[1] Dayton *v.* Hooglund, 39 Ohio St. 671. [2] 32 Gratt. 518.

Bright,[1] the parties were introduced to each other by a mutual acquaintance, who said that the plaintiff wanted copper for sheathing a vessel, and that he had recommended the defendants as persons who might be depended on, to which the defendants answered that they would supply him well. The plaintiff's shipwright then chose from among the copper lying in the defendants' warehouse "such sheets as he thought fit," and they were subsequently delivered to the plaintiff, with an invoice describing them as "copper for the ship Isabella." The sheets were used in coppering the bottom of the vessel, which went on a voyage to Sierra Leone, and on her return the copper was found to be so much corroded as to be unfit for further service. The plaintiff then brought a suit for the breach of an implied warranty that the copper was fit for sheathing, and the jury found that it was unfit for that purpose in consequence of an intrinsic defect, and a verdict was entered for the plaintiff. Best, C. J., said, in discharging the rule for a new trial, that it had been asserted that the invoice, which was the only written evidence, did not sustain the declaration, and that the defendants ought not to be bound by a loose conversation. An invoice was frequently not sent till long after the contract was completed, and was altogether unlike a broker's note, which does set forth the contract; but if the invoice alone was considered, it would be seen that the copper was expressly for the ship Isabella. He did not, however, narrow his judgment to that single point, but thought, that where the whole passes in parol, all that passes may sometimes be taken as forming part of the contract, though not always, because matters talked of at the commencement of a bargain may be excluded by the language used at the termination. Whatever, therefore, formed part of the contract, as distinguished from the preliminary negotiation or exchange of views, might be taken into consideration. In a contract of this kind it was not necessary that the seller should say "I warrant." It was enough if he said that the article which he sold was fit for a particular purpose. Hence, when the person who introduced the parties to each other said that the plaintiff was in

[1] 5 Bing. 533.

want of copper for sheathing a vessel, and one of the defendants answered they would supply him well, and there was no further communication, that constituted a contract and amounted to a warranty. The case might, however, be securely rested on the broad ground that a man who sells an article thereby warrants that it is merchantable, that is, that it is fit for some purpose. If he sells it for a particular purpose, he thereby warrants it fit for that purpose.

The decisions touching the sale of horses turned on the same principle. A man who sells a horse generally warrants no more than that it is a horse. The buyer puts no questions, and perhaps gets the animal cheaper; but if he asks for a carriage-horse or for a horse fit to carry a female or a timid or infirm rider, he who knows the qualities of the animal and sells, undertakes, on every principle of honesty that it is fit for the purpose indicated. The selling upon an inquiry for a horse with particular qualities is an affirmation that it possesses those qualities. So it had been decided that the sale of beer for exportation to Gibraltar was an affirmation that it would bear the voyage. Whether or not an article was sold for a particular purpose was, indeed, a question of fact; but if sold for such a purpose, the sale was an undertaking for its fitness. The law then resolved itself into this, that if a man sells generally he undertakes that the article sold is fit for some purpose. If he sells it for a particular purpose he undertakes that it shall be fit for that particular purpose.

Such, as I have already stated, is undoubtedly the rule where the choice is left to the vendor, and he selects or offers a specific thing as that which will suit the purchaser, but not where the purchaser chooses for himself,[1] although the purpose for which he buys is known to the vendor.[2] This is the underlying question which, though sometimes treated as one of law, is, as the Chief Justice intimated in Grey *v.* Coxe, really one of fact, and as such necessarily embarrassing under a

[1] Park *v.* Morris Axe Co., 4 Lansing, 103; Murray *v.* Smith, 4 Daly, 277; Gerst *v.* Jones, 32 Gratt. 524; Beals *v.* Olmstead, 24 Vt. 114.

[2] Deming *v.* Foster, 42 N. H. 165; Hight *v.* Bacon, 126 Mass. 10; Dounce *v.* Dow, 64 N. Y. 411.

system which administers the law through the jury-box; but it may be said in this as in most other instances, that the expectations on either side are no part of the contract in the absence of a stipulation that they shall be fulfilled.

In Dounce *v.* Dow,[1] the defendant wanted soft and malleable iron to be used in making agricultural implements; but his purpose, though known to the plaintiff, was not set forth in the written order, which was simply for "XX pipe iron." The words "pipe iron" had reference to the furnace where the iron was smelted, while the brand was supposed to indicate the quality, which both parties believed to be good and suitable for such purposes. The plaintiff forwarded iron so produced and branded which was accepted without trial, but was subsequently discovered to be hard, brittle, and quite unfit for any use requiring malleability and toughness. The court held that the plaintiff had forwarded what the defendant had ordered, and although both parties were under the impression that it would answer the end in view, there was no such stipulation or undertaking. The contract, therefore, was performed, and the defendant must bear the loss arising from his mistaken belief that the iron which he sent for was the article which he required. Had the order been for "XX pipe iron, tough, soft, and fit for manufacturing farming implements," the case would have worn a different aspect; and it might then have been the vendor's duty, under Day *v.* Pool,[2] to forward iron which not only was of that particular brand, but would meet the other requirements of the purchaser.[3]

Agreeably to some of the American decisions all that can safely be inferred from the exhibition or forwarding of an article as suited to a particular purpose, is that the seller has good reason to believe that it will answer the end in view, and he is consequently not answerable for latent defects which he has no sufficient means of discovering unless he is the manufacturer as well as vendor, and therefore answerable for the workmanship and materials, and not merely for sound

[1] 64 N. Y. 411. [2] 52 N. Y. 416.

[3] The cases of Port Carbon Iron Co. *v.* Groves, 18 P. F. S. 149, and Mason *v.* Chappell, 15 Gratt. 572, are to the same effect.

judgment and due diligence in the selection or choice.[1] If, as the dicta in Jones *v.* Bright intimate, the warranty does not reach beyond these bounds in the case of a horse, it should be equally limited in that of other chattels; but the judgment in Randall *v.* Newson [2] goes further and to the extent of throwing the entire responsibility on the vendor.

The rule in Pennsylvania differs from that followed in England, and generally in the United States. In Lord *v.* Grow,[3] the plaintiff inquired whether the defendants, who were dealers in grain, had any good "seed spring wheat," and received an affirmative reply; and they gave him an order on their miller for three bushels of wheat, omitting the descriptive words. The plaintiff went with the order in his hand to the mill, and was shown wheat which the miller said was the spring wheat which the defendants had brought with them from the West. This he took to his farm and sowed; but it proved to be winter wheat, and the result was an entire failure of the crop. There were various kinds of wheat at the mill, and the judge left the case to the jury on the evidence, with a charge that if the defendants sold the wheat as "seed spring wheat," and it was not such in fact, they were answerable for the loss. The judgment was reversed on the ground that the sale was on inspection which negatived the inference that might otherwise have been drawn. The buyer saw the wheat and got what he saw; and there was consequently no implied warranty that it was properly described by the name given by the vendor.

In Kirk *v.* Nice,[4] one who had agreed to deliver fifty tons of bar iron, of Centre County metal, was held with still less reason not to be answerable on an implied undertaking that the article should be of good quality and merchantable, although the contract was executory, and the duty of selection devolved upon him; but this case is at variance with the general course of decision, and even with the narrow rule which prevails in Pennsylvania.

[1] Bragg *v.* Morrill, 49 Vt. 45; Mann *v.* Everton, 32 Ind. 355; Gaylord Man. Co. *v.* Allen, 53 N. Y. 515; Brown *v.* Sayles, 27 Vt. 227.

[2] L. R. 2 Q. B. Div. 102; *ante*. [3] 8 Wr. 88. [4] 2 Watts, 367.

What a sale under a particular name or denomination implies, is an undertaking not for quality but kind; and hence the purchaser cannot reject the bales or hogsheads because the contents are inferior or unsound, unless the deficiency is such that they cannot fairly be thrown into the market and disposed of as that for which they were bought.[1]

The purchaser of a specific parcel of Manila sugar must consequently accept and pay, if the commodity be what is customarily known in commerce as "Manila," although it proves when delivered to contain more impurities than are ordinarily found in the sugar which passes by that name.[2]

In Whitney *v.* Boardman,[3] a sale of "Cawnpore buffalo hides," was held on like grounds to impose no obligation as to quality, save that the goods should not have lost their distinctive character as hides; and the contract was held to be fulfilled, although the hides had not been properly cured or packed and were in fact unmerchantable.

In like manner, the obligation arising from a sale of mackerel as No. 1 and No. 2 implies that the kegs or barrels were duly examined by the inspector, and so marked and branded; and the vendor will not be answerable for a deterioration arising from the lapse of time.[4]

The better opinion nevertheless is, that when a commodity is sold by description, or as being of a particular kind or denomination, it must not only be such in species, but the quality or soundness must come up to the trade standard for which the purchaser stipulated, unless the circumstances justify the inference that he relied on his own judgment, and not on the representations made or account given by the vendor.[5]

The test is, Could the purchaser, after discovering the defect honestly dispose of the thing by the name or description

[1] Fraley *v.* Bispham, 10 Barr, 320; Lamb *v.* Crafts, 12 Met. 353; Mixer *v.* Coburn, 11 id. 559; Kirk *v.* Nice, 2 Watts, 367.

[2] Gossler *v.* Sugar Refining Co., 103 Mass. 331.

[3] 118 Mass. 242.

[4] Winsor *v.* Lombard, 18 Pick. 57.

[5] See Jones *v.* Just, L. R. 3 Q. B. 197; Gardiner *v.* Gray, 4 Camp. 144; Story on Contracts, § 834; Rodgers *v.* Niles, 11 Ohio St. 48.

under which it was sold? for if such a resale would render him answerable in an action for deceit, he obviously has not got what he bargained for and is entitled to compensation.[1]

In Gardiner *v.* Gray samples of silk which had been recently imported from France and was still on shipboard, were exhibited with a view to sale. The bargain was then made, and a sold note given in which the article in question was described as "waste silk." The sale took place in London, and on the delivery of the goods in Manchester they were found to be inferior to the sample and of a quality not salable under the denomination of "waste silk." Lord Ellenborough said that it was not a sale by sample, and that the sample had been shown merely to afford the buyer an opportunity to form a reasonable judgment of the commodity. He was nevertheless entitled to expect a salable article answering to the description in the contract. Where there was no opportunity for inspection, the maxim *caveat emptor* did not apply. The question was, Could a commodity of such a quality be brought into the market for sale as "waste silk?"

In Mody *v.* Gregson,[2] the defendants sold the plaintiffs 2500 pieces "gray shirtings" according to a sample that had previously been exhibited, each piece to weigh seven pounds. The plaintiffs accepted the goods, and shipped them to Calcutta, where it was discovered that the shirtings had been made to weigh seven pounds per piece by the addition of more than fifteen per cent of "china clay" in the process of manufacture, and were, in consequence, unmerchantable. The court held that the stipulation as to weight could not be fulfilled by substituting a foreign material for that which should properly have been employed. The defendants had no more right to make each piece weigh seven pounds by incorporating china clay with the fabric than they would have had to sprinkle the shirtings with china clay or deliver it separately in a bag.

The cases were reviewed by Willes, J., in delivering judgment; "The first state of circumstances already dealt with

[1] See Merriam *v.* Field, 24 Wis. 640; Cornelius *v.* Molloy, 7 Barr, 293, 297.

[2] L. R. 4 Ex. 49.

by decision is that of a sale by sample of goods in which, unknown to the seller and buyer, there was a defect, by reason of a fraudulent act of the producer of the goods done to increase the apparent weight, such defect not being discoverable by the sample, though it afterwards developed heat in the bulk so as to make it unmerchantable. That was the case in Parkinson *v.* Lee,[1] where there was a sale of hops by sample, which the grower had fraudulently watered in order to increase their weight. This fact was unknown to the seller, though the fraud was of a sort known to the trade; and of this both buyer and seller were aware. The sample being taken from the centre of the pocket and exposed to the air did not suffer from the damp, and it would not be discovered in the bulk until it was disclosed by the gradual process of heating. The hops were bought in January, and delivered on the 8th of July. By the end of July the effects of the heating were apparent in all the pockets; one of them was found to be unsalable a few days after delivery, and the rest between that time and the 18th of October following. The jury found that the bulk answered in fact to the sample at the time of the sale without fraud, and that the seller had then no knowledge of the latent defect of the commodity. They, however, found for the plaintiff under the direction of the judge, upon the count alleging an implied warranty of merchantableness. That direction, which certainly went a very long way when it is considered that, as the sample was sound and the bulk answered the sample at the time of the sale, the hops must have been good at that time, was overruled by the court, and a new trial granted upon the ground that "the buyer had bought the pockets upon samples fairly taken in the usual way, and the seller merely sold what he had before bought upon the same mode of examination." Laurence, J., said, "I know of no authority which makes the seller liable for a latent defect where there is no fraud, and no representation was made by him on the subject to induce the buyer to take the thing. In 1 Rolle Abr. 90, P. 3, it is said, that if a merchant sell cloth to another, knowing it to be badly fulled, an action on the case in nature

[1] 2 East, 314.

of deceit lies against him, because it is a warranty in law. But there is no authority stated to show that the same rule holds if the commodity sold have a latent defect, not known to the seller." So that in Parkinson *v.* Lee[1] (the authority most relied upon for the defendants), the sample was fair, the bulk purchased was ascertained and existing, it did at the time the bargain was made and the property passed in fact answer the description in the contract, and was the very thing bargained for; and the secret defect which afterward developed itself and made the bulk unmerchantable, was not known to the seller nor caused by any act of his.

Another class of cases is that of goods bought under a specified commercial description, either by sample, or even after inspection of bulk. In such cases it is an implied term, notwithstanding the sample or inspection, that the goods shall reasonably answer the specified description in its commercial sense. The sample in such cases is looked upon as a mere expression of the quality of the article, not of its essential character; and notwithstanding the bulk be fairly shown, or agree with the sample, yet if, from adulteration or other causes not appearing by the inspection or sample though not known to the seller, the bulk does not reasonably answer the description in a commercial sense, the seller is liable. Thus in Nichol *v.* Godts,[2] where the sale was of foreign refined rape-oil, warranted only equal to sample, the jury found that the oil tendered was the same as the sample, but that it was not "foreign refined rape-oil," but a mixture of foreign refined rape-oil and another oil. It was held by the Court of Exchequer that the sample must be considered as referring to quality only, and could not control the contract in respect of the essential character of the article to be delivered. As Pollock, C. B., said: "It is not exactly a warranty; but if a man contracts to buy a thing he ought not to have something else delivered to him."

The cases approved in Jones *v.* Just[3] by the Court of Queen's Bench "establish beyond question that neither inspection of bulk nor use of sample absolutely excludes an inquiry whether

[1] 2 East, 314. [2] 10 Ex. 191. [3] L. R. 3 Q. B. 197.

the thing supplied was otherwise in accordance with the contract, and that if the sellers in this case had agreed to deliver merchantable gray shirting according to a sample, and not disclosing that it was unmerchantable by reason of the mixture of china clay, they would have been liable. The question, therefore, is whether the facts of the case showed that the contract was for merchantable gray shirting; and this must depend upon the fair inference to be drawn from the contract itself, and the circumstances under which it was made, so far as they are relevant to explain it. The goods were not specified, nor ascertained, nor inspected. They were bought by a sample which did not disclose any defect. That sample was made by the seller to represent the article, and, as we must assume against the seller, to represent it fairly to the buyer. It did, in fact, represent to the buyer a merchantable article. The article itself was stipulated for in terms 'each piece to be of seven pounds weight,' which if properly complied with, and no foreign material introduced, would have insured a merchantable article. The superadded stipulation for each piece to weigh seven pounds was descriptive of the goods, and asserted their essential character for commercial purposes. Agreement with the sample as to quality would not satisfy this term of the contract. If the pieces delivered had weighed but six pounds, though they had agreed with the sample, the contract would have been broken. It was the feigned and colorable performance, not real fulfilment of the stipulation as to weight, that caused the goods to be unmerchantable."

In this instance, as in Nichol *v.* Godts, the defect arose from adulteration, and might therefore justly be regarded as one of kind; but the principle is the same where a sale is made by description in the ordinary course of trade and the goods are unmerchantable from an inherent fault or a supervening decay or deterioration.

In Jones *v.* Just,[1] the defendant sold certain bales described in the sold note as "Manila hemp" (and specifically marked and numbered), "to arrive per Richard Cobden," which were

[1] L. R. 3 Q. B. 197.

delivered to the purchaser, but proved when opened and examined, to have been so much damaged by salt water as to be unmerchantable, although the contents had not lost the character of hemp. Blackburn, J., left two questions to the jury: Was the article in fact Manila hemp? secondly, Was it merchantable? They found for the purchaser, and the court sustained the verdict, although the seller had never seen the goods (which were still at sea when sold), and was ignorant of their true condition.

It results from these decisions that where specific goods are sold as being of a particular kind, they must not only answer the description, but must also be merchantable and salable under that description.[1] In the words of Lord Ellenborough, in Gardiner *v.* Gray, "without any particular warranty there is an implied trust in every such contract which it is incumbent on the seller to fulfil."[2] Such confessedly is the rule with regard to contracts to make or furnish, and this may be fulfilled by the delivery of anything answering to the terms prescribed;[3] and it implies, although for a different reason, where the agreement is two-fold, — for a specific thing, and that it shall be of a certain kind.

It is generally conceded, as the cases cited imply, that in considering whether the thing delivered is what the vendor agreed to sell, regard must be had to the mercantile rather than the literal meaning of the terms employed, and that if it would be regarded as the same among merchants and for the purposes of trade, it matters not how widely it may differ in point of fact.[4] If the article be commercially, it need not be chemically or botanically pure, and may on the contrary contain ingredients which though foreign in one sense do not affect its identity for the purposes of sale. The vendee was accordingly held answerable, in Jennings *v.* Gratz,[5]

[1] McClung *v.* Kelly, 21 Ia. 508.

[2] Jones *v.* Just, L. R. 3 Q. B. 197; Mody *v.* Gregson, L. R. 4 Ex. 49, 52; Laing *v.* Fidgeon, 4 Camp. 169; 6 Taunt. 108.

[3] Mann *v.* Everton, 32 Ind. 355; Gaylord Man. Co. *v.* Allen, 53 N. Y. 515; Gerst *v.* Jones, 32 Gratt. 524.

[4] Swett *v.* Shumway, 102 Mass. 365.

[5] 3 Rawle, 168.

for the price of tea which had been sold as Young Hyson, although it was adulterated with the leaves of plants which could not properly be rated as teas. The court said: "The teas were proved to be adulterated with certain leaves, which, it is believed, do not belong to the tea family. But it was also shown, that no teas of the same denomination are entirely free from adulteration by admixture of these same leaves, and if a small degree of adulteration were permitted to affect the question of specific character, there would seldom be a binding sale. Wines are constantly adulterated with brandy; in fact, it is in some degree a constituent part of the finest Madeira, and brandy itself passes in the market, although notoriously adulterated with alcohol in a cheaper form. Drugs, chemicals, paints, dye-stuffs, and a countless number of other commodities, are constantly purchased by dealers or consumers with full knowledge that they are not entirely free from admixture. The pigment called white lead is frequently purchased by house-painters when they are apprised that it contains a portion of Spanish whiting, which is not supposed to affect the denomination of the article, but its quality and price." Adulteration may, however, be carried so far as to destroy the distinctive character of the thing altogether, and in doubtful cases there is perhaps no practical test but that of its being merchantable under the denomination affixed to it by the seller.

If the meaning of the descriptive words is ambiguous, witnesses may be called to prove in what sense the term or phrase is used and understood by persons conversant with the trade or business.[1] In the case first cited, Scott & Co.'s mess pork was shown by such means to signify pork cured and packed by Scott & Co., as distinguished from pork coming from their warehouse, or sold and consigned by them; while in the second, the plaintiff was allowed to prove that the word "bale" had a particular signification in the gambier trade, and meant a compressed package weighing about two hundred

[1] Powell *v.* Horton, 2 Bing. N. C. 668; Gorrissen *v.* Perrin, 2 C. B. N. S. 681, 700; Smith *v.* Wilson, 3 B. & Ad. 728; Pike *v.* Fay, 101 Mass. 134; Swett *v.* Shumway, 102 Mass. 365.

weight. The doctrine was carried still further in Smith *v.* Wilson, by the admission of evidence that, agreeably to the usage of the district where the sale took place, one thousand rabbits meant twelve hundred rabbits.

The inquiry when the deterioration in quality or fitness is such that the commodity can no longer be regarded as the same in kind, is one that cannot easily be answered, because kind is but a name for an assemblage of qualities which are usually found together and constitute a species. The question arose in Barr *v.* Gibson,[1] on a deed poll, by which the defendant, in consideration of £4,200, "granted, bargained, sold, and set over to the plaintiff, all that ship called the Sarah, of Newcastle." The deed was set forth in the declaration, and it was averred that at the time when the same was executed and the consideration paid, the ship was wholly lost and destroyed, and could not, therefore, be sold or transferred to the plaintiff as the defendant had covenanted. It appeared from the evidence given at the trial, under a traverse of this averment, that the ship was at the time of the sealing and delivery hopelessly stranded in the Gulf of St. Lawrence, without the knowledge of either party, and could not be got off or repaired under the existing circumstances; but that she was, save in this regard, still in existence as a ship and might, had the requisite means been within reach and the season of the year different, have been floated and rendered seaworthy. Pattison, J., left it to the jury to say whether the vessel was, at the time of the sale, a ship or a mere bundle of timbers. They found that she was not a ship; whereupon a verdict was entered for the plaintiff with leave to move for a nonsuit. Such a motion having been made and argued before in the court in banc, Parke, B., said, in delivering judgment, that no warranty is implied in the bargain and sale of an existing chattel, but the bargain and sale of a chattel as being of a particular description does imply a contract that the article sold is of that description. Hence the sale of a ship implies a contract that the subject exists in the character of a ship, which will be broken if it has been physically destroyed, or

[1] 3 M. & W. 390.

has ceased to answer to the designation of a ship; but if it still bears that character there is no breach of the contract, although the ship be damaged, unseaworthy, or incapable of being beneficially employed. The question depended upon the condition of the vessel, and not on the collateral circumstances. If it did not, it might happen that the same identical thing in the same state of structure, would or would not be a ship, according to the facilities and conveniences that existed at the place and time. The question whether a vessel retained the character of a ship might sometimes be attended with much difficulty, but in the case in hand the court was clearly of opinion that the ship was capable of being transferred as such, though she might be totally lost within the meaning of a policy of insurance, where the contract was as much broken, if the thing was lost for beneficial purposes, as if it was physically destroyed. The contract under consideration was one of sale, and the subject was not less a ship because from the force of circumstances it was incapable of being usefully employed. It followed that the verdict which had been entered for the buyer, must be set aside.

This judgment is not easily reconcilable with the doctrine laid down in Gardiner *v.* Gray and applied in Jones *v.* Just.[1] If the designation of the subject-matter of a sale as "waste-silk" implies an undertaking that the article exists in a condition to be merchantable under that designation, why is not such an undertaking equally implied when the thing sold is designated as a ship; that is, a three-masted vessel built for the purpose of navigation, and capable of being so used? Or if hemp ceases to exist as such when so much damaged by salt-water as to be unmerchantable as hemp, why does not a ship equally cease to exist when stranded on a reef from which she cannot be extricated; or not without a cost that would exceed her value when afloat? True, the loss is due in one case to the condition, in the other to the situation of the thing; but this would be equally true of a vessel sunk a hundred fathoms deep in the middle of the sea. That cannot be said to be merchantable which, if the truth were known, no

[1] L. R. 3 Q. B. 197; *ante.*

one would think of offering under its appropriate denomination, and no one would agree to buy.

The effect of a failure to examine, in precluding complaint that the goods do not answer to the name under which they were purchased, is a point about which the authorities do not agree. It is generally conceded that such an omission on the buyer's part will not exonerate the seller when there is an entire difference of kind, and the thing cannot be disposed of as that for which it was sold.[1] A man who has bought beans cannot be compelled to accept and pay for peas, because he neglected to open and inspect the sack. If such be the rule, it should apply when the commodity is so mixed or adulterated that, taken as a whole, it is not what it was called by the vendor. Such is the view taken by the English courts, and in numerous instances in the United States.[2]

The inclination of the American authorities, nevertheless, is that unsoundness or an inferiority of quality however great, will not authorize a rejection of the contract or a demand for compensation, unless an examination is impracticable, and that when the goods are or might be seen the purchaser will be presumed to take the risk, although they fall below the commercial standard and cannot be disposed of as that for which they were sold.[3]

Such a modification of the rule is not easily reconcilable with any consistent or established principle, because if a sale by description, or under a specific name or denomination, is an implied undertaking that the goods shall correspond, the purchaser is entitled to rely on the assurance given by the vendor and need not look further or exercise his own judgment, and should certainly not be regarded as in default in not making an examination when from the circumstances, or nature of the defect, it would lead to no good result.

Whether the defect be latent and not discoverable by in-

[1] Mody *v.* Gregson, L. R. 4 Ex. 49; *ante.*

[2] See Nichol *v.* Godts, 10 Ex. 191; Wieler *v.* Schilizzi, 17 C. B. 619; Hawkins *v.* Pemberton, 51 N. Y. 198; Reggio *v.* Braggiotti, 7 Cush. 166; Wolcott *v.* Mount, 36 N. J. L. 262, 267; 38 id. 496.

[3] Barnard *v.* Kellogg, 10 Wallace, 383.

spection, or an inspection is impracticable, the effect is the same, and the vendor should equally be liable on an implied undertaking that the goods are merchantable under the name or description by which they are sold.[1] It is of little consequence that the hidden fault might have been ascertained, if it could not be ascertained by ordinary means, or without a delay and expense that would be incompatible with the effectual transaction of business. To require the purchaser to proceed to an examination under such circumstances, is to require him to do that which is impracticable, and may therefore be regarded as impossible relatively to the end which both parties seek to attain.[2]

The point has been adjudged in several instances, and the argument applies, for a stronger reason, when the defect is occasioned or concealed by a trick or artifice which an honest man would be slow to suspect, and against which caution may not be a sufficient guard.[3]

The preponderance of the American authority, notwithstanding, is that sales by description follow the general rule, that the buyer takes the risk, as regards quality and soundness, wherever an examination is or might be made, although it would not reveal the fault or answer any useful purpose, without the aid of analysis or a resort to means that are foreign to the usual course of business.[4]

The law was so held in Hyatt *v.* Boyle, although tobacco which had been sold in kegs as "Parkins' Brand" proved,

1 Rodgers *v.* Niles, 11 Ohio St. 48; Rose *v.* Beatie, 2 N. & McC. 539; Merriam *v.* Field, 24 Wis. 640; 29 id. 592; 39 id. 578; Lewis *v.* Rountree, 78 N. C. 325; Cornelius *v.* Molloy, 7 Barr, 293, 297. See Waring *v.* Mason, 9 Wend. 18; 18 id. 425; Dayton *v.* Hooglund, 39 Ohio St. 671.

2 Mody *v.* Gregson, L. R. 4 Ex. 49, 54; Rodgers *v.* Niles, 11 Ohio St. 48; Schuchardt *v.* Aliens, 1 Wallace, 359; Lewis *v.* Rountree, 78 N. C. 325.

3 See Heilbutt *v.* Hickson, L. R. 7 C. P. 438; Josling *v.* Kingsford, 13 C. B. N. S. 447; Mody *v.* Gregson, L. R. 4 Ex. 49; Henshaw *v.* Robbins, 9 Met. 83; Boorman *v.* Jenkins, 12 Wend. 566, 575.

4 Hyatt *v.* Boyle, 5 Gill & J. 110; Hight *v.* Bacon, 126 Mass. 10; Salisbury *v.* Stainer, 19 Wend. 159; Dickinson *v.* Gay, 7 Allen, 29; Barnard *v.* Kellogg, 10 Wallace, 383.

when opened, to be unfit for use; and the decisions in Pennsylvania are to the same effect.[1]

Agreeably to the view taken in the case last cited, a buyer who neglects to examine can have no redress, although the commodity is so impure or adulterated that the foreign ingredients impair the distinctive character of the whole and render it unmerchantable. Wool was shipped in bales from Buenos Ayres to a commission merchant in Boston, who made advances to the shippers, and placed the bales in the hands of a broker, with instructions not to sell unless the purchaser saw and examined for himself. The broker sent samples to the plaintiffs, who wrote offering to buy at fifty cents per pound if equal to the samples, and were informed in reply that their offer was accepted, if they would examine the wool on the succeeding Monday and decide whether they would take it. The plaintiffs called at the broker's office, were shown four bales, and told that they might open and examine the others if they saw fit. They declined to do so, and bought the entire lot without further inquiry. The bales were delivered, and remained unopened until some months afterwards, when it was discovered that they had been fraudulently packed with rotten and damaged wool and "tags" enveloped in fleeces of good quality.

The case was tried without a jury, and the court below found that under a usage common to New York and Boston, the vendor of wool in bales warrants that it has not been fraudulently packed, and that although an examination of the contents was possible, it would have been attended with so much labor and delay as to be in the business sense of the term impossible. It was held to follow that, although the sale was not by sample, and the vendor was innocent of the fraud, he was still answerable for the loss which had been sustained by the purchaser.

The judgment was reversed by the Supreme Court of the United States on the ground that whenever the buyer can examine he must do so or take the risk, and that usage cannot

[1] Fraley *v.* Bispham, 10 Barr, 320; Carson *v.* Baillie, 7 Harris, 375; Boyd *v.* Wilson, 2 Norris, 319; Barnard *v.* Kellogg, 10 Wallace, 383.

operate to vary a contract or introduce new terms, although it may help to explain what is already there. "No principle of the common law," said Davis, J., "has been better established or more often affirmed, both in this country and in England, than that in sales of personal property, in the absence of express warranty, where the buyer has an opportunity to inspect the commodity, and the seller is guilty of no fraud, and is neither the manufacturer nor grower of the article he sells, the maxim of *caveat emptor* applies. Such a rule, requiring the purchaser to take care of his own interests, has been found best adapted to the wants of trade in the business transactions of life. And there is no hardship in it, because if the purchaser distrusts his judgment he can require of the seller a warranty that the quality or condition of the goods he desires to buy corresponds with the sample exhibited. If he is satisfied without a warranty, and can inspect and declines to do it, he takes upon himself the risk that the article is merchantable. And he cannot relieve himself and charge the seller, on the ground that the examination will occupy time and is attended with labor and inconvenience. If it is practicable, no matter how inconvenient, the rule applies."

This judgment seems to have taken for granted, what is by no means clear, that it was practicable to have examined the bales, contrary to the finding of the court below, and that delay, cost, and inconvenience may not amount to a moral impossibility where the physical obstacles might readily be overcome. Such an inference is at variance with the obvious truth, — that when the transaction is pecuniary, and the object gain, the means must be consistent with the end, and the parties cannot reasonably be required to incur an expense that will absorb the profits which they anticipated. That which cannot be effected save at a greater cost than it is worth, is therefore, in cases of this description, impracticable; and impracticable is legally as well as to the eye of a business man, synonymous with impossible, because the law will not require an essay that will result in loss even if it succeeds. It is on this ground that a stranded vessel, which cannot be got off without an outlay that would exceed her value when afloat, is considered as totally lost.[1] "In matters of business," said Maule, B., in Moss *v.* Smith,[2] "a thing is regarded as impossible when it is impracticable, and impracticable when it can only be done at an excessive or unreasonable cost. A man may be said to have lost a shilling when he has dropped it into deep water, though it might be possible by some very expensive contrivance to recover it."

A sale of bales or packages which cannot be effectually examined without opening them, and "tearing them to pieces," is enumerated in Story on Contracts as governed by the rule which prevails when the goods are still at sea, or stowed away in the hold of a vessel; and the purchaser is equally entitled in both cases that they shall be merchantable under the description given by the vendor.[3]

The reasons given in Barnard *v.* Kellogg,[4] tend to the conclusion that a purchaser who fails to examine will be bound, although bales of hay are sold as cotton, or a cask of cider as claret. A difference of kind is not less real because it is partial, and some of the mass corresponds with the description given by the seller. Had the bales which were offered as wool contained nothing but tags, the court would presumably have held that the contract failed; and yet an adulteration which renders the whole impure and unmerchantable is the same in principle. In Josling *v.* Kingsford,[5] proof that a commodity sold as oxalic acid contained ten per cent of sulphate of magnesia, was held to give the purchaser as much right to redress as if the difference of kind had been entire.

A man who is misled, as was the buyer in Barnard *v.* Kellogg, may moreover be entitled to damages on another ground. There can be little doubt that the consignors knew or had notice that the cotton was fraudulently packed, and the conduct of the consignees was hardly consistent with good faith.

[1] Moss *v.* Smith, 9 C. B. 94; Peele *v.* Merchants' Ins. Co., 3 Mason, 27; Brig Sarah Ann, 2 Sumner, 206; 2 Am. Leading Cases, 5 ed. 703.

[2] 9 C. B. 94.

[3] See Rodgers *v.* Niles, 11 Ohio St. 48; Lewis *v.* Rountree, 78 N. C. 325.

[4] 10 Wallace, 383.

[5] 13 C. B. N. S. 447.

Had they communicated the instructions under which they were acting to the purchaser, he would have been put on his guard, and proceeded to an examination that would have disclosed the truth. An officious declaration that the goods are at hand and may be examined, if it is thought desirable, is a ready means of allaying distrust and preventing the inquiry which it is seemingly intended to promote.

The just inference seems to be that while the law does not imply a warranty against latent faults, and the buyer is no more entitled to indemnity for defects which are not discoverable than for those which are, yet when a failure to examine is relied on as excluding an undertaking that would otherwise arise from the contract read as a whole, or in the light of the circumstances, it may be a sufficient reply that the defect was not visible and could not be ascertained by examination in the ordinary course of business. Such was the ground taken in Mody *v.* Gregson;[1] and it obviates the necessity for inquiring whether the purchaser could and ought to have chosen for himself instead of relying on the assurance given by the vendor.

Whatever the law may be under other circumstances, it seems to be generally conceded on both sides of the Atlantic that where the sale is of a specific thing, as distinguished from the sale of a thing specifically described, the buyer must accept and pay although the commodity is unmerchantable and its defects could not be detected by ordinary means;[2] and the rule applies even where as in the case of provisions, the commodity can be put only to one use, and must be thrown on the dunghill if it proves unsound.[3]

[1] L. R. 4 Ex. 49.

[2] Rinschler *v.* Jeliffe, 9 Daly, 469; Hyatt *v.* Boyle, 5 Gill & J. 110; Hart *v.* Wright, 17 Wend. 267, 275; Parkinson *v.* Lee, 2 East, 314; Emmerton *v.* Matthews, 7 H. & N. 586; Barr *v.* Gibson, 3 M. & W. 390; Jones *v.* Just, L. R. 3 Q. B. 197, 202.

[3] Emmerton *v.* Matthews, 7 H. & N. 586; Ryder *v.* Neitge, 21 Minn. 70; Boyd *v.* Wilson, 2 Norris, 319.

CHAPTER XX.

SALE BY SAMPLE.

Inference from the Exhibition of a Sample. — Subsequent Inspection of the Goods by the Vendee. — Effect of a Written Memorandum. — Kind and Quality. — Rule in Pennsylvania.

THE exhibition of a sample at or before the sale amounts, when coupled with words or circumstances which indicate that it was so intended and understood, to a warranty or assurance that it was fairly taken, and that the goods will when delivered correspond in every material particular, including both quality and kind.[1] The case is therefore analogous to that of a sale of a commodity answering a certain description, and the goods may be rejected and a recovery had in damages if the undertaking be not fulfilled or accepted, and the default compensated by a corresponding deduction from the price, or through a cross-action if the defect be not discovered until after the payment has been made.[2]

Accordingly, when cotton is guaranteed in writing as about equal to samples, and the samples are "long staple Salem,"

[1] Pope *v.* Allis, 115 U. S. 363, 372.

[2] Mody *v.* Gregson, L. R. 4 Ex. 49; Williams *v.* Spofford, 8 Pick. 250; Schuchardt *v.* Allens, 1 Wallace, 359; Heyworth *v.* Hutchinson, L. R. 2 Q. B. 447; Azemar *v.* Cassella, L. R. 2 C. P. 431; Wells *v.* Hopkins, 5 M. & W. 7; Russell *v.* Nicolopulo, 8 C. B. N. S. 362; Pope *v.* Allis, 115 U. S. 363, 372; Bagley *v.* Cleveland, 21 Federal Rep. 159, 165; Dayton *v.* Hooglund, 39 Ohio, 671; Bradford *v.* Manly, 13 Mass. 139; Dickinson *v.* Gay, 7 Allen, 29; Hubbard *v.* George, 49 Ill. 275; Webster *v.* Granger, 78 id. 230; Gunther *v.* Atwell, 19 Md. 157; Osborn *v.* Gantz, 60 N. Y. 540; Waring *v.* Mason, 18 Wend. 425; Oneida Mfg. Co. *v.* Lawrence, 4 Cow. 440; Dailey *v.* Green, 3 Harris, 118, 125; Maute *v.* Gross, 6 P. F. S. 250; West Republic Mining Co. *v.* Jones, 15 Weekly Notes of Cases, 491.

the cotton is as effectually guaranteed to be "long staple Salem," as if those words were inserted in the contract. The undertaking here was for kind, but may equally well be for quality; and hence when the samples are "fine, white cotton," and the bulk proves to be damaged and unmerchantable, the vendor will be answerable for the resulting loss.[1]

The bare fact that a sample is shown by one party and is relied on by the other is not proof or necessarily evidence of a warranty of its genuineness, or that the goods are the same, and all that it implies is a representation that the bulk is like in kind and quality, which may render the seller liable on the ground of fraud, but not if he is acting in good faith and believes the sample to be accurate.[2]

The question is nevertheless one of intention, depending on what is done as well as on what is said or written, and slight circumstances may turn the scale. Conceding that the exhibition of a sample is *prima facie* a representation, still like other representations it will operate as a promise, if so made and understood. The stipulation is not, as seems to have been supposed in Hargous *v.* Stone,[3] a warranty, but is an undertaking for identity, analogous to that which arises when goods are sold as answering to a description or being of a certain kind.[4] When a specimen is shown as such, and the bargain concluded without more, the purchaser is seemingly as much entitled to say that what he bought and the seller agreed to deliver was a commodity having the qualities of the sample, as if he had seen and approved the bulk and a different article were substituted or tendered.[5] On the other hand, an examination of the goods subsequently to the exhibition of the sample may be evidence that the purchaser relied on his own judgment, and agreed to take them as they were, although it may still be for the jury to consider whether he trusted to

[1] Azemar *v.* Cassella, L. R. 2 C. P. 431; see Waring *v.* Mason, 18 Wend. 425.

[2] Waring *v.* Mason, 18 Wend. 425, 438; Hargous *v.* Stone, 1 Selden, 73, 85; Beirne *v.* Dord, id. 95; Ames *v.* Jones, 77 N. Y. 614.

[3] 1 Selden, 73, 87.

[4] Dailey *v.* Green, 3 Harris, 118, 125.

[5] Schuchardt *v.* Allens, 1 Wallace, 359; Boorman *v.* Jenkins, 12 Wend. 566.

the sample and was misled.[1] In Waring *v.* Mason[2] the offer was of cotton packed in bales. The plaintiffs said that they would buy if it was equal to the sample exhibited by the broker, and requested him to procure and bring fresh samples, which was done and the purchase made. The court held that the evidence was properly left to the jury, and sustained a finding that the sale was by sample and the vendor liable for the inferiority of the bales, which had been fraudulently packed and did not correspond with the parcel shown.

The doctrine is accurately stated in Gunther *v.* Atwell[3] in accordance with the view taken many years since in the American edition of Smith's Leading Cases. "Strictly speaking, a contract of sale by sample is not a warranty of quality, but an agreement of the seller to deliver, and of the buyer to accept goods of the same kind and quality as the sample. The identity of the goods sold in kind, condition, and quality with that of the sample is of the essence of the contract, and where the goods sold do not correspond with the sample, there would seem to be no performance of the contract.[4] The rule recognized in these cases as governing sales by sample, seems to be founded on or to be a simple application of the principle, that to fulfil a contract of sale the seller must deliver that which he has agreed to sell, and that if he does not, the purchaser may rescind the contract, or receive the goods and claim a deduction for their relative inferiority in value. In order that this principle may be applied, it is necessary in making the sale that the sample should be so used between the buyer and seller as to express or become a part of the contract, or in other words, that the sample should amount to and take the place of an express averment by the seller of the condition and quality of the goods sold, upon which the buyer relies in making the purchase. The mere exhibition of a

[1] Borrekins *v.* Bevan, 3 Rawle, 23, 38; Jones *v.* Wasson, 59 Tenn. 211.

[2] 9 Wend. 20; 18 id. 425.

[3] 19 Md. 157, 169.

[4] Young *v.* Cole, 3 Bing. N. C. 724; Mondel *v.* Steel, 8 M. & W. 858, 871; Williams *v.* Spofford, 8 Pick. 250; Bradford *v.* Manly, 13 Mass. 139; Beirne *v.* Dord, 1 Selden, 93; Hargous *v.* Stone, ib. 73; Waring *v.* Mason, 18 Wend. 425; 1 Sm. L. C. 5 Am. ed. 256, 257, 258.

sample by the seller and examination of it by the buyer, does not amount to such an averment, unless from all the facts or circumstances in the case, it can be presumed that an understanding is arrived at between the parties that the bulk is to correspond with the sample.[1] The reasonable deduction from the cases is, that to effect a sale by sample so as to bind the seller for a correspondence in bulk, it must be shown that the seller adopts the sample as his own description of the bulk, and that the buyer concludes the purchase upon the faith and credit of the description so given. Upon this theory, it is obvious that in making sales samples may be exhibited and examined without implying as a part of the contract of sale any obligation that the bulk shall correspond with the sample."

If the goods correspond with the sample the obligation is fulfilled, and the vendor will not ordinarily be answerable for any defect that is common to both, unless there is an express warranty, or such a difference of kind that the goods do not answer to the name or denomination under which they were sold;[2] and the rule was applied in Parkinson *v.* Lee, although the hops which were the subject-matter had been fraudulently watered by the prior vendor to increase the weight, and the defect which was latent at the time and would have rendered the hops unmerchantable if known, did not become perceptible until after they had been accepted by the buyer.[3]

The authorities are not less clear that, as the exhibition of a sample is designed to aid the buyer and enable him to form as correct a judgment as if he had seen the goods, so it will not preclude any course that would have been open had the bulk been exhibited instead of the sample; and he may consequently require that the commodity shall not only correspond with the sample, but be of the kind or description as

[1] Beirne *v.* Dord, 1 Selden, 93; Hargous *v.* Stone, id. 73; Waring *v.* Mason, 18 Wend. 425, 434.

[2] Parkinson *v.* Lee, 2 East, 315; Sands *v.* Taylor, 5 Johns. 395; Dickinson *v.* Gay, 7 Allen, 29; Mody *v.* Gregson, L. R. 4 Ex. 49; Dickson *v.* Zizinia, 10 C. B. 602.

[3] *Ante.*

and for which it was sold, and be free from any latent fault that will render it unsalable by that name or denomination in the ordinary course of business.[1] In other words, while the contract will be broken if the bulk differs from the sample, its conformity does not necessarily prove that the contract has been performed.[2]

The principle was stated by Lord Ellenborough in Gardiner *v.* Gray,[3] and has been applied in numerous instances. In Josling *v.* Kingsford,[4] an article which had been sold by sample as oxalic acid proved to be unmerchantable under that name in consequence of being adulterated to the extent of ten per cent with sulphate of magnesia, and the vendor was held answerable, although he had declined to warrant the strength of the acid, and the purchaser not only examined the sample but the bulk, and found both the same. So in Nichol *v.* Godts[5] the rejection of rape oil as not answering to the denomination of "foreign refined," under which it had been sold, was approved by the court although it had been warranted in writing as only equal to samples with which the bulk agreed. Baron Parke told the jury that the undertaking implied in a sale by sample related solely to quality, and was therefore entirely consistent with the existence of a collateral stipulation that the goods should be of a certain kind; and this interpretation was approved by the court in banc. It would apparently be more accurate to say that although a sale by sample is a contract that the commodity is the same in kind and properties, it may also be a contract that both bulk and sample are such as they were described as being or sold for. What the learned judge no doubt intended is, that whether the goods are shown or merely a sample, they must answer to the name or description given by the vendor, and if they differ in any material particular, the contract will be as completely broken as though no part were the same. A pur-

[1] Meyer *v.* Everth, 4 Camp. 22; Powell *v.* Horton, 2 Bing. N. C. 668; Bannerman *v.* White, 10 C. B. N. S. 844; Josling *v.* Kingsford, 13 id. 447; Nichol *v.* Godts, 10 Ex. 191; Schuchardt *v.* Allens, 1 Wallace, 359.

[2] Mody *v.* Gregson, L. R. 4 Ex. 49.

[3] 4 Camp. 144; *ante*.

[4] 13 C. B. N. S. 447.

[5] 10 Ex. 191.

chaser of oxalic acid is not bound to accept sulphate of magnesia because he saw and approved a sample; and the principle applies when the character of the mass is altered by an admixture or adulteration.

It has been decided in some instances that where there is a bill of sale or other written memorandum of the contract, it is the only test of what the vendor agrees to deliver and the purchaser to receive, and it is immaterial that the goods differ from a sample which was exhibited at or before the conclusion of the sale. The writing is no doubt conclusive as regards all that it sets forth or specifies, but does not necessarily preclude inquiry as to points that lie beyond its sphere.[1] A memorandum that A has sold and B purchased a hundred bales of hemp, leaves the question whether the sale is of specific hemp or for the delivery of any hemp answering to the terms employed, as much open as if the contract were oral, and proof that the purchaser examined a sample is seemingly not less admissible than proof that he examined the bulk.

To preclude oral and extrinsic evidence the writing should be so full and specific as to warrant the inference that it is meant to cover the entire ground, which cannot ordinarily be predicated of an informal instrument like a sold note or bill of parcels.[2] Moreover, if the undertaking implied in a sale by sample be, as Parke, B., declared in Nichol *v.* Godts,[3] for quality, it may well be legitimately used to supplement a writing which speaks only of kind.

In Boorman *v.* Jenkins[4] the buyer was allowed to recover on proof of a usage of trade that when a sample is exhibited the bulk must correspond, although the sale was not stated to be by sample in the broker's note; and the same point may be found in Syers *v.* Jonas.[5]

It has also been held that where the goods are examined before the completion of the contract, or the buyer has an opportunity for inspection and declines, the presumption that

[1] Bradford *v.* Manly, 13 Mass. 139; Hogins *v.* Plympton, 11 Peck. 99; Pike *v.* Fay, 101 Mass. 134.

[2] Atwater *v.* Clancy, 107 Mass. 369.

[3] 10 Ex. 191.

[4] 12 Wend. 566.

[5] 2 Ex. 111.

the purchase is made in reliance on the sample is repelled;[1] and the doctrine was applied although the bales in question had been fraudulently packed, and the trick could not be detected without ripping them open and examining the contents. The inquiry is nevertheless one of fact: Does the examination indicate that the buyer relied on his eyes and not on the sample; or simply that he used them as a measure of precaution and without waiving his right to hold the seller answerable for hidden or undiscovered defects? and if the latter is the true interpretation he will be as much entitled to enforce the implied warranty for conformity, as if it were express.[2]

Agreeably to the view taken in New York, and as it seems in Pennsylvania, the exhibition of a specimen is not evidence of an undertaking that the goods correspond, if they are accessible and might be examined, and it will make no difference that the defect is latent and could not be discovered without the use of means that would involve delay and expense, or would as in the case of preserved vegetables or fruits, deform the cases or packages and render the contents unmerchantable.[3]

The maxim *caveat emptor* is, according to these decisions, as applicable as though the sample were not shown, and if an examination is from distance or other cause impracticable when the contract is made, it must take place on delivery and before acceptance, or the default will be waived,[4] and the purchaser must pay the entire contract price; or according to Shields *v.* Pettee, the market rate although amounting to a larger sum. The commercial, like the common law, is as we have seen the other way and that the acceptance of something less or different is not, in the absence of an agreement to that effect, a waiver or satisfaction of the right to

[1] Salisbury *v.* Stainer, 19 Wend. 159; Barnard *v.* Kellogg, 10 Wallace, 383.

[2] Williams *v.* Spofford, 8 Pick. 250.

[3] Hargous *v.* Stone, 1 Selden, 73; Beirne *v.* Dord, id. 95; Boyd *v.* Wilson, 2 Norris, 319.

[4] Hargous *v.* Stone, 1 Selden, 73, 92.

indemnity for a failure to deliver the thing stipulated for or prescribed.[1]

The rule in Pennsylvania deviates still more widely from the general course of decision, and would seem to be peculiar to that State. In Boyd *v.* Wilson[2] a broker who had been commissioned to sell eight hundred and fifty cases of preserved corn, called on the defendants and exhibited a can as a sample. They asked for two more cans for examination, which were furnished and proved to be good, sweet, and sound in every respect. The defendants then made an offer for the entire lot, which was accepted and the goods delivered. It was subsequently discovered that a large number of the cans were unlike the sample, sour, greasy and unfit for food. The defendants requested the sellers to take back so many of the cans as they had not sold, and make a deduction for the residue. This proposition was declined, and a suit brought for the purchase-money. Here both acts and language pointed to a single inference that what the defendants agreed to buy was corn equal to the sample, and that they might consequently return the cans and claim damages for the breach of contract. The Supreme Court, nevertheless, held that the only contract arising under such circumstances is, that the goods shall be the same in kind and simply merchantable. If they are salable the contract is fulfilled, and their inferiority to the sample is not a ground of recovery or defence.

The buyer was in like manner held answerable in Selser *v.* Roberts,[3] although the boxes which he opened contained sound and undamaged peaches, and many of those delivered were mouldy and unsound. A sale by sample was said to be simply a guaranty of kind, which did not include quality unless the difference was so great as materially to affect the kind. The court below had erred in instructing the jury that although the goods might be "very inferior in quality to the sample," they must yet be "merchantable," that is, "sound goods, not damaged or spoiled, and fit for the use for which they are generally intended."

It is thus established that provisions are merchantable under

[1] 2 Sandf. 262. [2] 2 Norris, 319. [3] 105 Pa. 242.

the commercial law of Pennsylvania, although they are unsound, damaged, and unfit for food; in short, such as no honest shopkeeper would send to his customers, no man buy for himself or for his family. This view is peculiar to that State, and the opposite of that taken in Nichol *v.* Godts,[1] that a sale by sample is an undertaking that the bulk shall correspond in quality, which however necessarily implies that it must not be so unlike as to be in effect different in kind. The true meaning of a sale by sample cannot well be in doubt. It is an undertaking for the identity of the specimen and the mass; that they are in all material respects the same.

It is, notwithstanding, held in Pennsylvania as elsewhere that if the seller gives an express assurance that the quality of the goods shall be equal to the sample he will be bound, and if it be not, he may be compelled to make compensation in damages or submit to a deduction from the price.[2]

Agreeably to a recent English decision, while the obligation resulting from the exhibition of a sample may be an integral part of the contract, and not only render the vendor answerable in damages if it be not fulfilled, but entitle the purchaser to reject the goods, it will still, where the contract relates to a specific chattel, ordinarily be interpreted as a warranty or collateral undertaking that does not authorize a rejection of the goods, although it may give rise to a cause of action.[3]

The question arose in Heyworth *v.* Hutchinson,[4] on the following memorandum: "Sold 413 bales of wool at 10 *d.* per lb., to arrive ex 'Stige,' or any vessel they may be transshipped in. . . . Guaranteed about similar to samples, and if any dispute arises it shall be decided by the selling brokers, whose decision shall be final." On the arrival of the wool it proved to be inferior to the samples, and was rejected on that ground by the buyer, although the brokers' award was that it should be taken with an allowance for the defect. The vendor brought

[1] 10 Ex. 191.

[2] West Republic Mining Company *v.* Jones, 15 Weekly Notes of Cases, 491.

[3] Shields *v.* Reibe, 9 Ill. App. 598; Doane *v.* Dunham, 65 Ill. 512.

[4] L. R. 2 Q. B. 447.

suit for the purchase-money, and was held entitled to recover, subject to the amount prescribed by the award. Cockburn, C. J., said: "This contract is for the sale of specific wools to arrive by a particular ship. They are earmarked, so as to prevent the contract applying to any other wools, and they are guaranteed as about similar to samples. If the matter stood there, this being a sale of specific goods, though with a warranty, there would not be any right or power on the part of the buyer to reject the goods on the ground of their not being conformable to the samples; but the buyer's remedy would be either by a cross-action on the warranty, or by giving the inferiority in evidence in reduction of damages. There is nothing in the contract to import a condition that the buyer shall be at liberty to reject the wools if not about similar to samples." Blackburn, J., added, "the wools are guaranteed about similar to samples. Such a clause may be a simple warranty or it may be a condition. Generally speaking, when the contract is as to any goods, such a clause is a condition going to the essence of the contract; but when the contract is as to specific goods, the clause is only collateral to the contract, and the subject of a cross-action or matter in reduction of damages, according to the case of Mondel *v.* Steel.[1] Here there is, I think, merely a warranty as distinguished from a condition."

There can be no doubt that when a sale of specific goods is executed and passes the title, such a clause as that above referred to is necessarily a warranty as distinguished from an integral part of the contract, which must be fulfilled in order to bind the purchaser, because, as Parke, B., observed in Mondel *v.* Steel, "the right of property is then vested indefeasibly in him, and will not revert in consequence of the non-performance of anything that remains to be done on either side." To justify the rejection or return of the goods, and a withholding or recovering back of the price, there must be an entire failure of consideration, which cannot be said when they are what the purchaser agreed to buy, although inferior in quality or different in kind.

[1] 8 M. & W. 858, 870.

It should nevertheless be remembered that the effect of such transactions depends on the subject-matter, that is on what the vendor agrees to deliver and the purchaser to receive; and if that be not merely the goods which the parties have in view, but such goods as will answer to the sample, both stipulations must be fulfilled to pass the title or entitle the vendor to the price.[1] A sale of specific goods as answering to a certain description, or being of a particular kind, does not, as we have seen, render it incumbent on the purchaser to accept and pay unless the agreement is exactly fulfilled, and the principle is the same whether the description is in terms, or symbolical by the exhibition of a specimen or sample.

In Azemar *v.* Cassella, the sale, as described in the written memorandum, was of 128 bales of cotton, to arrive in London per "Cheviot," from Madras, guaranteed equal to sample. "Should the quality prove inferior to guaranty a fair allowance to be made." The sample was "long staple Salem," and the cotton proved, on arrival, to be Western Madras, and though of exceptionally good quality, inferior in value and length of fibre to "Salem." The decision was that the title did not pass, and that the purchaser was not bound to accept the cotton. Wilde, J., said that whether the defendants were right in their ground of rejection, namely, that the 128 bales by the "Cheviot" was not the cotton they had contracted to receive and pay for, depended on the terms of the contract, which were that the Messrs. Barber, acting as agents for both parties, had bought for the defendants of the plaintiffs 128 bales of cotton marked "D. C.," expected to arrive per "Cheviot" from Madras, at 25*d.* per pound. Had the writing stopped there it would have been a bargain for the purchase of that number of bales arriving so marked. There was, however, a further clause, "the quality guaranteed about equal to sealed sample in our possession," which completed the description, by showing that the bargain was made with reference to a sample in the hands of the brokers who signed for both sides. This, when looked at, was long staple Salem, and it was

[1] Azemar *v.* Cassella, L. R. 2 C. P. 431.

therefore obvious that the defendants bargained for long staple Salem. It followed that the difference was of kind, and that the defendants were not bound by the stipulation for an allowance which related solely to quality. It was also clear that the right of property was not intended to pass by the mere operation of the contract. Had it been otherwise, the defendants would have been obliged to take the goods and resort to a cross-action on the warranty. As the matter stood, they were no more bound to accept a kind of cotton different from that stipulated for in the contract than a man who has bargained for hay is bound to accept straw.

It results from this decision that the inference from the exhibition of a sample may vary with the circumstances and the language held on either side, and the difficulty is, as in cases where the goods are designated orally or in writing, to ascertain the subject-matter, that is, what one party agreed to sell and the other to receive. The sale may be (1) an agreement for the delivery of any goods corresponding with the sample;[1] (2) an agreement to deliver a parcel designated as that from which the sample was taken, and substantially the same, and therefore not obligatory on the purchaser unless such parcel exists and is tendered;[2] (3) a sale of a specific parcel, subject to a warranty of its identity with the sample that will render the vendor answerable if it is broken, without entitling the purchaser to reject the goods;[3] (4) the sample may be exhibited as a statement or representation of the vendor's belief or opinion as to the identity of the bulk, not entering into or forming a part of the contract, and that will not sustain an action unless it is intentionally false.[4]

In the first two cases the contract is executory, and the purchaser should have such a reasonable opportunity for examination as will enable him to ascertain whether the goods correspond with the sample, and may not only decline to accept and pay if they do not, but recover compensation for

[1] Hargous *v.* Stone, 1 Selden, 73, 92.
[2] Azemar *v.* Cassella, L. R. 2 C. P. 341.
[3] Heyworth *v.* Hutchinson, L. R. 2 Q. B. 447.
[4] Hargous *v.* Stone, 1 Selden, 73; Beirne *v.* Dord, id. 95.

the default.[1] His only redress in the third is by a cross-action on the warranty, or defalking the loss occasioned by the inferiority from the price;[2] while in the fourth and last, an action for deceit will lie, or the contract may be rescinded on proof that the sample was shown fraudulently with knowledge that gave a false idea of the bulk. Which interpretation should be adopted depends not on any inflexible rule of law, but on the object which the parties have in view, and the means taken for its attainment; and an executory contract for the sale of specific merchandise may, as in the sale of land, be attended with a stipulation which will survive the execution of the contract and render the vendor answerable in damages if it be not fulfilled. A sale by sample of goods then at sea may consequently be either a contract that such goods are on board the vessel, and will be delivered if she comes into port, or a sale of the goods on board with a warranty that they correspond with the sample; and while the purchaser will be bound to accept and pay the price in the latter case, and may maintain trover or replevin whether the warranty is broken or fulfilled, his only liability or remedy in the former is through an action for damages.

When the sale is executory and the right of property remains in the vendor, the buyer is entitled to a reasonable opportunity to ascertain whether the bulk corresponds with the sample, and if that is denied, may decline the goods without rendering himself liable whether they are or are not identical as regards kind or quality.[3] For like reasons the buyer is not bound to accept a tender in closed packages or barrels which the seller refuses to open. This is a general rule applying to all executory sales, and consequently to sales by sample.[4] It is not less clear, on the one hand, that delivery and receipt are not necessarily such an acceptance as will pre-

[1] Grimoldby *v.* Wells, L. R. 10 C. P. 391; Lorymer *v.* Smith, 1 B. & C. 1; Kein *v.* Tupper, 52 N. Y. 550; Parker *v.* Palmer, 4 B. & Ad. 387; Bradford *v.* Manly, 13 Mass. 139; Pope *v.* Allis, 115 U. S. 363, 372.

[2] Heyworth *v.* Hutchinson, L. R. 2 Q. B. 447.

[3] Lorymer *v.* Smith, 1 B. & C. 1.

[4] Isherwood *v.* Whitmore, 11 M. & W. 347.

clude a return of the goods for an after-discovered difference between the sample and the bulk, and on the other, that acceptance with a knowledge of the defect is not a waiver of the right to compensation in damages where it would otherwise exist.[1]

A sale by sample may like other contracts be impeached for fraud even when reduced to writing, and in Maute *v.* Gross[2] a contract for the delivery of "sixteen barrels of good lubricating oil of the quality of a sample this day placed in the custody of J. F. Slagle," was set aside on proof that the seller falsely represented that the bottle contained oil of his own manufacture, and such as he had previously delivered to a third person.

[1] Dailey *v.* Green, 3 Harris, 118; Pope *v.* Allis, 115 U. S. 363, 372; Heilbutt *v.* Hickson, L. R. 7 C. P. 438; Mody *v.* Gregson, L. R. 4 Ex. 49; *ante.*

[2] 6 P. F. S. 250.

CHAPTER XXI.

WARRANTY.

Definition. — Distinction between Warranty and Representation. — Implied Warranty.

A WARRANTY is an undertaking as distinguished from a statement or representation. It is therefore in one sense an integral part of the contract, while in another it resembles the covenants for title in a grant of land, as being intended to survive the execution of the contract and be obligatory after the title has vested in the grantee. As was accurately observed by Chief Justice Gibson in McFarland *v.* Newman[1] "a sale is an executed contract on which no action can be brought, and if an action will lie on a warranty it is because it is a collateral and independent covenant, and no more a part of the sale than a covenant of warranty in a deed is part of the conveyance."

The distinction was stated by Lord Abinger in Chanter *v.* Hopkins.[2] "Confusion," said he, "has arisen from the unfortunate use made of the word 'warranty.' Two things have been confounded together. A warranty is an express or implied statement of something which the party undertakes shall be part of the contract, and though part of the contract yet collateral to the express object of it. But in many of the cases, some of which have been referred to, the circumstance of a party selling a particular thing by its proper description has been called a warranty, and a breach of such contract a breach of warranty; but it would be better to distinguish such cases as a non-compliance with a contract which a party has engaged to fulfil, — as if a man offers to buy peas of another and he sends him beans, he does not perform his contract; but that is not a warranty; there is no warranty that he should

[1] 9 Watts, 55.

[2] 4 M. & W. 399.

sell him peas; the contract is to sell peas, and if he sells him anything else in their stead it is a non-performance of it. So, if a man were to order copper for sheathing ships, that is, a particular copper prepared in a particular manner, if the seller sends him a different sort, in that case he does not warrant, and while this may have been ranged under the class of cases relating to warranties, yet it is not properly so."

The line is also clearly drawn in the following citation from the notes to Smith's Leading Cases.[1] "A warranty properly so called can only exist where the subject-matter of the sale is ascertained and existing, so as to be capable of being inspected at the time of the contract, and is a collateral engagement that the specific thing so sold possesses certain qualities; but, the property passing by the contract of sale, a breach of the warranty cannot entitle the vendee to rescind the contract, and revest the property in the vendor without his consent.[2] . . . But when the subject-matter of the sale is not in existence, or not ascertained at the time of the contract, an engagement that it shall, when existing or ascertained, possess certain qualities, is not a mere warranty but a condition,[3] the performance of which is precedent to any obligation upon the vendee under the contract, because the existence of those qualities, being part of the description of the thing sold, becomes essential to its identity, and the vendee cannot be obliged to receive and pay for a thing different from that for which he contracted."[4]

Agreeably to these definitions, which are generally accepted

[1] Vol. ii. 8 Am. ed. p. 20.

[2] Dixon *v.* Yates, 5 B. & Ad. 340; Gilmour *v.* Supple, 11 Moore, P. C. C. 566.

[3] The commentator here substitutes "condition" for Lord Abinger's explicit declaration that if a man sells peas, and tenders beans, the contract is not performed. This seems to be one of the not infrequent instances in which the study of the civil, has perplexed writers on English law. The office of a condition is to suspend or vacate, while the sale of peas or any other commodity by its distinctive name is an undertaking which renders the vendor liable if it be not fulfilled.

[4] See Chanter *v.* Hopkins, 4 M. & W. 399; Barr *v.* Gibson, 3 id. 390; Gompertz *v.* Bartlett, 2 E. & B. 849; Lucy *v.* Mouflet, 5 H. & N. 229.

as exact,[1] a warranty is an assurance that something is or is not true of a chattel which the warrantor offers to sell and the opposite party desires to buy, and although ordinarily found where the contract is executed and passes the title, may be an incident to an executory sale of a specific thing, though not of an agreement to sell things of a certain kind, unless the intention is that the purchaser shall be bound to accept the goods if they agree in kind, and look to the vendor for compensation for any deficiency that may exist as regards the quality. Whether the vendor warrants the quality of a hundred barrels of flour standing by themselves in his warehouse, or of a hundred barrels forming part of a larger lot, he is equally bound, the difference being that the warranty cannot take effect as such in the latter case until the goods are set apart as the purchaser's or delivered to him, and if this be not done, and the seller is in default, the remedy is on the contract as a whole, and not for the loss that would have arisen from the breach of the warranty had the sale been consummated. It was accordingly said with much truth, in a recent New York decision, that a warranty is an incident only of a consummated and completed sale;[2] that is, that while the warranty may be given while the title is still in the vendor, it cannot be enforced by suit until the goods become the purchaser's.

It results from what has been said, that where the contract does not relate to a specific chattel and may be fulfilled by the delivery of any article which it describes, no undertaking which it contains can operate as a warranty or be other than a description of that which must be delivered in order to charge the buyer. Whether the seller offers to supply soft malleable iron, or iron warranted to be soft and malleable, the agreement is in effect the same, and if iron of a different kind is tendered it may be declined and damages recovered for the default.

On the other hand, while the offer or description of a specific chattel as being of a certain quality or kind is *prima*

[1] See Benjamin on Sales, § 600.

[2] Osborn *v.* Gantz, 60 N. Y. 540.

facie a warranty, and does not justify the rejection or return of the article if unfulfilled, it may still when such is the design, qualify the contract by showing that it is not merely for the sale and delivery of the thing, but of the thing as described. The test is, Do the parties intend the title to pass, whether the commodity does or does not correspond to the name or description under or by which it is sold? A sale of five hundred bales Sea Island cotton on board the "Rhone" will not be satisfied by a tender of that number of bales of any Sea Island cotton, nor necessarily of the cotton alleged to be a part of the cargo of the "Rhone," but only of cotton which is at once part of her cargo and Sea Island, and if there is no such cotton the contract is broken as soon as made. Still, the question is one of intention, and descriptive words may operate as a warranty if so designed. Thus, the purchaser in a case like that above supposed may prefer, in view of the state of the market and his own needs, that his title to the cotton shall not depend on the contingency of its being Sea Island, and that he shall, on the contrary, be entitled to claim it as his own, and maintain trover or replevin if it is withheld although it proves to be "upland" or of some other growth; and the contract will then not be executory for the delivery of cotton described as Sea Island and on board the ship in question, but executed for the cotton in her hold with a warranty that it is Sea Island. So a lady who buys a shawl on the faith of the shopkeeper's assurance that it is "genuine Cashmere," ordinarily intends that it shall be hers as absolutely as if the contract contained no such clause, with a right of recourse against the shopkeeper should the assurance prove to be untrue; but she may, if she thinks proper, stipulate for and agree to purchase a genuine Cashmere shawl of the texture and pattern exhibited by the seller, and will then, instead of acquiring a right of property, simply be entitled to damages if the property be not as described; or finally the sale may be on condition that the shawl is "Cashmere," and leave both parties free if it was woven elsewhere.

The authorities agree that in the absence of fraud a naked affirmation will not render the seller answerable for its truth or sustain a recovery in damages, unless it is intended as a warranty or so worded as to convey that impression.[1]

The principle is clear, and applies whether the representation is oral or contained in the written instrument of contract, the difference being that in the former case the question is one of fact for the jury under proper instructions, while in the latter it must be determined by the court.[2]

"Properly speaking," said Williams, J., in Behn *v.* Burness, "a representation is a statement or assertion, made by one party to the other before or at the time of contract, of some matter or circumstance relating to it. Though it is sometimes contained in the written instrument, it is not an integral part of the contract; and consequently the contract is not broken though the representation proves to be untrue, nor (with the exception of the case of policies of insurance, at all events, marine policies, which stand on a peculiar, anomalous footing) is such untruth any cause of action, nor has it any efficacy whatever, unless the representation was made fraudulently either by reason of its being made dishonestly, or with a reckless ignorance whether it was true or untrue."[3]

It is not necessary to say "I warrant" an undertaking, for the quality or character of the thing sold will operate as a warranty by whatever words expressed,[4] and may result from the vendor's assent to an inquiry or request from the purchaser.[5] It is accordingly settled, in accordance with the view taken by Lord Holt, in Cross *v.* Gardner,[6] and Medina *v.* Stoughton,[7]

[1] Jackson *v.* Wetherill, 7 S. & R. 480; McFarland *v.* Newman, 9 Watts, 55; Eagan *v.* Call, 10 Casey, 236; Worth *v.* McConnell, 42 Mich. 473.

[2] See Behn *v.* Burness, 3 Best & Smith, 751, 754; McFarland *v.* Newman, 9 Watts, 55.

[3] See Elliott *v.* Von Glehn, 13 Q. B. 632; Wheelton *v.* Hardisty, 8 E. & B. 232.

[4] Hopkins *v.* Tanqueray, 15 C. B. 130; Hopkins *v.* Hitchcock, 14 C. B. N. S. 65; Jones *v.* Quick, 28 Ind. 125; Hawkins *v.* Pemberton, 51 N. Y. 198; Patrick *v.* Leach, 8 Neb. 530; Robinson *v.* Harvey, 82 Ill. 58; Daniells *v.* Aldrich, 42 Mich. 58.

[5] Jones *v.* Bright, 5 Bing. 533.

[6] Carthew, 90.

[7] 1 Lord Raymond, 593.

that an assertion made by the seller with regard to the thing sold, for the purpose of influencing the purchaser and inducing him to buy, is a warranty if so understood and relied on by the purchaser.[1]

The rule holds good in pleading as well as in evidence, and an averment that the vendor affirmed or undertook and promised that the horse was sound, is equivalent to an averment that he warranted the horse.[2]

No precise rule can be laid down for the solution of a problem which varies with the circumstances of each successive case; but it may be said in general that whether a representation made during the sale is a warranty, or in other words, a promise or assurance as distinguished from an expression of the vendor's knowledge or belief, which merely renders him answerable for its good faith, is a question of intention depending not so much on the vendor's meaning as on the sense which the words were calculated to convey, and which would naturally be attached to them by the purchaser.[3]

The line was accurately drawn in Hawkins *v.* Pemberton, as follows: "It is not true, as sometimes stated, that the representation, in order to constitute a warranty, must have been intended by the vendor as well as understood by the vendee as a warranty. If the contract be in writing, and it contains a clear warranty, the vendor will not be permitted to say that he did not intend what his language clearly and explicitly declares; and so if it be by parol, and the representation as to the character or quality of the article sold be positive, not mere matter of opinion or judgment, and the vendee understands it as a warranty, and he relies upon it and is induced by it, the vendor is bound by the warranty, no matter whether he intended it or not. He is responsible for the language he

[1] Pasley *v.* Freeman, 3 T. R. 51; Ruff *v.* Jarrett, 94 Ill. 475; Pennock *v.* Stygles, 54 Vt. 226; Houghton *v.* Carpenter, 40 id. 588; Robinson *v.* Harvey, 82 Ill. 58; Morrill *v.* Wallace, 9 N. H. 111; Osgood *v.* Lewis, 2 Harris & Gill, 495; Henshaw *v.* Robins, 9 Met. 83; Cross *v.* Gardner, Carthew, 90; Claghorn *v.* Lingo, 62 Ala. 230.

[2] Chapman *v.* Murch, 19 Johns. 290; Smithers *v.* Bircher, 2 Mo. Ap. 499; Cross *v.* Gardner, Carthew, 90; McClure *v.* Williams, 65 Ill. 390.

[3] Hawkins *v.* Pemberton, 51 N. Y. 198.

uses, and cannot escape liability by claiming that he did not intend to convey the impression which his language was calculated to produce upon the mind of the vendee." This decision is in accordance with the general principle that language which admits of two interpretations shall be taken in the sense in which it would naturally be understood by the person to whom it was addressed.[1]

The rule, as above stated, leaves a wide margin for interpretation, and it is not surprising that the cases should, as Chief Justice Gibson pointed out in McFarland *v.* Newman, be not only divergent, but irreconcilable. Still, it must be remembered that in the greater number of instances in which the subject has been judicially considered, the controversy was not as to the proper inference but whether the case should have been withheld from or left to the jury; questions which have no necessary connection at common law, where as Woodward, J., observed, in Philadelphia & Wilmington Railroad Company *v.* Cowell,[2] it may be the duty of a court of error to sanction an inference which they would not have drawn, or to reverse a judgment which they would have pronounced if the question were before them as a matter of fact, because it was withheld from the constitutional tribunal in the court below and decided as one of law.[3]

In Wetherill *v.* Neilson,[4] a reiterated assurance by the vendor's broker, that soda ash, then afloat in the harbor, was "48 per cent English test Johnson's Brand," was held not to be a warranty, or evidence of one, although in the highest degree material to the quality and value of the commodity, and given with the view of inducing the purchaser to buy. The judgment might have been rested on the secure ground that no such words appeared in the bought note, which was the written evidence of the contract; but the court saw fit to decide as

[1] 2 Am. Leading Cases, 5 ed. 45, 139; 2 Sm. L. C. 7 Am. ed. 470; Mason *v.* Pritchard, 12 East. 227; see Douglass *v.* Reynolds, 7 Peters, 113; Lawrence *v.* McCalmont, 2 How. 426, 450; Hogg's Appeal, 10 Harris, 479.

[2] 4 Casey, 329; *ante*.

[3] Schuchardt *v.* Allens, 1 Wallace, 359.

[4] 8 Harris, 448.

a matter of law that a statement so made was not a warranty, and did not bind the vendor in the absence of fraud. So in Whitaker *v.* Eastwick,[1] there was said to be nothing from which the jury could infer a warranty, although the cargo of coal, which had been bought without inspection while still on board the canal boat, on the faith of a representation that it was of good quality and well adapted for generating steam, contained twenty per cent of dirt was unmerchantable and did not answer the purpose for which it was sold.

When, however, the question arose soon afterwards, in Warren *v.* Philadelphia Coal Co.,[2] an opposite conclusion was drawn from testimony which, if more explicit, was like in kind. The purchaser inquired particularly as to the quality of the coal on board a canal-boat, and was told that it was good, and the same as that which he had been buying. He replied, "You may put it on the wharf; but unless it is good I will not buy;" and the judgment of the court below was reversed, because the case had been withdrawn from the jury, instead of leaving it to them to say whether the representation amounted to an undertaking for the quality of the coal and that it was like that previously delivered.

The question was critically examined in Wolcott *v.* Mount,[3] where the Chief Justice said that the recent adjudications tended to put this subject on a reasonable footing. Starting from the admission that, in the absence of fraud and of a warranty, the rule of *caveat emptor* applies, the effort is, not to elevate particular expressions contained in a given contract into a general rule of law, but to regard each case in the light of its own circumstances, and with respect solely to the understanding of the parties. Whether the representation or affirmation accompanying a sale shall be regarded as a warranty, or as *simplex commendatio*, is a question to be solved by a search for the intention of the contracting parties.

The two cases of Jendwine *v.* Slade,[4] and Power *v.* Barham,[5] are conspicuous examples of this rule. In the former there was a sale of two pictures, the catalogue of the auction de-

[1] 25 P. F. S. 229. [2] 2 Norris, 437. [3] 38 N. J. L. 496, 498.
[4] 2 Esp. 572. [5] 4 A. & E. 473.

scribing one as a sea-piece by Claude Lorraine, and the other, as a fair by Teniers. This description was held by Lord Kenyon to be no warranty that the pictures were the genuine works of the artists referred to, but merely an expression of the opinion of the vendor to that effect. In the other case, it appeared that, at a sale of four pictures, they were described as "four pictures, views in Venice, Carnaletti," and it was left to the jury to decide whether the intention was to warrant the pictures as authentic, the court distinguishing this case from the former one by the circumstance that Carnaletti was comparatively a modern painter, the authenticity of whose works was capable of being known as a fact, while, with respect to the productions of very old painters, an assertion as to their genuineness was necessarily a matter of opinion.

In these instances the respective affirmations of the vendor were of equivalent import, intrinsically considered; but it was left open, as a matter of inference, whether they were to have the same signification when used under variant circumstances. The question consequently is, in every case of this kind, whether the conditions were such that the vendee had the right to understand, and did so understand, that an affirmation or representation made by the vendor was meant as a warranty. And for the determination of this question, Mr. Benjamin, in his admirable treatise on sales,[1] says: "A decisive test is, whether the vendor assumes to assert a fact of which the buyer is ignorant, or merely states an opinion or judgment upon a matter of which the vendor has no special knowledge, and on which the buyer may be expected also to have an opinion, and to exercise his judgment. In the former case there is a warranty; in the latter, not."

It has been held on like grounds, in Tennessee, that a representation made to influence the sale, and that has that effect, is equivalent to a warranty if loss ensues, and the vendor will be answerable whether he spoke ignorantly or knew that what he said was false.[2]

[1] p. 499.

[2] Hogg *v.* Cardwell, 4 Sneed, 151; Waterbury *v.* Russell, 8 Baxter, 159, 166.

Notwithstanding the weight due to the above view, it seems questionable in one particular. The question is not, Was the statement made as matter of fact or matter of opinion? but Did the vendor undertake that it was true? To hold otherwise is to efface the line which separates warranty from representation, and hold that an unqualified assertion is equivalent to a promise. One who is intimately convinced of a fact may obviously state it without affecting a doubt which he does not feel, and yet not be answerable in damages should his impression be erroneous. The test is, Would the buyer, were the contract reduced to writing, be entitled to require that the representation should be embodied as the promise or description under or subject to which the sale was made? for if not, there can be no warranty, and the vendor is not answerable unless the representation be fraudulent. In other words, that is a warranty which is so worded as to create and justify the belief that it is intended to enter into and qualify the contract.[1]

The law was accurately stated by Gibson, C. J., in McFarland *v.* Newman:[2] "Though to constitute a warranty requires no particular form of words, the naked averment of a fact is neither a warranty itself, nor evidence of it. In connection with other circumstances, it certainly may be taken into consideration; but the jury must be satisfied from the whole that the vendor actually, and not constructively consented to be bound for the truth of his representation. Should he have used expressions fairly importing a willingness to be thus bound, it would furnish a reason to infer that he had intentionally induced the vendee to treat on that basis; but a naked affirmation is not to be dealt with as a warranty merely because the vendee had gratuitously relied on it, for not to have exacted a direct engagement, had he desired to buy on the vendor's judgment, must be accounted an instance of folly. Testing the vendor's responsibility by these principles, justice will be done without driving him into the toils of an imaginary contract."

[1] See Richardson *v.* Grandy, 49 Vt. 22; Thorne *v.* McVeagh, 75 Ill. 80.

[2] 9 Watts, 55.

The divergence is seeming rather than real; both courts agreeing on the material point that a representation made during the negotiation for a sale should be read in the light of the circumstances, and if these indicate that it was designed to enter into and qualify the contract it will operate as a warranty.

In determining whether a representation is a warranty, regard may be had to the nature of the defect, for if that is so far patent or known to the purchaser that he can equally with the seller judge of its probable effect, the statements of the latter may reasonably be supposed to have been made and understood as an expression of opinion, and not as an undertaking on which he can be held answerable in damages.[1]

A warranty cannot be given after the sale without some new consideration;[2] but it may well arise from a previous assurance which is present to the minds of the parties when they finally agree.[3] If the buyer says, "I will give so much for the horse, if it is sound," and the offer is accepted, it is a warranty although nothing more is said about quality on either side; and so if the vendor describes the animal in such terms as will naturally be understood as a promise and the bargain is concluded subsequently in reliance on his words,[4] for if the whole be in effect one transaction, it matters not how far the beginning and conclusion are apart in point of time.

When the contract is reduced to writing, everything that the writing does not contain is presumably excluded from the contract, and evidence is not admissible that the vendor warranted the goods orally during the previous negotiation or

1 See Henshaw *v.* Robbins, 9 Met. 83; Margetson *v.* Wright, 7 Bing. 603; Pennock *v.* Stygles, 54 Vt. 226; Benjamin on Sales, 616.

2 Hogins *v.* Plympton, 11 Pick. 97; Roscorla *v.* Thomas, 3 Q. B. 234; Vincent *v.* Leland, 100 Mass. 432; Summers *v.* Vaughan, 35 Ind. 323; *ante.*

3 Lysney *v.* Selby, 2 Lord Raymond, 1118; Jones *v.* Bright, 5 Bing. 533; Driesbach *v.* Lewisburg Bridge Co., 32 P. F. S. 177; Wilmot *v.* Hurd, 11 Wend. 584; Falconer *v.* Smith, 6 Harris, 130.

4 Hopkins *v.* Tanqueray, 15 C. B. 130; Wilmot *v.* Hurd, 11 Wend. 585; Bannerman *v.* White, 10 C. B. N. S. 844, 860; Falconer *v.* Smith, 6 Harris, 130; Hogg *v.* Cardwell, 4 Sneed, 151.

when the instrument was executed;[1] or even that the sale was by sample and the bulk does not correspond.[2]

The opposite conclusion has been reached in Tennessee,[3] on the ground that the representations made on either side are inducements which do not enter into or form part of the contract, and need not appear in the writing though one is drawn up and signed. This is no doubt true where a representation is adduced in proof of fraud, but a warranty is essentially contractual, — a promise or undertaking, as distinguished from an affirmation,[4] and hence, when the parties reduce the agreement to writing, nothing that is not set forth in the instrument can operate as a warranty.

To call the rule into operation, the writing must nevertheless be so worded as to indicate that it is intended to set forth or express the entire understanding or agreement;[5] and an oral warranty at the commencement of the negotiations may be binding on the vendor, although they are subsequently conducted or brought to a close by letters;[6] or although he gives a written receipt, invoice, or bill of parcels which does not note the warranty, and simply sets forth or enumerates what is delivered, or acknowledges the payment of the price.[7]

In the absence of express words, a warranty may be implied. Thus, one who sells a thing for a particular purpose thereby impliedly undertakes that it is fit for that purpose, either as a term of the contract which must be fulfilled to render it incumbent on the buyer to accept and pay, or as

[1] Van Ostrand *v.* Reed, 1 Wend. 424; Peltier *v.* Collins, 3 id. 459; Reed *v.* Wood, 9 Vt. 288; Lamb *v.* Crafts, 12 Met. 253; Kain *v.* Old, 2 B. & C. 627.

[2] Harnor *v.* Groves, 15 C. B. 667; Hogins *v.* Plympton, 11 Pick. 97; Pike *v.* Fay, 101 Mass. 134.

[3] Hogg *v.* Cardwell, 4 Sneed, 151; Waterbury *v.* Russell, 8 Baxter, 159.

[4] Behn *v.* Burness, 3 Best & Smith, 751, 753.

[5] Houghton *v.* Carpenter, 40 Vt. 588.

[6] Jones *v.* Bright, 5 Bing. 533; Filkins *v.* Whyland, 24 N. Y. 338.

[7] Driesbach *v.* Lewisburg Bridge Co., 32 P. F. S. 177; Hersom *v.* Henderson, 21 N. H. 224; Perrine *v.* Cooley, 39 N. J. L. 449; Allen *v.* Pink, 4 M. & W. 140; Hazard *v.* Loring, 10 Cush. 267; Boardman *v.* Spooner, 13 Allen, 353; Frost *v.* Blanchard, 97 Mass. 155; Atwater *v.* Clancy, 107 id. 369.

a warranty which imposes a liability in damages but it is not a condition precedent to the passage of the title.[1] So it has been held that the sale of goods under circumstances which preclude inspection or render it impracticable, is subject to an implied warranty that they are merchantable; and the rule was applied, in Merriam *v.* Field,[2] to the sale of planks, which though lying in the stream were in the form of a raft, and were found on delivery to consist to a large extent of refuse.

Such an undertaking may be implied, though the contract is reduced to writing, and merely stipulates for the delivery of goods of a certain kind; and it does not necessarily vary the case that it contains an express warranty, unless it is so drawn as to negative the inference that would otherwise be drawn from the contract as a whole.[3]

The sale of provisions should seemingly give rise to a warranty that they are fit for consumption, as being their appropriate use, and the one to which they must ultimately be applied unless they are thrown on the dunghill for manure;[4] but what a sale in the course of trade imports according to the weight of authority, is in the case of provisions as of other merchandise, simply that the commodity answers in kind to the description given by the seller, and is not so defective in quality as to be unmerchantable;[5] because when the object of the buyer is to sell again, what the seller guarantees is that the article is of the kind described, and merchantable under the name by which it was bought. Thus, a sale of "cargo beef" in barrels imports that the contents are not merely beef, but beef so cured and packed as to come under that denomination.[6]

1 Reggio *v.* Braggiotti, 7 Cush. 166.

2 24 Wis. 640.

3 Bigg *v.* Parkinson, 7 H. & N. 955; Merriam *v.* Field, 24 Wis. 640; Shepherd *v.* Pybus, 3 M. & G. 868.

4 See Van Bracklin *v.* Fonda, 12 Johns. 468; 3 Bl. Com. 164, 165.

5 Emerson *v.* Brigham, 10 Mass. 197; French *v.* Vining, 102 id. 132; Winsor *v.* Lombard, 18 Pick. 57; Humphreys *v.* Comline, 8 Blackf. 516; Moses *v.* Mead, 1 Den. 378; 5 id. 617; Hol *v.* Sanborn, 21 N. Y. 552; Ryder *v.* Neitge, 21 Minn. 70; Burnby *v.* Bollett, 16 M. & W. 644; Emmerton *v.* Matthews, 7 H. & N. 586.

6 Bailey *v.* Nikols, 2 Root, 407.

It is not less well settled that selling provisions for domestic use is not only an affirmation that they are sound and fit for food, which renders the dealer answerable if he knows it to be untrue, but an implied warranty of soundness on which a recovery may be had without proof of a scienter.[1]

Agreeably to the weight of authority in the United States, a usage that a warranty shall be implied generally, or where the sale is made without an opportunity of inspection, is invalid, and will not be allowed to impose any obligation that would not otherwise exist.[2] Such evidence would it has been said, vary the contract by adding a term to which the parties did not agree, and contravene the legal principle which throws the risk on the buyer in the absence of an express stipulation that it shall be borne by the seller.[3] The rule has been applied even where the custom might seem altogether reasonable, as, for instance, that cotton sold in bales shall be fairly packed and merchantable.[4]

Usage is, nevertheless, one of the means by which public opinion corrects the defects of the law, or shapes it to meet the existing wants of trade, and may justly be employed to supplement, though not to contradict what the parties have said or written.[5]

It results from what has been said in this and the foregoing chapters, that the descriptive words used by the vendor, as, for instance, where the sale is of unsulphured hops, may be, (1) an executory undertaking for the delivery of any hops corresponding to its terms, which must be exactly fulfilled in order to charge the purchaser or exonerate the vendor; (2) a sale of a specific parcel of hops with a representation that they have not been sulphured, which will be inoperative unless it is fraudulent, and misleads the purchaser; (3) a warranty

[1] See Van Bracklin *v.* Fonda, 12 Johns. 468; Moses *v.* Mead, 1 Den. 378; Hoover *v.* Peters, 18 Mich. 51.

[2] Thompson *v.* Ashton, 14 Johns. 316; Dickinson *v.* Gay, 7 Allen, 29; Dodd *v.* Farlow, 11 id. 426; Coxe *v.* Heisley, 7 Harris, 243; Wetherill *v.* Neilson, 8 id. 453; overruling Snowden *v.* Warder, 3 Rawle, 101.

[3] Barnard *v.* Kellogg, 10 Wallace, 383, 390.

[4] Barnard *v.* Kellogg, 10 Wallace, 383; Beirne *v.* Dord, 1 Selden, 95.

[5] 1 Sm. L. C. 8 Am. ed. 934, 950.

that sulphur was not used, which will entitle the purchaser to damages if broken, but not to reject the hops; (4) a condition that may exonerate the purchaser without charging the vendor, as where the purchaser agrees to take the hops if unsulphured; (5) an executory contract for the delivery of a specific parcel of "unsulphured" hops, which can no more be fulfilled by a tender of sulphured hops than of an article of an entirely different kind; and as the right of property does not pass under such a sale, the purchaser cannot maintain trover or replevin before acceptance, although he may recover the difference between the contract price and what the hops would have been worth had they been as described.[1]

[1] See Owens *v.* Sturges, 67 Ill. 366.

CHAPTER XXII.

REMEDIES OF THE VENDEE.

Breach of Executory Contract of Sale by Tender insufficient in Time, Quality, Amount, or Kind. — Vendee's Option to accept or reject the Goods. — Measure of Damages. — Vendor's Liability for, resulting from Defective Goods. — Time of Rejection. — Description may be Stipulation, Condition, or Warranty. — Action for Breach of Warranty may be Case or Assumpsit. — Measure of Damages.

When the thing tendered under an executory contract differs as regards time, quality, amount or kind, from what the buyer agreed to receive, it may be declined and the breach treated as entire,[1] or it may be accepted as so much on account of what the contractor agreed to do or render and an action brought for the amount by which the performance falls short of the promise.[2] In the former case, the measure of damages is the sum by which the market value of that which the vendor failed to deliver exceeds the contract price at the stipulated time and place;[3] in the latter, the difference between the benefit actually conferred and that which would have resulted from the fulfilment of the contract, as deduced from the actual or selling value of both.[4] In other words, while regard must be

[1] Hart *v.* Wright, 17 Wend. 267, 277; Howard *v.* Hoey, 23 id. 350; Doane *v.* Dunham, 65 Ill. 512; 79 id. 131; Youghiogheny Iron and Coal Co. *v.* Smith, 16 P. F. S. 340; Pope *v.* Allis, 115 U. S. 363, 371.

[2] Lewis *v.* Rountree, 78 N. C. 323; Cox *v.* Long, 69 id. 7; Polhemus *v.* Heiman, 45 Cal. 573; Borrekins *v.* Bevan, 3 Rawle, 23, 44.

[3] Fessler *v.* Love, 12 Wr. 407; Smethurst *v.* Woolston, 5 W. & S. 106; Blanchard *v.* Ely, 21 Wend. 342; Smith *v.* Harris, 12 Ill. 462; Whitmore *v.* Coates, 14 Mo. 9.

[4] Hadley *v.* Baxendale, 9 Ex. 341; Wolcott *v.* Mount, 36 N. J. L. 262, 266; Mondel *v.* Steel, 8 M. & W. 858, 870; Dailey *v.* Green, 3 Harris, 118; Borrekins *v.* Bevan, 3 Rawle, 23; Howard *v.* Hoey, 23 Wend, 350; Hastings *v.* Lovering, 2 Pick. 214; Mixer *v.* Coburn, 11 Met. 559; Ketchum *v.* Wells, 19 Wis. 26; Morehouse *v.* Comstock, 42 id. 626; Osgood *v.* Lewis,

had in both cases to the value of that which the buyer would have received had the contract been fulfilled, the result depends in the one on the excess of such value over the contract price, in the other on the sum by which it exceeds the market value of the goods actually delivered by the seller and accepted by the buyer,[1] with a right in either case to compensation for such consequential losses as can be definitely established by proof. If the buyer accepts the goods he will be answerable for the purchase-money, and may either pay it in full, and proceed against the seller for the damages as ascertained by the above rule, or wait until the seller sues, and recoup the damages from the amount due under the contract.[2] If the former course be adopted, the costs will be thrown on the vendor, while in the latter they will devolve on the purchaser; and he must also, agreeably to the English rule as established prior to the Judicature Act, but which did not obtain in the United States, forego the consequential damages or make them the subject of a cross-suit.[3]

The rule may be illustrated by examples. Let the stipulated price be $1,000; the market value of the goods, as contracted for, $1,200; and that of the goods actually tendered or delivered, $800. If the goods are rejected the breach is entire, and the buyer may recover the $200 which he presumably would have gained had the contract been fulfilled, together with so much of the purchase-money as has been paid in advance, and compensation for such consequential losses as can properly be brought into court.[4] If they are accepted,

2 Harris & Gill, 495; Kellogg *v.* Denslow, 14 Conn. 411; Boughton *v.* Standish, 48 Vt. 594; Douglass Axe Man. Co. *v.* Gardner, 10 Cush. 88; Flanders *v.* Putney, 58 N. H. 358.

[1] Youghiogheny Iron and Coal Co. *v.* Smith, 16 P. F. S. 340; Buffington *v.* Quantin, 5 Harris, 310.

[2] Dayton *v.* Hooglund, 39 Ohio St. 671; Hirshhorn *v.* Stewart, 49 Ia. 418; Mackey *v.* Swartz, 60 id. 710; Barton *v.* Kane, 18 Wis. 262; Defenbaugh *v.* Weaver, 87 Ill. 132; Doane *v.* Dunham, 65 id. 512; 79 id. 131; Dennis *v.* Stoughton, 55 Vt. 371.

[3] Mondel *v.* Steel, 8 M. & W. 858; Sm. L. C. 8 Am. ed. vol. i. p. 360, vol. ii. p. 19.

[4] Heilbutt *v.* Hickson, L. R. 7 C. P. 438, 440.

the buyer will be answerable for the purchase-money, and entitled to $400 damages which may be deducted from the price, or if that has been paid recovered from the seller.[1]

The account may be stated in another form. The purchaser owes the vendor $800 on an implied obligation to pay as much as the goods actually received are worth; but the vendor has broken the express contract and is indebted to the purchaser in the sum of $200, — the amount by which the value of such goods as he agreed to deliver would exceed the contract price, and which deducted from $800, leaves a balance of $600 in favor of the vendor. Both methods lead to the same arithmetical result. The difference is that while one proceeds on the idea that the acceptance gives rise to a new contract, it is agreeably to the other a waiver of the right to insist that there is an entire breach of that originally made; and the latter view is sustained by the weight of authority in England and in the United States. The vendor's failure to fulfil the contract, attended if there be a tender with a rejection of the goods, leaves two courses open to the buyer, — who may either proceed on the contract for damages, or rescind it and demand back the purchase-money or so much of it as has been paid. Rejection does not necessarily imply rescission; although it is essential to the adoption of that course, and depends on the buyer's right to insist on a strict fulfilment of the agreement and decline whatever differs in any particular from that for which he has stipulated.[2] By demanding damages the buyer treats the contract as subsisting, and affirms the right of the seller to the price, less the loss occasioned by the default which may be trivial; by rescinding it he waives his right to damages, but entitles himself to withhold or recover back the consideration.

It is immaterial as regards the application of the principle, that the price is paid in advance and the goods come to a falling market so that the value is less than the buyer gave, and that he is a loser by the whole amount of the difference, as

[1] Loder *v.* Kekule, 3 C. B. N. S. 128.

[2] Honck *v.* Muller, L. R. 7 Q. B. Div. 92; Wolcott *v.* Mount, 36 N. J. L. 262, 266.

well as of the damage resulting from their failure to correspond to the terms of the agreement.[1]

In the case first cited, the defendant bought and paid for one hundred casks of tallow, which was described in the sold note "Ukraine Y. C.," but proved on delivery to be an inferior and less valuable commodity. The purchaser offered to return the tallow, but the vendor declined. It was then sold for the vendor's account, and brought £595 less than it would have brought had it been according to the contract. The court held that this sum was the measure of the damages, although it did not, when added to the proceeds of the sale, reimburse the purchaser, because the loss was due to a fall in the price of tallow that had nothing to do with the breach of contract, and for which the vendor was not responsible.

"Where," said Rogers, J., in Smethurst *v.* Woolston, "the vendor fails to deliver the article bought, the purchaser may elect to rescind the contract and recover back the money paid, or he may bring suit on the agreement and recover the value at or about the time it ought to have been delivered. And this is a just rule; for if it has risen in value he has the advantage of the increased price; if it has decreased, why should he when he adheres to the contract recover more from the vendor than for the injury he has sustained by the non-performance of the agreement? And the vendee has the less reason to complain, because he may, as before stated, rescind the bargain and place himself in the same situation as before it was made."

Although the measure of the buyer's liability on acceptance is ordinarily the contract price, whether the contract be or be not fulfilled, the rule meets with an exception where he accepts a thing of a different kind, knowing that it bears a higher price, and he may then be compelled to pay for it at that rate subject to an abatement for the damages resulting from the breach of the contract. In Dennis *v.* Stoughton,[2] the law was so held where the buyer kept and used an "at-

[1] Loder *v.* Kekule, 3 C. B. N. S. 128; Smethurst *v.* Woolston, 5 W. & S. 106; Wilkinson *v.* Ferree, 12 Harris, 190.

[2] 55 Vt. 37.

tachment cider-press," which was sent to him by mistake, instead of a "counter-attachment cider-press" which he had ordered.

The difference between the market and contract price is ordinarily the measure of damages, because the purchaser may presumably buy from other persons at the market rate, and ought not to make the seller answerable for losses which he could not anticipate, and that might have been avoided with due care. The rule does not, therefore, apply where there is no shop or market within reach where such goods can be procured, and the seller knows or is informed of the purpose for which they are bought; and the buyer may then be entitled to compensation for the injurious consequences of the default, — as for instance, his inability to run his mill or fulfil the contracts which he has made with third persons, from the want of the machinery or materials which he ordered and the seller promised to make or furnish.[1]

For like reasons, where the goods do not answer the description under or the purpose for which they were sold, the seller may be answerable for the injurious consequences of their use in ignorance of the defect, to an amount far exceeding the value of the commodity or the contract price. A man who sells a carriage pole which is unsound from a latent defect, may consequently be compelled to respond heavily in damages for a consequent injury to the carriage or its occupants.[2] So also, a manufacturer who uses materials in the belief that they are such as he ordered and the defendant agreed to furnish, is entitled to compensation for the failure of the process in consequence of their inferiority or difference in quality or kind; and it is not an answer that the defect might have been discovered by analysis, or by means that lie outside of the ordinary course of business.[3]

It was said in the case last cited, that where the injurious

[1] Benton *v.* Fay, 64 Ill. 417; Ramsey *v.* Tully, 12 Ill. App. 463; Parsons *v.* Sutton, 66 N. Y. 92; Taft *v.* Tiede, 55 Ia. 370; Cockburn *v.* Ashland Lumber Co., 54 Wis. 619.

[2] Randall *v.* Newson, L. R. 2 Q. B. Div. 102; *ante.*

[3] Bagley *v.* Cleveland Rolling Mill Co., 21 Federal Rep. 159.

effects of a breach of contract can be avoided by reasonable care and forethought, a party who is wanting in this regard is not entitled to indemnity for a loss which is due wholly or in part to his own inactivity or negligence. Had, therefore, the plaintiffs had any just reason to suppose that the steel was unfit for the purpose for which they used it, they would have forfeited their right to compensation. But they might well assume, in the absence of evidence to the contrary, that the defendant had fulfilled his contract, and were not bound to institute an investigation or make experiments to ascertain whether such was or was not the case.

The right of rescission has its root in equity rather than in the common law, and cannot be exercised where the buyer has dealt with the goods as his own with a knowledge of the deficiency, nor where, although without such knowledge, he has done any act that renders it impracticable to reinstate the vendor; nor where he has been wanting in the exactitude and diligence which are requisite to protect the seller's interests as well as his own.[1] Such is the established rule where the contract is rescinded as fraudulent;[2] and it applies in the analogous case of a suit brought to recover back the purchase-money on the ground of failure of consideration. In neither instance can the purchaser single out part and decline the rest, but must keep all or none;[3] although the case is essentially different where a seller who has been paid in advance, apportions the consideration by a partial delivery or performance, and fails to tender or fulfil the residue; and assumpsit for money had and received may then be maintained for the amount, if any, which has been paid in excess of the value of what has actually been received.[4]

[1] Harnor *v.* Groves, 7 Bing. 743; Heilbutt *v.* Hickson, L. R. 7 C. P. 438, 451; Chapman *v.* Morton, 11 M. & W. 534; Wolf *v.* Dietzsch, 75 Ill. 205.

[2] Clarke *v.* Dickson, 1 E. B. & E. 148.

[3] Harnor *v.* Groves, 7 Bing. 743; Clark *v.* Baker, 5 Met. 452; Morse *v.* Brackett, 98 Mass. 205; 10 id. 494; Mansfield *v.* Trigg, 113 id. 350; Voorhees *v.* Earl, 2 Hill, 288; Lyon *v.* Bertram, 20 How. 149; Buchenau *v.* Horney, 12 Ill. 336; Bowen *v.* Schuler, 41 id. 192; Wolf *v.* Dietzsch, 75 id. 205; Harzfeld *v.* Converse, 105 id. 534.

[4] Freeman *v.* Skinner, 3 Ired. 32; Devaux *v.* Conolly, 8 C. B. 640.

Rescission is, as I have already intimated, *summi juris*, and will be precluded by an unreasonable delay on the part of the purchaser, who is not entitled to wait on the course of events, but should be prompt in ascertaining the defect, and acting as soon as it is discovered.[1] What is a reasonable time is a mixed question of fact depending on circumstances, and it has been said that an unexplained delay of four months, with full knowledge of the facts, is an absolute bar;[2] although, agreeably to recent English decisions, the purchaser may keep the question open so long as he does nothing to affirm the contract, and no change occurs on either side to vary the position of the parties or render the exercise of the right inequitable.[3]

Reasonable promptitude and diligence are not less requisite where goods which have been tendered or delivered are rejected or returned, not as a rescission of the contract but on the ground that it has not been fulfilled, and with a view to obtaining compensation in damages for the default.

Delivery and receipt are not necessarily such an acceptance as will defeat the right to reject articles which do not correspond with the terms of the agreement, and the buyer is on the contrary entitled to a reasonable time and opportunity to ascertain whether he is bound to receive and keep what the seller tenders.[4] He will not, therefore, lose the right to return the goods and sue for damages or the purchase-money by storing them in a public warehouse, or in his own cellar, until they can be subjected to such examination or analysis as will disclose whether they correspond with the samples exhibited by the vendor, or the description given in the contract of sale.[5]

[1] Clarke *v.* Dickson, 1 E. B. & E. 148; Matteson *v.* Holt, 45 Vt. 336; Hammond *v.* Pennock, 61 N. Y. 145; Buchenau *v.* Horney, 12 Ill. 336; Wolf *v.* Dietzsch, 75 id. 205; Prickett *v.* McFadden, 8 Ill. App. 197; Gatling *v.* Newell, 9 Ind. 572.

[2] Boothby *v.* Scales, 27 Wis. 626; Barnett *v.* Stanton, 2 Ala. 181; Hirshhorn *v.* Stewart, 49 Ia. 418; Whitcomb *v.* Denio, 52 Vt. 382.

[3] Clough *v.* Railway, L. R. 7 Ex. 26; Morrison *v.* The Marine Ins. Co., L. R. 8 Ex. 40, 197.

[4] Shields *v.* Reibe, 9 Ill. App. 598; Doane *v.* Dunham, 65 Ill. 512; Okell *v.* Smith, 1 Stark. 107; Street *v.* Blay, 2 B. & Ad. 456; Pope *v.* Allis, 115 U. S. 363, 372.

[5] Bannerman *v.* White, 10 C. B. N. S. 844; Webster *v.* Granger, 78 Ill. 230.

It is not essential to an effectual rejection that the buyer should incur the risk or expense of sending back the goods or placing them in a neutral custody, and his duty will ordinarily be fulfilled by depositing them in some building or receptacle suited to the storage of such things and notifying the vendor;[1] and it will then be incumbent on the latter to call for his property and take it away, and if he omits to do so and loss ensues it must be borne by him.[2]

The precise limits of the right and the time within which it must be exercised cannot be easily defined, and while it may be lost at once through an unconditional acceptance with a knowledge of the circumstances, it will endure until the defect can be discovered by such means as are usual in the course of business,[3] unless the buyer has in the mean time done something which alters the condition of the goods or renders it impracticable to reinstate the seller, when, from the nature of things, he will be compelled to seek redress in an action for damages or by way of recoupment or set-off.[4]

"When," said Bell, J., in Dailey *v.* Green, "the contract is executory, as it always is when a particular article is ordered without being seen, from one who undertakes that it shall be of a given quality or description, and the thing sent as such is never completely accepted, the buyer is not bound to keep or pay for the article on any terms, though no fraud was intended by the vendor.[5] But then he must return the goods as soon as he detects the deficiency, or at least give notice of his intention not to accept them." In this instance, lumber that had been sold by a sample to which it did not correspond and delivered to the purchaser, was left by him in an insecure position without notifying the vendor and swept away by a flood; and the court held that he had made the lumber his

[1] Bannerman *v.* White, 10 C. B. N. S. 844; Lucy *v.* Mouflet, 5 H. & N. 229; Grimoldby *v.* Wells, L. R. 10 C. P. 391.

[2] Okell *v.* Smith, 1 Stark. 107; Heilbutt *v.* Hickson, L. R. 7 C. P. 438; Rood *v.* Priestley, 58 Wis. 255, 260; Dailey *v.* Green, 3 Harris, 118; Youghiogheny Iron and Coal Co. *v.* Smith, 16 P. F. S. 340.

[3] Pennock *v.* Stygles, 54 Vt. 226; Webster *v.* Granger, 78 Ill. 230.

[4] Heilbutt *v.* Hickson, L. R. 7 C. P. 438.

[5] Hibbert *v.* Shee, 1 Camp. 113; Street *v.* Blay, 2 B. & Ad. 456.

own, and might give the inferiority of quality in evidence to reduce the verdict though not as a complete defence.

If the seller declines to send for or take back the goods on being duly notified, the purchaser is not bound to keep them indefinitely, and may, as in other cases where a man is needlessly burdened with chargeable or perishable property belonging to another, disburden himself by a sale as the seller's agent and on his behalf, and the account may then be balanced by charging the buyer with the net proceeds, and crediting him with the difference between the contract price and what the goods would have been worth had the contract been fulfilled.[1] The sale should be made with due notice to the vendor, and on his account, and if these precautions are not observed it is an acceptance of the goods, and the purchaser will be answerable for the purchase-money less the damages resulting from the breach.[2] Such at least is the view generally taken in the United States,[3] although it was rejected in Buffington *v.* Quantin,[4] on grounds that are not clear.

Latent defects stand on a different footing from such as are discoverable by inspection, and the question is not how much time has elapsed, but was the delay unreasonable in view of the circumstances;[5] and in determining this question regard may be had to the conduct of the vendor, and whether his manner or language was such as to induce the purchaser to prolong the trial or omit any step that might have led to an earlier discovery of the fault.[6]

In Heilbutt *v.* Hickson, shoes which had been sold by sample with a knowledge that they were intended for use in the French army during a winter campaign, were tendered

[1] Powell *v.* Horton, 2 Bing. N. C. 668.

[2] Loder *v.* Kekule, 3 C. B. N. S. 128; Chapman *v.* Morton, 11 M. & W. 534, 540.

[3] See Sands *v.* Taylor, 5 Johns. 395; Pollen *v.* Le Roy, 30 N. Y. 549; Girard *v.* Taggart, 5 S. & R. 19.

[4] 17 Pa. 312.

[5] Bannerman *v.* White, 10 C. B. N. S. 844; Woodle *v.* Whitney, 23 Wis. 55; McCormick *v.* Basal, 50 Ia. 523; Pennock *v.* Stygles, 54 Vt. 226.

[6] Adams *v.* Richards, 2 H. Bl. 573; Heilbutt *v.* Hickson, L. R. 7 C. P. 438, 452.

inspected and received in London, and the purchase-money repaid. They were subsequently forwarded to Lille and rejected by the military authorities there, because a large number of the soles proved on examination to contain paper fillings, and were unfit for army use. The purchasers thereupon required the sellers to take back the shoes, and on their refusal brought an action for the non-fulfilment of the contract, and claimed the amount paid as damages, together with the cost of forwarding the shoes to Lille, and the profits that would have been made had they been accepted by the French government. It was contended for the defence that the acceptance in London was absolute and vested a right of property in the purchasers, which nothing that occurred subsequently could defeat. The plaintiffs had their attention directed to the question whether the soles contained paper, and might have ripped a sufficient number to ascertain the truth. A purchaser moreover, had no right to reject unless he could place the seller *in statu quo;* and here the purchasers had, by sending the goods to Lille, and the consequent delay, so altered the condition of things that they could not reasonably return the shoes.

The court held that this view would have been correct, had not the defendants, while the inspection and delivery were taking place in London, and the bulk of the shoes were still there, written to say that they would take back such shoes as might be thrown on the buyer's hands in consequence of paper in the soles. The plaintiffs were not therefore, limited to the difference between the value of the shoes actually delivered and what would have been their value had they been according to the contract, but might recover the entire amount which they had paid for the shoes, with such other damages as were the legal consequences of the breach. Brett, J., dissented from so much of the judgment as implied that a recovery could not have been had on the original agreement. The defendants knew that the shoes would be inspected by the authorities at Lille, and declined if the soles were found to be defective, and had, with this knowledge, made the shoes personally or through their servants with a secret fault that could not be discovered by an inspection made in the ordinary course of business. It followed that the inspection at Lille was substituted for that contemplated in the contract, and became the test whether the shoes were or were not according to the samples.

The principle applies to a breach arising from a failure to deliver at the appointed time, as well as when it consists in a defect of kind or quality, and is stated in the following judgment of the Illinois Court of Appeal: "A voluntary acceptance without objection of a purchased article where there are no compulsory circumstances necessitating such acceptance, and no special damages to be occasioned thereby, may properly be regarded as evincing an intention to waive the time specified for delivery. But where the circumstances are such as to show that the acceptance can in no just sense be regarded as voluntary, but rather as compulsory, the presumption of an intention to waive does not arise. The appellants were engaged in the construction of a public work, for the completion of which they had given bonds. The work was but half finished, and they could obtain bricks of the requisite quality nowhere but from the appellees. They notified them of their necessities, and requested them to comply with their contract. To say that an acceptance after the time for delivery had passed, under such circumstances, was voluntary in such sense as to evince an intention to waive their right to claim damages for the delay, would be a perversion of language. They did the best they could in the situation in which they found themselves placed."[1] A like view was taken in Hansen *v.* Kirtly,[2] as to the effect of a subsequent acceptance on the right to compensation for the loss occasioned by a failure to deliver at the day.[3]

Agreeably to the recent course of decision in New York and some of the other States, the acceptance or retention of an

[1] Ramsey *v.* Tully, 12 Ill. App. 463; Havana, Rantoul & East R. R. Co. *v.* Walsh, 85 Ill. 58.

[2] 11 Ia. 565.

[3] See Priestly *v.* Northern Ind. and Chic. R. R. Co., 26 Ill. 205; Haven *v.* Wakefield, 39 id. 509; Tobey *v.* Price, 75 id. 645, to the same effect.

article which does not satisfy the terms of the contract is a waiver of the default, which precludes the right to return it or even to make a counter claim for damages.[1] The rule has been applied in some instances to reclamations for defects of quality, and in others when the variance was in species or kind. As stated in Gaylord Manufacturing Company *v.* Allen,[2] it is as follows: "In the absence of fraud or latent defects an acceptance of the article sold upon an executory contract, after an opportunity to examine it, is a consent and agreement that the article is satisfactory and as conforming to the contract, and bars all claim for compensation for any defects that may exist in the article. The party cannot, under such circumstances, retain the property, and afterwards sue or counter-claim for damages, under pretence that it was not of the character and quality or description called for by the agreement."[3]

Accordingly, where the defendant purchased all the lumber at the plaintiff's mill at a certain rate for prime, at another rate for merchantable, and at still another rate for refuse, and gave a receipt on delivery after an opportunity for inspection, for so many thousand feet of "prime," so many of "merchantable," and so many of "refuse," evidence that all the lumber for which the plaintiff sought to recover as prime, and a large portion of that claimed to be merchantable was in fact refuse, was rejected as inadmissible as a defence or in mitigation of damages. It was decided on like grounds in Comstock *v.* Sanger[4] that "acceptance with an opportunity for examination" is, under the authorities and on principle, a waiver of the right to compensation, and Chapman *v.* Morton[5] and Parker *v.* Palmer[6] were cited in support of the proposition, al-

[1] Reed *v.* Randall, 29 N. Y. 358; Gaylord Man. Co. *v.* Allen, 53 id. 515; Dounce *v.* Dow, 57 id. 16; 64 id. 411; Dutchess Co. *v.* Harding, 49 id. 321; Gilson *v.* Bingham, 43 Vt. 410; Sprague *v.* Blake, 20 Wend. 61; Hargous *v.* Stone, 1 Selden, 73; Mackey *v.* Swartz, 60 Ia. 710; Haase *v.* Nonemacher, 21 Minn. 486.

[2] 53 N. Y. 519.

[3] Dutchess Co. *v.* Harding, 49 N. Y. 321; M'Cormick *v.* Sarson, 45 id. 265; Reed *v.* Randall, 29 id. 358, and cases cited.

[4] 51 Mich. 497.

[5] 11 M. & W. 534, 541.

[6] 4 B. & Ald. 387, 393.

though they simply show that the buyer becomes answerable on acceptance for the contract price without losing the right to recoup the damages.

These decisions can hardly be said to have been rendered with a due regard for the exigencies of trade. A manufacturer who has ordered the coal on which he depends for motive power, or the materials without which his wheels and spindles cannot be profitably employed, may be obliged to accept an inferior article or sustain a greater loss, and should not be denied compensation for any injury that may result from the vendor's default.[1] Such is the undoubted rule where the cause of action is a breach of warranty, and the difference between such cases and an executory contract for the delivery of goods of a certain kind or answering to a sample, is technical rather than real.[2] A tender made not under or as a fulfilment of the contract, but in satisfaction and so accepted, will undoubtedly preclude the purchaser from recovering damages for the breach; but such an agreement ought not to be implied in the absence of proof, and the presumption is, until the contrary is shown, that the vendor means to abide by the agreement and do what he can to carry it into effect.[3]

In Day *v.* Pool,[4] the plaintiffs ordered rock-candy syrup, with a stipulation that it must not crystallize, and the defendants filled the order with a warranty that the syrup would answer the terms prescribed. The syrup was delivered in parcels and found to crystallize; but the plaintiffs used it in their business with a knowledge of the defect, and brought suit for the damages resulting from the breach of the contract. The court held that although they might have been precluded by the acceptance of the syrup had the contract simply been for the delivery of syrup of a certain kind or quality, yet they

[1] Merrill *v.* Nightingale, 39 Wis. 247; Bishop *v.* Price, 24 id. 480; Ramsey *v.* Tully, 12 Ill. App. 463; *ante.*

[2] Dayton *v.* Hooglund, 39 Ohio St. 671; Cooch *v.* Money, 5 Del. 177; Bagley *v.* Cleveland Rolling Mill Co., 21 Federal Rep. 159, 165.

[3] See Coit *v.* Schwartz, 29 Kan. 344; Ramsey *v.* Tully, 12 Ill. App. 463; McArdle *v.* Atha, 29 Hun, 219; Camors *v.* Gomila, 9 Miss. App. 205; Croninger *v.* Paige, 48 Wis. 229.

[4] 52 N. Y. 416.

were entitled to judgment on the express undertaking given by the defendants.[1] It was well settled that where the sale was executed the purchaser might keep the goods and enforce the warranty, and there was no reason why the principle should not apply to executory contracts. Such a distinction is not easily reconcilable with principle, and would seem to subordinate the sense to a merely formal difference. For as a warranty is an incident of a consummated and completed sale, and its proper office in an executory contract is simply to define what one party is bound to render and the other entitled to demand, it can have no greater effect in this connection than any other plain, descriptive words.[2] Whether the undertaking is for the delivery of uncrystallizable syrup, or of syrup with an undertaking that it will not crystallize, the contract is substantially the same and should lead to the same result. The case of Day *v.* Pool would, therefore, seem to be an endeavor to get back by a side path to the main line of decision, which had been abandoned without sufficient cause. It was accordingly held in Ketchum *v.* Wells,[3] that since the bolts in question were necessary for stocking the defendant's mill and keeping it in operation, and could not be returned without inconvenience, the bare fact that they were kept and used did not operate as a waiver of the right to prove that they were not such as the contract called for, and recoup the damages from the price.

When, however, the same argument was used not long afterward under analogous circumstances, it was disregarded, and the court held that the purchaser had forfeited the right to compensation for the insufficiency of the wood that had been delivered to him under an executory contract, by accepting it without objection, although it was essential to the fulfilment of agreements which he had entered into with third persons, in reliance on that which the defendants had broken. Save when the defect was latent, or there was no opportunity for

1 Reed *v.* Randall, 29 N. Y. 358; McCormick *v.* Sarson, 45 id. 265.

2 Cooch *v.* Money, 5 Del. 177; Bagley *v.* Cleveland Rolling Mill Co., 21 Federal Rep. 159; Dayton *v.* Hooglund, 39 Ohio St. 671.

3 19 Wis. 26.

inspection, the seller must be notified at once or within a reasonable time of the insufficiency of the goods, and a failure to adopt this course would preclude the buyer from returning them subsequently or enforcing a claim for damages.

In the subsequent case of Morehouse *v.* Comstock,[1] there was another shift in the current of decision. Apples which had been forwarded in obedience to a written order were delivered to the buyer, who received them, paid the freight, and commenced selling them by the barrel without examination. His customers complained, and it was found that a considerable portion of the apples were unmerchantable. These facts were communicated to the seller some twenty days afterward, but without an offer to return the fruit. The court held, on the authority of Bonnell *v.* Jacobs,[2] that acceptance is not a waiver of the right to damages, unless the defect is patent and there is a full opportunity for examination, and the purchaser may maintain an action for damages or recoup them from the price, without offering to return the goods or notifying the vendor that they are defective.

Whatever the rule may be under other circumstances, it is clear that where a trial is requisite to ascertain whether the contract has been fulfilled, or the article will answer the object for which it is purchased,[3] it may be kept and put to its appropriate use without losing the right to compensation for any defect that may subsequently appear.[4] It is consequently unnecessary to return a furnace which has been bought for the purpose of warming a house, or to notify the seller before bringing suit. In like manner seed which has been sold as being of a particular kind or of an early growth, may be sown, and the vendor held answerable for a loss of the crop arising from a defect of quality or kind.[5]

So it is not reasonable to require a retail dealer to open the packages which are forwarded to him, forthwith, and he may,

1 42 Wis. 626.

2 36 Wis. 59.

3 McCormick *v.* Basal, 50 Ia. 523.

4 Bonnell *v.* Jacobs, 36 Wis. 59; Woodle *v.* Whitney, 23 id. 55; Craver *v.* Hornburg, 26 Kan. 94.

5 Van Wyck *v.* Allen, 69 N. Y. 61.

on the contrary, keep them on his shelves without examination until they are called for by his customers, or there is an opportunity for disposing of them in the course of trade; although he should, agreeably to the American decisions, notify the vendor as soon as he discovers or has reason for suspecting the defect.[1]

The following extract from the judgment in Lewis *v.* Rountree,[2] gives a succinct and accurate exposition of the law, save in terming that a warranty which was of the essence of the contract. "The defendants agreed to deliver 517 barrels of strained rosin, which clearly amounts to a warranty that the article which they deliver is of that specific description. It may be called a condition precedent, and so it is, for the purpose that the vendee is not obliged to receive the article unless it comes within the description. But it is more than that; for it is held, as will presently be seen, that after the vendee has received and retained the articles, he may recover damages if they do not come within the specific description; the description must therefore be a warranty or what practically is equivalent to it.[3] Of course, it is not meant that words of description are always a warranty. But the cases in which that is held have all something special to take them out of the rule, and to show that in those cases it was not so intended. That the plaintiffs had an opportunity to inspect the rosin before or when it was delivered, and did in fact select the particular barrels out of a large number, did not amount to a waiver of the warranty that it should be of the specific description. This is reasonable. It is almost impossible, or at least very difficult, to tell from any inspection of a barrel of rosin short of breaking it up into fragments, whether it contains dross — that is chips, dirt, etc. — or not. And to break it up makes it unfit for transportation and unmarketable.

"In Jones *v.* Just,[4] Mellor, J., says, 'In general, on the sale of goods by a particular description, whether the vendee is able to inspect them or not, it is an implied term of the con-

[1] Doane *v.* Dunham, 65 Ill. 512; Morehouse *v.* Comstock, 42 Wis. 626.

[2] 78 N. C. 323.

[3] Benjamin on Sales, §§ 600, 647.

[4] L. R. 3 Q. B. 197.

tract, that they shall reasonably answer such description, and if they do not it is unnecessary to put any other question to the jury.' . . .

"It is said, however, that as soon as the plaintiff discovered that a part of the rosin did not come within the description of strained rosin, which he did after it arrived in New York, he was bound to notify the defendants of the defect, and to offer to return the rosin to them. We think this is answered by the case of Poulton *v.* Lattimore.[1] In that case Littledale, J., said, 'I am of opinion that where goods are warranted, the vendee is entitled, although he do not return them to the vendor or give notice of their defective quality, to bring an action for breach of warranty, etc.' It is true in that case the plaintiff declared upon a breach of warranty as to quality; but there can be no difference in principle between such a warranty and one as to the identity of the article.[2] The only result of a failure to offer to return the goods, or to notify the vendor of their defective quality, is to raise a presumption that the complaint of the quality is not well-founded. In this case the plaintiff had paid for the goods, and the property had passed to him. The defendant was under no obligation to receive them back and return the price. The case of Cox *v.* Long[3] supports this view. The plaintiff had contracted and paid for shingles of certain dimensions, and had received and used those delivered with knowledge that they did not correspond to the warranty, without having offered to return them, and it was held that he was entitled to recover damages for breach of the warranty."

The better opinion is in accordance with this decision: that a buyer does not forfeit the right to compensation, by using or selling the goods without making an examination for the purpose of ascertaining whether the description is true, although a failure to complain or notify the seller may afford ground for an inference that a subsequent reclamation is unfounded.[4]

1 9 B. & C. 259.

2 Benjamin on Sales, §§ 897, 899, note r.

3 69 N. C. 7.

4 Cooch *v.* Money, 5 Del. 177; Bagley *v.* Cleveland Rolling Mill, 21 Federal Rep. 159, 165; Dayton *v.* Hooglund, 39 Ohio, 671; Story on Sales,

Pleading is the test of legal principles, and on referring to Lilly's Entries and other authentic treatises we shall find that the proper mode of declaring is to describe the subject-matter in the terms of the contract, and then aver that the seller did not and would not deliver such goods, though the buyer was ready to accept and pay.[1] Hence in a case like Bannerman *v.* White, the count should set forth that the defendant agreed to sell and the plaintiff to buy the defendant's crop of unsulphured hops, but that the defendant failed to supply such hops as aforesaid, and on the contrary tendered hops which were contaminated with sulphur. The kind, quality, time, and place of growth would each be a part of the undertaking that must be fulfilled in order to exonerate the seller and bind the purchaser, and the difference between such a sale and a contract for the next year's crop is that one would relate to specific goods and the other to goods not yet in existence.

It results, from what has been said in this and the foregoing chapters, that where the contract is executory, and the title remains in the seller, three demands or causes of action may grow out of the tender or delivery of goods which do not correspond with the terms prescribed.

First, the goods may be accepted, the price paid, and a suit brought for the amount by which their actual value falls short of what they would have been worth had the agreement been fulfilled; or the price may be withheld, and a sufficient amount recouped or deducted to cover the loss. Secondly, they may be rejected, and a recovery had in damages for the excess of the market value of such goods as the seller agreed to deliver over the contract price. Thirdly, the contract may be rescinded on the ground of failure of consideration, and indebitatus assumpsit maintained for the recovery of the purchase money, or so much of it as has been paid. Which course should be adopted depends on the circumstances; but the third is obviously advisable where the purchaser has made a disad-

§ 405; Benjamin on Sales, §§ 825, 859; Shields *v.* Reibe, 9 Ill. App. 598; Doane *v.* Dunham, 65 Ill. 512.

[1] See Lilly's Entries, 16; 2 Chitty's Pleadings, 270.

vantageous bargain by giving more than he would have made had the contract been fulfilled, and will consequently be a gainer by setting it aside.[1]

The language held in some of the recent English cases is scarcely reconcilable with the doctrine of Mondel *v.* Steel[2] that the acceptance of goods which do not correspond with the terms of an executory contract gives birth to an implied agreement to pay as much as they are worth, which must be enforced through a *quantum valebat* as distinguished from a suit on the contract.[3]

In Behn *v.* Burness, cited and approved in Heilbutt *v.* Hickson,[4] the law was stated as follows: "In cases where the thing sold is not specific, and the property has not passed by the sale, the vendee may refuse to receive the thing proffered to him in performance of the contract, on the ground that it does not correspond with the descriptive statement, or, in other words, that the condition expressed in the contract has not been performed; still, if he receive the thing sold and has the enjoyment of it, he cannot afterward treat the descriptive statement as a condition, but only as an agreement for a breach of which he may bring an action to recover damages." And in the last edition[5] of the notes to Williams' Saunders,[6] the result of several of the cases is thus stated by the learned editor. "When it appears that the consideration has been executed in part, that which was before a warranty or condition precedent loses the character of a condition, or, to speak more properly, ceases to be available as a condition, and becomes a warranty in the narrower sense of the word, namely, a stipulation by way of agreement for the breach of which a compensation must be sought in damages." This language may convey an erroneous impression. Mutual promises by the seller to deliver, and by the pur-

1 Smethurst *v.* Woolston, 5 W. & S. 106, 109; Wilkinson *v.* Ferree, 12 Harris, 190.

2 8 M. & W. 858.

3 Shields *v.* Reibe, 9 Ill. App. 598; Doane *v.* Dunham, 65 Ill. 512; Behn *v.* Burness, 3 Best & Smith, 751.

4 L. R. 7 C. P. 438.

5 1871.

6 Vol. i. p. 554.

chaser to accept and pay for goods answering a certain description, or of a certain kind, are not conditions, save as every contract is conditioned for the fulfilment of the consideration on which it depends. If the thing tendered be not the thing described, it may be declined not as a repudiation of the agreement, but because the purchaser is entitled to require that the agreement shall be performed. And in determining this question, the descriptive words should be regarded as a whole and no one term singled out as a condition without sufficient cause. A sale of the vendor's last year's growth of unsulphured hops, is an undertaking on his part to deliver hops which are the produce of his own vineyard and unsulphured; and there is no more reason for holding that the term "unsulphured" is a condition if the hops are rejected, or a warranty if they are accepted, than there is for attaching a like signification to the entire clause, or so much of it as designates the subject-matter as hops grown by the seller or gathered from his vines. Each and every part of such a stipulation is an undertaking from the beginning and retains that character to the end, whether the article be accepted or declined, the difference being that in the latter case the buyer elects to treat the breach as partial instead of entire. Instead therefore, of terming the descriptive words a condition that may be converted into a warranty by acceptance, it seems more accurate to say that they are an undertaking which may be treated as a condition if not fulfilled.[1]

The function of a promise is to bind, that of a condition to suspend or annul; and if promises may operate as conditions, it is owing to an equitable interpretation of the contract as a whole, and because the failure of the consideration may involve the failure of the obligation, and not from the form of words employed on either side.

Mutual and concurrent promises on one side to do or render, and on the other to pay or compensate, were accordingly so far from being regarded as conditions at Rome that even when the contract was consensual each had an independent existence, and might be enforced, notwithstanding a failure to

[1] See 3 Best & Smith, 761, note, Am. ed.

fulfil the other.[1] Such also was the rule at common law where both promises were to be performed simultaneously until it was set aside by Lord Mansfield.[2]

The distinction between stipulations which are designed to impose, and stipulations which are designed to suspend or modify obligations is essential, and cannot be overlooked without a liability to error.[3] Whether the contract is to deliver goods of a certain kind by a particular vessel, or that they shall be delivered if the vessel arrives with the goods, the purchaser is not bound unless she arrives and brings the goods; but while the vendor's obligation is absolute in the former case, it is conditional in the latter, and he may plead that the vessel did not come into port or that she had no such cargo.

A sale of goods to arrive by a particular ship is subject to two contingencies, — that the ship shall reach her destination, and that the goods shall be on board, — and unless both stipulations are fulfilled the contract fails.[4] So a contract for the sale and delivery of a given kind and quantity of merchandise, "to arrive" at a certain time, will fail unless the entire quantity arrives within the time prescribed, and the seller will not be answerable for withholding a smaller quantity which actually comes to hand.[5]

Such contracts are clearly conditional, as depending on contingencies for which the vendor does not undertake to be answerable, and by which both parties agree to abide. A description of the goods as "now on passage," or "on board," is, on the other hand, an undertaking which binds the vendor,

[1] Maynz, §§ 177, 210, 218; Accarias, No. 612; Ortolan, Explic. Histoire des Inst. tome 3, p. 282, cited Benjamin on Sales, § 410.

[2] Gower *v.* Capper, Croke Eliz. 543; Nichols *v.* Raynbred, Hobart, 88; Bettisworth *v.* Campion, Yelv. 134; Thomas *v.* Cadwallader, Willes, 496; Langdell, Summary, §§ 140, 141.

[3] See Davis *v.* Shields, 24 Wend. 322, 326, where the line was drawn, and Shields *v.* Pettee, 4 Comst. 122, where it seems to have been overlooked.

[4] Dike *v.* Reitlinger, 23 Hun, 242; Lovatt *v.* Hamilton, 5 M. & W. 639; Johnson *v.* MacDonald, 9 id. 600; Shields *v.* Pettee, 2 Sandf. 262.

[5] Russell *v.* Nicoll, 3 Wend. 112; Alwyn *v.* Pryor, Ry. & M. 406; Boyd *v.* Siffkin, 2 Cowper, 326; Idle *v.* Thornton, 3 Camp. 274.

and entitles the purchaser to damages, if the ship arrives without the goods; and if the purchaser is discharged it is on the ground of the failure of consideration.[1]

In Gorrissen *v.* Perrin,[2] the sale, as set forth in the bought note, was of "1170 bales gambier, now on passage from Singapore, and expected to arrive at London, namely, per Ravenscraig, 805 bales; per Agnes Duff, 365." Both vessels arrived with bales, which though answering to the language of the contract were the property of third persons, and with other bales which though belonging to the seller were deficient in point of weight, and rejected on that ground. It was contended for the defence that the words "now on passage" were like "expected to arrive," a condition which invalidated the contract if broken, and not a stipulation that must be fulfilled. The court held that although the contract was conditioned on the arrival of the vessel and would have failed if she were lost during the voyage, it was absolute that such bales as it described had been laden and formed part of the cargo. "Now on passage" might be a condition precedent to the buyer's liability, but was an undertaking which the seller was bound to fulfil.

In like manner, while an undertaking to pay for a patent, or value received in any other form, "in such manner as shall be mutually agreed," is so far a condition that the seller cannot maintain indebitatus assumpsit until such an agreement has occurred, it is also an undertaking to use every reasonable effort to come to terms; which will be broken if the buyer declines the terms proposed by the seller without making any reasonable proposal of his own.[3]

It is of little consequence how the descriptive terms of the contract are designated if their true import be steadily kept in view; but classifying them as conditions may convey the idea that they are nothing more, and, if broken, will not only exonerate the seller but deprive the purchaser of all right under the contract, and may place him in a less favorable position than if it had been fulfilled.

[1] Hale *v.* Rawson, 4 C. B. N. S. 85; Simond *v.* Braddon, 2 id. 324.

[2] 2 C. B. N. S. 681.

[3] Hall *v.* Conder, 2 C. B. N. S. 22, 53.

Such was the ground taken for the defence in Gorrissen *v.* Perrin; and it was successfully maintained in Shields *v.* Pettee,[1] where the question arose on the following memorandum: "Sold, . . . 150 tons Gartshemi pig-iron No. 1, at $29 per ton, . . . on board 'Siddons.'" The ship, which was then at sea, arrived some days afterward with iron which turned out to be of inferior quality not answering to the description No. 1, Gartshemi. Sixty tons were delivered to the purchasers, who on discovering the defect refused to accept the residue, or pay more for what they had received than the contract price, after deducting the loss resulting from the default. The seller brought suit, and it was held that the words "on board," were a condition on which the entire obligation turned. When the ship came into port without the iron for which the purchasers had stipulated the contract was at an end; and the subsequent delivery and acceptance of iron of a different kind, gave rise to a new implied agreement to pay the market price of the iron which they had received, although owing to an accidental rise it considerably exceeded the rate originally fixed. It was not a sale, but an undertaking, that if 150 tons of Gartshemi pig-iron of the quality denominated No. 1 came by the "Siddons," one party would deliver and the other would receive it, at a certain price per ton. The iron so called for did not arrive, but iron of a different quality, and the cause of action arose on a new implied contract that had nothing in common with that which had failed. It is not easy to coincide with this decision. The contract of sale was seemingly subject to only one contingency, and when that was satisfied by the arrival of the vessel, became as absolute as if "now in store" had been written instead of "on board;" and the result was a surprise on the purchaser, who naturally expected in accepting the sixty tons, that he would be entitled to an allowance for the inferiority of quality, and was not aware that he was entering into a new agreement on less favorable terms.

It is not therefore surprising, that in Davis *v.* Shields,[2] the court arrived at a different conclusion from premises which

[1] 2 Sandf. 262; 4 Comst. 122.

[2] 24 Wend. 322.

were nearly the same. The contract there was "Sold, . . . 50 tons of English bar-iron, . . . to arrive on board brig Anna, said iron to be in good order or no sale." The vessel brought a cargo of English bar-iron to a rising market, and the vendors disposed of it to third persons, on the ground that it was not in good order and they might consequently treat the contract as void. This construction was summarily overruled. "It is," said Cowen, J., "in plain English this: I have broken my promise, and therefore the promisee has no right to recover damages against me. It is of the essence of a contract that the promisor or covenantor should be bound, and not have it in his power to discharge himself at pleasure."

Such is the established rule with regard to stipulations intended for the benefit of the covenantee; and even when it is expressly provided that the agreement shall be void in the event of non-performance he may waive the forfeiture and recover compensation for the breach.[1]

In Dike *v.* Reitlinger,[2] the contract was executory for the sale of goods "to arrive," with a clause providing that they should be equal in quality to a sample which had been exhibited to the purchaser. The vessel came into port with goods on board of a like kind with the sample, but inferior in quality; and it was decided that while "to arrive" was a condition that would have annulled the contract had no such goods been on board, the stipulation as to quality was an undertaking which bound the seller and rendered him liable in damages for the breach. The court endeavored to distinguish the case from Shields *v.* Pettee, but both appear to be substantially the same.

The effect of the non-fulfilment of the provisions of a contract of sale in exonerating the party who suffers from the breach, depends in general on how far it involves a failure of consideration. We have seen that where the thing tendered under an executory agreement does not correspond with its terms as regards time, quality, or kind, the breach is

[1] See 1 Sm. L. C. 7 Am. ed. 112; Jones *v.* Carter, 15 M. & W. 718; Clark *v.* Jones, 1 Den. 517.

[2] 23 Hun, 242.

complete, and the buyer equally entitled to reject the goods, whether the variance is confined to a single point, or extends to all, because an entire consideration is broken in every part if each be not fulfilled.[1]

In like manner, if the buyer be not ready to pay in full at the appointed time and place, the seller may treat the breach as complete, and a subsequent tender will come too late. An entire consideration which fails partially, fails wholly; and the court has no jurisdiction to inquire into the extent of the difference, or whether justice would be done by allowing the plaintiff to recover with an allowance for the loss.[2]

Consideration is nevertheless, as I have elsewhere stated, the result of agreement, and may be either performance, a promise to perform, or a promise followed by performance. In the ordinary case of a sale on credit, the consideration on one side is actual delivery, on the other the buyer's word; or he may conversely agree to pay in advance and trust the vendor for the goods.

In like manner, when goods are sold with warranty, the buyer impliedly agrees to rely on the seller's assurance that they are such as described, and to accept and pay whether it be or be not fulfilled. A breach on the seller's part does not therefore discharge the buyer, and he must seek redress in an action for damages, or according to the recent practice through an abatement of the contract price on equitable grounds.[3] Or, to state the principle somewhat differently, inasmuch as the right of property vests indefeasibly in the buyer, and the seller becomes entitled to the price immediately on the completion of the contract, so the one can no more return the goods because the warranty is broken, than the other can maintain trover or replevin for a default in the payment of the price.[4]

[1] Chanter *v.* Leese, 5 M. & W. 698; 4 id. 295; Giles *v.* Edwards, 7 T. R. 181.

[2] Smith *v.* Lewis, 40 Ind. 98; Bowes *v.* Shand, L. R. 1 Q. B. Div. 470; 2 id. 112; 2 App. Cases, 455, 467; Devaux *v.* Conolly, 8 C. B. 640; Norrington *v.* Wright, 115 U. S. 188, 204; Brawley *v.* The U. S. 96 id. 168.

[3] Mondel *v.* Steel, 8 M. & W. 858, 871.

[4] Thornton *v.* Wynn, 12 Wheat. 183; Houghton *v.* Carpenter, 40 Vt. 588; Voorhees *v.* Earl, 2 Hill, 288; Cary *v.* Gruman, 4 id. 625; Muller

A different view prevails in Massachusetts where a warranty may be treated as a condition subsequent at the election of the buyer, who may on the discovery of the breach, rescind the contract and recover back the price.[1] A like view prevails in Maryland and some of the other States,[2] although it is essential to success in such a suit that the plaintiff should have been diligent, and have done all in his power to replace the vendor in the position which he held before the sale.[3]

It was said in Bagley *v.* Cleveland Rolling Mill Co.[4] that "there is no distinction in principle, as to the rights and remedies of a purchaser, between a cause of action arising out of a breach of contract by the vendor to deliver an article of a specified quality or description, or out of the breach of a representation which is collateral to the contract, or out of such a breach when the representation or warranty is implied instead of being expressed. In either case there is an agreement in substance and purport to the same effect; in either, the same presumption of fact arises from an acceptance of the article after discovery of its defects; whether the cause of action is for a breach of a contract or for the breach of a warranty is a mere matter of nomenclature,[5] and the breach of a promise implied by the law works the same consequences, imposes the same obligations, and creates the same rights as a breach of an express promise."

Such, undoubtedly, is the rule as regards contracts *in genere*, for the delivery of things of a certain kind; but it is not necessarily applicable to the sale of a specific chattel, and

v. Eno, 14 N. Y. 597; Kase *v.* John, 10 Watts, 107; Freyman *v.* Knecht, 28 P. F. S. 144; Owens *v.* Sturges, 67 Ill. 366; Walls *v.* Gates, 9 Mo. App. 241.

1 Perley *v.* Balch, 23 Pick. 283; Dorr *v.* Fisher, 1 Cush. 274; Bryant *v.* Isburgh, 13 Gray, 607; Boardman *v.* Spooner, 13 Allen, 353.

2 Hyatt *v.* Boyle, 5 Gill & J. 110; Franklin *v.* Long, 7 id. 407; Taymon *v.* Mitchell, 1 Md. Ch. 496; Horn *v.* Buck, 48 Md. 358; Rogers *v.* Hanson, 35 Ia. 283; Jack *v.* The Des Moines R. R. Co., 53 id. 399; Birdsall *v.* Carter, 11 Neb. 143; Marston *v.* Knight, 29 Me. 341; Warder *v.* Fisher, 48 Wis. 338.

3 Dorr *v.* Fisher; Horn *v.* Buck; Warder *v.* Fisher.

4 21 Federal Rep. 165.

5 Hastings *v.* Lovering, 2 Pick. 214.

the question then is one of intention, — Did the purchaser agree to become the owner and answerable for the price at all events, or only in case the article conforms to the description given by the vendor? In the latter case he must abide by his bargain, and seek indemnity through a cross-action or in a deduction from the price; in the former, he may either treat the breach as an entire failure of consideration and reject the goods, or pay what they are worth, as measured by the difference between what they ought to have been and what they are.

The buyer may maintain assumpsit on the warranty, or proceed in tort under the doctrine of the earlier common law, that the breach of a promise by which another has been induced to act may be a ground for a recovery in case, although the promise itself was not consciously false or under seal, and could not have been enforced in an action strictly *ex contractu*.[1] Whichever form is adopted it is not requisite to aver that the misrepresentation was intentional; and if the *scienter* be averred it may be treated as surplusage.[2] The safer method, consequently, is to declare in case on the warranty, adding a count for an intentional deceit, by representing the goods to be as the vendor knew they were not, and a recovery may then be had on the latter count on proof of the *scienter*, or on the former although there is no evidence that the vendor knew the warranty to be false.

"The ancient remedy for a false warranty was an action on the case sounding in tort.[3] The remedy by assumpsit is comparatively of modern introduction. In Williamson *v.* Allison, Lord Ellenborough said it had 'not prevailed generally above forty years.' In Stuart *v.* Wilkins, Lord Mansfield

[1] *Ante;* Williamson *v.* Allison, 2 East, 446; Jones *v.* Bright, 5 Bing. 533; Wood *v.* Smith, 5 M. & R. 124; Vanleer *v.* Earle, 2 Casey, 277; Evertson *v.* Miles, 6 Johns. 138; Freyman *v.* Knecht, 28 P. F. S. 144; Booth *v.* Northrop, 27 Conn. 325; Beeman *v.* Beech, 3 Vt. 53; Vail *v.* Strong, 10 id. 457; West *v.* Emery, 17 id. 584; Pennock *v.* Stygles, 54 id. 222; Blanton *v.* Wall, 4 Jones (N. C.), 532; 1 Sm. L. C. 7 Am. ed. 344; Notes to Chandelor *v.* Lopus.

[2] Osgood *v.* Lewis, 2 Harris & Gill, 495.

[3] Stuart *v.* Wilkins, 1 Douglas, 18; Williamson *v.* Allison, 2 East, 447.

regarded it as a novelty, and hesitated to give it the sanction of his authority. It is now well settled, both in English and American jurisprudence, that either mode of procedure may be adopted. Whether the declaration be in assumpsit or tort it need not aver a *scienter*. And if the averment be made it need not be proved." [1]

We have seen that the English law regarded a breach of warranty as a delict, that could not be given in evidence as a defence or set-off, and for which redress must be sought through an action on the case.[2] Until the change made by the recent Judicature Act the rule remained on this basis, with two considerable modifications; one, already noted, that assumpsit might be substituted for case in a suit on the warranty; the other, that the buyer might give the breach in evidence when sued for the purchase-money.[3] The right to rely on a breach of warranty as a defence was nevertheless confined to proving how much less the goods were worth as they were, than they would have been worth as warranted; and if the buyer desired compensation for consequential losses it was necessary to bring a cross-action, because set-off was unknown to the common law, and the statutes by which it was authorized did not include unliquidated damages.[4] Hence the purchaser of a ship might, agreeably to the rule as stated in Mondel *v.* Steel, give a defect in the workmanship or materials in evidence as a defence to an action for the price, but could not prove the loss which he had sustained in consequence of her inability to carry freight, or the damage to the cargo from her unsound condition.

The limit thus imposed on the right of set-off was logical rather than just, and tends to increase costs and litigation by compelling the buyer to make that which is in effect a whole the subject of two distinct inquiries.[5] Thus where a rope, which had been sold with an express or implied

[1] Schuhardt *v.* Allen, 1 Wallace, 359.

[2] *Ante;* Mondel *v.* Steel, 8 M. & W. 858, 870.

[3] Mondel *v.* Steel, 8 M. & W. 858, 870.

[4] Mondel *v.* Steel, 8 M. & W. 858, 871.

[5] Whitbeck *v.* Skinner, 7 Hill, 53, 56.

warranty of its fitness to raise heavy weights, broke under the strain of a cask of wine, all that the jury could deduct, under the common-law rule, in a suit brought for the purchase-money, was the amount by which a sound rope would exceed the value of that actually delivered, and the buyer was obliged to submit to the loss of the wine or seek redress in a cross-action. The distinction between diminution of value and damages is therefore generally discarded in the United States as technical, and the loss occasioned by a breach of warranty, false representation, or failure to comply with an executory contract, allowed to be deducted from the price; or to state the rule in the general terms in which it is applicable to every species of agreement, the defendant in an action *ex contractu* may prove that the plaintiff has violated the same contract, and thus preclude a recovery for more than the balance if any due the plaintiff.[1]

The rule applies whether the contract is executed or executory, under seal or by parol, to render services or for the sale or lease of land or chattels,[2] and includes damages growing out of a fraudulent representation or deceit in the making or fulfilment of the contract, as well as damages occasioned by a breach of warranty or the delivery of goods of a different kind.[3]

The principle is carried still further in Pennsylvania, where it was established, at an early period of Colonial history, that the defendant may not only defalk an unliquidated cross-demand, growing out of the same or another transaction, but have a certificate that the balance is in his favor, and proceed thereon to judgment and execution.[4]

[1] Whitbeck *v.* Skinner, 7 Hill, 53, 55; Davis *v.* Talcott, 2 Kernan, 184; Deen *v.* Herrold, 1 Wr. 150; Havana R. R. Co. *v.* Walsh, 85 Ill. 58; Withers *v.* Green, 9 How. 213; Epperley *v.* Bailey, 3 Ind. 72.

[2] The Mayor *v.* Mable, 3 Kernan, 151; Avery *v.* Willson, 81 N. Y. 341; Ives *v.* Van Epps, 22 Wend. 155.

[3] McAllister *v.* Reab, 4 Wend. 489; Muller *v.* Eno, 4 Kernan, 597; Green *v.* Bell, 3 Mo. App. 291; Van Epps *v.* Harrison, 5 Hill, 64; Steigelman *v.* Jeffries, 1 S. & R. 477; Heck *v.* Shener, 4 id. 249.

[4] Uhler *v.* Sanderson, 2 Wr. 128; Hunt *v.* Gilmore, 9 P. F. S. 450, 454; Preston *v.* Finney, 2 W. & S. 53.

Here, as in some other matters of greater moment, Pennsylvania led the way in a reform, which has been followed on both sides of the Atlantic, and the defendant may, under the law as codified in New York and some of the other States, maintain a counter-claim, or cross-action, and recover whatever amount is due to him in the transaction, considered as a whole.[1] Such, also, is now the English practice under the authority conferred by the Judicature Act.[2]

In the absence of consequential injuries, or where they are not admissible in evidence, the measure of damages for a breach of warranty is, as in the case of the acceptance of goods which do not correspond with the terms of an executory contract, the difference between the value of the goods as they actually are, and as they would have been had the warranty been fulfilled,[3] or in other words, how much less they will sell for in consequence of the defect which constitutes the breach;[4] and while the contract price may be given in evidence as indicating the estimate formed on either side at the time of sale,[5] it is not conclusive, and should be disregarded if at variance with the market or selling rate.[6]

"The rule," said Comstock, J., in Muller *v.* Eno,[7] "rests upon a comparison of value, and not of the price at which the article is bought and then sold again. The cases which establish the rule admit, as I certainly do, that the price agreed upon on a sale of goods with warranty is strong, and in the absence of other proof, controlling evidence of their value estimated as

[1] See McKnight *v.* Devlin, 52 N. Y. 399; Gillespie *v.* Torrance, 25 id. 306; Batterman *v* Pierce, 3 Hill, 171.

[2] See Benjamin on Sales, § 1353. Mersey Steel & Iron Co. *v.* Naylor, 9 Q. B. 648; 9 App. Cases, 434.

[3] Marsh *v.* McPherson, 15 Otto, 709; Wright *v.* Roach, 57 Me. 600.

[4] Shultz *v.* Christman, 6 Mo. App. 338; Hersey *v.* Long, 30 Minn. 114; Voorhees *v.* Earl, 2 Hill, 288; Cary *v.* Gruman, 4 id. 625; Muller *v.* Eno, 4 Kernan, 597, 606.

[5] Blanchard *v.* Ely, 21 Wend. 342, 347; Clare *v.* Maynard, 7 Car. & Payne, 741.

[6] Cothers *v.* Keever, 4 Barr, 168; Stetson *v.* Croskey, 2 P. F. S. 220; Lane *v.* Lantz, 27 Md. 211.

[7] 4 Kernan, 597.

sound. The price, however, comes in aid of the rule, but does not furnish it. So the price which a purchaser obtains on a resale is evidence against him of the actual value, if on such resale the defects are known, and of the sound value of similar goods, if the defects are not known. But the evidence which may be given under the rule must not be confounded with the rule itself."

The reason, as given in Seigworth *v.* Leffel,[1] is that a purchaser who has made a bad bargain is not entitled to throw the consequences of his own want of judgment on the vendor by holding him answerable for the loss arising not from a breach of the warranty, but because he gave too much for the goods. The question is not, therefore, Did the plaintiff lose or gain by the sale; but, What is the injury resulting from the non-fulfilment of the undertaking which is the cause of the suit?

If, for instance, a horse warranted sound, and that would be worth $200 if the warranty were true, is sold for $400, and labors under a defect or unsoundness that reduces its value by one half, the purchaser can recover only $100, and must bear the remaining loss, which is due to his having paid $200 more than the horse was worth. So if a bale of cotton sold for $800, and warranted sound, but which would be worth only $400 if the warranty were true, proves to be rotten, and will not sell for enough to cover costs and charges, the damages are $400, and the vendor may sue for and recover the rest of the purchase-money; as to which there is no defence. Conversely, the purchaser is not less entitled to damages because he is a gainer by the sale; and a man who gives $300 for a lame horse on the faith of a warranty, and which is worth that sum notwithstanding the defect, may recover $300 on proof that the horse would sell for $600, if it were sound, and thus in effect get the animal for nothing.

Where there is no definite or market price recourse must necessarily be had to other standards, and one measure of inferiority of value is what it would cost to place the buyer in

[1] 26 P. F. S. 476.

the same position as if the contract had been fulfilled.[1] If a machine which has been sold as perfect, proves to be out of repair, the buyer may consequently recover the amount requisite to put it in good order; and while one who has bought with a warranty that the article may be used without infringing a patent, is entitled to the amount for which a license may be obtained from the patentee, he will not be allowed to recover a larger sum.[2]

[1] See Whitney *v.* Allaire, 4 Den. 554; Parsons *v.* Sutton, 66 N. Y. 92; Benton *v.* Fay, 64 Ill. 417; Ramsey *v.* Tully, 12 Ill. App. 463.

[2] Croninger *v.* Paige, 48 Wis. 229; Barnhill *v.* Haigh, 3 P. F. S. 165.

CHAPTER XXIII.

PERFORMANCE.

Performance in respect to Quantity, Quality, Time, and Place. — Breach of an Executory Contract by Non-delivery of an Instalment. — Breach by Non-payment for an Instalment.

PERFORMANCE is, as the term implies, such a thorough fulfilment of a duty as puts an end to obligations by leaving nothing more to be done. The chief requisite consequently is that it shall be exact. The very terms of the agreement must be pursued, and if they are not the default cannot be excused on the ground that the difference is immaterial and occasions no appreciable injury.[1] Where a contract for the sale of land fixes a day for the execution of the deed, it must be strictly followed and a subsequent tender will be too late.[2]

In Jordan *v.* Cooper,[3] the court held that the delivery of a conveyance after the day prescribed and its acceptance by the vendee, was not such a fulfilment as would entitle the vendor to recover the purchase-money in an action of covenant on the agreement as originally made, nor without alleging that the time which it named had been waived and another substituted; and if a chancellor does not regard punctuality as essential in sales of land, it is because the contract being for a specific thing is self-executing and confers an equitable interest as

[1] Clark *v.* Wright, 5 Phila. 439; Young *v.* White, 5 Watts, 460; Norrington *v.* Wright, 115 U. S. 188, 189; Lowber *v.* Bangs, 2 Wallace, 728; Bowes *v.* Shand, 7 Q. B. 470; 2 id. 112; 2 App. Cases, 455, 463, 480.

[2] Sansom *v.* Rhodes, 5 Bing. N. C. 261; Seaward *v.* Willock, 5 East, 198, 208; Cornish *v.* Young, Selwyn N. P. 177; Hill *v.* Fisher, 34 Me. 143; Tilley *v.* Thomas, L. R. 3 Ch. App. 61, 67, 69; Sugden on Vend.

[3] 3 S. & R. 564.

soon as it is made, which will not fail through a subsequent default in the absence of a condition to that effect.[1]

Contracts for the manufacture or sale of chattels are subject to the same principle, and the purchaser will not be bound to accept and pay unless the contract is fulfilled as regards quantity, quality, place and time.[2]

The ruling principle is that each and every stipulation which enters into the description of that which is to be done or rendered, is equally material with every other, as tending to identify the subject-matter; and if any particular remains unfulfilled the entire contract is broken, and the party in default will not only be liable in damages but may be precluded from enforcing the promises on the other side.[3]

An excess may be as prejudicial in this regard as a deficiency, and if more is sent than the purchaser agreed to buy, he may decline the risk and trouble of selecting part and return the whole.[4] A man who orders 300 bales of rags is not bound to accept 360 bales;[5] and qualifying words, as, for instance, "about," or "more or less," will in the case of an executory contract be presumed to have been used to guard against slight and accidental variations, and not with a view to preclude the operation of the rule.[6] So where the contract is for the delivery of grain, "say not less than one hundred quarters," a smaller quantity than the minimum may be declined.[7] The goods must correspond in form as well as substance, because either may affect their selling value and the

[1] See 2 Leading Cases in Equity, 4 Am. ed.

[2] Norrington *v.* Wright, 115 U. S. 188, 203; Cash *v.* Hinkle, 36 Ia. 623; Foos *v.* Sabin, 84 Ill. 564; Young *v.* White, 5 Watts, 460; 2 Parsons on Contracts, 660; Addison on Contracts, 185, 188.

[3] Lowber *v.* Bangs, 2 Wallace, 728; Filley *v.* Pope, 115 U. S. 213; Behn *v.* Burness, 3 Best & Smith, 751; Bowes *v.* Shand, 1 Q. B. 470; 2 id. 112; 2 App. Cases, 455, 467.

[4] Rylands *v.* Kreitman, 19 C. B. N. S. 351; Levy *v.* Green, 1 E. & E. 969; Cunliffe *v.* Harrison, 6 Ex. 903; Rommel *v.* Wingate, 103 Mass. 327; Norrington *v.* Wright, 115 U. S. 188, 205.

[5] Cross *v.* Eglin, 2 B. & Ad. 106.

[6] Cross *v.* Eglin; Brawley *v.* The United States, 96 U. S. 168; Norrington *v.* Wright, 115 id. 188, 204.

[7] Bear *v.* Harnish, 3 Brews. 113; Leeming *v.* Snaith, 16 Q. B. 275.

court cannot treat as immaterial anything that the parties have agreed on, and a contract for the delivery of a commodity in packages or cases of a particular kind will not be fulfilled by a delivery in bulk.[1] So a sale of merchantable pine lumber, assorted in lengths and each kind piled separately by itself, imposes the duty of assortment and piling on the seller, and if he fails the buyer will be discharged.[2] The question is one of law, and it is error to instruct the jury to inquire whether the variance is essential and if in their opinion the contract is substantially performed, to find a verdict for the vendor with an allowance for the loss occasioned by the default.[3]

As Lord Blackburn observed in Bowes *v.* Shand,[4] "The parties for reasons best known to themselves have chosen to say, 'We bargained to take rice shipped in this particular region, at that particular time, on board that particular ship;'" and "before the defendants can be compelled to take anything in fulfilment of that contract, it must be shown not merely that it is equally good, but that it is the same article as they have bargained for."

It results from the same principle that when a day is fixed for the fulfilment of an executory contract of sale, the purchaser will be discharged if the goods are not ready for delivery or tendered at the time prescribed.[5] Punctuality is a requisite of the first importance in business, and the parties may enforce it by making time of the essence of the contract.[6]

Accordingly, where the contract is for 300 tons of Madras rice, to be shipped during the months of March and April, and the larger part is put on board in February, and the residue in March, the buyer is not bound to accept the rice,

[1] Clark *v.* Wright, 5 Phila. 439.

[2] Hill *v.* Chipman, 59 Wis. 211.

[3] Clark *v.* Wright, 5 Phila. 439. See Norrington *v.* Wright, 115 U. S. 188, 209.

[4] L. R. 2 App. Cases, 455.

[5] Reuter *v.* Sala, 4 C. P. Div. 239; Young *v.* White, 5 Watts, 460; Cleveland *v.* Sterrett, 20 P. F. S. 204.

[6] Gath *v.* Lees, H. & C. 558; Russell *v.* Nicoll, 3 Wend. 112; Norrington *v.* Wright, 115 U. S. 188, 203; Lowber *v.* Bangs, 2 Wallace, 728.

although no real injury has ensued and the breach is seemingly of the letter of the agreement. The thing sold is not 300 tons of rice, generally or in gross; it is 300 tons of Madras rice to be put on board at Madras during the particular months named, and unless the seller shows that each term of the description is fulfilled, he does not "launch" his case and the suit will be dismissed.[1] In like manner when the agreement provides that the goods shall be delivered on or before a given day and at a certain place, a partial delivery at the time and place will not suffice, although the residue are ready and tendered soon afterwards, and no loss appears to have resulted from the delay.[2]

The port from which the shipment is to be made will, if the parties so provide, be as material as the place where or the time when they are to be delivered, and where the terms of the sold note were "shipment from Glasgow as soon as possible," and the goods were put on board some ninety miles away at Leith, the court held that there was a fatal variance, although the effect was to expedite the shipment which could not have been made without expense and delay from Glasgow.[3] So also an agreement for the shipment of iron from Great Britain to New York will not be fulfilled by the purchase of iron of the kind and quality prescribed in New York, and tendering it at the appointed time.[4]

A tender may be made on either side down to the last hour of the last day fixed for the performance of the contract;[5] but after that, all right under the contract will be gone at law, and equity will not relieve when chattels are in question as it may in the case of land.[6] If it is agreed

[1] Bowes *v.* Shand, 2 App. Cases, 455. See Norrington *v.* Wright, 115 U. S. 188, 207; Welsh *v.* Gossler, 89 N. Y. 540; Hill *v.* Blake, 97 id. 216.

[2] See Davenport *v.* Wheeler, 7 Cow. 231; Roberts *v.* Beatty, 2 Penrose & Watts, 63; Russell *v.* Nicoll, 3 Wend. 112.

[3] Filley *v.* Pope, 115 U. S. 213.

[4] Cunningham *v.* Judson, 30 Hun, 63.

[5] Conawingo Petroleum Co. *v.* Cunningham, 25 P. F. S. 138; Startup *v.* McDonald, 6 M. & G. 593.

[6] Coddington *v.* Paleologo, L. R. 2 Ex. 193.

that delivery shall begin on the 17th of April and terminate on the 13th of May, some portion of the goods must be ready on the 17th of April, and if they are not, a subsequent tender of the whole may be rejected although made before the day fixed for the completion of the contract. So where the agreement was for the purchase of 667 tons of iron, to be shipped from Sweden in about equal proportions in each of the months of June, July, and August, the court held that time was of the essence of the contract, and as the vendor only shipped 23 tons in June the purchaser was neither bound to accept thus much, nor the residue though offered before the summer had gone by.[1]

In Gath *v.* Lees[2] the defendant agreed to buy a quantity of cotton "to be delivered at seller's option in August or September, 1864, payment within ten days from date of invoice." The seller afterwards gave notice that the cotton was ready for delivery on a certain day in August and that the invoice would be dated from that day. It was held that the plaintiff having exercised his option was bound to make delivery in August, and that the non-delivery in that month was a good defence to an action for not accepting the cotton in September. When no time is fixed, the delivery or performance must take place within a reasonable time, and if this is allowed to pass without fulfilment, a subsequent tender will come too late whether the delay is or is not injurious.[3]

The rule is not less applicable to contracts to build or manufacture, and a man who agrees to erect a house or bridge or construct a machine can recover nothing unless the contract is substantially fulfilled, although the structure stands on the defendant's land and is occupied by him.[4]

When the consideration is entire, it should seemingly make no difference as regards the duty to be exact and punctual, whether the whole is to be rendered at once or in succes-

[1] Hoare *v.* Rennie, 5 H. & N. 19.

[2] 3 H. & C. 558.

[3] Hirshhorn *v.* Stewart, 49 Ia. 418.

[4] Allen *v.* Curles, 6 Ohio St. 505; Goldsmith *v.* Hand, 26 id. 101; Mehurin *v.* Stone, 37 id. 49; Lewis *v.* Smith, 40 Ind. 98; Olmstead *v.* Beale, 19 Pick. 528; Smith *v.* Brady, 17 N. Y. 173; Tompkins *v.* Dudley, 25 id. 272; Jones *v.* Dermott, 2 Wallace, 1.

sive parcels, because if any delivery is withheld or behindhand the performance does not answer to the promise and the injured party is absolved.[1] Whether the contract is for the delivery of ten bales of cotton at the same time, or at the rate of one bale per diem for ten successive days, the purchaser is equally entitled to ten bales and ought not to be compelled to accept or pay for nine; and if in the case last supposed the second delivery fails he is not less entitled to reject the third, because he accepted the first in the belief that the second would be forthcoming at the appointed time.[2] This is not on the ground of a rescission of the contract, but because though still subsisting it has not been fulfilled,[3] and the purchaser may not only decline to receive the remaining parcels but hold the vendor answerable in damages.[4] It will not do to say that since part of the consideration has been received there can be no right to treat the residue as unfulfilled, because consideration is the result of agreement, and so long as any part of what the contract calls for has not been performed, nothing has been performed.[5] What is voluntarily received and kept must be paid for notwithstanding the failure to deliver all; but this depends on a waiver arising from the acceptance of a substituted performance, or may be referred to an implied promise to pay what the benefit conferred is reasonably worth.[6]

In Catlin *v.* Tobias,[7] the principle was carried to the extent of denying the right to compensation even for what has been delivered and received, unless it appears that the purchaser knew that the rest would not be forthcoming, and

[1] Hoare *v.* Rennie, 5 H. & N.; 19 L. R. 7 Ex. 259; Honck *v.* Muller, L. R. 7 Q. B. Div. 92; Reuter *v.* Sala, 4 C. P. Div. 239; King Philip *v.* Slater, 12 R. I. 82; Van Buren *v.* Digges, 11 How. 461; Norrington *v.* Wright, 115 U. S. 188, 203.

[2] Norrington *v.* Wright, 115 U. S. 188, 202; Catlin *v.* Tobias, 26 N. Y. 217.

[3] Honck *v.* Muller, L. R 7 Q. B. Div. 92.

[4] See Mansfield *v.* Trigg, 113 Mass. 354; Osborn *v.* Gantz, 60 N. Y. 540.

[5] Norrington *v.* Wright, 115 U. S. 188.

[6] See Bradley *v.* King, 44 Ill. 339; Smith *v.* Lewis, 40 Ind. 98.

[7] 26 N. Y. 217.

accepted part as so much on account of the whole. The contract was for the manufacture and delivery of bottles in April, May, and June, and the defendant gave his note in April for the articles delivered up to that time. The plaintiffs became insolvent soon afterward and were unable to deliver the rest of the bottles, and it was held that the breach was entire and constituted a defence to the suit. There was no waiver because the defendant had no reason to suppose that the residue would not be delivered, or to anticipate a default that had not occurred when the note was given. The case was therefore simply that of a partial performance succeeded by a failure to complete the whole, which was in legal effect as though nothing had been done.

So, conversely, although the point is one about which the authorities differ, when a particular delivery is to take place and be paid for before the day named for the next delivery, and the buyer fails to accept or pay, the seller will be discharged, not merely technically, but from the natural presumption that he relied on the payment as the means of carrying out the agreement;[1] and such also speaking generally is the rule where a partial payment is to be made while the deliveries are going on.[2]

It has notwithstanding been contended in England, that when the goods are to be furnished in parcels or instalments, and paid for on delivery or in proportion to the quantity received, the consideration cannot be regarded as entire and the failure to make or to accept and pay for one delivery, will not authorize the injured party to rescind the contract or refuse to proceed in accordance with its terms, unless the effect is an entire frustration of the purpose which the latter presumably had in view. Accordingly, where the defendant agreed to furnish 6,000 to 8,000 tons of coal from his mines, to be delivered in equal monthly portions throughout the year into wagons which the plaintiff undertook to send, and the wagons sent during the first month would not hold more than half the stipulated amount, a majority of the judges held that

[1] Honck *v.* Muller, L. R. 7 Q. B. Div. 92.

[2] Robson *v.* Bohn, 27 Minn. 333.

the defendant could not on that account rescind the contract, or refuse to fill the wagons which were sent during the succeeding months.[1] The case was, in their opinion, within the doctrine of Pordage *v.* Cole,[2] that when the promise which has been violated goes to part only of the consideration, and the breach is compensable in damages, there is not such a failure of consideration as will discharge the opposite party, and he must perform the promises on his part and seek redress by suit. If such was the ground of the decision, it went beyond the rule which is not absolute, but depends on the relation of what has been done under the contract to the residue which remains unfulfilled.[3]

This case was followed in Roper *v.* Johnson,[4] as the authoritative decision of a co-ordinate tribunal which was not open to debate; but when the question arose soon afterwards in Honck *v.* Muller,[5] Simpson *v.* Crippin was shaken if not overruled; and the court reverted to the doctrine of Hoare *v.* Rennie,[6] that a failure to make one of several deliveries or payments in accordance with an executory contract, is in effect equivalent to a failure to pay or deliver all, because the opposite party is not bound to accept less than he stipulated for, or at a different time.[7] The suit was brought on a contract for the sale and purchase of 2,000 tons of pig-iron at forty-two shillings a ton, to be delivered in November, 1879, or equally over November, December, and January. The purchaser failed to take any of the iron in November, though requested to do so, and the seller wrote on the 1st of December that he regarded the contract as cancelled, and subsequently refused to deliver in December or January. The plaintiff then brought suit for the difference between the contract and market price of 666⅔ tons, being the amount of the deliveries which were withheld. Bramwell, L. J., likened the case to an order for a suit of clothes, the cost being £7,—£4 for the coat, £2 for the trousers, and £1 for the waist-

[1] Simpson *v.* Crippin, L. R. 8 Q. B. 14.
[2] 1 Wms. Saund. 319.
[3] *Post.*
[4] L. R. 8 C. P. 167.
[5] L. R. 7 Q. B. Div. 92.
[6] 5 H. & N. 19; L. R. 7 Ex. 259.
[7] Honck *v.* Muller, L. R. 7 Q. B. Div. 92, 99.

coat, — where the buyer could not be made to take the coat only, whether all were to be delivered together, or the trousers and waistcoat first. So the plaintiff, having agreed to take 2,000 tons, had no right or power to demand $1333\frac{2}{3}$ tons and decline the residue. Where no part of a contract has been performed by one party to it, and the other party refuses to perform the entirety to be performed by him, there is no difference in principle whether the delivery is to be at different dates, or the whole is to be sent at once. Suppose a purchase of one hundred yards of silk at so much a yard, and that the buyer came for fifty yards only, could he insist on it? Would it make any difference, if fifty yards were to be taken and paid for on Monday and fifty on Tuesday, and the Monday's delivery was not taken but the Tuesday's demanded? Or suppose a contract to supply bread for a year to a workhouse from the 1st of January, and the contractor says he will not supply any in January, can he insist on supplying for the other eleven months, or can he fail during eleven months and insist on supplying in December? "The party to a contract so broken has a right, not to rescind the contract, for rescission is the act of both parties, but a right to declare that he will not perform a part only of his contract, namely, what would remain to be performed if the other party had performed his part and so enabled the performance of the whole. If indeed the contract has been in part performed and cannot be undone, then it must be proceeded with without the power of declaring off." If the plaintiff had taken the November delivery, but had refused the December, the defendant would have been bound to make the January delivery. Such was the case of Simpson *v.* Crippin, which was distinguishable from Hoare *v.* Rennie, because there had been a part-performance. The consequence of an opposite conclusion was, if the November delivery had been a profit to the defendant, and the December and January deliveries were losses, he must bear the loss and have no security that he would get the profit. This reasoning would, no doubt, apply where there was a part-performance, but there the hardship could not be avoided.

Baggallay, L. J., concurred. But for the authority of Simpson *v.* Crippin, he would have no doubt that the refusal to take the first delivery was a justification for the refusal to make the remaining ones. The decision in Simpson *v.* Crippin was irreconcilable with Hoare *v.* Rennie, except in the manner pointed out by Bramwell, L. J., but the judgment was not based on any such distinction and the principles enunciated in the latter case were more in accordance with reason and justice.

It is not easy to coincide with the conclusion reached in Simpson *v.* Crippin, or the supposed effect of the acceptance of one parcel in precluding the right to rely on the rejection of a subsequent parcel as a justification for a refusal to deliver the remaining parcels. If, as Bramwell conceded in Honck *v.* Muller, the loss and inconvenience from the non-payment of the money on which the seller relies for the execution of the contract, and his reason to apprehend that a subsequent tender will meet with the fate of that already made, are the same whether a previous delivery was or was not accepted, he should be equally entitled in either case to proceed no further, and look elsewhere for a customer. The motive for parcelling the deliveries and apportioning the payments is convenience, — that the goods and money may be forthcoming when they will be needed, and not to enable either party to decide capriciously how much he will receive or render. If the parties were asked on entering into such an agreement whether any parcel could be rejected without forfeiting the right to insist on the delivery of the remaining parcels, they would answer, No.[1] Accordingly, when the question arose in The Mersey Steel & Iron Co. *v.* Naylor,[2] Bramwell's dictum in Honck *v.* Muller was criticised by Sir George Jessel, and disavowed by its author in delivering judgment in the House of Lords.

The doctrine of Hoare *v.* Rennie, that exactitude is not less requisite because performance is to take place by parcels, was

[1] See Mr. McMurtrie's article, "Rescission of Divisible Contracts," 15 Am. Law Review, 623, 632.

[2] L. R. 9 Q. B. Div. 648; 9 App. Cases, 434.

followed in the King Philip Mills Co. *v.* Slater,[1] and again by the Supreme Court of the United States in Norrington *v.* Wright,[2] on a careful review of the authorities. The contract in the latter case was as follows: —

PHILADELPHIA, January 19, 1880.

Sold to Messrs. Peter Wright & Sons, for account of A. Norrington & Co., London, five thousand (5,000) tons old T iron rails, for shipment from a European port or ports, at the rate of about one thousand (1,000) tons per month, beginning February, 1880, but whole contract to be shipped before August 1, 1880, at forty-five dollars ($45) per ton, of 2,240 pounds custom-house weight, ex ship Philadelphia, settlement cash, on presentation of bills accompanied by custom-house certificate of weight. Sellers to notify buyers of shipments, with vessels' names, as soon as known by them. Sellers not to be compelled to replace any parcel lost after shipment. Sellers, when possible, to secure to buyers right to name discharging berth of vessels at Philadelphia.

The plaintiff shipped from various European ports 400 tons by one vessel in the last part of February, 885 tons by two vessels in March, 1,571 tons by five vessels in April, 850 tons by three vessels in May, 1,000 tons by two vessels in June, and 300 tons by one vessel in July, and notified the defendants of each shipment. The defendants received and paid for the February shipment upon its arrival in March, and in April gave directions at what wharves the March shipments should be discharged on their arrival, but on May 14, about the time of the arrival of the March shipments, and having been then for the first time informed of the amounts shipped in February, March, and April, gave written notice that they should decline to accept the shipments made in March and April, because none of them were in accordance with the contract.

Judgment was rendered for the defendants on the following grounds: —

"The contract sued on is a single contract for the sale and purchase of 5,000 tons of iron rails, shipped from a

[1] 12 R. I. 82. [2] 115 U. S. 189.

European port or ports for Philadelphia. The subsidiary provisions as to shipping in different months, and as to paying for each shipment upon its delivery, do not split up the contract into as many contracts as there shall be shipments or deliveries of so many distinct quantities of iron.[1] The further provision that the sellers shall not be compelled to replace any parcel lost after shipment, simply reduces, in the event of such a loss, the quantity to be delivered and paid for. The times of shipment, as designated in the contract, are 'at the rate of about 1,000 tons per month, beginning February, 1880, but whole contract to be shipped before August 1, 1880.' These words are not satisfied by shipping one sixth part of the 5,000 tons, or about 833 tons, in each of the six months which begin with February and end with July. But they require about 1,000 tons to be shipped in each of the five months from February to June inclusive, and allow no more than slight and unimportant deficiencies in the shipments during those months to be made up in the month of July. The contract is not one for the sale of a specific lot of goods, identified by independent circumstances, — such as all those deposited in a certain warehouse, or to be shipped in a particular vessel, or that may be manufactured by the seller, or may be required for use by the buyer in a certain mill; in which case the mention of the quantity accompanied by the qualification of 'about,' or 'more or less' is regarded as a mere estimate of the probable amount, as to which good faith is all that is required of the party making it. But the contract before us comes within the general rule. 'When no such independent circumstances are referred to, and the engagement is to furnish goods of a certain quality or character to a certain amount, the quantity specified is material, and governs the contract. The addition of the qualifying words "about," "more or less," and the like, in such cases, is only for the purpose of providing against accidental variations, arising from slight and unimportant excesses or deficiencies in number, measure, or weight." [2]

[1] Mersey Steel and Iron Co. *v.* Naylor, L. R. 9 App. Cases, 434, 439.

[2] Brawley *v.* United States, 96 U. S. 168, 171, 172.

"The seller is bound to deliver the quantity stipulated, and has no right either to compel the buyer to accept a less quantity, or to require him to select part out of a greater quantity; and when the goods are to be shipped in certain proportions monthly, the seller's failure to ship the required quantity in the first month gives the buyer the same right to rescind the whole contract, that he would have had if it had been agreed that all the goods should be delivered at once. The plaintiff, instead of shipping about 1,000 tons in February, and about 1,000 tons in March, as stipulated in the contract, shipped only 400 tons in February, and 885 tons in March. His failure to fulfil the contract on his part in respect to these first two instalments, justified the defendants in rescinding the whole contract, provided they distinctly and reasonably asserted the right of rescission. The defendants immediately after the arrival of the March shipments, and as soon as they knew that the quantities which had been shipped in February and in March were less than the contract called for, clearly and positively asserted the right to rescind, if the law entitled them to do so. Their previous acceptance of the single cargo of four hundred tons shipped in February was no waiver of this right, because it took place without notice or means of knowledge that the stipulated quantity had not been shipped in February. The price paid by them for that cargo being above the market value, the plaintiff suffered no injury by the omission of the defendants to return the iron, and no reliance was placed on that omission in the correspondence between the parties."

It has notwithstanding recently been declared in England that the material inquiry in such instances is not, Has the consideration been fulfilled? but, Does the language or conduct of the party in default amount to such an absolute refusal to perform his part as would constitute a rescission if he had the right? for if it does, the opposite party may take him at his word and bring the obligation to a close at once. "Non-payment on the one hand, or non-delivery on the other, may amount to such an act, or may be evidence for a jury of an intention wholly to abandon the contract and set the other party free." [1]

If this proposition is not in accordance with the doctrine of consideration, or the civil-law theory of fault, it is intelligible and might lead to definite results were it not that, as the reversal of The Queen's Bench Division in Mersey Steel and Iron Co. *v.* Naylor indicates, there is no certain rule for ascertaining what defaults manifest an intention to rescind. If three thousand tons of iron are sold deliverable in three successive parcels in March, April, and May, does the failure to deliver the first parcel within the time constitute an abandonment of the contract, or if it does not, should such an inference be drawn if the second is also behindhand, and will the result be affected in either case by a declaration that the seller purposes to be punctual in May? If this problem can be solved, what is to be said when a partial delivery is tendered in each of the three months; and will the acceptance of the first or second preclude the right to reject the third?

The test is still more unsatisfactory when the breach is non-payment. A failure to pay for one of several successive deliveries may obviously arise from a want of will or want of means, and is consistent either with a sincere purpose and expectation to provide punctually for the next instalment, or with a dishonest intention to get the goods and put the seller to the expense and delay of a suit. Which interpretation should be adopted depends on facts and circumstances which may be known only to the buyer, and is immaterial as regards the seller, whose loss and inconvenience from not receiving the amount due do not depend on the causes which actuate the buyer, and may be equally great whether the latter does or does not intend to abandon the contract.

The question arose in Freeth *v.* Burr, out of an agreement on the 28th of November, for the sale of 250 tons of pig-iron, half in two weeks, the remainder in four, payment to be made in fourteen days after each delivery. The first delivery was

[1] Freeth *v.* Burr, L. R. 9 C. P. 208; Mersey Steel and Iron Co. *v.* Naylor, L. R. 9 Q. B. Div. 648, 657; 9 App. Cases, 434. See Norrington *v.* Wright, 115 U. S. 188, 189.

not begun until the 15th of February, nor completed before the 29th of May, and the buyer declined to pay for it unless the second was delivered punctually, or a deduction made for the delay. This led to a refusal by the seller to deliver the second parcel, which was the cause of action. Here the evidence seemingly admitted of but one conclusion. There was an entire breach of the contract on the seller's part by the failure to deliver either parcel at the appointed time, which no subsequent default on the other side could excuse, and which not only entitled the buyer to damages, but to withhold the purchase-money until the account was adjusted.[1] Judgment was rendered for the buyer, not on these grounds, but because the non-payment did not under the circumstances indicate an intention to abandon the contract, or authorize the seller to treat it as at an end.

A like view was taken in Bollman *v.* Burt,[2] where the court held that a failure to pay for one delivery would not, save exceptionally, authorize the seller to treat the contract as at an end; but that such a right would result from such repeated failures as would defeat the purposes and object of the contract. In the case at bar there were successive defaults in January and February, and, although these were condoned, the purchaser might well when a breach occurred in March rescind the contract by a notice given before the May delivery, although a rescission when or after that was tendered would have been too late.

In the subsequent case of Mersey Steel & Iron Co. *v.* Naylor,[3] the contract was "for five thousand tons of steel blooms, to be delivered on board at Liverpool by instalments of one thousand tons monthly, commencing with January, 1881, payment to be made in three days after receipt of shipping documents." Partial deliveries, amounting in all to 350 tons, took place and were accepted in January and February, but the purchaser withheld the price under the advice of counsel, on the ground that a petition had been presented to wind up the company and that it was doubtful whether the payment

[1] Bradley *v.* King, 44 Ill. 339.

[2] 61 Md. 415.

[3] 9 Q. B. Div. 648, 657; 9 App. Cases, 434.

could be made with safety before a hearing. The company then went into the hands of a liquidator, who refused to make any further deliveries in consequence of the delay in payment, and brought a suit for the price of the blooms which had been already sent.

The defendants filed a counter-claim averring that, before any act to be done on their part under the contract, the plaintiffs broke the same by delivering 1,331 tons instead of 1,000 tons, and afterwards wrongfully refused any further performance, and demanding £2,500 as damages for the breach. The Queen's Bench Division overruled the counter-claim on the ground that the refusal to pay for the amount actually received was an implied refusal to proceed under the contract, which terminated the obligation on the other side. The case was then carried before the Privy Council, and subsequently to the House of Lords, where the plaintiffs contended that the question was not whether the non-payment manifested an intention to abandon the contract, which might be doubtful on the evidence, but had the agreement been so far fulfilled as regarded the money, as to give a right to call for the goods. Such contracts were made on the assumption that each parcel would be paid for punctually, and in time to put the manufacturer in funds to provide for the preparation and delivery of the succeeding parcels; and if the buyer failed in this material point the seller was absolved. This contention was overruled by the Privy Council, and afterwards in the House of Lords. Lord Selborne observed that no particular payment could be a condition precedent to the entire contract, because payment was in each instance to be made subsequently to delivery, and the controversy was therefore reduced to whether the defendants had so conducted themselves as to give the sellers an option to proceed no further under the contract. Such an inference could not be drawn under the circumstances, and it followed that the decision in the Privy Council in favor of the buyers should be affirmed.

What these decisions establish is that when the several deliveries are to be made on credit, and the consideration is not payment but the buyer's promise to pay, the obligation to furnish the goods is independent of that to render the purchase-money, relatively to each instalment and therefore as to all, and a failure to pay for one instalment will not excuse a refusal to tender the others. The distinction was not, as seems to have been supposed in Norrington *v.* Wright,[1] between payment and performance, but that where payment is to succeed performance it cannot be a condition precedent. It is therefore inapplicable where both acts are to be done simultaneously, and neither can be exacted without a tender or fulfilment of the other.

It may also be observed that in both the above cases the deliveries fell short of the amount called for by the contract, and the result might have been different but for the default on the seller's part. The argument that withholding a payment which is not to take place until after delivery does not justify a refusal to make a subsequent delivery, may be logical but would hardly occur to a business man; and the motive for stipulating that payment shall take place between the deliveries presumably is, not only to afford the purchaser time to procure the money but to put the seller in funds to provide the goods; and both considerations should be kept in view in deducing the intention of the parties and the effect of the breach.[2]

The principle laid down in Freeth *v.* Burr is abstractly true, many authorities determining that an unqualified refusal to perform is not less a breach because the time for fulfilment has not arrived.[3] The difficulty is to know how there can be room for the principle in instances like that to which it was applied. If the thing omitted to be done on one side is the whole or an essential part of the consideration for performance on the other, the injured party is discharged regardless of the intention of the party in default; if it is not, an abandonment of the contract cannot justly be inferred.

[1] 115 U. S. 188, 210.

[2] See Bollman *v.* Burt, 61 Md. 415; Robson *v.* Bohn, 27 Minn. 333.

[3] Lilly *v.* Elwin, 11 Q. B. 742, 755; Cort *v.* Ambergate R'y Co., 17 id. 127; Hochster *v.* De la Tour, 2 E. & B. 678; Lilly *v.* Erwin, 11 Q. B. 742, 755. See Smith *v.* Lewis, 24 Com. 624; Lovell *v.* The Ins. Co., 111 U. S. 264.

Accordingly, where the owner of a peach-orchard sold his crop, and agreed to have the baskets of fruit at the wharf ready for delivery every market-day throughout the season to be then and there received and paid for, the court held that he was not bound to incur the risk of delay, and might on the failure of the purchaser to appear and pay on any of the days so named, dispose of the entire remaining stock to a third person.[1] Here the perishable nature of the commodity was a material element in the transaction, and made it reasonable to infer that the parties intended that the contract should be entire, and depend for its obligation on the readiness and willingness of the buyer to render the stipulated equivalent for each parcel when it arrived.

[1] Reybold *v.* Voorhees, 30 Pa. 116.

CHAPTER XXIV.

DEPENDENT AND INDEPENDENT COVENANTS AND PROMISES.

Presumption of Dependence from Order of Performance. — Performance as a Condition Precedent. — Inference from Failure to fix the time of Performance. — Simultaneous Payment and Delivery. — Sale and Conveyance of Land. — Part-performance.

In construing contracts for the delivery of a gross amount of merchandise in successive parcels payable at or after delivery, it is requisite to advert to the dependence of mutual promises, as implied from the order of time in which they are reciprocally to be performed, and to the effect of the breach of one of several promises which together constitute the consideration, in discharging the obligation on the other side.

Two consequences may follow from the doctrine that performance must be full and punctual, — one, that a party who fails in either regard will be answerable for the damages; the other, that he cannot enforce the contract against the party who is injured by the default. The former rule is universal save when an exception is implied from the nature of the subject-matter; but the latter is a question of intention as deduced from the wording of the contract. When there is but a single promise on either side, and both are to be performed simultaneously, there can be no room for doubt.[1] For although the consideration in such cases is the promise and not performance, still, if the promise remains unperformed there is a failure of consideration, which constitutes a defence. Such is the constantly recurring case where a seller agrees to deliver and the buyer to accept and pay, and neither can enforce the contract against the other unless he

[1] Marsden *v.* Moore, 4 H. & N. 500; Weichardt *v.* Hook, 83 Pa. 434; Hartley *v.* Decker, 89 id. 470.

himself was ready and willing at the time prescribed.[1] It does not necessarily vary the case that the larger part of what was agreed on has been done, and that what remains is comparatively trivial. If the partial performance has been beneficial, and was voluntarily accepted and enjoyed, with notice that the residue was not and would not be fulfilled, a recovery may be had on the ground of waiver or of a new implied undertaking, but not on the contract as originally made.[2]

The case is obviously different when by the terms of the agreement performance is to precede payment, or payment performance. Such is the common case of a sale on credit, or where the whole or a part of the purchase-money is to be paid in advance. If the delivery is to take place on the first of December, and payment on the first of the new year, and the goods are not sent at the day the buyer may sue at once without averring that he was ready with the price; but no recovery can be had by the seller because the failure to pay is excused by his default. Under these circumstances the promises are said to be independent; but it is more accurate to say that the seller's obligation is independent of the buyer's, the buyer's dependent on the seller's.

Covenants were divided by Lord Mansfield — and the remark applies to simple contracts — into three classes: 1. Such as are mutual and independent, where separate actions lie for breaches on either side; 2. Covenants which are conditions and dependent on each other, in which the performance of one depends on the prior performance of the other; 3. Covenants which are mutual conditions to be performed at the same time, as to which the party who would maintain an action must, in general, offer or tender performance.[3]

[1] The courts did not arrive at this conclusion until near the close of the last century; and it was originally held that since the promises were the consideration the contract might be enforced though they were not performed, subject to the right of the injured party to maintain a cross-action for the damage resulting from the breach. Langdell, Summary, §§ 140, 141. See Thorpe *v.* Thorpe, 12 Mod. 455; Nicholas *v.* Raynbred, Hobart, 88; Martindale *v.* Fisher, 1 Wilson, 88; Gower *v.* Capper, Croke Eliz. 543.

[2] See Mehurin *v.* Stone, 37 Ohio St. 49, 57; *ante.*

[3] See Jones *v.* Barkley, Douglas, 390; Northrop *v.* Northrop, 6 Cow. 296.

The principles which govern in cases of this description were reduced by Sergeant Williams to rules which, with some modifications, are still followed by the courts.[1]

"If a day be appointed for payment of money, or part of it, or for doing any other act, and the day *is* to happen, or *may* happen, *before* the thing which is the consideration of the money, or other act, is to be performed, an action may be brought for the money, or for not doing such other act *before* performance; for it appears that the party relied upon his *remedy*, and did not intend to make the *performance* a condition precedent: and so it is where *no time* is fixed for performance of that, which is the consideration of the money or other act."[2]

"But when a day is appointed for the payment of money, etc., and the day is to happen *after* the thing which is the consideration of the money, etc., is to be performed, no action can be maintained for the money, etc., before performance."[3]

The rule may be stated generally as follows: —

That which will or may precede cannot depend on that which is to follow; that which follows is *prima facie* dependent on what goes before.[4] Things which are to be done at the same time are reciprocally dependent unless a contrary intention appears.[5]

There is a qualification that where the promise on one side is to be performed at or after the period named for the fulfil-

[1] Notes to Pordage *v.* Cole, 1 Wms. Saund. 319.

[2] Edgar *v.* Boies, 11 S. & R. 445; Stevenson *v.* Klippenger, 5 Watts, 420; Putnam *v.* Mellen, 34 N. H. 71; Keenan *v.* Brown, 21 Vt. 86.

[3] 1 Salk. 171; Thorpe *v.* Thorpe, 2d Resolution; 12 Mod. 462; 1 Lord Raymond, 665; 1 Lutw. 251; Dyer, 76, *a.* pl. 30.

[4] Negley *v.* Stewart, 10 S. & R. 207; Neale *v.* Ratcliffe, 15 Q. B. 916; Goodwin *v.* Lynn, 4 W. C. C. 714; Grant *v.* Johnson, 1 Selden, 247, 250; Langdell, Summary, § 122.

[5] See Keenan *v.* Brown, 21 Vt. 86; Kettle *v.* Harvey, id. 301, 305; Bean *v.* Atwater, 4 Conn. 4, 13; Roach *v.* Dickinsons, 9 Gratt. 154, 160; Adams *v.* Williams, 2 W. & S. 227; Johnson *v.* Wygant, 11 Wend. 48; Williams *v.* Healey, 3 Den. 363, 366; The Bank of Columbia *v.* Hagner, 1 Peters, 455, 465; Gardiner *v.* Carson, 15 Mass. 500; Dana *v.* King, 2 Pick. 155; Couch *v.* Ingersoll, id. 292, 301; Howland *v.* Leach, 11 id. 151; Kane *v.* Hood, 13 id. 281.

ment of two or more promises on the other side, and would be dependent under the above rule, a recovery may notwithstanding be had on the performance of one of them, if its importance and the relation it bears to the contract as a whole, are such that it cannot reasonably be supposed that the parties intended that compensation should be denied for what is done under it unless the others are fulfilled.[1] Thus when an agreement for the sale of land, and that the purchaser shall have a right of way over an adjacent field, is partially performed by the delivery of a deed, the seller may be entitled to recover the purchase-money, notwithstanding his inability to give the right of way, and leave the buyer to seek redress by recouping the damages or a suit for compensation, because he ought not to keep the land and withhold the purchase-money.

It results from the principles already stated that when performance is to precede payment a partial or substituted performance will not ordinarily entitle the plaintiff to compensation, although the larger part has been done, or the thing tendered is more useful or valuable than that for which the defendant stipulates.[2]

The rule applies with equal or greater force where the promises on both sides are for performance, because acts are less susceptible of apportionment than money.[3] Accordingly, where a lessee agreed to keep the premises in repair, the same being first put in repair by the lessor, and the jury found that part only had been put in repair by the landlord and part left out of repair by the tenant, judgment was entered for the latter on the verdict.[4]

Agreeably to the judgment in Pordage *v.* Cole,[5] when a time is fixed for payment and none for doing that which is the consideration for the payment, an action may be brought for

[1] Grant *v.* Johnson, 1 Selden, 247, 250; 2 Sm. L. C. 8 Am. ed. 11.

[2] Smith *v.* Brady, 17 N. Y. 173; Mehurin *v.* Stone, 37 Ohio St. 49; Witherow *v.* Witherow, 16 Ohio, 238; Champlin *v.* Rowley, 13 Wend. 258; Harris *v.* Liggett, 1 W. & S. 381; Martin *v.* Schoenberger, 8 id. 367.

[3] Ellen *v.* Topp, 6 Ex. 424; Lowber *v.* Bangs, 2 Wallace, 720.

[4] Neale *v.* Ratcliffe, 15 Q. B. 916.

[5] 1 Saund. 319.

the money without averring performance.[1] For as one party is under these circumstances confined to a definite period and the other left at large, the court will not infer an intention different from that which has been expressed.[2] A covenant on one side to pay on or before a certain day, and on the other to convey without naming the time, are therefore agreeably to the letter of this rule independent, and the seller may recover the price without tendering a deed, or the buyer have damages for a refusal to convey without averring payment.[3]

The rule is technical, and as applied in Pordage *v.* Cole may defeat intention.[4] As was observed in the King Philip Mill Co. *v.* Slater,[5] persons of ordinary intelligence would probably infer on entering into such an agreement as that considered in Pordage *v.* Cole, that although the money was to be paid at a particular time while no time was prescribed for the delivery of the deed, yet as it was stated and admitted that the payment was to be for the land, the purchaser should not be compelled to pay unless he got the land or knew that it could not be conveyed by that time, and agreed with his eyes open. After all, said Jervis, C. J., in Roberts *v.* Brett,[6] "the rule in Pordage *v.* Cole only proposes to give the result of the intention of the parties, and where on the whole it is apparent that that which is to be done first is not to depend on the performance of the thing to be done afterwards, the parties are relying on their remedy and not on the performance of the condition, but when you plainly see that it is their intention to rely on the condition and not on the remedy, the performance of the thing is a condition precedent." It followed in the case at bar, that although the day appointed for performance on the defendant's part might happen before that on which the plaintiff covenanted to give a bond, still looking at

[1] Thorpe *v.* Thorpe, 1 Lord Raymond, 662; Wilks *v.* Smith, 10 M. & W. 355; Mattock *v.* Kinglake, 10 A. & E. 50.

[2] Bailey *v.* Clay, 4 Rand. 346; Cunningham *v.* Morrell, 10 Johns. 204.

[3] Mattock *v.* Kinglake, 10 A. & E. 50.

[4] Roberts *v.* Brett, 18 C. B. 561, 572; 11 H. L. 337; Cunningham *v.* Morrell, 10 Johns. 204.

[5] 12 R. I. 82, 86.

[6] 18 C. B. 561, 572; 11 H. L. Cases, 337; Langdell, Summary, § 127.

the object of the latter stipulation which was security, it must be regarded an indispensable preliminary to the right of suit.

In considering the effect of a failure to fix the time, it should be remembered that where no time is prescribed the law implies a reasonable time, which in the case of a sale is that the buyer shall be ready with the money when the goods are to be delivered;[1] and he cannot maintain an action against the seller unless the condition is fulfilled. On the other hand when the contract is for work, as for instance to build a house, performance is an implied prerequisite to payment, and a recovery may be had against the contractor without averring readiness to pay the price, while he is entitled to nothing until the work is completed.[2]

In general, where a conveyance is to be made, a mortgage or note surrendered, or other act done on payment, the inference is that both are to take place simultaneously and the money cannot be recovered without a tender or delivery of the deed or thing.[3] But this inference will not be drawn when the payment is to be made or thing rendered to a third person, and it will then be sufficient to aver that the plaintiff was ready and willing to pay or perform whenever the defendant showed that he had fulfilled his side of the agreement.[4] Hence, where two joint owners agree that each shall pay his share of the incumbrances without prescribing the time, the covenants will from the nature of the case be independent, and either party may recover for a failure to pay on the other side without proving payment on his own.[5]

[1] Tipton *v.* Freitner, 20 N. Y. 423; Withers *v.* Reynolds, 2 B. & Ad. 882; Knight *v.* The New England Worsted Co., 2 Cush. 271, 288.

[2] Harris *v.* Liggett, 1 W. & S. 301; School Trustees *v.* Bennett, 3 Dutch. 515; Smith *v.* School Dist., 20 Conn. 313, 320; Tompkins *v.* Dudley, 25 N. Y. 272; Sinclair *v.* Bowles, 9 B. & C. 92.

[3] Bollman *v.* Burt, 61 Md. 415; Slocum *v.* Despard, 8 Wend. 615, 619; Johnson *v.* Wygant, 11 id. 48; Roach *v.* Dickinsons, 9 Gratt. 154, 160; Adams *v.* Williams, 2 W. & S. 227; Goodisson *v.* Nunn, 4 T. R. 761.

[4] Northrop *v.* Northrop, 6 Cow. 296; Slocum *v.* Despard, 8 Wend. 615.

[5] Breden *v.* Agnew, 3 W. & S. 300; Roberts *v.* Brett, 18 C. B. 561, 572.

Much may depend on the nature of the acts to be done on either side, and the relation which they bear to the contract as a whole.[1] A covenant to pay the purchase-money of land on the delivery of the deed, will be interpreted as binding the parties to a simultaneous performance,[2] while a man who covenants to pay on the erection of a building, need not have the money ready until the work is done. So a stipulation for security is presumably a condition precedent which must be specifically performed, because the parties manifestly do not intend to rely on their remedies or each other's word, and as the damages for the breach will be nominal or no more than would be recoverable on the contract as a whole, such a clause would if differently interpreted be merely futile.[3]

On the other hand, where land is sold for a sum to be paid at the expiration of four years, and interest in the mean time half yearly, the vendor may recover the interest without tendering a conveyance, because he would otherwise be compelled to wait for the interest, or to part with the land and rely on the purchaser's willingness and ability to pay the price.[4]

The natural inference that payment and delivery are to occur simultaneously, and that neither seller nor buyer can treat the other as in default without performing or tendering the equivalent for which he stipulated, is one that should not be disregarded without sufficient grounds, and has been generally drawn in England and the United States.[5]

"It is," said Hosmer, C. J., in the case last cited, "a primary and fundamental rule concerning contracts, that their

[1] See Porcher *v.* Gardner, 8 C. B. 461.

[2] Johnson *v.* Wygant, 11 Wend. 48; Adams *v.* Williams, 2 W. & S. 227; *ante.*

[3] Roberts *v.* Brett, 18 C. B. 561, 572, 11 H. L. 337; see Dakin *v.* Williams, 11 Wend. 68, 71.

[4] Wilks *v.* Smith, 10 M. & W. 360.

[5] King Philip Mill Co. *v.* Slater, 12 R. I. 82, 86; Cunningham *v.* Morrell, 10 Johns. 204; Roach *v.* Dickinsons, 9 Gratt. 154; Morton *v.* Lamb, 7 Tenn. 125; Glazebrook *v.* Woodrow, 8 id. 366; Bollman *v.* Burt, 61 Md. 415; Atkinson *v.* Smith, 14 M. & W. 695; Head *v.* Baldy, 6 A. & E. 459; Bankart *v.* Bowers, L. R. 1 C. P. 484; Bean *v.* Atwater, 4 Conn. 4.

construction must be according to the intention of the parties; and so paramount is this rule, that to such intention, even technical words must give way.[1] When the inquiry is in relation to their dependence or independence, this is to be collected from the evident sense and meaning of the parties; and however transposed they may be in the instrument, their precedency must depend on the order of time in which the intent of the transaction requires their performance.[2] If the language of a contract will admit of it, justice and general convenience incline to the construction of a simultaneous performance; but if a man will agree to pay his money before he has the thing for which he ought to pay it, and will rely upon his remedy, this is a law of his own making and his agreement he ought to perform. On the other hand, courts should carefully endeavor to avoid compelling a person to give credit, when he did not intend it."

Agreeably to the fifth and fourth rules laid down by Sergeant Williams, when mutual covenants go to the whole consideration on both sides they are mutual conditions, and performance must be averred.[3] These rules are as follows: —

"Where two acts are to be done at *the same time*, as where A covenants to convey an estate to B on such a day, and in consideration thereof B covenants to pay A a sum of money on the *same day*, neither can maintain an action without showing performance of, or an offer to perform his part, though it is not certain which of them is obliged to do the first act.[4] This particularly applies to all cases of sale, when the common understanding is that one thing is to be exchanged for another,[5] and consequently if no time be set that payment

[1] Porter *v.* Shephard, 6 T. R. 668; Campbell *v.* Jones, 6 id. 570; Morton *v.* Lamb, 7 id. 125; 1 Wms. Saund. 320 n.; Gazley *v.* Price, 16 Johns. Rep. 267.

[2] Jones *v.* Barkley, 2 Douglas, 684.

[3] Large *v.* Cheshire, 1 Ventris, 147; Duke of St. Albans *v.* Shore, 1 H. Bl. 270; Dakin *v.* Williams, 11 Wend. 68; Dermott *v.* Jones, 2 How. 231.

[4] 1 Wms. Saund. 548, notes.

[5] Goodisson *v.* Nunn, 6 T. R. 665; Marsden *v.* Moore, 4 H. & N. 500; Atkinson *v.* Smith, 14 M. & W. 695; Bollman *v.* Burt, 61 Md. 415; Bankart *v.* Bowers, L. R. 1 C. P. 484.

and delivery are to be concurrent;" and generally whenever both parties are to do or render at the same place and time.[1]

"Where the mutual covenants go to the *whole consideration* on both sides, they are mutual conditions, and performance must be averred."

None of the above rules is conclusive and all are subordinate to intention and when it appears on the face of the contract or by a necessary legal intendment that mutual promises are so unequal in amount or value that one cannot be the equivalent for the other, the presumption of dependence that might otherwise arise from the order of time will be repelled, and neither party need aver performance in order to maintain a suit.[2] In Christie *v.* Borelly the promise on the plaintiff's part was that certain bills of exchange amounting to £162 should be retired by the drawer, and on the defendant's part that £300, due by a third person for goods sold to him by the plaintiff, should be paid, and the plaintiff was held to be entitled to judgment on the latter promise although the bills had not been "retired," because the damages for the breaches on either side were so different that the parties could not have intended that the performance of one stipulation should be a condition precedent to the performance of the other. In this case, however, as in that of an agreement to accept a smaller sum in satisfaction of a larger, the principle does not apply unless the inadequacy appears as the result of computation; and the performance of a promise to give a peppercorn may well be a condition precedent to the obligation of a promise to pay £100.[3]

Concurrent acts can seldom be literally simultaneous, and neither party is absolutely bound to put himself in the power of the other by beginning. If the vendor parts with the goods he will lose his lien, if the purchaser pays he may not get the goods; and so of the delivery of the cargo of a vessel and the payment of the freight.[4] Accordingly, when

[1] Paynter *v.* James, 1 L. R. 2 C. P. 348.

[2] Christie *v.* Borelly, 7 C. B. N. S. 561.

[3] *Ante.*

[4] Black *v.* Rose, 2 Moore, P. C. N. S. 277; Paynter *v.* James, 1 L. R. 2 C. P. 348, 357; *ante.*

the question arises on a sale of goods the purchaser must produce the money, but need not part with it till the thing is transferred; and so of the vendor's duty to deliver the thing sold.[1] It is not necessary therefore to aver performance, but simply readiness and willingness to perform; and the question which party was playing fast and loose, and is answerable for the breach, is one of fact for the jury.[2]

"Where two acts," said Smith, J., in Paynter *v.* James, "are to be concurrent there must be a concurrent readiness on both sides; on the one to deliver and on the other to pay; each party is entitled to see that the other is ready to do his part, and it is for the jury to say which is in default. Here there was abundant to satisfy the jury that the plaintiffs were ready and willing to deliver the timber, and that the defendants were neither ready nor willing to pay the freight. I therefore think that the plaintiffs were entitled to succeed. It is clear that when two acts are concurrent, actual performance is not necessary to enable one party to maintain an action, and that it is enough to show a readiness to perform his. For this the note to Pordage *v.* Cole is a sufficient authority."[3]

It was declared in like manner, by Storrs, C. J., in Smith *v.* Lewis,[4] that "as the agreement required only that the acts of both the parties should be done at the same time, neither was obliged to do the first act or actually to perform his part of the agreement before the other. The plaintiff, in order to sustain this action, need only to show that he did what the law required of him; and all that it required was that he should be ready and willing to perform on his part, if the defendant was ready to perform on his." This opinion was cited and followed in Clark *v.* Weis.[5]

The case is more complicated when as in the sale of land the contract is to be carried into effect by a conveyance,

[1] Merrit *v.* Rane, 1 Strange, 458.

[2] 2 Sm. L. C. 8 Am. ed. 12; Ransom *v.* Johnson, 7 East, 203; Paynter *v.* James, L. R. 2 C. P. 348; Black *v.* Rose, 2 Moore, P. C. N. S. 277; Smith *v.* Lewis, 24 Conn. 624. See Langdell, Summary, § 142.

[3] 1 Wms. Saund. 320, c. 5.

[4] 24 Conn. 624; 26 id. 110.

[5] 87 Ill. 438.

which must be drawn with care and deliberation, and the preparation of the instrument may then be a necessary preliminary to the fulfilment of the agreement and the right of suit. This duty devolves in the United States on the vendor, who must not only have the deed ready for execution, but tender it to the purchaser before he can treat the latter as in default for the non-payment of the purchase-money.[1] Such also was the rule in England until the simplicity of the common law gave place to the elaborate conveyancing of modern times,[2] when it became usual "to submit an abstract of the numerous instruments relating to the title to the purchaser's counsel," and for him "to prepare the conveyance."[3] The usage became general and acquired the force of law; and in Stephens *v.* De Medina,[4] the court held that for the sake of uniformity it ought to prevail even when the thing sold is stock, and the "form of the conveyance simple and prescribed by an act of Parliament."[5] This rule has the advantage of simplifying the transaction by rendering it incumbent on the buyer to take the initiative as to both the acts which are requisite to complete the sale, namely, conveyance and payment. It is nevertheless essential in England, where conveyances are not registered, that the vendor should prove his right and power to convey by exhibiting his title-papers or an abstract of them to the purchaser, and until this preliminary step is taken the latter is neither able nor bound to prepare a conveyance and tender it for execution.[6]

[1] Green *v.* Reynolds, 2 Johns. 207; Parker *v.* Parmele, 20 id. 130; Johnson *v.* Wygant, 11 Wend. 48; Kane *v.* Hood, 13 Pick. 281; Tinney *v.* Ashley, 15 id. 546; Welch *v.* Matthews, 98 Mass. 131; Mervin *v.* M'Faden, 2 Watts, 132; Love *v.* Jones, 4 id. 455; Adams *v.* Williams, 2 W. & S. 227; Dubois *v.* Baum, 46 Pa. St. 537; Taylor *v.* Longworth, 14 Peters, 172.

[2] See Goodisson *v.* Nunn, 6 T. R. 665.

[3] Sugden on Vend. ch. IV. s. 54, p. 241.

[4] 4 Q. B. 422.

[5] Stephens *v.* De Medina, 4 Q. B. 422; Bowlby *v.* Bell, 3 C. B. 284, 2 Ex. 549; Poole *v.* Hill, 6 M. & W. 835; Taylor *v.* Longworth, 14 Peters, 172, 175.

[6] Sugden on Vend. Ch. V. s. 4, No. 37, p. 239; Brymer *v.* The Thames Dock Co., 2 Ex. 549; 5 id. 696.

In this country, on the other hand, the title is ordinarily recorded and open to inspection, and the purchaser informs himself without calling on the seller;[1] although if the title is defective or does not appear of record, it may be incumbent on the vendor to supply the missing links at his own expense.[2]

In sales of real as of personal property an actual tender is not essential, and a recovery may be had on proof of an offer on the plaintiff's part to pay or perform, attended with the will and the power to carry it into effect, and such language or conduct on the part of the defendant as amounts to a refusal to proceed under the contract in good faith.[3] For as payment and delivery are to be concurrent, the buyer is not bound to pay the price without obtaining the land, nor the vendor to part with the land until he is sure of the money, so all that either need show is that he was ready and willing to fulfil the agreement and would have done so but for the other's bad faith and laches. In Smith *v.* Lewis, the conveyance was drafted by an attorney in pursuance of a mutual agreement to that effect, and that the parties should meet at the attorney's office for the execution of the instrument and the payment of the price, but when the vendor called at the time and place the purchaser could not be found, and it appeared on inquiry that he had gone out of town, and it was held that the vendor might recover although he had not executed or tendered a deed.[4]

[1] Langdell, Summary, § 170.

[2] Mowat's Estate, 6 W. N. C. 239.

[3] Smith *v.* Lewis, 24 Conn. 624; 26 id. 110, 119; Tinney *v.* Ashley, 15 Pick. 546; Williams *v.* Bentley, 27 Pa. St. 294; Zents *v.* Legnard, 70 id. 192.

[4] "Some misapprehension or confusion," said Storrs, C. J., in Smith *v.* Lewis, "appears to have arisen from the mode of expression used in the books in treating of the necessity of a tender or offer by the parties, as applicable to the case of mutual and concurrent promises. The word 'tender,' as used in such a connection, does not mean the same kind of offer as when it is used with reference to the payment or offer to pay an ordinary debt due in money, where the money is offered to a creditor who is entitled to receive it, and nothing further remains to be done, but the transaction is completed and ended; but it only means a readiness

In Tinney *v.* Ashley,[1] the covenant sued on was that the defendants would execute and deliver a good and sufficient warranty deed on the surrender of a certain bond; and the question arose on an averment that the plaintiff demanded the deed and was then and there ready to deliver up the bond, yet the defendants never executed and delivered the deed but neglected and refused so to do. The declaration was held sufficient on the following grounds, as stated by Wilde, J.: "Where concurrent acts are to be performed by the parties at the same time, the party suing for damages for the non-performance by the other party is only required to aver that he was ready and willing to perform the agreement on his part, and that the defendant was requested to perform the agreement on his part but refused or neglected so to do. This was decided in the case of Rawson *v.* Johnson,[2] in which the former cases were considered, and such an averment was held to be sufficient. It was argued for the defendant, that it was not enough to be ready and willing to perform, unless that was made known to the other party; but this objection was overruled, and, as we think, upon sound and satisfactory reasons.

and willingness, accompanied with an ability on the part of one of the parties, to do the acts which the agreement requires him to perform, provided the other will concurrently do the things which he is required by it to do, and a notice by the former to the latter of such readiness. Such readiness, ability, and notice are sufficient evidence of, and indeed constitute and imply, an offer or tender in the sense in which those terms are used in reference to the kind of agreements which we are now considering. It is not an absolute, unconditional offer to do or transfer anything at all events, but it is in its nature conditional only, and dependent on, and to be performed only in case of, the readiness of the other party to perform his part of the agreement. Hence the declaration states what amounts to a tender or offer by the plaintiff, as properly understood in reference to this subject. The authorities fully sustain the principles which we have laid down, and nearly in the same terms, and most explicitly sanction the mode of declaring adopted in this case. A reference to them only is necessary. Morton *v.* Lamb, 7 T. R. 125; Rawson *v.* Johnson, 1 East, 203; Waterhouse *v.* Skinner, 2 Bos. & P. 447; Ferry *v.* Williams, 8 Taunt. 62; Norwood *v.* Read, Plowd. 180."

[1] 15 Pick. 546, 552.

[2] 1 East, 208.

"When one party demands of the other the performance of a mutual agreement, by which concurrent acts are to be performed by each party, an offer on the part of the party making the demand to perform his part of the agreement is implied and understood; and when the other party refuses to comply, he thereby dispenses with any other offer. And where he neglects to comply, without offering any reason for his non-compliance, the legal effect is the same. In the fourth count, however, a neglect and refusal are both alleged.

"As to the other part of the objection, that it was incumbent on the plaintiff to prepare a deed for the defendants to execute, we think it clearly was not. The defendants contracted to execute and deliver a good and sufficient deed, and it was incumbent on them to do whatever was necessary to the performance of their contract. If the law in England is otherwise, it must be founded on custom and practice, and not on any legal principle independently of practice."

The rules above considered depend on the order of time in which the acts in question are to be done; but the problem is as we have seen more complicated, where a party who has agreed to do several things which, though tending to the same end are yet distinct, performs some of them and seeks to recover the compensation which he has not fully earned. One of the rules[1] which governs under these circumstances is given by Sergeant Williams, in the note to Pordage *v.* Cole: "Where a covenant goes only to *part* of the consideration on both sides and a breach of such covenant may be paid for in damages, it is an independent covenant, and an action may be maintained for a breach of the covenant on the part of the defendant without averring performance in the declaration." The reason, as stated by the learned commentator, is that "where a person has received a *part* of the consideration for which he entered into the agreement, it would be unjust to enjoy that part without either paying or doing anything for it: therefore, the law obliges him to perform the agreement on his part, and leaves him to his remedy to recover any damages he may have sustained in not having received the whole consideration."

[1] The Third Rule.

As thus stated, the rule may appear entirely just; but when carried out, it led to results that were not consonant with justice. It might seem equitable that a contractor, who has received a part of the stipulated compensation in advance, should be required to do the work, notwithstanding a want of punctuality in the payment of the residue; but it followed that a recovery might be had against him without averring that the whole was paid, and conversely that the employer might be compelled to pay although the contractor had left the work unperformed.[1]

So construed, the rule ceased to be a guide to intention, and became a canon which must be strictly followed, although the consequences were such as the parties could not reasonably be supposed to have anticipated; and the existence on either side of a promise going to a part of the consideration rendered the promises on both sides independent, however clearly the language or the order of time indicated that such was not the design.[2] If any promise was independent all were independent, and might be treated for the purpose of suit and recovery as so many distinct contracts, and not as parts of a whole.[3]

This view is now generally discarded, and the independence of one or more promises will not give that character to other promises in the same contract which do not reasonably admit of such an interpretation, nor will a vendor or contractor be allowed to recover the entire price without tendering a deed or performing the work, because part was by the terms of the agreement to be paid in advance.[4]

"It is contended," said Lawrence, J., in Glazebrook *v.* Woodrow,[5] "that where one promises to another to perform

1 Terry *v.* Duntze, 2 H. Bl. 389; Seers *v.* Fowler, 2 Johns. 272; Havens *v.* Bush, id. 387.

2 See Glazebrook *v.* Woodrow, 8 T. R. 372.

3 Terry *v.* Duntze, 2 H. Bl. 389; Cunningham *v.* Morrell, 10 Johns. 203.

4 See Cunningham *v.* Morrell, 10 Johns. 203; Roach *v.* Dickinsons, 9 Gratt. 154; Allen *v.* Sanders, 7 B. Monroe, 593; Bean *v.* Atwater, 4 Conn. 3; Glazebrook *v.* Woodrow, 8 T. R. 372; The King Philip Mills *v.* Slater, 12 R. I. 82, 88; Grant *v.* Johnson, 5 N. Y. 247.

5 8 T. R. 372.

a certain thing in consideration of several matters to be performed by himself, he is entitled to maintain an action against the other for non-performance of his engagement if he himself has performed any one of the things stipulated by him to be done. Therefore, that in this instance the plaintiff, who has covenanted to put the defendant in possession and convey the premises to him in consideration of a certain sum, is entitled upon performance of one of those things to maintain his action for the consideration-money. But it is clear that if the agreement appear to be that the whole of what the plaintiff engaged for was to be done before the money was to be paid, it will not follow that because a part only has been performed he can recover the money, and leave the defendant to his remedy upon the agreement for the breach of the other part. For whether one promise be the consideration of another, or whether the performance, and not the mere promise, be the consideration, must be gathered from and depends entirely upon the words and nature of the agreement."

In like manner, while an indenture covenanting to assign a patent and teach the assignee how to use it, may well be construed as entitling the assignor to the price on proof that the former undertaking was performed, although the latter remains unfulfilled,[1] such an interpretation cannot reasonably be put on covenants to give the buyer of land possession and execute a deed, because so long as the title remains in the vendor the purchaser cannot be secure.[2] So when the instruction which the plaintiff agrees to give is essential to the performance which he seeks to enforce, he cannot withhold it and treat the defendant as in default.[3]

In considering whether the receipt of part of the consideration will preclude the right to rely on the non-performance of the residue as an answer to an action brought for the defendant's failure to perform his side of the agreement, regard may be had to the following inquiries: —

[1] Campbell *v.* Jones, 6 T. R., 570; Ellen *v.* Topp, 6 Ex. 424, 441.

[2] Glazebrook *v.* Woodrow, 8 T. R., 371; Grant *v.* Johnson, 5 N. Y. 252.

[3] Pittsburgh B. S. R. Co. *v.* Hinckley, 17 Federal Rep. 584.

1. Was the partial performance contemporaneous with the execution of the contract, or accepted subsequently with knowledge of the default?[1] 2. Is the promise which has been kept so material relatively to that which has been broken and to the contract as a whole, as to warrant a recovery of the entire compensation, notwithstanding the breach?[2] 3. Is the damage occasioned by the breach susceptible of being estimated in money and a pecuniary compensation?—for if such be not the case, it is more just that the party who is in default should forfeit all right under the contract, than that the opposite party should be compelled to pay in full for a partial performance.[3] If these requisites are fulfilled, a recovery may be had on the performance of one of the plaintiff's promises, although he has broken another promise in the same agreement, and both were to be performed before or at the time fixed for the performance of the promise on which the suit is brought.[4]

The principle can best be illustrated by instances. In Graves *v.* Legg,[5] the declaration set forth an agreement on the part of the plaintiffs to sell and of the defendants to buy fleeces to be shipped from Odessa, and laid down in good order in Liverpool, the names of the vessels to be declared, and that the fleeces arrived in good order, but the defendants declined to accept and pay. The plea averred that the defendants had agreed to buy the fleeces with a view to a resale, which as the plaintiffs well knew could not be effected unless they had notice of the shipment and the name of the vessel; but that the plaintiffs failed to give such notice within a reasonable time, or until the market price of wool had declined. Here the name of the vessel might seem trivial, and the shipment the main object which the parties had in view, but the court was of opinion that as the one was essential to the bene-

[1] See Grant *v.* Johnson, 5 N. Y. 247.

[2] Ellen *v.* Topp, 6 Ex. 424, 441. See Lowber *v.* Bangs, 2 Wallace, 278; Stavers *v.* Curling, 3 Bing. N. C. 355; Graves *v.* Legg, 9 Ex. 709.

[3] See Roberts *v.* Brett, 11 H. & L. 337.

[4] See Chanter *v.* Leese, 4 M. & W. 294; 5 id. 698.

[5] 9 Ex. 709.

ficial operation of the other, the contract was virtually unperformed, and as the default had not been waived by acceptance, nothing was due. So in Ellen *v.* Topp,[1] a covenant to take the defendant's son as an apprentice, and instruct him in the art of an auctioneer, appraiser, and corn-factor, was held to be so far entire that the plaintiff's relinquishment of the trade of a corn-factor precluded a recovery for the refusal of the apprentice to serve out his term. An analogous decision was made in Martin *v.* Schoenberger.[2]

For like reasons, the case will not fall within the principle unless the performance of the promise which is kept goes so far towards the fulfilment of the object which the parties had in view on entering into the agreement that a part can equitably be allowed to stand for the whole; or, as Pollock, C. B., observed in Ellen *v.* Topp,[3] "The rule does not apply to every case in which a covenant by a plaintiff forms only a part of the consideration, and the residue of the consideration has been had by the defendant. That residue must be the substantial part of the contract." Hence, where the vendor agrees to give possession, and also to execute a deed, the performance of the former covenant will not entitle him to the purchase-money unless the latter has also been fulfilled, because possession is necessarily precarious until assured by a conveyance.[4]

When, on the other hand, the non-fulfilment of one of the plaintiff's promises does not materially impair the benefit derived from the performance of the others, and the loss occasioned by the breach may be compensated in damages, he may be entitled to recover the stipulated compensation and leave the defendant to seek redress in a cross-action.[5]

In Stavers *v.* Curling, the plaintiff agreed that he would take command of the defendant's vessel, secure a cargo of sperm oil, or "as great a proportion thereof as might under the circumstances be within his power," and return with it

[1] 6 Ex. 424. [2] 8 W. & S. 367. [3] 6 Ex. 424, 441.

[4] Grant *v.* Johnson, 5 N. Y. 247.

[5] Weaver *v.* Sessions, 6 Taunt. 154: Stavers *v.* Curling, 3 Bing. N. C. 355; Long *v.* Caffrey, 93 Pa. 526; Fame Hose Co.'s Appeal, 83 id. 396, 413.

to London, would obey instructions, be frugal of provisions, and would not smuggle or trade on his own account, or permit any one on board to do so. The defendants pleaded that the plaintiff had broken the contract in not paying strict attention to the stores belonging to the ship, by engaging in trade on his own account, and by going into port when there was no necessity to do so; and also was drunk at divers times during the voyage. Chief Justice Tindal said that the question depended on the meaning of the parties as expressed in the instrument, and on the application of common sense to each particular case. When the intention is discovered, all technical forms of expression must give way. In the case in hand, the necessary inference was that the parties did not intend that the fulfilment of any of the covenants entered into by the plaintiffs should be essential to the recovery of the stipulated remuneration. If, for instance, the covenant to "procure a cargo of sperm oil, or as great a proportion," etc., were interpreted as a condition precedent, the slightest carelessness would occasion the loss of all that he was to receive from the voyage; whereas, if the breach were made the subject of an action by the defendants, their compensation would correspond exactly to the amount of the loss. Judgment would consequently be rendered in accordance with what appeared to be the intention of the parties, namely, that the ship-owner should have redress in damages on the captain's covenants, but should not be allowed to make a full and literal performance on his part a prerequisite to the fulfilment of the obligation which they had waived.

How much the question is one of proportion and circumstances appears from Jones *v.* Marsh,[1] which though falling literally within the rule as stated by Sergeant Williams, was contrary to its spirit. The plaintiff agreed to take all the cheese made by the defendant during the ensuing summer, on the first of October,— $50 to be paid at once and the residue on delivery. The defendant brought the cheese, but the plaintiff was not ready with the money; and when he tendered it soon afterwards, the defendant had disposed of the cheese.

[1] 22 Vt. 144.

The court held that the plaintiff was not entitled to damages, or even to the $50 which he had laid down. If the amount paid in advance by a purchaser who failed to pay in full could be recovered back in any case, there was no such right where, as in the case under consideration, it fell short of the damage occasioned by the subsequent default. In the cases which were cited for the plaintiff, the principal part of the consideration had been received and enjoyed. To warrant a recovery in the absence of full performance, there must have been such an acceptance of part as rendered it fraudulent to rely on the non-fulfilment of the rest, which could not be said when, taking the benefit with the injury, there was a loss. The case of Allen *v.* Sanders,[1] is to the same effect.

That the contract is for several things will not vary the case, or render a partial performance a ground for compensation if it is entire in terms, and there is nothing in the language of the contract or the nature of the subject-matter that makes it divisible, or authorizes the court to resolve it into as many promises as there are acts to be done.[2] In Chanter *v.* Leese, the declaration set forth that it was agreed between the plaintiff and the defendant, that the latter should have the exclusive use of six several patents, and should, in consideration thereof, pay £400 a year. A plea alleging that one of the patents was invalid, was sustained by the court below, and in the Exchequer Chamber. Chief Justice Tindal observed that the patents had not been assigned, and the whole matter rested in contract. One of them was confessedly void, but the plaintiff's contention was that the others were valid, and might be used by the defendants, and that they were bound to perform their part of the agreement by paying the annuity and must bring a cross-action for damages in respect to the one void patent. This reasoning would undoubtedly apply if the consideration were divisible, and the money payable by the defendants had been apportioned by the contract to the different parts of the consideration. But in the case at bar,

[1] 7 B. Monroe, 593.

[2] Chanter *v.* Leese, 4 M. & W. 294; 5 id. 698; Lowber *v.* Bangs, 2 Wallace, 728; Ellen *v.* Topp, 6 Ex. 424.

the enjoyment of all the six patents was the consideration for every part of the defendants' promise, and the annuity was neither apportioned by the contract, nor capable of being apportioned by a jury. All the patents but one were admitted by the pleadings to be valid, but there was no admission that they had been enjoyed by the defendants or averment to that effect in the declaration. The consideration was consequently entire, and by failing in one particular, failed as a whole. Had it appeared affirmatively that the other five patents were enjoyed, the court would still have thought that no action could be maintained on the agreement for the annuity, whatever question might be raised in some other form as to some right of compensation for such enjoyment.

For like reasons, one at least of the plaintiff's promises must have been fully performed; a partial performance of some or of all of them will not suffice, because the case is then virtually the same as if he had made a single promise which had remained unfulfilled.[1] So when that which has not been done is essential to the beneficial operation of that which has been done, both are virtually unperformed and will not sustain a suit.[2]

The case of Lowber *v.* Bangs,[3] may be thought to carry this principle to an extreme. A vessel was there chartered while on her way to Melbourne, for a voyage from Calcutta to the United States, and the charter contained a stipulation that she should proceed from Melbourne to Calcutta "with all possible dispatch." Before the master could be informed of this agreement the vessel had left Melbourne for Manilla, which is out of the direct course to Calcutta, and did not reach Calcutta as soon as she would have done but for the deviation. Freights had fallen during the interval, and the charterers hired another vessel, and refused to accept or load the "Mary Bangs." A suit having been brought for damages, it was contended that the undertaking "to proceed direct" was an independent covenant that might be compensated by money,

[1] See Grant *v.* Johnson, 5 N. Y. 247.

[2] Graves *v.* Legg, 9 Ex. 709; Martin *v.* Schoenberger, 8 W. & S. 367.

[3] 2 Wallace, 728.

and did not entitle the defendants to treat the contract as at an end. This argument was overruled by the court, and judgment rendered in their favor on the ground that time was of the essence of the contract, and the delay fatal to the right to compensation.

It may be observed, with regard to this decision, that although what occurs subsequently cannot vary the meaning of the parties as expressed at the time,[1] a subsequent event may be taken into view in determining whether their purpose has been carried into effect.[2] When by the terms of the agreement various things are to be done for the attainment of an end, it may reasonably be supposed that the intention was that the right to compensation should depend, not on the literal fulfilment of every one of them, but on whether enough was done to produce the desired result; and that if the object was substantially accomplished the contractor should be entitled to payment: if it failed through his default, he should have nothing.[3] Such was in effect the judgment in Stavers *v.* Curling,[4] and although the principle was questioned in Behn *v.* Burness,[5] and may not be so logical as that which was applied in Bangs *v.* Lowber, it tends to a more equitable result;[6] and should seemingly, as Chief Justice Cockburn intimated, be enacted by the Legislature if it cannot consistently be sanctioned by the courts.[7]

Several contracts may be embodied in the same instrument which, though growing out of the same transaction, are yet so far distinct that each may stand alone; and hence when various acts are to be performed by one party and compensated by

[1] Behn *v.* Burness, 3 Best & Smith, 751, 757; Lowber *v.* Bangs, 2 Wallace, 728, 738.

[2] See Ellen *v.* Topp, 6 Ex. 424, 441; Freeman *v.* Taylor, 8 Bing. 124; Dimech *v.* Corlett, 12 Moore, P. C. C. 199, 224, 227.

[3] See Behn *v.* Burness, 1 Best & Smith, 865, 887.

[4] *Ante.*

[5] 1 Best *v.* Smith, 877: 3 id. 750.

[6] See Freeman *v.* Taylor, 8 Bing. 124; Clipsham *v.* Vertue, 5 A. & E. N. S. 265; Tarrabochia *v.* Hickie, 1 H. & N. 183; Dimech *v.* Corlett, 12 Moore, P. C. C. 199.

[7] 1 Best & Smith, 877, 887.

the other, at a rate specifically designated for each, the performance of one of them may give a right to compensation, although the rest have not been performed, and all have a common object which fails in consequence of the non-fulfilment of the contract as a whole.[1]

In Knight *v.* The New England Worsted Co.[2] the agreement was twofold — that the plaintiff should give and the defendants take a lease of the plaintiff's mill at a certain rent, and also for the sale and delivery of the wool and yarns on the premises at so much a pound. The defendants entered into possession of the mill and goods and sold some of the yarns on their own account, but the mill and stock were destroyed by fire a few days afterwards and before the lease was executed. The court held that though the contract was entire, the stipulations with regard to the real and personal estate were so far independent that the defendants became owners of the goods and answerable for the price on delivery, and the plaintiff's inability to give a lease could not be relied on as a defence. If the contract was entire in its origin relatively to the purpose for which it was made, it was divisible in its operation, and although one branch remained unfulfilled, there was a complete performance of another which gave rise to a definite obligation that might be enforced in indebitatus assumpsit. A like conclusion was reached in Stone *v.* Rogers.[3]

In Todd *v.* Summers,[4] an equitable result was attained by treating covenants as independent, which to ordinary apprehension were links in the same chain. The plaintiff there agreed to sell to the defendants his interest in a tract of land; for which they were to make him 50,000 staves by the next Christmas, 25,000 more by the first of May, 1839, and a like number before the close of the year, he sawing the stuff to their hands. They went into possession, and made from 18,000 to 25,000 staves out of timber sawed and furnished by the plaintiff, but he failed to saw the residue of the timber, and they consequently could not make the staves. The court held

[1] Tipton *v.* Feitner, 20 N. Y. 423.

[2] 2 Cush. 271.

[3] 2 M. & W. 443.

[4] 2 Gratt, 67.

that while he was to take the first step by furnishing the materials, and the defendants' covenant to make the staves would consequently be dependent looking solely to the order of time, yet the effect of such a contention would be to deprive the plaintiff of all remuneration for the land, because the defendants were to perform the work during the year, and as their obligation to make the staves depended on his to furnish the lumber, they could not be required to fulfil it after the time had gone by. The plaintiff was entitled to as much as the staves would have been worth allowing for all losses growing out of his own failure to supply the materials. Covenants, though dependent in form, might be construed as independent when necessary to prevent a failure of justice, and a party who has agreed to do two things, allowed to recover on proof of performance of one of them.

Here the choice lay between denying the plaintiff compensation in any form, and compelling the defendants, who may have had neither means nor credit, to pay in money instead of the work which they agreed to do, and would have performed but for the plaintiff's failure to furnish the materials. The latter alternative may have been the more equitable, but it certainly was not what the parties intended when they entered into the agreement.

There can be little doubt as to the true inference where the larger part of the consideration passes at the time, and what remains is a promise that will not, if unfulfilled, impair the value of that which has been received by the defendant, because it cannot reasonably be supposed that the plaintiff is to have nothing unless he performs all, or that the defendant can retain the benefit without making the stipulated compensation. A failure of title to part of the land, rights, or goods conveyed with an express or implied warranty or covenant for title, will not, therefore, as Lord Abinger pointed out in Chanter *v.* Leese,[1] debar the vendor from maintaining an action for the price, although it may be a reason for deducting the amount of the loss;[2] and the principle applies when a breach

[1] 4 M. & W. 294.

[2] Goodman *v.* Meriden Brit. Co., 50 Conn. 139.

of the landlord's promise to make improvements or fulfil a collateral covenant in the lease, is relied on as a defence to an action for the rent.[1] So when the agreement is that the plaintiff shall furnish materials and the defendant work them up, a failure to furnish the quantity stipulated for will not justify the defendant in refusing to finish those already received.[2]

The case of Boone *v.* Eyre,[3] where the principle was laid down by Lord Mansfield, is in conformity with this view. The plaintiff conveyed a plantation and stock of slaves, with a covenant that he had a good title to both, in consideration of a covenant on the defendant's part to pay £500, and an annuity of £400 yearly; and a plea that the plaintiff was not legally possessed of the slaves was overruled by Lord Mansfield, on the ground that if such a defence was allowed the failure of a title to a single negro would operate as a forfeiture of the entire purchase-money.

Such were the circumstances under which the doctrine was originally advanced, and we may doubt whether there are any others where it can properly be applied.[4] Although the question is, what the parties meant when the contract was made, and nothing that occurs afterwards can affect the inference to be drawn from the language used at the time,[5] a subsequent event may preclude the assertion of a right that would otherwise be valid, and a man who accepts a benefit under a contract with notice that it has been broken, will be held to his choice, and cannot treat the contract as void although he may still be entitled to damages. The better opinion would consequently seem to be that when the contract is purely executory, and nothing is done or given when it is made, the subsequent performance of one of two or more promises on

[1] Obermeyer *v.* Nichols, 6 Binn. 159; Liggett *v.* Smith, 3 Watts, 331; Weaver *v.* Sessions, 6 Taunt. 154.

[2] Mill Dam Foundry *v.* Hovey, 21 Pick. 417.

[3] 1 H. Bl. 273.

[4] See Graves *v.* Legg, 9 Ex. 709; Carter *v.* Scargill, 10 Q. B. 564; Bean *v.* Atwater, 4 Conn. 4; Jones *v.* Marsh, 24 Vt. 148; Tompkins *v.* Elliott, 5 Wend. 496.

[5] Grant *v.* Johnson, 1 Seld. 252; Lowber *v.* Bangs, 2 Wallace, 278.

the plaintiff's part, will not warrant a recovery on a promise on the defendant's part which in the order of time is dependent on both, unless the benefit so conferred is accepted by the defendant, with notice that the residue of the consideration has not been or will not be fulfilled.[1]

As was observed in Grant *v.* Johnson, much of the confusion in the books arises from confounding the doctrine of waiver with a rule of construction applicable to the agreement as it came from the hands of the parties.[2] A defendant may waive performance by the plaintiff, and thus in the case of a covenant clearly dependent render himself liable in some form of action,[3] but it is only when the consideration is divisible and the payments are apportioned by the agreement to the different parts of the consideration, that the covenant becomes independent and a recovery can be had on the original contract without averring performance or an excuse for non-performance.

If we now revert to the question mooted in Simpson *v.* Crippin, and Honck *v.* Muller,[4] it will appear that unless an agreement to deliver a gross amount, — say two thousand tons of iron, — in three successive parcels at so much per ton, is to be regarded as three contracts for the delivery of the respective parcels, contrary to the view taken by Lord Selborne in Mersey Steel & Iron Co. *v.* Naylor, and by the Supreme Court of the United States in Norrington *v.* Wright, the acceptance of the first parcel will not preclude the purchaser from relying on a failure to deliver the second parcel as a reason for rejecting the third, because there is no such relation between what has been done and what remains unperformed, as justifies an inference that the end which the parties had in view has been substantially attained, and the acceptance cannot operate as a waiver of a default that has not yet occurred.

[1] See Grant *v.* Johnson, 5 N. Y. 247, 252; Jones *v.* Marsh, 22 Vt. 128; Ellen *v.* Topp, 6 Ex. 424, 441; Legg *v.* Graves, 9 id. 709; Lowber *v.* Bangs, 2 Wallace, 278.

[2] Havelock *v.* Geddes, 10 East, 555.

[3] Mitchell *v.* Darthez, 2 Bing. N. C. 555; Lucas *v.* Godwin, 3 id. 737.

[4] *Ante*, p. 576.

So when delivery is to take place in parcels and the payments are to be made *pro rata*, a failure to pay for any one parcel at the appointed time and place, should preclude the buyer from maintaining an action for a refusal to deliver the rest, because the seller may not only be in want of the money on which he relied for the completion of the contract, but have his wares left on his hands and be unable to find another purchaser;[1] and as this consequence may ensue from a failure to pay for the second parcel, whether the first has or has not been accepted, the rule should be the same in either event.[2]

The rules which have been laid down for determining whether a promise is independent, that is, susceptible of being enforced without averring performance, tend to the solution of a single question: Did the defendant agree to accept the plaintiff's promise as the equivalent for his own, and seek redress in damages if it were not fulfilled? because if he did, he obtained what he stipulated for, and if the non-fulfilment of the plaintiff's promise is a defence it must be on some other ground than that of failure of consideration.[3]

While the obligation of a parol contract is due in every instance to the consideration, and becomes extinct if that be not fulfilled, the application of the principle depends on what constitutes the consideration in the case in hand. Consideration is the result of agreement, and may be either performance, a promise to perform, or a promise attended with performance. The question is, Did the defendant stipulate for a reciprocal engagement, or that the plaintiff would not only promise but perform at or before the period named for the fulfilment of the defendant's promise?[4] In the one case the contract is on trust or credit; in the other, if the consideration be pecuniary for cash. Which interpretation should be adopted depends on

[1] Withers *v.* Reynolds, 2 B. & Ad. 882; Honck *v.* Muller, L. R. 7 Q. B. Div.; Robson *v.* Bohn, 27 Minn. 333.

[2] *Ante.*

[3] Mattock *v.* Kinglake, 10 A. & E. 50; Wilks *v.* Smith, 10 M. & W. 355; Campbell *v.* Jones, 6 T. R. 570.

[4] Mattock *v.* Kinglake, 10 A. & E. 50; Wilks *v.* Smith, 10 M. & W. 355, 358.

the language of the parties as read in the light of the circumstances. In the ordinary case of the sale of a specific chattel, the right of property passes immediately on the completion of the contract, while the vendor is left to his right of action for the price with a lien on the goods if they have not been delivered, showing that the consideration is not payment but the buyer's promise to pay. If the buyer has not done all that the contract requires, he has done all that constitutes the consideration, properly so called, — namely, that for which the seller stipulated as the condition on which he was willing that the thing sold should cease to be his and become the purchaser's; and hence a failure to pay at the time prescribed will not annul the contract or preclude the purchaser from making a subsequent tender of the purchase-money and bringing trover, if the goods are withheld. The question, nevertheless, is one of intention, and when that is that payment shall be essential to the passage of the title, the contract will be executory on both sides, and if the purchase-money be not forthcoming the seller is no longer bound, and may dispose of the goods as he thinks proper, and proceed to recover damages for the breach.

The principle is still clearer when the sale is professedly on credit, because the seller agrees to give not only title but possession, and take the purchaser's promise as an equivalent; and as the consideration is complete as soon as the contract is executed it cannot fail through a subsequent default in payment.

The rule is the same as regards executory contracts for the sale of goods of a certain kind, although somewhat differently applied. An agreement to deliver in consideration of a promise to pay in advance, or when the goods are tendered, is obviously a very different thing from an agreement to deliver them in consideration of a promise to pay at a subsequent period. In the latter case, the seller's obligation is absolute immediately on the execution of the contract; in the former it depends on the purchaser's punctuality; and if he is behindhand although but for a single day, he will lose all claim against the vendor and be liable in damages for the excess of the price over the market value of the goods. On the other hand when delivery is to precede payment, a failure to tender the goods at the appointed time will render the seller answerable and discharge the purchaser.

Although promises which in terms or by implication are to be performed simultaneously, will ordinarily be interpreted as dependent, and sales for cash are seemingly within the principle, it does not apply when the title passes on the completion of the contract. For as the seller under these circumstances impliedly agrees to take the buyer's promise to pay the price as an equivalent for the ownership, and seek redress by suit if it be not fulfilled, he cannot rely on a failure to pay at the day as a reason for refusing a subsequent tender, or treating the sale as at an end. The effect is the same when an executory contract is so far fulfilled by delivery and acceptance as to vest the right of property in the purchaser, for as this cannot take place without the consent of both parties, prior breaches are waived so far as they relate to the end in view, and a subsequent default will not operate as a defeasance, unless it grows out of the non-performance of some stipulation which is worded as a condition, or so designed. Hence the acceptance of goods which are delivered under an executory agreement will vest the right of property indefeasibly in the purchaser, whether they are or are not such as he agreed to buy,[1] unless he is ignorant of the defect and returns them as soon as it is discovered, although it will not preclude a claim for compensation for the injury actually occasioned by the default.

The principle is clearly stated in Addison on Contracts. "When the sale is of quantity of things of a certain kind, and may be fulfilled by the delivery of any goods answering to the terms prescribed, the right of property does not pass from the vendor to the purchaser, and time will in general be of the essence of the contract so long as the contract remains executory; and the purchaser will not be bound to accept and pay for the goods if they are not tendered on the day specified. But if the sale is of specific, ascertained chattels, and the

[1] Parker *v.* Palmer, 4 B. & Ald. 387; Chapman *v.* Morton, 11 M. & W. 534.

ownership and right of property in the thing sold have been transferred by the bargain to the purchaser, time is not of the essence of the contract, and the vendor cannot repudiate the sale and revest the right of property and the ownership in himself, and refuse to deliver the goods at a subsequent period on a tender of the price, on the ground of the non-payment thereof at the time appointed,[1] unless the sale has been made conditional for payment at the time named, and it appears to have been the intention of the parties that the sale should be at an end, and the vendor entitled to sue for damages in case of the non-payment of the purchase-money at the appointed period."[2]

It is established, in accordance with these principles, that the failure of the buyer of a specific chattel to pay the price will not defeat the title which passed on the completion of the sale, or preclude him from tendering the money subsequently and maintaining trover or replevin; and it is immaterial in this regard whether the sale is for cash or on credit, or that payment is by the terms of the agreement to precede delivery.[3]

In Martindale *v.* Smith, certain stacks of oats were sold with an agreement that they should be paid for in twelve weeks, but might remain on the premises for four months, and should then be called for and removed by the buyer. The latter did not pay at the time prescribed, but made a subsequent tender, which was declined by the vendor who treated the sale as annulled by the default, and sold the oats to a third person. The buyer brought trover; and it was contended for the defence that the failure to pay cancelled the obligation to deliver, and authorized the vendor to deal with the property as his own. Lord Denman said, in giving judgment, "Having taken time to consider of our judgment, owing to the doubt excited by a most ingenious argument whether the vendor has not a right to treat the sale as at an end and revest the property in himself by reason of the vendee's failure to pay the price at

[1] Martindale *v.* Smith, 1 Q. B. 295; Wilmshurst *v.* Bowker, 7 M. & Gr. 792.

[2] Addison on Contracts, 235, Am. ed.

[3] Martindale *v.* Smith, 1 Q. B. 395. *Ante.*

the appointed time, we are clearly of opinion that he had no such right, and that the action is well brought against him. For the sale of a specific chattel on credit, though that credit may be limited to a definite period, transfers the property in the goods to the vendee, giving the vendor a right of action for the price and a lien upon the goods if they remain in his possession, till the price be paid. But a default in payment does not rescind the contract. Such is the doctrine cited by Holroyd, J., from Comyns's Digest, in Tarling *v.* Baxter,[1] and it will be found consistent with all the numerous cases referred to in the course of the argument. In a sale of chattels, time is not of the essence of the contract unless it is made so by express agreement, than which nothing can be more easy by introducing consistent words into the bargain."

It is a consequence of the same principle that a vendor may maintain an action for the price, notwithstanding a breach of warranty, or in other words of an undertaking for the quality, kind, or fitness of the chattel which is the subject of the sale. For, as under these circumstances the purchaser agrees to buy the very thing which is offered or exhibited, and trusts the vendor's word for its quality or kind, the title passes as soon as the thing is delivered or set apart, whether the warranty is broken or fulfilled.

Mutual and dependent promises are sometimes said to be conditions, but it would be more accurate to say that they not unfrequently operate as if such were the case.[2] Promises bind; conditions suspend, modify or vacate; and promises on one side to sell, and on the other to accept and pay, are not conditions in the sense either of the common or the civil law, even when each is presumably made in consideration of the performance of the other, and will fail if it be not fulfilled. Such is the established rule with regard to parol contracts, and failure of consideration may also be a defence to a covenant, on the equitable ground that a man ought not to be allowed to enforce a promise without giving the equivalent stipulated for by the promisor, whether it is, or is not set forth in the instrument.

[1] 6 B. & C. 360, 362.

[2] Behn *v.* Burness, 1 B. & S. 877; 3 id. 750.

CHAPTER XXV.

ENTIRE AND DIVISIBLE CONTRACTS.

Contracts to pay by Instalments for a single Act or Thing. — Waiver of Default by Acceptance. — Structures imperfectly erected on another's Land. — Recovery upon substantial Performance with Compensation for Defects. — Destruction of the subject-matter before the Completion of an entire Contract.

THE rule that an entire contract must be fulfilled in every particular to give a right to compensation is inapplicable where the performance is divisible, and the consideration apportioned to the several parts.[1] The contract does not cease to be entire, but the language indicates an intention that an equivalent shall be given for what is done or rendered without waiting for the completion of the whole.[2]

Such a case may, agreeably to the view taken in some instances, grow out of an agreement to serve for a year at so much per month, or to furnish merchandise payable by the load or ton,[3] or where a builder stipulates for *pro rata* payments at certain stages, as the work proceeds, and under these circumstances a failure to complete the whole will not, it has been said, forfeit the right to what has been already earned.[4] Hence, when goods are sold deliverable by instalments, and it is incumbent on the buyer to pay for each parcel when received, he cannot resist an action brought for the

[1] Simpson *v.* Crippin, L. R. 8 Q. B. 14; Oxendale *v.* Wetherell, 9 B. & C. 386; Tipton *v.* Feitner, 20 N. Y. 423; Lucesco Oil Co. *v.* Brewer, 66 Pa. 351; Morgan *v.* McKee, 77 id. 229. See Scott *v.* The Kittatanning Coal Co., 89 Pa. 231; Bollman *v.* Burt, 61 Md. 415.

[2] The Anglo Egyptian Co. *v.* Rennie, L. R. 10 C. P. 271; Grant *v.* Johnson, 5 N. Y. 247. See Mersey Steel and Iron Co. *v.* Naylor, L. R. 9 App. Cases, 434; Norrington *v.* Wright, 115 U. S. 188, 204.

[3] Button *v.* Thompson, L. R. 4 C. P. 330; Withers *v.* Reynolds, 2 B. & Ad. 882; Tipton *v.* Feitner, 20 N. Y. 423.

[4] Cunningham *v.* Morrell, 10 Johns. 203; Bean *v.* Atwater, 4 Conn. 4.

amount because a subsequent delivery is not made at the appointed time.[1]

Such an inference will not, however, ordinarily be drawn because delivery is to be made in parcels, unless it also appears that each parcel is to be paid for on delivery.[2] The motive presumably is convenience, and not to authorize the plaintiff to choose how much or how little he will perform, and then ask a court or jury virtually to make a new contract by fixing the amount which he is entitled to recover.[3]

In the case last cited, an agreement to deliver "800 tons of coal, at $6.00 per ton, on board vessels as sent for, during the months of August and September," was held to be entire, and to impose no obligation on the purchaser to pay for each cargo, or until the whole was fulfilled. His refusal to pay for the first cargo consequently did not exonerate the vendors, or constitute a defence to an action for their failure to forward the residue. Sharswood, J., said that if the intention was that each shipload should be paid for on delivery, nothing could be easier than to have expressed it in terms. There might be, no doubt, as Best, C. J., observed, in Mavor *v.* Payne,[4] a principal contract which was entire, and subordinate contracts for the several parcels. Such was not the case before the court; but if it were, the suit was on the entire contract, and the vendors had brought suit and recovered on the subordinate contract in another court.

Agreeably moreover to the weight of authority, a stipulation that the price shall be paid by instalments as the goods are delivered or the work proceeds, will not render a contract for an entire thing, — as, for instance, to build a house or furnish a given weight or quantity of merchandise, — divisible, or so apportion the consideration to the several parts as to dispense with an exact fulfilment of the whole;[5] and if the

[1] Withers *v.* Reynolds, 2 B. & Ad. 882; Tipton *v.* Feitner, 20 N. Y. 423, 426.

[2] Catlin *v.* Tobias, 26 N. Y. 217; Harris *v.* Liggett, 1 W. & S. 301.

[3] Shinn *v.* Bodine, 60 Pa. 182.

[4] 2 C. & P. 91.

[5] Norrington *v.* Wright, 115 U. S. 188, 204; Mersey Steel and Iron Co. *v.* Naylor, L. R. 9 App. Cases, 434, 439.

contractor fails to do all, he will not only be precluded from recovering what remains unpaid, but may be compelled to refund the sums which he has already received; and it will make no difference that the default arose without negligence on his part, from the destruction of the building by fire, a tornado, or other insuperable cause.[1]

The true theory in such cases appears to be, not that the failure to complete the work is a forfeiture of the amount already earned, but that it entitles the employer to the difference between what is and what ought to have been done, which, in the case of a total loss by fire, is the entire value of the building, less so much of the price as remains unpaid.

Contracts to repair or alter an existing thing stand in this regard in marked contrast to contracts to construct, in being subject to an implied condition that the thing shall continue to exist; and if it perishes before the work is completed, the contractor will not only be exonerated, but may be entitled to compensation for what has been actually rendered or performed.[2]

Although a man need not take less or other than he stipulated for, he is still free to choose, and the acceptance of a substituted performance will defeat the right to rely on the breach as an entire failure of consideration, although it will not preclude a claim for compensation for the difference between what is and what ought to have been performed.[3] Such is the established rule when the merchandise delivered under an executory contract does not correspond with its terms;[4] and if Tindal, C. J., inclined to an opposite view in Chanter *v.* Leese,[5] his language was at variance with that held in the court below,

[1] Tompkins *v.* Dudley, 25 N. Y. 272; Adams *v.* Nichols, 19 Pick. 275; Superintendent, &c. *v.* Bennett, 3 Dutch. 513; Shaw *v.* The Turnpike, 3 Penrose & Watts, 454; The School District *v.* Dauchy, 25 Conn. 530; Jones *v.* Dermott, 2 Wallace, 1; Fildew *v.* Besley, 42 Mich. 100.

[2] Anglo Egyptian Co. *v.* Rennie, L. R. 10 C. P. 271; Lord *v.* Wheeler, 1 Gray, 282; Rawson *v.* Clark, 70 Ill. 656.

[3] Richardson *v.* Dunn, 2 Q. B. 218; McCombs *v.* McKennan, 2 W. & S. 216.

[4] *Ante.*

[5] 5 M. & W. 698.

and may be regarded as an *obiter dictum*, because the point did not arise on the pleadings.

It is, nevertheless, essential to such a result that the party should be aware of the default which he is alleged to have condoned; and while one who accepts goods on the 1st of July, which ought to have been sent on the 1st of June, cannot rely on the delay as a reason for rejecting a subsequent delivery under the same contract on the 1st of August, the case is widely different when the first parcel arrives at the appointed time, and the second is too late.[1] Accordingly, where the contract was for the sale of a specific quantity of corn, to be delivered within a designated period and paid for subsequently, proof that part of the corn had been forwarded and accepted during the time prescribed, was held not to entitle the seller to the whole or any part of the price.[2] So in Champlin *v.* Rowley[3] the plaintiff agreed to deliver one hundred tons of pressed hay before the close of navigation, for which the defendant was to pay $100 down, and the residue when the whole should be delivered. He paid the amount due in advance, and received and used or sold half of the hay; but the delivery was interrupted by the ice and not resumed until the following spring. The court held that the defendant was not answerable for the whole or any part of the hay. He did not by receiving part, when there was no reason to suppose that the rest would not be sent, waive a default that had not occurred. These decisions contravene the doctrine enunciated in Honck *v.* Muller,[4] that renunciation comes too late after part has been received, though under the belief that the whole will be fulfilled.

The acceptance must also be voluntary under circumstances which leave the defendant free to choose.[5] A man who keeps and uses goods knowing that they are sent with a view to remuneration, may be compelled to pay although he never ordered them or they are not such as he agreed to take; but

[1] Catlin *v.* Tobias, 26 N. Y. 217; Kein *v.* Tupper, 52 id. 550.

[2] Witherow *v.* Witherow, 16 Ohio, 238.

[3] 13 Wend. 258.

[4] L. R. 7 Q. B. Div. 92, 99; *ante*.

[5] Olmstead *v.* Beale, 19 Pick. 528; Faxson *v.* Mumford, 2 Mass. 407.

he is not bound to refrain from using his land because it is occupied by a building or other structure, which however useful or beneficial does not conform to the terms of the agreement.[1]

In Ellis *v.* Hamlen[2] a builder who had not fulfilled the contract as regarded some of the joists and materials, sought to recover under the common counts on the ground that the defendant having received a benefit, was liable on an implied promise to pay what it was worth. A nonsuit was entered at the trial, and the court refused a motion to take it off. "The defendant," said Sir James Mansfield, "agreed to have a building of such and such dimensions. Is he to have his ground covered with buildings of no use, which he would be glad to see removed, and is he to be forced to pay for them besides? It is said he has the benefit of the houses, and therefore the plaintiff is entitled to recover on a *quantum valebant*. To be sure, it is hard that he should build houses and not be paid for them; but the difficulty is to know where to draw the line, for if the defendant is obliged to pay for one deviation from the contract, he may equally be obliged to pay for anything, how far soever distant from what the contract stipulated for."

It was decided in like manner in Mehurin *v.* Stone[3] that "when the stipulations which are conditions precedent in a contract for the erection of a structure on another's land have not been substantially fulfilled, the party in default cannot maintain an action either on the contract originally made, or on an obligation arising out of the use and occupation of the building as incident to the possession and ownership of the land. No recovery can be had upon a *quantum meruit*, because, where the contract is express, none can be implied

[1] Munroe *v.* Butt, 8 E. & B. 738; Smith *v.* Brady, 17 N. Y. 173; Tompkins *v.* Dudley, 25 id. 272; Glacius *v.* Black, 50 id. 145; Miller *v.* McCaffrey, 9 Pa. 245, 249; Bryant *v.* Stilwell, 24 id. 314; Brewer *v.* Tysor, 3 Jones (N. C.), 181; Mehurin *v.* Stone, 37 Ohio St. 49; Olmstead *v.* Beale, 19 Pick. 528; Hartupee *v.* Pittsburgh, 97 Pa. 107; Shaw *v.* Turnpike Co., 3 Penrose & Watts, 454; Fildew *v.* Besley, 42 Mich. 100.

[2] 3 Taunt. 52.

[3] 37 Ohio St. 49.

relating to the same subject-matter. The principle that conditions precedent to the right to compensation for labor done or materials furnished must be substantially performed, in order to put the other party in default, is of universal application, admitting of no exceptions."

So nothing is due for the partial fulfilment of an agreement to act as mate of a vessel during an entire voyage, or to haul a pile of wood for coaling. There may be a benefit, but there is no acceptance, because it is not in the power of the employer to render back what he has received.[1] In Lantry *v.* Parks, the contract was for six months' service, at $20 per month. The plaintiff worked for a month, and left without any better reason than his own pleasure or convenience, and the decision was that his employer owed him nothing. The courts, nevertheless, in cases of this description incline to avoid the hardship that might result from the letter of the rule, by laying hold of any circumstance that tends to show an understanding that the compensation should be in the ratio of the time,—as for instance, that the wages were paid by the week or month,[2]—and was carried in Britton *v.* Turner to the extent of deciding that the plaintiff, who after agreeing to work for a year had left the defendant's service without cause at the expiration of six months, might recover on a *quantum meruit* for the time during which he was actually employed.

It was declared at one period in Massachusetts, that even where there is such a failure in the performance of the work or character of the materials, that the contractor cannot maintain an action on the agreement, he may yet, where "they are of some value and benefit to the other contracting party, recover on a *quantum valebant* for the materials." It is, agreeably to this view, "conformable to justice, that the party who has the possession and enjoyment of the labor and materials of another shall be held to pay for them, so as in all events

[1] Cutter *v.* Powell, 6 T. R. 320; 2 Sm. L. C. 1; Harris *v.* Liggett, 1 W. & S. 301; Larkin *v.* Buck, 11 Ohio, 561; Badgley *v.* Heald, 4 Gilman, 64; Lantry *v.* Parks, 8 Cow. 63; Miller *v.* Goddard, 34 Me. 102.

[2] See 2 Sm. L. C. 8 Am. ed. 43.

that he shall lose nothing by the breach of the contract."[1] This doctrine has been recognized or applied in some other States;[2] but was virtually overruled in Olmstead *v.* Beale,[3] and is contrary to the weight of English and American authority.[4] What constitutes such a waiver or acceptance as will render the defendant answerable, notwithstanding a failure of performance, was clearly shown by Comstock, C. J., in Smith *v.* Brady.[5] "No doubt," said he, "a person may voluntarily accept a benefit under a contract of which the conditions precedent have not been performed by the other party, and he may do this in such circumstances that a new obligation to pay for the benefit will arise. Thus, if A should agree to manufacture and deliver to B a carriage of a particular kind, and should make a different one, B may elect whether he will take it or not. Until he so elects, he has no property in the fabric. If he voluntarily accepts the article, he thereby either waives the objections which he might make to it and is liable to pay for it according to his contract, or a new assumpsit arises from the act of acceptance as though no previous agreement had existed. The case cited on the argument of Vanderbilt *v.* The Eagle Iron Works,[6] was determined very distinctly upon these principles. But the rule, as it is well settled with us, allows a party to retain without compensation the benefits of a partial performance, where from the nature of the contract he must receive such benefits in advance of a full performance, and by its terms or just construction he is under no obligation to pay until the performance is complete. Thus, if a person engages to perform a year's labor for another, and payment is to be made when the labor is

[1] Hayward *v.* Leonard, 7 Pick. 181; Smith *v.* The First Cong. Meeting House, 8 id. 178.

[2] McKinney *v.* Springer, 3 Ind. 69; Britton *v.* Turner, 6 N. H. 481.

[3] 19 Pick. 528.

[4] Mehurin *v.* Stone, 37 Ohio St. 49; Smith *v.* Brady, 17 N. Y. 73; McMillan *v.* Vanderlip, 12 Johns. 165; Thorpe *v.* White, 13 id. 53; Jennings *v.* Camp, 3 id. 94; Champlin *v.* Rowley, 13 Wend. 258; 18 id. 187; Paige *v.* Ott, 5 Den. 406; Pike *v.* Butler, 4 Comst. 360; Pullman *v.* Corning, 5 Seld. 93.

[5] 17 N. Y. 73.

[6] 25 Wend. 665.

done, in such a case the employer necessarily receives the benefit of each day's service when it is performed; yet if the laborer without just cause abandons the service at any time however short, before the year has expired, he can recover no part of his wages.[1] So the contract may be to sell and deliver goods at different times, to be paid for when the whole are received. If the vendor refuses to perform entirely without good cause, the purchaser is neither bound to pay for nor to return the goods received in part performance.[2] If A should agree to plow the field of B, consisting of twenty acres, at a given price for the whole service, or at so much per acre to be paid when the service is done, and after plowing nineteen acres should abandon the contract, he can recover nothing for his work. The owner of the field may enter, sow it with his grain and reap the harvest, thus enjoying fully the benefits of the part performance. In so doing he waives nothing, because he cannot reasonably do otherwise. He is not obliged to abandon his field in order to be enabled to insist upon the condition of the contract. Closely analogous is the case of a building contract. The owner of the soil is always in possession. The builder has a right to enter only for the special purpose of performing his contract. Each material as it is placed in the work becomes annexed to the soil, and thereby the property of the owner. The builder would have no right to remove the brick or stone or lumber after annexation, even if the employer should unjustifiably refuse to allow him to proceed with the work. The owner, from the nature and necessity of the case, takes the benefit of part performance, and therefore by merely so doing, does not necessarily waive anything contained in the contract. To impute to him a voluntary waiver of conditions precedent from the mere use and occupation of the building erected, unattended by other circumstances, is unreasonable and illogical, because he is not in a situation to elect whether he will or will not accept the benefit of an imperfect performance. To be enabled to stand upon the contract, he cannot reasonably be required to tear down and destroy the edifice if he prefers it to remain. As

[1] Cases *supra*.

[2] Champlin *v.* Rowley, *supra*.

the erection is his by annexation to the soil, he may suffer it to stand; and there is no rule of law against his using it without prejudice to his rights."

A waiver may also be inferred from evidence that the defendant's attention was called to a change in the mode or plan of the work, or the character of the materials, and that he signified his assent or failed to object to the alteration. To render silence equivalent to assent, it must, nevertheless, be incumbent on the party to speak; and in Pike *v.* Butler,[1] the court held that where the buildings erected by a tenant during his lease did not correspond with its terms, the landlord was not bound to pay for them, although he knew of the deviation while the work was going on and did not object, because it is the duty of the person who does the work and not of him for whom it is done, to see that the agreement is fulfilled. A waiver or estoppel cannot justly be deduced from standing by or looking on without objecting, unless the opposite party was proceeding ignorantly and it became a duty to set him right. If a man wilfully builds on my land, or breaks his contract with me, my acquiescence at the time will not preclude an action for redress.[2]

It is, moreover, essential to a waiver that the party should have knowledge or notice of the default which he is alleged to have condoned; and the fact that the defendant paid large sums of money while the work was going on, in pursuance of a satisfactory report from an engineer in his employ, will not debar him from relying on the non-fulfilment of the contract as a defence, unless the default is so obvious that the engineer not only might, but must be presumed to have been aware of its existence.[3]

It has been held in various instances that a waiver cannot be given in evidence unless it is set forth in pleading, so that the defendant may come prepared to meet the issue.[4] Such,

[1] 4 Comst. 360.

[2] 2 Sm. L. C. 8 Am. ed. 891; Young *v.* White, 5 Watts, 460; Hartupee *v.* City of Pittsburgh, 97 Pa. 107.

[3] Hartupee *v.* City of Pittsburgh, 97 Pa. 107.

[4] Mehurin *v.* Stone, 37 Ohio St. 49; Palmer *v.* Sawyer, 114 Mass. 1; Alexander *v.* Hoffman, 3 Harris, 382.

no doubt, is the rule where the plaintiff declares specifically on the contract, though not when the question arises under the common counts unless there is a variance from the bill of particulars.

It is not less well established, on grounds which are equitable rather than logical, that where the agreement is substantially performed as regards form, workmanship, and materials, the contractor may be entitled to recover notwithstanding slight or immaterial deviations which do not impair the value or usefulness of the structure as a whole.[1] The rule was stated in Hayward *v.* Leonard,[2] in terms that were criticised in Smith *v.* Brady as much too broad, but the language held subsequently in Olmstead *v.* Beale[3] accords with the view presented above and the general course of decision.

"Formerly," said Okey, J., in Kane *v.* The Stone Co., "there could be no recovery on a contract like this, unless the agreement was strictly performed. But the rigid rule upon this subject has been relaxed, and now, where the builder acts in good faith, there may be such recovery, although there may not have been literal performance.[4] What is essential and indispensable to a recovery is substantial compliance with the agreement. This is not a suit on a *quantum meruit*, but an action on the contract. No evidence was offered as to the value of the work or materials, but evidence was offered as to damages that may have been sustained by the failure to strictly comply with the agreement. The action is properly prosecuted on the contract, and the measure of recovery is the sum stipulated in the agreement, less the damages sustained by a failure to strictly perform."[5] A like measure of damages was applied in McKinney *v.* Springer.[6]

[1] Goldsmith *v.* Hand, 26 Ohio St. 101; Mehurin *v.* Stone, 37 id. 49; Kane *v.* Stone Co., 39 id. 1; The Danville Bridge *v.* Pomeroy, 3 Harris, 182; Ellis *v.* Lane, 85 Pa. 265; Preston *v.* Finney, 2 W. & S. 53, 55; Nolan *v.* Whiting, 88 N. Y. 648; Johnson *v.* DePeyster, 50 id. 666; Glacius *v.* Black, 50 id. 145; Phillip *v.* Gallant, 62 id. 256.

[2] 7 Pick. 181.

[3] 19 Pick. 528.

[4] Goldsmith *v.* Hand, 26 Ohio St. 101; Mehurin *v.* Stone, 37 id. 49.

[5] Nolan *v.* Whitney, 88 N. Y. 648.

[6] 3 Ind. 59.

The latitude thus given does not warrant any material departure from the plan or specifications either as regards materials or design; and if such a deviation occurs it cannot be excused on the ground that the change is beneficial, and adds to the beauty or stability of the work.[1] The owner is entitled to the thing he contracted for and no other; and if the contractor gives him a different thing though it be more valuable or useful, the goodness of his intentions and the benefit conferred do not constitute a legal ground for remuneration.[2]

It was accordingly declared in Olmstead *v.* Beale, that the equitable principle advanced in Hayward *v.* Leonard,[3] and other cases belonging to the same category, is of recent growth, and only extends "to unimportant accidental and unintentional deviations, which from the differences of opinion that so often exist in relation to the exact requisition in the details of a special contract, had become indispensable to the administration of justice in such cases. But where there is an important and voluntary deviation or omission from the contract, the doctrine of Faxon *v.* Mansfield[4] will apply, and the contractor can have no remedy for the materials furnished and the services performed."

Every one, said Comstock, C. J., in Smith *v.* Brady,[5] "has a right to build his house, his cottage, or his store after such a model and in such style as shall best accord with his notions of utility, or be most agreeable to his fancy. The specifications of the contract become the law between the parties until voluntarily changed. . . . If the owner, having regard to strength and durability, has contracted for walls of specified materials, to be laid in a particular manner, or for a given number of joists and beams, the builder has no right to substitute his own judgment or that of others. Having departed from the agreement, if performance has not been waived by the other party, the law will not allow him to

[1] Goddard *v.* Bebout, 40 Ind. 114.

[2] Mehurin *v.* Stone, 37 Ohio St. 49; Smith *v.* Brady, 17 N. Y. 173; Olmstead *v.* Beale, 19 Pick. 528.

[3] 7 Pick. 181.

[4] 2 Mass. 147.

[5] 17 N. Y. 182.

allege that he has made as good a building as the one he engaged to erect. He can demand payment only upon and according to the terms of his contract; and if the conditions on which payment is due have not been performed, then the right to demand it does not exist. To hold a different doctrine would be simply to make another contract, and would be giving to parties an encouragement to violate their engagements, which the just policy of the law does not permit."

The difficulty in cases of this description is to know what constitutes a substantial performance, or distinguish a technical and unimportant deviation from one which is material; and unless the question is regarded as one of law instead of being thrown into the jury-box, the principle is of little worth. It seems to have been regarded in the former aspect in Mehurin *v.* Stone, where the court said that if the facts had appeared on the face of the pleadings judgment would have been entered for the defendant; and the result should be the same when they are proved or admitted at the trial. Agreeably to the New York authorities, what is material may be a legal question; but whether a specific breach or deviation comes within the rule must be left to the jury as matter of fact.[1]

Under the view taken in Pennsylvania, and which generally prevails, the substantial performance which entitles the plaintiff to recover is not inconsistent with the existence of defects, which give the defendant a right to compensation; and the verdict should then be for the contract price, less such a sum as will afford compensation for what remains undone or has been ill performed.[2]

The line is closely drawn in the following citation from the judgment in Mehurin *v.* Stone,[3] though not more strictly than is requisite to hold men to their agreements. "In the present case the deviation from the contract above-mentioned cannot

[1] Johnson *v.* DePeyster, 50 N. Y. 666; Glacius *v.* Black, id. 145; Phillip *v.* Gallant, 62 id. 256; Nolan *v.* Whitney, 88 id. 648.

[2] Monocacy Bridge Co. *v.* American Iron Bridge Mfg. Co., 83 Pa. 517, 524.

[3] 37 Ohio St. 49.

be regarded as slight or non-substantial. The defendant — as the contract must be construed unaided by any light that extrinsic proof may have thrown around it — stipulated for a solid bed of stone, well cemented together, for a foundation for the vault; and for its front he stipulated for a marble slab or block for the space immediately below the roof, that would materially add to its beauty, if not to its strength and durability. To the fulfilment of these stipulations he was clearly entitled. It is quite immaterial whether, in the judgment of the plaintiffs or others, the structure as completed was as durable as the one contracted for or not. It was the right of the defendant to consult his own judgment and tastes, and to provide for the construction of a vault that would best accord therewith; and having provided, by the specifications of his contract, for a foundation of a given character, and for one block of marble to fill the gable of the vault, he was entitled to a substantial compliance by the plaintiffs before he would be called upon to pay any part of the agreed compensation."

The rule that so long as anything remains to be performed under an entire executory contract nothing is done, applies, although the agreement is to manufacture or construct a thing which is nearly finished and would be completed but for a hurricane, fire, or other inevitable accident, and although, as in the case of a building contract, the structure is erected on the land of the person for whom the work is done, and therefore seemingly within the maxim, *res perit domino*. There may be no fault on the builder's part, but so long as he is or ought to be in charge the responsibility is his; and as the owner is not benefited and has no means or opportunity to guard against the loss, it cannot equitably be thrown on him, or the case treated as an exception to the general rule that nothing is done on an executory contract until it is fulfilled. The builder must consequently begin again and restore what has been injured or consumed, and if he fails to do so will not only be unable to maintain an action for the price, but may be compelled to refund what he has received in advance or as a part-payment. Impossibility is not a defence at common law, and if it were there is no impossibility but merely increased labor and expense, which must be borne by the contractor as incident to the obligation incurred by entering into the agreement. The law has been so held in various instances,[1] and was applied in Tompkins *v.* Dudley, although the house was under roof, and floored and plastered when the fire occurred, and what remained to be done would not have cost more than $50. In like manner, where the building falls, or is in an unsafe and dangerous condition in consequence of the marshy and treacherous nature of the soil, the contractor must secure a firm foundation by driving piles, and should that prove impracticable will still be answerable for the loss arising from a risk which he voluntarily assumed.[2]

The question arose in Adams *v.* Nichols,[3] on an action against a surety for the failure of the principal contractor to finish a house which had been destroyed by fire when near completion; and it was said to be clear that had the article to be made been a coach or a vessel, or a chattel of any kind, the materials in the first instance, and the article itself in every stage of its progress towards completion would have been at the risk of the builder, and the principle was not less applicable because the thing to be manufactured was attached to the freehold.[4]

A like decision was made in The School District *v.* Dauchy.[5] The defendant there agreed to build a school-house for the sum of $2,469 by the 1st of May, 1854, the price to be paid by instalments as the work progressed. The first instalment of $1,000 was paid, and the school-house was nearly finished, when it was struck by lightning and consumed. The defendant having declined to erect another building in the place of that destroyed, the plaintiff brought suit for the non-performance of the contract, and was held entitled to recover back the amount paid in advance, although the accident might

[1] Tompkins *v.* Dudley, 25 N. Y. 272; Adams *v.* Nichols, 19 Pick. 275; School District No. 1 *v.* Dauchy, 25 Conn. 530; Fildew *v.* Besley, 42 Mich. 100.

[2] Superintendent and Trustees of Public Schools of Trenton *v.* Bennett, 3 Dutch. 513; Jones *v.* Dermott, 2 Wallace, 1.

[3] 19 Pick. 275. [4] Kein *v.* Tupper, 52 N. Y. 550. [5] 25 Conn. 530.

have been an answer to a claim for damages for the failure to complete the school-house at the appointed time.

The rule applies with equal strictness to executory contracts of sale, whether they are *in genere* or for the delivery of specific chattels; and if any of the goods perish before all is done that is requisite to pass the title to the whole, no portion of the purchase-money can be recovered, although some of them were weighed, measured, or sampled, and set apart for the buyer before the loss occurred.[1]

The rule was strictly followed in Kein *v.* Tupper. The plaintiffs there contracted, on the 3d of July, 1868, to sell, and the defendants to purchase, 119 bales of A. cotton, described by marks, at 31¼ cents per pound, payable in cash on delivery. The sale was negotiated through brokers, who acted for their principals, and bought and sold notes were delivered reciprocally. The sale was to be by sample, the cotton to be weighed and samples taken and compared with the original samples in the hands of the brokers. The plaintiffs gave the defendants' broker an order on the warehouse where the cotton was stored for the 119 bales, and the broker's clerk indorsed upon the order a direction to re-store on account of defendants. On the 15th of July, 70 bales of the cotton were taken out of the warehouse, weighed and sampled, and returned to the warehouse in accordance with the indorsement. On account of the lateness of the hour, the weighing and sampling of the residue was deferred until the next day. That night the warehouse was burned, and its contents damaged, or destroyed. Seventy-eight of the bales which had been weighed and sampled were saved in a damaged condition, tendered to the defendants, rejected by them, and subsequently sold for their account at auction with notice. The 49 bales that had not been weighed were so much injured as to be unmerchantable. It was held that the title to both parcels was still in the vendor, and that he must bear the loss.[2]

[1] Kein *v.* Tupper, 52 N. Y. 552.

[2] Church, J., said "It is conceded that the loss occasioned by the fire must fall upon the party who, at the time, had the legal title to the cotton, and such is the well-settled rule. 8 N. Y. 291. The contract of sale

Executory contracts for the sale or delivery of a specific thing are, nevertheless, subject to an implied condition that

and purchase did not pass the title. When anything remains to be done by the seller to ascertain the identity, quantity, or quality of the property, no title passes. 5 Den. 379 ; 25 N. Y. 525, and cases there cited.

"Assuming that this was a sale of a quantity of specific cotton, which I think we may do, and which is the most favorable view for the plaintiffs, yet as the cotton was to be weighed by the vendors to ascertain the quantity, and sampled by both parties to ascertain the quality, no title would pass until these acts were done.

"The question was presented on the trial in various forms, that the delivery was not complete as to any part of the cotton ; but the court held and ruled that if the jury found that the direction to re-store was given by the defendants, and the broker was authorized to accept a delivery of the cotton for the defendants, then that as a matter of law, what took place in weighing and sampling the 70 bales amounted to a delivery of that quantity. In this, I think, the learned judge erred. If the broker had full authority, and that authority was conferred upon Bolton, the sampler, it was an authority to receive 119 bales, and not 70 or 42, or any other number. Neither of them had power to accept a less number, or waive the delivery of any part of the cotton purchased. 41 Barb. 446; Hill & Den. Suplt. 75.

"But neither of them assumed to accept unconditionally 70 bales of the cotton. The acceptance, as far as it went, must be construed as conditional upon the delivery of the balance. The bales weighed were pronounced satisfactory, but were received subject to the delivery of the remainder. Besides, the sampling of the 70 bales was not complete until the samples taken out were compared with the original samples, which were at the broker's office. This was the business of the broker, who passed upon the quality upon such comparison. The sampler exercised his judgment as to the quality; but the final decision, it seems, was to be made by the broker.

"Until this was done the 70 bales were not ready for delivery even, much less delivered and accepted. The direction to 're-store' for the defendants, on the back of the order, must be construed to mean a direction to re-store when the cotton was all delivered. It did not apply to each bale as it was weighed, and, in fact, there was nothing done by the warehouseman to change the storage. All that can be predicated of the transaction of the fifteenth of July is, that the parties had commenced the performance of acts as to some of the cotton necessary to enable a delivery to be made, but had not completed them, and as to the balance of the cotton nothing had been done. I think the court should have held that there was no delivery of any part of the cotton.

"But if there was a delivery of 70 bales, the action could not be

it shall continue to exist until the time for performance arrives, and if it perishes during the interval, the obligation on both sides is at an end and neither party can maintain an action against the other.[1]

A different view prevailed at Rome, where the doctrine of consideration was unknown, and the breach of a contract to sell, to manufacture, or to construct a specific thing neither rendered the contractor answerable, nor precluded him from recovering the price, unless it arose from his fault as distinguished from the operation of causes which he could not control.[2]

This seeming anomaly is referred by Maynz to a principle, which he states as follows: "Justice demands imperiously, that a debtor, whose misconduct renders it impossible to execute the obligation which he has assumed, should answer for

sustained. The contract was entire, and the plaintiffs must prove performance to entitle them to recover. The defendants purchased 119 bales, to be paid when delivered. Until the delivery of the whole quantity no action accrued to the plaintiffs.

"While the destruction of the subject-matter of the contract, without fault of the plaintiffs, would relieve them from an action for damages for not performing the contract, yet it would not enable them to enforce a part-performance against the defendants. 47 N. Y. 62. The rule is well settled in this State, that upon a contract for the delivery of a specified quantity of property, payment to be made on delivery, no action will lie until the whole is delivered. 13 Wend. 259; 16 id. 632; 3 id. 112; 21 N. Y. 397; 2 id. 153.

"The English rule, that a recovery may be had for the portion delivered, if retained until after the time for full performance, as held in 7 B. & C. 387, and other cases, has never been adopted, but expressly repudiated, by the courts of this State. Id. That rule rests upon no solid foundation, and in effect enables courts to alter the terms of contracts as made by parties.

"A vendee may accept a delivery of a part of the property, and waive the delivery of the remainder, and this may be shown by circumstances, but in this case there is not the slightest circumstance tending to establish such acceptance and waiver. Both parties expected to perform the contract in full. The unfortunate accident prevented it before the title had passed from the vendors, and the misfortune is theirs."

[1] Dexter *v.* Norton, 47 N. Y. 62.

[2] Maynz, ii. §§ 177, 210, 218; *ante*.

the resulting loss. On the other hand, it is equally just not to hold him responsible for a breach occasioned by a fortuitous event, that is to say, by an occurrence in which he has no share and which is not in any respect imputable to him. . .

"It is accordingly a general rule that no one shall be answerable for a default occasioned by a force which he could not resist, and especially that a debtor shall not be obliged to compensate the creditor for losses arising from such a cause. This rule applies as well to obligations in which both parties are reciprocally bound, as to those in which one alone is answerable to the other.

"Hence if an irresistible force renders it impossible for one of the parties to a bilateral contract to do what is incumbent on him, he will be freed from all responsibility without losing the right to demand the performance of what is due from the opposite party by virtue of the same contract."[1] It is said by the same author, to follow from these principles, as applied to the contract of sale, that "If the thing sold perishes, or is damaged before delivery from a purely fortuitous cause, the buyer though he has received nothing, or has received a damaged article, is nevertheless bound to pay the price agreed without having a claim for compensation against the opposite party, because the seller, although he owes the thing, is still only answerable for such acts as can justly be imputed to him."[2]

In considering what is here said, it is necessary to remember that "obligation" was a generic term, comprising every case where compensation was due for a wrong attended with injurious consequences, whether the default consisted in a tortious act, or was simply a failure to comply with an engagement.

It was not the contract, nor yet the duty which it imposed, that constituted the obligation, but the intervention of the law to compel the performance of the duty, or rather to redress the injury resulting from the default.[3] Hence if one who was charged with a breach of contract proved that it was due to

[1] See Maynz, ii. § 173, p. 14; § 218.

[2] See Maynz, ii. § 177, p. 38.

[3] Institutes 3. 13.

causes that could not be controlled, it was a defence to the suit. This consideration may explain why a vendor was not answerable for the non-delivery of a chattel which perished in his hands subsequently to the sale, but it does not show that the purchaser could justly be compelled to pay for that which he did not receive. It may be just not to hold me accountable for a default which no care or skill would have enabled me to avoid, but it is not just that my misfortune should be made a ground for compelling another to compensate me for a service which I have not rendered, or for goods which I have been unable to deliver.

The difficulty will be less if we reflect that the forms of contracts prescribed or recognized by Roman law had the efficacy which the common law ascribes to a covenant, and that failure of consideration consequently was not a defence, unless the circumstances were such as to render it inequitable to insist on the fulfilment of the obligation; or as the principle is stated by Ortolan, although both obligations, that of the seller to deliver and that of the buyer to pay, are founded in consent, they yet, when once contracted have independent existence, and if the former is modified or extinguished by the deterioration or loss of the thing sold, the latter will none the less subsist unchanged.[1]

It might therefore reasonably be held that a buyer who suffered the chattel which he had agreed to buy to remain in the vendor's custody, should bear all losses that could not be foreseen or guarded against; but it does not follow that a like rule could equitably be applied in every instance where one of the parties to a mutual contract was unavoidably prevented from rendering the equivalent for which the other had stipulated.

A reference to the commentators will accordingly show that if contracts falling under the head of *locatio operis*, — as, for instance, to build or manufacture, — were within the principle, it was subject to qualifications which limited its operation, and the contractor could not recover for work which

[1] Ortolan, Explic. Hist. des Inst. Tome, 3, p. 282, as cited Benjamin on Sales, § 410. Accarias, No. 612.

he did not perform, on the ground that the failure was due to accident without fault on his part, nor unless he could show that it was occasioned by a *vis major*, — or to use an English equivalent, "the act of God or the king's enemies."[1]

The doctrines taught in the above citations have little or no place in a system of jurisprudence which like our own, classes torts and contracts under different heads, and deduces the obligation of the latter, when not under seal, from the consideration for which they are conditioned. At common law, one who enters into an agreement takes the risk of every event that may interfere with its fulfilment, and will be equally answerable whether the breach is wilful or the result of an unforeseen and irresistible force. Impossibility is not therefore an excuse for non-performance, and still less will it entitle a party who has not fulfilled his promise to compel the opposite party to give an equivalent for what he has not received.

The common law is, nevertheless, as we have seen, so far analogous to the civil law that when the covenants in a bilateral agreement are independent, either party may sue without alleging that he has fulfilled his part of the agreement, and proof that it has been broken will not be a defence unless it is admissible under the statutes conferring or regulating the right of offset.

[1] Accarias, No. 621; Maynz, ii. §§ 173, 177 p. 40, note 11; § 218, p. 249, note 15.

CHAPTER XXVI.

IMPOSSIBILITY.

Impossibility as an Excuse from Performance. — Effect of Previous Knowledge of Impossibility. — Distinction between Things that Cannot be, and Things that Cannot be Accomplished. — Warranty of Possibility. — Impossibility subsequently resulting through no Fault of the Promisor. — Distinction between Impossibility and Inconvenience. — Contract for Impossibility may operate as Insurance. — Contract for Act forbidden by Law Invalid.

Agreeably to the Roman law, impossibility might modify or annul the obligation of an agreement in various ways: 1. A contract to do that which is impossible in fact or in law, — as, for instance, to touch the sky with one's finger, or to convey a thing which does not exist, or is insusceptible of being transferred, was void.[1] 2. If performance became impossible through a supervening cause without fault on the part of the promisor, he was discharged. 3. Such a supervening impossibility might in the case of a mutual contract not only exonerate the party in default but leave him free to enforce the contract against the opposite party, because as the obligation arose not from the consideration but from the promise, the failure of the consideration was not a defence.[2]

[1] Gaius, iii. § 97; Institutes 3. 19. 12. "Il faut que la prestation soit physiquement et légalement possible. Il est d'abord évident que nous ne pouvons nous obliger à une prestation physiquement impossible, par exemple, à toucher le ciel du doigt, à donner à un autre une chose qui lui appartient dejà, à faire partiellement une prestation indivisible, à prester le fait d'un autre; pas plus que nous ne pouvons promettre un *genus* qui n'existe plus ou n'a jamais existé. Il en est de même des choses qu'il est légalement impossible de donner ou de livrer, notamment des choses hors du commerce." Maynz, ii. § 199.

[2] Maynz, ii. §§ 173, 177, 210, 288; Benjamin on Sales, § 410; *ante*. See Wharton on Contracts, § 296, for an exhaustive examination of the subject.

To warrant the application of the principle, the impossibility must consist in the nature of the thing to be done, and not in the inability of the party to do it; or as it is sometimes termed, be an *impossibilitas rei* as distinguished from an *impossibilitas facti*. If the thing could be accomplished by any one with proper means and the requisite skill and knowledge, the promisor was not less answerable because it was impossible to him.

These distinctions were logical under the Roman law which held that there could be no liability where there was no fault,[1] but have no place in a system where the obligation of a contract arises from what is done or promised on the faith of the assurance which it holds forth, and the inquiry is not Was the defendant to blame for not doing as he agreed? but Was the promise made, and did it induce the plaintiff to change his position for the worse? This reasoning may not apply to agreements under seal, which depend for their effect on the solemnity with which they are executed, but it is as true of them as of parol contracts, that the expectation which they excite in the mind of the covenantee may be as real, and the disappointment if they are broken equally great, whether the agreement can or cannot be carried into effect.

An owner who sends his ship to a distant port in reliance on a covenant to load her when there, or provide a pass that will enable the master to procure a cargo, is obviously entitled to compensation if the undertaking be not fulfilled, whether the default be wilful or owing to causes that cannot be controlled.[2]

The common-law rule, accordingly, is that a man who agrees to do that which is contrary to the nature of things, or insusceptible of being performed, as for instance to construct a "perpetual motion," or deliver a larger quantity of barley than the world contains, cannot rely on the impossibility as a defence.[3]

1 *Ante.* Maynz, §§ 177, 218. Accarias, Nos. 662, 663.

2 Kirk *v.* Gibbs, 1 H. & N. 820.

3 Thornborow *v.* Whitacre, 2 Lord Raymond, 1164; Wild *v.* Harris, 7 C. B. 999; Jones *v.* St. John's College, L. R. 6 Q. B. 115.

In Thornborow *v.* Whitacre,[1] the plaintiff declared, upon an agreement between him and the defendant, that the latter in consideration of 2*s.* 6*d.* in hand paid, and of £4 17*s.* 6*d.*, to be paid upon the defendant's performing the agreement, would deliver two grains of rye corn on Monday, the 29th of March, and four grains of rye corn on Monday then next following, and eight grains of rye corn on Monday next after the Monday last mentioned, and sixteen grains of rye corn on Monday next after the said third Monday, and double the number of grains of rye corn, namely, thirty-two grains of rye corn on Monday next after, being the fifth Monday, *et progressu sic deliberaret quolibet alio die Lunæ successive infra unum annum, ab eodem* 29 *Martii bis tot grana secalis quot die Lunæ proximo precedente respective deliberanda forent, etc.* The defendant demurred, and Salkeld contended on his behalf that the agreement appeared upon the face of it to be impossible, the rye to be delivered amounting to such a quantity as all the rye in the world was not so much, and being impossible was void, and the defendant was not bound to perform it. There were three sorts of impossibilities: *Impossibilitas legis*, such are all immoral actions, as to murder J. S., etc. Secondly, *impossibilitas rei*, such as are all natural impossibilities which cannot be done from the nature of the thing. Thirdly, *impossibilitas facti*, namely, such an impossibility, as though there is nothing in the nature of it impossible to be done, yet it is impossible for a man to do, as to touch the heavens or go to Rome in a day. And a covenant or condition to do any of these impossibilities is void. Though relief be by law to be paid immediately upon the death of the tenant, yet if the relief be a rose or a bushel of roses, if the tenant die in winter, the lord shall not distrain for his relief till the season that roses come, because *lex non cogit ad impossibilia;* and the law takes notice that roses cannot be kept; but otherwise of wheat, etc., which may.[2] If a man be bound by his deed to do things which cannot be done by reason of impossibility (although it was his folly), yet the deed is void; but a man is liable to do as far as can be done by the power of a man.[3]

[1] 2 Lord Raymond, 1164. [2] Litt. § 129. [3] Y. B. 40 Edw. III. 6 a.

Hence, a covenant to leave a wood in as good plight as it was when leased, is not broken if the trees are uprooted by a tempest, although it would be otherwise in the case of a house, because it is possible to rebuild the house, but not to make the trees grow as they were before.[1] The demurrer was overruled: Lord Holt saying that *impossibilitas rei* and *impossibilitas facti* are all one, and simply come to this — that the contractor promised more than he can perform. "If a man will for money undertake to do an impossible thing, an action shall lie against him for not performing it." So it was declared in Jones *v.* St. John's College[2] that "if people will bind themselves to absurd regulations as to matters that appear to be impossible to be performed within the time, they must take the consequences of it, and therefore if you make such a bargain it is clear you cannot imply a condition which is unconnected with it."

To warrant a recovery in assumpsit, it must nevertheless appear not only that the defendant promised, and the plaintiff took the course which the promise was calculated to induce, but that he did so in reliance on the defendant's word, or, as it was customarily set forth in the declaration, *Fidem adhibens assumptioni.*[3] Regard may consequently be had under this head to the nature of the promise, and if it is one which no sane man could have credited, a necessary element is wanting and the action will fail. The question is not as to the defendant's good faith, or whether he knew that his undertaking was impossible, but — Did the plaintiff believe that the agreement could be fulfilled? The contract may be such, as in the instance given in the Institutes of a promise to touch the sky with one's finger, as to leave no room for doubt; but there are cases where the answer depends on the knowledge and intelligence of the person who brings the suit or relies on the breach as a defence. The validity of an agreement to procure or deliver a hippogriff, unicorn, or other fabulous beast for exhibition in a circus or menagerie should, therefore,

[1] F. N. B. tit. Covenant; Perkins, § 738.

[2] L. R. 6 Q. B. 115, 124.

[3] Yard *v.* Eland, 1 Lord Raymond, 368; Clark *v.* Russel, 3 Watts, 283.

depend on whether the showman knew that no such animals exist, and if the jury found that he entered into the contract in good faith he would be entitled to judgment, although the damages might be nominal or only such as would compensate him for the loss of time or the amount expended with the view of carrying it into effect. Had the defence been based on such grounds in Thornborow *v.* Whitacre it might have prevailed. A line has accordingly been drawn between that which cannot be, and that which cannot be accomplished, and an undertaking which falls within the latter category, as for instance that it shall not rain to-morrow, or that the Pope shall be at Westminster by a certain day, treated as not less valid because there are insuperable obstacles to its fulfilment.[1]

The principle was so far recognized at Rome that while a stipulation for the delivery of a temple, a forum, or other consecrated or public edifice was merely void, a consensual sale of such a place or building entitled the buyer to compensation if he was deceived; or according to Accarias, though he was not, because the vendor was fraudulent if he knew the truth, and negligent if he did not inquire. If, on the contrary, the thing sold was one which nature does not produce, the sale was as invalid as the stipulation, because both parties were presumed to have notice and to be equally in fault.[2] The principle is the same whether the impossibility of performance arises from the want of any legal means of carrying the contract into effect or from any other cause, and a covenant to obtain or perfect a patent may consequently be valid although the parties are aliens, and the right to such an exclusive privilege is confined by the law to citizens.[3] So it is not a defence for the non-fulfilment of a covenant to supply the master of a ship with the pass which will enable him to procure a cargo, that it is arbitrarily withheld by the government of the country where the contract is to be performed.[4]

[1] See Beebee *v.* Johnson, 19 Wend. 500; Superintendent and Trustees *v.* Bennett, 3 Dutch. 513, 519.

[2] Institutes, 3. 23. 5; Sandars's Justinian, 419; Accarias, No. 602.

[3] Beebee *v.* Johnson, 19 Wend. 500.

[4] Kirk *v.* Gibbs, 1; H. & N. 810.

It is immaterial as regards the result whether the contractor is aware of the obstacle and might have guarded against it with due care, — as in the case of an undertaking to erect a building within a year that will require three, — or meets with an unexpected obstacle; and a builder who agrees to finish an edifice by a given day, including such alterations as may be directed while the work is going on, or forfeit a given sum, must pay the penalty if he is behindhand although the directions are such as cannot possibly be complied with before the time expires.[1] So a breach of a positive undertaking by the lessee of a coal mine to raise a given quantity of coals in each year, or by the owner of a vessel to procure and load a cargo of guano at a certain island, cannot be excused on the ground in the one case that there were no coals to be got, or in the other that all the guano was dug and carried away before the ship arrived;[2] and the rule was applied in the case last cited, although the instrument contained a clause discharging the defendant from liability if the vessel was lost, or any other unforeseen cause prevented the fulfilment of the charter-party.

Conversely a charterer may, according to the view taken in Lowber *v.* Bangs,[3] excuse his failure to furnish a cargo, on the ground that the ship did not proceed to the designated port with despatch and by the shortest route, as stipulated in the charter-party, although when the instrument was executed she was on the other side of the globe, and the master could not possibly be notified in time to enable him to comply punctually with the agreement, and although the delay did not frustrate the object of the voyage or cause any real detriment. In like manner it is not a justification for the breach of an agreement to build a house or forward goods to their destination by an appointed time, that performance became impossible through a breach in the canal which was the only means of transportation;[4] or that the building was destroyed when

[1] Jones *v.* St. John's College, L. R. 6 Q. B. 115.

[2] The Marquis of Bute *v.* Thompson, 13 M. & W. 487; Hill *v.* Sughrue, 15 id. 253, 263. See Clifford *v.* Watts, 5 C. B. N. S. 579, 587.

[3] 2 Wallace, 728.

[4] Harmony *v.* Bingham, 12 N. Y. 99.

near completion by a fire or hurricane, or even that the walls fell through the shifting and marshy character of the soil, and the impossibility of obtaining a secure foundation.[1]

In Jones *v.* St. John's College[2] the controversy arose out of a contract to erect a building before the 15th of March next ensuing, with a proviso that if the work was not done by that time the contractor should forfeit £3 as liquidated damages for each day that it remained unfinished. The contractor sued for the price, and the defendants pleaded that the building was not finished by the 15th of March, nor for many days thereafter, and that £800 was due as compensation for the delay, which they claimed as an offset. The plaintiff replied that while the work was going on, the defendants had directed various alterations which rendered it impossible to complete the building within the appointed time. The rejoinder was that by the terms of the agreement all such alterations as the college clerk and bursar might order were to be made as if they formed part of the original plan, and without any enlargement of the time, and that the alterations in question took place in pursuance of such an order. The court held that had alterations been ordered that were not contemplated by the agreement, or had the order come at an unreasonable time, the case would have worn a different aspect, but that a man who agrees absolutely to do such work as another may direct, by a given day, is answerable in damages whether it be or be not possible to comply.[3]

It results from the above decisions that when the contractor warrants the possibility of performance, or what comes to the same thing, that the agreement shall be fulfilled at all events, impossibility is not a defence. The rule is nevertheless subject to a qualification, that if the agreement relates to a specific thing and cannot be performed if that ceases to

[1] The School District *v.* Dauchy, 25 Conn. 530; Tompkins *v.* Dudley, 25 N. Y. 272, 277; Superintendent and Trustees *v.* Bennett, 3 Dutch. 513; Dermott *v.* Jones, 2 Wallace, 1; Harmony *v.* Bingham, 12 N. Y. 99.

[2] L. R. 6 Q. B. 115, 124.

[3] See Roberts *v.* The Bury Commissioners, L. R. 4 C. P. 755; 5 id. 310.

exist, the parties will be discharged if the thing is destroyed or perishes before the time for fulfilment arrives.[1]

Such is the established doctrine of the common law with regard to executory contracts for the sale of a house or chattel, because the contract will be presumed to have been made subject to the continued existence of the subject-matter.[2] The Roman law was the same relatively to the seller, if the thing sold perished before delivery without fault on his part, but differed in holding the buyer answerable for the price.[3] Contracts for the delivery of things of a certain kind, that may be satisfied by tendering any goods answering to the descriptive words, stand on the same footing under both systems, and impossibility, caused by a failure of the contemplated means of supply, is not an excuse.[4]

The question arose in Dexter *v.* Norton,[5] under a contract for the sale and delivery of 607 bales of cotton, designated by marks and numbers. A large number of the bales had been delivered, when a fire occurred which destroyed the residue, without fault or negligence on the part of the seller. Cotton had risen in price in the interim, and the buyer brought a suit for the loss of the bargain, which was defended on the ground that the contract being for the delivery of specific things was subject to an implied condition that they should be in existence when the time arrived for its fulfilment. This view was sustained by the court in the following judgment: —

"This action was brought by the purchaser against the vendor to recover damages for the non-delivery of cotton, and the important and only question in the case is whether upon an agreement for the sale and delivery of specific articles of personal property, under circumstances where the title to the

[1] Taylor *v.* Caldwell, 3 B. & S. 826; Howell *v.* Coupland, L. R. 9 Q. B. 462; 1 Q. B. Div. 258; Anglo-Egyptian N. Co. *v.* Rennie, L. R. 10 C. P. 271; Lakeman *v.* Pollard, 43 Me. 463; Spalding *v.* Rosa, 71 N. Y. 40.

[2] Dexter *v.* Norton, 47 N. Y. 62; Appleby *v.* Myers, L. R. 2 C. P. 651; Howell *v.* Coupland, L. R. 9 Q. B. 462; Rugg *v.* Minet, 11 East, 218.

[3] *Ante;* Institutes, 3. 23, § 3; Accarias, No. 612.

[4] Accarias, No. 612, note 1; Youqua *v.* Nixon, 1 Peters, 221; Gilpins *v.* Consequa, ib. 91.

[5] 47 N. Y. 62.

property does not vest in the vendee, and the property is destroyed by an accidental fire before delivery without the fault of the seller, the latter is liable upon the contract for damages sustained by the purchaser. The general rule on this subject is well established, that where the performance of a duty or charge created by law is prevented by inevitable accident without the fault of the party, he will be excused, but where a person absolutely contracts to do a certain thing not impossible or unlawful at the time, he will not be excused from the obligations of the contract unless the performance is made unlawful, or is prevented by the other party. Neither inevitable accident, nor even those events denominated acts of God will excuse him; and the reason given is that he might have provided against them by his contract.[1] But there are a variety of cases where the courts have implied a condition in the contract itself, the effect of which was to relieve the party when the performance had, without his fault, become impossible; and the apparent confusion in the authorities has grown out of the difficulty of determining in a given case whether it required or justified such an implication, and also in some cases in placing the decision upon a wrong basis. The relief afforded to the party in the cases referred to is not based upon an exception to the general rule, but upon the construction of the contract. For instance, in the case of an absolute promise to marry, the death of either party discharges the contract, because it is inferred or presumed that the contract was made upon the condition that both parties should live."

The same rule has been laid down as to property: "As if A agrees to sell and deliver his horse Eclipse to B on a fixed future day, and the horse die in the interval, the obligation is at an end."[2] In replevin for a horse, and judgment of *retorno habendo*, the death of the horse was held a good plea in an action upon the bond.[3] In Taylor *v.* Caldwell,[4]

[1] Paradine *v.* Jane, Alleyn, 27; Harmony *v.* Bingham, 12 N. Y. 99; Tompkins *v.* Dudley, 25 id. 272.

[2] Benjamin on Sales, 424.

[3] Carpenter *v.* Stevens, 12 Wend. 589.

[4] 3 B. & S. 826.

A agreed with B to give him the use of a music hall on specified days, for the purpose of holding concerts, and before the time arrived the building was accidentally burned; held, that both parties were discharged from the contract. Blackburn, J., at the close of his opinion, lays down the rule as follows: "The principle seems to us to be that in contracts in which the performance depends on the continued existence of a given person or thing, a condition is implied that the impossibility of performance, arising from the perishing of the person or thing, shall excuse the performance." And the reason given for the rule is, "because from the nature of the contract, it is apparent that the parties contracted on the basis of the continued existence of the particular person or thing."

The rule does not apply conversely, and the loss from causes beyond control of that which the vendor has agreed to sell is not under our system, as it was at Rome, so far an excuse for non-delivery as to warrant a recovery of the price.[1]

The case is substantially the same where the contractor is prevented by disease or death from doing an act or rendering a service which, as in the case of an engagement to sing at a concert or appear at court at the day named in a recognizance, is so far personal that no one else can fill the place.[2]

Such is the position of an artist who becomes blind while working at the picture which he has been employed to paint, or of an author who is overtaken by illness in the midst of his work, and the default will be excused in both cases, — or rather there is no default, although there may be an obligation to refund any amount that may have been paid in advance for the unfinished work.[3]

It may accordingly be stated as a general principle, that where from the nature and wording of the contract it cannot be carried into effect if some specific thing or person ceases

[1] *Ante;* Kein *v.* Tupper, 52 N. Y. 550.

[2] Boast *v.* Firth, L. R. 4 C. P. 1; Hall *v.* Wright, 3 E. B. & E. 746; Anglo-Egyptian N. Co. *v.* Rennie, L. R. 10 C. P. 271; Scully *v.* Kirkpatrick, 29 P. F. S. 381.

[3] See Hall *v.* Wright.

to exist or is disabled by disease, the parties will be presumed to have contemplated the possibility of such an event, and to have intended that if the contingency occurred the obligation should be dissolved. Whether, therefore, the impossibility arises from the death or illness of the person by whom the agreement is to be performed, or the destruction of the place where, or means through which alone it can be fulfilled, there is equally a breach of an implied condition, and the contract cannot be enforced.[1]

It is therefore a sufficient answer to an action for the non-fulfilment of an agreement to erect machinery in a shop or mill, that the premises were destroyed by fire before the work could be finished; and a contractor who agrees to repair a house may claim the protection of the same principle, if the house is consumed before the work is finished.[2] When the agreement is for work on a particular thing belonging to another, which is partly performed, and the thing perishes before the whole is performed, the contractor is not only discharged but may be entitled to retain any sums that have been paid in pursuance of the contract while the work was going on; and the rule is not less applicable because part of the work is to be done in the contractor's shop, and then supplied or fitted to the thing in question.[3] A general undertaking by a lessee to keep in repair stands on a different footing, as being in effect to maintain; and if the premises are destroyed by fire or swept away by a flood they must be rebuilt, at whatever cost.[4]

"There seems," said Blackburn, J., in Taylor *v.* Caldwell, "no doubt that where there is a positive contract to do a thing not in itself unlawful, the contractor must perform it or pay damages for not doing it, although in consequence of

[1] Taylor *v.* Caldwell, 3 Best & Smith, 826, 833; Hall *v.* Wright, 3 E. B. & E. 746; Thomas *v.* Knowles, 128 Mass. 22; Field *v.* Brackett, 56 Me. 121.

[2] Lord *v.* Wheeler, 1 Gray, 282.

[3] Lord *v.* Wheeler, 1 Gray, 282; Anglo-Egyptian N. Co. *v.* Rennie, L. R. 10 C. P. 271.

[4] See The Brecknock Co. *v.* Pritchard, 6 T. R. 750; Walton *v.* Waterhouse, 2 Wms. Saund. 422.

unforeseen accidents the performance of his contract has become unexpectedly burdensome or even impossible. The law is so laid down in 1 Roll. Abr.,[1] and in the note to Walton *v.* Waterhouse,[2] and is recognized as the general rule by all the judges in the much-discussed case of Hall *v.* Wright.[3] But this rule is only applicable when the contract is positive and absolute, and not subject to any condition, either express or implied; and there are authorities which, as we think, establish the principle that where from the nature of the contract, it appears that the parties must from the beginning have known that it could not be fulfilled, unless when the time for the fulfilment of the contract arrived some particular specified thing continued to exist, so that, when entering into the contract, they must have contemplated such continuing existence as the foundation of what was to be done; there, in the absence of any expressed or implied warranty that the thing shall exist, the contract is not to be construed as a positive contract, but as subject to an implied condition that the parties shall be excused in case before breach, performance becomes impossible from the perishing of the thing without default of the contractor."

Agreeably to a recent decision, a covenant by a lessee to dig not less than one thousand tons of clay on the demised premises in each and every year throughout the term is within this principle, and a plea that no such quantity of clay existed or could be found on the land may be a good defence.[4] The case of the Marquis of Bute *v.* Thompson[5] might appear to be at variance with this decision, but was distinguished on the ground that the contract there was in effect in the alternative, to mine the coals or pay a certain rent, and on the failure to fulfil one branch the defendant became answerable on the other.

It may be observed in this connection that a lease is an irrevocable sale or transfer of the right of property during the term for a yearly return, instead of a sum payable in

[1] 450, Condition (G).
[2] 2 Wms. Saund. 421 a, 6th ed.
[3] E. B. & E. 746.
[4] Clifford *v.* Watts, L. R. 5 C. P. 577.
[5] 13 M. & W. 487, *ante.*

gross, which makes the tenant as much the owner while his interest lasts as if he were a purchaser. And as he will reap the benefit should the bargain prove advantageous, so he should bear the loss if his expectations are disappointed by the event. Such is confessedly the rule with regard to the lease of a farm, a manufactory, or a ship, and it is seemingly not less applicable to the lease of a mine. If the failure of the ore in a mine is a defence, why may not a like plea be urged where a house which has been let is destroyed by fire?

In Walker *v.* Tucker,[1] the question arose on a plea to an action brought for the rent reserved in a lease of certain mines, that they "became and were wholly exhausted and incapable of yielding sufficient coal to pay for working said mines." The court held that where, from the nature of the covenant, it is apparent that the parties contracted on the basis of the continued existence of a given person or thing, a condition is implied that if the performance becomes impossible from the perishing of the person or thing, that shall excuse such performance. Had, therefore, the plea stopped short after alleging that the mines became wholly exhausted, it would have been good; but the subsequent qualification showed that these words did not mean exhausted of coal, but only of such coal as would, with due diligence, pay for working the mines. This might be, and yet the most valuable portion of the mines remain untouched. It was incumbent on the defendants to know, and the presumption was that they did know, when they made the covenant, the difficulties to be encountered in performing it. "It is elementary law that when the contract is to do a thing which is possible in itself, the promisor will be liable for a breach thereof, notwithstanding that it was beyond his power to perform it; for it was his own fault to run the risk of undertaking to perform an impossibility, when he might have provided against it by his contract."[2] Impossible is here used in the sense in which it is synonymous with impracticable; or, in other words, with that which cannot be done because it

[1] 70 Ill. 527, 542.

[2] 1 Chitty on Contracts, 11th Am. ed. 1074.

will cost more than any benefit that can be derived is worth.[1]

In the foregoing instances the agreement was specific for the delivery of a particular thing, or that it should be done in a way prescribed, and the principle does not apply to contracts *in genere* for goods of a certain kind, or to perform an act without specifying the means. There is an obvious difference between a contract to forward goods by a particular ship and a contract to forward them without naming the vessel; and it will not be an answer in the latter case that the contractor relied on a ship then in port which perished before the cargo could be put on board, and that he could not procure another. In the instance first above supposed, the contract is as specific as a sale of a designated bale of merchandise or of a horse,[2] and the destruction of the thing terminates the obligation; in the second, it is as general as an undertaking for the delivery of goods of a certain kind, and if the means originally prepared or relied on fail, the contractor must provide others at his peril.

The failure of a usual and advantageous means of performance which the parties contemplated will not therefore be a defence unless it is specified in the contract, or is the only means of carrying it into effect, and was so regarded on both sides.[3]

In the case last cited, the question arose on an agreement for the carriage of merchandise from New York to New Orleans within a given time, with a deduction of ten cents per one hundred-weight from the freight for every day during which the carriers were in default. It appeared in evidence that the goods were forwarded in the usual course of business to Columbia, in the interior of Pennsylvania, to be carried thence by a canal which was rendered unnavigable by a violent and unexpected freshet, so that it was necessary to wait until it could be repaired, or bring the goods back to

[1] See Moss *v.* Smith, 9 C. B. 94. [2] *Ante.*

[3] Hand *v.* Baynes, 4 Wharton, 204; Beebee *v.* Johnson, 19 Wend. 500; Harmony *v.* Bingham, 1 Duer, 210; 12 N. Y. 99; McDonald *v.* Gardner, 56 Wis. 35; Eugster *v.* West, 35 La. An. 119.

the seaboard which would have been attended with delay and expense. The carriers were held liable to the penalty. It did not appear that the goods could not have been sent in time by sea, and they had, by making the contract, incurred the burden of doing all that was requisite to carry it into effect at whatever cost, or of making compensation for the delay.

For like reasons it is not an answer to an agreement to erect a house that the ground was from latent defects so treacherous and unsound that the walls fell when the building was near completion, and could not be rebuilt without driving piles or the use of some other costly and artificial means of obtaining a secure foundation, which would exceed the contract price;[1] and a contractor who fails to proceed under such circumstances will not only lose the right to compensation, but may be held answerable in damages or compelled to refund the sums which have been paid in advance.

In Lovering *v.* The Buck Mountain Coal Co.[2] the defendants agreed to deliver four thousand tons of coal from their mines in Lehigh County from time to time as required, at their wharf in Philadelphia. The only route by which the coal could be transported to the place of delivery was the canal of the Lehigh Navigation Company, which was swept away by a freshet soon after the first order had been filled, and the defendants were consequently unable to comply with the subsequent orders. When the canal was again in working order they offered to deliver the residue, which was declined on the ground that the time had gone by; and a suit brought for the previous default. The court held that the plaintiffs must be presumed to have been aware of the place whence the coal was to come, and of the means through which alone it could be shipped, and to have agreed, subject to an implied condition that the canal should continue in such working order as would render it possible to fulfil the

[1] Superintendent and Trustees *v.* Bennett, 3 Dutch. 513; Dermott *v.* Jones, 2 Wall. 1.

[2] 54 Pa. 291.

contract. The obligation was consequently suspended while the break continued, and all that could reasonably be required of the defendants was that they should be, as they actually were, ready and willing to forward the coal as soon as the canal was repaired. When their offer to do so was declined, there was no longer any liability on either side, because the plaintiffs were not bound to accept the coal at a later period, nor the defendants for an inevitable delay. The case consequently fell within the doctrine of Appleby *v.* Myers,[1] that when the completion of a contract to supply and put up machinery for the defendants' mill, was prevented by a fire, which consumed the premises after part of the work had been performed, there was a common misfortune but no fault, and the contractor was not entitled to compensation for the work already done, nor the owner to damages for the failure to complete the whole.

It may be observed with regard to the decision, that if the question in Appleby *v.* Myers was analogous, it was not the same. If the thing stipulated for ceases to exist, the contract is at an end, but it does not follow that the failure of that which is not stipulated for will have the same effect because it is the only means by which the contract can be fulfilled. Where, as in Lovering *v.* The Buck Mountain Coal Co., the contract is for delivery at a remote point, there is an implied condition that the seller shall have a reasonable time, and any event by which the transit is unavoidably delayed is admissible to show that he is not in default. The case went to the jury on this ground in the court below, and the judgment seemingly establishes nothing more.

The question is throughout one of intention, and if a man will warrant that which is beyond human power, as, for instance, life, or that a building or growing crop shall not be damaged by hail or consumed by fire, he will be answerable as an insurer, if on no other ground. A man may by apt words bind himself that it shall not rain to-morrow, or he will pay damages,[2] and the contracts by which ships are insured against the perils of the seas, houses against fire, and vine-

[1] L. R. 2 C. P. 651.

[2] *Ante;* Canham *v.* Barry, 15 C. B. 619.

yards from the devastating hail-storms which arise in France, may be referred to this principle, and would be invalid without its aid.

The intention to insure need not be expressed in terms; it is enough that the language of the contract read in the light of the circumstances, indicates that the party meant to bind himself absolutely and at all events, or to render a pecuniary compensation if the thing itself cannot be performed.[1] Thus when the plaintiff executed a deed and took a collateral agreement from the grantor to deliver a wooden stable on the premises whenever it should be demanded, in as good a condition as it then was, the court held that the undertaking was unconditional, and that the destruction of the building by fire was not a defence.[2]

It is immaterial in this regard whether the cause which precludes performance is or is not what is commonly called an act of God. The *actus Dei* of the law books is simply such a violent and extraordinary manifestation of the natural forces which are constantly at work in a less degree, as can neither be guarded against nor foreseen, and no more the result of divine causation, than any other event in the appointed order of the universe; and therefore as much within the scope of a contract to be answerable should it happen, as if it were of every-day occurrence.

A covenant to do an immoral act, or one contrary to law, is illegal and void *ab initio;* and the effect is the same when a statute forbids that which was lawful when the agreement was made, because the law will neither enforce what it has prohibited nor hold the covenantor answerable in damages for refraining in obedience to its command;[3] or as the rule was stated in Brewster *v.* Kitchell,[4] if the covenantor agrees not to do an act or thing which it was lawful to do, and an Act of Parliament comes after and compels him to do it, the

[1] Goddard *v.* Bebout, 40 Ind. 114. [2] 40 Ind. 114.

[3] Brewster *v.* Kitchell, 1 Salk. 198; Brown *v.* The Mayor of London, 9 C. B. N. S. 726; Baily *v.* De Crespigny, L. R. 4 Q. B. 180; Jones *v.* Judd, 4 Comst. 412; Brick Presbyterian Church *v.* New York, 5 Cow. 538.

[4] 1 Salk. 198.

statute repeals the covenant. So if he covenants to do a thing which is lawful, and an Act of Parliament comes in and hinders him from doing it, the covenant is repealed. This is not on the ground of impossibility but illegality; and hence a subsequent prohibition by a foreign government is not necessarily a defence, although the act is to be done within its territory.[1]

When the act stipulated for is innocent in itself, the plaintiff may be entitled to damages, although it is rendered illegal by circumstances of which he is ignorant, and in Wild *v.* Harris,[2] compensation was awarded for the breach of a promise of marriage, although the defendant was a married man, on proof that the fact was unknown to the plaintiff.

The validity of a guaranty against an alteration of the law, as for instance, that Congress will not depreciate the currency, or lay such a duty on wool with a view of encouraging American industry as will render the manufacture of broadcloth impracticable, is a question of purpose and circumstances, that admits of an affirmative reply when the object is indemnity or insurance.[3] A contract to do an act, notwithstanding any laws that may be made to the contrary, is, if taken literally, invalid.

I may add in this connection that a clause in a lease providing that the tenant's goods shall not be exempt from distress by virtue of any subsequent statute, is valid in Pennsylvania as a waiver of a right conferred for his benefit, and that cannot be abrogated retroactively consistently with the Constitution of the United States.[4] Such also is the rule with regard to clauses in notes or other contracts, exempting property to a certain amount or value from execution. An opposite view prevails in New York.[5]

[1] See Barker *v.* Hodgson, 3 M. & S. 267; Kirk *v.* Gibbs, 1 H. & N. 810; Ford *v.* Cotesworth, L. R. 4 Q. B. 127; 5 id. 544; Knowles *v.* Dabney, 105 Mass. 437.

[2] 7 C. B. 999.

[3] Brown *v.* The Ins. Co., 1 E. & E. 853; The Mayor *v.* Oswald, 1 E. & B. 295.

[4] McKinney *v.* Reader, 6 Watts, 34; Case *v.* Dunmore, 23 Pa. 93; Lauck's Appeal, 24 id. 426; Bowman *v.* Smiley, 31 id. 225.

[5] Kneetle *v.* Newcomb, 22 N. Y. 249.

The inquiry may be summed up as follows: — A contract involving an impossibility may be viewed as an undertaking that the impossibility shall be specifically performed; that it shall be performed as an equivalent for something which the opposite party is to do or render; or as a guaranty that if the event, though beyond human control, occurs and is attended with injurious consequences, the contractor will make compensation. Viewed in the first aspect it is necessarily invalid; in the last two, the contractor may be answerable in damages to an amount equalling the value parted with or loss sustained.

INDEX.

INDEX.

A.

B.

D.

E.

F.

J.

L.

Q.

R.

S.

V.

W.